PROMOTIONAL MANAGEMENT

Norman Govoni
Babson College

Robert Eng
Babson College

Morton Galper
Babson College

PRENTICE-HALL, INC., ENGLEWOOD CLIFFS, N.J. 07632

Library of Congress Cataloging in Publication Data

Govoni, Norman A. P.
    Promotional management.

    Bibliography: p.
    Includes index.
        1. Marketing.   2. Sales promotion.
I. Eng, Robert J.   II. Galper, Morton.
III. Title.
HF5415.G6243   1985   658.8'2   85-9423
ISBN 0-13-731019-6

Editorial/production supervision and
    interior design: Eve Mossman
Cover design: Whitman Studio, Inc.
Cover photo by Lou Odor Photography
Manufacturing buyer: Ed O'Dougherty

Printed in the United States of America

10 9 8 7 6 5 4 3 2 1

ISBN 0-13-731019-6   01

Prentice-Hall International (UK) Limited, *London*
Prentice-Hall of Australia Pty. Limited, *Sydney*
Prentice-Hall Canada Inc., *Toronto*
Prentice-Hall Hispanoamericana, S.A., *Mexico*
Prentice-Hall of India Private Limited, *New Delhi*
Prentice-Hall of Japan, Inc., *Tokyo*
Prentice-Hall of Southeast Asia Pte. Ltd., *Singapore*
Editora Prentice-Hall do Brasil, Ltda., *Rio de Janeiro*
Whitehall Books Limited, *Wellington, New Zealand*

To Terry, Eva, and Judy

Contents

PART TWO   The Setting for the Promotional Effort

PART THREE Advertising and Advertising Management 153

PART FOUR Personal Selling and Sales Management 293

PART FIVE   Sales Promotion and Public Relations   382

PART SIX Promotional Management: Broad Perspectives 486

Preface

This book is aimed toward accomplishing four major objectives: (1) to foster an understanding of the role of promotion in overall marketing strategy, (2) to identify the key elements of promotional management, (3) to show the interaction among the several variables in the promotional program, and (4) to present a framework for analyzing the important promotion decisions.

The text is organized into six parts. Part One, "Promotional Management: Foundations," is designed to establish the foundation upon which a study of promotional management rests. Discussion centers on the role of promotion and the relationship between promotion and marketing. Following this is an overview of promotional management in which attention is directed to how the promotional effort might be organized and put into effect. The discussion then focuses on the communications process, the cornerstone of any promotion program.

Part Two, "The Setting for the Promotional Effort," presents several major topics, the understanding of which is essential for an effective analysis of the promotional effort: consumer decision making, market segmentation and product positioning, and promotion objectives and budgets. Parts One and Two set the stage for a discussion of the major promotion activities and procedures in the next three parts.

Part Three, "Advertising and Advertising Management," is the first in-depth analysis of a major ingredient of the promotional mix—advertising. Emphasis is placed on managing the advertising program, the development of a media strategy, the characteristics of the various media available to carry the advertising message, and the advertising message itself.

Part Four, "Personal Selling and Sales Management," focuses on another vital element of any promotional program—the selling function. Starting with a discussion of the role of personal selling, selling activities, the personal-selling process, and ways to improve selling performance, attention then shifts to developing and executing sales strategy.

In Part Five, "Sales Promotion and Public Relations," the spotlight is on the final two major forms of promotion. Emphasis is first on building and managing an effective sales promotion program (with special treatment given to sales promotion activities directed at consumers, the trade, and the sales force). Then the focus shifts to public relations and publicity, and the many ways that these important activities contribute to a successful promotion effort.

Part Six, "Promotional Management: Broad Perspectives," zeroes in on the total promotional program and its evaluation and control, followed by a detailed discussion of two important topics that serve to make the investigation of promotion complete—namely, the regulation of promotion and the social aspects of promotion.

The plan of this book permits an excellent understanding and appreciation of this essential element of a total marketing program.

Acknowledgments

A book of this magnitude requires contributions from many sources. Indeed we owe a large debt of gratitude to many people. Certainly our present and former students have provided us with much insight and enthusiasm for the project. Also, the many authors and businesspeople who contributed their work deserve our thanks. We are indebted to the reviewers who provided us with candid appraisals and invaluable suggestions for improving the manuscript. We truly appreciate the efforts of Professors Alan Bush (Texas A&M University), V. Glenn Chappell (East Carolina University), Wayne D. Hoyer (The University of Texas at Austin), Cecil Hynes (University of Maryland), Thomas Leigh (Pennsylvania State University), and John Wagle (Northern Illinois University). To Richard P. Flanagan, Professor of English at Babson College, who edited the entire manuscript, go our deepest thanks for his first-rate effort to make the text more readable. To Henry N. Deneault, Dean of the Graduate Programs at Babson College, goes our great appreciation for his contributions to several of the chapters. We owe special thanks and appreciation to our secretaries, Joan Brawley and Marion Power, beyond what words could adequately describe. Our heartfelt gratitude is extended to our colleagues in the Marketing Division at Babson College, each of whom had significant input into the project at one time or another. The graduate assistants helped make our tasks roll more smoothly. We thank Vicki Delbono, Pat Millen, Carol Poirier, and Connie Stumpf, word-processing specialists at Babson College, for their help in typing the manuscript, often faced with impossible deadlines but always coming through. For providing continual and expert assistance, we have great praise and admiration for the following Prentice-Hall personnel: Elizabeth Classon, editor-marketing; Eve Mossman, production editor; Marie Lines, copy editor; and Gloria Schaffer, assistant to Ms. Classon. And, most important, to our wives for their encouragement and understanding throughout this entire project—*thanks!* Obviously this book would not have been a reality without the contributions of these and many other people. But we ourselves must accept full responsibility for any shortcomings.

Norman Govoni
Robert Eng
Morton Galper

Babson Park, Mass.

1

Promotion
and
Marketing

The Hanes Corporation began test-marketing the pantyhose called L'eggs.[1] By the end of the first year, retail sales in markets representing only 3.5 percent of the United States totaled $9 million. In the next year, sales rose to $54 million in just one-third of the U.S. market. L'eggs had become the best-selling brand of hosiery in the country. Two years later, with full distribution, L'eggs had retail sales of $150 million. In recent years, L'eggs has enjoyed a market share of 20 to 25 percent with sales in excess of $340 million, the leader of the industry.

How can we explain this extraordinary accomplishment? Had the entire market for hosiery grown so dramatically in those four years? No! Overall, the hosiery market declined during that period. Had major competitors dropped out of the business? No! Hanes' two largest competitors increased their marketing activity over the same period.

The explanation is both simple and complex. L'eggs succeeded because of a brilliant marketing strategy devised by people who recognized the needs of pantyhose customers and the characteristics of the marketing environment. Easy to say. The hard part is developing such a strategy, wherein all the elements harmonize with and reinforce each other.

In a totally different domain, two young engineers combined their technical skills with an adaptive, insightful marketing strategy to give birth to a new multibillion-dollar industry. In 1976, starting in a backyard garage with $1,500 and an idea,[2] Apple Computer, Inc., would ultimately develop and produce the Apple I, which became the touchstone for the personal computer (PC) revolution. Apple's first-year sales of $100,000 were quite respectable,[3] but very small when compared with the company's subsequent growth. By 1979 the firm had established itself as the leader in the personal computer industry and had achieved sales of $75 million.[4] Two years later Apple posted sales of $335 million, representing a 23 percent market share.[5] By 1984 Apple had relinquished its leadership position to IBM but still commanded a market share of 20 percent, with a total of $1.5 billion in sales.[6]

Since promotion, the topic of this book, is part of overall marketing strategy, we will begin our exploration of promotion with a brief review of the nature of marketing strategy and then identify the specific strategic decisions that Hanes and Apple made in developing their marketing and promotional programs. We will then consider the relationship between promotion and the other marketing mix elements. We will also look at the various environments that influence the development of promotional strategy.

MARKETING STRATEGY

Marketing strategy is the foundation on which marketing programs are built. It involves allocating resources to meet specified goals. The major decision elements of *marketing strategy* are *selection of the target market* and *development of the appropriate marketing mix* to reach the goals.[7] The target market is the segment or group of potential customers the company elects to serve. Since not all customers within the total market for a product have the same needs and characteristics, the selection of a particular segment defines the needs and characteristics to which the marketer must respond. Determination of the appropriate marketing mix means choosing the right combination of product, price, distribution, and promotion to match the needs, interests, values, and other characteristics of the selected target market. Success here requires a deep knowledge of the target market, an understanding of the attributes of each marketing mix component, and a sensitivity to the environment within which the firm will operate.[8]

THE L'eggs MARKETING PROGRAM[9]

Target Market

The target market Hanes chose was young, convenience-minded, active women who wanted to be attractively dressed. This target market was a significant growth opportunity for four reasons: (1) changing demographics made young women (18–35) the fastest-growing sector of the population; (2) increasing numbers of women were entering the labor market in professional and semi-professional positions, where being appropriately dressed was a desirable personal characteristic; (3) a study of trends showed that women in this group were moving away from the "anything goes" casualness of the sixties to a greater fashion orientation in the seventies; and (4) career responsibilities made convenience an increasingly valuable attribute for these consumers. To serve this market, Hanes had to make basic choices about each element of its marketing mix.

Marketing Mix

The Right Product

Hanes used a newly developed yarn that would stretch or contract to fit the body. A single size gave most women a snug fit. An egg-shaped package coordinated with the name to give L'eggs a unique and memorable image.

The Right Price

L'eggs sold for $1.39 a pair, expensive when compared with other hosiery products that sold in supermarkets for a dollar or less. The primary competition for L'eggs, however, was the pantyhose and stockings sold in department stores and women's specialty shops, and these competitive offerings sold in the $3.00 range. Thus L'eggs was positioned between the two sets of competing products—superior in quality (fit, wearability, and consistency) to traditional supermarket hosiery and more attractive in price than department store offerings.

The Right Distribution

The convenience-minded, active woman would find L'eggs in the most convenient outlets: supermarkets and drugstores. Six hundred L'eggs saleswomen in their distinctive trucks maintained the uniquely designed boutique displays in some seventy thousand retail outlets. The display fit into just two square feet of a store's high-traffic areas. Retailers liked the high volume of sales, and they loved their 35 percent profit margin.

The Right Promotion

Some of the promotional elements in the L'eggs strategy are already obvious: unique name and package, distinctive trucks and sales force, efficient and attractive displays. Two other factors dominated the promotion. The distinctive theme "Our L'eggs fit your legs" introduced L'eggs in one region after another. A heavy advertising expenditure (equivalent to $10 million nationally) pushed the L'eggs message in magazines and newspapers and on prime-time television. The second factor was the extensive distribution by direct mail of twenty-five-cent discount coupons. These two promotional efforts made L'eggs the leading promoter in the entire hosiery business.

THE APPLE MARKETING PROGRAM

Target Market

Apple's initial target market was the home user, who would use the low-cost small computer to play games, teach children some basic skills, and perform occasional personal financial analysis.[10] However, Apple quickly realized that professionals (e.g., doctors, lawyers, stockbrokers, accountants) and small retail outlets and offices with fewer than ten employees were the most important market segment.[11] In recent years the company's target market has expanded to include colleges and universities, as well as individual managers within large and medium-sized firms.

Marketing Mix

The Right Product

Apple used its brand name to create a memorable image of simplicity and friendliness.[12] A complete Apple II system (its first widely recognized machine) consisted of a keyboard, a processor with internal storage, a monitor (TV screen), disk drives (external storage), a printer, and software. It has been Apple's approach to software development that has provided a tremendous boost to its prospects. In late 1979, of the more than one thousand programs widely available for the Apple II, over 90 percent had been developed by Apple users.[13] By providing a vehicle for distributing user-developed programs and encouraging the growth of Apple "users clubs" to stimulate the exchange of programs and programming ideas, the company benefited significantly. Today more than twelve thousand programs for Apple computers are distributed through computer stores and other retail outlets, only a small fraction of which have been developed at company expense.

The Right Price

The price for the Apple II processor and keyboard was positioned in the $1,200–$1,500 range,[14] while a full system as described above totaled about $3,000–$3,500. Apple's pricing approach has been based around being a value leader (computing power per dollar) rather than a price leader. Subsequent models of the Apple II family (e.g., IIe, IIc) remained in the same price range while offering significantly enhanced performance capability and features.

The Right Distribution

To reach the 140 million potential customers worldwide that Apple executives envisioned required something different from the traditional direct sales approach.[15] Utilizing a network of independent computer stores supported by wholesale distributors, both independent and company owned, Apple expanded from five hundred specialty outlets in 1978[16] to nearly two thousand in 1984.[17] Department stores have been added to the retail outlets carrying Apple products.[18] Offering attractive discounts and a full range of support tools (sales training, cooperative advertising, dealer seminars, promotions, etc.), Apple developed and retained an enthusiastic and loyal retail network.

The Right Promotion

With its most unusual name for a "high-tech" company, followed by Dick Cavett's memorable bites of apple on national television, Apple Computer launched one of the most aggressive promotional campaigns ever undertaken by a computer manufacturer. Starting with a $400,000 advertising budget in 1977, and expanding it to $15 million in 1981 to hold off an army of new competitors,[19] Apple in 1983 was spending at a $40 million rate.[20] By 1985 there was another big increase in advertising spending by Apple, to $100 million.[21] Indicative of the aggressive promotional push by Apple was its sole sponsorship of *Newsweek*'s special election issue in November 1984. With IBM's entry into the market, Apple positioned itself as the prime alternative to IBM. It appealed to baby-boom professionals and businesspeople through a series of lifestyle ads that more than successfully defended its position in the industry.[22]

The L'eggs and Apple strategies are excellent examples of how well-coordinated and integrated marketing programs can produce outstanding results. Our objective in examining these case histories, however, is not to discover their implications for the development of marketing strategy but to focus on one element of that strategy—namely, the promotional aspect—and thereby gain some insight into the development and execution of promotional programs within an overall marketing plan. A successful promotional program does not arise in isolation; it must fit with the other strategic elements and take into account the environment in which the firm operates. When all pieces of the puzzle fit together, excellent results are possible.

INTERACTION BETWEEN PROMOTION AND OTHER MARKETING MIX ELEMENTS

As mentioned earlier, promotional strategy is but one element in the overall program that the marketing manager develops, implements, and controls. The manager, however, cannot make the critical judgments in this or in any other policy area without recognizing the impact of these decisions on each of the other strategic elements, especially because marketing is a system of interacting parts.[23] Let us now examine each of the elements of marketing strategy to see how they interact with and affect promotional strategy.

Product

The *product* aspect of the marketing mix refers to the company's offerings, either goods or services. The concept of the product means the total bundle of attributes being offered to a specific set of prospective customers. It incorporates not only the basic physical aspects, size, weight, and horsepower in automobiles, for example, but also special features such as AM–FM radios, radial tires, and tinted windshields. In addition, it includes services such as warranty, maintenance, and repair service supplied by the dealer. Finally, it includes intangibles such as image, reputation, and prior experience.

From this bundle of product attributes the marketing manager selects one or two characteristics that will be crucial in positioning the product in the marketplace. These attributes will stand out in all forms of communication the company will use to establish and reinforce its message. The selected attributes ideally represent product characteristics the target market wants, and they clearly differentiate this product from competitive offerings. Calling 7-Up "the Uncola" and using the lonely, unneeded Maytag serviceman to indicate good quality are two examples of how these important product attributes become effective positioning statements and themes. Many products are developed to have the specific attributes that will give them the desired positioning in the marketplace. The interaction between product policy decisions and promotional strategy is substantial, and sophisticated marketers will take note of it.

Price

The *price* element of the marketing mix may appear to be a straightforward concept, but it too has several dimensions. In the first place, the right price must clearly relate to the value of the bundle of attributes the product offers, as the customer sees it. If these are not consistent—a price too high or too low relative to perceived value—then either the customer will not purchase the product or the company will be giving up a profit it could earn. Other considerations in pricing involve such areas as credit terms; quantity discounts; prices for various sizes, models, and styles; and rental versus purchase prices.

Consumers often think of price as being a good guide to product quality. Therefore price also has a promotional influence. The content, style, mood, and orientation of advertising, sales promotion, packaging, and other aspects of promotional activity must communicate the same sense of quality to the consumer as the price suggests. An inconsistent message creates uncertainty and hesitation, providing the buyer with reasons to delay or cancel a purchase decision.

Another aspect of the necessary integration of price and promotion decisions lies in sales promotion. Sales promotion activities often entail the offer of a price concession (such as discount coupons) to the consumer. This form of price reduction ensures that the lower price in fact goes to the consumer and not to the retailer in the form of higher margin. Price reductions of this nature are usually temporary. Price and promotion must go together in strategic decision making or else one risks consumer misperceptions or ineffective pricing moves.

Distribution

The third element of the marketing mix, *distribution*, concerns the selection of distribution channels. Clearly, the choice of retail outlets relates to both the product offering and its price. We do not expect to find automobiles for sale at the local supermarket or meat and produce in a hardware store. Some brands are available only in discount stores, others only in specialty stores, and some in both. Why is this? Price may be one of the reasons, store image may be another, and the retailer's desires may be a third.

The structuring of a distribution channel involves choice and decisions by two parties—the manufacturer and the distribution outlet. Each selects or rejects the other, and promotion plays a major role in these choices.

Some retailers will only select brands that are heavily advertised and have strong brand followings to help attract customers to their store. Others place great weight on the promotional allowances and cooperative advertising programs that suppliers offer. Still others prefer to promote their own store brands, which they acquire from smaller manufacturers under private-label arrangements.

On the other side, some manufacturers will sell only to outlets whose image and position in the marketplace are consistent with their own. Others choose retailers known for their support of manufacturers' promotional programs, such as in-store displays and demonstrations. Some prefer to eliminate retailers altogether, opting for direct consumer sales.

Both the manufacturer's and the retailer's promotional programs are important influences on the distribution decision. Conversely, the distribution strategy also has a material impact on promotional actions.

Once more we see the close linkage between promotional strategy and a key element of marketing strategy. We have attempted here to demonstrate the importance of integrating promotional strategy with all the other key ingredients of marketing strategy. This process of combining the strategic elements into a unified and consistent whole is vital to the development of a successful strategic direction. Another crucial consideration in the creation of effective programs is an understanding of environmental influences on promotional activities. Let us now examine the environmental factors.

ENVIRONMENTAL CONTEXT OF PROMOTION

A promotional strategy cannot be effective unless the strategy accounts for and is responsive to the environment in which the product business will have to operate. The environment may enhance or constrain the strategic options available to the marketer, or it may facilitate or restrict the success of a given strategy. Furthermore, the environment is not static; one of its key characteristics is its dynamism. It is constantly changing, providing new opportunities to some businesses, delimiting the prospects for others.

We can view the *environmental context* on two levels, determined by the degree of control the company may exercise over individual factors. (See Exhibit 1-1 for a diagram that identifies these two levels.) The outer ring is the *external environment*, uncontrollable by the individual company or organization. These environmental factors can have considerable influence on the way the company operates. The second level, represented by the interior ring, is the *operating environment* of the company, semicontrollable, since actions by the organization can affect or change the key elements within this environment. These changes may take place over the long term, rarely in the short term. Let us now examine the individual factors and their influence on promotional decisions within these two environments.

EXHIBIT 1-1 The Environmental Context of Promotion

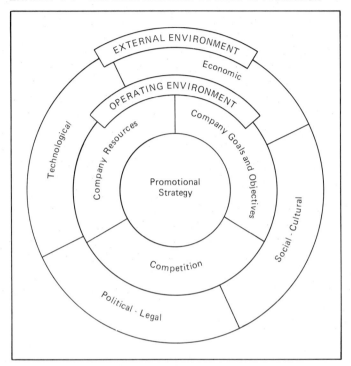

External Environment of Promotion

There are four factors (see Exhibit 1-1) in the external environment, and the marketing manager must be conscious of these in developing promotional strategy.

The *economic* environment is the first factor, and we only need to recall how a recession affects the sale of houses, automobiles, appliances, and other consumer durables to realize the impact of this factor on the marketing manager's plans. The devastating effect of high interest rates during the early 1980s on automobile sales is ample evidence of the significance of this variable. Sales promotions involving discounted interest rates on consumer car loans and rebates were widely used to counteract the difficult economic climate. These were initially successful in increasing short-term sales but did not change the overall sales level or the consumers' attitudes. Unit sales dropped to prepromotional levels once the rebates and special promotions had stopped.

The *social* and *cultural* environment is also important in developing promotional strategy. The increased popularity of jeans, cowboy hats, and boots during the late 1970s reflects a more casual, back-to-nature lifestyle emerging during that period. Television advertising for feminine hygiene products has been made possible by a significant shift in attitudes about the discussion, in public media, of our bodily functions.

The *political* and *legal* environment, as evidenced by tax laws, environmental rules, and Federal Trade Commission regulations and rulings, to name a few, influences the decisions of marketing managers. The FTC's insistence on documentation of advertising claims, the Food and Drug Administration's labeling requirements, and the Federal Communications Commission's specific limitations on the available TV advertising time are three examples. These effects may also be felt in overseas markets as our international relations provide opportunities for or constraints on business dealings with other countries. In addition, their regulation of promotional activity may be even more restrictive than our own. For example, in France, TV advertising time is very limited and is permitted only at the completion of a program; in Germany, comparative claims are not permitted in advertising copy.

The final variable in the external environment, *technology*, can lead to the creation of entirely new industries (pocket calculators, computers, satellite communications, solar energy) and to the demise of others (vaudeville, buggy whips, slide rules, and passenger trains). Technological changes have created new media (cable TV systems), altered the character of others (direct mail campaigns with the aid of computers are increasingly being personalized), and fostered entirely new methods of personal communications (telemarketing techniques provide many of the advantages of personal selling at a much lower cost). This may be the most difficult factor for the marketing strategist to assess. Historically, the technology with the most significant impact on an existing business has come from outside the industry (passenger trains replaced by autos and airplanes; slide rules superseded by pocket calculators; vaudeville made obsolete by movies and radio). Development of an effective strategy depends nonetheless on awareness of this critical environmental factor.

Each of these external uncontrollable factors has many dimensions. The marketing manager must keep informed and up to date on the changes occurring within the dimensions most vital to his or her business. Making the right strategic adjustment to a short-term external condition or the appropriate shift in response to a fundamental long-term environmental change will enhance the company's performance and its prospects over time. Successful marketers understand this well. Others have learned the lesson at great cost.

Operating Environment of Promotion

As we noted earlier, the operating environment consists of those factors that relate directly to the particular product business of the company (see Exhibit 1-1). The most widely recognized variable in the operating environment is *competition*. It shapes and influences the company's promotional strategy in the most direct way. Increases or decreases in the number of competitors, changes in competitive strategy, new sales promotions, sales force expansions, changes in product positioning, and so on, can all have a substantial near-term impact on the company. Marketing managers keep very close track of competitors' actions and reactions.

Note that we are describing competition in the narrowest sense, *direct competitors*—those products and companies that seek to serve the particular market need with essentially the same type of product (Texas Instruments, Hewlett-Packard, and Sharp all produce pocket calculators). Other competitors can influence a company's promotional strategy but do not make or offer similar products. These companies are known as *indirect competitors*— those products and companies that seek to serve the particular market need but with different product concepts (Hertz, General Motors, and the local transit system all provide transportation services to commuters—if the local transit system extends its lines to new locations, changes its service frequency, or aggressively promotes special fares, this will have an effect on the purchase of new cars and on car rental activity in its service area). And, finally, there is competition from everything else—all the competing goods and services the potential customer could buy with his or her money (a new car competes with washing machines, stereos, furniture, and a trip to Bermuda). The marketing manager should view competition in the broadest context. Too narrow a perspective can lead to faulty judgments and failures in the marketplace.

The next variable in the operating environment is the company's *goals* and *objectives*. In general these do not, nor should they, change very often or very quickly, and therefore they serve as boundaries or constraints for the marketing executive in the development of strategy. The goals and objectives of the company are long-range guideposts. They can be expressed as sales levels, market shares or profits, return on investment (ROI) or earnings per share (EPS). They can be defined in human as well as financial terms, as in employee turnover rates or personnel development. In any event, they provide the decision-making framework that governs *all* key management decisions.

Equally important, as a constraint and guidepost, are the company's *resources*. We tend to view these as essentially financial attributes. This is only partly valid. There are two other dimensions to the concept of company resources. One is the physical resource dimension—the plants, equipment, tools, trucks, and so on. These define the limits of the company's capacity to produce. Obviously these can grow, but generally not in the short run. The other is the human resources—the skills and abilities of the manager, marketing staff, engineers, production personnel, and the rest who represent the company's capacity to develop, produce, and market its offerings effectively. Together these resources—financial, physical, and human—define and constrain the company's ability to respond to any particular market challenge or opportunity.

We have described the operating environment as semicontrollable. A company can change those key elements in response to either its internal needs or shifts in the external environment. Executive action can modify the company's goals, but maintaining a steady course over time yields significant benefits. The company's resources can grow through recruiting new personnel, seeking additional funds in the capital markets, or initiating the construction of facilities. None of these actions is likely to produce significant short-term results but may lead to longer-term improvements in resources. Competitors are influenced by the company's decisions just as the reverse is true, and the company can take steps to change the competitive environment. Despite these substantial opportunities for control, in the short run, these factors tend to restrict the strategic choices marketers may exercise.

In summary, the marketing executive defines, develops, and executes promotional strategy within environments, both external and operating. Failure to account for all these elements, in pursuing a marketing objective, carries serious risk. In the discussion to this point we have sought to augment the reader's general knowledge of the nature and content of promotional activity. We will expand that perspective somewhat and then examine the key ingredients in promotional strategy in the remainder of the text.

PROMOTIONAL STRATEGY

Promotional strategy is the process of developing and maintaining a communications mix that utilizes company resources to their full potential in a way that is competitively attractive to target markets while contributing to the company's short-run and long-run marketing and organizational goals. Promotion is undoubtedly the most visible element of the marketing mix. There are few people, be they marketing professionals or members of the general public, who do not have strong opinions about their likes and dislikes in promotional activity. Yet, despite this high level of awareness, there is much that is not understood about this vital aspect of marketing strategy.

Promotion, often called marketing communications, is all those means by which marketers communicate to their target market. In general terms, the *purposes of marketing communication are to inform, to persuade, or to remind*: to inform consumers, that is, about the availability of a new detergent, say, to persuade them that this detergent is better in some respects than others, and to remind them to buy more when the last cup has been poured into the washing machine. All of this must go forward against a continuous background of competing communications, both promotional and nonpromotional. Without an effective promotional effort the best-conceived products, at the most-attractive prices, will often gather dust on retailers' shelves. Realistically, consumers do not make purchase transactions simply because a company believes that it has designed and manufactured a valuable product. Potential buyers must be informed that the product exists, given the reason or reasons why it is better than competing products, and persuaded that they should buy as soon as possible. This is the role promotion plays in marketing strategy. And designing the proper promotional mix is a complicated process involving, among other things, a knowledge of what promotion can and cannot do and a knowledge of the nature of each promotional tool.[24]

In short, many benefits can flow from an effective promotional effort when promotion communicates product advantages to potential consumers, helps to increase sales of existing products, establishes awareness and favorable attitudes toward new products, helps to create brand preference among consumers and to secure distribution in outlets, helps to obtain greater cooperation and support from middlemen, generates greater effort from the sales force, and helps to build a favorable corporate image.

With that general perspective on what promotion can and should do for the marketer, let us consider for a moment what it cannot and should not be expected to do. It cannot create buying activity for a product that serves no consumer need; it cannot persuade consumers that a product is superior when consumer experience with the product reveals the opposite; it cannot influence consumers to pay a higher than reasonable price when there is no greater value perceived by them; it cannot convince buyers to make extraordinary shopping efforts when competitive products are readily available at local outlets. A promotional strategy, then, no matter how brilliantly conceived, no matter how creatively executed, cannot be expected to overcome fundamental weaknesses in the rest of the marketing strategy.

To this point we have discussed promotion as if it were a single item. Of course, it is not. Promotion as a strategic variable consists of four elements, which must be coordinated to form the overall promotional strategy. These elements are advertising, personal selling, sales promotion, and public relations. We will describe them only briefly here, recognizing that we will discuss each in depth in subsequent chapters. As a frame of reference, Exhibit 1-2 shows the relationship between promotional strategy and overall marketing strategy.

Advertising

Advertising is fundamentally impersonal mass communications. It presents a standard commercial message simultaneously to a large dispersed audience through media. The media may be broadcast (radio and television), print (newspapers and magazines), or other (mail, billboards, or transit).

Advertising decisions involve a combination of analysis and creativity. The analysis determines which media will reach the selected target audience most efficiently, which theme or message will be most in tune with the

EXHIBIT 1-2   Promotional Strategy and Overall Marketing Strategy

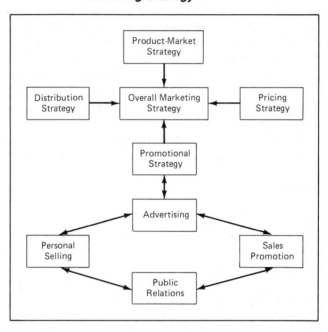

customer's buying motivation, which execution of the theme will be most attention getting and memorable. Creativity brings the art and copy together to develop the desired product image, with visual images to capture the audience's imagination, and with music and backgrounds to provide a mood.

Advertising decision making also involves research and testing at many stages in the process. This requires rigorous thinking as well as careful and appropriate use of various research methodologies and statistical techniques.

The true measure of advertising effectiveness is not whether the commercials or ads are beautiful or funny or even win awards. The real measure is highly pragmatic—Do they produce the desired results at the expected cost?

Personal Selling

Personal selling contrasts sharply with advertising. It is personal, individualized communication that transmits a tailored, highly adaptive commercial message to a small, very select audience. Personal selling takes place via direct contact between buyer and seller, either face-to-face or through some form of telecommunications.

The management decisions here also require a variety of skills and insights, both analytical and interpersonal. Key decision issues that sales managers face include such matters as what type of sales organization to use, how to build and train a sales force, what size the sales force should be, how to deploy the sales force in territories, how to keep salespeople motivated, what degree of supervision is needed, what the compensation programs should involve, and how to measure sales performance. Obviously, personal selling has far-reaching implications for the overall promotional program.

Sales Promotion

Sales promotion is an extremely diverse form of commercial mass communications, the purpose of which is to provide additional motivation for customers to make buying decisions now. A few examples will highlight the range of activities encompassed by this promotional area: product samples (used aggressively by Procter & Gamble for new-product introductions); discount coupons (mailed or included in advertising); point-of-purchase displays (a supermarket favorite); and premiums (be the first in your crowd to have an Adidas gym bag). As we will see later, there is wide latitude here for creative initiative.

The variety of techniques available adds to the challenge of the management task. The audience selected, whether company sales force, middlemen, or ultimate consumers, will have a bearing on the approaches one might use. Other factors such as the stage of the product's life cycle, competitive activity, industry practice, and company strategy will also be influential. As with other promotional elements, analysis and creativity will both contribute to effective sales promotion decisions.

Public Relations

Public relations is also a multifaceted form of communication. Its intent is to foster a positive company or product image in a nonsponsored framework. This attribute of nonsponsorship enhances the credibility of the message and cloaks the company with the respectability of the source, which may be viewed by the audience as either the spokesperson or the medium. It may be as personal as a speaker at a PTA meeting or as impersonal as a magazine article. It may be as commercially indirect as the sponsorship of a Little League team or as direct as a new-product release in a trade magazine. Even sophisticated marketing organizations sometimes underuse this kind of promotion, but it can be a highly effective means of establishing both awareness and credibility of a product offering or a company.

The management of public relations is not as linear as other communications approaches, since it depends in many instances on the willingness of others to take action. Submitting a new product release to a trade publication does not guarantee that it will appear; calling a press conference does not ensure that the desired media will attend or ever use the material provided. These are but two examples of the circumstances that make a successful public relations effort dependent on the combined capability of interpersonal skills and a solid understanding of the internal workings of the media.

At this point it should be evident that there is a wide range of activities that constitute the promotional area of marketing. Clearly, the importance of developing an integrated and coordinated strategy is no less vital in promotional planning than it is in other strategic areas.[25] In fact, the very diversity of promotional activities and the distribution of promotional management responsibilities across a wide spectrum of functional areas make effective decision making and planning all the more critical. We stress this point throughout the book.

PLAN OF THE BOOK

Now that we have established the framework within which the promotion and marketing functions are implemented, and have outlined the relationships between promotional activities and marketing activities, we will proceed to other key topics in an overview of the promotional function. The remainder of Part I, "Promotional Management: Foundations," provides a survey of promotional planning and the nature of communications.

Part II, "The Setting for the Promotional Effort," emphasizes areas essential to the development of sound promotional programs. Buyer behavior, market segmentation and positioning, and promotional objectives and budgets occupy our attention. The discussion of consumer decision making and market segmentation and positioning will show why it is important to understand the market and zero in on a target market. That will lead us to a consideration of promotional objectives and budgets, a natural outgrowth of consumer and market factors.

Part III, "Advertising and Advertising Management," begins our discussion of the major components of the promotional mix. This part is devoted to advertising management, creative strategy in developing the advertising message, media strategy, and a description of the various media available to carry the advertising message.

In Part IV, "Personal Selling and Sales Management," another vital element of the promotional effort is spotlighted. The personal-selling function, as well as the many aspects of developing and executing a sales strategy, will be discussed.

Part V, "Sales Promotion and Public Relations," covers the other two major forms of promotion. We will see what is involved in managing sales promotion activities and what sales promotion can do for consumers, trade customers, and the sales force. And we will return to a full consideration of the role of public relations in promotional strategy.

The last part of the book—Part VI, "Promotional Management: Broad Perspectives"—focuses on the evaluation and control of complete promotional programs. In addition, it will address the legal and social aspects of promotion, since they represent important dimensions of any promotional program.

SUMMARY

Promotion, encompassing many different activities, is an essential part of virtually every organization doing business, whether the organization operates in the consumer or industrial market, produces a product or a service, is profit-seeking or not-for-profit, or is in the public or private sector. As a key ingredient in marketing strategy, promotion must relate to other elements of that strategy, notably product, price, and distribution.

Promotional strategy consists of four major elements: advertising, personal selling, sales promotion, and public relations. The effective communications program is the one that integrates these four elements as planning develops. Promotional decisions are made within complex and changing environments, both external and operating, that serve as constraints on (and at the same time opportunities for) decision making.

Development of a successful promotional strategy requires sound analysis, creative concepts, and effective management practice. In this book we endeavor to provide the reader with a good understanding of how one meets these requirements.

Above all, a successful promotional strategy requires planning, and we now turn to this crucial matter.

REVIEW AND DISCUSSION QUESTIONS

1. *It has been mentioned that marketing strategy consists of two basic decision elements: selection of the target market and determination of the appropriate marketing mix. Explain.*

2. *The marketing mix is comprised of four major elements. What are they and how do they work together in a company's marketing program?*

3. *Identify and explain the factors associated with the external environment of marketing.*

4. *How does the social and cultural environment affect marketing strategy? Give examples.*

5. *What is meant by the operating environment of marketing? What elements make up the operating environment?*

6. *Explain the relationship between the external and the operating environment of marketing.*

7. *Marketing has been described as a process of adjusting "controllables" to "uncontrollables." What do you think is meant by this? Explain your reasoning.*

8. *How does competition affect the marketing strategy of a company? To what extent should competition determine the particular way a company formulates its marketing strategy?*

9. *What is the role of the product in marketing strategy? Price? Distribution? Promotion?*

10. *Explain what promotion can do.*

11. *What are the similarities and differences in the way promotion might be used for*

   a. *A company selling coffee compared with a company selling heavy-duty packaging machinery?*

   b. *A company selling a tangible consumer product compared with one selling a service, such as investment counseling?*

   c. *A profit-seeking company compared with a not-for-profit organization?*

   d. *A large company compared with a small company?*

12. *Why is promotion referred to as marketing communications?*

13. *Identify the elements that constitute promotion. Explain each element in terms of what it contributes to the overall promotional mix.*

14. *What are some of the key promotional decisions management has to make?*

15. *Explain why promotion should be thought of as a process involving several interrelated elements.*

NOTES

1. From the case L'eggs Products, Inc., by Harvey N. Singer and F. Stewart DeBruicker in E. Raymond Corey, Christopher H. Lovelock, and Scott Ward, *Problems in Marketing* 6th ed. (New York: McGraw-Hill Book Company), 1981, pp. 341–357. Copyright © 1975 by the President and Fellows of Harvard College. Used with permission of the Harvard Business School.

2. "The Hot New Computer Companies," *Dun's Review*, January 1979, p. 55.

3. Ibid.

4. "Apple's Pie," *Forbes*, August 20, 1979, p. 55.

5. "Test of Time, As Competition Grows, Apple Computer, Inc. Faces Critical Period," *Wall Street Journal*, November 11, 1981, pp. 1, 25.

6. Brian Moran and Cleveland Horton, "Marketing Methods Bring Apple Back," *Advertising Age*, December 31, 1984, p. 22.

7. E. Jerome McCarthy and William D. Perreault, Jr., *Basic Marketing*, 8th ed. (Homewood, Ill.: Richard D. Irwin, 1984), p. 43. *Also see* William M. Pride and O. C. Ferrell, *Marketing*, 4th ed. (Boston: Houghton Mifflin, 1985), pp. 18–26, 32–65.

8. For two excellent discussions of the importance of marketing strategy and the need to apply fresh thinking to traditional approaches to marketing strategy, see George S. Day and Robin Wensley, "Marketing Theory with a Strategic Orientation," *Journal of Marketing*, Fall 1983, pp. 79–89; and Yoram Wind and Thomas S. Robertson, "Marketing Strategy: New Directions for Theory and Research," *Journal of Marketing*, Spring 1983, pp. 12–25.

9. This description is based on material excerpted from the case "L'eggs Products, Inc.," by Harvey N. Singer and F. Stewart DeBruicker, in *Problems in Marketing*, 6th ed., ed. E. Raymond Corey, Christopher H. Lovelock, and Scott Ward (New York: McGraw-Hill, 1981), pp. 341–57. Copyright © 1975 by the President and Fellows of Harvard College. Used with permission of the Harvard Business School.

10. "The Hot New Computer Companies," p. 55.

11. "Apple's Pie," p. 55.

12. Ibid.

13. Ibid.

14. Ibid.

15. "Personal Computer Market Barely Tapped, Says Apple Exec," *Merchandising*, June 1982, p. 62A.

16. "The Hot New Computer Companies," p. 55.

17. Moran and Horton, "Marketing Methods," p. 1.

18. "Personal Computer Market Barely Tapped," p. 62A.

19. "Test of Time," p. 25.

20. "Mass Marketing the Computer," *Fortune*, October 31, 1983, p. 63.

21. Moran and Horton, "Marketing Methods," p. 1.

22. "Mass Marketing the Computer," p. 63.

23. Victor P. Buell, *Marketing Management* (New York: McGraw-Hill, 1984), p. 28.

24. Philip Kotler, *Marketing Management*, 5th ed. (Englewood Cliffs, N.J.: Prentice-Hall, 1984), p. 623.

25. Ibid., pp. 632–33.

2

Promotional Management: An Overview

The promotional plan is the blueprint describing the role of communications in achieving an organization's marketing objectives. We have identified the individual elements of the promotional effort, and although we have not yet discussed them in detail, there is evidently a need for an *integrated* approach to communicating with the target market.

As we will see in succeeding chapters, each element of the promotional program has particular strengths and weaknesses making it more suitable or less suitable for accomplishing particular tasks or achieving certain objectives. The most effective promotional program recognizes these advantages and limitations and deploys the available resources accordingly. Management distributes promotional activities among many departments and many individuals. This diffusion of responsibility contains the potential for serious discrepancies and conflicts in the planning and execution of the program. Two significant areas of risk are the *content* of the promotional efforts, which may communicate conflicting messages to the target audience; and the *timing* of the promotional activities, which may render parts of the plan substantially less effective because of delayed availability of necessary promotional materials. To minimize these risks while striving for the objectives in an efficient and effective manner, we must have a carefully developed promotional plan.

To convey the importance and complexity of an integrated approach in effective communications, this chapter provides an overview of promotional management. We start by considering the circumstances under which programs are developed, and we then review promotional decisions including the establishment of objectives, determination of budget, implementation of activities, and evaluation of results.

WHEN ARE PROGRAMS DEVELOPED?

There are three separate occasions for creating promotional plans: when a new product is being introduced, when changes in the market environment indicate that a revised marketing strategy is appropriate, and during the annual planning and budgeting cycle. Let us examine some major characteristics of the promotional planning effort during each of these situations.

New-Product Introductions

The successful introduction of new products is the lifeblood of growing organizations. Considerable time and attention, not to mention promotional resources, flow to these endeavors. Typically, extensive marketing and advertising research programs are cornerstones of the planning effort, since there is often little direct experience in the particular product market. The absence of firsthand operating knowledge increases the risk of failure through oversight, misinterpretation, or unavailability of market information. For similar reasons, the market size and sales forecasts generally have a wide band of possible outcomes. Interpreting research and test data is an important skill that managers of promotional programs for new products should cultivate.

The task of planning a new-product promotion campaign is a complex one. There are many targets to be considered, and the timing of such efforts as advertising, personal selling, sales promotion, and public relations is critical. For example, enthusiasm for a new product must be generated among the company's sales representatives, its distribution channels, and, of course, the ultimate consumers. First, steps must be taken to ensure that the sales force supports the product. The company's sales reps may require incentives before they take time from selling existing successful brands and devote it to what they view as a risky situation. Then the channel members including merchant wholesalers and retailers must be convinced that the new product is likely to move off the store shelves before they allocate limited money and effort for a product with virtually no sales track record. Finally, promotion must persuade the consumers to give the new product a try. Therefore a new-product promotion campaign requires considerable time and attention.

Revised Marketing Strategy

Two conditions will precipitate an extensive revision of the marketing strategy: failure to meet the established program objectives (sales, market share, or profitability goals) or a substantial change in the market environment (change in number of competitors, legislation, technological developments). (Chapter 1, as you will recall, discussed the market environment.) In both conditions there are operating data at hand, useful to the manager in examining alternative promotional strategies. The thrust of the promotion program may have to be changed to be consistent with the new marketing strategy. For example, the targets of communication may have to be redefined, or the balance among efforts including advertising, personal selling, sales promotion, and public relations may have to be reformulated. Careful analysis of available data to determine the reasons for unsatisfactory performance or to infer the likely effects of the environmental change is an important element in the review process. Managers with good diagnostic skills can make a significant contribution to the development of promotional programs in these circumstances.

Annual Planning and Budgetary Cycle

In contrast with those two situations, program development during a regular planning and budgeting cycle is incremental. Typically, it involves small modifications and fine tunings of existing programs rather than the breaking of new strategic ground. The routine nature of this type of program development may lead the promotional manager to be less than diligent in his or her review of past results and the present and anticipated market environment. Incipient but significant changes in the market environment, visible but not yet influential, often escape notice, leading to a misinterpretation of trends. Managers who can improve the efficiency of the promotional effort, as well as those who have a keen sense of market evolution, are important in this milieu.

ORGANIZING FOR PROMOTION

Since the 1960s when Chandler published his insightful research on the relationship between business strategy and organizational structure,[1] there has been a growing recognition that the form of an organization can have a significant impact on the successful development and implementation of

EXHIBIT 2-1   Functional Organization Structure

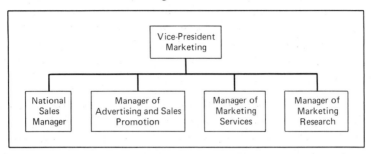

corporate, functional, and subfunctional strategy. This perspective is also valid for marketing in general and the promotional activities in particular.

There are two common organizational structures for marketing activities: functional and product. The traditional functional structure is shown in Exhibit 2-1. This was the dominant form in the early 1950s.[2] Exhibit 2-2 illustrates one form of product organization structure that the large packaged goods organizations (like Procter & Gamble) initiated, and it has become the dominant structure in all types of firms—consumer, industrial, and service.

There is one quite common variation in both types of structure. In many organizations, sales and marketing are separate and parallel functions, each headed by a senior executive who reports directly to the president. This form came about in companies marketing industrial products and spe-

EXHIBIT 2-2   Product Organization Structure

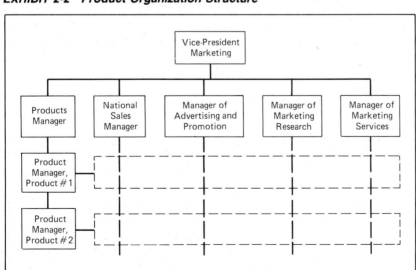

cialty consumer goods, where personal selling is the foremost means of marketing communications. Let us now examine the carrying out of responsibilities for planning, execution, and control of the promotional program in each of the organizational approaches.

Functional

The *functional organization structure* (Exhibit 2-1) clearly places responsibility for planning and controlling the promotional strategy for all products on the marketing vice-president. He or she receives information and recommendations from the managers of the subfunctions, but the ultimate decisions rest with this executive. This approach seeks to ensure that the strategic decisions made about product emphasis and promotional efforts will be in harmony with both marketing and corporate objectives. To achieve this end requires that the marketing vice-president be heavily involved in overseeing the execution phase of the promotional program. The assignment and management of specific functional tasks lie with the individual functional managers, but responsibility for coordination of these efforts for each product line and across product lines resides with the senior marketing executive. This responsibility becomes even more complex if a different senior executive directs the sales force.

Clearly, the essential weakness of this organization lies in the amount of detail coordination and decision making that involves the marketing vice-president. These day-to-day operating demands and pressures can only detract from the time and attention given to longer-range strategic issues. Furthermore, in organizations with relatively narrow product lines serving common and concentrated markets, this structure can be highly effective. It is only when either product or market scope expands and diversifies that the inherent weakness surfaces.

Product

As we might expect, the development of the other form of organization (Exhibit 2-2) is a direct outgrowth of the rapid expansion of the product and market scope of major companies. In the *product organization structure*, the product manager, in some situations, assumes the position of a general manager with full responsibility for the profitability of his or her product line. In other situations, the product manager may have a much more limited scope; he or she would primarily be responsible for developing promotional programs and coordinating the marketing research, advertising, sales promotion, and marketing services efforts for the specific product line. Either way, the product manager is the focal point for the planning, coordination, and control of a major portion of the promotional program.

This form also has limitations. The product manager must obtain the services of the functional specialists in a timely and appropriate manner while having no direct line authority over these specialists. He or she must fulfill certain responsibilities through logical argument, goodwill, professional competence, and other indirect forms of authority. In a multi-product environment, these specialists have numerous calls on their time and expertise, and they make commitments and personnel assignments based on their own sense of priorities. The vice-president of marketing may be called upon frequently to adjudicate conflicting priorities among product managers or between a product manager and a promotional specialist.

On a day-to-day basis, this organizational structure provides focus on and attention to the marketing efforts for individual product lines. It also relieves the senior marketing executive of the detailed coordinative responsibilities. Furthermore, it increases the demands for this executive to make resource allocation decisions among product lines, among the major promotional areas, and within each promotional element. These responsibilities are strategic in nature and are the appropriate purview of the vice-president of marketing.

Use of Outside Services

The planning and execution of promotional strategies are rarely undertaken with the involvement of company personnel alone. The tasks are sufficiently diverse and specialized that outside service organizations play a major role. Outside firms that one might typically call upon to contribute to promotional programs include advertising agencies, marketing research firms, and public relations counselors.

Developing an effective working relationship with *outside services* is not an easy task. It is important that these resources function as an integrated part of the company's marketing team, yet they may be unwilling or unable to do so. Outside agencies serve many clients, and sometimes the pressure to work on the account of one client imposes a barrier to an effective working relationship with another. For example, outside agencies tend to serve the more important clients (usually determined by the fees a service expects to receive) while limiting attention to the smaller ones. On the other hand, too heavy a commitment to one client may not be an ideal condition. It can create vulnerability that strips the outside service of its objectivity and independence, two important factors in providing a client with an effective promotion plan. In other instances, an effective working relationship between the outside service and the client firm may be inhibited by personal differences between individuals of each party. For example, a marketing manager with a conservative philosophy in terms of marketing decisions may be unable to work effectively with an agency representative who prefers to take daring, innovative approaches. Managing the relationship between the company and its outside support services, then, is a sensitive and challenging responsibility. Given this background, let us now examine the role of each service in promotional campaigns.

Advertising Agencies

Although we discuss advertising agencies in detail in Chapter 7, we will introduce them here to show their role in planning. *Advertising agencies* range in scope from full-service organizations that provide all the services associated with promotional activity to highly specialized firms that concentrate on one particular facet. Typically, the marketing strategist retains agencies to provide creative services—conceptualization, layout, artwork, and copy writing of advertisements for both print and broadcast media; media services—analysis, evaluation, selection, and scheduling of appropriate media in which to present the company's message; and production services—creative development as well as procurement of production quantities of collateral promotional materials (catalogs, specification sheets, hang tags, displays, and so on).

An account executive serves as the liaison between the agency and the client company to ensure proper execution of the company's programs and to coordinate the agency's activities with those occurring within the company and elsewhere. This executive will also frequently participate in the strategic-planning phase of the promotional effort.

A company will usually engage an advertising agency on a continuing basis so that it can participate in the entire process of planning, implementing, and evaluating the promotional program. Compensation for agency services has traditionally been a combination of fees for certain analytical, creative, and production services, with commissions on media placements covering media administration and other agency services. The growth of the specialist agency that concentrates exclusively on one service area or another (like creative services or media buying) has led to a fee-based compensation arrangement.

Marketing Research Firms

Marketing research organizations provide the fundamental market data essential to the effective development, execution, and evaluation of promotional programs. The contributions of marketing research specialists range from the evaluation of new segmentation approaches to the conduct of focus group sessions, to the pretesting and posttesting of various advertising concepts. Sound research is the cornerstone of any successful promotional campaign. The outside research firm supplies expertise in particular research methodologies as well as in the development, execution, analysis, and reporting of research projects. It may also serve as a supplement to an internal research operation to handle either peak loads or highly specialized tasks.

Research services are contracted for on a project-by-project basis; however, long-term relationships between these marketing research firms and their client organizations tend to develop as a result of successful performance.

Public Relations Counselors

Companies retain *external public relations counselors* to provide advice and practical assistance in their public relations efforts. Many of these companies may also have an internal PR staff, but as with all promotional services, expertise in particular areas of effort can often be of immense value. The PR firms may make contributions through relationships with particular media (local newspapers), knowledge of certain publics (financial analysts and investors), or experience in a type of public relations activity (as in staging special events). The PR counselors may be retained on a continuing basis or hired project by project. The best results generally derive from continuing relationships where mutual respect and trust between the PR firm and the senior executives of the company have had time to develop.

PROMOTIONAL DECISIONS

There is a wide range of diverse but related decisions that marketing managers make in developing a promotional strategy. To put these many facets of promotional decision making into perspective, it helps to have a structure that defines both the sequence and the content of these decisions. Ray outlined a marketing communications framework well suited for this purpose.[3] We have modified that framework and present it as Exhibit 2-3. The model illustrates a decision sequence incorporating several major elements. Let us now look briefly at these important factors.

Company Situation

The first step is the *analysis and evaluation of the company situation*. Fundamental to the decision process, the situation analysis involves an assessment of company strengths and weaknesses, the specific product attributes, customer needs and attitudes, and competitive activity, as well as trade needs and support.[4] An evaluation of the environmental factors also enters into this background analysis. The first stage of the decision process is essential to the creation and execution of a successful promotional plan. The detailed description of the market conditions facing the business provides crucial information to the marketer as he or she seeks to determine suitable goals for the business and the appropriate promotional actions to achieve those goals. The background information can be derived from internal sales records, ongoing market-monitoring activities, or special marketing research projects.

EXHIBIT 2-3   Sequence of Marketing Communications Decisions

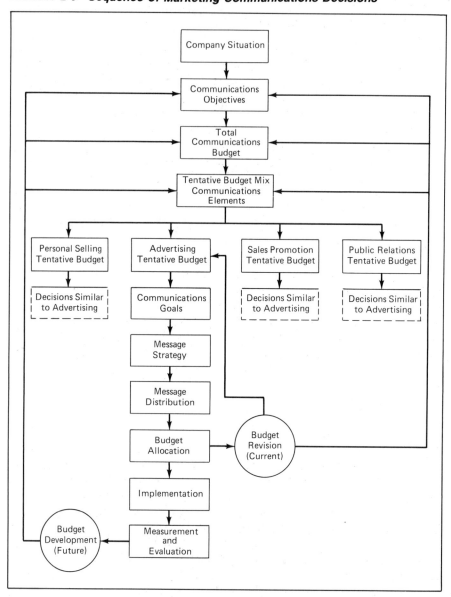

Adapted from Michael Ray, "A Decision Sequence Analysis of Developments in Marketing Communications," *Journal of Marketing*, January 1973, p. 31.

The more complete the situation analysis, the sounder the information base for subsequent decisions, with the net result being better decisions.

Communications Objectives

The *determination of promotional objectives* follows the situation analysis activities. Setting objectives is perhaps the most important element in the sequence of communications decisions, since the objectives provide the fundamental directions toward which the efforts are guided. The objectives are also the standards by which success or failure of the promotional strategy is determined.

Good objectives are the result of much work. For example, it is easy for the marketing manager to define sales and profit goals that represent a modest increment above last year's performance. But is it appropriate or realistic? Can the marketer achieve these gains in light of the product's stage in the life cycle, its market acceptance, the competitive activity, the economic climate, or the resources the company is likely to make available to this business? Goal setting should define the possible in light of the conditions and circumstances that have been determined in the situation analysis. The ultimate goal sought by the marketer is purchase by the consumer. As a means to that end, though, the marketer may seek to put something in the consumer's mind, change the consumer's attitude, or get the consumer to take a specific action.[5]

Total Promotional Budget

The *determination of the size of the total promotional budget* is the first reality test of the defined objectives. Functional areas of the business compete with each other for company resources. The total communications budget made available to a particular area is a clear measure of the corporate commitment to and expectation of a particular activity. As a result of this decision, upward or downward revisions of the goals established earlier may be necessary. To this point no one has made any decisions on specific promotional actions. The marketing manager operating in consultation with other senior executives has determined the goals and objectives of the particular business in light of the market situation and the promotional resources allocated.

Tentative Budget Mix:
Communications Elements

At this point management makes a *tentative allocation of the communications resources* available to each of the communications elements in the program: personal selling, advertising, sales promotion, and public relations. The marketing manager makes this allocation in light of his or her knowledge and understanding of the effectiveness of each element in achieving the specified marketing objectives. In making these tentative decisions, the manager seeks to reflect the likely market response to each of these promotional elements individually, as well as the expected synergistic impact of the various promotional mixes. In other words, the marketing manager seeks to formulate a coordinated plan that uses each promotional element most effectively. Note that these are tentative allocations, subject to later change as information on the specific actions and their costs becomes available. The manager may also adjust them to account for new insights gained from fresh assessments of the market environment.

Detailed Decisions: Each Promotional Element

The fifth step involves a series of *detailed decisions about each promotional element*. Typically, specialists in each field provide detailed plans and decisions within each promotional area. The manager must play a key role in coordinating these activities to keep them consistent with the overall objectives and within the budget allocations. These decisions embrace the selection of the target audience, the communications goals, the message content and distribution, and the resultant allocation of the particular element's budget to these specific tasks. Since each element will probably play a different role in the overall promotional plan, the specific details noted above may be quite distinct for each promotional activity. For example, personal selling may aim at the central buying office of major chains with the objective of achieving certain levels of stocking, whereas advertising for the same product may address users to build awareness and induce initial trial. Of course, the message content and distribution in each of these elements would also differ.

Feedback

The sixth step injects *feedback* into the sequence. In light of the detailed plans and their anticipated costs and market responses, management may have to make changes in key decisions. These changes could involve the overall marketing goals, the total budget, the promotional mix, or the detailed plans for each promotional element. The marketing manager would intend to reconcile and integrate the detailed plans for each promotional activity with overall goals and financial constraints. Usually, the manager will adjust the tentative budget mix or the detailed plans; on rare occasions he or she may have to change the marketing objectives or the overall budget to reconcile discrepancies between desired results and available resources.

Implementation

The next step is the *implementation* or execution *of the promotional plan,* as management has finally determined it in the previous phase. We often naively assume that since the plans have now been made and approved, someone will carry them out in the prescribed manner. However, this is not the way it usually works. Now a key responsibility of the marketing manager is to coordinate the activities in many parts of the organization to ensure that individuals accomplish these tasks in a thorough, professional, and timely manner. It is easy to envision how small details that have been overlooked can limit the effectiveness of the most creative programs (a beautiful four-color sales brochure that contains no company address or phone number except on an order form separate from the brochure, or an in-ad coupon so small that it is nearly impossible to fill out). Keeping track of the details may be a deadly bore after the challenges of the planning stages, but it is a vital step if the goals are to become reality. To get a sense of the implementation activities, let us look at the basic sequence of activities.

Developing the Creative Concept

The *creative concept* or message is a direct outgrowth of the situation analysis and communications goals. Miller Lite's "Tastes Great, Less Filling," Ford's "Quality Is Job 1," Allstate Insurance's "You're in Good Hands with Allstate," and Wheaties' "Breakfast of Champions" are examples of themes that derive from well-defined positioning strategies. This is a challenging creative task, since the most effective messages or themes must be simple, clear, appropriate, and easily communicated in a variety of forms and media. (Chapter 10 examines message formulation.)

Executing the Theme

The *execution of the theme* in a consistent and coordinated manner in each of the promotional forms—advertising, personal selling, sales promotion, and public relations—is the next significant stage in the implementation process. It involves the preparation of such things as print and broadcast ads, point-of-purchase displays, catalogs, brochures, sales presentations, news releases, and a host of other specific materials to deliver the principal message properly. In one sense this is an effort to translate and adapt the theme to the specific advantages and constraints of each promotional element. It is at this stage that contradiction between strategy and execution most often occurs.

Preparing the Final Materials

The *preparation of final materials* is an integrating effort to ensure that each of the elements of the promotional program is complete and that together they present a consistent and coherent message and image to the selected market. It is here that the manager makes any corrections and adjustments before committing the substantial resources to initiate the full program.

Initiating the Program

The *initiation of the program* can take place in one of two modes—either in a *rollout approach* where the program goes into effect region by region or on a *one-shot basis* where a national or worldwide introduction goes forward at one time.

Most of the large packaged goods companies (Procter & Gamble, General Foods, Coca-Cola) use the rollout approach extensively, whereas the major industrial firms (IBM, Xerox, Norton) tend to make national introductions. A rollout strategy allows further testing and tuning of the program, risks fewer promotional dollars, permits a slower buildup of production capacity to meet demand, and contains self-financing potential in that sales from one region provide cash flow for subsequent regional introductions. The national approach limits opportunity for competitive response even before a definite establishment of one's own market position minimizes negative customer reaction, since the product is available equally to all customers, and it provides a most efficient use of promotional resources because appropriate media are likely to be national in coverage.

The initiation stage is the final phase of the implementation process. On the other hand, since the development and execution of promotional programs are ongoing, repetitive processes, it is also the first stage for data input from which the development and execution of subsequent promotional strategies will proceed. This will occur if the organization is measuring and monitoring the results of its efforts and taking the necessary steps to change, redirect, or otherwise adapt, based on the information provided by the monitoring process. Promotional program evaluation and control is the subject of Chapter 18, and we will discuss it in depth at that time. Yet we should not leave the discussion of the implementation process without emphasizing its continuous, adaptive nature as it regularly assimilates new information from an active and effective monitoring system.

Measurement and Evaluation

The final step is the *measurement and evaluation of the communications program*, as implemented. Measurement or assessment of the level of performance should begin as soon as the program has been launched to monitor progress toward goals. Tuning and adjustments may then be possible even while the program is in progress. The marketing manager must gauge sales and communications effects to evaluate the accomplishments of the promotional elements individually and collectively as well as to provide insight for the planning and execution of the next period's program. The information can be obtained from the company's sales records, from outside services such as A. C. Nielsen and SAMI, or by special studies to determine communications effects (such as awareness, recall, and attitude changes). Other measurable forms of response may be inquiries received or coupons redeemed. There are many ways to track performance; the key action for the marketing manager is to establish the measurement system and use the data it provides to improve the promotional strategy in subsequent periods.

Testing and evaluating at each stage should clearly be an integral part of the implementation process. Since the company is about to commit significant resources—financial, human, and physical—to a promotional program, it is prudent for management to test and evaluate the market response to the program and each element thereof as carefully as possible before expending these resources.

The form of the testing should fit the specific aspects under examination and should go forward with serious regard for the quality and utility of the results. A range of techniques will meet the defined needs, including focus groups, deep personal interviews, laboratory experiments, split-run tests, media tests, and full-scale test marketing in selected areas. The reader can find detailed discussions of these research techniques in several marketing research texts, a few of which we suggest as references.[6]

We must highlight another consideration. Research is only valuable if it proceeds in a professional and competent manner and decision makers respect its findings and incorporate them into the decision process. The responsible managers must be willing to modify their approach if the research dictates such action. There is no greater futility or waste of precious resources than a serious research effort whose findings are ignored. Individuals responsible for promotional activities must be open minded to the contributions of research before undertaking major efforts.

The process we have described above and shown in Exhibit 2-3 is fundamental to the development of a sound promotional strategy. The sequence of decisions may vary, the review and revision process may be more or less formal, and the degree of detail may differ, but the most successful organizations give careful consideration to each of these specific decisions. To make the necessary choices leading to an effective and efficient promotional strategy requires sound analysis, creative concepts, and well-conceived management practices.

Beyond the steps we have highlighted above, there are two other factors we must spell out: (1) the assignment of tasks and responsibilities to both departments and individuals and (2) the establishment of the program schedule and timetable. Too often these important details receive only lip service, after the "heady wines" of market analysis and strategy formulation have been deeply drunk. Still, it is likely that one can trace a program's success or failure to these tactical plans as well as to the strategic concept.

Assignment of Tasks and Responsibilities

In most organizations, the assignment of particular elements of a promotional program to a specific department is a rather straightforward decision; in others it may not be so. Problems can arise when promotional elements require a joint effort of two or more departments.[7] The preparation of product catalogs, sales manuals, point-of-purchase displays, and application notes are typical examples. The department responsible for layout, artwork, or photography may not be the same one responsible for writing copy. Furthermore, when a subordinate takes the responsibility assignment one level of detail further to the individual who will perform the task, another issue surfaces. How does that person determine what priority should be given to which assignment, as most promotional specialists must time-share their efforts among multiple projects? Effective coordination of the overall promotional program, as well as those activities that require joint participation, suggests very strongly that management must clearly define the task and responsibility assignments.

Establishment of Program Schedule and Timetable

As we have seen, promotional programs involve many diverse elements, the responsibilities of numerous individuals both inside and outside the company. To achieve the objectives at the time specified, within the budget established, *synchronization of the major elements of the promotional strategy is essential*. For this, each of the steps or stages leading to the completion of a particular promotional activity must be fulfilled in a timely and efficient manner. The more comprehensive the program at hand, the greater the number of pieces of the puzzle that must be fitted together. To help define and coordinate the relationships among these various subtasks, several planning techniques have been developed, among them Gantt charts and PERT networks (Program Evaluation and Review Technique). Such techniques allow management to graphically plot a specific activity or series of activities, from start to completion date. Management can then compare actual progress with the plan. By showing when the sequential steps of a project should be completed to achieve a predetermined objective, these devices help management make sure that activities are performed on schedule. For complex projects like complete promotional programs that include many activities, some of which can occur simultaneously while others must be completed before others can start, techniques such as Gantt charts and PERT networks can be invaluable planning tools.[8]

SUMMARY

Managing the promotional effort involves several different activities. Planning is fundamental to the promotional program. Management must plan for the introduction of a product, for the revision of marketing strategy, and during the annual planning and budgeting cycle. To implement a plan, the proper organization must be in place. The two most common organizational types are the functional and product forms. Promotional strategies rarely go forward using only company personnel. Outside services such as advertising agencies, marketing research firms, and public relations counselors provide valuable assistance.

Actual development of promotional strategy involves a wide range of activities and decisions, including analyzing the company situation, establishing objectives, setting the budget, deciding on the specific elements of the promotional mix (requiring decisions on advertising, personal selling, sales promotion, and public relations), executing the plan, and monitoring results. And all of this has to be done with consumers and target markets in mind. Efficiency comes from properly assigning tasks and responsibilities to departments and individuals and from establishing program schedules and timetables.

Execution of the promotional strategy requires considerable skill and strict attention to an orderly process of developing the creative message, executing the theme, preparing the final materials, and initiating the program.

All of what we have said justifies this conclusion: Managing a promotional program, from planning through execution, entails a great deal of work. The planner must have extensive understanding of the capabilities of the separate promotion areas: advertising, personal selling, sales promotion, and public relations. The manager achieves maximum effect when each element complements the others, and when the right communications tool comes into play at the right time. The successful manager has learned how to juggle all these activities—and not drop any of them.

REVIEW AND DISCUSSION QUESTIONS

1. Explain the concept of a promotional program.
2. Describe the two major risks involved when several promotional efforts are occurring simultaneously in one total program.
3. When are promotional programs likely to be developed?

4. *A new promotional program may be necessary when the marketing strategy changes. When does this occur? Explain.*

5. *Why is the organizational structure important to the promotional program?*

6. *Compare and contrast the two major types of organizational structure for promotion. What are the advantages and disadvantages of each?*

7. *In your opinion, what role should the product play in developing a promotional program? Explain.*

8. *What are some of the contributions that outside agencies make to a company's promotional program? How would you go about searching for outside services?*

9. *Describe the major outside services used in developing a promotional program.*

10. *Give an overview of the development process for a promotional program.*

11. *Explain the importance of synchronization of individual promotion efforts. How is this achieved?*

12. *What are the four stages in the implementation process? Give an example of each stage.*

13. *What is meant by a rollout strategy? Cite examples.*

14. *Compare and contrast rollout and national strategies, including the advantages and limitations of each.*

NOTES

1. Alfred D. Chandler, Jr., *Strategy and Structure* (Cambridge, Mass.: MIT Press, 1962).

2. R. W. Ackerman, "How Companies Respond to Social Demands," *Harvard Business Review*, 51 (1973), 88–99.

3. Michael Ray, "A Decision Sequence Analysis of Developments in Marketing Communications," *Journal of Marketing*, January 1973, pp. 29–38. For an excellent discussion of an alternative promotion decision sequence, see David J. Luck and O. C. Ferrell, *Marketing Strategy and Plans*, 2nd ed. (Englewood Cliffs, N.J.: Prentice-Hall, 1985), pp. 414–31.

4. Victor P. Buell, *Marketing Management* (New York: McGraw-Hill, 1984), pp. 210–12.

5. Philip Kotler, *Marketing Management*, 5th ed. (Englewood Cliffs, N.J.: Prentice-Hall, 1984), p. 611.

6. Harper W. Boyd, Ralph Westfall, and Stanley F. Stasch, *Marketing Research*, 6th ed. (Homewood, Ill.: Richard D. Irwin, 1985); Raymond Barker, *Marketing Research* (Reston, Va.: Reston, 1983); David J. Luck, Hugh G. Wales, Donald A. Taylor, and Ronald S. Rubin, *Marketing Research* (Englewood Cliffs, N.J.: Prentice-Hall, 1983); Thomas Kinnear and James R. Taylor, *Marketing Research* (New York: McGraw-Hill,

1983); Donald R. Lehmann, *Marketing Research and Analysis*, 2nd ed. (Homewood, Ill.: Richard D. Irwin, 1985); and Pamela L. Alreck and Robert B. Settle, *The Survey Research Handbook* (Homewood, Ill.: Richard D. Irwin, 1985).

7. Alan Dubinsky, Thomas Barry, and Roger A. Kerin, "The Sales Advertising Interface in Promotion Planning," *Journal of Advertising*, 10, No. 3 (1981), 35–41.

8. For a comprehensive discussion of Gantt, PERT, and other project-planning tools, see M. Spinney, *Elements of Project Management: Plan Scheduling and Control* (Englewood Cliffs, N.J.: Prentice-Hall, 1981); and Clifford F. Gray, *Essentials of Project Management* (Princeton, N.J.: Petrocelli Books, 1981).

3

The
Communications
Process

The rage of the 1983 Christmas season was Coleco's Cabbage Patch Kids. Pushing, shoving customers grabbed the dolls as soon as they appeared on the selling floor. A parent flew across the Atlantic to London to get one!

The phenomenal success of the Cabbage Patch Kids did not result from a string of lucky events but from a series of timely, effective marketing and communications activities. In August 1982 Coleco bought the rights to mass-produce the dolls after learning of the intense popularity of the limited number of the original, custom-made ones. Monitoring activities in the marketplace allowed the company to identify an opportunity, but the mere ownership of the doll rights did not guarantee financial rewards. The conversion of potential to actual sales depended on how well the company promoted the Cabbage Patch Kids. Coleco went to a logical source for ideas; it conducted informal group interviews with consumers in the fall of that year, listened closely to comments and suggestions, and came away with some valuable promotion ideas. The consumers were not the only important audience in a promotion campaign. Retailer cooperation and enthusiasm were essential to ensure high visibility and availability of the product. The Cabbage Patch Kids were heavily promoted in a February 1983 New York trade show. A publicity campaign was launched shortly after February. Advertising, well before the holiday season, presented the doll to children. The distinctive facial features and accompanying adoption papers were so impressive that the doll made almost every live kid's Christmas list. Once these lists got to Santa Claus, Christmas sales of Coleco's doll soared to over $20 million.[1]

Communications—the flow of information from one party to another—is essential for marketing success. Without it, there can be no transactions among manufacturer, middlemen, and marketplace. Obviously a buyer cannot purchase a product or service if its existence and its attributes are unknown. A seller cannot put together an attractive offering without listening to the needs and wants of the marketplace. Effective distribution networks cannot occur if manufacturers do not communicate with middlemen. *Communications is the activity that produces interaction between the marketer and the market.*

Effective marketing communications requires an understanding of the process. In this chapter we describe the process at two levels. First we present some typical *marketing communications systems*, the information networks that exist for the purpose of facilitating exchange or transaction between firms and their customers. Then we present a model to explain the major factors that influence the effectiveness of *communications between two elements* (like a sales rep and a client prospect) in the system.

MARKETING COMMUNICATIONS SYSTEMS

As we noted in Chapter 1, success of the *entire* promotion campaign is based on coordination of the individual promotion activities including, for example, advertising to the ultimate purchaser, personal selling directed toward wholesalers, sales promotion in support of retailers, and public relations to build goodwill. Success requires coordination in terms of *what* to do, *whom* to contact, and *when* to contact. With that in mind, we can clearly state that the promotion manager must fully understand the process of information flow.

The marketing information flow can be simple or it can be complex depending on the number of parties and their linkages. Our presentation will concentrate on the relationships between and among three basic units—the manufacturer, the middleman, and the marketplace. To simplify our presentation, we will define *manufacturer* as any producer or originator of a product or service. The *middleman* unit represents any and all intermediaries including agents, merchant wholesalers, retailers, and so on. The *marketplace* includes not only the buyer but also the users who may not have bought but still came into possession of the product.

Exhibit 3-1 graphically illustrates three possible communications systems. While there may be other scenarios, these three represent the range of communications possibilities.

Simple Systems

In some marketing situations, the major communications activity is that between the manufacturer and the marketplace. This is fairly common in industrial marketing where the number of potential customers is limited

EXHIBIT 3-1 *Marketing Communications Systems*

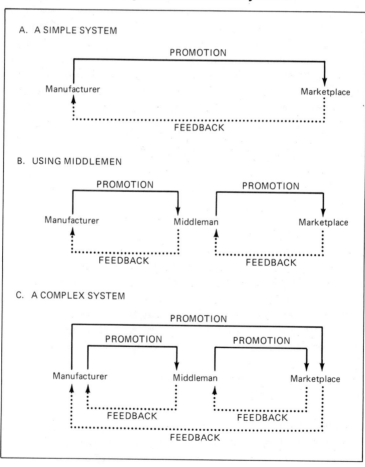

or the value of the sale is sufficiently high that direct market contact is effective and cost efficient. For example, Xerox uses its own sales force and business advertising to solicit business from its commercial customers. The expense and time required to contact prospects is offset by the sizable revenue that comes from the sale of a copying system.

In consumer marketing, manufacturer-marketplace contact without the benefit of intermediaries takes place at a national level, although it is more likely to occur when a company operates in a limited geographical market. Direct contact with the national marketplace can be costly because of the number and geographical dispersion of customers, but some companies find this approach quite successful. Many of them depend on advertising; others use personal selling. L. L. Bean, the Maine-based manufacturer of outdoor apparel and footwear, relies on its catalog to reach and sell to markets across the country. On the other hand, the Encyclopedia Britannica uses personal selling as the principal means of presenting its relatively expensive product.

Use of Middlemen

Sometimes the manufacturer cannot effectively communicate with the marketplace. It may not have the financial resources to underwrite such an extensive promotion effort, or it may lack capabilities such as a trained sales force. An intermediary comes into play when direct contact between manufacturer and marketplace is not feasible.

The second diagram in Exhibit 3-1 illustrates one role that an intermediary can play in the communications process. The manufacturer's communications effort aims toward the intermediary, who in turn communicates with the marketplace.

This is typical of undifferentiated items in both industrial and consumer marketing. A manufacturer of materials-handling equipment such as conveyor systems is likely to use independent sales agents and brokers to reach its end market. Conveyor systems do not differ significantly from one company to another, so the manufacturer would find it difficult to develop market insistence for that product. Since conveyor system purchases are infrequent, and the purchasers are numerous and dispersed geographically, the maintenance of a company sales force to ensure complete market coverage is too expensive. The intermediary then becomes critical in creating an exchange. Agents and brokers give the manufacturer necessary market coverage. They know their territory, they know their customers, and therefore they are much more effective communicators than the manufacturer. The manufacturer's promotion effort, through trade advertising and possibly salespersons, strives to stimulate agent and broker willingness and enthusiasm in representing the company's line. We can visualize the communications network as follows:

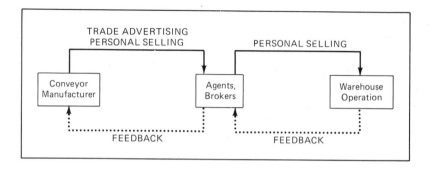

Complex Systems

Communications lines may be numerous, as we see in the third diagram in Exhibit 3-1. The manufacturer not only attempts to solicit middleman business but also communicates with the marketplace in support of intermediaries. Concurrently, the intermediaries communicate with the marketplace.

The communications environment for a national producer of frozen foods might be as follows:

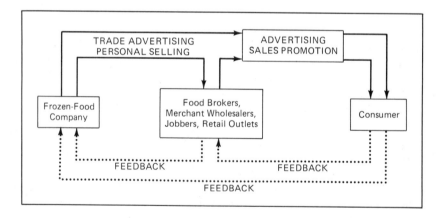

The producer must get the cooperation of such middlemen as brokers, merchant wholesalers, rack jobbers, and retail outlets. To accomplish this, company sales reps visit the middlemen, there is advertising in trade publications, and there are promotional incentives such as special point-of-purchase displays. Simultaneously, consumer advertising and sales promotion such as couponing or free samples move toward the marketplace. Retail stores will initiate their own promotion, newspaper advertising for example, or special coupon redemption policies.

Understanding the System
Is Important

The marketing communications process can be simple or complex. The degree of complexity depends largely on the conditions for marketing exchange activity. Companies operating in industrial markets with distinctive products may find that direct communication with the marketplace is effective. On the other hand, low-priced, consumer convenience goods may be marketed in a setting where there is extensive communications activity among the manufacturer, intermediaries, and marketplace.

Regardless of the degree of complexity, the exchange of goods and services in the marketplace results from cooperation among the major parties. The cooperation comes from effective communications. Cooperation may result from the manufacturer's listening to the marketplace and then persuading it that the manufacturer offers something appropriate for its needs and wants. Or in a complex system, cooperation must come about between the manufacturer and intermediaries, manufacturer and marketplace, and intermediaries and marketplace.

In the next section we present a general model of the communications process. In doing so, we look at the major determinants of effective communications between the source of messages and the receiver of messages.

THE INTERPERSONAL
COMMUNICATIONS PROCESS

We have presented an overview of various marketing communications networks, trying to make it clear that effective communication is essential to marketing exchange. In this section we take a closer look at the communications process between two units. Exhibit 3-2 depicts the framework for this discussion.

The communications process begins with a source or communicator. This source has an idea or concept to convey to a receiver. To ensure that the receiver—the communications target—will, in fact, receive the idea, the source formulates or encodes a message expressing the idea in words, sounds, or visuals significant to the receiver. Upon completion of encoding, the sender causes the message to be transmitted through a medium such as television, newspapers, or a sales representative. Upon receipt of the message, the process of interpreting or decoding the source's message begins. The receiver's understanding of the message generates an action or response.

There is the possibility of distortion during the communications process. "Noise" is an external factor interfering with the fidelity of message transmission, a disruptive factor not controllable by the marketer. For example, an advertiser buys space in a newspaper and the editor places the ad

EXHIBIT 3-2 A Communications Model

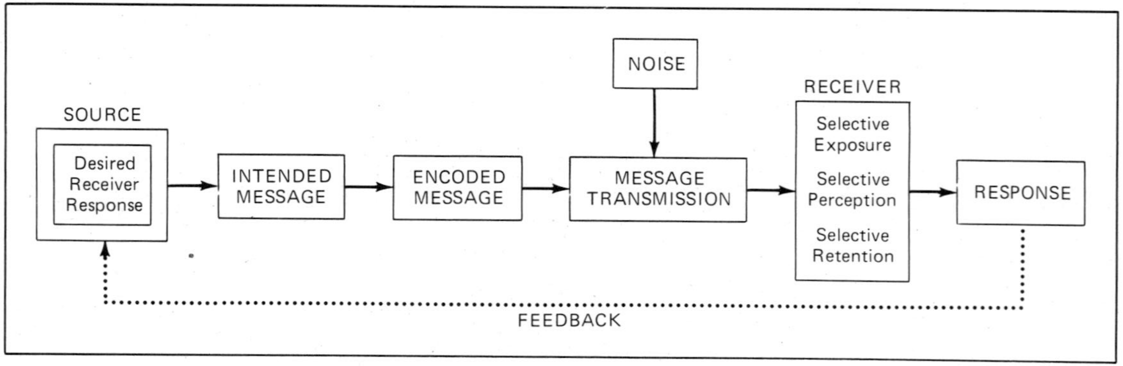

in a section that has poor readership. A radio commercial loses its effectiveness because the listener is engaged in other activities such as homework assignments and has the radio on only for background entertainment.

Let us now consider some detailed descriptions of factors that enhance or restrict the quality of communications.

The Source

Since the audience or message recipient is the pivotal element in the success or failure of communications, our definition of the source must be based largely on the perspective of the message recipient if we are to fully understand influences in the communication process. The *source* is the originator and advocate of the message idea as the receiver sees it. The perceived source may be an individual like a salesperson or celebrity endorser, it may be an organization like Underwriters' Laboratories, or it may be an advertising vehicle like *Good Housekeeping*.

Often the perceived source may not be the same as the actual source. A person watching a television commercial about Chevrolet automobiles would probably correctly perceive the message source to be Chevrolet. In an advertisement for a consumer food product like decaffeinated coffee, however, the audience may perceive the message source to be a celebrity spokesperson rather than the actual seller of the product.

Why is it important to recognize that a message may be perceived as coming from sources other than the actual sponsor? As we will see in the subsequent paragraphs, persuasion to accept a message is facilitated or hindered by the *believability*, or lack of it, attributable to the source. In situations where persuasion is necessary, the marketer may facilitate the task by engaging a source considered believable by the audience. For example, Franklin, relatively unknown to the marketplace for its boxing gear, enlisted the services of the famous boxer Sugar Ray Leonard, someone with a high-credibility factor (probably much more than just the company's name) in promoting such equipment. Let us now look at this issue of source credibility more closely.

The Importance of Source Credibility

The extent to which the originator of a message must be believable relates to two factors: the communications objective and the background of the audience.

The communications objective. Believability—the extent to which ideas will be accepted by the receiver based simply on their source—is especially necessary when the communications objective is persuasion or attitude change.[2] The marketer seeks to bring about such change by presenting as many favorable opinions about the product or product performance as possible, hoping to affect brand choice by the consumer.

In that connection, the marketer knows that the opinion a buyer holds about the advocate of a message can affect the opinion one holds about the message itself. Consider the consumer who is thinking about buying a color television set. A recommendation to "buy the Sony Trinitron" will be more acceptable coming from *Consumer Reports*, the publication of an independent testing organization, than from a magazine advertisement paid for by the Sony Corporation.

As we will see in Chapter 7, many marketing communications activities do not set out to persuade but to raise awareness and disseminate simple factual information. The aim of advertising for a convenience item like a candy bar is to instill brand familiarity. The name that comes to mind readily directs product choice, not the complicated processing of product attributes. In such a case, persuasion is not necessary and the importance of source credibility for an effective campaign is low.[3]

Audience background. If a person does not have the knowledge or skills to evaluate a message, then he or she is likely to determine the acceptability of that message because of the believability of the source behind the message. For example, consider two different persons in the market for a personal computer. One person is an electrical engineer with a knowledge of computer science, while the other person operates a small retail pet store. The pet store operator will probably be more dependent on the words and thoughts of a salesperson than our engineer. Our engineer, because of a computer-related background, is able to analyze by himself or herself all the "bits and bytes" information a salesperson presents. The pet store owner's acceptance or rejection of recommendations will probably not depend on knowledge of facts but on how much the pet store owner believes the salesperson. Persons who have a high degree of uncertainty in their decision making are likely to rely on credible external sources of information for reducing doubt and assisting in the final judgment.[4]

Determinants of Credibility

When one needs *source credibility*, the marketer must ask, What makes for credibility? Source credibility is a function of two major characteristics, trustworthiness and expertise.[5] *Trustworthiness* is the degree of confidence that a receiver attaches to the source's intent, whereas *expertise* refers to the perception of the source's qualifications to make valid or correct statements. One sees a source as highly credible when the source is considerate of the interests of the receiver and has the knowledge and experience to present the facts accurately.

Trustworthiness. In attempting to persuade someone to accept a position on an issue or engage in a certain behavior, the sender of the message must bear in mind that the receiver is not only evaluating the merits of the arguments presented in the message but also making judgments about the motives and considerations of the sender.[6] Sources who project a high degree of trustworthiness are more likely to be successful in persuasion than sources who do not project such an image. The implication for the marketer is rather obvious. To increase the chances of getting the market to like the product and ultimately purchase it, the sponsoring company and its representatives should have or develop an image of trust among the target audience.

The audience is likely to consider a source trustworthy if it holds the following perceptions:

> The source is objective and informative rather than biased and manipulative.
>
> The source is one who understands the receiver's interests and situation.
>
> The source's principal concern in having the receiver adopt the advocated position is the interest and welfare of the receiver.

If a seller were to tell a prospective customer that his product is the best product that money can buy, there might be a little skepticism about the message. What else would one expect to hear from a company whose intent is to make money? On the other hand, if an organization or a person, independent of the seller, were to make a similar statement, then the chances of message acceptance would increase. Chicken of the Sea tuna once advertised itself as "the only leading tuna with the U.S. government seal of approval." The ad went on to say that it was the only brand that voluntarily submitted to Department of Commerce inspection. The implication of the ad was that the claims of top quality and wholesomeness were not mere advertising puffery but a clear statement of fact.

Without the element of trust, market transactions cannot take place. One of the major hurdles a salesperson encounters is the natural tendency on the part of the prospective client to be defensive. By definition, the salesperson is one whose sole objective is to get a sale at the expense of the buyer's budget, and the buyer knows it. Attempts to portray salespersons as persons who are trustworthy include the use of titles such as account executive, the use of letters of recommendation from satisfied clients, and the selection and assignment of salespersons who are familiar with the needs and wants of the prospective customers. Additionally, salespersons who are perceived to be similar to the prospect are more likely to be successful in persuasion than salespersons who are not. Similarity may be determined along a variety of dimensions including physical characteristics (e.g., race and age), group affiliation (e.g., the Masons and Chamber of Commerce) and interests (e.g., music and golf).

In an effort to show the audience that they can trust the message claims, some advertisers use the testimonies of "real" consumers. Examples of this approach are television commercials using the "hidden camera," "overheard conversations," or "man-on-the-street interviews." Such commercials have included on-the-scene laundromat tests of detergents, supermarket taste tests for soft drinks and peanut butter, and informal conversations recorded during laboratory tests. The main characters in such commercials are very similar to the audience of the message and generally give the impression that their comments on product performance are spontaneous and unrehearsed. For example, some of Tylenol's television commercials after the 1982 cyanide poisoning incidents used on-the-street settings in which the interviewed consumers expressed confidence in the product.

Expertise. In general, sources perceived as having high levels of expertise are likely to be more persuasive than those without. An *expert* is a person one considers to be very competent on a subject; he or she is capable of delivering accurate information.

The marketer who can project an image of expertise in a product, industry, or problem area is in a position to influence what the marketplace considers good or bad. If a consumer sees someone as an expert, the consumer will listen when that expert speaks on topics that call on that expertise. And when one needs information to solve a problem, one seeks out the expert on that subject for immediate help as well as for assistance in making decisions. Consider again the area of computers. A company contemplating the purchase of computer equipment is very likely to place IBM on the list of potential vendors automatically. Why? Because of the product expertise that IBM has developed in that area.

To be acknowledged as an expert, a source must have proper credentials. People use a number of criteria to judge the competence of an individual. Sometimes demographic characteristics such as age or educational status influence the audience's perceptions. For example, a prospective client's assessment of a sales representative's ability to solve a highly technical production problem will be different if the sales representative is a former engineer, 45 years old, with over twenty years of relevant industry experience, rather than 22 years old and fresh out of college with a degree in history.

Experience is one of the most popular measures of expertise. Race car drivers endorse a wide range of automotive products like tires, oil, and batteries; professional sports celebrities are spokespersons for tennis rackets, football gear, and basketball shoes.

Where experience is not entirely obvious to the audience, professional titles or certifications may help. The insurance industry designates qualified persons with C.L.U., Chartered Life Underwriter; the accounting profession has the CPA, Certified Public Accountant; and the legal profession certifies a lawyer's competence through admittance to the bar.

The Message

The response of the receiver depends very much on the *message*. The right response will probably take place if the source of communications has taken steps to ensure that the information the receiver gets is the right information.

To understand the critical phases in communications, one should visualize the development of messages as consisting of two distinct but complementary stages. The first stage calls for the source to determine what should be conveyed to trigger a response in the appropriate audience. This is the intended message or idea. Then one must find the best form for that intended message. The result is called the encoded message.

Since Chapter 10 discusses message development in detail, we will provide just an overview here.

The Intended Message

The communicator's objective is to get the receiver to respond in a particular manner. And the *intended message*—the idea that the communicator wishes to convey to and have accepted by the receiver—should be the direct cause of the desired results. If the objective is to raise awareness, then the message should increase the receiver's familiarity with the brand. If the objective is to change attitudes, then the message should cause the receiver to reformulate his or her opinions.

The identification of the appropriate intended message comes from market analysis. Such analysis researches the underlying determinants of decisions by the target audience. The manufacturer of toothpaste might determine the intended message in the following manner. Research into toothpaste purchase patterns determines, for example, that the target group selects a toothpaste for decay prevention. To influence the group's brand choice, an advertisement would stress decay prevention capabilities.

We cannot overemphasize the importance of identifying the right message idea. If the communicator totally misunderstands the market and chooses an ineffective theme, no amount of creative expression will lead to successful communications.

The Encoded Message

The communicator may achieve effective expression of the intended message by the careful selection of symbols—perceptible elements like colors or sounds as representations of abstractions like joy or nostalgia—and the manner of presenting the message theme. The process of *encoding the message* is the process of selecting the right symbols to represent the message idea.

These symbols, when seen, heard, felt, sniffed, or tasted, should convey the intended meaning.

Written or spoken words play a major role in transmitting ideas. A copywriter with an extensive vocabulary and a creative way with words can produce a memorable slogan, an attention-getting headline, or a suggestive brand name for a new product. An articulate salesperson can take a highly abstract product idea and express it in a concrete way.

Visual symbols such as color, size, shape, and texture are sometimes necessary because the written or spoken word is not adequate for communications, especially when the message is a mood or feeling. For example, it is easier to *show* a person savoring a freshly brewed cup of coffee than it is to describe it with words. The notion of "Miller Time" comes across best through the visual images we see on the television screen. Illustrations enhance the point that words might deliver.

The use of sound can be to the communicator's advantage. Catchy jingles and background sound effects contribute to fuller expression of the message.[7]

The appeal to the sense of taste to convey the benefits of food products is a common technique. It is not unusual to see professional demonstrators at supermarkets handing out taste samples of such items as crackers or cheese spreads.

The receiver's ability to interpret scents has been the focus of some communications efforts. A few years ago the seller of powdered mixers for alcohol promoted its pina colada product with the use of scratch-and-sniff swatches in magazine ads.[8]

Message presentation. The message idea can be presented in a number of different ways that we will classify according to their appeal and the tone of their appeal. Appeal can be emotional or rational. The tone can be light or serious.

	Appeal			
	Emotional		Rational	
	negative	positive	simple	complex
Light				
T O N E				
Serious				

Emotional appeals stir up feelings within the audience by presenting the message through psychological or social motivators. Rational appeals present the message in factual, objective terms. Emotional appeals can be cast in either negative or positive form. For example, an ad for life insurance may stress the dire financial consequences to one's dependents upon the death of the underinsured, principal wage earner. Or it may stress the feeling of security and responsibility experienced by someone who is adequately insured. The message (buy life insurance) is the same in both instances, but its presentation is different.

Rational appeals can be simple or complex. A telephone directory ad is an example of a simple rational appeal. The information is straightforward— the name of the company, a general classification of its products or services, its telephone number, and its address. On the other hand, a sales rep's presentation to a prospective multimillion dollar purchaser of industrial robots will include technical specifications about the company's product and a detailed comparison with those of competitors.

The emotional or rational appeal can assume a light or a serious tone. IBM used a rational appeal with a light tone, a presentation in a cheery or humorous setting, in advertising the IBM PC microcomputer. The Charlie Chaplin-like character in various business situations created an enjoyable and entertaining atmosphere in which to present the product attributes. In contrast, the Smith Barney, Harris & Upham Company advertisement used a spokesperson who thoughtfully and soberly talked about the investment house's making money the old-fashioned way—earning it.

The combination of appeal and tone in communications should reflect the decision process one wants to influence. As we will see in Chapter 4, differences in decision making are considerable—sometimes uncomplicated, sometimes not. If the decision maker is not interested in devoting time and effort to processing information, an ad that presents product facts in a serious tone will not attract and hold interest. A light, entertaining ad with simple information may. On the other hand, some decision makers, such as those searching for a new family car, are highly involved in information processing. They are attentive to product information. And they would most likely be willing to pay attention to a presentation of product attributes in a serious tone.

Message Transmission

The *transmission decision* is the selection of the proper vehicle for delivering the message. In advertising, the transmission decision revolves around the selection of media. In personal selling, the transmission decision involves selecting the salesperson. Since subsequent chapters go into detail about the major channels and vehicles for communications, we will present an overview here of the factors that influence the selection of transmission channels.

There are three major categories involved in the selection of channels of communication: the audience, the message, and the characteristics of the channels under consideration.

Different people have different information-processing habits, reflected in the media to which they pay attention and the occasions on which they make themselves available to communications.[9] For example, individuals who are especially interested in home improvements are likely to subscribe to *Popular Mechanics*. The avid photographer will read a publication such as *Modern Photography*. Not only does the background of the audience reflect the type of media it turns to for information, the background may also determine the time when it seeks information. For example, the daily routine of commuting to and from work by automobile means that radio's largest audiences occur during the morning and afternoon rush hours.

The implication of the varying media habits across audiences is that a significant portion of the communications campaign's efficiency depends on whether the message goes over the right channels at the right time. Arbitrary development of a plan to transmit a message, without a careful consideration of the audience's media habits, may mean that the audience will not get the message. The communicator must answer a fundamental question, Where and when is my audience going to look for information about the topic I am promoting?

Characteristics of the intended and encoded message affect the choice of transmission vehicles. Sometimes legal and social constraints on the message topic dictate the availability of channels. For example, manufacturers of cigarettes cannot promote their product on television. Sometimes the creative expression of the message precludes or dictates certain vehicles. A message relying heavily on action-oriented visuals will not go on radio. Or an ad that must make use of scratch-and-sniff material must appear in print.

Finally, the characteristics of the channels under consideration determine the effectiveness of message delivery. As we will see in Chapter 9, each channel has its strengths and weaknesses. A medium's technical limitations and its role as a source of information for an audience determine whether a vehicle is right for the communications plan. For example, a major technical limitation of newspapers is that they provide relatively poor color reproduction. This drawback as a communications vehicle is offset by the fact that many people consider the newspaper a primary information source for current events, including announcements of special sales.

The Receiver: Getting the Message

So far in this survey of the communications process, we have described the impact of the source, the message, and the transmission channel. Let us now concentrate on the target of all the communications effort, the *receiver*. First we will discuss the determinants that lead a receiver to attend to, interpret, and retain the message. Then we will briefly survey the influences that shape the receiver's response to the message. The response process is discussed in depth in the next chapter.

Perception of the Message

Success in communications cannot occur unless the receiver perceives the existence of the message and interprets the message in the desired manner. Two perceptual concepts are important in the planning of communications: perception is selective, and perception is subjective.

Individuals do not pay attention to each of the thousands of messages present and available every day. Think of all the billboard ads, the promotional signs in store windows, the radio commercials, and the announcements of sales in newspapers that you never notice. Think of all the television commercials you elect not to watch in favor of a trip to the refrigerator. Or think about a recent automobile trip where the radio played song after song and commercial after commercial, of which you recall only a handful.

Selective exposure and *selective attention* protect the receiver from an overload of information. A person, no matter how intelligent, has a limited capacity to store information and as a result seeks and pays attention to only useful information.

The concept of selective exposure means that a person, because of actual choice or certain restrictions in lifestyle, will be available to some communications channels but not others. A woman who is interested in the latest trends in fashion may choose to subscribe to *Cosmopolitan* magazine. Because of the route that she uses to go to work, this same woman may not see the billboard ads for cosmetics positioned along the major highway leading into the city. For the marketer who targets this woman, the billboard space would not be a wise media buy.

Transmitting the message through a vehicle favored by the audience does not necessarily mean that the message will surely be noticed. Confronted with a large amount of information, the receiver will pay attention to some but either consciously or unconsciously ignore the rest.[10] If a marketer wants to reach executives, *Fortune* magazine is a good choice; executives select that source of information. The fact that an advertisement appears in that magazine, however, does not mean that all executives will notice it. Attention to one ad instead of another may be due to the degree of reader interest in the message content. For example, a personnel manager planning an off-site executive training program is likely to be vigilant for information pertaining to conference facilities. On the other hand, that same manager may gloss over ads dealing with items like storage bins, items that hold no interest.

Additionally, a message may fail to be noticed because of its execution. Perhaps the words and visuals of the ad are not sufficiently creative to catch a reader's eye.[11] Think about how you flip past the ads in a magazine until you get to something that arouses your curiosity. Perhaps you notice the message for an instant, but nothing in the words or artwork sufficiently arouses your curiosity and you turn the page.

Interpretation of the Message

If a receiver decides that a message merits attention, the receiver then goes about interpreting or deducing the meaning of the message. Either consciously or unconsciously, the receiver converts the symbols, the appeal, and the tone of the message into impressions. These impressions are what the receiver considers to be the communications intent of the source. In advertisements, the words, illustrations, sounds, movements, or textures contribute to the understanding of the message. In personal selling, the sales representative's impact on the prospective client might be due not only to the content of the presentation but also to such factors as the tone of voice in delivery, the mannerisms and gestures accompanying the presentation, and the general physical appearance of the representative.

Why does the receiver assign particular meaning to different elements of a message? The interpretations spring from learned associations. This learning may be formal, such as the committing to memory of definitions in school. Or this learning may come without formal training but through experiences. For example, the receiver's interpretation of the phrase "new and improved" might depend on vocabulary development in elementary school. When you see the color scheme of red and white on a soft-drink bottle, however, you probably think of a cola, an association process that did not come from any formal education but from an accumulation of experiences over time.

Persuasion is unsuccessful when the interpreted message is much different from the intended message. This happens because the communicator has expressed the message using elements to which the receiver does not attach meaning or attaches an incorrect meaning. For example, a finance manager participating in a buying committee for a computerized assembly line might understand a payback analysis produced by a sales rep but might not be able to evaluate a report on a machine's technical specifications. The receiver may misinterpret the message when the message elements are ambiguous. For example, an ad stating "Our product is cheap" may confuse the audience as to what is actually meant. Communications may fail when the message elements have meanings quite different from those intended.

The marketer can increase, through research, the chances that the *decoded message* is similar to the intended message. The source of ideas for expressing the message should be the receiver. Whenever possible, the receiver should be contacted either in the development of the creative ideas or in the evaluation of the creative ideas before they are approved. It is not unusual for a marketer to conduct "brainstorming" sessions, called focus group interviews, presenting ideas to a group similar to the audience and encouraging the participants to describe and evaluate the idea or product in their own words. Before launching an advertising campaign, significant amounts of testing take place.

Retention of the Message

Assuming for the moment that the receiver attends to a message, the concern of the source is the time span the receiver will retain the message. *Selective retention* is likely to occur—only a fraction of the messages noticed are retained. We discard information quickly if there is no use for it in the immediate or distant future. And we discard a great deal of information because we see it as trivial and not worth retaining.

The task of getting the receiver to retain information for a length of time is easier to deal with than the problem of the receiver's purposely discarding it. Repetition over time can facilitate retention. Or if the receiver is interested in the sender's information but is not likely to remember it at the right time, the sender can provide the information on "external storage." For example, a salesperson who leaves a product brochure and a business card is providing the customer with an opportunity to keep information and use it when necessary; the salesperson does not have to worry about the problem of the customer's forgetting information.

If a receiver purposely does not retain information, then either the marketer has targeted the wrong audience or the development of the message was not appropriate. Either way, a serious problem exists in the fundamental plan and a revision in the campaign strategy is necessary.

Receiver Response

By capturing the receiver's attention, the communicator has created an opportunity to influence behavior. *If the right message has gone forward in the right fashion, the desired communications effect will occur*. The effect of communications may simply be the raising of brand awareness and familiarity with an established brand such as Coca-Cola. Communications activity may produce some comprehension of product facts, as with a new-product promotion. Communications may shape judgments or attitudes toward a product. And communications in the form of sales promotions such as price rebates may produce sales.

The actual communications effect depends on the objectives. These objectives in turn reflect the decision processes of the audience of interest. The next chapter details these various processes.

SUMMARY

Communication is essential for marketing transactions, which may occur in many ways. The manufacturer may deal directly with the marketplace, as in mail orders. Manufacturers must generate support among middlemen. Middlemen often direct promotion to end markets, that is, consumers. In this chapter we provided a model, a framework for understanding the communications process illustrated in Exhibit 3-2.

Where persuasion is the communications task, source credibility is necessary. To be believable, the originator or advocate of the message should be perceived as trustworthy and competent with respect to the message content.

The intended message is the idea that the source wishes the receiver to understand. This idea, correctly determined, should be the catalyst for the desired receiver response.

Communications effectiveness rests on the source's ability to express the intended message properly. In the encoding process, the communicator selects the proper symbols (words, colors, etc.) and the appropriate manner of presentation.

The channel of transmission is the means for delivering the message. In this decision, the communicator must consider the audience's likelihood of experiencing the channel, the characteristics of the intended and encoded message, and the characteristics of channels.

If the receiver attends to, interprets, and retains the message, there will be a response, perhaps simple awareness of the message content, perhaps comprehension, an opinion formed toward the message content, or overt action such as a purchase. In the next chapter we will take a hard look at the receiver's decision process.

REVIEW AND DISCUSSION QUESTIONS

1. Identify and explain the elements of the interpersonal communications model.

2. In an interpersonal communications situation, source credibility has a major impact on persuasion. What is source credibility? How might it apply to personal selling situations?

3. Using the concept of source credibility, select a famous spokesperson whom you would want in advertisements for the following products: (a) an economy automobile, (b) a low-priced camera, (c) a home computer, and (d) a lawn maintenance service. Justify your selections.

4. Explain the importance of the message encoding process in effective

communications. What are the chief means by which a message is encoded?

5. *Assume that you are marketing a brand of deodorant. Describe how an ad for your product might appear with a rational appeal, a fear appeal, and an emotional appeal. Which would you use? Why?*

6. *You are the public relations official for the local electric company. Your plant had been emitting pollutants into the air because of unknown equipment failure. You are scheduled to address an open meeting which has been called to determine whether your company should be fined. Assuming that the crowd will be hostile, how might you structure your message to convince the audience that the pollution was a justifiable accident?*

7. *Explain the process by which an individual attaches meaning to an encoded message. What might be the implications of such a process for a marketer designing a package for a new breakfast cereal?*

8. *What are the major factors to consider when selecting a channel of communications?*

9. *Explain what is meant by (a) selective exposure, (b) selective attention, and (c) selective retention.*

10. *What can the marketer do to increase the chances that the decoded message is similar to the intended message? Explain.*

NOTES

1. James Forkan, ". . . along with Toys," *Advertising Age*, December 5, 1983, pp. 1ff; and "Top Products of '83," *Advertising Age*, January 2, 1984, p. 27.

2. Ruby Roy Dholakia and Brian Sternthal, "Highly Credible Sources: Persuasive Facilitators or Persuasive Liabilities?" *Journal of Consumer Research*, March 1977, pp. 223–32; and Brian Sternthal, Ruby Roy Dholakia, and Clark Leavitt, "The Persuasive Effect of Source Credibility: Tests of Cognitive Response," *Journal of Consumer Research*, March 1978, pp. 252–60.

3. Richard Olshavsky and Donald Granbois, "Consumer Decision-Making: Fact or Fiction?" *Journal of Consumer Research*, September 1979, pp. 93–100.

4. Calvin Duncan and Richard Olshavsky, "External Search: The Role of Consumer Beliefs," *Journal of Marketing Research*, February 1982, pp. 32–43.

5. Gerald Zaltman and Melanie Wallendorf, *Consumer Behavior: Basic Findings and Management Implications* (New York: John Wiley, 1983), pp. 237–38. For an excellent discussion of source effects in marketing communications, as well as other message, media, and consumer effects, see Henry Assael, *Marketing Management* (Boston: Kent, 1985), pp. 317–46.

6. Richard Settle and Linda Golden, "Attribution Theory and Advertiser Credibility," *Journal of Marketing Research*, May 1974, pp. 181–85.

7. Al Ries and Jack Trout, "The Eye vs. the Ear," *Advertising Age*, March 14, 1983, pp. M27–M28.

8. "Marketers Expand Scratch 'n Sniff Applications," *Marketing News*, March 6, 1981, p. 1.

9. *A Study of Media Involvement* (New York: Magazine Publishers Association, 1982); and Nancy Stephens, "Media Use and Media Attitudes Change with Age and with Time," *Journal of Advertising*, 10, No. 1 (1981), 38–47.

10. William Bearden, Robert Headen, Jay Klompmaker, and Jesse Teel, "Attentive Audience Delivery of TV Advertising Schedules," *Journal of Marketing Research*, May 1981, pp. 187–91; and Wolfgang Schafer, "Selective Perception in Operation," *Journal of Advertising Research*, February 1979, pp. 59ff.

11. Richard Sparkman and Larry Austin, "The Effect on Sales of Color in Newspaper Advertisements," *Journal of Advertising*, 9, No. 4 (1980), 39ff; and Lawrence Soley and Leonard Reid, "Industrial Ad Readership as a Function of Headline Type," *Journal of Advertising*, 12, No. 1 (1983), 34–38.

4

Consumer Decision Making

In the preceding chapter we provided an overview of the communications process with emphasis on the potential effects of the source, the message, and the transmission channel on the receiver. In this chapter we look more closely at the reactions and attitudes of the consumer and at their implications for promotion. The purpose of this chapter is not so much to provide a comprehensive exposition of all factors affecting consumer decisions; we leave this task to formal courses on consumer and buyer behavior. Rather, the purpose is to identify some of the major factors in consumer decisions and impress upon the reader that markets are indeed complex entities that need to be thoroughly analyzed and understood for an effective promotion campaign.

Why is it necessary to understand the consumer decision process? The nature of the decision process determines the nature of the promotion effort. Let us look at the promotional strategies for two contrasting products. Assume that you want to introduce your division's new brand of cheese crackers nationally. Promotional strategy calls for an intensive cents-off couponing through local newspapers. In the major metropolitan areas, free samples are distributed at supermarket entrances. Concurrently, you schedule a saturation campaign of television commercials in a one-week period. The company's sales force will ensure the display of point-of-purchase materials in the supermarkets. Within six weeks you will have a strong sense of whether the brand will be as successful as the two years of product and market tests suggested. Six weeks is ample time for consumers to show how they react to your product.

Think of this scenario in contrast with another. You are in charge of promotion for a new videocassette recording (VCR) system with a list price of $1,200. The system is innovative and unique and is not compatible with available equipment. The promotional strategy calls for a major publicity campaign especially directed toward reviewers working for major newspapers and electronic entertainment magazines. Print advertisements set out to educate; they are filled with information about product features and performance. Additionally, these ads list a toll-free number that interested readers may call for more information and the name of the nearest dealer. Colorful, informative brochures go out to retailers so that prospective buyers can take something home to look over in making their decisions. You arrange for major retailers to set up special demonstration displays of your VCR. Your company makes special literature available to the stores' salespersons so that they can handle virtually all buyer inquiries. Unlike the preceding cracker situation, here you cannot judge the promotion's success or failure quickly. Consumers must have time to learn about the product, form an opinion, develop a preference, and then make a choice. You may have to allow a year or two to pass before the full market response is known.

The promotional activities and their timing are based on the decision process one wants to influence. In the first case, the decision process leading to purchase of crackers is simple and short; the promotional plan reflects that. In the second case, the consumer decision to spend $1,200 warrants considerable time and effort, and the promotional plan must adapt to that reality.

In this chapter we will first discuss the major social factors that shape decision making. Then we will take a close look at two major decision processes. The chapter concludes with an overview of the relationship between promotion plans and the decision processes they seek to influence.

SOCIAL INFLUENCES
ON CONSUMER DECISIONS

To live and function in this world, you must interact with others. This interaction is necessary because of mutual needs, wants, and personal objectives. You associate with friends because you share common interests. Or

EXHIBIT 4-1   Social Influences on Consumer Decision Making

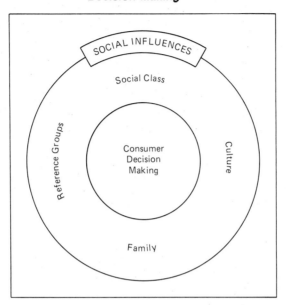

you work with fellow students on projects because you have the same learning goals. Social interaction affects an individual's behavior. In other words, consumer decisions are subject to *external influences*, influences that come from people and situations surrounding the individual. Exhibit 4-1 illustrates this. While these influences cannot be directly controlled or influenced by the marketer, they must nevertheless figure in the marketer's planning because they do affect the results of promotion effort. By understanding the impact of social influences on consumer decisions, the marketer can avoid barriers to effective communications and can find opportunities otherwise unseen.

In this section we survey the impact of four types of *social influences* on consumer decision making: reference group, culture, social class, and the family.

Reference Group Behavior

Reference group behavior refers to the fact that a decision maker may designate a particular group's values—beliefs and opinions about what is desirable—or actions as benchmarks or standards for his or her own attitudes and conduct. A *reference group* is a source of product information and guidelines or norms for how an individual should act under particular circumstances.[1]

Influence on Consumer Decisions

A group may influence an individual's reaction to the generic product category, or it may even move an individual toward a product or specific brand of a product.[2] For example, in one group members may want to own a stereo system but not any particular manufacturer label. In another group a person may want to own only the particular stereo system that the reference group considers acceptable. A framework for viewing such influences appears in Exhibit 4-2. Influence on product and brand choice is strong for such public luxuries as golf clubs and snow skis, whereas influence on decisions is weak for such private necessities as a floor lamp or a mattress.

The Occurrence of Reference Group Behavior

Why does reference group influence occur? A consumer may turn to others because he or she needs advice or information to resolve uncertainties. For example, someone searching for a cordless telephone and confused over the array of features in alternative brands may approach a friend who has gone through such a purchase process. The principal purpose of this reference group behavior is to obtain information or knowledge.

EXHIBIT 4-2   Reference Group Influence on Brand and Product Choice

COMBINING PUBLIC-PRIVATE AND LUXURY-NECESSITY DIMENSIONS
WITH PRODUCT AND BRAND PURCHASE DECISIONS

	Public	
Product / Brand	Weak reference group influence (−)	Strong reference group influence (+)
Strong reference group influence (+)	*Public necessities* Influence: Weak product and strong brand Examples: Wristwatch, automobile, man's suit	*Public luxuries* Influence: Strong product and brand Examples: Golf clubs, snow skis, sailboat
Weak reference group influence (−)	*Private necessities* Influence: Weak product and brand Examples: Mattress, floor lamp, refrigerator	*Private luxuries* Influence: Strong product and weak brand Examples: TV game, trash compactor, icemaker

Necessity — ————————————————— Luxury

Private

Reprinted with permission from William O. Bearden and Michael J. Etzel, ''Reference Group Influence on Product and Brand Purchase Decisions,'' *Journal of Consumer Research*, September 1982, p. 185.

Additionally, group influence may occur if a purchase decision seems likely to affect the individual's relationship with the group and the individual values that relationship highly.[3] Consider a college student contemplating the purchase of a pair of skis. If the student expects that skiing companions will think more of him or her because of the choice of equipment, and that student deeply cares about the opinions of companions, the final purchase may be what the friends actually recommend or what the student perceives that the group approves.[4] When the risk of negative social consequences from an incorrect product decision is high, reference group influence occurs.[5]

Characteristics of Reference Groups

The major characteristics of a reference group include the following:

1. It can be a formal or an informal organization.
2. It can be actual or aspirational.
3. It can be positive or negative.

A formal group is one whose organizational structure and activities are self-evident, like a national trade association, a union, or a civic organization. Much of the nature of a formal group may be known from its established guidelines for conduct. For example, doctors who belong to the American Medical Association adhere to its rules and guidelines for professional conduct. A pharmaceutical manufacturer would have a good idea of how to approach physicians in the marketing of a new drug simply by consulting the American Medical Association policies.

An informal group does not have specified roles for its members, nor does it have specified activities. Any distinctive conduct probably evolves over time as the individuals interact. The behavior patterns of an informal group become evident only through observation of activities. An informal group may consist of friends, fellow students, or neighbors.

An individual may be guided by the norms of actual or aspirational group membership. For example, if you belong to a fraternity or sorority, there are certain rules to which you must adhere as a brother or sister. Any major deviation from accepted conduct may jeopardize your standing with that group. On the other hand, conduct is sometimes directed by the behavior of a group to which one does not actually belong but with which one may wish to associate. For example, *The Wall Street Journal* ran a series of ads featuring top executives. In these ads, the executives said that regular reading of the *Journal* had contributed to their success. The obvious suggestion of the ads was that aspirants to executive positions should read *The Wall Street Journal*.

While much of the group influence derives from maintaining or obtaining affiliation, sometimes an individual's behavior is determined by the values or actions of a group from which he or she wishes to be disassociated. That is, on some occasions a particular group's behavior is a reference for what the individual should not do. In marketing communications, appeals often refer to groups to which the audience does not wish to belong. Some insurance ads cite examples of people affected by the untimely death of the main wage earner, mouthwash ads depict the offensiveness of people who did not use the product, or the American Cancer Society describes in strong terms the health conditions of persons who smoke heavily. The intent of such ads is to identify behavior characteristics of an undesirable group. The reference groups in such instances are negative reference groups.

What implications does reference group influence have for the promotion manager? First, a reference group may affect consumer behavior; it may serve as a source of information or a source of persuasion. Second, if the promotion manager knows that reference group influence is operative in a particular purchase situation, he or she may be able to use it to produce the right communications effect. For example, if a promoter of athletic footwear for young teens finds the target market to be susceptible to opinions of sport stars on equipment, the promoter may influence the purchases by using celebrity sportspersons as endorsers in an advertising campaign. While the existence or nonexistence of reference group behavior on consumer decision making is clearly not determined by the marketer, the marketer can still use it to facilitate communications.

Cultural Group Influence

A *culture* is a group within which individuals have shared knowledge, beliefs, and customs, learned and internalized over time. Such a group instills in individuals opinions about what is to be appreciated and desired. These opinions or values provide the fundamental base for all conduct by the group members. These shared values encourage and discourage certain types of behavior.

Culture Affects Lifestyles

Different cultures are distinguished by the manner in which they live or exist as reflected by special activities, interests, and opinions. In turn, these lifestyle differences show up in different purchase patterns. Exhibit 4-3 lists the results of an attitude survey conducted in several cultures. The implication of the varying attitudes for the marketer is that the marketing opportunities differ across cultures. For example, based on the results shown in Exhibit 4-3, the opportunities for the marketing of furniture polish are much greater in Italy than in the United States, while it appears from the

EXHIBIT 4-3   Cross-Cultural Attitudes Toward Housecleaning, Children, and Deodorants

"A HOUSE SHOULD BE DUSTED AND POLISHED THREE TIMES A WEEK."	"MY CHILDREN ARE THE MOST IMPORTANT THING IN MY LIFE."	"EVERYONE SHOULD USE A DEODORANT."
100% Agreement	*100% Agreement*	*100% Agreement*
86% Italy	86% Germany	89% U.S.A.
59% U.K.	84% Italy/French	81% French Canada
55% France	Canada	77% English Canada
53% Spain	74% Denmark	71% U.K.
45% Germany	73% France	69% Italy
33% Australia	71% U.S.A.	59% France
25% U.S.A.	67% Spain	53% Australia
	57% U.K.	
	56% English Canada	
	53% South Africa	
	48% Australia	

Source: Joseph T. Plummer, "Consumer Focus in Cross-National Research," *Journal of Advertising*, Spring 1977, pp. 10–11.

data that Americans, compared with consumers in most countries, have the strongest attitudes about using deodorants.

For the promotion manager, an understanding of a group's lifestyle dictates the development of persuasive communications. A product or idea presented as being consistent with the existing lifestyle may be more attractive to an audience. Let us look further at the influences of culture on communications.

Culture Affects Communications

Cultures differ in the way they understand and process information. What bears meaning in one culture may not in another. The initial attempt by the leading U.S. soup company, Campbell Soup, to penetrate the British soup market was disappointing. One major reason was the general unfamiliarity among British housewives with condensed soup, and another was that the British considered the youth-oriented commercials, which were so effective in the U.S. market, too fanciful and unrealistic.

Cultures communicate through the use of such symbols as words, illustrations, and mannerisms. People interpret these symbols and attach meanings to them. Problems in marketing communications sometimes arise because the marketer has used the wrong symbols and the real message does not get across. For example, directly translating the General Motors' phrase

"Body by Fisher" into French would result in something equivalent to "Corpse by Fisher," or loosely translating "Schweppes Tonic Water" into Italian would produce something equivalent to "Bathroom Water."

Communication symbols have different meanings for different groups. In many western countries, the color white is used on joyous occasions, while in many oriental countries white is used during occasions of mourning. The swastika clearly has negative connotations in western cultures, while some eastern religions consider the swastika a symbol of good fortune. The holding of hands between two males is acceptable as a sign of friendship in the Middle East, but not usually in the United States.

Satisfactory promotion is difficult unless the communicator understands the culture's values and the manner in which ideas are transmitted. Boy-girl romance themes, widely used in the U.S. television commercials for products such as mouthwash and toothpaste, are generally not acceptable in Islamic cultures such as Iran. Or China's popular brand of men's underwear, named Pansy after the flower, would probably have to be rebranded for successful export to the United States.[6]

It should be clear by now that each culture has its distinctive way of life and its distinctive manner of communications. Effective communications is built on a foundation of understanding a culture's set of values. We will now take a closer look at a culture that most of us will probably market to in the future—the U.S. culture.

The U.S. Culture

While there are many different values characteristic of the U.S. population as a whole, patterns have emerged and the major ones relevant to the marketer include the following:[7]

> Individualism—there is a value on independence and freedom, and to a certain extent one is encouraged to "be your own self."
>
> Materialism—the economic system of the United States emphasizes ownership and consumption of goods to the extent that one's status in society equates with the quantity and worth of one's possessions.
>
> Personal Achievement—Americans believe in continually bettering themselves. Purchases of products and services are often considered signs of and rewards for achievement of goals.
>
> Progress—there is value placed on continual innovation, especially of goods that improve the standard of living. Preference for the modern over the traditional is customary.
>
> Activity—Americans value effort whether directed toward leisure or business. Americans work hard and they play hard. The pace of life is relatively hectic compared with that of many other cultures.
>
> Youthfulness—Americans place a high value on being young and on such youthful characteristics as unconventional clothing styles.

Cultural values are relatively stable, but they do change slowly. As cultures evolve, some observers try to foresee the major trends in values. Some believe that the significant lifestyle themes for the 1990s will be

Self-indulgence
Emphasis upon leisure time
Immediate gratification of desires
Desire for security and avoidance of risk
Enhancement of physical and psychological self
Cosmopolitanism
Escape from everyday pressures[8]

Why is it important to track trends in values? Cultural values are often expressed in the products that are bought and the reasons for buying them. For the marketer, the tracking of values may mean the identification of product and promotion opportunities. For example, the increasing value on enhancement of the physical self has led to the recent boom in the sales of physical health products like weights, rowing machines, and tread-mills. Promoters of other products have built campaigns around fitness themes. Campbell's Soup advertises itself as an important source of nutrition for fitness.

Although we have just presented a survey of major trends in the United States, these values are not exact characterizations of every U.S. resident. Indeed, we can expect variations across individuals. This diversity reflects individuals' associations and interactions with groups within the mainstream U.S. culture. These groups are sometimes called *subcultures*. Let us look at some of them.

U.S. Subcultures

Within a large culture, there are likely to be groups of subcultures. These subcultures belong to the mainstream, but they have characteristics that differentiate them from others. It is important that the marketer be cognizant of these differences, which are often reflected in differences across purchase and consumption behavior. Just as we would expect distinctive behaviors across major cultures, we should also acknowledge the existence of distinctive lifestyles across subcultures. What are some of these subgroups and their lifestyles?

For the marketer, the major categories of subcultures can be defined according to ethnic, age, and regional characteristics. *Ethnic* subcultures are those groups generally characterized by national origin, race, or religion. *Age* subcultures are those groups whose lifestyles are related to stages in life. *Regional* subcultures are those defined by geographical areas.

Many ethnic subcultures in the United States are significant to the marketer because of their size or their distinctive purchase and consumption patterns. Their distinctive characteristics may represent marketing and promotion opportunities. Two ethnic subcultures that cannot be ignored when searching for opportunities are the black and Spanish-American groups, representing about 11 and 6 percent of the total U.S. population, respectively.[9] Beyond the size of these markets, the marketers may be attracted to these groups because of distinctive purchase behavior. Research has found patterns in product purchases among blacks and Spanish-Americans. For example, blacks usually spend a greater portion of their income than whites with comparable wages on clothing and personal-care items,[10] whereas Spanish-Americans usually spend a greater portion of their income on packaged food products like canned foods and beverages.[11] In addition to the black and Hispanic subcultures, there are smaller but also lucrative markets. For example, the maker of Planter's Peanut Cooking Oil realizes that its product is popular in Chinese cooking. To penetrate the Chinese-American market, the one-gallon cans of cooking oil stocked in Chinatown grocery stores have Chinese characters as well as English words describing the product.

There are significant variations in values and behavior based on age. Leisure and recreation activities appeal to the youth market, which is attractive to marketers because of its large amount of discretionary income and its willingness to spend that money.[12] Observers forecast that the senior group (65 years or older) will be a significant market opportunity by the year 2000 when it will constitute close to 20 percent of the population.

Regional differences in the United States are often quite sharp. These differences range from colloquial differences to substantial differences in lifestyles. For example, the term *tonic* used by a Bostonian may prove baffling to a Chicagoan who would use the word *pop* to refer to the same item, a soft drink. Beyond simple vocabulary differences, there are differences in patterns of behavior. Exhibit 4-4 contrasts some regional behaviors that came into and went out of vogue in 1983.

We should point out that we have only surveyed some of the major characteristics of cultures. The important point in this section is that there are distinctive lifestyles across groups, and these lifestyles do affect purchase and consumption behavior. To effectively market to and communicate with these groups, the marketer must carefully study their activities, interests, and opinions. Let us turn to another influence on consumer decision making, social class influence.

Social Class Influence

Social class refers to a position or standing within a society. An individual's social position often derives from characteristics or achievements considered valuable by others. An individual with greater levels of those desirable traits has a higher standing in a community than one with lesser levels. We will now consider various indicators or determinants of social positions.

Determinants of Social Class

An individual's social class comes not from any single factor but from a set of factors. Income, by itself, appears to be an inconsistent classifier. A college instructor at a well-known university may earn $25,000 annually while a bus operator for a public transit system may earn $30,000. Even though the bus driver draws greater pay, society may view the college instructor as being higher on the social ladder. Factors in classification include income, occupation, education, house type, and dwelling area. Of all the determinants studied, it appears that occupation is the most reliable indicator of status, although one should not use it alone in the description of social class.[13]

The most widely used system of classification is Warner's Index of Status Characteristics.[14] With a combination of occupation, source of income, house type, and dwelling area, the system suggests six distinct classes. These six classes and their percentages of the U.S. population are as follows:

Upper-upper class—1.4%
Lower-upper class—1.6
Upper-middle class—10.2
Lower-middle class—28.1
Upper-lower class—32.6
Lower-lower class—25.2

What is the significance of the existence of classes? Persons within a class generally exhibit similar purchase and consumption behavior. We will look at some of these patterns in the following two sections.

Social Class Affects Consumer Behavior

The relevance of the social class concept to the marketer does not lie in the idea of social hierarchy across groups. That one group has more prestige than another is not the basic issue in planning a campaign. Rather, the relevance is in the commonality of habits and attitudes that characterize individuals in a class. This commonality may reflect itself in the form of predictable purchasing and consumption patterns for particular products.[15] Specifically, individuals within a social class or individuals aspiring to a group are likely to have product preferences and make purchases appropriate for that group. Some of these products attributable to higher classes are

EXHIBIT 4-4 *Regional Differences in Lifestyle*

NEW YORK	CHICAGO	ATLANTA	HOUSTON
IN	**IN**	**IN**	**IN**
Raw-milk cheeses, salt-free foods, Cajun cooking	Gourmet popcorn, chocolate	Owning your own business	One-piece bathing suits, dressy satin clothes
Brass, jewel-tone fabrics in home decorating	Double-breasted suits for men, sweat-shirt material for women	"New music" (mellow disco)	Gravity-guidance units for hanging upside down
Black in women's clothes, bold necklaces	Walking fast, squash for exercise	Light wine, wine spritzers	Playing the stock market
Formal sit-down dinners	Caffeine-free colas, champagne	Marriage, premarital contracts	Lipectomy (suction-assisted removal of body fat)
"Break dancing," as seen in the film "Flashdance"	Vacations in Mexico	Short-hair styles	Bible study
Sugar-free iced-tea mixes	Master-of-business-administration degrees	Pedal pushers for teens, Marilyn Monroe jeans	Luke Skywalker, John Wayne, Humphrey Bogart
Mink and sable	'50s music	Salt-free diets	Vacations at the Dominican Republic's Casa de Campo resort
Natural-bee-pollen tablets	Q*Bert (videogame)	Picnics at music festivals	
Military look in teen clothes	Convertibles, luxury cars	Videocassettes	Small, elegant patio homes
Monogamy	Fancy Murphy beds	Health clubs	Home video cameras
			Cream liqueurs, imported beers
OUT	**OUT**	**OUT**	
Brie, artificially dried fruits and nuts	Croissants	Climbing the corporate ladder	**OUT**
Chrome, lucite, glass	Preppy look, Western look	Disco	Urban-cowboy look, sloppy look
Pastels	Jogging, racquetball	Bourbon, Long Island iced tea	Roller skates, skateboards
Sit-on-the-floor wine-and-cheese parties	Regular colas, white wine	Quick pickups	Collectibles, money-market funds, certificates of deposit
Sneakers	White-water rafting in Colorado	Bikinis, Calvin Klein jeans	
Tea in cans	Law degrees	Fried fish	Unpierced ears
Fake furs	Country and Western music	Real estate as a profession	Cults
Vitamin pills	Pac Man	Time-share condos	Real-life heroes
The '50s look for teenagers	Boxy economy cars	Ballad records	Vacations in the Middle East
Promiscuous sex	Water beds	Marijuana	Houses with big lawns
			Home movie cameras
			Scotch, bourbon, sweet wines

SAN FRANCISCO	LOS ANGELES	DENVER	WASHINGTON, D.C.
IN	**IN**	**IN**	**IN**
Romance	Brie, low-sodium cheese	Computer books	White-chocolate mousse,
Cajun dishes, pizza topped	Plastic tubs for bathing ba-	Big cars	homemade pasta, smoked
with caviar	bies	Plaid and striped men's	meat
"Hunks"—sexy men	Sushi bars	shirts, suspenders	Bold, glittery clothes
Running shoes worn with	Pasta machines	Classy casual look for	Hair-coloring products for
business suits	Soap operas	women	men
Mutual funds	Gray, pastels, especially	Continuing education	Tea, aperitifs
Imported beer	pink	Art-deco bars and restaur-	Entertaining with gourmet
Computer literacy	Cambridge diet	ants	carryout food
Lipectomy	Individual retirement ac-	High-tech stocks, real-estate	Elegant townhouses, condo
Porsche-Carrera sunglasses	counts	investments	apartments
Fixing up city neighborhoods	Aerobics, Jane Fonda work-	Breakfast meetings	Rubberized material in
	outs	Weight lifting for women	purses, belts, shoes
OUT	Vacations in Acapulco	Weekends in Santa Fe, va-	Convertibles
Promiscuity		cations in British Virgin	Running with weights, jump-
Croissants, gooey desserts	**OUT**	Gorda	ing on small trampolines
Men's open collars and gold	Beef, pork, veal		Vacations in Morocco
chains	Bathinettes for babies	**OUT**	
Certificates of deposit	Health-food restaurants	How-to sex books	**OUT**
White wine	Yogurt machines	Small cars with no extras	Marinated foods, heavy Ital-
Wall-to-wall carpeting	TV game shows	Cowboy boots, big handbags	ian dishes
Jeans, valley-girl look	Bright colors	College activism	Tightly fitted garments,
Herpes jokes	Beverly Hills diet	Country and Western bars	clothes with designer sig-
Cambridge diet (with high-vi-	Condo investments	Money-market funds, oil and	natures
tamin powder)	Jogging	gas investments	Suntans
Moving to the suburbs	Vacations in Las Vegas	Vegetarian food	Hard liquor
		Racquetball	Living together without mar-
		Suburbs	riage
		Vacations in Mexico, Las Ve-	Houses with big lawns
		gas	Longhaired furs
			Big black limousines
			Jane Fonda exercises
			Vacations in France

Reprinted from *U.S. News & World Report* issue of August 1, 1983. Copyright 1983, U.S. News & World Report, Inc.

commonly referred to as *status symbols*. Many in those strata would consider that ownership of products and services such as a bathroom telephone, Gucci apparel, Rolls-Royce car, and private club memberships characterize upper-class individuals.

A social group's distinctive consumption behavior may derive from (1) an ability to buy, (2) a preferred lifestyle, or (3) a social pressure to buy. A high-priced sable coat is within the economic abilities of those in the upper classes but would certainly be a financial burden for those in the lower. For this product, upper-class status with the appropriate income qualifies the consumer for purchase. Purchase patterns come about, however, not only from one's ability to buy but from one's desire to buy. An annual subscription to the *New Yorker* or the *Smithsonian* may be within the financial reach of most classes, but only certain groups are apt to find the content harmonious with their lifestyles and interests. Finally, purchase behavior may be normative, that is, an individual feels bound to buy a particular product to maintain membership in a group. For example, an individual may frequent an exclusive department store in order to maintain prestige and status in the eyes of others.

Social Class and Media Habits

Media usage differs across classes.[16] There are differences in the types of media that social classes use and in how they use them as sources of information for decision making. Commentators may generalize, for example, that newspapers and magazines are popular media among the middle-to-upper classes, while television viewing is more popular among the lower classes. Additionally, the middle-to-upper classes tend to read more printed material while deciding upon a durables purchase than does the lower class. The lower class is more likely to depend on information at the purchase location, displays and salespeople, in its decisions.

Knowledge of media habits allows the marketer to select the vehicles for effectively communicating with his or her market. The *New Yorker* magazine's audience is dominated by the middle-to-upper classes. It therefore serves as a more effective means of reaching that audience than does the *National Enquirer*, which delivers an audience with more lower-class people.

Family Influence

An individual's decision making, although influenced by others, is not always focused only on his or her own use or consumption. Quite a number of products are purchased for, used by, and/or consumed by persons other than the principal decision maker. For example, a parent's decision to choose one brand of cold breakfast cereal over another is influenced by the expressed desires of the child. Or the purchase of a washing machine is not for the express benefit of any one person but for the benefit of the family unit as a whole. The presence of *family influence* and considerations in the marketplace is quite extensive; over 65 percent of the U.S. adults are married, representing almost 105 million persons.[17] Let us look at some implications of family influence.

For the marketer, the importance of studying family influence is based on two facts. First, each family member is likely to have some involvement in and impact on a major purchase; and second, the nature and intensity of participation will vary by product. The marketing of a product by the manufacturer is easier if there is an understanding of how the family interacts in making a purchase decision. This understanding leads to the development of effective communications campaigns.

Family Influence on Decision Roles

As indicated in Exhibit 4-5, the relative husband-wife influences differ across products. With family vacations and schooling for the children, decisions are equally shared and the marketer must address the information needs of both individuals. On the other hand, husbands dominate decisions concerning insurance matters, and wives assume responsibility for kitchenware decisions; here, the marketer can concentrate on one spouse.

To develop an effective communications campaign for a family decision group, the marketer must address the following questions:

1. Who participates in the decision?
2. What role does each assume in the decision process?

In a decision with many interactions, a person may be characterized in one or more of the roles of

Initiator—the person who starts the decision process

Influencer—the person whose opinions have a major impact on the evaluation of product information

Purchaser—the person who engages in the act of buying

User—the person who consumes or uses the product

Information gatherer—the person who gathers and provides facts or data used in the decision process

For example, in the purchase of toys for a two-year old, the parents assume the roles of initiator, influencer, information gatherer, and purchaser. The decision to buy a toy may start with their recognition that little Johnny or Judy needs certain objects to develop particular motor skills. They ask

EXHIBIT 4-5 Husband-Wife Roles in Family Decisions by Product Category

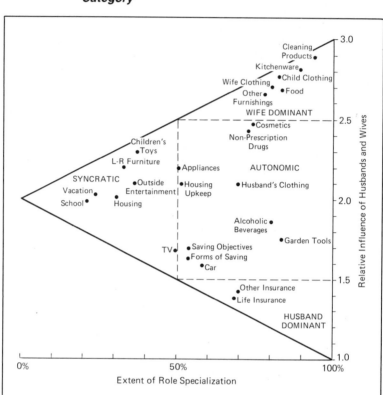

Reprinted with permission from Harry L. Davis and Benny P. Rigaux, "Perception of Marital Roles in Decision Processes," *Journal of Consumer Research*, June 1974, p. 54.

friends with similar-aged children for advice; they read advertisements by different toy manufacturers. They evaluate the facts and then purchase the preferred item. Little Johnny's or Judy's role is limited to that of a user. On the other hand, children between the ages of six and twelve may serve as initiator, information gatherer, influencer, and user while the parents serve only as purchasers. Knowledge of the roles among the different family members assists the promoter in providing the right information at the right time to the right person.

We have just surveyed one distinct characteristic of family decision making, the existence and variety of roles in product purchases. We now turn to another important aspect of the family that is reflected in items bought and used, the family life cycle.

The Family Life Cycle

Family purchase and consumption patterns can be characterized by the stage in the *family life cycle*. The family life-cycle concept proposes that a family changes over time. The number of members may change, and each member undergoes a development process whereby activities, interests, and opinions change. These changes are reflected in the kinds of products and services people buy and use. Exhibit 4-6 lists and describes the different stages in the life cycle. Note that the consumption pattern in the first stage, the bachelor stage, focuses on recreation, clothing, vacations, and courtship. On the other hand, in all the full-nest stages, a significant amount of the spending goes for the care and upbringing of the children.

The promotional implication of the life-cycle concept concerns the manner in which the marketing strategist will present a product in advertisements. For instance, the manner in which the strategist presents financial planning services to a young married couple with a small child will be different from that for a near-retirement head of household. An appeal emphasizing security against financial catastrophe may be effective for the first, while the concept of guaranteed immediate income might be more appealing for the second. Clearly, if a promoter's audience is known to be in a particular stage of life, this knowledge can be used to facilitate the audience's acceptance of the message.

Social Influences Affect
Consumer Decisions

We have surveyed four major social influences—reference groups, culture, social class, and family. In our discussion of each, we observed that some social or external influences on consumer decision making may be *direct* (there is an explicit, deliberate consideration of that influence by the decision maker) or they may be *indirect* (the influence exists but the decision maker is not consciously aware of it). Reference groups and family members can be viewed as sources of direct influence on decision making. Such influence when it occurs is obvious; for example, one spouse consults the other when contemplating a big-ticket item like an automobile, or a college student planning Friday's evening of entertainment and leisure may turn to a friend for advice about a movie being shown at the local theater. On the other hand, the effects of culture and social class are relatively subtle. Culture and social-class factors lay the foundation for much of the consumer's decisions by shaping the basic manner in which one lives. More specifically, products are purchased because they fit with a fundamental set of values and influences. For example, a young professional working couple purchasing a microwave oven may consult with each other in the decision process; there is clearly direct family influence. The effect of culture and social class

EXHIBIT 4-6   Family Life-Cycle Stages

BACHELOR STAGE

Although earnings are relatively low, they are subject to few rigid demands, so consumers in this stage typically have substantial discretionary income. Part of this income is used to purchase a car and basic equipment and furnishings for their first residence away from home—usually an apartment. They tend to be more fashion and recreation oriented, spending a substantial proportion of their income on clothing, alcoholic beverages, food away from home, vacations, leisure time pursuits, and other products and services involved in the mating game.

NEWLY MARRIED COUPLES

Newly married couples without children are usually better off financially than they have been in the past and will be in the near future because the wife is usually employed. Families at this stage also spend a substantial amount of their income on cars, clothing, vacations, and other leisure time activities. They also have the highest purchase rate and highest average purchase of durable goods, particularly furniture and appliances, and other expensive items, and appear to be more susceptible to advertising in this stage.

FULL NEST I

With the arrival of the first child, some wives stop working outside the home, and consequently family income declines. Simultaneously, the young child creates new problems that change the way the family spends its income. The couple is likely to move into their first home, purchase furniture and furnishings for the child, buy a washer, dryer, and home maintenance items, and purchase such products as baby food, chest rubs, cough medicine, vitamins, toys, wagons, sleds, and skates. These requirements reduce family savings and the husband and wife are often dissatisfied with their financial position.

FULL NEST II

At this stage the youngest child is six or over, the husband's income has improved, and the wife often returns to work outside the home. Consequently, the family's financial position usually improves. Consumption patterns continue to be heavily influenced by the children as the family tends to buy food and cleaning supplies in larger sized packages, bicycles, pianos, and music lessons.

FULL NEST III

As the family grows older, its financial position usually continues to improve because the husband's income rises, the wife returns to work or enjoys a higher salary, and the children earn money from occasional employment. The family typically replaces several pieces of furniture, purchases another automobile, buys several luxury appliances, and spends a considerable amount of money on dental services and education for the children.

EXHIBIT 4-6   (Continued)

EMPTY NEST I

At this stage the family is most satisfied with its financial position and the amount of money saved because income has continued to increase, and the children have left home and are no longer financially dependent on their parents. The couple often make home improvements, buy luxury items, and spend a greater proportion of their income on vacations, travel, and recreation.

EMPTY NEST II

By this time the household head has retired and so the couple usually suffers a noticeable reduction in income. Expenditures become more health oriented, centering on such items as medical appliances, medical care products that aid health, sleep, and digestion, and perhaps a smaller home, apartment, or condominium in a more agreeable climate.

THE SOLITARY SURVIVOR

If still in the labor force, solitary survivors still enjoy good income. They may sell their home and usually spend more money on vacations, recreation, and the types of health-oriented products and services mentioned above.

THE RETIRED SOLITARY SURVIVOR

The retired solitary survivor follows the same general consumption pattern except on a lower scale because of the reduction in income. In addition, these individuals have special needs for attention, affection, and security.

may not be so obvious; the specific purchase of a microwave oven may be based on values placed on convenience and timesaving, basic values learned from a culture or acquired from social group interaction.

Whether the social influence is obvious or subtle, there is an effect on the individual consumer decision. This section surveyed some of those effects and suggested that social influences do affect the promotional decision. If the influences are known to exist, perhaps through marketing research, the promoter can take them into account and facilitate communications.

Let us now consider the decision processes themselves. In the following section we will examine the decision-making stages phase by phase and their implications for promotion.

AN OVERVIEW
OF DECISION PROCESSES

At the beginning of this chapter and in Chapter 3 we emphasized the importance of understanding the manner in which the audience behaves when putting together an effective communications plan. More specifically, a marketing communications campaign should be planned with the consumer's decision process in mind. A promotional plan, if it is to ultimately influence consumer behavior, must take into account *how* purchase decisions are made. Knowledge of the activities and thought processes leading up to and after the act of purchase determines *what* type of promotion effort is needed and *when* it is needed. For example, if we are planning a promotion campaign for a breakfast cereal and find that our target audience deliberates about the nutritional qualities of food items before determining choice, we may wish to mount a campaign with a primary goal of dissemination of information about our distinctive ingredients. This promotion effort contrasts with the effort where the target audience is spontaneously influenced in its cereal choice by what comes to mind while walking down the store aisle. In this case, the promotion effort may rely on attractive, attention-getting displays at the point of purchase, the store shelf.

The remainder of this chapter describes two major types of consumer decision processes—the *low-involvement* and *high-involvement* processes—and the implication of each for promotion. The differences between the two processes stem from the kinds and numbers of activities the consumer will engage in and the sequence of these activities. Exhibit 4-7 contains schematics of each. Our discussion will begin with the high-involvement decision process, not because it is the more common process, but because it is the more complex one.

The High-Involvement Process

A simplified model of the high-involvement decision process is shown in Exhibit 4-7A. The decision-making process begins with recognition of a problem. The consumer conducts a search for alternative solutions, evaluates these alternatives, and makes a choice. Finally the consumer experiences the outcome of his or her choice.

The process is extensive when an individual views the consequences of a decision as serious and important. Hoping to avoid the serious consequences of a poor decision, the consumer commits himself or herself to a high level of personal involvement. Time and effort are focused on gathering and evaluating all the relevant information. For example, a person in the market for a $150,000 house will engage in high-involvement decision making. The risks of making a wrong decision (financial loss, inferior school system for the children, and so on) are great. Large commitments of time

EXHIBIT 4-7 Two Types of Decision Processes

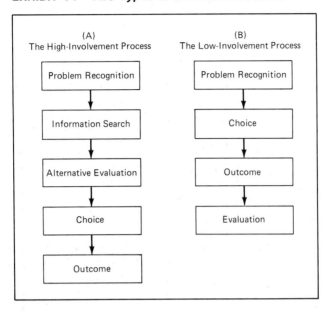

and effort are justified. The potential buyer gathers and evaluates information about property taxes, town services, value of neighboring properties, structural characteristics of houses, and the like. The process of information gathering and analysis will continue until the decision maker is satisfied that additional time and effort will not yield a better decision.

Problem Recognition

A parent with a daughter who plans to go to college reads a newspaper advertisement by a brokerage firm promising returns on investment higher than those obtainable from a bank. Concerned about the future financial demands of a college education, the parent responds to the ad.

A young executive comes back to her apartment at 9:30 P.M. Another late night at the office has forced her to miss the television network news, one of her favorite broadcasts. While reading a magazine later that evening, she sees an advertisement for a videocassette recorder. She recalls the many occasions when she has missed her favorite programs because of commitments at the office. And television viewing is her principal means of unwinding after a hard day. The following weekend she begins her search for a recorder.

Both of the above examples illustrate a consumer decision process initiated by problem recognition, an awareness that the actual situation was less than what was desired. With the parent of a college-bound daughter, the problem took the form of an opportunity to improve on the current financial status. Our young executive realized that she was suffering inconveniences as her job responsibilities grew. She was then motivated to find a solution.

The decision process begins, therefore, with *problem recognition*. The recognition of a problem may arise from within the individual consumer, or it may be that the marketer will stimulate awareness of a problem that is not obvious. Regardless of the source, awareness of a problem is a necessary condition for consumer action.

The role of needs. A need serves as a catalyst for action. It produces an uncomfortable tension within the individual, and the individual acts to satisfy the need. If we view the consumer as a problem solver, we can say that decision making begins only when a need exists. Decision-making activity concentrates on finding satisfaction of the need.

A need can be *physiological* or *psychological*. Hunger, thirst, and fatigue are overt signs of the existence of physiological needs, that is, physical or biological needs. On the other hand, the desire for the respect of others and the desire to feel loved are psychological needs, that is, emotional needs.

A need can be *conscious* or *subconscious*. A conscious need is one of which the individual is aware. A subconscious need affects behavior without the cognizance of the individual. For example, your car roars every time you accelerate, and it dawns on you that you have a faulty exhaust system. You understand the dangers from exhaust fumes and purposely look for a muffler shop. You may *unknowingly* choose the nationally franchised shop over the local ones because that shop satisfies your subconscious need for security. Here, both conscious and subconscious needs are at work, although you, the decision maker, may only be aware of fulfilling the conscious ones.

At any time, *several needs may be present* within the individual, and each may be competing against the others for the consumer's attention. This conflict complicates the process of decision making. A young man visits a clothing store because he needs apparel suitable for his friend's wedding. Because he does not anticipate too many other situations in which he will require formal attire, he does not wish to spend too much money. He sees a sports coat with a matching pair of slacks at a reasonable price, but he worries about whether those in attendance will view the outfit as too casual. In addition to the sports coat and slacks, he sees a well-styled, designer-label suit, but the price is about $80 more than he planned to spend. What should he do? He must resolve the conflict of needs so that he can make a proper choice.

An individual will typically address the more important needs rather than the less. One establishes a *priority ranking of needs*, and this ranking reflects the degree of importance attached to the need's resolution. Let us return to our young man facing the apparel decision. If he needs to save money more than he needs to have the contemporary image projected by the designer suit, then his purchase is likely to be the sports coat and slacks set.

Implications for promotion. The decision process leading to purchase begins with recognition of a problem. Problem or need recognition may arise from within the individual or from prompting by promotional activity. A formidable task faced by a salesperson soliciting new business is persuading the prospective client that a problem exists and needs to be addressed. Unless this is accomplished, the prospect clearly has no reason to purchase. Consider the television ad for a mouthwash depicting a person who unknowingly offends others with bad breath; the suggestion in the message is that the audience may have halitosis (and a need for the mouthwash) and not know it.

Efforts to stimulate problem recognition are not limited to addressing a single need. In many instances, the promoter may instigate action by appealing to a combination of needs. For example, a marketer of women's winter coats may appeal to the physiological need for warmth and simultaneously use a famous female model as a spokesperson in order to appeal to a subconscious, ego-related need, like the desire for prestige. It is presumed that an appeal to the combination is more effective than an appeal to just one.

Successful marketing communication requires an understanding of the prevalent needs of the marketplace. The focus of the communications campaign is to show the consumer that the product or service promoted addresses a need of some significance.

Search

The existence and awareness of a problem, as we noted earlier, produces an uncomfortable tension within the individual, who undertakes action to relieve this tension by finding a solution to the problem.

Two kinds of *search* may occur. The consumer may conduct an *internal* search for solutions. That is, the consumer may draw upon personal experiences for a solution. Or the consumer may rely on *external* sources of information. For example, a consumer recognizes that her only means of transportation, a nine-year-old car, has been incurring high repair and maintenance bills. What should she do? Should she continue to put money into the car? Should she look for a repair center that charges less money? Should she keep the car? Her search for solutions may entail recall of her own past experiences and information. She may project from past repairs what future garage bills will be, she may consider public transportation because she knows that there is a bus route conveniently near her residence, or she may think about car pooling, as some of her friends have done. If she feels that she has enough knowledge of available alternatives and the skills necessary to analyze alternatives, then she may conduct an information search that is largely internal. If she feels that her own information is inadequate or that she is incapable of conducting a satisfactory analysis of alternatives, she may conduct an external search.[18] She may be more alert to automobile ads. She may visit the automobile showrooms to seek salespersons' advice. She may consult with the mechanic of the garage that services her present car. Or perhaps she will consult reports of independent testing agencies.

Information gathering about available alternatives and the procedures for evaluating those alternatives stem from the desire to make right decisions and avoid wrong ones, or at the least the desire to make a satisfactory choice among different alternatives. When a consumer perceives the consequences of an incorrect decision as serious, and does not have confidence in the quality of his or her own information, that consumer is likely to engage in a more intensive search for external information than if the perception of decision consequences and the quality of internal information were otherwise.

Implications for promotion. When the consumer is willing to search for external information, the marketer now has an opportunity to provide information on how its product might solve the consumer's problem. To take advantage of this opportunity, there are two major considerations, the message and the channels for delivery of the message. First, the marketer's message should convey the product attributes in an appealing manner. The message must characterize the product as providing benefits, taking care of relevant needs of the consumer. Second, the marketer must use the right channel of communications. As we will see in Chapter 9, some media are more effective than others. The morning commuter audience can be reached more effectively with radio and outdoor advertising than with any other media. On the other hand, the at-home audience can be reached best through evening network television broadcasts.

Alternative Evaluation

The consumer's fact-finding activities help form opinions or attitudes toward *alternatives*. As our owner of the nine-year-old car with the high repair bills gathered information about alternatives, ranging from keeping the car and doing nothing to buying a brand new car as a replacement, she may have determined the pros and cons of each alternative.

An *attitude* is a summary judgment reflecting a predisposition or feeling. It comes from *beliefs* or *perceptions* formed about the product according to specific attributes known as *evaluative criteria*. Beliefs are what the decision maker considers to be facts about product performance. The evaluative criteria are those characteristics that a decision maker considers relevant and important in judging a product. For example, if you are shopping for a watch, you may view price and style as the two relevant and important bases on which you will make a selection. These two, then, are evaluative criteria. Subsequently, for each watch under consideration, you take the effort to look at the style carefully and check out the price tag. This effort allows you to formulate beliefs or perceptions about a watch's stylishness and reasonableness of price.

The manner in which beliefs are processed can vary from consumer to consumer and decision to decision. Research has suggested many categories of attitude formation processes; we will discuss two: compensatory and non-compensatory processes.

Compensatory processes. In compensatory processes, alternatives with specific weaknesses may still receive an overall favorable judgment. Weaknesses are permitted and may be compensated for by strengths as one applies other criteria.[19] A popular compensatory model is the weighted linear model of the following form:

$$A_i = \sum_j B_{ij} W_j$$

where

A_i = attitude held toward alternative i
B_{ij} = belief about alternative i performance on criterion j
W_j = importance or weight given to criterion j

In this process, one creates beliefs about product performance along specific dimensions. The impact of each belief on the overall attitude arises from the importance of the dimension. Let us look at an example of how this would work. For the sake of simplicity, assume that we are evaluating coats A, B, and C on only three attributes—color, price, and manufacturer's name. The following table contains quantitative expressions of the attitude components:

ATTRIBUTE	ATTRIBUTE IMPORTANCE (W_j)	BELIEFS (B_{ij})		
		Coat A	Coat B	Coat C
Color	2	1	3	4
Price	4	5	3	3
Manufacturer's name	1	3	3	3
Attitude score = $\sum_j B_{ij} W_j$		25	21	23

Our perceptions about the coats on each dimension are expressed on a 1-to-5 scale where 1 is very poor and 5 is very good. The importance of each dimension is also expressed on a 1-to-5 scale where 1 is very unimportant and 5 is very important.

Coat A may have impressed us with its very low price and generates the belief rating of 5. On the other hand, the color is an unappealing bright purple and our disappointment is shown with a belief score of 1. We know nothing about the manufacturer and have no strong belief in one direction or another. Coat B has no weaknesses, but then it has no distinctive positive points. Coat C has a good color but not much appeal on the other two attributes.

If our attitude formation follows this compensatory model, our attitude toward coat A, in spite of its poor color, is more favorable (we have constructed our example so that higher total scores reflect more favorable opinions) than our attitude toward coats B and C. Coat A's price and the importance of price to us compensated for our dislike of purple.

For those who insist that there is no way a purple coat would do even though the price is right, we agree. Not everyone is willing to trade off weaknesses against strengths. Some demand that a product be absolutely perfect, while others, not so strict, only require that there be no deficiencies. Many individuals probably use a noncompensatory process to evaluate alternatives. Let us look at how it works.

Noncompensatory processes. Alternatives frequently come into play only if they meet the minimum acceptable performance on each attribute. Unlike the compensatory situation, no weaknesses are permitted. We can express this with the following model:

$$A_i = \sum_j B_{ij} W_j, \text{ for } B_{ij} \geq m_j$$

where

A_i, B_{ij}, W_j are as defined in the compensatory model
m_j = minimum acceptable level for attribute j

For our coat example, assume that we will consider only alternatives with at least average performance (a 3 rating on our 1-to-5 scale) on all three attributes.

ATTRIBUTE	ATTRIBUTE IMPORTANCE (W_j)	BELIEFS (B_{ij})		
		Coat A	Coat B	Coat C
Color	2	1	3	4
Price	4	5	3	3
Manufacturer's name	1	3	3	3
Attitude score = $\sum_j B_{ij} W_j$		Not considered	21	23

Under our noncompensatory model, we would not even consider the purple coat despite a very strong attribute in price. We would evaluate only coats B and C, with the more favorable attitude held toward C.

Implications for promotion. An understanding of the attitude formation process increases the likelihood of persuasive communications. Our presentation of these processes suggests that persuasion may come about through control of consumer perceptions about product performance, the importance attached to attributes, or the types of attributes entering into the evaluation process. Let us see how promotion of coats A, B, and C might try to influence attitudes.

Beliefs about product performance are affected by promotional messages. Favorable perceptions about product attributes lead to favorable attitudes. For example, promoters of coat A may improve the customer's attitude by altering the perception about any one of the three attributes. Under the noncompensatory process, coat A dropped from consideration because of its less-than-average color appeal. The promoters may mount a campaign to convince the market that purple is not such a bad color after all. If they are successful in favorably changing the opinion about purple (from the present rating of 1 to a rating of 3), coat A not only would qualify for purchase but would clearly be the one with the most favorable attitude score.

Promotion may aim at changing the weight placed on evaluative criteria. For example, coat C may be able to take advantage of its superior color appeal by convincing the audience that color should have more weight in the decision process than it currently has. Looking at the scores under the compensatory process, the original attitude toward coat C was less favorable than that for coat A. Coat C may improve its chances of selection if it can convince the audience to be more concerned with color than it now is, which might change the original importance score of 2 to a higher one like 3. If this were to happen, then the overall attitude toward coat C would be more favorable than that for coat A.

The attitude toward coat B in our discussion always fell below that for A or C. This is clearly because it did not have any significant advantages in the three attributes used in evaluation (the belief scores were all 3). Coat B could improve its position by persuading the market to incorporate an additional attribute into its evaluation, an attribute that gives B a distinct advantage. For example, the coat may be made of material far superior to that of A or C. Promoters of B might then influence attitudes by getting the customer to consider the quality of material. This consideration would lead to a favorable increase in attitudes.

The evaluation process results in assignment of preference to alternatives. The order of preference flows from the relative order of the attitudes held toward the alternatives. The most-preferred alternative is most likely to be the choice.

We have given only brief examples of how attitudes might be changed. There is additional discussion in Chapter 10, which covers the formulation of advertising messages.

Choice

The preceding section on attitudes may have given the impression that the product or brand toward which the most favorable attitude is held will indeed be the item chosen. This is definitely not the case. Attitudes in general are not reliable indicators of purchase behavior; an attitude is simply a reflection of a person's feeling toward an item based on product-related information available at that time. What attitudes do not necessarily reflect are considerations of the situation and circumstance leading up to, and including, purchase. For example, you may have the highest opinion of the Mercedes-Benz car. However, you may not intend or plan to buy one as your next purchase. Why? One major reason (we assume your net worth is similar to that of most college students) is a financial one; you cannot afford it. Only if you had the money would you have serious intentions to buy. If circumstances are right, then favorable attitudes will lead to intentions to buy. If circumstances are right, the customer's intentions will find fulfillment and he or she will *choose the marketer's product*. But what are these circumstances? These circumstances include product availability, conditions of purchase such as delivery and after-sale agreements, store location, shopping hours, and the like. The aim of marketing is to set up those conditions that facilitate the realization of intention.

Implications for promotion. While promotion is traditionally a persuasive activity prior to purchase, it may also be useful in a choice situation. For example, point-of-purchase display materials can generate awareness or reinforce beliefs at the purchase location. Special discount coupons may be the effort that convinces the consumer that it is the right time to buy. Direct mail marketing, like a catalog, provides a means for customers to immediately select and order products they have just read about. Salespersons are sometimes responsible for getting orders. Telemarketing may work for simple transactions; it is a convenient means for placing orders.

Outcome

After selecting an alternative, the consumer then experiences the results of the solution. A woman who purchases and accepts delivery of a new car experiences the performance as she drives around. She notices that the braking is precise, that the transmission shifts smoothly, and that the ride is quiet. Or she may hear an unlocatable rattle, feel some hesitation in acceleration, and see misalignment of body parts. These experiences remain in her memory for reference in similar decision-making situations.

Satisfaction or a positive experience will result when the outcome is perceived to be equal to or greater than expectations prior to purchase. In contrast, dissatisfaction will result when product performance is viewed as less than expected. Finally, a consumer may not yet have formed impressions one way or another. In our car purchase example, the new owner may not be sure about what to conclude; she may be uncertain because there appears to be no clear-cut good or bad performance. Let us look at the implications for promotion.

Implications for Promotion. Dealing with the customer does not stop after the completion of a sale. Where there are opportunities for repeat business or additional business derived from that sale (like after-sale servicing or word-of-mouth recommendations to the buyer's friends), ongoing communications may be necessary. Satisfactions should be reinforced. Dissatisfactions should be detected and reduced, if not completely eliminated.

For high-involvement products such as a car, absolute certainty within the buyer of making the best buy is rare. The choice will entail some lingering doubts. Dissonance—uncertainty over the wisdom of the purchase action—is likely. Promotion can be used to provide reinforcing information. For example, a common tactic among automobile manufacturers and their dealers is the mailing of after-sale literature congratulating the recent buyer on a wise purchase.

The Low-Involvement Process

You are walking through a supermarket. As you reach the spices-and-condiments aisle, you realize that you must replace that near-empty bottle of catsup (you intended to get a bottle on the previous two trips but have somehow forgotten each time). Your usual purchase is a sixteen-ounce Heinz-brand bottle, but on this occasion the store has run out of your brand. Do you go through a lengthy, thorough evaluation of all other alternatives? Do you wait a couple of days to determine an acceptable substitute brand? The answer to both questions is probably no. You pick up another familiar brand, such as Hunt's. Past experience may have told you Hunt's is an acceptable substitute for Heinz, or if you have never tasted Hunt's before, you still get Hunt's because the risk of a poor selection is insignificant.

For many consumer purchases, little if any time and effort go into decision making.[20] Chances are good that the consumer does not spend much time selecting a soft drink, a candy bar, a loaf of bread, or a package of hot dogs. The consumer is unwilling to expend time and effort in the purchase decision. These types of decisions are called low-involvement decisions.

In low-involvement decisions, the consequences of quick decision making do not seem to be serious. The consumer, moreover, does not expect that additional effort will mean any significant improvement in the quality of the decision. Many low-involvement products are similar, and extended evaluation of competing brands would not identify a significantly better item among alternatives. Continuing with our catsup example, spending additional time and energy visiting other stores and talking to people will probably not yield a significantly better choice than Hunt's. And if the Hunt's brand does turn out to be a poor substitute for Heinz, you can throw it away and not suffer any serious financial loss.

The decision process commences with problem recognition, and choice may occur before one conducts any alternative evaluation. The experiences with the choice outcome provide the basis for formulating an attitude toward a product. Return to Exhibit 4-7B for an illustration of the low-involvement decision process.

Problem Recognition

Problem recognition is temporal. It fades quickly from memory because more important thoughts take its place. In our catsup example, you recognized the need for a replacement bottle on at least two earlier occasions, but you forgot it in the time between recognition and the purchase opportunity. Since that need is not a pressing one, attention may move away from it to other needs like driving carefully in traffic, getting to work on time, or calling a plumber to fix a big leak.

Implications for promotion.   The probability of action to fulfill a need diminishes rapidly after recognition. Unless purchase opportunities occur at the time of problem recognition, it may be that no action will take place. Since the need is relatively unimportant, one can postpone action and eventually just forget the need. Thus advertising for low-involvement products may not lead directly to purchase. Such advertising will build recognition of product benefits only after significant repetition.

Marketers can take advantage of a given situation to stimulate problem recognition and immediate action. For example, point-of-purchase display materials are effective in attracting attention to a product and aiding recall of needs for low-involvement products. Some marketers facilitate the purchase of low-involvement goods by offering convenient catalog or telephone ordering.

Choice

Choice is influenced by easily recallable information that an individual has stored in memory. Let us return, in our catsup example, to the moment when you have realized that the Heinz brand is not available. You are willing to find a substitute immediately because it is a low-involvement product. Your first step is to think of what are possible substitutes. You scan the shelves and you see Hunt's and Del Monte brands along with several others. You unhesitatingly reach for Hunt's. Why? Because you have seen it advertised recently on television and its name seems more familiar to you than any other.

Implications for promotion. Recognition of the brand is a key factor in the choice among low-involvement items. Since there is little importance attached to the product, little or no serious product evaluation takes place. Consequently, items with distinctive features such as unusual package shapes, eye-catching colors, or memorable brand names have an edge over competitors' products, since choice is often directed toward the item that comes to mind first.[21]

Consider a typical promotional effort for a supermarket item. The manufacturer uses repetitive advertising to build up a high level of awareness of the product. This awareness alone does not necessarily prompt the consumer to run down to the store. But this awareness along with the right situation may lead to purchase. Sales promotion support at the stores in the form of point-of-purchase displays and other merchandising devices is designed to trigger recall of the advertised product. The availability of the product and the immediate recall of the advertised product combine to lead to purchase.

Outcome and Evaluation

After selecting and using a product, the consumer has a chance to assess the results. Attitudes toward that product come from those experiences. If a product performs satisfactorily, the buyer forms a favorable opinion.

Implications for promotion. A favorable attitude influences future product choice but does not ensure that brand insistence will take place. A consumer may continue to buy a brand that is delivering satisfactory benefits. This loyalty is a spurious one at best. The consumer stays with a brand not because it is indeed outstanding relative to others (for most low-involvement goods, it is difficult to detect comparative product advantages) but because the consumer is content with its performance and does not wish to spend time looking for better alternatives.

Brand switching can easily be triggered by aggressive promotion efforts (cents-off coupons, free samples, premiums, and the like) to encourage product trial. Marketers of low-involvement products must devote attention to three types of promotional efforts. First, they must conduct promotion that maintains the presence of the brand name in consumers' minds. Even for an established brand like Coca-Cola, promotion is necessary to ensure that the brand is at the top of the buyer's mind at the point of a purchase decision. Second, they must be vigilant against competitors' efforts to lure customers away. When brands are viewed as being essentially similar, competitive advantages are often sought through sales promotions like rebates or free premiums. When sales promotions are launched into the marketplace, brand switching may occur rather quickly. Unless marketers are vigilant about these activities, they may be surprised by a serious erosion of their sales. And third, they must engage in activities to encourage switching by users of competing brands. Growth opportunities exist not only in getting *present* customers to buy and use more of the product; this can be accomplished by maintaining a high level of brand familiarity. Growth opportunities also exist in luring *customers of rival brands* to switch over.

DECISION PROCESSES AND THE
PROMOTION PLAN: AN OVERVIEW

We have described two major decision processes and presented implications for specific promotional activities in each major phase. We will now take a look at the broader issue of how the promotion plan is affected by the way the target market makes its decisions. (After a detailed discussion of market segmentation and positioning in the next chapter, we will examine the relationship between promotional objectives and the target market's decision process.)

Exhibit 4-8 illustrates promotional tasks for different decision processes. For the high-involvement decision, graphic 4-8A suggests that consumer purchase action is conditional on the achievement of a series of tasks. These tasks assume that the consumer wants to and needs to go through information processing activity before purchase. First comes product awareness, followed by comprehension of product features. The beliefs about product performance are the foundation for development of feelings about a product. If these feelings are sufficiently positive, then purchase can take place.

Graphics 4-8B and 4-8C suggest two possible promotion plans for low-involvement products. In both of these plans (1) the development of a positive feeling or attitude toward a product is not necessary prior to its purchase, and (2) attitudes come about after the buyer experiences the outcome of his or her action.

Since familiarity affects choice, instilling product awareness and a simple level of comprehension are often the first tasks of promotion. Then

EXHIBIT 4-8 Promotion Tasks Adapted for Different Consumer Decision Processes

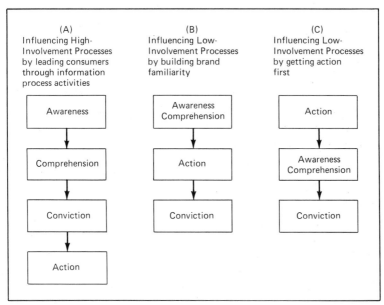

(A) Influencing High-Involvement Processes by leading consumers through information process activities	(B) Influencing Low-Involvement Processes by building brand familiarity	(C) Influencing Low-Involvement Processes by getting action first
Awareness	Awareness Comprehension	Action
↓	↓	↓
Comprehension	Action	Awareness Comprehension
↓	↓	↓
Conviction	Conviction	Conviction
↓		
Action		

Michael L. Ray, *Advertising and Communication Management*, © 1982, pp. 184–188. Adapted by permission of Prentice-Hall, Inc., Englewood Cliffs, N.J.

come efforts to generate consumer action. The final task is to ensure that favorable experiences lead to favorable attitudes that may influence future purchase. Graphic 4-8B suggests this promotion process.

Sometimes consumer action will be the first task of the promotion effort. For example, taste demonstrations or sample packets of new products encourage usage. Upon usage, awareness of the brand arises and attitudes take shape, as Graphic 4-8C suggests.

SUMMARY

Effective promotion requires an understanding of the decision process one wants to influence. In this chapter we covered the major social influences that shape consumer decision making and then discussed the two major processes, the high-involvement and the low-involvement decisions.

Our discussion of social influences included reference groups, culture, social class, and the family. Reference groups provide the individual with benchmarks or standards for behavior. These groups can be formal or informal, actual or aspirational, and positive or negative.

Through culture an individual acquires knowledge, beliefs, and customs. Culture affects not only purchase habits but the way in which communication takes place. Cultural values are relatively stable, but they do change over time. Some current trends appear to be emphasis on leisure time, immediate gratification of desires, enhancement of physical self, and desire to escape from everyday pressures.

Social class refers to social order. The relevance of the concept is that there are relationships between class and purchase tendencies and between class and media habits.

We looked at two major characteristics of the family: the difference in decision roles, and the life cycle concept and its effect on buying habits.

In the second section we looked at the high-involvement and low-involvement processes. These processes differed in terms of the time and effort devoted to decision making.

High-involvement decisions begin with problem recognition. Because of the serious risk of making an incorrect decision, a consumer will gather information about alternatives. With such information, the consumer develops attitudes toward these alternatives. When the consumer is ready to take action, choice will emerge from the relative order of preference across alternatives.

Promotion can influence the process. It can generate awareness of problems or opportunities. It provides information on product performance and can affect consumer feelings or opinions about alternatives.

Low-involvement decisions are low risk and thus much simpler than high-involvement ones. Problem recognition is temporal. The consumer may forget the need quickly but recall it when prompted by factors on the scene. Choice can take place without any information processing. Attitudes will take shape after purchase.

Through promotion activities at the point-of-purchase, the marketer can stimulate problem recognition and offer immediate solutions. Since choice comes from familiarity, promotion should aim at raising and maintaining brand awareness.

In the last section we showed how promotion tasks could differ according to the decision process one wants to influence. For a high-involvement process, promotion raises the market's awareness of the product, delivers product information, influences consumer preferences, and then stimulates consumer purchase and consumption. On the other hand, the promotion of low-involvement products need not cultivate favorable attitudes to get sales. Product awareness along with special incentives to act may be all that is necessary.

We move now to a discussion of market segmentation and product positioning. This will provide an additional understanding of market characteristics, an understanding we consider essential to sound promotion decisions.

REVIEW AND DISCUSSION QUESTIONS

1. Why is it important that the promoter understand the decision-making behavior of the market?

2. What are the different social influences affecting buyer behavior?

3. What are the characteristics of a reference group? Name three products for which the decision is influenced by a reference group. Justify your answers.

4. Differentiate between an actual and an aspirational reference group. Give examples.

5. Assume that you are marketing an all-weather overcoat. How might an ad utilizing an associative reference group appeal differ from an ad with a disassociative reference group appeal?

6. Why is cultural analysis essential when marketing U.S. products overseas?

7. Based on the U.S. lifestyle trends cited in this chapter, list some marketing opportunities. Explain your selections.

8. What is the usefulness of the social class concept to the marketer?

9. To a marketing communications manager, what are the implications of joint decision making?

10. Define each of the following: (a) initiator, (b) influencer, (c) purchaser, (d) user, (e) information gatherer.

11. What are the stages in the high-involvement consumer decision process?

12. Problem recognition initiates the consumer decision-making process. Describe some ways in which a manufacturer of smoke alarm systems could get the consumer thinking about buying such a product.

13. One stage of the high-involvement decision-making process is the search for information. What generally occurs in this activity, and how could a marketer benefit from such activity?

14. In what ways can a marketer influence the opinion that consumers form toward its product?

15. Intentions to buy a product often go unfulfilled because of situational factors. What are some situational factors that prevent the fulfillment of the desire to buy a stereo system?

16. What types of products fall into the category of low-involvement decision making? Explain your answer.

17. As a marketer of a low-involvement product, what would you consider to be critical factors in influencing consumer choice? Give some examples.

18. The decision process for high-involvement products is extended. Why?

19. Which of the following product purchases are low-involvement decisions? High-involvement? Why?

a. Coffee

b. Running shoes

c. A weekly news magazine

d. Spark plugs for a do-it-yourself tuneup

e. A dog food

20. Assume that you are marketing a new sports car to the young professionals. This car will list for $13,000. What risks do you think the market will see in such a car? How would you address such risks in an advertising campaign?

NOTES

1. C. Whan Park and V. Parker Lessig, "Students and Housewives: Differences in Susceptibility to Reference Group Influence," *Journal of Consumer Research*, September 1977, pp. 102–10.

2. William O. Bearden and Michael J. Etzel, "Reference Group Influence on Product and Brand Purchase Decision," *Journal of Consumer Research*, September 1982, pp. 183–94.

3. A. Benton Concanougher and Grady D. Bruce, "Socially Distant Reference Groups and Consumer Aspirations," *Journal of Marketing Research*, August 1971, pp. 379–81.

4. James E. Stafford, "Effects of Group Influence on Consumer Behavior," *Journal of Marketing Research*, February 1966, pp. 68–75.

5. Jeffrey D. Ford and Elwood A. Ellis, "A Reexamination of Group Influence on Member Brand Preferences," *Journal of Marketing Research*, February 1980, pp. 125–32.

6. "Chinese Commit Faux Pas Too in Export Marketing," *Marketing News*, October 14, 1983, p. 13.

7. David L. Loudon and Albert J. Della Bitta, *Consumer Behavior: Concepts and Applications* (New York: McGraw-Hill, 1984), pp. 174–80.

8. "Analyze Lifestyle Trends to Predict Future Product/Market Opportunities," *Marketing News*, July 10, 1981, p. 8.

9. U.S. Bureau of the Census, *Statistical Abstract of the United States 1982–83* (Washington, D.C.: U.S. Department of Commerce, 1982), p. 15.

10. Raymond Bauer and Scott Cunningham, "The Negro Market," *Journal of Advertising Research*, April 1970, pp. 3–13.

11. Mark Watanabe, "A Profile Grows to New Heights," *Advertising Age*, April 6, 1981, pp. 5–23.

12. Ben Bodec, "Marketing Paradox: Fewer Teens, More Spending," *Marketing and Media Decisions*, April 1981, p. 77.

13. James F. Engel and Roger D. Blackwell, *Consumer Behavior* (New York: Dryden Press, 1982), pp. 113–14.

14. W. Boyd Warner, Marchia Meeker, and Kenneth Eells, *Social Class in America : Manual of Procedure for Measurement of Social Status* (New York: Harper & Brothers, 1960).

15. Michael J. Munson and W. Austin Spivey, "Product and Brand User Stereotypes among Social Classes," *Journal of Advertising Research*, August 1981, pp. 37–46.

16. Henry Assael, *Consumer Behavior and Marketing Action* (Boston: Kent Publishing, 1984), p. 350.

17. U.S. Bureau of the Census, *Statistical Abstract*, p. 39.

18. Calvin P. Duncan and Richard W. Olshavsky, "External Search: The Role of Consumer Beliefs," *Journal of Marketing Research*, February 1982, pp. 32–43. For an excellent discussion of search processes and how search fits into the overall consumer decision process, see David J. Reibstein, *Marketing* (Englewood Cliffs, N.J.: Prentice-Hall, 1985), pp. 140–60.

19. Assael, *Consumer Behavior*, p. 187.

20. Richard W. Olshavsky and Donald H. Granbois, "Consumer Decision Making—Fact or Fiction," *Journal of Consumer Research*, September 1979, pp. 93–102.

21. "Pilot Study Finds Final Product Choice Usually Made in Store," *Marketing News*, August 6, 1982, p. 5.

5

Market Segmentation and Product Positioning

In a nation with almost 230 million persons, a large number will exercise some freedom of choice in the marketplace. They will not all act in exactly the same way. Unique sets of activities, interests, and opinions characterize each person. Among your friends and acquaintances, some prefer a Heineken to a Budweiser beer; some would rather drive a sports car than a subcompact; some would rather attend a symphony performance than a rock concert; and some would rather watch college football than professional football.

The marketing concept states that profitability comes from satisfying consumer needs and wants, but there is a limit beyond which this concept cannot be applied. Realistically, limited resources prevent any firm from satisfying all consumers. Even the Baskin-Robbins Ice Cream Store, with over one hundred flavors and more than two thousand outlets throughout the United States, Europe, and Asia, cannot capture 100 percent of the market. Budget and labor constraints limit the scope of product, price, promotion, and distribution policies.

To have an effective campaign, the promotion planner must know whom to contact and what to say to them. Assume that you are responsible for promoting a very dry, imported red wine for which your company has the exclusive U.S. distribution rights. The first thing you should realize is that not every adult drinks alcoholic beverages, not every alcohol consumer drinks wine, and not every wine drinker likes a dry, red wine. You want to spend money directing a campaign toward those who do drink such a wine now or those who, if they do not now, could be persuaded to drink it. Finally, to get your target to select your brand, your campaign must present your wine in an appealing fashion.

In this chapter we describe three related activities critical to the planning of a promotion campaign: market segmentation, target selection, and product positioning. These activities are not unique promotion-planning activities. Instead they are part of the overall marketing planning that guides promotional strategy as well as product, pricing, and distribution tactics.

MARKET SEGMENTATION

Market segmentation is the partitioning of a large market with diverse needs and wants into submarkets or segments. These segments consist of individuals with similar needs and wants.[1] These segments, then, represent the set of plausible alternatives from which a marketer will select a target. More specifically, the segmentation process creates groups according to certain criteria:

1. A relatively distinctive behavior characterizes each group.
2. One may describe each group by referring to measurable and understandable dimensions.
3. The market potential has an appropriate size.
4. There is a means of communicating with the segment.

The following paragraphs examine each of these criteria.

Groups with Distinctive Behavior Patterns

A campaign's ultimate objective is to cause some type of change in the marketplace. The marketer may seek to achieve such goals as greater awareness, more favorable attitudes, or higher purchase rates. The extent to which changes in the marketplace will occur depends largely on two factors. First, there must be a *potential for change* inherent in the market. Second, the design of the marketing effort can in fact bring about change.

What do we mean by potential for change? Different people will react differently to a marketer's appeals. As a result, the diversity of markets represents the variety of opportunities for success. For example, a few years ago Ocean Spray Cranberries, Incorporated, sought to increase the sales of its cranberry sauce.[2] A fundamental question prior to the development of a marketing strategy was, Where were the opportunities to increase sales? That is, What individuals would be the most receptive to the idea of consuming more cranberry sauce? Four distinct segments emerged from data collected in segmentation analysis. One segment used cranberry sauce because of its convenience of preparation. Another segment used it because of their general enthusiasm about cooking. A third segment used it because of its colorful, decorative qualities. The fourth segment used the product on limited occasions and showed some indifference to the product itself. Each of the four segments represented a very different opportunity for the increase of sales, since data showed that the consumption rates varied considerably. The highest usage rate, and thus the greatest potential for change in the form of increased sales, was among the enthusiastic cooks.

In creating the different segments, the marketer is actually categorizing the market by its tendencies to respond or react to marketing efforts. Exhibit 5-1 shows how advertising strategies differ across market segments. In that exhibit you can see descriptions of five different segments for five South Carolina vacation spots. Note how the proposed advertising headlines, illustrations, copy, and magazine selections vary across the locales and segments. These variations reflect the different segment response tendencies.[3]

Exhibit 5-2 lists some of the major response tendencies around which the marketer creates segments. They are purchase patterns, usage patterns, propensity to respond, and product benefits sought.

Let us look at how purchase and usage patterns apply to the segmentation of the beer market. *Purchase patterns* describe the purchase rate for the product class according, say, to the number of twelve-ounce cans of beer people bought in the last two weeks. The purchase rate for a particular brand is the number of twelve-ounce cans of that brand, say Schlitz, people bought in the last two weeks. A market may also be segmented by the situation under which purchase occurred. For example, the beer market may be segmented by purchase location, a discount store, a supermarket. *Usage patterns* will describe the amount of the product class consumed (number of twelve-ounce beers per week), the volume consumed by brand (number of twelve-ounce Schlitz per week), or the usage situation (percentage of beer consumed at home).

For campaigns where the objective is to encourage brand switching or maintain brand preferences, segmentation by *brand loyalty characteristics* is useful. The objective is to identify those people who tend to stick with a brand and those who tend to purchase multiple brands. One might describe loyalty according to the number of times a person bought a particular brand in the last ten purchases. A beer purchaser whose last ten purchases consisted only of Schlitz obviously has less tendency to switch than someone whose last ten purchases consisted of Schlitz and three other brands.

Sometimes the objective of a promotional campaign is to influence the processes leading to a product purchase decision rather than the immediate purchase or consumption. This is customary for high-involvement products where a long decision process precedes purchase. Here, one segments a market according to *stages in the decision-making process*. For example, an automobile manufacturer may look to new markets, rather than previous customers, for sales growth. To influence the ultimate automobile choice, the manufacturer may have to guide the prospective customer through the decision process. Some persons may be more easily guided to a choice than others. How? The manufacturer may group customers by those who have only heard of the manufacturer but hold no attitudes, those who have some opinions about the manufacturer's car but have not test-driven it, or those who have test-driven the car but have not purchased. You will notice that each group represents persons at different stages in a purchase decision. Some are closer to making a choice than others. For those who have not even heard of the car model, promotion effort and time must be expended to both inform and persuade. On the other hand, for those who have test-driven the model and have been impressed, promotion only needs to reinforce positive opinions.

Benefit segmentation stratifies the market according to benefits that individuals seek.[4] This type of segmentation rests on the premise that the desire for specific product performance is a major determinant of purchase behavior, and that it makes sense to group people around this desire. For example, consider the various priorities people may have as they search for a watch. Each of the following may be a high priority and thus a principal motivator in choosing a watch: low price, durability, precise timing, prestigious brand name, and distinctive styling. Each is a product benefit valued by a group of individuals, a characteristic that will move people within the designated group to make a purchase.

Segment Descriptors

Marketplace potential achieves reality when the marketer is able to locate and communicate with the consumers.[5] One needs a profile of the target group. For example, a marketer has determined that increases in its sales will come from attracting the occasional users of a competitor's brand. To transmit a message to those light users, the marketer must first know what the light user looks like. Without a clear idea of who is a qualified prospect and who is not, the marketer's message may be wasted on individuals who have little or no interest in the product. Without profile specifica-

EXHIBIT 5-1 Market Segments and Proposed Advertising Strategies

PREIDENTIFIED MARKET SEGMENTS AND ADVERTISING STRATEGIES

Market segments	The beach vacationer	The colonial sightseer	The fisherman	The highlands vacationer	The second home vacationer
Predicted profiles	Married couples with children under 19 living at home. The head of the household is probably a blue collar worker. They enjoy the ocean along with new exciting activities. Life typically revolves around the family. Travel party size is usually four or more and summer travel is preferred. Median education, middle socioeconomic status, and young to middle age.	Married couples with no children living at home. Upscale white collar worker interested in America's historical growth and development. May be retired. Travel party size is usually two and spring or summer travel is preferred. Enjoy dining out. College educated, middle to upper socioeconomic status, and middle age or older.	Married couples with one or no children living at home and more likely to be 35 to 55 or older than other segments. They enjoy fishing and viewing the scenic beauty of the outdoors. Travel party size is usually less than four. They prefer to travel during the spring and summer. High school education and middle socioeconomic status.	Married couples with children under 19 at home. They enjoy the outdoors, camping, and the scenic beauty of the mountains. Travel party size is usually four or more. Prefer to travel during the spring or summer. High school education, middle socioeconomic status, and young to middle age. Head of household is probably a blue collar worker.	Married couples with no children living at home and probably in the latter stages of a professional/ managerial career or retired. They enjoy the ocean and solitude of their second home. Travel party size is usually small. Prefer to travel during the summer. College educated, upper socioeconomic status, and beyond middle age.

	Myrtle Beach	Charleston	Santee	The mountains	The Sea Islands
Ad headlines	"Water slides, roller coasters, arcades, whirling, spinning, playing, winning. And we throw in the Atlantic Ocean . . . free."	"Nearly 300 years ago one of the best ways to see it was by horse and buggy. It still is."	"Here the Stripers, Catfish, Crappie, and Largemouth have one thing in common. They're big."	"There's just one way to ride the Chattooga. Downstream. And fast."	"We have 17 sea islands where you can find beaches, sun-drenched resorts, catamaran sailing and horseback riding. Or solitude."
Advertising illustration	A young girl on a waterslide with the beach in the background.	A couple and driver in a carriage on a cobblestoned street with a colonial house in the background.	Striped Bass, Channel Catfish, Black Crappie, and Largemouth Bass.	Four people in a raft on the Chattooga River.	Dunes with marshes in the background.
Advertising copy	"Uninterrupted Beach" "Amusement Park" "Action and Excitement"	"Museum of Colonial America" "Open-air Market" "European Cuisine"	"They come out fighting" "One of the world's top freshwater fishing spots"	"Camp near a waterfall" "Unspoiled South Carolina mountains"	"Vacationers have found a mecca" "Rare wildlife and waterfowl" "Room for the solitary beachcomber"
Magazines	*Better Homes & Gardens, Family Circle, Good Housekeeping, Glamour, Redbook*	*Better Homes & Gardens, Woodall's, Smithsonian, Travel, House Beautiful*	*Fishing World* (Two insertions)	*Camping Journal* and *Popular Science*	*Natural History, New Yorker, Southern Living, Woman's Day, Smithsonian*

Arch Woodside and William Motes, "Sensitivities of Market Segments to Separate Advertising Strategies," *Journal of Marketing*, Winter 1981, pp. 64–65.

EXHIBIT 5-2   Response Indicators for Segmentation

PURCHASE PATTERNS	
Product purchase rate:	The amount of a product class that is bought
Brand purchase rate:	The amount of a specific branded item that is bought
Purchase situation:	The circumstances under which an item is bought
USAGE PATTERNS	
Product usage rate:	The amount of consumption over a period of time
Brand usage rate:	The volume of a specific branded item that is consumed
Usage situation:	The conditions under which the product or brand is consumed
PROPENSITIES TO RESPOND	
Brand loyalty levels:	The propensity to remain with or switch to a brand
Decision process stages:	The stage or point in the product purchase decision
PRODUCT BENEFIT DIMENSIONS	
Benefits sought:	Product attributes that are primary motivators of brand choice

tions, it is difficult to sort out target from nontarget customers; it is difficult, at best, to have a cost-effective campaign.

Criteria for Selecting Descriptors

The major considerations in the description of each segment are as follows: The descriptors for any segment must be characteristics common to individuals of that segment, the set of descriptors for any segment permits the marketer to discriminate clearly between segment and nonsegment individuals, and the descriptors must be measurable and understandable dimensions.

We will demonstrate the process of profiling segments using data generally available through market research bureaus. Exhibit 5-3 contains data drawn from the *1980 Study of Media and Markets* by the Simmons Market

EXHIBIT 5-3   Soaps and Detergents for Regular Laundry: Usage (Female Homemakers)

	HEAVY USERS	LIGHT USERS
Total:	22,005,000	26,004,000
Age: 18–24	8.9%	13.3%
25–34	27.7	16.5
35–44	28.9	8.6
45–54	19.2	11.0
55–64	10.1	17.1
65 or older	5.3	33.4
	100%	100%
Household Income:		
$35,000 or more	15.0%	6.5%
25,000 to 34,999	22.2	8.5
20,000 to 24,999	16.9	7.9
15,000 to 19,999	16.3	10.3
10,000 to 14,999	16.6	24.1
5,000 to 9,999	9.3	21.4
Under $5,000	3.7	21.2
	100%	100%
Urban:		
Metro Central City	29.3%	33.0%
Metro Suburban	41.9	41.6
Non Metro	28.8	25.4
	100%	100%

Source: Simmons Market Research Bureau, Inc., 1980 Study of Media and Markets.

Research Bureau.[6] These data reveal some information about heavy and light users of laundry detergent.

Common characteristics. Age, household income, and locality identify dominant characteristics *within* each age group. Individuals belonging to each group can be characterized by an age category. Over 56 percent of the heavy users are between the ages of 25 and 44, while over 61 percent of the light users fall into the category of 45 and over.

Each group can be described by income and residential characteristics. More than 54 percent of the heavy users have annual household incomes of $20,000 or more, while 77 percent of the light users have annual household incomes of less than $20,000. Both the heavy and light users are concentrated in the metropolitan suburban localities.

The fact that all three dimensions identify prominent characteristics of heavy and light users means that they qualify as segmenting variables.

Let us now look at the data to see whether they meet another need, clear discrimination among users.

Discriminating characteristics. Only age and income distinguish among user groups. The data indicate that there is a helpful separation of users on the basis of age; heavy users are younger than light users. And heavy users have higher incomes.

Locality is not helpful in differentiating among users. Both the heavy and light users are concentrated to the same degree in metropolitan suburbs with similar distributions in the city and nonmetropolitan areas. Locality is a useful descriptor for each group, but it does not discriminate one user from another.

Measurable, understandable characteristics. Age and income meet our third criterion for segmentation descriptors. They are characteristics, qualities, that we can assess and quantify. Furthermore, the quantitative expression of age and income characteristics is understandable. That is, the meaning is easily grasped. For example, when we describe someone as being 24 years old, it is quite clear as to how much time has elapsed since that person's birth.

We will now look at some descriptors of segments.

Demographic Descriptors

The dimensions in the preceding example were only three of many possible dimensions like occupation, education, household size, and so on. These dimensions make up the category of demographic dimensions customary in segmentation. The term *demographics* means those objectives and commonly known dimensions we use to describe the population. Exhibit 5-4 lists the popular demographics in segmentation.

Demographic descriptions of market segments are very common and are almost the standard language of the communications community. For example, a marketer must determine which media offer audiences that match target specifications. To match up media audiences with the target market, there must be common dimensions for audience and target specifications. Virtually all the media describe their audience in terms of demographics. Thus in order to determine whether a medium can deliver a desired audience, the marketer must have demographic descriptors about its target.

Demographics are popular because they are easy to understand and quantify. A person who is asked his or her age can readily respond because it is a known datum, expressible in numerical terms with a meaning that everyone can easily understand.

A major weakness of demographics is that they are often inaccurate predictors of marketplace behavior. They characterize and qualify segments

**EXHIBIT 5-4   Commonly Used
Demographic Variables
for Segmentation**

Age

Sex

Income (individual and household)

Occupation

Education

Marital status

Race

National origin

Household size

Number of children

Age of children

Housing status (own or rent)

Value of home

Geographical region

Residence location (urban or nonurban)

Employment status

as prospective purchasers, but figures do not automatically predict behavior. For example, over 40 percent of the purchasers of Cadillacs have annual household incomes of over $35,000, while less than 20 percent of Chevrolet purchasers are at that level. Above-average income qualifies someone to buy a Cadillac, then, as compared with a Chevrolet, but an above-average income by itself does not lead a person to a Cadillac. One may choose a Lincoln, a BMW, a Peugeot . . .

Nondemographic Descriptors

The search for appropriate segment descriptors leads to a desire for dimensions that reflect what actually takes place in the market, dimensions that will direct the marketer toward the right promotional strategy.

Marketers often turn to *lifestyle* or *psychographic* dimensions to supplement the demographic descriptions of segments. Lifestyle dimensions reflect the manner in which people spend their time, and come from studies of activities, interests, and opinions.[7] Exhibit 5-5 lists some of the measures.

The use of lifestyle descriptors rests on the theory that a person purchases a product because of its compatibility with his or her way of life. For example, lifestyle influences the selection of a make and model of automobile. The person who does the weekly grocery shopping, hauls trash to

EXHIBIT 5-5 Lifestyle Measures

ACTIVITIES	INTERESTS	OPINIONS
Work	Family	Themselves
Hobbies	Home	Social issues
Social events	Job	Politics
Vacation	Community	Business
Entertainment	Recreation	Economics
Club membership	Fashion	Education
Community	Food	Products
Shopping	Media	Future
Sports	Achievements	Culture

Source: Joseph Plummer, "The Concept and Application of Life Style Segmentation," *Journal of Marketing*, January 1974, p. 34.

the dump on weekends, and transports children to activities like football or baseball practice needs a different car than someone who spends considerable time camping during the summer and skiing during the winter.

Groups with an Appropriate Size

Segments should define *distinctive* groups with distinctive habits, but that is not all. They should also define groups having *sufficient demand* to warrant marketing effort. In most instances, a group's demand emerges not from population size alone but from its purchasing power. Assessing these two factors, a firm can determine potential revenue. Assume that you must assess the potential of two segments. One segment consists of fifty thousand people; the other of ten thousand. Without further analysis, you might consider the former to have greater potential. If those in the first segment can and are likely to buy $10 worth of your product, the potential revenue is $500,000 ($10 times 50,000 persons). If those in the second segment are likely to buy $60 worth of your product, then they represent a segment with a potential of $600,000.

Groups with Accessibility

While segments may be identifiable, sizable, and composed of people who have essentially similar market response tendencies, the marketer must also discover effective and efficient means for tapping this potential. For example, the potential for selling items targeted solely for left-handers is extremely large. Unfortunately, it is difficult to reach these left-handers at a *reasonable* cost. Why? There is currently no medium that aims principally at left-handers. Selection of any medium to reach left-handers would mean that you would be paying to reach audiences composed principally of right-handers, persons from whom you receive no revenue and for whom you should not be expending your promotional money.

Accessibility is a primary concern in formulating promotion plans. To communicate ideas, there must be a means of making contact. Without it, there is no channel for information delivery. If an advertising campaign is to deliver a message to a selected audience, it must find the newspapers and magazines it reads, the radio stations it tunes in, or the television programs it watches. A sales rep for forklifts cannot hope to get a company's business unless he or she identifies and contacts the right decision makers in the organization.

TARGET MARKET SELECTION

After segmenting the market and identifying the opportunities within it comes the task of choosing one or more segments as the targets of the marketing effort. Target market selection is the result of assessing the identified segments as to their potentials for the achievement of marketing and corporate goals. This analysis and its occurrence in the market segmentation process is depicted in Exhibit 5-6.

Effective target selection results from the following four efforts conducted simultaneously:

1. Determination of the marketing effort to be expended by the firm to properly serve the segments under consideration
2. Approximation of the cost required by the necessary effort
3. Analysis of the competitive environment in the segments
4. Estimation of the company performance in the competitive situation cited in item 3 as a result of the effort noted in item 1

Determining the Appropriate Effort

Recall that effective segmentation identifies segments with different response tendencies. A marketer must tap each segment's potential with a specific marketing effort. Part of this effort will be the promotion campaign. For example, two common segments in the toothpaste market are the decay prevention and economy segments. To tap the potential of the former segment, a company's marketing effort will center on the product benefit of decay prevention. The fundamental message in any promotion directed at this group will extol the product's decay prevention attributes. The other segment will respond to a campaign promising product value. Finally, the delivery of a message to each group may call for the use of different media, one by radio but the other with magazines.

EXHIBIT 5-6　The Market Segmentation and Target Selection Process

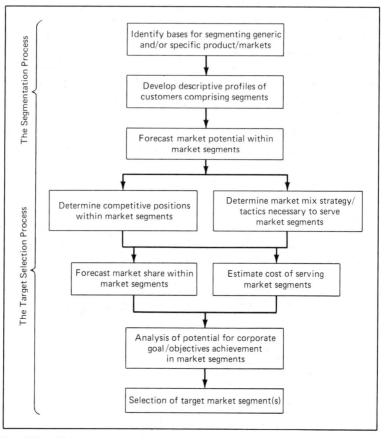

Cundiff/Still/Govoni, *Fundamentals of Modern Marketing*, Transparency Masters, 4th ed., © 1985. Reprinted by permission of Prentice-Hall, Inc., Englewood Cliffs, N.J.

How do we know which promotion efforts to employ? These efforts should be and are often determined by research and analysis. Returning to the toothpaste example in the preceding paragraph, we might survey a sample of each segment in order to gauge their relative enthusiasms with respect to decay prevention and the value aspects of toothpaste. Additionally, we may pose questions to determine the television programming they watch or the local radio station they tune in.

Assessment of the Costs

Different marketing efforts require different budgets. If a segment can be tapped with point-of-purchase display materials, the cost to the marketer will be much less than the cost of a campaign directed toward a segment that can be reached only with national prime-time television ads. The marketer must define the cost of the efforts necessary to produce the desired market response from a segment. In some instances, the costs necessary to develop the segment response may outweigh the returns from the segment.

Analysis of the Competitive Environment

In a highly developed market economy such as the United States, a company will seldom be the sole seller in the marketplace. More likely, a company will encounter competition for consumer dollars from companies with somewhat similar offerings. A valid assessment of the potential contributions of a segment includes an evaluation of the competitive environment. This evaluation focuses on the number of competitors selling to a segment, their market share, and the degree of loyalty that competitors establish within the segment. A large number of companies currently marketing to a segment may not be a deterrent to a company wishing to enter if it turns out that no single supplier or group of suppliers dominates the market. For that matter, the fact that a single company dominates the segment may not be a barrier to entry if one determines that those customers will probably switch brands if a better alternative comes along.

Projection of Performance

The assessment of the competitive environment together with the identification of the cost and effort needed to penetrate a segment help to predict accomplishment. The projected achievements can be expressed in the form of sales, market share, profitability, or some combination. If one projects that a segment will meet or exceed established goals for sales, market share, or profitability, then the company selects that segment.

PRODUCT POSITIONING

Identifying potential buyers and consumers by itself does not necessarily ensure the success of a marketing campaign.[8] If a target market is to buy a marketer's product, it is logical to assume that in the consumer's mind, the product is appealing not only in and of itself but also in comparison with other available products.[9] Consider the misunderstood prune. The traditional perception of the prune is that it is a dark fruit eaten solely for its laxative properties. This unappealing image has been an impediment to successful prune sales. In 1983 the California Prune Board, representing most of America's prune producers, launched a promotion campaign to improve the product image. Television commercials sought to convince viewers that the prune is a delicious, nutritious change from the usual breakfast and snack foods. The activity that led to the promotional campaign was product-positioning analysis.

Product-positioning analysis determines the product image—the impression of a product held in the consumer's mind—that one wants to communicate to the target market. This image, if it is appealing and distinctive, occupies a place or niche in the mind and has a strong influence when a product choice occurs. When you think of computers, you think of IBM. When you are in the market for a home sewing machine, you think of Singer. When you want a bullish stockbroker, you think of Merrill Lynch. When you order dessert gelatin in a restaurant, you are quite likely to ask for Jell-O. In each instance, a distinctive image has made an impression on your mind. And when you think of the product class, the specific brand or company image comes to mind.

The product-positioning decision is especially important for promotional strategy. Promotion communicates ideas, and these ideas in turn influence market response. The basic message idea about the product or service, whether delivered through advertising, personal selling, publicity, or sales promotion, depends on the product image, those impressions about the promoted product that influence choice. Positive, distinctive impressions about a product increase the chances of its selection among a number of options.

In the remainder of this section we will describe the major types of product images, and then we will look at the process of identifying and selecting an image.

Types of Positioning

A product's image arises from one or more of the following considerations: product attributes, symbolic projections, and competitive positioning.

Product Attribute Images

Many brands appeal to consumers because of benefits that stem directly from product features. The Sears Diehard car battery promises dependable cold-weather starts from its power-packed, long-life cells. Parents are confident that their children will take aspirin with little coaxing because of the chewable, flavored ingredients of St. Joseph aspirin. You do not have to worry about your next washload (especially ring around the collar) if you use Wisk with its special cleaning agents. The promotion message, each time, concentrates on the consumer gains resulting from product performance.

Images Based on Symbolism

There are many products for which differentiation among product attributes is either insignificant or nonexistent. This may be true of technically simple products like a candy bar or of products for which consumers do not spend much time making decisions. For such products, the position arises from broad symbolisms rather than specific product performance. Beer marketing is an example of such positioning. Most beers do not differ significantly across such product characteristics as taste and aroma. If there are differences, average drinkers cannot detect them. Brand images, therefore, do not emerge from product attributes but from associations with the moods or feelings projected from the advertisement settings.[10] Budweiser's image is not product based; it is an image of a beer for blue-collar men. Its entertaining television commercials show construction workers, policemen, firemen, and Olympic hopefuls engaged in activities. The association of Bud with the impressions of these settings produces the brand image.

Direct Competitive Positioning

In a highly competitive setting a product may not be successful simply by being distinctive. It may have to convince consumers explicitly that it has advantages over competitors' products.

An image can be established with respect to the position of a competitor. In this approach, a product's position uses the competitor's position as a reference point. Burger King's advertising in 1982 delivered the message that its hamburger tasted better than McDonald's. Pepsi-Cola directly compares itself with Coca-Cola; 7-Up positions itself as an uncola. The Paperboard Packaging Council claimed that milk in paper cartons contained more vitamins than milk in plastic ones.

The Product-Positioning Process: An Example

The underlying rationale for product-positioning decisions consists of the following:

1. The segmentation process has identified groups with different market response tendencies.
2. Different response tendencies are reflected in the differences of product preference.
3. A brand has the potential to assume many images.
4. A segment's perception of a brand is determined largely by what is communicated.
5. A segment will select the brand its members perceive as coming closer than any other to satisfying their preference.

To understand this process, let us consider the job of positioning a new bar of soap on the basis of product benefits. We must first segment the market, and we will begin by asking a simple question, What possible benefits can a consumer look for in a bar of hand soap? Assume that market research tells us that people generally consider one or more of the following qualities:

> Moisturizes the skin
> Deodorizes
> Cleans
> Accents the decor of the bathroom
> Alleviates skin problems . . .

If we assume that these factors are major determinants in the choice of a brand of soap, we can segment the market according to the values held by different individuals. For example, there may be individuals who are more concerned with the moisturizing contents of soap than with the decorative aspects. There may be a sufficient number of these individuals to constitute a sizable segment. And it is with them in mind that the marketer decides what position or image the new brand should assume.

Let us develop our example further. For simplicity, assume that only two dimensions—moisturizing ability and decorative quality—are relevant to consumers. To determine the value that the individuals might place on each of these two dimensions, we might use a questionnaire with the following request:

> Please indicate the degree of importance that each factor has in your evaluation of a bar of soap.

	Very Unimportant				Very Important
Moisturizing ability	1	2	3	4	5
Decorative qualities	1	2	3	4	5

Responses by individuals to this request provide information on the desired qualities of the product. We could graphically display the response of any and all individuals, as we show in Exhibit 5-7. Assume that the points in Exhibit 5-7 (the product space) represent individuals' sets of responses. There are those who want soap that is both highly decorative and moisturizing. They are graphically represented as points in the upper-right portion. On the other hand, those whose responses indicate a strong desire for moisturizing but some degree of indifference to decoration are plotted in the upper-left area. We can see that there are three general clusters of responses; they are highlighted by circles. These clusters are market segments.

Segment A consists of individuals who place heavy emphasis on the moisturizing and decorative qualities of soap. Individuals who are concerned about moisture content but are relatively indifferent about the aesthetics

EXHIBIT 5-7   Graphic Illustration of Positioning Alternatives

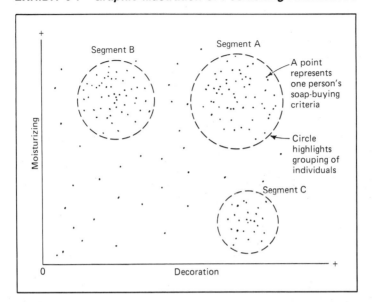

of soap constitute segment B. And segment C represents those who choose soap largely on decorative potential.

After identification of the market preferences, the next step is to determine the position that our product should occupy. Specifically, which combination of product attributes do we wish to project in our soap? Should the projected image be consistent with the preference of segment A, high-moisture content with good decorative qualities? Or should we concentrate our efforts only on promotion of a highly decorative soap?

Selection of the specific image is intertwined with the target selection decision and depends on the answers to these two questions:

Which benefits can the product actually deliver?

Which segment position is the most profitable?

The marketer can probably get a significant number of target consumers to try a product because of promised benefits, but the retention of customers depends on the fulfillment of expectations. The inability to deliver on promised benefits not only leads ultimately to the product's failure but jeopardizes the credibility of future campaigns. For example, a manufacturer may target segment A. Consumers from that segment may initially be lured by the company advertising promises of an excellent moisturizing soap with appealing appearance. However, if the soap does not deliver according to customers' expectations, the likelihood of repurchase diminishes.

The determination of profitability calls for an analysis of the potential revenue represented by a segment, the strengths of competitive products in a segment, and the cost incurred to develop a product image.

For the soap example, one analysis would be the potential sales in each segment, estimating the total volume purchased and multiplying that volume by a price figure. In mathematical terms, the potential sales are

$$S_i = V_i \times P$$

where

S_i = dollar sales potential from segment i
V_i = total volume of purchases by segment i
P = price per unit

Thus one would calculate market potentials for segments A, B, and C. This calculation provides a preliminary indication of the relative magnitude of opportunities.

Realistically, no single company operating in a competitive environment is likely to reach the total market potential. With companies competing for shares of a segment, the marketer must assess the strengths of rivals in each segment. More specifically, the marketer's sales will be based on the total potential of the market and the share that is captured:

$$\text{Sales}_{ij} = S_i \times M_{ij}$$

where

Sales_{ij} = dollar sales in segment i for company j
S_i = total dollar potential from segment i
M_{ij} = market share for company j in segment i

From the preceding mathematical formula, we can easily conclude that the projection of company sales is sensitive to the estimation of market share. While there is no foolproof method for generating market-share estimates, there are general guidelines. First, the historical and current market shares of competitors must be considered. As a rule, sizable market share concentrated in the hands of one or a few competitors for a length of time may suggest a formidable task in trying to capture sales. In such a case, it is logical to reason that those competitors have found a way to hold on to their customers. However, although historical and current competitive share data indicate strength (or lack of it) in the marketplace, they *do not necessarily* predict the trend for the future. A second major consideration in forecasting market share is the intensity of brand loyalty among the competition's customers. If the loyalty of competitors' customers is high, let us say nine of the last ten product purchases have been competitors' brands because they actually like the product performance, then getting market share through brand switching may be difficult. Where competitive loyalty is high, the marketer will find switching resistance and thus should reduce market-share expectations.

Projections of sales potential and market share provide a measure of revenues. But revenue projection is only one-half of the elements needed to estimate profitability. The final element in the determination of profitability is a realistic assessment of the costs of a successful marketing campaign for each segment. The marketer must consider the funds required to support the appropriate advertising strategy, the sales promotion campaigns, the personal-selling activities, and the necessary publicity work. The marketer compares these costs with the expected revenues to estimate profitability. The decision rule is that a company chooses the segment product position with highest profitability expectations.

Repositioning

A brand does not have to be stuck with the image the company chooses at the outset. The nature of the marketplace changes because of competitive conditions and consumers' lifestyles. Repositioning will sometimes give new life to the sales of a brand, usually the result of a broader appeal to either existing segments or new segments. Arm & Hammer Baking Soda's market share had seriously eroded in the late 1960s owing to the introduction of numerous cleansers, deodorizers, and personal hygiene products with heavy promotional backing.[11] To turn things around, Arm & Hammer repositioned itself in the homemaker's mind as an economical, natural cleanser and deodorant. As a substitute for chemical products, Arm & Hammer portrayed itself as an effective deodorizer for problem areas such as the refrigerator and the bathroom, as well as a cleanser for the swimming pool. The repositioning worked.

The need for *repositioning* is often evident in declining market share and/or market potential figures. Changes in market share provide a direct indication of competitive standing, while market potential data may reflect the expansion, contraction, or stability of industry volume. Exhibit 5-8 suggests a few alternatives in light of market share and market potential trends. In the face of a declining market, the long-term objective would be to reposition into other markets, markets with significant potential. Additionally, in the short-term, a declining share would suggest defensive strategy where the current positioning is reevaluated to determine the best approach to stemming the erosion of competitive standing. If market share has been increasing, it indicates a strong position which should be maintained as long as the market has significant potential.

EXHIBIT 5-8   Repositioning Alternatives Based on Market Share and Market Potential Trends

	MARKET SHARE	
	Decline	Growth
MARKET POTENTIAL — Decline	Short term: Stem the erosion of share by reviewing current position Long term: Look for positioning in other markets	Short term: Maintain current position for competitive edge Long term: Look to reposition in other markets
MARKET POTENTIAL — Growth	Short term: Review current position Long term: Stay in the market	Short term: Maintain current position Long term: Stay in the market

An expanding or growing market represents additional opportunities in the long term. Repositioning may be necessary when share in a growing market declines. Such a decline suggests that the brand is not getting additional sales in proportion to what it had in the past. In the case of an increasing share in an expanding market, the brand is clearly positioned well. The objective then is to maintain the successful positioning strategy.

SUMMARY

No single company has the resources to satisfy the needs and wants of everybody. There is too much diversity among a large population, and this diversity means that efforts to satisfy everybody would be very costly.

Market segmentation is the partitioning of a large market with diverse needs and wants into submarkets. These submarkets or segments are groups of individuals with similar marketplace habits.

Effective segmentation creates groups describable along measurable and understandable dimensions, of an appropriate size, and accessible for communications.

From the identified segments, the marketer selects a target market, the focus of the marketing effort. Profitability—projected by evaluation of the effects of competitive actions, the efforts required of the marketer, and the cost of that required effort—determines the final target selection.

To penetrate a market segment, that segment must find the product appealing. The extent of the appeal depends on the positioning of the product. There are two objectives in positioning: creation of a product image that is distinctive, and development of an image whose advantages are superior to those of competitors.

With this understanding of the marketplace and its opportunities, the promotion planner is ready to think about the activities needed to capitalize on those opportunities. Let us now look at two planning areas that determine the nature of promotional activities: the objectives and the budget.

REVIEW AND DISCUSSION QUESTIONS

1. Explain the philosophy underlying the concept of market segmentation.

2. Why is market segmentation essential to the success of so many marketing campaigns?

3. Explain the importance of creating groups with homogeneous behavior.

4. In selecting descriptors for market segments, what criteria should be employed?

5. Even though demographics are not precise predictors of marketplace behavior, they are still popular as dimensions for segmentation. Why are demographics imprecise predictors of marketplace behavior? How do you explain the popularity of demographics for segmentation given their imprecise predictions?

6. What is meant by psychographics and why are they useful in segmentation? Give examples.

7. What is meant when it is said that a market segment should be an appropriate size to warrant the attention of the marketer?

8. Unless market segments are easily accessible, they may not represent any opportunity for the marketer. Explain.

9. Describe the process by which a marketer selects a target market after going through the segmentation process.

10. When is it likely that a marketing communications campaign will have more than one target?

11. What is meant by product positioning? Cite an example of product positioning that you have recently seen or heard about.

12. Why is product positioning critical in a highly competitive environment?

13. Assume that you are responsible for positioning a new brand of mouthwash. Describe the process that you would go through to identify your brand's image. Begin the task by listing all the characteristics that make a brand of mouthwash attractive to a consumer. Be specific about the type of information that you would need to make a decision.

14. Repositioning is one means for injecting new life into a product. What do you think repositioning involves? Cite some examples of products that have been successfully repositioned.

NOTES

1. Ronald E. Frank, W. F. Massy, and Y. Wind, *Market Segmentation* (Englewood Cliffs, N.J.: Prentice-Hall, 1972), pp. 4–6.

2. Jan-Erik Modig and F. Stewart DeBruicker, "Ocean Spray Cranberries, Inc. (A): The Fruit Positioning Study," in *Cases in Consumer Behavior*, ed. F. Stewart DeBruicker and Scott Ward (Englewood Cliffs, N.J.: Prentice-Hall, 1980), pp. 137–61.

3. Arch Woodside and William Motes, "Sensitivities of Market Segments to Separate Advertising Strategies," *Journal of Marketing*, Winter 1981, pp. 63–73.

4. Russell Haley, "A Benefit Segmentation: A Decision-Oriented Tool," *Journal of Marketing*, July 1968, pp. 30–35.

5. Henry Assael and A. Marvin Roscoe, Jr., "Approaches to Market Segmentation Analysis," *Journal of Marketing*, October 1976, pp. 67–76.

6. *The 1980 Study of Media and Markets* (New York: Simmons Market Research Bureau), Vol. P-23.

7. Joseph Plummer, "The Concept and Application of Life Style Segmentation," *Journal of Marketing*, January 1974, pp. 33–37.

8. Theodore Leavitt, "Marketing Success Through Differentiation—of Anything," *Harvard Business Review*, January-February 1980, pp. 83–91.

9. Jack Trout and Al Ries, "The Positioning Era: A View Ten Years Later," *Advertising Age*, July 16, 1979, pp. 39–42.

10. "Marketing Emphasis Is on Consistent Imagery When Selling Beer: Stroh Exec.," *Marketing News*, March 4, 1983, p. 10.

11. Jack Honomichi, "The Ongoing Saga of 'Mother Baking Soda,' " *Advertising Age*, September 30, 1982, pp. M2ff.

6

Establishing Promotional Objectives and the Promotional Budget

In this chapter we address two important and related steps in the development of a promotional campaign. The first is the establishment of objectives for the communications strategy, and the second is the determination of the budget to carry out that strategy. We will discuss these facets individually with the full realization that there is a vital interaction between these decision areas. In practice, that interaction may require an iterative process of objective setting and budget determination, as indicated in Exhibit 6-1.

ESTABLISHING PROMOTIONAL OBJECTIVES

Promotional objectives are the goals of the promotional activities. They should not only be statements of what management desires from the effort but also be practical expectations of what will occur in the marketplace if the mix of the communications elements realizes its full potential.

The establishment of objectives not only facilitates the planning of a

EXHIBIT 6-1   Interaction of Promotional Objectives and Budget

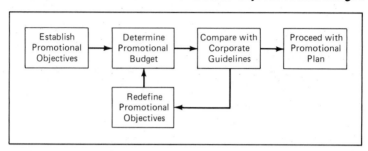

promotional campaign but also provides the foundation for the evaluation of the campaign effort. The objectives of the campaign also indicate the direction in which the resources of the communications departments will flow. In essence, the objectives are clear statements of the results that management rightfully expects from those who develop and execute the communications strategy.

In this section we discuss the criteria by which we can judge whether an objective is sound. We will elaborate on these criteria through the use of a working example, which will focus on the objectives of an overall promotional effort. The development of objectives for each of the specific promotional elements will be covered in the individual discussions of advertising, personal selling, sales promotion, and public relations. Clearly, as we note here and several times throughout the text, the coordination and integration of objectives, plans, and actions among the various forms of promotional effort are vital ingredients in mounting a successful promotional strategy.

Characteristics of Good Objectives

Good promotional objectives do not happen by chance. Although an organization may, for some period of time, find a successful set of working objectives through a haphazard, arbitrary, or intuitive process, the likelihood of continued success that way is slim at best. Objectives set in this manner provide poor guidelines for channeling the organization's efforts. Good promotional objectives come from extensive consideration of the factors that affect the welfare of the organization in general and the promotion department in particular. Good promotional objectives emerge from what is beneficial for the firm, what is desirable, and what is achievable. While the details of objective statements may differ across industries, firms, and product lines within a firm, there is a set of dimensions that underlies any good promotional objective. Valid promotional objectives have the following characteristics in common:

1. They rest on an awareness of the corporate and marketing objectives.
2. They depend on a clear understanding of the target audience and its response tendencies to different levels of communications.
3. They are quantifiable.
4. They reflect as much as possible the actual effects of promotion activity.
5. They are demanding, yet achievable.
6. They articulate realistic time frames.

Let us now examine each of these characteristics.

The Relationship between Corporate, Marketing, and Promotion Objectives

Good promotional objectives must encompass more than the narrow perspective of the promotion group. They must embody an understanding of how the communications efforts contribute to the *company's overall interests*. Valid objectives are the result of a thorough analysis of all the factors that affect the company's welfare. These factors include the response tendencies of the marketplace to the communications elements, the competitors' communications efforts, the company's overall objectives and resources, and environmental factors such as political, legal, social, and ethical constraints. In short, the development of promotional objectives must extend to considerations outside the promotion department.

The promotion manager does not have complete freedom in establishing objectives for his or her department. A good manager realizes that there is more to consider than his or her immediate areas of responsibility. The company's ultimate success or failure depends on how well the individual departments understand their contributions to the enterprise's performance and the extent to which these departments relinquish some of their independence for the purpose of coordinating and balancing activities. Departments that do not integrate their efforts with others may very well increase their own performance at the expense of the company as a whole. The promotion manager may arbitrarily establish a goal of having awareness of the brand name among 95 percent of the population, and this goal by itself appears appropriate for the promotion department. But if the company does not have the financial capability to support such an objective, it may be hurt by the promotion department's attempts to maximize its performance.

Exhibit 6-2 illustrates the priority of objectives. We see that the corporate objectives take precedence over the objectives of all other areas of the firm. Marketing's objectives must contribute to the achievement of the firm's mission as well as its own, and the promotion department's objectives in turn must find their proper scale within the larger goals. While the objectives

EXHIBIT 6-2   The Hierarchy of Objectives

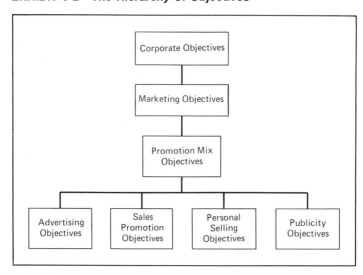

within the organization appear to be separate, they are actually complementary. The establishment of objectives within and across various areas of the firm calls for exchange of ideas about what each area seeks to do and is capable of doing.

To illustrate what we have said so far and to help the reader understand concepts in subsequent sections, let us develop a working example. Assume that the stated corporate objective is to raise the earnings per share by two dollars. Marketing may contribute to the achievement of that objective, increasing the firm's revenue by increasing the share of the market by three percentage points. How can the promotional group assist in the achievement of the marketing objective of boosting market share? We would begin by getting together with the marketing planners, and we would explore with them their ideas and our ideas on how the promotional mix can accomplish the goal. Let us assume that after extensive discussion, we all agree that market-share increases will come from the new uses for the product. Thus our preliminary objective might be:

To communicate the new uses of the company's product

While this statement of objective is not necessarily in its final form, it is a good starting point. It began with a consideration of what the promotional department can do for the marketing department and ultimately for the firm. The subsequent sections will show how to improve the objective statement as we examine the other characteristics of a valid objective statement.

Definition of the Target Audience and the Audience Response

Well-formulated promotion objectives are those that aim toward *well-defined market opportunities*. In no uncertain terms, the manager must identify the target audience that represents the market opportunity. This identification emerges from the market segmentation process we described in Chapter 5.

In addition to a description of the target audience, there should also be a corresponding statement of the expected response from that audience. Simply saying whom the promotion effort aims at is not enough. The manager must add a declaration of the expected reaction of that audience upon experiencing the communications effort. This projection emerges from a clear understanding of the consumer decision process and the promotion mix's influence on that process.

Returning to our working example, we now see that we must clearly describe the target market with which we wish to communicate. We will improve our original version of the objective statement when we have investigated the segments the marketing planners wished to reach. We will then have a clear idea of which audience is to be the recipient of our messages. Thus an improved statement of objectives might read:

To communicate the new uses of our product to an audience that is female, between the ages of 18 and 25, and has at least a high-school education

The specific demographic descriptors we have used are incidental to the point of this section. What is important is that we have been very explicit about who it is that we want to receive our messages.

At this point we can further refine our statement to reflect our analysis of how our communications efforts will affect the consumers of the target group. To do this, we would include in the objective a statement of the expected audience response.

Returning to our example, we have a decision to make. Do we look for a heightening of awareness level of our product uses, do we expect people to change attitudes toward the product itself, or do we expect to have an impact on the intentions to buy our product? Assume for the moment that research has indicated that the target audience already holds a favorable attitude toward the brand and does indeed purchase it, but the purchase rate is low because of the limited number of situations in which people can use the product. Educating the audience about new applications would then be a valid objective. For example, the makers of Windex, a cleaning solution, sought sales increase by informing consumers that Windex cleans not only windows but also the metal and glass exteriors of household appliances.

An improvement of our working example might take the following form:

To instill awareness of the new uses of our product in an audience that is female, between the ages of 18 and 25, and has at least a high-school education

Where is the improvement? We have become more precise in the meaning of "communicate." We now understand that the desired and expected communications effect is on the consumers' awareness level. The persons who execute the promotion plan now know that they are not charged with changing attitudes; they also know that the expected communications effect is not increased sales.

Can we enhance the statement of objective further? Yes! We believe we can!

Quantified Terms

Up to this point we know whom we want to reach and the type of response we want to generate from the audience. The question that we will deal with now is, *How much do we want of the desired response?* Specifically, what is the extent to which we wish to raise awareness of product uses among the target group? Do we want 5 percent of the audience to be aware of the uses? Is it possible to hope for 20 percent? Is 45 percent awareness level among the target group reasonable?

We must be as precise as possible in specifying our objectives. The degree of precision with which we can *assess performance* is determined largely by the extent to which we have *quantified* the established objectives. Therefore we could further refine the working example of objectives this way:

To instill awareness of the new uses of our product to 40 percent of our audience, which is female, between the ages of 18 and 25, and has at least a high-school education

We will assume that our arbitrary use of 40 percent rests on some rational grounds. In actuality, the quantification of goals is not an easy task. Typically, research would lay the groundwork, assessing the current status so that the manager could measure real gains from promotion. In our example, we might wish to ascertain the current level of awareness of different uses among the target prior to the campaign. Quantified expectations of promotion performance would then be based on evidence about promotion effects.

Valid Measures of Performance

Whenever benchmarks are used to assess performance, they must be *valid measures of performance*. Otherwise the manager cannot obtain a true picture of the results of specific actions. Since promotional objectives serve as reference points for the evaluation of the communications effort, these objectives must concentrate on areas for which the promotional program can probably be held accountable. These objectives should also represent as closely as possible what is clearly the effect of promotional effort, not the effect of other variables in the marketing mix like pricing and distribution.

Good objectives must provide measures of performance so that the manager can confidently assign responsibility for results. In an ideal case, these measures neither overrate nor underrate the accomplishment. Such measures depend on a thorough understanding of the effect of promotional effort on the mechanics of the marketplace. And that understanding is reflected in the detailed definition of the objectives. In a realistic setting, it is virtually impossible to identify a *truly* valid measure. The marketplace environment, which includes competitive actions, economic uncertainties, and the like, is so complex that the best researchers can only approximate, not isolate, promotion effects.

In our working example, we have yet to elaborate in our definition exactly what we mean by the term *awareness*. We can achieve this improvement by stating exactly how to measure the concept of awareness, and there are many ways to do it. There is an awareness level known as *unaided recall*, where the audience spontaneously calls to mind the message of the campaign without prompting. Here is an example: "Please describe three advertisements you have recently seen." Or awareness can be defined as *aided recall*, where the audience is able to recall the message after prompting with some message-related clue. An aided recall measure for an airline promotion might take this form: "What airline advertisements have you seen lately?" The list of different measures of awareness is quite formidable, and it is not our purpose in this book to identify all of them. We simply want to point out that the manager must be careful to be conceptually precise in defining the objectives. Our working example would be strengthened by the addition of a phrase that defines awareness:

To instill awareness, as measured by unaided recall, of the new uses of our product in 40 percent of our audience, which is female, between the ages of 18 and 25, and has at least a high-school education

Achievable yet Demanding

With the achievement of valid goals, the manager can be sure of having tapped the maximum potential of his or her department. *Goals should demand a full effort*. A sales manager, for example, in setting quotas for a salesperson, sets a level that brings out all the skills. Otherwise opportunities may be missed and the company pays for services not used.

Goals that are too easy or goals virtually impossible to reach contribute nothing to the efficiency and effectivensss of an organization. Readily attainable goals result in wasted resources and a false view of the organization's ability. Goals set too high are demoralizing to those held accountable. Knowledge that goals cannot be attained even with the strongest of efforts damages the credibility of the leadership.

Time Horizon

Success in the marketplace is rarely an overnight phenomenon. Success is merely one phase in a process. A series of intermediate gains will usually precede the achievement of ultimate success. The gain in one phase is predicated on the accomplishment or gain in a prior phase. *Long-term* success flows from a series of *short-term* successes.

The development of promotional objectives must recognize that communicating with the public is a process. One transmits messages over time, and time is required for the messages to have an impact. Changing attitudes must begin with awareness of the message. Then comes comprehension of the message before people can develop the attitudes the firm desires. Good objectives not only detail the expected effects but also state when the effects should show up among the target audience.

In our working example, we have not yet established a time horizon or schedule for the objectives. Clearly, the communications will take place over time, and we must establish when the awareness will come about:

To instill, within twelve months, awareness, as measured by unaided recall, of the new uses of our product in 40 percent of our audience, which is female, between the ages of 18 and 25, and has at least a high-school education

The insertion of the time element into the objective statement recognizes that we measure an organization's efficiency not only by what results it obtains but also by when those results occur. The insertion of a time element acknowledges that the response of the marketplace is the result of a sequence of events of which the communications program serves as the catalyst or spark. In our example, we might have chosen a twelve-month time horizon with something like this rationale: The product to promote is a consumer food item, cheese. To communicate the new ways to serve our cheese, we will use ads in a national magazine and in-store demonstrations. Ad insertions in several issues may be necessary before the consumer takes notice of just one. In addition, in-store demonstrations of cheese preparations depend on the willingness of supermarket managers to allot valuable floor space. Our sales force may need time to build retailer cooperation.

OBJECTIVES AND
THE PROMOTION MIX

We have stressed something very basic but very important—valid objectives are the focal point in planning promotional strategy. Now we will take a look at how promotion objectives affect the mix of promotion elements. Earlier we said that objectives should be based on an understanding of how communications will affect the audience and its decision making. With that in mind, our discussion of promotion objectives will center on the two major types of decision processes: high-involvement and low-involvement.

High-Involvement Product Promotion

Let us assume that we are putting together a mix for the promotion of a new, expensive lawn mower-tractor. Exhibit 6-3 sets the framework for our discussion.

The long-term and ultimate objective of the campaign is to stimulate purchases. Prior to that, we must develop awareness of the product's existence, comprehension of its attributes, and favorable opinion toward it. The nature of the promotional objectives and the activities appropriate to their achievement, therefore, will change over time.

**EXHIBIT 6-3   Objectives and Promotion Mix Over
Time: A High-Involvement Product**

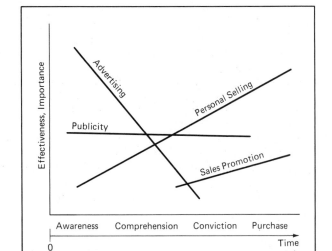

Larry J. Rosenberg, *Marketing*, © 1977, p. 407. Adapted by permission of Prentice-Hall, Inc., Englewood Cliffs, N.J.

At the outset, we must create market awareness of the product. Advertising is especially effective and will play a major role. It reaches many people quickly and at a reasonable cost. Advertising space in lawn and garden publications will be one avenue of market contact. Concurrently, publicity releases will go out to media with content in praise of the product. For example, we may send a new-product announcement to the editor of *Flower & Garden* magazine.

Interested prospective customers need information about product performance to make a decision. Advertising is an important source of information about product features and their benefits. At the same time, publicity articles can highlight our product benefits to their interested readers. The role of personal selling by retail salespeople increases as interested consumers visit the showrooms to get a better idea of the tractor.

When we want persuasion and attitude change, personal selling takes over as the most important element. Until now, personal selling has played a relatively minor role. It is an individualized communications activity and very inefficient for reaching large numbers of people to convey a simple message. By this time, however, interested consumers should be familiar with the product's attributes. The tailored, adaptive communications of personal selling shape consumer attitudes about product performance. Advertising, because it is an impersonal medium, has only minor persuasive effects for this high-involvement consumer decision, but it may still reinforce or add to consumers' knowledge of the product. Finally, the promotion campaign directs its attention to conversion of favorable attitudes into sales. The importance of personal selling increases, to reinforce favorable attitudes and eliminate uncertainties. At the same time, sales promotion activities may stimulate people to purchase. We may want to motivate retailers by offering bonuses. Or we may entice the consumer with a limited-time offer of a free mulching attachment.

Low-Involvement Product Promotion

We have just discussed the relationship between objectives and promotion activities for a high-involvement product. The objectives and corresponding activities would differ for other situations. For instance, the promotion campaign for a new brand of canned green beans, a low-involvement product, we would portray in the graphic form shown in Exhibit 6-4. Since extended information processing does not precede purchase, we do not need a campaign to develop awareness, followed by comprehension and attitude change. We need a campaign that first generates awareness. But opinions about the product do not follow from product awareness or knowledge. Rather, experience of the product may be the more effective means for shaping consumer opinions. Product trial is the major objective, and we will achieve that through an intensive sales promotion effort including coupons for free samples, in-store taste samples, and so on. After the initial

**EXHIBIT 6–4   Objectives and Promotion Mix Over
Time: A Low-Involvement Product**

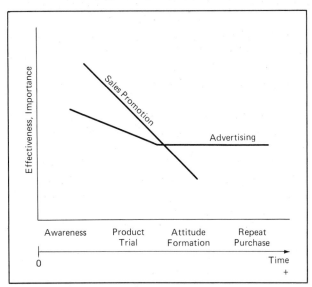

Larry J. Rosenberg, *Marketing*, © 1977, p. 407. Adapted by permission of Prentice-Hall, Inc., Englewood Cliffs, N.J.

trial period, we reinforce consumer attitudes and repeat purchases by reminder advertising. This also ensures a high degree of product familiarity, a familiarity that influences subsequent choices.

OBJECTIVES ARE IMPORTANT

We cannot overstate the importance of well-planned objectives. Sound promotion objectives provide direction for the communications effort and benchmarks for the assessment of performance. Good promotional objectives contribute to the achievement of corporate and marketing goals; they demand maximum effort from the promotional group; they depend on audience analysis; they are very clear in the definition and quantification of the goals; and they derive from an understanding that the communications process takes place over time. With this foundation, our attention now turns to the budget.

DETERMINING THE PROMOTIONAL BUDGET

In this section we deal with one of the most significant issues of promotional strategy—determining the promotional budget. Yet, despite its importance, it is probably the least understood of the key strategic decisions.

Some managers see budgeting as a routine, distracting, number-crunching exercise that one does more for the benefit of the controller than for the marketers. This view, prevalent in some organizations, is decidedly inaccurate. Budgeting is an important and vital activity for the marketing manager. Let us examine some of the values that derive from a careful budgeting effort:

1. It is the quantification of the marketing plan and strategy that the marketing organization will execute.
2. It defines in compatible terms (dollars) the relative commitments to each of the promotional activities in order to achieve the established marketing goals and objectives.
3. It provides an opportunity for managers of individual promotional activities to integrate their plans with each other and to adjudicate any discrepancies.
4. It is a benchmark that allows marketing and promotional managers to measure progress toward the established goals through the monitoring of the input (action) side of the performance equation.
5. It serves as an input to the company's financial-planning process, which is essential to a healthy and viable organization.

The reader may wish to refer to Chapter 1 for the overview discussion of promotional decisions to see how this vital area fits into an overall strategic context.

Procter & Gamble has a well-earned reputation as a successful marketer. Its internal budget guideline for promotional activities for new products is to spend in the first year an amount equal to the expected first year's sales. If this is true, how did P&G determine that this is the appropriate amount? Would this rule of thumb work for everyone? If not, why not?

Hanes, when it introduced L'eggs (see Chapter 1), spent at the national rate of $10 million for advertising and $5 million for consumer sales promotion, and it established an extensive route sales force to cover each outlet directly. These expenditures were more than double the amount the entire industry spent for promotional support of branded hosiery.[1] How did the Hanes management make these decisions? Were they good decisions?

In addressing the budgeting issue, we are seeking to find answers to two fundamental questions regarding funds for efforts to achieve promotional objectives:

1. How much should we spend for *all* promotional activities for the company or product line?
2. How should we allocate the expenditure among the various promotional elements available?

We will answer these two questions by exploring the traditional approaches to these spending decisions and some recently developed methods that hold promise for improving the effectiveness of these decisions. Before embarking on the detailed discussion of budgeting techniques, we must present the theoretical framework for the promotional budgeting decisions.

Theoretical Framework

Every business decision has at its root the achievement of some company objective or goal. The most widely accepted goal among business executives is the maximization of company profits. The teachings of many economists and organizational behaviorists reinforce this position.

The Theory of Profit Maximization

If we accept *profit maximization* as the primary long-term goal of our promotional decisions (and marketing as a concept certainly supports this view), then as managers we are seeking to expend promotional dollars of such an amount and in such a way as to achieve the maximum dollar profit for the company or the product line. If we follow the guidelines of classical economics, we will continue to spend for promotional activities up to the point where the additional (marginal) cost (promotional expense) equals the additional (marginal) revenue (profit contribution). In other words, economic theory suggests that the marketer continue to add promotional effort so long as the profit contribution from the additional sales is greater than the cost of the promotional effort. The marketer would also maintain the effort at the level where the additional costs and the additional profit contribution were equal. Exhibit 6-5 portrays this condition.

This description rests on two reasonable assumptions: (1) that sales returns for each incremental unit of promotion effort decrease (as a market is increasingly penetrated, additional sales opportunities become harder to locate); and (2) that each incremental unit of promotion effort costs more (efficient promotion vehicles are always selected first, the remaining vehicles are the less-efficient ones). Ultimately these two curves intersect, producing the "optimum" operating point where total profit contribution has reached its peak. There are, of course, other conditions and assumptions (like level marginal revenues), but these conceptualizations would only add complexity to the fundamental theoretical concept without really changing it.

Sales Response Considerations

Still, there is one further refinement to the theoretical framework that we cannot ignore. As we consider the implications of the above discussion, we should realize that both the total and the marginal profit contributions

EXHIBIT 6-5   Profit Maximization Based on Marginal Analysis

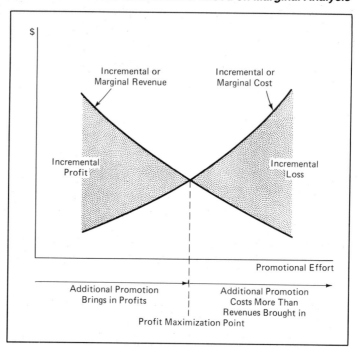

are determined by the level of sales activity. Therefore we are principally interested in the sales level that results from a given amount of promotional expenditure. This relationship between sales level and promotional expenditure is known as the *sales response function*. Exhibit 6-6 depicts four common perspectives on the nature of this relationship.

The earliest viewpoint of the relationship between promotional effort and sales is a linear response, as Exhibit 6-6A shows. In this perspective each increment of promotion produces an identical amount of sales gain. If these were profitable sales, then the logic of this approach dictates ever-increasing promotional budgets and expenditures, which would result in ever-increasing sales and profits. This view, carried to the extreme, implies promotional efforts and sales in excess of the gross national product. In its defense, it is not unreasonable to project that over some range of expenditures the market would in fact respond in this manner.

The second viewpoint (Exhibit 6-6B), identified as the threshold effect, has been most vigorously supported by Krugman of General Electric.[2] The basic premise here is that individual buyers in the market have to receive a minimum number of exposures to the promotional message before any significant buying action takes place. This would certainly seem to be valid for newly introduced products, complex items, and infrequently purchased

EXHIBIT 6-6   Different Perspectives of the Sales Response Function

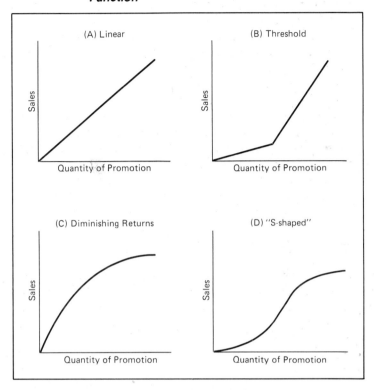

products (e.g., automobiles, appliances, furniture, etc.). Still left unanswered by this conceptualization is the question of what happens to the relationship after the threshold has been reached.

The third view, *diminishing returns* (Exhibit 6-6C), seeks to deal with the inherent weakness of the linear relationship. Here the manager speculates that each subsequent increment of promotional effort produces a reduced level of sales response. In this view the first promotional activity generates the highest level of additional sales, while later efforts may produce little or no incremental sales response. The approach recognizes that markets are finite in size and that consumers reach a saturation point in product usage. Additional promotional efforts, rather than adding to sales volume, may in fact do just the opposite.[3]

We may take exception to the idea that the sales response starts to decline from the very beginning, since it ignores the argument expressed earlier on threshold effects. On the other hand, this conceptualization deals reasonably well with the factors of saturation and market size.

Inspection of the fourth—"S-curve"—response function (Exhibit 6-6D) reveals that this is actually a *composite* of the three previous sales response concepts. It implies that the character of the market response changes over various ranges of promotional effort and at various levels of sales. In short, it incorporates the major contributions and perspectives of the other three viewpoints. We believe that there is a close parallel between the development of this theoretical framework and the parable of the blind people and the elephant.[4] Each researcher in this field has observed only his or her small piece of the overall picture but is claiming to have identified the whole elephant. This "S-curve" concept seeks to integrate the three apparently divergent perceptions into a unified framework.

Before moving on to the more specific task of discussing how promotional budgets are and should be determined, we should clarify certain aspects of the preceding discussion. First, let us acknowledge that we have been explaining relationships that people have conceptualized theoretically but have not yet proven by formal research or empirical data. Second, the reader should note that in Exhibits 6-6A through 6-6D there are no scales on any of the axes; therefore these depictions are conceptual representations, not quantitatively defined relationships. Finally, these sales response relationships rest on two assumptions: (1) that the market environment is essentially stable in terms of both market size and competitive activity, and (2) that the company has made no other changes in its marketing strategy.

In summary, the theoretical economic approach to budget setting rests on two underlying concepts: First, managers of individual businesses seek to maximize the total profit for that business and should therefore continue to make promotional expenditures as long as the profit contribution from the resultant sales is greater than the cost of the promotional effort. Second, profit contribution is clearly related to the sales generated by the promotional effort, and these sales are a function of how the particular market responds to various levels of promotional activity.

As we will see below, these ideas, although intriguing, have certain limitations that make them difficult for managers to apply.

Determining a Budget:
Common Approaches

Marketing managers and other marketing executives who are responsible for establishing budgets have experienced great difficulty in applying the preceding theoretical frameworks in their expenditure decisions. Many factors contribute to this situation, but two are most significant:

1. There are few or no data readily available to quantify the relationship between promotional expenditure and sales response. In addition, the time and cost required to collect appropriate data make it prohibitive for most companies.

2. The sales response relationships we have described are based on certain assumptions of stability in terms of both the market environment and the company's marketing strategy. Most experienced marketing personnel find this constraint difficult to accept as reasonable.

As a result of these difficulties, a number of approaches have evolved over the years in an attempt to establish a workable procedure for determining the level of expenditures for the total program or individual elements. A description of the five most widely used systems follows.

SALT (Same-As-Last-Time)

One of the more common bases by which a firm might establish promotional budgets is the SALT (*same-as-last-time*) approach. This method produces an expenditure level that is the same as the previous budget period, subject only to adjustments for special circumstances such as product introductions or special promotional activities. (This year's budget was $500,000, but next year the company is planning a major product introduction at a cost of $100,000. The next year's budget would be $600,000.)

One might argue that this is a reasonable approach in a stable market environment where the firm is generally satisfied with its sales and profit performance. Two other reasons support this system: It is relatively simple to prepare, and it is also easy to sell to management, since it is based on prior experience, requires no change in the role of promotion, and does not rely on future performance expectations.

The major problem with this approach is that it permits a setting of the budget without a serious analysis of the relationship between expenditures and returns. In an environment that is dynamic because of competitive actions or changing consumer tastes, the firm may miss opportunities or overlook inefficiencies.

Percentage of Sales

Percentage of sales is an adaptation of the procedure we described above, also based on a historical relationship: the previous periods' ratio of promotional expenditure to sales. This is perhaps the most widely used approach. In one survey, 27 percent of the firms responding indicated that they used this method.[5] In establishing the promotional budget for example, the marketing manager would take next year's sales forecast, apply the historical percentage, and arrive at a budget: Sales forecast = $1 million; ratio of promotional expense to sales in prior years = 10 percent; therefore, next year's promotional budget = $100,000.

This also has the advantages of simplicity and ease of selling we noted above, but in addition it recognizes changes in the market environment as well through the sales forecast. If next year's sales forecast is higher than this year's sales, then the budget would go up; conversely, if the forecast were lower, the budget would go down.

This approach is open to serious criticism—it is clearly arbitrary and misrepresents the cause-and-effect relationship between promotion and sales. This approach suggests that sales lead to promotion expenditure when the proper concept is that promotion expenditures affects sales levels. In using the percentage-of-sales approach, there is the implicit assumption that sales levels are somewhat independent of promotion levels.

All-That-Can-Be-Afforded

In contrast to the approaches described above, the *all-that-can-be-afforded* procedure is not based on historical relationships but on current financial circumstances. It treats the promotional program not as an effort that produces current sales but as an investment in future sales performance. With this philosophy, advocates believe they can reduce, defer, or even eliminate these expenditures in the interest of short-term profitability. On the other hand, when the company's short-term profit performance is strong, then they can justify greater expenditure on promotional activities. The promotional budget this procedure suggests would depend on what was available ("left over") after incorporating some base level of profit into the financial plan.

This concept has merit on two grounds. First, it is essential that the organization realize some minimum level of profitability in order to survive and to support its growth. Second, to a certain extent, current promotional expenditures do create a future value. This may permit a company, in a relatively stable market environment, to reduce its promotional expenditures for a short time without losing its market position. Experiments conducted by Anheuser-Busch produced findings that support this view.[6] One must also remember that sufficient prior promotional investment makes this beneficial result possible.

The major weakness in the all-that-can-be-afforded method is that it does not require a full understanding of the promotion effects. The funds available are established independently of what promotion can produce. Thus the approach runs the risk, of course, of spending beyond what is necessary or not spending enough to take advantage of opportunities.

Competitive Position

The *competitive position* procedure comes from a different notion of the role of promotion than those we have discussed so far. Here promotion is as much as a weapon in a competitive battle as it is a means of communicating with potential customers. In many product markets, particularly in packaged consumer goods, advertising share and market share of each of the competitors are closely related. As a result, each supplier in these markets seeks to improve or at least maintain its relative position by adjusting the advertising and promotional budget to the moves of the major competitors. One need not spend as much as competitors to achieve parity; it is only essential to maintain the relative position. The well-known consumer goods marketer Procter & Gamble generally seeks promotional dominance as its strategy, a scheme proven over the years to be highly successful. To implement this budgeting procedure, the manager must have accurate and current competitive data.

There are major limitations. It is possible to carry the concept of competitive parity to an extreme, whereby the product business becomes unprofitable for all participants. In this instance, the marketer with the biggest bankroll will likely succeed if the firm has the will to stay on the course. Second, this approach assumes that the competition's budgeting has some sound basis. If the competition is budgeting in an arbitrary manner or if the conditions under which competition has set its budget differ, a company will be following the wrong lead.

Objective-Task

The *objective-task* method of establishing promotional budgets has been widely adopted by both consumer and industrial marketers. It is a straightforward management concept of establishing very specific goals and objectives for the promotional effort for the period (number of new customers or dealers, level of consumer awareness, number of repeat orders, and so on). Once these have been determined, management defines the actions necessary to achieve these goals. The promotional budget derives from the cost of these particular actions. In addition, a measurement system monitors progress against these objectives.

This approach has several attractive characteristics. First, it forces the marketing manager to specify, in detail, what the goal is. As a result, a much clearer picture of how the goal is to be achieved emerges. Second, it requires the establishment of an information system to measure progress. Third, it provides feedback, which allows for improvements in the budgeting process either in goal setting or in action planning. This is an attractive procedure where short-term results are important and the impact of the company's actions (promotional programs) stands apart from changes in other factors in the market environment (competitors' actions, economic activity, technological change). Promotion by retailers and direct consumer marketers has these favorable characteristics.

The major impediment to widespread use of this approach is the difficulty of its execution. Effective application requires an understanding of the relationship between the goals and the corresponding activities or tasks that the goals dictate. If inappropriate tasks are assigned, then goals will not be met. The identification of goal-task relationships comes from solid research, an activity that is difficult, time consuming, and sometimes expensive.

Summary of Budgeting Concepts

Before discussing the manner in which elements of the promotion mix fit into the total budget, a few summary observations on the approaches, with the exception of the objective-task method, are in order. On the one hand, they all share certain common advantages for marketing managers who wish to maintain the current situation. They are relatively easy to implement (do not require extensive research or analysis). They are so widely used that they can be sold with little difficulty to top management. Finally, they avoid to a large extent the responsibility for relating promotional expenditure to the achievement of sales and profits.[7]

On the other hand, it is these very advantages, particularly the last one, that makes them less attractive to marketing managers who desire to improve their organizations' performance. These budgeting methods do not in any way suggest what a manager might do to improve sales and profit performance either through an increase or a decrease in the levels of expenditure. In addition, they do not provide insight or guidance as to how to respond promotionally to a dynamic market environment. Nor do they provide direction on the issue of allocating promotional expenditures among product businesses within the company.

One final observation: Promotional budget planning that flows from a general satisfaction with prior performance and historical precedents does not, in our judgment, challenge the marketing organization. It does not call upon it to improve its contribution to the organizational well-being through creative insight, research and analytical skill, and acceptance of reasonable business risk. In short, these approaches are defensive and reactive rather than aggressive and proactive.

Now that we have discussed the budgetary process for the *total* effort, let us consider the budgeting for the *individual* elements of the promotion mix.

Budgeting within the Mix

We can look at the funding of individual elements in the total budget from three perspectives. These perspectives are distinguishable from the budgeting procedures described earlier. We can apply the methods discussed in the previous section (SALT, percentage of sales, all-that-can-be-afforded, competitive position, and objective-task) to the budgeting of individual promotional elements as well as to the promotional budget overall.

This section focuses on the processes that determine the relationship of one activity's budget to budgets of other activities and the total budget. More specifically, this section deals with the manner in which one promotional element's funding may be more or less than another's. It also looks at the process by which individual budgets flow from the total budget and vice versa.

The Total Budget Built up by Tasks

One of the more widely used procedures for defining budgets for individual promotional elements (like advertising) is on a *task-by-task* basis. The manager of the particular functional area determines the task that he or she expects to perform over the budget period. These tasks are translated into specific costs, and the total then becomes the budget for that promotional activity. All areas of promotional activity can generate budgets in a similar manner. These individual totals are then combined to produce the overall promotional budget. Exhibit 6-7 illustrates this process.

Build-up is attractive because it is task related, is fairly straightforward to develop, and comes from the individual manager's knowledge of what it takes to accomplish specific tasks within his or her area of expertise. There is one major and frequent problem, however. What does the manager do when the total dollars budgeted by individual promotional functions exceed the total promotional budget planned? Adjustments often entail the elimination of some activities that contribute to achievement of objectives.

Individual Budgets Come from the Top

One way of avoiding such adjustment questions is for the marketing manager or other senior marketing executives to make an *overall budget allocation* to each functional area that does not, in the aggregate, exceed the predetermined total. The managers in the functional areas, knowing what is available, proceed to distribute these funds to the tasks at hand with an understanding of the overall marketing plan. Exhibit 6-8 contains a graphic representation of this approach.

Clearly a key advantage here is the involvement of senior marketing management. They have the best understanding of the overall marketing strategy and can make the necessary trade-offs among the functional areas. Despite this positive element, we are still left with two areas of concern. The first is how management makes this division. Is it by a historical relationship, current needs, personal bias and experience, or expected market response? The choice will have a bearing on the decision's effectiveness. The second is how the individual functional manager translates his or her total budget into specific tasks and actions. Is the allocation the same as that envisioned by the marketing manager in product areas, activities, tasks?

EXHIBIT 6-7 *The Task-by-Task Approach to Promotional Budgeting*

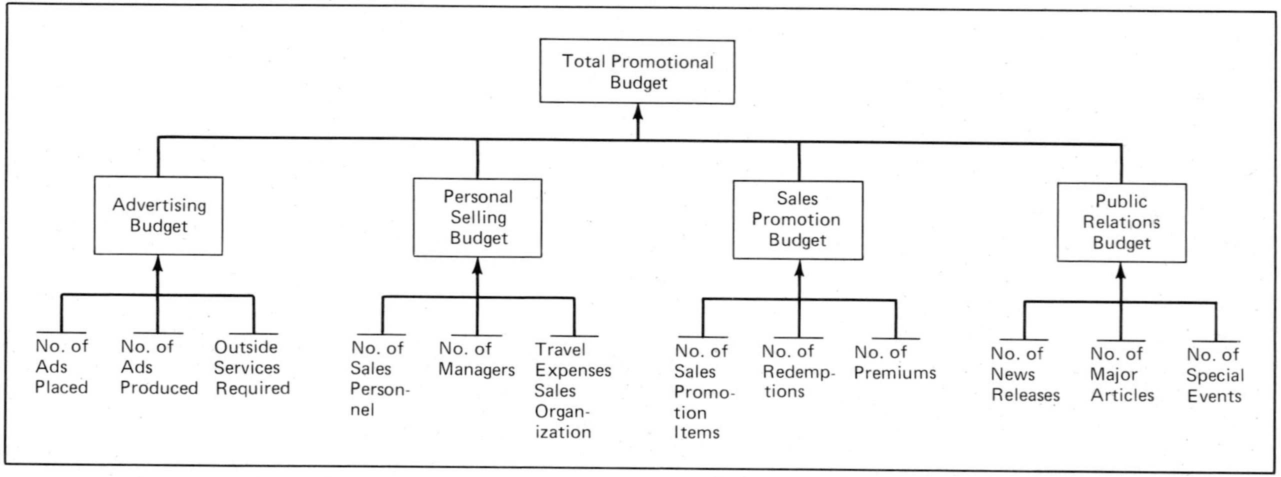

Total Promotional Budget

Advertising Budget
- No. of Ads Placed
- No. of Ads Produced
- Outside Services Required

Personal Selling Budget
- No. of Sales Personnel
- No. of Managers
- Travel Expenses Sales Organization

Sales Promotion Budget
- No. of Sales Promotion Items
- No. of Redemptions
- No. of Premiums

Public Relations Budget
- No. of News Releases
- No. of Major Articles
- No. of Special Events

EXHIBIT 6-8 The Top-Down Approach to Promotional Budgeting

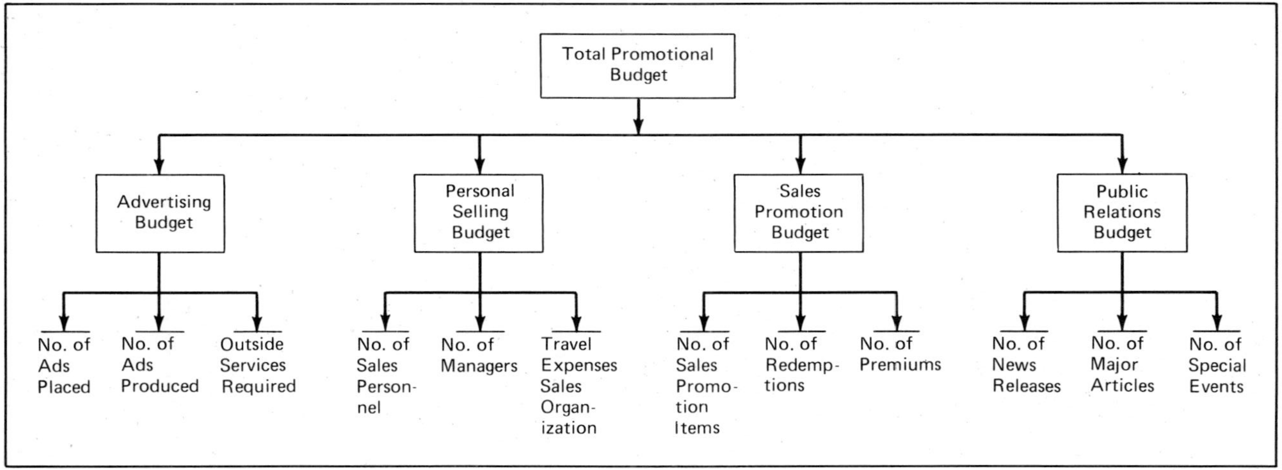

Total Promotional Budget

Advertising Budget
- No. of Ads Placed
- No. of Ads Produced
- Outside Services Required

Personal Selling Budget
- No. of Sales Personnel
- No. of Managers
- Travel Expenses Sales Organization

Sales Promotion Budget
- No. of Sales Promotion Items
- No. of Redemptions
- No. of Premiums

Public Relations Budget
- No. of News Releases
- No. of Major Articles
- No. of Special Events

How does this allocation relate to the activities of the other promotional functions? There is a strong likelihood that the plans will not relate closely without further review and coordination.

Organizational Power

The budgets within the promotional mix may be influenced by *organizational power*, which we define in this context as the ability to influence decision making. It may reside in either a functional area or in an individual and may come from force of personality, close relations with senior management, expertise and knowledge, or prior performance and accomplishment. Functional areas led by managers with power and influence in the organization will often receive a greater share of the budget than those that are not. Functional areas where performance is perceived to be more measurable will also gain in the budgeting process. These allocation decisions may be appropriate, or they may not. What is disquieting is that corporate power governs the process, rather than the clear analysis of the marketplace or strategic needs. Organizational power could be used to further the interests of individuals at the expense of effective promotional effort.

Budgeting Is Not Easy

Some additional observations about budgeting are in order before we discuss the quantitative techniques for determining budgets. As difficult as it is to determine the total budget, the task of setting and coordinating budgets among the many separate activities is even greater. There are of course several reasons for this:

1. It involves more political and organizational power dimensions.
2. There is less general background knowledge and research available to aid in determining a suitable allocation.
3. It is difficult to isolate the effects of individual promotional actions; they tend to be undertaken in an integrated fashion, which makes interpretation highly subjective.
4. Exhaustive testing is not feasible, as the number of variations in a mix that could be explored is enormous.

The approaches we have described represent the current practice. Each approach has its strengths and weaknesses. Very often an approach is selected with these positive and negative characteristics in mind. An approach is certainly not used because it is flawless. Rather, it is used cautiously with an understanding of its weaknesses. Sound management seeks to enhance the best effects and control the negative aspects.

QUANTITATIVE TECHNIQUES
FOR BUDGETING

Researchers in the field of study that deals with quantitative techniques for budgeting have developed specific ways to handle the limitations we have just noted.[8] Their efforts aim toward the expression of quantitative relationships between promotion expenditures and *overall* sales measures like revenue, unit volume, or market share. We will look at three categories of techniques: those that draw inferences from historical data, those that use data from experimentation, and those that rely on subjective estimates. In this section we simply describe the variety of quantitative techniques available for budgeting. We leave to marketing research and management science books the deeper discussion of specific techniques.

Historical Data—Using Regression Analysis

The most popular category of techniques for analyzing data on past sales and promotion expenditures is *regression analysis*. The many forms of regression analysis (simple regression, multiple regression, nonlinear regression, to name a few) differ in their ability to incorporate the complexities of the market environment, but they all address the same questions: Does there appear to be *any* pattern between changes in promotion effort and changes in sales; and if there is a pattern, what is the *degree of intensity* of this relationship? More specifically, regression analysis looks for the direction and degree of correspondence in changes between promotion and sales. When promotion effort has gone up, have sales gone up, have they basically remained constant, or have they even declined? Additionally, when promotion effort has changed and has become either higher or lower, *how much* have sales reacted to that change?

Regression in its simple form produces a mathematical model like this:

$$\text{Sales} = a + b \text{ (promotion effort)}$$

where

$$\text{Sales} = \text{market response}$$
$$\text{Promotion effort} = \text{expenditure level}$$
$$a \text{ and } b = \text{coefficients produced by regression analysis}$$

The model essentially says that the amount of change in sales will be equal to the amount of *change* in promotion effort factored by the value of the coefficient b. For example, if sales and promotion effort were measured in millions of dollars and the value of b were 2.3, then the model states that sales will change by $2.3 million for every $1.0 million in promotion.

Analysis of historical data offers two major advantages in budgeting. First, it can be relatively inexpensive compared with other quantitative techniques. Especially if data can be drawn from existing internal company records, there will be significant savings over techniques that require data collection. Second, it may be easy to process. The availability of computerized, user-friendly statistical packages permits the processing of sizable data bases in a short period of time.

Despite the advantages, analysis of historical data through regression is not widely employed. First, the type of data needed to account for marketplace complexities such as competitive activities, consumer attitudes, and shipping schedules may not be readily available or in usable form. Without such data, it is not possible to isolate the relationship between promotional expenditures and sales. Second, the *past* relationship between sales and promotion may not be a fair representation of the *present* and *future* relationships. Many things in a dynamic marketing environment (number of competitors, government regulations, economic conditions) may have changed or are likely to change and substantially alter the earlier relationship.

Data from Experimentation

Experimentation eliminates many of the problems with historical data. In conducting a marketplace experiment, promotion expenditures as well as other marketer-controlled influences like prices and product availability are systematically varied. These variations are assigned to test locations like entire cities or sections of a metropolitan area, selected on the basis of predetermined market environment criteria including popular demographics, competitive strengths, and economic conditions. A properly designed experiment in the marketplace will give data that are timely and will also isolate the sales effects of promotion. These are possible because the aim of experimentation is to account for or control all influences on sales.

The major disadvantages in the use of field experimentation are the time, expense, and difficulty of controlling the environment. The use of a natural setting requires the experimenter to engage in typical promotion activities like production of sample packages, scheduling of media, waiting for the printing of coupons, and so on. All of these are time consuming, and the wait for a significant data base to model the sales-promotion relation can be lengthy. In addition to the direct costs of conducting experiments, experimentation is expensive because the need for variations in budget levels means that excessive amounts will be spent in some locations and insufficient amounts in others. Finally, conditions in the field are difficult to control, especially for lengthy tests. Climates may affect distribution, local economic conditions may change, and disruptive competitive actions like a special cents-off promotion may have confounding effects on sales data and reduce the validity of projecting from test results to normal conditions. In the face of these difficulties, relatively few companies wish to devote the necessary time, money, and effort. One company, Anheuser-Busch, did and permitted publication of its findings.[9] The results were quite dramatic, providing, in this case at least, a strong justification for the research commitment and effort.

Subjective Estimates—Using a Decision-Calculus Approach

The *decision-calculus approach* pioneered by John Little seeks to minimize the problems we raised above by using judgmental rather than empirical data.[10] In contrast to the relationships determined by regression analysis or experimentation, the parameters or coefficients of this model derive from managers' opinions. Here is how it works:

1. Managers state their beliefs about the impact of promotion on sales.
2. A researcher translates the beliefs into quantitative forms suitable for modeling.
3. The model using the preliminary inputs describes the sales-promotion relationship.
4. The managers review the results to see if they conform to their expectations.
5. If necessary, the model parameters are adjusted or "fine tuned" using new insights from management.

This approach can be very powerful if applied thoughtfully. It permits the incorporation of management expertise not possible with historical or empirical techniques alone.

Its greatest weakness, of course, is the judgmental estimates that are essential to the model formulation. The validity of the model depends on the degree to which managers have internalized the promotion-sales relationship, their ability to articulate it, and the researcher's ability to express opinions in quantitative terms.

Some Generalized Results

Methods involving generalized results have been used by individual companies for their own purposes. The proprietary nature of the results restricts their publication, but even if they were made known, the extent to which they might apply to another organization's situation is questionable.

There have been published results of a general nature.[11] These studies survey diverse industry groups. The researchers collected, in addition to

sales and promotion data, data on such product factors as quality and technical complexity, on such market factors as number of end users and customer
concentration, and on such strategic factors as product life cycle and marketing aggressiveness. Some of the results showing positive and negative relationships with promotional effort are listed in Exhibits 6-9 and 6-10. For
example, both exhibits suggest that the promotional efforts for products
made to order are less intense than the efforts for products that are not.

A note of caution is necessary at this point lest the reader believe
that the results in Exhibits 6-9 and 6-10 are the "holy grail" of promotion
budgeting. The results only *describe* past and current management practices.
They do not *explain* what organizations should do. Since the data came from
different companies operating under different conditions, they do not yield
information that can prescribe budgets for any single organization.

**EXHIBIT 6-9   Factors Related to Advertising and Sales Promotion
Intensity (Profit Impact of Marketing Strategies—PIMS—
Data Base)**

	EXPENDITURE INTENSITY—ADVERTISING AND SALES PROMOTION EXPENDITURES AS PERCENTAGE OF SALES	
FACTOR	Industrial products	Consumer products
Number of end users	+	+
Product made to order	−	−
Purchase frequency	+	+
Purchase amount	−	−
Importance of auxiliary service	+	+
Market share	−	−
Relative price	+	+
Contribution margin	+	+
Percent capacity utilized	−	−
Percent of sales from new products	+	+
Percent of sales direct to end users	−	−

Key
+ = Expenditure intensity increases with increase in variable.
− = Expenditure intensity decreases with increase in variable.

Adapted from Paul W. Farris, *Determinants of Advertising Intensity: A Review of the Marketing
Literature,* Working Paper, No. 77-109 (Cambridge, Mass: Marketing Science Institute, September 1977); and Paul W. Farris and Robert D. Buzzell, *Relationship between Changes in Industrial
Advertising and Promotion Expenditures and Changes in Market Share,* Working Paper No.
76-118 (Cambridge, Mass: Marketing Science Institute, December 1976).

EXHIBIT 6-10   Factors Related to Promotional Expenditures (ADVISOR Data Base)

FACTOR	TOTAL PROMO-TIONAL EXPENDITURES *Industrial products*	ADVERTISING & SALES PROMOTIONAL EXPENDITURES *Industrial products*
$ Sales	++	++
Number of potential users and specifiers	++	++
Customer concentration	−	−
Stage of life cycle	−	−
Aggressive plans	+	+
Product complexity	+	NA
Perception of product quality	−	NA
Product made to order (%)	−	−

Key
+ = Expenditure increases with increase in variable.
− = Expenditure decreases with increase in variable.
++ = Variable with primary effect on expenditure level.
NA = Not available.

Adapted from Gary Lilien, "A Study of Industrial Marketing Budgeting Descriptive Analysis—Final Report," Working Paper (Cambridge, Mass.: Massachusetts Institute of Technology, February 1978).

Despite the limitation, the findings do have merit. First, they represent the collective wisdom and insight of a varied group of managers, planning for a diverse set of businesses, concentrated on the important determinants of promotional spending. Second, they provide an external benchmark, however rough, against which the manager can assess a company's current spending plans. Finally, they foster and facilitate a detailed appraisal of a business's marketing environment in terms of the variables, their degrees of influence, and the direction of their influence.

THE BUDGETING PROCEDURE: AN OVERVIEW

As we said at the beginning of this chapter, the budget is the quantification for some defined period of time of the promotional strategy the marketing manager developed. Any viable budgeting procedure starts with the marketing strategy as senior management has articulated it. Two essentially different approaches can then determine the overall promotional budget, the individual departmental budgets, and finally the specific activity budgets. Either a top-down or a build-up procedure similar to those we described earlier may be appropriate.

The top-down approach starts with the senior marketing executive's decision as to the size of total promotional budget for the company, the business unit, or the product line. Similarly, after discussion and consultation with the managers of the various promotional activities comes the allocation of the budget to each of the functional areas. The promotional managers will then take their overall budget and distribute it to various activities within their departments. The budget process in this approach goes from a general expenditure pool down to the specific promotional actions.

For example, the marketing manager for a $20 million product line may decide (based on one of the approaches discussed earlier) that objectives dictate that the overall promotional budget for the coming year will be $3 million. This manager then determines that $2 million will go for the sales organization and the balance will fall equally to advertising and sales promotion. The national sales manager will then determine how many field salespeople, how many regional managers, how many offices and administrative personnel, and so on, he or she can support, given tentative budget allocation. The advertising manager will be making similar decisions about the number and type of ads, media, frequency of appearance, and the like, that can be justified in the context of a $500,000 expenditure. Managers of other promotional functions make similar judgments. Any one of them may find that the dollars allocated are insufficient to achieve the goals. At this stage, an interaction between the senior executive and the promotional manager takes place to resolve the apparent discrepancy. There are three possible results—the budget stays the same; the budget goes up for a particular activity and another goes down to offset it; or the overall budget goes up to accommodate the increment.

In the build-up approach, each promotional manager determines the activities he or she will undertake to achieve the objectives of the strategic plan. The manager estimates the costs of these actions, summarizes them into an overall departmental budget, and submits it to the senior marketing executive. The marketing manager reviews these documents and if satisfied compiles the individual submissions into an overall promotional budget, which then goes to the executive committee for integration into the annual financial plan. If changes are necessary, the process is reversed and individual promotional managers will have to adjust their plans to fit the available funds.

Once a final promotional budget both in total and in detail has been approved, the managers can then begin to execute their particular section of the promotional plan. Clearly, the process does not end at this point, as the managers monitor both their expenditures and their results against the prescriptions of the budget. If adjustments are necessary to bring the results and the expenditures more into balance, managers effect them as soon as possible, and the budget as well as other financial documents will undergo modification at the next cycle to reflect the current conditions.

Before we conclude this section on budgeting procedure, two general observations are worth making:

1. Regardless of which process (top-down or build-up) is the primary technique to determine the promotional budget, the other ought to be employed to supplement and strengthen the overall review procedure. Detailed promotional budgets only make sense if they fit within a well-defined overall financial plan. Similarly, overall promotional budgets are only helpful when they are sufficient to carry out the specific promotional tasks. Both budgeting techniques work to good effect in a comprehensive budgeting procedure.

2. The budget is the quantification of the promotional strategy. It is not an absolute, unchangeable commitment. Shifts in the market environment may require changes in strategy, which in turn change budgets. Regular review and evaluation steps should be part of the budget procedure to keep it well tuned to the current environment and the needs of the marketing and promotional strategy.

Once the manager has established the budgets, everyone can go about planning and executing specific activities. We take up these topics in the next chapters.

SUMMARY

Valid objectives are necessary for the success of the promotion program. They coordinate promotion activities with those in marketing, they identify the target and specify in precise terms *what* to accomplish and *when*, and they are challenging.

Promotion objectives affect the composition of the communications mix. Certain objectives can be better achieved with some activities than with others. Advertising is effective in disseminating information for consumer awareness and comprehension but weak in persuasion. On the other hand, sales-promotion activity may spark purchases but is too costly for a simple awareness campaign.

After the definition of objectives, the manager faces two issues: the amount to be spent for the total promotion effort and the funding levels for the individual mix elements. We described five traditional approaches: same-as-last-time, percentage of sales, all-that-can-be-afforded, competitive position, and objective-task. The first four are popular because of their ease of application, but they do not require a serious evaluation of the relationship between sales and promotion expenditures. The objective-task method looks at goals and their indicated activities, the costs of which dictate the budget.

Finally, we looked at some quantitative techniques useful in the budgeting task. These techniques might rest on historical, experimental, or subjective inputs. Each type has its strengths and weaknesses. Historical data are relatively inexpensive, but they may not be available in the form necessary for analysis. Experimental data are timely but expensive, and collecting them requires considerable time and effort. Subjective estimates incorporate management expertise, but their nature does not permit easy verification of their accuracy.

Once the objectives and budgets have been set, the task of planning and executing specific activities commences. These activities consist of advertising, personal selling, sales promotion, and public relations. Over the next eleven chapters we will be examining these activities. We begin with advertising.

REVIEW AND DISCUSSION QUESTIONS

1. Explain the relationship between the marketing budget and the promotional budget.

2. What is the interaction between promotional objectives and the promotional budget?

3. How do promotional objectives influence promotional strategy? Be specific.

4. What are the characteristics of good objectives? Give examples.

5. What is meant by the concept of a hierarchy of objectives?

6. "Since the ultimate objective of any business effort is to generate profits, promotion should always be responsible for sales improvements." Comment.

7. How are priorities set for objectives?

8. Explain what is meant by the statement "Objectives should be achievable, yet demanding."

9. Why is it important to express objectives in quantitative terms?

10. "Long-term success is based on a series of short-term successes." Comment.

11. The budgeting task addresses two questions. What are they? Give examples.

12. What benefits can be derived from a careful budgeting effort?

13. How does economic theory aid our understanding of promotional budgeting?

14. Describe the concept of the sales response function.

15. Distinguish between the linear, threshold, diminishing returns, and S-shaped views of the sales response function.

16. Identify and explain the common approaches to setting the size of the promotional budget. Which do you recommend as the "best" approach? Why?

17. Would you agree with the notion that the larger the promotional budget, the greater the opportunity to take advantage of unforeseen market conditions? Why or why not?

18. Under what conditions does it make sense to use the competitive parity method of setting the promotional budget? Give examples.

19. State the advantages and limitations of the following approaches to promotional budget setting: (a) SALT, (b) percentage of sales, (c) affordable, (d) competitive parity, and (e) objective-and-task.

20. What are the advantages of the build-up method of allocating the promotional budget? The limitations?

21. Explain the advantages and limitations of the top-down approach to promotional budget allocation.

22. How does organizational power influence the way in which the promotional budget is allocated? Explain.

23. Explain the promotional budgeting procedure.

24. "The budget is the quantification of the promotional strategy." Explain.

NOTES

1. Harvey N. Singer and F. Stewart DeBruicker, "L'eggs Products, Inc.," in *Problems in Marketing* (6th. ed.) ed. E. Raymond Corey, Christopher H. Lovelock, and Scott Ward (New York: McGraw-Hill, 1981), pp. 341–57.

2. Herbert E. Krugman, "Why Three Exposures May Be Enough," *Journal of Advertising Research*, December 1972, pp. 11–15.

3. Russell L. Ackoff and James R. Emshoff, "Advertising Research at Anheuser-Busch, Inc. (1963–1968)," *Sloan Management Review*, Winter 1975, pp. 1–15.

4. Three blind people were led to an elephant, an animal that none had ever encountered. Each was asked to describe the animal. One, feeling only the leg, said, "An elephant has the shape and texture of a tree; it is rough on the outside and grows straight up." Another, having grabbed the trunk, said, "An elephant is like a big snake; it's long and can coil itself up." The third one, feeling one tusk, declared, "An elephant is like a long rock; it is hard and cool to the touch."

5. *The Gallagher Report*, September 1975.

6. Ackoff and Emshoff, "Advertising Research," pp. 1–15.

7. Task method is a partial exception because it is specifically goal-oriented. Usually, the goals established and measured are not sales or profit goals.

8. Robert D. Buzzell and Paul W. Farris, "Marketing Costs in Consumer Goods Industries," Working Paper 76-111 (Cambridge, Mass.: Marketing Science Institute, 1976); Buzzell and Farris, "Industrial Marketing Costs: An Analysis of Variations in Manufacturers Marketing Expenditures," Working Paper 76-118 (Cambridge, Mass.: Marketing Science Institute, 1976); Gary L. Lilien, "ADVISOR 1: A Descriptive Model of Advertising Budgeting for Industrial Products," MIT Sloan School Working Paper, WP 974-78 (Cambridge, Mass.: Massachusetts Institute of Technology, February 1978); Lilien, A Study of Industrial Marketing Budgeting Descriptive Analysis—Final Report (Cambridge, Mass.: Marketing Science Institute, February 1978); John D. C. Little, "Aggregate Advertising Response Models: The State of the Art," MIT Sloan School Working Paper, WP 1048-79 (Cambridge, Mass.: Massachusetts Institute of Technology, February 1979); Darrall G. Clarke, ed., Cumulative Advertising Effects: Sources and Implications (Cambridge, Mass.: Marketing Science Institute, September 1977); Leonard M. Lodish, "Sales Territory Alignment to Maximize Profit," Journal of Marketing Research, February 1975, pp. 30–36; David B. Montgomery and Alvin J. Silk, "Estimating Dynamic Effects of Marketing Communications Expenditures," Management Science, June 1972, pp. B485–501; Kristian S. Palda, "Sales Effects of Advertising: A Review of the Literature," Journal of Advertising Research, September 1964, pp. 14–16; and Palda, "The Measurement of Cumulative Advertising Effects," Journal of Business, April 1965, pp. 162–79.

9. Ackoff and Emshoff, "Advertising Research," pp. 1–15.

10. John D. C. Little, "Models and Managers: The Concept of a Decision Calculus," Management Science, April 1970, pp. B466–85.

11. Paul W. Farris and Robert D. Buzzell, "Why Advertising and Promotion Costs Vary: Some Cross-Sectional Analyses" (working paper, 1979); and Lilien, Study of Industrial Marketing Budgeting Descriptive Analysis.

7

Advertising Management

The sequence of the preceding chapters has shown that the development of an effective promotion plan is a systematic process. Let us briefly look at that process again. It begins with an understanding of promotion's contribution to the whole marketing effort. Since promotion's customary role is to influence marketplace behavior, market analysis that yields a better understanding of the nature of the market is essential. This understanding in turn is the foundation for the objectives and budget of the promotion mix. And advertising, personal selling, sales promotion, and public relations arise from the objectives and budget.

We will now concentrate on particular elements of the promotion mix, beginning with an overview of *advertising*, the mass-media component of that mix. We will look at the management of an advertising program. Chapters 8 and 9 will describe the development of media plans and the characteristics of the major media. Chapter 10 discusses the development of messages.

THE IMPORTANCE
OF ADVERTISING

Enormous expenditures, all by themselves, suggest the importance of advertising in the United States. In 1983 over $75 billion was spent for advertising space and time, and by 1990 these expenditures may exceed $147 billion.[1] If the estimates are accurate, the delivery of commercial messages will cost some $625 per person per year.

Procter & Gamble spends over $800 million a year just to buy print space and broadcast time. No doubt P&G spends considerable millions for other advertising costs, such as the creating of messages and the planning and implementing of a campaign. Advertising expenditures at firms like P&G are clearly major investments in their marketing efforts.

We know that the images most of us have of popular brands such as Ivory Soap or Lite Beer come primarily from successful advertising. Furthermore, advertising programs often generate support and cooperation from wholesalers and retailers while stimulating demand resulting in sales for these middlemen. And even beyond that, advertising can maintain the goodwill of a market. When Tylenol underwent the ordeal of the cyanide incident, McNeil Labs used advertising to reassure the public by being forthright about the problem and by announcing its refund program. Effective management of the advertising program makes a significant contribution to such successes.

AN OVERVIEW OF ADVERTISING
MANAGEMENT

Advertising management entails analysis, planning, implementation, and control activities directed toward objectives, budgets, message development, and media decisions. Exhibit 7-1 gives a graphic overview of advertising management. The substance of Exhibit 7-1 reminds us of the management principles presented in the first chapter. The nature of effective management is consistent across most decisions whether they involve advertising, personal selling, sales promotion, or public relations.

For illustration, consider *The Wiz*. After runs in Baltimore, Detroit, Philadelphia, and a few days on Broadway, it became clear that *The Wiz*, an all-black stage version of *The Wizard of Oz*, would turn out to be a bomb unless some dramatic action brought in the crowds. Professional theater critics had given it mixed reviews, and their opinions apparently influenced the ticket sales.[2]

Market research produced some interesting results. Those who had attended the musical were considerably different from the traditional audience. They were younger, showed up at weekend rather than weekday per-

EXHIBIT 7-1 An Overview of Advertising Management

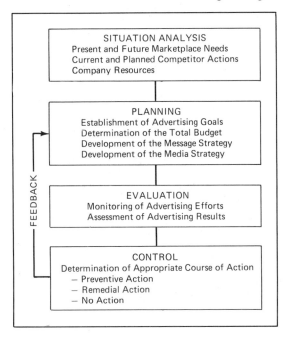

formances, were likely to bring children, and consisted of a large percentage of minorities. Moreover the research indicated that they saw *The Wiz* because of strong recommendations from friends who had seen the musical.

The producers saw a chance to stimulate demand among the nontraditional theater audience through an intensive advertising campaign. They reasoned that the traditional communications of critics' columns and announcement ads in newspapers reached traditional theater crowds. To reach a nontraditional, mass-market audience, lively commercials saturated the New York television and radio market for two weeks. They gave a taste of the action and excitement in the musical. Ticket sales increased dramatically and ensured a long Broadway run.

Success in the marketplace does not come easily. With *The Wiz*, analysis and planning identified opportunities not otherwise known. Effective campaign plans start with a solid understanding of the operating environment. In general, analysis assesses the opportunities in existing and expected marketplace needs, the current and planned actions of competitors, and the availability of resources for the campaign.

Situation analysis uncovers the hidden market opportunities, while planning produces the framework for action to exploit those opportunities. The responsibility of the advertising manager is to identify the kind of effort needed to realize the marketplace potential. The ad plans contain

A clear statement of the advertising goals

A budget prescribing the financial resources required to achieve the goals

The message strategy

A media plan for the transmission of the message

For good plans to produce the desired results, there must be action. When the blueprints for the campaign are ready, the manager's responsibility is to launch the program and coordinate its various elements like the development of advertisements and the scheduling of media vehicles. As the campaign sets sail, the task of monitoring performance also commences: identifying and correcting existing problems, forestalling potential problems.

Throughout these management activities, the manager may enlist the services of outside organizations, specialists in some or all of the facets of the campaign and able to facilitate its management. Although such firms generally call themselves advertising agencies, we will see later that agencies vary widely in the services they offer their clients.

ADVERTISING OBJECTIVES

Advertising objectives are the tasks the campaign must accomplish, the goals that dictate all elements of the advertising program. Furthermore, they reflect the areas of accountability for those who administer the promotion.

Correct and clear objectives are crucial for a successful campaign. Improper objectives lead to inappropriate plans, and no matter how well the plans are carried out, the final results spell an unsuccessful campaign. In turn, improper advertising goals may jeopardize the effectiveness of the entire promotion mix. For example, the salespeople's efforts to bring in new business may depend heavily on advertising's ability to generate sufficient awareness of the company and product before a sales call. Failure to achieve such awareness hinders the salespeople's job.

The relationship of objectives to advertising performance can be stated simply. The campaign must concentrate on doing the right things rather than merely doing things right. Good performance without being directed at the right goals does not result in satisfactory achievements. With this in mind, let us look at advertising objectives more closely.

Valid Objectives

Since Chapter 6 described in some depth the characteristics of valid objectives, this section will provide only a general statement of the determinants of valid objectives for advertising. Appropriate advertising objectives are based on

A concise definition of the target audience

A clear statement of the response or responses to be generated among the target audience

An expression of goals in quantitative terms

A projection of achievements attributable to advertising

An expressed understanding of advertising's role with respect to the rest of the promotion program

An acknowledgement that the goals are demanding yet achievable

An expression of the time constraints

The reader should refer to Chapter 6 for a full explanation of each criterion.

In his classic 1961 book, *Defining Advertising Goals for Measured Advertising Results*, Russell Colley stressed the importance of understanding what advertising can and should be held responsible for.[3] He held that advertising is a communications activity and should be held accountable only for communications effects and not sales results. His reasoning was that sales are the culmination of a variety of other promotional, marketing, and corporate activities such as personal selling, a fairly priced product, and efficient production, and that advertising simply effects communication between the marketer and the market. According to Colley, the following communications factors might lead to sales:

Awareness	There is awareness of the existence of the brand or company.
Comprehension	There is understanding of what the product is and the benefits that it provides.
Conviction	There is mental disposition to buy the product.
Action	There is action, such as a call to a sales rep, a visit to a dealer, or a purchase.

While subsequent research on advertising effects has displaced many of Colley's specific ideas, his work is useful to the advertising profession even today in understanding the fundamental task of setting objectives. *The manager must be specific about who will be the focus of communications, what will be the desired effect of communications on that person, and when that effect should become evident.*

Considerations in Setting Ad Objectives

The specific objectives selected for any advertising campaign generally depend on four major factors: the target market, the product, the other marketing efforts by the firm, and the competitive conditions.

Target Market Considerations

The entire marketing program endeavors to guide the decision of the *target market* toward purchase of the product or service, and the objective set for advertising should flow from knowledge of the market's use of advertising as a factor in decision making. A poor objective for an advertising program would be to aim for attitude change where the target market relies very little on advertisements for evaluating alternatives. For example, in the extended decision to buy a house, the buyer uses advertising to identify alternatives but is likely to rely very little on advertising promises in making final decisions.

Product Considerations

The nature of the *product* or *service* sometimes determines the nature of the consumer decision process. Chapter 4 notes that in some products, the consumer sees large risks looming in a wrong decision. For these high-involvement products, decision making is often lengthy, and advertising's role may be to provide knowledge of critical features and benefits. On the other hand, very little decision making enters into the purchase of some products. Here the degree of familiarity with a brand's name can make the difference. With such products, the objective of advertising is to increase that level of awareness.

Other Marketing Efforts

Advertising's influence on a seller-buyer exchange often stems from *other marketing and promotion variables*. A product such as the prune, which has a poor image in the minds of consumers, might depend heavily on advertising to change attitudes. On the other hand, the objective of advertising may simply be to inform a market of the presence of a product inherently attractive to the target audience and widely available in distribution outlets. This was the case in the early 1980s for some home arcade games such as PAC MAN; the market eagerly awaited the products, and advertising's role was simply to announce where and when they could be purchased.

Competitive Considerations

Competitive actions often dictate the role of advertising. Aggressive advertising by competitors will frequently call for a direct response in order to protect market position. In the autumn of 1983 Toro launched an advertising campaign announcing a creative sales promotion. A purchaser of a Toro snowblower could get as much as 100 percent of the manufacturer's suggested list price refunded if the snowfall for that winter fell below the average. Simplicity, a major competitor of Toro in the snowblower market, responded with comparative advertisements. Simplicity's ads asserted the benefits of Simplicity's equipment over Toro's and commented on the probabilities of receiving refunds as Toro's program promised. Competitive considerations affected Simplicity's advertising just as they affect the advertising of McDonald's and Burger King or Coca-Cola and Pepsi-Cola.

Summary

One may easily conclude, then, that goals of different campaigns may vary considerably. An advertising campaign may be expected to bear the responsibility for actually bringing in sales; the advertising manager fully expects the promotion to be the principal factor in leading to consumer purchase. Or the goal of a campaign may be very simple: to generate awareness about the company's and its product's existence while other factors such as sales promotion, personal selling, price, product, and retailers bring about a sale.

The choice of a valid objective requires an understanding of the nature of each objective. We will now classify the various objectives into two frameworks—first theoretical, then practical.

Categories of Advertising Objectives

Advertising objectives reflect the anticipated response in the marketplace and thus can be expressed in a variety of ways (see Exhibit 7-2). The effect in the marketplace may simply be the creation of awareness of a product where no awareness existed before. Or the desired effect may be purchase or consumption behavior. Thus any conceptual framework for categorizing ad objectives should be related to the spectrum of possible responses by the target market.

Our discussion will be organized according to the major stages common to many consumer decision-making processes—awareness, comprehension, conviction, and action. Bear in mind that the actual sequence of these stages varies across decision situations, such as Chapter 4 described. The flow here should *not* be considered a reflection of the process for all decisions.

Awareness Objectives

An ad campaign charged with raising *awareness* in the marketplace attempts to acquaint the target market with the existence of a product or service. Such a campaign generally falls into one or more of the following categories:

1. Increasing or reinforcing the awareness of an existing product or service to an existing target market
2. Creating awareness of a new offering in a current target market
3. Achieving awareness of an existing offering among new target customers
4. Instilling awareness of a new product or service in a target that has not been approached before

Awareness campaigns are associated with well-established products as well as new products. For example, in the case of a well-known product such as Coca-Cola or Marlboro cigarettes, advertising's role is to reinforce the brand name in the minds of the public. Such ads are often very simple

EXHIBIT 7-2   Common Advertising Objectives

Perform the complete selling function
Close sales to prospects already partly sold through past ad efforts
Announce a special reason for "buying now"
Remind people to buy
Tie in with some special buying event
Stimulate impulse sales
Create awareness of product existence
Create a brand image
Provide information regarding product benefits
Correct false impressions
Build familiarity with a product or trademark
Build confidence in a company
Place advertiser in a position to select preferred dealers
Secure universal distribution
Establish brand recognition
Hold market share against competition
Convert competitions' customers to advertiser's brand
Convert non-users of the product to users of the product and the brand
Increase usage rate among present customers
Advertise new uses for the product
Persuade the prospect to visit a showroom
Induce the prospect to sample the product
Aid the salesforce in getting accounts and orders
Build morale of the salesforce

Source: Russell Colley, *Defining Advertising Goals for Measured Advertising Results* (New York: Association of National Advertisers, 1961), pp. 62–68.

in layout with the brand name dominating the advertisement. In the intro-duction of a new product, a campaign sets out to announce the availability of the innovation with the expectation that additional information may come through other promotion channels such as personal selling or point-of-purchase displays. For example, the ad shown in Exhibit 7-3 announces the availability of a new product with the expectation that consumers can obtain more information by visiting a dealer or writing to the company.

Underlying most awareness campaigns is one of the following assump-tions about the step leading to consumer purchase:

1. Awareness of the product is sufficient to lead to purchase
2. Awareness of the product is all that advertising can do to promote the product during the campaign period

In the case of low-involvement or convenience products, a high level of awareness may be sufficient to lead to product purchase. The decision-making process for such products is relatively simple: If a consumer thinks about the product and if the product is readily available, he or she will buy with little hesitation. For these products, the consequences of poor judgment are minimal. Consider the case of a shopper impulsively throwing a new brand of soap into the shopping cart. The shopper may have seen a television commercial announcing the brand, and the sight of an end-of-aisle display reinforced this awareness. Perhaps the recognition of this new brand name, along with an introductory price offer, leads to purchase. No extended decision making takes place because there is no great loss (only a few cents) if a poor decision is made.

Where there is product familiarity and perhaps existing purchase be-havior, advertising need only remind and reinforce. In the case of established brands and companies like Kool-Aid or IBM, the objective is often to keep the name at the top of customers' or prospective customers' minds.

In the case of high-involvement products, advertising's major role is that of calling attention to a product. Information dissemination, persuasion, and ultimately consummation of a sale may be better achieved through elements like personal selling and sales promotion. For example, industrial products like machinery or office equipment are often advertised in trade publications. These ads are often designed to announce a product's availabil-ity. Additional information or product demonstration is left to sales reps who may be contacted with the business-reply forms that often accompany such advertising.

Comprehension Objectives

Advertising can be designed to convey specific details about product features and benefits. The intended result is that the target audience will

EXHIBIT 7-3 *An Ad to Get Potential Customers to Start an Information Search*

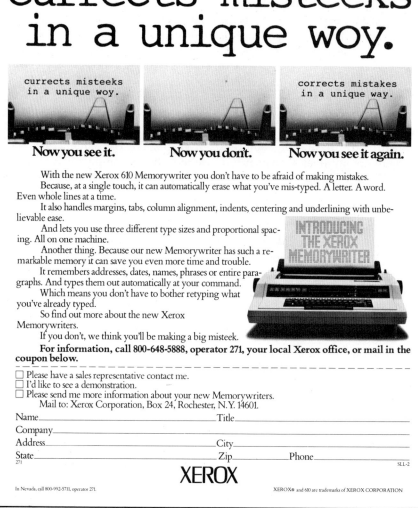

Courtesy Xerox Corporation.

not simply be aware of the availability of the sponsor's product but will retain product information useful for their decision making.

Knowledge objectives often characterize so-called educational campaigns. Such campaigns view advertising's role as dissemination of product facts with the effect that the audience's beliefs are influenced in the advertiser's direction. The expectation is that those beliefs are the foundation for favorable opinions or attitudes about the advertised product and that some other marketing effort will lead the consumer to purchase. Such an ad campaign may have one of the following tasks:

1. Provide the target audience with new information
2. Correct false impressions that an audience may have
3. Reinforce beliefs to prevent forgetting

A product undergoing repositioning or a modified product will probably engage in an educational campaign. For example, the ad shown in Exhibit 7-4 calls the customer's attention to an aspect of the product with which he or she is not familiar; that is, Knox Gelatine, a food product, is also excellent for plant growth. This is an obvious attempt to increase purchase rates by informing the customer of new applications for a current product.

Ad campaigns are sometimes called upon to clarify what the marketplace believes about certain products. For example, consumers perceived Maxim, a freeze-dried coffee, as very expensive (fewer cups per jar than instant coffees) and a bit too strong in taste. Research by General Foods indicated that coffee drinkers, accustomed to the weaker instant coffees, were putting heaping spoonfuls of the highly concentrated Maxim granules into regular-size cups. Thus they were getting fewer servings and stronger coffee than with instant coffee. The marketplace clearly had incorrect knowledge about product usage, and the campaign, as shown in Exhibit 7-5, set about to educate the user that a "spoonful makes a mugful" if it is Maxim.

Conviction Objectives

Sometimes an ad campaign aims at *shaping specific beliefs* about a product, the bases for the consumer's overall opinion or attitude. Its primary mission is to transmit information that contributes to, but may not solely direct, the audience's judgments.

The Pepsi-Cola television advertising campaign "Take the Pepsi Challenge" set out to shape the attitudes of cola drinkers by giving them certain facts. The commercials explicitly reported the results of comparative taste tests in which Pepsi won out over its major competitor, Coca-Cola. The commercials ultimately shaped beliefs and led to favorable opinions about Pepsi as compared with Coke.

An ad campaign may have the goal of stimulating or reinforcing the

EXHIBIT 7-4   Informing the Consumer of New Uses

Reprinted by permission of Knox Gelatine, Inc.

EXHIBIT 7-5 Educating the Consumer about Product Use

TED BATES & COMPANY
Advertising

Client: GENERAL FOODS
Product: MAXIM
Title: "FLORIST"
Comm'l No.: GFMX-1100
Date: MARCH 31, 1982

FLORIST: Hey! My coffee cup!

JINGLE: A spoonful makes a mugful

when it's Maxim.

FLORIST: That's rich!

CHEF: My coffee cup!

JINGLE: A spoonful makes a mugful

when it's Maxim!

CHEF: That's rich!

ANNCR: (VO) Compared to this other leading freeze-dried coffee, Maxim concentrates 27% more coffee

into every spoonful. Instead of a cup. . .Maxim makes a mugful!

STUDENTS: My cup!

JINGLE: A spoonful makes a mugful

when it's Maxim.

STUDENTS: Mmmm. That's rich.

ANNCR: (VO) Maxim. The spoonful rich enough for a mugful!

audience's existing feeling about a product. Audience interest may rise as the audience receives information not previously available. For example, in the early 1980s many consumers wanted to buy automobiles but were reluctant to pursue deals because of high interest rates for financing auto purchases. Exhibit 7-6 shows an ad touting a very favorable financing rate. Note that the ad addresses those "waiting to buy."

Action Objectives

Sometimes advertising objectives take the form of *action* directives. These actions may or may not be aimed directly at purchase. Advertisements might contain reply cards for customer inquiries, or they might offer toll-free numbers for product information.

Then again, an ad campaign may have responsibility for sales results even though its actual effect on the consumers may only be awareness or comprehension. An advertiser expects that the content of the campaign alone or perhaps acting as a catalyst for other marketing factors will lead to purchase. For example, advertising for a low-involvement item may be held accountable for sales because brand selection depends so strongly on brand familiarity enhanced by advertising.

Unless advertising has a strong impact on purchase behavior, it is not realistic to hold advertising accountable for sales. Advertising, for example, often provides valuable information for a car purchase, but ultimately the purchase derives from many factors, such as price, product quality, and dealer performance. In such an instance, a sales objective is not appropriate.

Summary

Factors that determine advertising objectives include target market characteristics, product characteristics, other marketing efforts, and the competition.

Advertising's chief contribution to the total promotion effort for most consumer goods, especially low-involvement ones, is increased awareness of the product and awareness of its existence and of its qualities. In the case of high-involvement items, advertising's primary aim is the dissemination of product information. Note, however, that advertising objectives may include not only what advertising actually does but also what results can be obtained beyond the immediate effects. Although the primary objective may be a direct effect such as awareness, a secondary objective may be an effect only indirectly attributable to advertising. If, for example, the campaign objective for a one-ounce candy bar is sales, the objective can only aim for an indirect effect because the advertiser cannot realistically expect to induce purchase solely through exposure to advertising. The purchase will derive from many factors, including retailer merchandising, an unspecified

EXHIBIT 7-6   An Ad Directed to Those with Intention to Buy

GOOD NEWS FOR CAR BUYERS

GMAC LOWERS CAR FINANCING RATE TO

13.8%

ANNUAL
PERCENTAGE
RATE

ON AUGUST DELIVERIES OF CHEVROLETS · PONTIACS · OLDSMOBILES BUICKS · CADILLACS

This can result in a savings of hundreds of dollars to you.*

Here's the best news you've seen in months. GMAC and your participating GM dealer are now offering GMAC car financing at only 13.8%.

That's right! You can finance any new General Motors car delivered in August at just 13.8%. And this means big savings to you.

Your participating GM dealer is ready now to offer you this new 13.8% financing rate on all new GM cars, including the new Chevrolet Cavalier, Pontiac J2000 and Cimarron by Cadillac.

So see your GM dealer today and pick out that new Chevy, Pontiac, Oldsmobile, Buick or Cadillac that you've been waiting to buy.

GMAC

*Actual savings will depend on the amount financed, the length of the contract and your State's automobile financing law.

THE FINANCING PEOPLE FROM GENERAL MOTORS

Courtesy General Motors Acceptance Corp.

desire for sweets, and, of course, familiarity with the product's name, thanks to advertising.

BUDGET DECISIONS

Since Chapter 6 set forth the requirements and techniques for determining a budget amount, we will simply highlight some of those factors as they appear in an advertising campaign.

The budget decision is important because of its potential impact on the effectiveness and efficiency of the campaign. The advertising planner, before formulation of the campaign, will usually pose two simple but important questions:

1. How much *should* we spend to achieve the defined objectives?
2. How much *have* we to spend?

The size of the budget defines the number and magnitude of alternative strategies from which the planner may select. A budget that is too small may preclude from consideration certain advertising efforts that could be most effective. On the other hand, a budget that provides for more funds than necessary may encourage wasteful spending in areas that make only minor contributions to the program.

The attempt to determine an optimum budget level often proves to be an impossible task for a number of reasons. Research may not be able to isolate the effects of advertising from the effects of such factors as price or stockout conditions. Variations in creative elements such as words and visuals often produce different results for the same levels of expenditures. And there is uncertainty about the effects of competitors' strategies on one's own campaign. For example, an ad that seemed to generate much interest in a laboratory test may be viewed as dull when actually placed against more creative ads of rivals.

It is not surprising, therefore, to find that budget figures vary across industries and across firms within a particular industry. Exhibit 7-7 lists the one hundred highest advertising media expenditures in 1983. Note that the total dollars spent (and, of course, expenditures as a percentage of sales) differ significantly across industries and firms. Differences across the budget reflect differences in the following areas:

1. The advertising objectives of the ad programs
2. The efforts needed to achieve those objectives
3. The ability or willingness of the firm to finance such efforts

In a survey of the top one hundred national advertisers, researchers found that a variety of methods were used in the budgeting process.[4] In contrast to survey results from a 1957 study which reported that few companies attempted precise budgeting efforts, it was found that over 60 percent of the leading advertisers attempted to systematically put together a budget with the objective-task method.[5] Still, over 50 percent in the study reported that budgets were based on anticipated sales levels, with almost 25 percent of the budgets based on an arbitrary or all-you-can-afford approach.

For a detailed review of budgeting techniques such as same-as-last-time, percentage of sales, all-that-can-be-afforded, and the objective-task method, you may wish to reread parts of Chapter 6.

MESSAGE STRATEGY AND ITS EXECUTION

Since advertising is a communications activity, its effect on the marketplace depends, logically, on the *form* and *content* of the communications. A major activity in advertising management is the development and execution of the message strategy. In this phase of planning, management selects the basic message or underlying theme of the advertising as well as the manner in which this message will be expressed through appropriate words or visuals or both.

This message strategy and its execution derive from the *copy platform*. The copy platform, arising from the objectives of the campaign, provides in turn the framework for the advertising theme and specifies the ideas to be stressed. The copy platform typically consists of

1. A full description of the relevant product characteristics to be promoted
2. A clear identification of those product features to be highlighted in advertisements
3. Guidelines for the explanation of the major product benefits to the audience
4. Identification of the general tone or mood of the message

Chapter 10 examines the development of the message and the various ways of delivering its full meaning.

MEDIA PLANNING

As part of the development of a program, the manager must select and schedule the means for delivering the message. He or she must select not only the type of medium—television, newspapers, magazines, and so forth—but also the specific vehicles in each medium, such as WABC–TV in New York or the *Washington Post*.

EXHIBIT 7-7 The Top 100 Advertisers in 1983

THE LEADING ADVERTISERS BY RANK ($000)

Rank	Company	Advertising	Rank	Company	Advertising	Rank	Company	Advertising
1	Procter & Gamble Co.	$773,618.3	35	Gillette Co.	$185,604.4	69	American Motors Corp.	$100,800.7
2	Sears, Roebuck & Co.	732,500.0	36	Mattel Inc.	179,934.8	70	Sony Corp. of America	97,283.2
3	Beatrice Cos.	602,775.4	37	Kellogg Co.	176,306.9	71	CPC International	96,627.3
4	General Motors Corp.	595,129.5	38	Sterling Drug	171,828.1	72	Miles Laboratories	89,063.8
5	R.J. Reynolds Industries	593,350.3	39	CBS Inc.	167,711.0	73	Union Carbide Corp.	88,000.0
6	Philip Morris Inc.	527,481.8	40	Tandy Corp.	156,728.0	74	S.C. Johnson & Son	86,970.3
7	Ford Motor Co.	479,060.0	41	Richardson-Vicks	150,813.9	75	Greyhound Corp.	83,564.0
8	American Telephone & Telegraph	463,095.5	42	Quaker Oats Co.	148,441.7	76	AMR Corp.	80,000.0
9	K mart Corp.	400,000.0	43	Batus Inc.	146,076.9	77	Kimberly-Clark Corp.	77,460.0
10	General Foods Corp.	386,134.2	44	Gulf & Western Industries	145,500.0	78	UAL Inc.	77,200.0
11	Nabisco Brands	367,530.4	45	American Cyanamid Co.	142,400.0	79	American Brands	75,590.1
12	PepsiCo Inc.	356,400.0	46	Chesebrough-Pond's	141,324.5	80	MCA Inc.	74,543.6
13	Warner-Lambert Co.	343,553.5	47	Eastman Kodak Co.	141,318.9	81	Mazda Motors of America	74,500.0
14	American Home Products Corp.	333,485.0	48	Loews Corp.	135,115.1	82	Stroh Brewery Co.	73,532.4
15	Unilever U.S.	324,865.8	49	ITT Corp.	134,229.0	83	Pfizer Inc.	72,084.3
16	McDonald's Corp.	311,378.0	50	Beecham Group p.l.c.	134,126.8	84	Brown-Forman Distillers	70,500.0

#	Company		#	Company	
17	Johnson & Johnson	295,328.8			
18	Mobil Corp.	294,932.5			
19	J.C. Penney Co.	292,451.0			
20	Anheuser-Busch Cos.	290,616.4			
21	Ralston Purina Co.	285,667.4			
22	Coca-Cola Co.	282,150.0			
23	General Mills	268,690.2			
24	Colgate-Palmolive Co.	268,000.0			
25	Warner Communications	251,049.6			
26	Bristol-Myers Co.	235,000.0			
27	Chrysler Corp.	230,020.1			
28	U.S. Government	228,857.2			
29	RCA Corp.	212,300.0			
30	Dart & Kraft	210,279.4			
31	H.J. Heinz Co.	202,400.0			
32	General Electric Co.	196,506.6			
33	Consolidated Foods Corp.	195,858.0			
34	Pillsbury Co.	190,944.3			
51	Texas Instruments	129,042.0	85	GTE Corp.	70,179.9
52	Campbell Soup Co.	126,000.0	86	Eastern Air Lines	70,000.0
53	Revlon Inc.	123,968.9	87	Cosmair Inc.	69,955.0
54	Nissan Motor Corp. in U.S.A.	122,848.0	88	Clorox Co.	69,429.0
55	Mars Inc.	120,350.5	89	Hershey Foods Corp.	68,257.4
56	Time Inc.	119,785.0	90	Wendy's International	64,445.0
57	Jos. E. Seagram & Sons	119,604.4	91	Wm. Wrigley Jr. Co.	63,948.2
58	International Business Machines Corp.	119,222.5	92	Delta Air Lines	63,944.3
59	Schering-Plough Corp.	117,914.2	93	Adolph Coors Co.	63,621.3
60	American Honda Motor Co.	115,182.3	94	Noxell Corp.	58,264.4
61	Nestle Enterprises	114,957.0	95	Canon U.S.A.	58,032.9
62	Toyota Motor Sales U.S.A.	113,649.0	96	Goodyear Tire & Rubber Co.	57,831.7
63	Volkswagen of America	112,500.0	97	GrandMet U.S.A.	55,566.2
64	IC Industries	112,100.0	98	Coleco Industries	55,216.4
65	Xerox Corp.	110,101.8	99	Carnation Co.	54,284.6
66	American Express Co.	107,571.0	100	American Broadcasting Cos.	49,167.5
67	Du Pont	102,637.0			
68	Trans World Corp.	101,503.3			

Figures are a composite of measured and unmeasured advertising.

In this phase of planning, the manager determines the times when the vehicles will broadcast or print the advertisements, the frequency with which an ad is transmitted, and the period of time for using the vehicles. *Media planning*, a complex process, is the subject of Chapter 8, which examines the major elements of that process.

EVALUATING PROGRAM PERFORMANCE

A major impediment to the development of successful ad campaigns is the inability to foresee all the factors that affect the campaign's performance. Things can go wrong in many ways. The color schemes that seemed so appealing in the planning stages may turn out badly in the newspaper printing process. Surprisingly intense competitor advertising may burst forth. The television programming selected as a setting for commercials may prove to be a major flop in audience viewership.

An important activity in the management of an ad campaign is the systematic evaluation of feedback on program performance. The fundamental questions throughout this tracking process are the following:

Are we getting the results that we had planned and expected?

Why are we getting the performance that we are?

In addressing these two questions at critical phases of the campaign, the advertiser can maintain control of the program. The comparison of results with expectations points out deficiencies that demand attention or superior performances that merit rewards. Analysis of the reasons leading to specific performances facilitates the remediation or prevention of problems. Or it may identify productive efforts to be reinforced and encouraged.

The responsibilities of the ad manager in setting up an evaluation system are (1) to establish the criteria or benchmarks to be used for judging performance and (2) to develop procedures for the accurate measurement of ad results. The basic structure of an evaluation process and the major technical details for carrying out that process are described in Chapter 18.

AN EXAMPLE OF ADVERTISING MANAGEMENT: THE STORY BEHIND THE FIRST NATIONAL ADVERTISING CAMPAIGN FOR WENDY'S OLD-FASHIONED HAMBURGERS[6]

So far we have discussed the management of an ad program in an abstract context. We will now fill in the conceptual framework underlying the management of an advertising program. In the following paragraphs we will look at the development and execution of Wendy's first national advertising campaign.

Company Background

"Does America need another hamburger chain?" That was the question as R. David Thomas opened the doors to his first Wendy's Old-Fashioned Hamburgers restaurant in downtown Columbus, Ohio, on November 15, 1969.

At that time many food industry experts and some skeptical observers commented that the fast-food growth curve had already peaked during the late 1960s . . . and that the rapid expansion of the industry had passed.

But this skepticism did not take into account the determination of R. David Thomas, who, at the age of 36, was soon to be referred to as the "David after the hamburger Goliaths." Thomas's early food service career had been varied but extensive. At the age of 12, he got his first restaurant job as a counterman, and he has been in the food service business ever since.

In the 25 years before starting Wendy's, Thomas had worked as a busboy, dishwasher, short-order cook, baker, fryman, assistant manager, manager, and corporate officer. At the age of 21, Thomas operated an enlisted men's club in the U.S. Army. As a franchise owner of Kentucky Fried Chicken (KFC), Thomas was one of the first to open a free-standing KFC store, and after selling his market area back to the parent company, he became a regional director for KFC. Thomas next played a major role in organizing the Arthur Treacher's Fish & Chips chain, but hamburgers remained his first love, and this prompted him to start Wendy's, naming the company after one of his daughters.

With the opening of his first restaurant, he introduced his "Cadillac hamburger," offered in one-quarter, one-half, and three-quarter pound portions, served hot off the grill on a "cooked-to-order" basis, and made of only 100 percent pure American beef pattied fresh daily. Thomas believed he had found a distinctive market of people who wanted his quality product. Quality was important to Thomas, so much so, in fact, that he incorporated it into his company's philosophy and in the Wendy's cameo logo and advertising slogan, "Quality Is Our Recipe."

During the company's first year of operation, the store achieved sales of approximately $300,000. This encouraged Thomas to open an additional restaurant in 1970, and two more in 1971, all successful and proving he had a winning concept.

In 1972 the company decided to franchise its limited menu, quality food, and fast-service concept and signed its first franchise agreement for the Indianapolis, Indiana, market area. Unlike its food-service competitors, who franchised individual restaurant locations, Wendy's granted its franchising rights on a market or regional basis, which entitled the franchise owner to develop multiunit operations based on the population density. This was unique for the food service industry, and it was a significant factor contributing to the company's rapid growth and expansion. By year-end 1972 there were nine Wendy's restaurants in operation with systemwide sales exceeding $2 million. The rapid growth cycle for Wendy's had now begun.

In 1976, with 520 stores in operation and systemwide sales totaling $187,683,000, Thomas initiated plans for the company's first national advertising campaign. To bring it into being, the company established the Wendy's National Advertising Program (WNAP), a nonprofit organization, to administer the national advertising and sales promotion programs. Both corporate personnel and franchise owners served as officers and trustees of WNAP. The operating funds for WNAP came from one percent of gross sales contributions from all franchised and company-owned stores. This amount would total approximately $3.8 million for Wendy's first national advertising campaign.

The Problem and Objectives

Although Wendy's had been promoting actively in its respective local markets, the promotional budget (3 percent of gross sales per restaurant) varied depending on the actual number of restaurants in each market area. Consequently, putting into effect a national advertising and promotion program would provide many benefits. It would (1) assist media buying efficiency, (2) help unify Wendy's image and positioning in the market, (3) increase the overall effectiveness in the local markets, and (4) facilitate the rapid development of new outlets.

Specifically, the objectives of Wendy's first national advertising program were to create greater consumer awareness, unify company identity, and create strong product acceptance.

The Campaign Budget

Wendy's two major competitors, McDonald's and Burger King, were spending approximately $120 million and $50 million respectively on their national advertising programs in 1976. By contrast, Wendy's was preparing to launch its first national advertising campaign with $3.8 million, a fraction of what its established competitors were spending.

Another influencing factor was the number of restaurants in operation. When Wendy's planned to air its "Hot 'n Juicy" campaign, there were approximately seven hundred restaurants in operation. That number, according to many observers, was far below the thousand restaurants thought necessary for an efficient and effective national advertising program.

Despite these limitations and disadvantages, the Wendy's marketing team was able to increase the impact of the national campaign by closely coordinating and integrating the local advertising and promotional efforts with the national program. The budget and allocation for both programs appear in Exhibit Wendy's-1. Wendy's advertising budget had two classifications: national (network television advertising) and local (the amount for each market area).

The Concept

While a number of operational and product differences existed between Wendy's and its major competitors, the consumer did not see these differences as unique. For example: (1) Wendy's used *fresh* meat, while its major competitors used *frozen* meat; (2) Wendy's served its hamburgers hot off the grill, while its competitors served their hamburgers precooked, pre-wrapped, and warmed under heat lamps; (3) Wendy's offered its hamburgers "cooked-to-order," with customer's choice of nine different condiments (cheese, tomato, lettuce, mayonnaise, catsup, mustard, pickles, relish, and onions), while its competitors served their hamburgers with standard condiments and offered variety only by "special request"; and (4) Wendy's offered fast and convenient service with its Pick Up Window, an innovation later copied by most of its competitors. The company had to make the consumer aware of these differences.

EXHIBIT WENDY'S-1   The Wendy's Ad Budget and Allocation

National*		
Media (network television buy)	$3,200,000	
Production of television commercials	600,000	
		$ 3,800,000
Local†		
Television (local placement)	$8,550,000	
Radio	1,710,000	
Print media	570,000	
Other	570,000	
		$11,400,000
Total advertising budget		$15,200,000

* Derived from 1 percent of gross sales contributions from all franchised and company-owned restaurants.
† Derived from 3 percent of gross sales contributions from all francished and company-owned restaurants.

The Execution

To make this campaign work, Wendy's used a team approach that combined the creative talent of Dick Rich, an established advertising industry professional; the network television buying expertise of Clifford A. Botway; and the local market-planning and execution capabilities of Stockton-West Burkhart, Wendy's advertising agency since 1973.

The product and service differences were translated into the advertising theme to make it a positive product benefit for the consumer. The Wendy's "Hot 'n Juicy" Hamburgers campaign, using television commercials that incorporated a hard-sell, entertaining approach, emphasized the company's product superiority over its competition. (See Exhibit Wendy's-2 for a television commercial.) In-store posters and employee buttons reaffirmed the benefit at the point of purchase.

The media schedule Wendy's purchased during the campaign's inaugural year emphasized sports programming (both baseball and football), primetime movies, and family shows to reach both family and adult male audiences. (See Exhibits Wendy's-3 and Wendy's-4 for examples of the national media buy.)

The Results

Nine months after the start of the "Hot 'n Juicy" national advertising campaign, the results were very evident and extremely favorable. System-wide sales in 1977 for the 905 Wendy's restaurants in operation totaled $425,847,900, up 227 percent from the previous year. In addition, the company had opened 385 new restaurants since the start of campaign planning.

The campaign helped "put Wendy's on the map," as consumer awareness continued to increase, enhancing company identity in the local markets, which in turn contributed to a faster growth curve in new restaurant openings. The campaign's advertising strength helped "presell" new market areas by creating consumers' demand for Wendy's products. No longer was the company only a "local advertiser." It now had established national representation for the company and its franchise owners.

The success of the "Hot 'n Juicy" national advertising campaign, combined with the company's unique franchising concept and innovative operations, no doubt helped the company reach and surpass its thousandth restaurant in operation, an impressive milestone. In a relatively short time, Wendy's had grown from one restaurant and a philosophy of quality into a national restaurant chain. This was a first, setting an unparalleled record within the food service industry.

The campaign's overall success registered in other ways too. As a national advertiser, the company could now more accurately assess its advertising effectiveness by conducting tracking studies and recall-comparison sur-

EXHIBIT WENDY'S-2 *Wendy's Television Ad Storyboard*

THE WENDY'S NATIONAL ADVERTISING PROGRAM, INC.

"WIPES II"
30 Second TV

(Music: "Wendy's Theme")
Wendy's presents, hot and juicy hamburgers.

If you've ever had a dry, chewy hamburger, you're gonna love Wendy's hot and juicy hamburgers.

Wendy's hot and juicy hamburgers.

Juicy meat. Juicy toppings. And lots of napkins.

EXHIBIT WENDY'S-3   *The Wendy's National Advertising Program: National Media Buy, Second Quarter*

DATE	PROGRAM	TIME	AUDIENCE
April 1	Chico and the Man	8:30–9 P.M.	26,760,000
April 3	The Big Event	9:30–11 P.M.	22,200,000
April 5	Kojak	9–10 P.M.	26,040,000
April 6	Good Times	8–8:30 P.M.	26,920,000
April 7	The Waltons	8–9 P.M.	29,460,000
April 10	ABC Sunday Night Movie	9–11 P.M.	28,040,000
April 11	ABC Monday Night Football	8:30 P.M.	17,940,000
April 16	NBC Major League Baseball	2:00 P.M.	9,540,000
April 18	ABC Monday Night Baseball	8:30 P.M.	17,940,000
April 18	NBC Monday Night at the Movies	9–11 P.M.	23,780,000
May 7	NBC Major League Baseball	2:00 P.M.	9,540,000
May 10	Police Woman	9–10 P.M.	27,340,000
May 10	One Day at a Time	9:30–10 P.M.	27,340,000
May 16	ABC Monday Night Baseball	8:30 P.M.	17,940,000
May 16	The Tonight Show	11:30 P.M.	10,960,000
May 29	The Wonderful World of Disney	7–8 P.M.	19,660,000
May 30	ABC Monday Night Baseball	8:30 P.M.	17,940,000
June 4	NBC Major League Baseball	2:00 P.M.	9,540,000
June 18	NBC Saturday Night at the Movies	9–11 P.M.	20,080,000
June 20	ABC Monday Night Baseball	8:30 P.M.	17,360,000
June 20	The Tonight Show	11:30 P.M.	10,960,000
June 25	NBC Saturday Night at the Movies	9–11 P.M.	20,080,000
June 27	ABC Monday Night Baseball	8:30 P.M.	17,360,000
June 27	NBC Monday Night at the Movies	9–11 P.M.	22,200,000
June 27	The Tonight Show	11:30 P.M.	10,960,000

veys with its competition. The results would be significant in future media planning and market strategies.

The "Hot 'n Juicy" theme received critical acclaim and numerous advertising and marketing awards, including the prestigious Clio Award. The campaign had "staying power" and established strong company identity for the consumer.

USING ADVERTISING AGENCIES

It should now be clear that advertising management is a complex matter. It entails a wide range of activities demanding many different skills, ranging from the managerial ability to define and coordinate objectives to the ability

EXHIBIT WENDY'S-4   The Wendy's National Advertising Program: National Media Buy, Third Quarter

DATE	PROGRAM	TIME	AUDIENCE
July 4	NBC Monday Night at the Movies	9–11 P.M.	18,360,000
July 6	Baretta	9–10 P.M.	22,640,000
July 9	Starsky & Hutch	9–11 P.M.	17,220,000
July 11	ABC Monday Night Baseball	8:30 P.M.	16,360,000
July 11	The Tonight Show	11:30 P.M.	10,520,000
July 14	Best Sellers	9–10 P.M.	19,220,000
July 23	NBC Major League Baseball	2:00 P.M.	9,680,000
July 25	ABC Monday Night Baseball	8:30 P.M.	16,360,000
August 1	ABC Monday Night Baseball	8:30 P.M.	16,360,000
August 7	The Big Event	9:30–11 P.M.	19,080,000
August 8	ABC Monday Night Baseball	8:30 P.M.	16,360,000
August 13	NBC Major League Baseball	2:00 P.M.	9,680,000
August 15	ABC Monday Night Baseball	8:30 P.M.	16,360,000
August 15	The Tonight Show	11:30 P.M.	10,520,000
August 22	NFL Monday Night Football	9:00 P.M.	17,800,000
August 27	NBC Saturday Night at the Movies	9–11 P.M.	18,780,000
August 29	NFL Monday Night Football	9:00 P.M.	17,800,000
August 29	The Tonight Show	11:30 P.M.	10,520,000
September 4	NBC Sunday Night News	6:30–7 P.M.	8,680,000
September 5	NFL Monday Night Football	9:00 P.M.	17,800,000
September 10	NFL Monday Night Football	9:00 P.M.	24,920,000
September 19	NFL Monday Night Football	9:00 P.M.	24,920,000
September 26	NFL Monday Night Football	9:00 P.M.	24,920,000

to generate, screen, and supervise the execution of creative work, to the familiarity with analytical techniques in program evaluation.

A successful campaign calls for an organization with significant depth in particular skills. Few organizations are sufficiently large to maintain a full staff with specialized skills across the range of management activities. An advertising agency provides the special services to assist in various phases of campaign management and execution.

In this section we summarize the services offered by agencies and the role they play in the several stages of an advertising program.

Ad Agency Functions

An advertising agency is essentially an organization that provides one or more of the skills necessary in the management of an advertising campaign specifically, and a promotion program in general. In serving a client, the agency may take charge of all responsibilities from the beginning to the end of a campaign, or it may be contracted for specific services to supplement the client's own advertising activity. The range of services that an advertising agency can provide a client is listed in Exhibit 7-8. As you can see, agency services are available to run not only an ad campaign but also an entire promotional program, with the exception of providing personal selling for the client.

Exhibit 7-9 illustrates the typical structure of an agency capable of assuming all the responsibilities of a campaign. This type of agency is called

EXHIBIT 7-8 Advertising Agency Services

Basic services	Product services
Planning	New product development
Copywriting	Product design
Layout	Creation of brand names
Media selection	Creation of trademarks
	Complete packaging design
Research services	
Market research	*Merchandising services*
Consumer research	Displays
Copy research	Package inserts
Media research	Banners, streamers
	Other point-of-purchase
Trade promotion services	material
Wholesaler promotions	
Dealer promotions	*Direct mail services*
Booklets, pamphlets, broadsides	Letters, folders, booklets
Catalogs, catalog sheets, specification	Brochures
sheets	Sampling
Exhibits	Couponing
Sales training services	*Other services*
Planning sales meetings	House organs
Salesman's manuals and portfolios	Premiums
Visual aids	Contests
	Instruction booklets
Publicity and public relations services	Calendars
New product publicity	Annual reports
News stories	Pricing
Company image building	
Consumer relations	
Employer-employee relations	

Richard E. Stanley, *Promotion: Advertising, Publicity, Personal Selling, Sales Promotion*, © 1977, p. 175. Reprinted by permission of Prentice-Hall, Inc., Englewood Cliffs, N.J.

EXHIBIT 7-9 Typical Organization of a Full-Service Agency

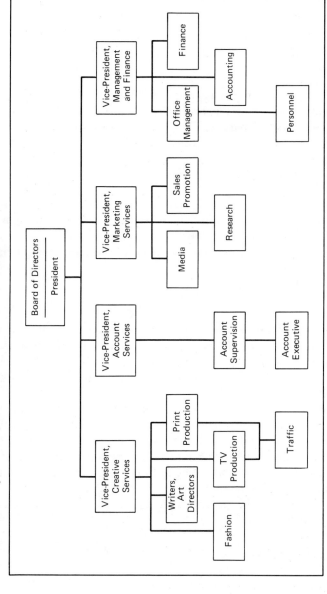

Kleppner/Russell/Verrill, *Otto Kleppner's Advertising Procedure*, 8th Ed., © 1983, p. 473.
Reprinted by permission of Prentice-Hall, Inc., Englewood Cliffs, N.J.

a *full-service agency* and usually consists of four major divisions. One division is responsible for the internal administration of the agency. Exhibit 7-9 shows that this area oversees office operations, finance, accounting, and personnel. The remaining three divisions—account services, creative services, and marketing services—directly address client needs.

Account Services

The *account services* division is responsible for client contacts and relationships. Usually, the account executive works with the client organization through its advertising manager. The role of the account executive consists of

1. Contributing to the development of the client's campaign goals and strategies
2. Acting as an intermediary between the client's needs and requests, and the agency's suggestions and responses to those needs during the preliminary stages of the campaign
3. Supervising and reporting to the client on the implementation of the campaign

Creative Services

In the *creative services* division are the writers and artists who create the copy and visuals for the campaign. The creative director guides the conceptualization of the ideas for expressing the message strategy. The actual production of the advertisements can be in-house or through subcontracts with outside shops.

The work of writers and artists goes beyond advertisements. Their talents may aid the development of trade promotions such as catalogs or booklets, publicity activities, and packaging.

Because of the number of activities that take place concurrently, there is need for a central coordinator. The traffic group is in charge of scheduling the production of the creative work. Their principal concern is that the production of the ads be in line with the timetables established for the entire campaign.

Marketing Services

According to Exhibit 7-9, the *marketing services* department includes the persons who buy and schedule time and space in the media, the persons who conduct research, and the persons who develop sales promotions to complement an advertising campaign. The media group's responsibilities are to identify the appropriate media vehicles and to arrange a schedule for presentation of the ads.

The research group provides input for a number of decisions in the management process. For example, they conduct consumer studies, analyze marketplace trends, test advertising copy, and monitor the performance of media.

Management

The *management* division is responsible for the administrative aspects of the agency—its internal functions—including the accounting system, the financial system, and personnel supervision.

The Client-Agency Relationship

Let us now focus on selecting an agency, working with it, evaluating its performance, and determining compensation.

Selecting an Agency

An organization usually seeks an agency when it recognizes that it lacks some essential strength for the development or management of an ad campaign. The task of selecting the right agency is complicated. Exhibit 7-10 presents a comprehensive list of points suggested by the American Association of National Advertisers for evaluating and selecting an agency. In seeking an agency, you would want to know an agency's background, the types of business it handles, the manner in which it works on an account, the creative skills it has to offer, and the manner in which it is compensated. We will discuss four major considerations in screening prospective agencies.

Size. The size of an advertising agency is often described in two ways: (1) the amount of media billings, representing the dollar value of print space and broadcast time contracted for the agency's clients; and (2) the income or actual revenues the agency received from clients. Exhibit 7-11 lists some of the largest advertising agencies.

Large agencies offer more services under one roof than small agencies. While small agencies may be able to subcontract services as necessary, they cannot match the large agencies' benefit of convenience, nor can they ensure the degree of service coordination promised by the large groups.

There are two possible disadvantages in working with large agencies. First, the size of their operations results in high overhead costs, and by setting minimum billing requirements, they tend to handle only large accounts. This obviously discourages low-budget advertisers. Second, a small-

EXHIBIT 7-10 *Selected Criteria for Evaluating Prospective Agencies*

I. THE AGENCY

a. The length of time the agency has been in business
b. General business experience
c. The types of accounts, clients and services the agency believes in or specializes in
d. The qualifications of the management of the agency
e. Method of evaluation, planning and execution to be employed in serving client's account

II. ANALYSIS OF ACCOUNTS

a. Accounts by name and product
b. Recent new accounts
c. Recent accounts lost
d. Billings of the smallest and largest account
e. Policy on account conflicts
f. Growth rates in billings in recent years
g. Evidence of success with accounts—sales results, market share, etc.

III. ACCOUNT MANAGEMENT

a. Who will work on account
b. The time to be devoted to the account
c. The planning, coordinating and review responsibilities of the account executive, service department heads and management

IV. CREATIVE

a. Agency philosophy on copy and creative activities
b. Backgrounds of key creative people
c. The responsibilities for the planning, development, execution and approval of creative work
d. Examples of past creative work

V. ADVERTISING EFFECTIVENESS RESEARCH

a. Methods used to check results
b. Studies made for clients
c. Use of outside research services

VI. BILLINGS AND FEES

a. Use of commission and/or fee system
b. Services provided within commissions
c. Fees for extra services

Selecting an Advertising Agency (New York: Association of National Advertisers, 1977), pp. 41, 47.

EXHIBIT 7-11   The Top 10 Agencies in Income

Rank	Agency	1983	1982
	TOP 10 AGENCIES IN WORLD INCOME		
	(GROSS INCOME IN MILLIONS)		
1	Young & Rubicam	414.0	376.6
2	Ted Bates Worldwide	388.0	356.1
3	J. Walter Thompson Co.	378.4	347.1
4	Ogilvy & Mather	345.8	315.1
5	McCann-Erickson Worldwide	298.8	276.1
6	BBDO International	289.0	238.3
7	Saatchi & Saatchi Compton	253.3	186.5
8	Leo Burnett Co.	216.5	221.2
9	Foote Cone & Belding	208.4	180.4
10	Doyle Dane Bernbach	199.0	185.0
	TOP 10 AGENCIES IN U.S. INCOME		
	(GROSS INCOME IN MILLIONS)		
Rank	Agency	1983	1982
1	Young & Rubicam	274.4	246.7
2	Ted Bates Worldwide	244.4	233.4
3	Ogilvy & Mather	204.1	176.9
4	BBDO International	199.0	155.0
5	J. Walter Thompson Co.	189.9	167.2
6	Foote Cone & Belding	158.9	129.2
7	Doyle Dane Bernbach	146.0	138.0
8	Leo Burnett Co.	135.0	136.0
9	Grey Advertising	125.1	109.0
10	McCann-Erickson Worldwide	95.4	82.5

budget client is constantly concerned that its account will not receive the attention accorded to bigger clients.

As a rule, the client should seek an agency with accounts similar in size to its own. The client's account should not dominate the agency's other business, nor should it be an insignificant part of the agency's activities.

Conflict accounts. Advertising agencies try to avoid handling the accounts of competing clients. In this way, conflict of interest is not likely to arise.

When conflicts of interest do arise, they are seldom intentional. Instead they stem from the differing perspectives between the client and the agency as to what constitutes a competitive account. For example, an agency may consider a tea account and a coffee account to be nonconflicting while the client of either account may view the other's product as a competing substitute among consumers.

Distinctive skills. An agency usually develops a distinctive competence either in an advertising function or in a product or service industry. Perhaps because of its experiences and the talent of its personnel, an agency may excel in an area such as creative copy, effective media scheduling, and brand name development. Or an agency may specialize in clients from specific products or services such as the computer industry or financial investment firms. Selecting an agency with an appropriate competence should result in more effective use of advertising dollars.

Past performance. While an agency's past successes will not ensure the success of current or future campaigns, the potential client may infer at least that the past successes indicate a degree of expertise. With that in mind, an agency's past record may be one valid basis for selection, providing of course that principals of that agency remain the same.

Working with an Agency

The client's interest is the framework for the agency's efforts. The agency applies its skills to obtain results the client wishes to see.

The client may rightfully expect a high degree of service from the agency and should make these expectations clear prior to the campaign. On the other hand, the client also has many responsibilities to the agency, including the necessary support in the form of funds and information. Although the advertiser does have the right to provide the agency with feedback on its satisfaction with performance, this should facilitate rather than interfere with the execution of the agency's work. There must be trust in agency judgment and sufficient latitude for the agency to exercise its skills.

A successful client-agency relationship results when each party understands the other party's tasks and interests.

Evaluating Agency Performance

Feedback to the agency is not a one-time activity. If there is a good working relationship between both parties, the agency will receive periodic feedback from the client during the course of the campaign. Although feedback is an ongoing process, there does come a time for review of the agency's overall performance.

The evaluation of an agency usually covers four major areas. The first question to ask, of course, is, How close to the campaign's goals are the campaign's results? Then one assesses the marketing-planning services, the effectiveness of the creative services, and the overall working relationship between client and agency. Exhibit 7-12 contains an agency evaluation form.

Agency Compensation

There are two methods by which an agency can generate revenue, the commission and the fee. Exhibit 7-13 shows that the *commission system* is by far the more popular approach. Under that system, an agency's income is usually some percentage of the contracted costs of media time and space. In some instances, income can also derive from billing the client for cost

EXHIBIT 7-12   Sample Agency Evaluation Form

AGENCY PERFORMANCE EVALUATION SUMMARY

_____ AGENCY

Biannual Review Dated

ITEM WEIGHT	ITEM PERFORMANCE EVALUATION	ITEM POINT SCORE (Item Weight x Evaluation)

Product Line ___ ___ ___ ___ ___
% Impm't Goal ___% ___% ___% ___% ___%

TOTAL SCORE

Share of Market Performance   (Range: 0 — 100% = Optimum)

60 (a) Percent Improvement Achieved   ___% ___% ___% ___% ___%
   (Memo) Actual Data: XXX
   Subtotal

Creativity   (Range: 0 — 100%; 100% = Optimum)
6 (a) Marketing Strategy Formulation   ___% ___% ___% ___% ___%
4 (b) Conceptual Ability (Defining & Solving Problems)
4 (c) Creative Ability in TV
4 (d) Creative Ability in Print   XXX
1 (e) Advertising Research Ability (Media & Copy)
1 (f) New Product Development
   Subtotal

Cooperation   (Range: 0 — 100%; 100% = Optimum)
10 (a) Overall Performance   ___% ___% ___% ___% ___%
5 (b) Service (Deadlines, Cost Control)   XXX
5 (c) Goal Achievement Efforts
   Subtotal

Total Individual Product Line Performance (100 Points = Optimum)

A. Planned Relative Profit Importance of Marketing Strategies   ___% ___% ___% ___% ___%   %

B. Total Agency Performance Score (100 Points = Optimum)

Reprinted with permission from the April 18, 1977 issue of *Advertising Age*. Copyright 1977 by Crain Communications, Inc.

EXHIBIT 7-13 Agency Compensation Arrangements

COMMISSION-RELATED ARRANGEMENTS	NUMBER OF MENTIONS	% OF 275 TOTAL
Traditional 15% media commission plus markup	168	61%
Reduced commission	11	4
Increased commission	3	1
Combination of hourly rates and commissions	4	1
Volume rebate	1	—
Minimum guarantee	12	4
Efficiency incentive compensation plan	7	3
Other	21	8
Total media commission-related	227	82%
STRICTLY FEE ARRANGEMENTS		
Cost plus profit	16	6%
Fixed fee (flat fee, fixed compensation)	18	7
Flat fee plus direct costs	6	2
Supplemental fees (project fees)	3	1
Other	5	2
Total fee	48	18%
Overall total	275	100%

Kleppner/Russell/Verrill, *Otto Kleppner's Advertising Procedure*, 8th Ed., © 1983, p. 478. Reprinted by permission of Prentice-Hall, Inc., Englewood Cliffs, N.J.

plus markup for ad production or market research or other extraordinary services.

The typical commission is 15 percent of the cost of the media. An agency that purchases $10,000 worth of space in a newspaper for its client would bill the client for $10,000 but forward only $8,500 to the publisher. The $1,500—15 percent of the cost of the space—is the agency's gross income. From this $1,500, the agency takes care of costs associated with the campaign, including the services of writers, artists, printers, and so on.

The commission system is simple for the client to understand, and the charge for agency services is easy to calculate. These are clear advantages. However, the simplicity of the commission reflects an inherent fault. The client's bill may not necessarily relate to the actual services. For example, an advertiser that elects to extend the use of a previously produced television commercial may request an agency to book air time. The agency would get 15 percent of the media billing without having provided the usual services beyond buying media.

For the agency, the convenience of the commission system is frequently offset by the uncertainty of the profitability of an account. For the most part, an agency that goes with commissions is responsible for assuming the costs associated with the management of a campaign. Sometimes there is difficulty in estimating the costs with any reasonable degree of precision. An agency that works solely on commission exposes itself to the risk that some accounts may engender unanticipated difficulties and expenses. For example, an imaginative theme may require such a unique combination of words and visuals that the creative services division devotes an inordinate number of labor-hours to meet a deadline.

The *fee system* provides revenue to the agency based on the services provided and the costs incurred. Many agencies that operate strictly on a fee basis credit the client's account with any commissions derived from media billings.

The advantage for the client is that there is an itemization of the bill from the agency. This identifies the services rendered along with the corresponding charge. The disadvantage of the fee system for both the client and the agency is that it may be rather complex. The agency's accounting system must do more work. In large campaigns, the final bill to the client may be somewhat complicated and confusing.

Specialized Agencies

The competitiveness of the marketplace has spun off agencies offering specialized services rather than the full range. While the use of a *full-service agency* may benefit from the synergism that arises from having all services coordinated by one management, the specialists may be more effective and efficient in complex advertising activities requiring highly skilled personnel. In recent years, two types of specialists, the media-buying service and the creative boutique, have become popular.

Media-Buying Services

A *media-buying service* selects and schedules media vehicles for its customers, who may themselves be small agencies or advertisers. These services have emerged because the factors in making good purchases have become so burdensome.[7] The substantial number of television vehicles, radio stations, and programs, the abundance of special-interest magazines, the complexities of rate structures, the variation in closing dates for ad placements, and so on, are just a few of the considerations in media buying. Media-buying services assume all the responsibility for developing or implementing a media plan.

Creative Boutiques

Creative boutiques are advertising agencies that offer only creative services and subcontract for other services—such as media buying—if necessary.

Boutiques exist because many advertisers do not need the extensive services (or the corresponding overhead) offered by a full-service agency. Boutiques offer expertise in creative ideas, copy, and artwork. The client may supply its own service in other areas or buy additional services as the need arises.

SUMMARY

Advertising management consists of the following activities: situation analysis, establishment of objectives, determination of the budget, design of the message strategy, development of the media plan, and evaluation of program performance. We emphasized the importance of valid objectives and presented some major objectives in both conceptual and operational form. We saw that budget decisions have two chief components: total amount to spend and allocation of that amount. We looked at the design of message strategy, embodying identification of key ideas for communications and execution of the strategy growing out of the copy platform of an ad campaign. Media planning involves the selecting and scheduling of communications vehicles. The ad manager makes decisions about times, frequency, and time interval for ad placement. The manager must monitor performance and effect necessary control measures for successful execution of the campaign. Finally, we considered the usefulness of advertising agencies, both full-service and specialty firms; and we stressed the importance of mutual responsibilities shared by client and agency.

REVIEW AND DISCUSSION QUESTIONS

1. Give an overview of the major activities in advertising management.
2. Explain what is meant by situation analysis. What types of information should be gathered when conducting an analysis of the advertising situation?
3. Explain the importance of objectives in an advertising campaign.
4. What are the characteristics of valid advertising objectives?
5. Compare and contrast advertising campaigns with the following objectives: (a) awareness, (b) comprehension, (c) conviction, and (d) action. Give examples of each.
6. In your opinion, how might the objectives of Coca-Cola's advertising differ from those of a new cola soft drink?
7. What are the implications of a budget that is too high or too low?
8. What is a copy platform, and how does it fit into the advertising process?

9. *What tasks are involved in media-planning activities?*

10. *What role does an advertising agency play in a company's advertising program? What functions does the agency usually perform?*

11. *What major guidelines would you recommend in selecting an advertising agency?*

12. *In what ways is an ad agency compensated? What are the advantages and disadvantages of each to the advertiser? To the agency?*

13. *Describe the responsibilities that an account executive has to a client.*

14. *What criteria would you establish for evaluating an advertising agency's performance? Explain.*

NOTES

1. See "U.S. Advertising Volume," *Advertising Age*, May 28, 1984, p. 50; and Christy Marshall, "Ad Spending Seen Climbing 13.8%," *Advertising Age*, December 19, 1983, p. 56.

2. "Twentieth Century-Fox—The Wiz," in *Cases in Advertising & Communications Management*, ed. Stephen A. Greyser (Englewood Cliffs, N.J.: Prentice-Hall, 1981), pp. 497–515.

3. Russell Colley, *Defining Advertising Goals for Measured Advertising Results* (New York: Association of National Advertisers, 1961). For another excellent discussion of advertising objectives and their significance for a successful advertising effort, see Joseph P. Guiltinan and Gordon W. Paul, *Marketing Management* (New York: McGraw-Hill, 1985), pp. 237–65.

4. Charles H. Patti and Vincent Blasko, "Budgeting Practices of Big Advertisers," *Journal of Advertising Research*, December 1981, p. 25.

5. Leading advertisers are increasingly using mathematical and computer-based budgeting techniques. For more information on such techniques and advertiser practices, see Edward Riordan and Fred Morgan, Jr., "A Taxonomic Evaluation of Advertising Budgeting Models," *Journal of Advertising*, 8, No. 1 (1979), 33–38; and Kent Lancaster and Judith Stern, "Computer-Based Advertising Budgeting Practices of Leading U.S. Consumer Advertisers," *Journal of Advertising*, 12, No. 4 (1983), 4–9.

6. Courtesy of Denny Lynch, Vice President, Communications, Wendy's International, Inc., Dublin, Ohio; research and editorial by D. A. James Associates, Columbus, Ohio.

7. For a discussion of major issues in media buying, see Herbert Zeltner, "Media Buying Calls for Tight Controls," *Advertising Age*, October 1, 1984, pp. 3ff.

8

Advertising Media Strategy

A message, no matter how good, will not have its full impact without the right delivery to the target audience. The media strategy is an essential component of an effective campaign.[1] Appropriate selection and scheduling of transmission channels ensure that the message reaches the right market at the right time and with maximum effect.

The specific details of media plans will vary with each advertiser, but the process and logic leading to the final plan are fairly consistent across plans. Exhibit 8-1 presents a graphic overview of the process. Analysis in four areas—communications objectives, target audience, message strategy, and competition—is the foundation beneath screening, selecting, and then scheduling.

In this chapter we focus on the decisions and considerations in planning media strategy. Specifically, we discuss the process of evaluating and selecting media vehicles and then the scheduling decision.

EXHIBIT 8-1   Overview of the Media-Planning Process

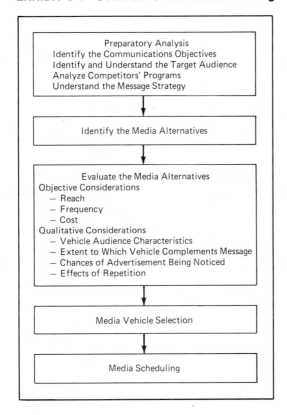

PREPARATORY ANALYSIS

The necessary first step is to review the marketing and promotion plans so that the goals of the media strategy fit into the overall effort. This first step is especially important because it establishes many of the criteria for evaluating the vehicles. For example, a media objective might be:

Deliver the message to the target audience at least five times a week for a period of one month.

This objective precludes the use of magazines because of their publication frequencies (typically weekly or monthly issues). Newspapers, radio, and television vehicles might be possible, but it would depend on their broadcast or printing schedules.

Media vehicles serve as channels for the flow of a message from the advertiser to the vehicles' audiences. Obviously an advertiser is successful only if the message flows to an audience that falls within this advertiser's target market. Knowledge of the target market discloses whether the audience of a specific vehicle is acceptable. Furthermore, analysis of the target market's media habits—Do they watch television? If so, when do they watch? What programs do they watch?—facilitates media selection and scheduling decisions.[2]

The media planner must also understand message strategy. Vehicles, by virtue of their individual characteristics, may enhance or lessen the impact of a message. For example, a manufacturer of automobile batteries has a theme that its batteries reliably start engines on the coldest of days. To convey this theme, television is used to broadcast graphic visuals that depict subfreezing conditions accompanied by distinctive sound effects. The message has the intended impact because television has both visual and audio capabilities. In Chapter 9 we will look more closely at the distinctive moods and characteristics of various media.

Finally, we have to keep in mind that competitors vie for the consumer's attention. Since the consumer has only limited attention capacities, his or her attention to one message may postpone or even preclude attention to another message. An analysis of competitive strategy provides the advertiser with an idea of the intensity and distribution of media effort necessary to be competitive. For example, knowledge that the strongest competitor intends to buy six minutes of air time during the broadcast of a television special may lead an advertiser to consider equivalent time during similar programs in order to protect market position.

MEDIA SELECTION FACTORS

After the preparatory analysis has been completed, the complex work of actually evaluating media vehicles begins. The planner must screen media on both quantitative and qualitative factors. *Quantitative* factors are those characteristics that are objectively measurable, such as audience size and cost to reach the audience. *Qualitative* characteristics are based on the subjective judgments of the planner; they often prove more difficult to assess and understand than the quantitative dimensions, but they are an essential consideration in an effective media plan.[3]

Quantitative Factors

Four quantitative criteria are customary in the evaluation of media vehicles: reach, frequency, gross rating points, and cost per thousand persons reached.

Reach

A vehicle's contribution to the success of a campaign is sometimes measured by the number of people that it contacts. In general, a vehicle that has a large audience is more desirable in a media plan than a vehicle that does not.

The term *reach* describes the ability of a vehicle to contact people. The reach of a vehicle is the number of people who experience the vehicle during a stated period, usually defined by its publication or programming frequency. For example, if the reach of a magazine is 2 million, it means that 2 million different persons read each issue.

While the concept of reach is rather simple, the actual measurement of it for a specific vehicle and for the plan as a whole may be confusing. Here is how the advertiser determines a vehicle's reach.

Measures of reach vary with media. The measure for newspapers and magazines is circulation and readership figures. In the broadest sense, total circulation refers to the number of copies distributed during a publication period. A newspaper with a circulation of 350,000 sends out that number of copies in one issue. Since circulation can be defined in so many different ways, circulation figures typically break down into the following major categories:

1. Paid circulation. These people actually purchase the publication.
2. Subscription circulation. These people have committed themselves to purchasing the publication over a period of time.
3. Newsstand circulation. This type of paid circulation is based on single-copy sales.

Circulation figures are available from the vehicles themselves, although there are organizations that verify circulation. The best known of these is the Audit Bureau of Circulations (ABC). Exhibit 8-2 shows an ABC report.

Readership, sometimes called total audience, takes into account the fact that not only the subscriber (the primary reader) but others, too, may read a single issue of a newspaper and especially a magazine. Readership figures incorporate a pass-along rate into the circulation figures. Thus a magazine with a circulation of 250,000 that usually passes on to two other people would have a readership of 750,000.

Audience exposure to television and radio vehicles generates two measures, the rating and the share. A rating figure for a radio or television program is the percentage of households owning sets in the broadcast area tuned into that particular program. The calculation is

$$\text{Program rating} = \frac{\text{Number of households tuned in}}{\text{Number of households with sets}}$$

EXHIBIT 8-2   An ABC Magazine Audit Report

ABC Audit Report: Magazine

TV GUIDE
Radnor, Pennsylvania

CLASS, INDUSTRY OR FIELD SERVED: Consumer Magazine about Television.

1. AVERAGE PAID CIRCULATION FOR 12 MONTHS ENDED JUNE 30, 1983:

Subscriptions:	7,901,941
Single Copy Sales:	9,184,375
AVERAGE TOTAL PAID CIRCULATION	17,086,316
Advertising Rate Base and/or Circulation Guarantee during Audit Period	17,000,000
Average Total Non-Paid Distribution	303,089

2. PAID CIRCULATION BY ISSUES: (Total of subscriptions and single copy sales)

ISSUE 1982			ISSUE 1982			ISSUE 1983			ISSUE 1983		
July	3	16,586,889	Oct.	2	17,424,221	Jan.	1	17,164,348	Apr.	2	17,569,718
	10	16,391,859		9	16,973,129		8	17,164,052		9	17,575,987
	17	16,564,169		16	17,047,666		15	17,018,477		16	17,252,941
	24	16,381,560		23	17,060,410		22	16,883,360		23	17,123,884
	31	16,417,120		30	17,081,457		29	17,108,427		30	17,300,799
Aug.	7	16,429,816	Nov.	6	17,152,658	Feb.	5	17,566,727	May	7	17,124,141
	14	16,569,026		13	17,194,129		12	18,116,734		14	17,119,062
	21	16,421,632		20	17,146,328		19	17,490,423		21	16,915,245
	28	16,484,708		27	17,059,583		26	17,513,186		28	16,915,780
Sept.	4	16,876,364	Dec.	4	17,401,815	Mar.	5	17,766,222	June	4	16,874,127
	11	18,198,473		11	17,426,841		12	17,555,521		11	16,771,446
	18	17,303,710		18	17,300,377		19	17,381,195		18	16,594,266
	25	17,010,719		25	16,646,642		26	17,650,373		25	16,420,715

AVERAGE PAID CIRCULATION BY QUARTERS for the previous three years and period covered by this report:

Calendar Quarter Ended	1979	1980	1981	1982	1983
March 31		19,419,735	18,412,467	17,846,747	17,413,773
June 30		18,184,616	17,662,540	17,084,196	17,042,932
September 30	18,907,284	17,763,979	17,549,213	16,741,234	
December 31	19,205,798	18,198,632	17,797,917	17,147,327	

AUDIT STATEMENT

The difference shown in average total paid circulation, in comparing this report with Publisher's Statements for the period audited, amounting to an average of 53,269 copies per issue, is accounted for by deductions made for: additional credit subscriptions cancelled for nonpayment, 42,600 copies per issue; additional newsdealer returns, publisher having underestimated returns in filing statements with the Bureau, 10,669 copies per issue.

The records maintained by this publication pertaining to circulation data and other data as reported for the period covered have been examined in accordance with the Bureau's bylaws, rules and auditing standards. Tests of the accounting records and other auditing procedures considered necessary were included. Based on ABC's examination, the data shown in this report present fairly the circulation data and other data as verified by Bureau auditors.

June, 1984.
(04-1285-0 - #137817 - DJMcC - SH)

Audit Bureau of Circulations
900 North Meacham Road, Schaumburg, Illinois 60196

Source: *ABC Audit Report: Magazine* (Schaumburg, Ill.: Audit Bureau of Circulations, June 1983).

For example, American Broadcasting Company's initial broadcast of the special miniseries, *Winds of War*, averaged a 39.3 rating. This means that 39.3 percent of all households owning televisions watched an episode.

The term *share* refers to the percentage of all viewing or listening households tuned into a program. The calculation is

$$\text{Share} = \frac{\text{Number of TV households tuned in}}{\text{Number of TV households with sets on}}$$

Winds of War averaged a 54 percent share per episode. This means that each broadcast drew 54 percent of all the households whose sets were on at the time of the broadcast.

Finally, let us consider the issue of reach as it applies to a total plan rather than individual vehicles. In assembling a package of vehicles, the advertiser wants the maximum audience coverage. We determine total reach by adding the reach of individual vehicles and then adjusting for duplication. For example, Magazine A and Magazine B have paid circulations of 250,000 and 100,000, respectively. They also share 25,000 readers. The effective reach for the package of A and B is 325,000. This 325,000 is the *unduplicated* or *net cumulative* audience for the total plan.

Frequency

Frequency is the number of times that an ad appears in the specified time period of a vehicle or media plan. An average rate per vehicle often serves to characterize a media plan. For example, a plan with an average frequency of 4 consists of vehicles in which an advertisement appears on the average four times. Frequency for a specific vehicle is simply the number of times that an advertisement appears in that vehicle. The term *insertion* means the same as frequency.

Frequency affects the media-planning process in three ways. First, the planner must determine the number of message repetitions necessary simply to produce initial exposure to the advertisement. He or she must answer the question, How many times must we transmit an ad before the prospective customer becomes aware of the ad's existence? Think about the number of television commercials you do not pay attention to because you viewed the commercial break as a chance to go to the refrigerator for a snack. Or think about the number of advertisements you skip over to read the featured articles in your favorite magazine. Second, the planner must consider the number of ad exposures needed, after initial customer awareness, to cause the desired effect, such as full understanding of the product's benefits, change of attitude, or intentions to buy; in general terms, then, the number of exposures necessary to accomplish the ad's objectives. Finally, the planner must select those vehicles or that package of vehicles that can deliver the necessary frequency over the course of the campaign. For example, the nature of the audience and the complexity of the message are such that seven exposures may be necessary over the course of a four-week campaign. This requirement would obviously eliminate any plan to use, say, only one monthly magazine. The objective may demand certain newspapers and even some broadcast vehicles.

Gross Rating Points

The *gross rating point* (GRP) is a summary measure of the impact of a media package. The GRP integrates the concepts of reach and frequency and is computed as follows:

$$GRP = \text{Average reach} \times \text{Average frequency}$$

with *reach* (often determined by a research service like A. C. Nielsen) expressed as a percentage of the total audience and *frequency* the number of times the ad will appear. The GRP score is a summary measure of the total effort delivered by the media plan under evaluation. While it typically describes television, radio, and outdoor media plans, the concept also works with other media.

In planning a campaign, the advertiser decides on the number of total GRPs needed for effective delivery of the message. Then the advertiser develops packages of television programs, magazine space, and the like, to meet the GRP needs.

A note of caution: The GRP level simply reflects the magnitude of the media effort on the assumption that the GRP figure is a reasonable measure of the effectiveness of a media plan. The effectiveness of the total effort is highly dependent on the way the GRPs are delivered; there can be considerable variation in the reach and frequency combination across GRPs. Typically, an advertiser relies on media planners to recommend a total media effort expressed in the form of GRPs, a figure that often comes from the planners' experiences of media efforts in similar campaigns and their perceptions of the results (while this is highly subjective, it is assumed that their opinions as experts are reliable ones). Within this GRP level, the media people assemble alternative schedules. Sometimes the schedules will contain time and space requests by the advertiser, such as time on the annual Miss America program or the inside front cover of *Time* magazine's Man-of-the-Year issue. Usually, the time and place of ad appearance depend on vehicle availability and the discretion of those in charge of vehicle production. For example, others may have reserved all the commercial minutes on a desired prime-time television program, so another program at another time must take its place. And if the substitute program differs from the desired one in reach, then attaining the same GRPs means adjusting the frequency.

A level of GRPs may be delivered with different schedules. Here are two possible ways that 100 GRPs can be delivered to the advertiser:

Package 1—Average reach: 25%
Average frequency: 4
GRPs = 25 × 4 =   100

Package 2—Average reach: 20%
Average frequency: 5
GRPs = 20 × 5 =   100

Assume for the moment that Packages 1 and 2 represent plans for the use of television and that the television households represent the targeted audience. Package 1 might then consist of a show with an average rating of 25 with four insertions, while Package 2 might be a less-popular show with a 20 rating and five insertions. Each delivers 100 GRPs to the advertiser.

Where a campaign uses different media, the advertiser computes the GRPs for each media group and then adds them. For example, calculating the GRP for a media plan consisting of television and magazines would proceed this way:

Calculate the GRP score for the proposed set of television programs.

Calculate the GRP score for the proposed magazine vehicles.

The GRPs for the complete plan will be the sum of the individual GRP scores.

Thus, if the television GRPs were 120 and the magazine GRPs were 76, the GRPs for the entire plan would be 196 (120 plus 76).

Theoretically, the selection from alternative packages with equivalent total GRPs would be based on the combination of reach and frequency factors that best met the advertiser's needs. In some instances, the advertiser may value reach over repetition. For example, reminder campaigns for well-established brands such as Coca-Cola may be effective by simply contacting people occasionally and thus maintaining extensive reach in a campaign. On the other hand, a complicated message involving a high-risk product such as life insurance may affect the audience only after much exposure and reinforcement. Here, frequency is desirable.

Although GRPs are popular summary statistics of plans among media planners, we should not conclude that GRPs are completely accurate measures of a plan's effectiveness. The major weakness of the GRPs is the difficulty of estimating the net or cumulative audience. If we consider that the total GRPs are simply the summation of the GRPs for each vehicle, there is the risk of overestimating the effect of the total plan because of duplicated audiences. For example, the GRPs of a media plan using the magazine *Sports Illustrated* and the television show "Wide World of Sports" may be overestimated because a good portion of the television program's audience may be readers of the magazine, resulting in a double count in the reach figures and an inflation of the GRP score. In such a case, the size of the duplication should be subtracted from the original reach figure for a more precise estimate of GRP.

Cost Per Return

Advertisers look at reach, frequency, and GRP measures to judge the effectiveness of media plans. To evaluate the efficiency of the media, they use *cost-per-coverage* measures. As a rule, advertisers prefer those media with lower costs per coverage.

A popular measure for evaluating the efficiency of a media buy is the *cost-per-thousand* (CPM). Historically, CPM has measured magazine vehicles, but it can easily be applied to other media. CPM is an indication of how much it costs the advertiser to reach a thousand persons. It is computed as follows:

$$CPM = \frac{\text{Media cost}}{\text{Circulation}} \times 1{,}000$$

Assume that we want to compare one plan, which costs $5,000 and reaches 250,000 persons, with another plan, which costs $3,000 but reaches 100,000 persons. The CPM rates are $20 for plan 1 and $30 for plan 2. If both plans reached the same audience, plan 1 would be the more efficient buy.

In directly comparing vehicles rather than plans, the advertiser must be certain to use standardized costs in the computation of CPM. The advertiser cannot make a valid comparison if the cost for one magazine is the full-page rate while the cost for the other magazine is the half-page rate.

Although the CPM is useful for many media, there are still some efficiency measures for a specific medium. The *milline rate*, for example, is specifically used for evaluating newspaper vehicles. Technically, the milline rate represents the cost of reaching a million persons. Realistically, newspapers are not likely to have circulations in the millions. The milline rate stems from tradition, and it does provide a standard for comparing newspapers. Here is the computation for the milline rate:

$$\text{Milline rate} = \frac{\text{Line rate}}{\text{Circulation}} \times 1{,}000{,}000$$

The *line rate* is a standard rate for newspaper advertising and measures one-fourteenth of an inch deep and one column wide.

When the advertiser measures media impact in GRPs, it calculates the *cost per point*:

$$\text{Cost per point} = \frac{\text{Media cost}}{\text{GRPs}}$$

Since GRP is used for several media including television, radio, and outdoor advertising, cost per point represents a standardized unit for comparing efficiencies of different types of media.

Qualitative Considerations

With the objective measures of reach, frequency, gross rating points, and cost per contact, the advertiser also incorporates subjective judgments on factors for which there are no objective or reliable measures. Experience dictates their consideration.

According to Gensch, subjective judgments occur chiefly in five areas:[4]

1. Target Market–Media Audience Match
2. Message Strategy–Vehicle Appropriateness
3. Advertisement Exposure Probabilities
4. Advertisement Perception Chances
5. Cumulative Frequency Effects

Target Market—Media Audience Match

The nature of a mass-media vehicle is such that its audience may include not only the marketer's target but also individuals not in the marketing plan. Since audience size determines media rates, the advertiser often pays, inescapably, for a portion of an audience that has little value. To minimize such waste, the advertising manager must evaluate the degree of match between the desired target market and the audience delivered by the vehicle. The media plan should consist of vehicles that provide the best match.

It is often difficult to determine the extent to which a vehicle's audience corresponds to the marketer's target. The more complex the advertiser's description of its target, the more difficult the evaluation of the target audience match. Complexity results from the number or type of descriptors. Let us consider a simple case. The advertiser, selling a potent vitamin tonic for senior persons, describes the market only on the dimension of age, anyone over 55, a single dimension easy to understand and easy to measure. Further-more, many vehicles maintain records of their audiences in terms of age. The advertiser will simply evaluate vehicles on one decision: Select the vehi-cle or set of vehicles in which persons 55 and older dominate the audiences.

When the target market has many attributes, and these attributes are not traditional measures such as demographics, the evaluation of the target-audience match becomes very subjective. If the advertiser above had specified that its market was persons 55 or older *with* incomes greater than $50,000 per year and extroverted personalities, it would have a difficult time evaluat-ing target-audience match. A vehicle may not have defined its audience by cross-tabulating age and income but may have described its audience on each dimension individually. Moreover, it is very uncommon for a vehicle to maintain personality statistics on its viewers, listeners, or readers. Any evaluation of target-audience match may have to rest on attributes only indirectly related to the marketer's interests.

Weilbacher suggests that media evaluation based on audiences' product usage characteristics may be a better means to effective media strategy than evaluations based on demographics or psychographics.[5] He argues that prod-uct usage is a logical and direct reflection of the consumer behavior that advertising is to influence. Thus it is understandable that past research has found demographics and psychographics to be inefficient in matching audi-ence with target markets.[6]

Message Strategy—Vehicle Appropriateness

Very often the effectiveness of a message depends on the environment the media vehicle creates. According to Gensch,[7] some of the major determi-nants of the appropriateness of a vehicle for delivering a message are

1. Editorial climate
2. Product fit
3. Technical capabilities
4. Competitive advertising

The *editorial climate* refers to the views and stories the vehicle presents. An audience finds attractive those vehicles that share its views and interests. In the summer of 1981, Procter & Gamble stated as a matter of policy that it would avoid placing spots on television shows characterized by sex or violence. P&G did not want its commercials and its products in those envi-ronments.

The *nature of the product* is important in selecting a vehicle. In some instances, a vehicle's editorial content and the audience it attracts may be more suitable for some products and brands than for others. For example, household-cleaning products are not suitable for Saturday morning television programming because of the prevalence of children's shows. Such products fit better in daytime programming when the homemaker audience is watching.

The *technical characteristics* of a vehicle affect the message's impact. Radio is not appropriate for ads relying heavily on visual effects. An ad that must convey dynamism will use television and avoid print media. For example, a few years ago Federal Express wanted to position its delivery service in the context of a "fast-paced world." It chose a television commercial that became a hit with viewers. In that commercial, an exceptionally talented actor played the role of a harried business executive carrying on a telephone conversation in a busy office setting complete with secretary, helpers, and such equipment as copiers and collators. What was it about this commercial that fascinated the viewers? It was the actor's ability to speak clearly at an incredibly fast pace with a deadpan face while office activities occurred routinely in the background. The impact of hearing and seeing the actor speak at an extreme speed contrasted with the "normal" pace in the background sparked curiosity and held the audience's attention. The impact could only have been delivered through television.

Only a small number of vehicles address audiences with special interests. Avid nature lovers, for example, can turn to only a few publications. This limitation poses a challenge to the advertiser to select a time or place where its message can stand out. During the late 1970s and early 1980s, the heavy demand for technical professionals resulted in a large number of competing help-wanted ads in the classified section of Sunday newspapers. In the Boston area, the section contained so many ads that any single advertisement might be lost. For a short time, Digital Equipment Corporation, hoping to avoid the heavy competition for attention, withdrew its ads from the Sunday editions of the *Boston Globe* and placed them in a special business section appearing on Tuesdays.

Competitive advertising strategy may preclude opportunities for the advertiser. For example, a competitor may have contracted for the back cover of a monthly magazine for the next half year. Since cover space is finite, other advertisers cannot include that preferred position in their media plans. They must then look elsewhere for space opportunities.

Advertisement Exposure Probabilities

Although a television program may transmit a commercial, or a magazine may present an advertisement, an audience member will not inevitably get the message. Anywhere from 50 to 80 percent of a viewing audience is likely to be out of the room or not paying attention during a commercial.[8] Some vehicles are more likely than others to give exposure to a message.

The audience for many of the special-interest magazines such as *Personal Computing* is actually interested in and seeks out ads.

The chances of exposure increase when the advertiser carefully picks the broadcast time or page position of its advertisements. Commercials for toys are more likely to reach a key decision maker, the child, on Saturday morning television than at any other time. Or a magazine audience is more likely to notice an ad on the inside or back cover than within the pages of the magazine. As we will see in the next chapter, sellers of vehicle space or time recognize that the probabilities of ad exposure depend on placement within the vehicle, and this in turn means additional charges for preferred positions or times.

Advertisement Perception Chances

Exposure to a message does not immediately lead to perception or conscious awareness of the message. For example, radio typically serves as background music for a person busy with other activities. A person may actually be within earshot of a commercial but, because of diverted concentration, not pick up the message. Or a newspaper reader, intently searching for the continuation of a story from a previous page, passes over many ads. Advertisements must use attention-getting techniques like bold headlines or vivid colors.

Cumulative Frequency Effects

People learn from repeated experiences. With advertising, there is a cumulative effect from repeated exposures to a message. Advertisers ponder the question of how great a frequency is necessary to produce the desired effect.

Research on the impact of frequency is scarce because of methodological complexities, but there are some interesting findings. Zielske conducted a well-known study with two groups of housewives.[9] One group received a mailing every week for thirteen weeks. Sixty-three percent of this group were aware of the advertising mailing after the thirteenth week but had almost completely forgotten it by the fifty-second week. The other group also received thirteen mailings, but these mailings were at four-week intervals over a fifty-two-week period. The percentage of awareness of the advertising mailing in the latter group increased steadily throughout the fifty-two-week period.

With media selection, the issue is whether a media vehicle or package of vehicles can deliver the necessary frequency over the desired time.[10] If the advertiser wants immediate effects on awareness, repetition should occur over a rather short time. On the other hand, if the advertiser wants retention, a distribution of ad insertions over time is desirable. In a later section of this chapter we will look at various scheduling patterns.

MEDIA SELECTION TECHNIQUES

It should be evident by now that the development of the media plan is complex and time consuming. A considerable number of quantitative and qualitative factors require consideration, including budget constraints, coverage offered by vehicles, their costs, and a large amount of intuition, often called expert judgment, about critical qualitative media factors. No wonder media selection often seems more an art than a science.

Some media planners feel comfortable about formulating media plans on the basis of their vast experience. And some of them do it very well. Many media planners, however, especially those responsible for a large ad budget, would like reassurance, beyond simple expert opinion, that they are spending money in some logical, systematic manner. In this section we identify some structured techniques that facilitate or have some potential to facilitate the media selection process. Our purpose is not to present a full demonstration of any technique but rather to familiarize the reader with the existence and use of media decision aids.

The application of management science techniques to media planning has been increasing in popularity since the early 1960s, largely because of their potential contribution to management decisions when used with computers, the need to assess the risk associated with large advertising investments, and the desire to ensure the optimum allocation of the budget. Management science techniques are essentially mathematical and statistical tools to assist the decision maker by applying some established and objective methods to managerial problem solving. In advertising, they serve to generate or assess alternatives.

In the following paragraphs we discuss the broad categories of techniques applied to media selection problems.

Linear-Programming Techniques

The development of a media plan is an effort to find the right combination of vehicles within the constraints of objectives, financial resources, and vehicle characteristics. Our media objective is to have as many as possible of the target market become familiar with our message. Of course, our budget establishes a parameter for our effort. We will include specific vehicles in our plan as we ascertain their individual costs. A package of higher-cost television time or magazine pages will have fewer vehicles than a media package with less-expensive vehicles under the same budget. As we weigh the merits of fewer or more vehicles, we must consider the extent to which vehicles would deliver the type of audience we want. The vehicles that become part of the media plan must also meet frequency requirements; if we wish to deliver six insertions to our target in a two-week period, a monthly magazine may be out of the question. And there are many other factors involved. The point should be clear—the development of a media plan is the result of numerous trade-offs. *Linear programming*, which evaluates the *concurrent* (simultaneous) constraints and yields a best choice, may be appropriate for such a task. In media planning, a typical objective is to obtain the most exposures, given such vehicle constraints as cost, circulation, frequency of issue, and target market-audience match. The end product of linear programming is that combination of media that accomplishes the objective most effectively.[11]

Linear programming held great promise as a media-planning tool when Batten, Barton, Durstine and Osborne (BBDO) offered it as a client service in 1963. Its performance over the years, however, has been disappointing because of the technique's inability to incorporate some basic conditions. Among the limitations are the model's assumption that a repeat exposure has the same impact as the first exposure, that media costs are constant with no discounts for volume, and that the audience of one vehicle does not duplicate the audience of another.

Sequential Techniques

Sequential or iterative techniques differ from linear programming in that they evaluate and select media vehicles *one at a time* rather than simultaneously. These techniques begin by selecting the best buy, determined by audience coverage, cost-per-thousand, and the like, from the set of possible vehicles. Then evaluation of the remainder singles out the next-best vehicle. This process continues within constraints such as media objectives and budget until a complete media plan results.[12]

Sequential techniques can take into account factors that are not possible in linear programming. For example, audience duplication may occur across vehicles, and when the advertiser wishes to maximize reach, this duplication is undesirable. In using a sequential technique, the advertiser can adjust the audience estimates of remaining vehicles for duplication after every selected vehicle. Since linear programming considers all vehicles at once, adjustment for duplication is difficult.

While the flexibility of sequential techniques provides advantages over more restrictive techniques such as linear programming, sequential techniques have their limitations. As with any quantitative decision tool, the actual entering of the elements is difficult, chiefly because of the absence of precise, quantifiable input. For example, sequential techniques generally permit the planner to adjust for the impact of repeated exposures, but precise data on cumulative frequency are rarely obtainable for the specific planning situation. The advertiser, for example, does not customarily know exactly how a third exposure may differ in effect from the seventh exposure.

Simulation

The preceding methods have the purpose of producing a media plan with an optimum return. To the extent that the media planner accepts the underlying assumptions and structure of the techniques, he or she may believe that the resulting plans are actually the best plans. In most instances, however, the rigidity of assumptions inherent in such techniques is difficult to accept.[13]

The media planner would ideally like to use a technique where he or she has a considerable amount of discretion in defining the technique's structure. Techniques such as linear programming have a prescribed structure, and the media planner must often redefine the nature of his or her problem to fit the technique.

In some instances, media planners have turned to constructing their own techniques. These techniques then reflect an analytical structure tailored to the situation at hand. A typical approach is the development of a quantitative, computer-based *simulation model* of the marketplace.

A simulation model of market reaction can be as complex or as simple as the planner sees fit. The objective of a simulation is a realistic representation of market response. Incorporating a few or a substantial number of factors accomplishes this realism. A well-constructed or realistic simulation takes a proposed media plan and produces a simulated target market reaction.

In the development of a simulation model, the planner first identifies the market's response to such factors as advertising exposure, repetition, theme, advertising copy, and competitive media strategies. Historical data and input from experts' opinions usually accomplish this end. With these response factors, the planner then evaluates specific aspects of a proposed media plan such as number of insertions per vehicle and audience coverage, ultimately generating a simulated market response in the form of sales, market share, profits, attitude change, and so forth.

The major attraction of simulations is that the planner can tailor simulated conditions to the advertiser's situation. They permit, too, the evaluation of a media plan under a variety of assumptions. The major limitation in using simulations is the difficult task of quantifying the variables. The accuracy of a simulation model depends on the precision with which the planner defines relationships. If critical factors in the simulation are not correct, the results are of questionable value.

The Value of Quantitative Techniques

Although the results of computer-based quantitative techniques have not matched the early expectations, the use of such techniques has nevertheless contributed to the media decision-making process. Their principal contribution is that they require the user to identify and articulate as precisely as possible the major determinants of media effectiveness. The ad planner must abstract and understand the essential elements of the promotion environment. In the course of such an effort, the advertiser gains a clearer and more-organized picture of the situation than if such an effort had not taken place.

With the current state of model development, the media-planning techniques described above at best provide insight to supplement the traditional analysis. Since models incorporate many but not all of the realities of a media selection situation, the results are useful but limited. Nonetheless, these results coupled with managerial insights do facilitate the media selection process.

MEDIA SCHEDULING

In addition to selecting the best vehicle buys, the media planner must detail *when* the placements will occur by using a *schedule* or calendar of events. The planner lays out the schedule visually on a media worksheet like the one shown in Exhibit 8-3, detailing the time of use for specific vehicles.

Factors in Scheduling

Scheduling takes into account vehicle factors, the nature of the target audience, and the competitive schedule. Two vehicle factors, issue frequency and vehicle contents, have a major impact on scheduling. Issue or appearance dates obviously affect the schedule because they determine vehicle availability. Use of a weekly magazine, as opposed to a quarterly, permits more flexibility in scheduling. Or an advertiser's willingness to place commercials in weekly television programming affects the media schedule much differently than if the advertiser insisted on sponsoring special programs such as the annual Miss America pageant.

The nature of the audience, especially in terms of media and purchase habit, affects scheduling. During the summer, television reruns and the lure of outdoor activities greatly reduce the audience size from that of the regular television season. A commercial appearing on "Dallas" in October will give greater audience coverage than the same commercial appearing on "Dallas" in the middle of July. Consumer habits also affect scheduling, since advertise-

EXHIBIT 8-3 Example of a Media Worksheet

Media	Month: Week:	Jan 1 2 3 4	Feb 1 2 3 4	Mar 1 2 3 4	Apr 1 2 3 4	May 1 2 3 4	June 1 2 3 4

ments should run in order to have the right effect at the right time in the decision-making process. The advertising schedule for many consumer products is particularly heavy in the last quarter of the year in order to influence holiday shopping. On the other hand, soft-drink bottlers develop schedules around strong summer sales.

Very often the competitors' schedules determine the advertiser's schedule, especially when a primary objective of the campaign is to hold or gain market position against specific companies. Sometimes the advertiser must schedule commercials to go head to head with the schedule of rivals and ensure that there is no domination of communications channels. An agency in a large eastern city purchased space in a trade publication to announce proudly that it had reached billings of $100 million, a significant achievement. This announcement would improve its image and attract clients. A rival agency, discovering that such an ad was scheduled, purchased ad space in the same issue. The rival's ad message was simple but effective; it extended congratulations to the recent $100 million agency from an agency that had already reached $100 million!

Scheduling Patterns

We have seen that a schedule can assume any of a variety of patterns. Exhibit 8-4 shows a classification scheme of major patterns.[14] In each of the twelve patterns, the horizontal axis represents time periods and the vertical axis represents the intensity of the advertising effort. Thus pattern 1 characterizes a schedule with equal intensity in each of a few periods, while pattern 12 characterizes a schedule extending the advertising effort over a number of periods with alternating intensity in each period.

As indicated in Exhibit 8-4, scheduling patterns differ on the basis of both the timing of vehicle usage and the message intensity when vehicles are used.

EXHIBIT 8-4   Major Media-Scheduling Patterns

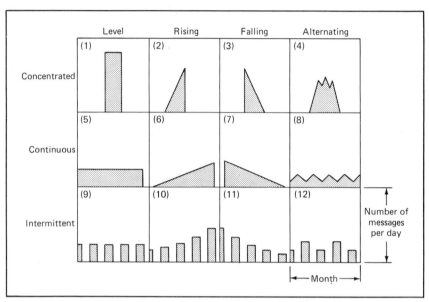

Philip Kotler, *Marketing Management*: Analysis, Planning, and Control, 5th Ed., © 1984, p. 654. Reprinted by permission of Prentice-Hall, Inc., Englewood Cliffs, N.J.

Timing of Vehicle Usage

Vehicle usage over time can be continuous or noncontinuous. *Continuous* schedules are those that use vehicles throughout the campaign, while *noncontinuous* schedules have time lapses between media usage.

One type of continuous schedule concentrates levels of expenditures on a specific medium or set of media over a relatively short period of time. An advertiser employs such a schedule to focus advertising effort for maximum effect. Perhaps seasonal factors will dictate such a strategy for the marketer of outdoor summer furniture. Or an advertiser may be working with a relatively small budget. To get any significant impact, the small-budget advertiser should consolidate the media effort rather than spread it over a long period of time.

Another type of continuous schedule discloses a somewhat uniform distribution of media effort over an extended period of time. See pattern 5 in Exhibit 8-4. Relatively stable media effort over time may be appropriate for products or services where continuous advertising is necessary but where upward variations in the level of media effort have little effect on market response. The company that services residences with clogged drains is not likely to raise demand significantly with advertising, but it must purchase ad space in the yellow pages throughout the year to attract business when the customers' needs arise.

Noncontinuous schedules, patterns 9, 10, 11, and 12, use vehicles intermittently when the need for advertising arises only at specific times. For example, a greeting card company may use national media on special occasions such as Valentine's Day, Mother's Day, Father's Day, and Christmas.

Message Intensity

The number of messages delivered by media over time can take on one of four possible trends: a constant level, increasing intensity, decreasing intensity, or alternating intensity.

Constant intensity, patterns 1, 5, and 9, may reflect a strategy with either high or low levels of effort. Constant, moderate levels are often used with established products or services where the objective is regular reminder or reinforcement advertising. A constant, high intensity over a period of time may be the result of a media dominance strategy where the advertiser seeks to focus spending on one medium or a few media to create an impact. In general, a constant level of effort over time is appropriate when variation of intensity does not significantly affect market response or when strategy calls for media dominance over time.

Very often a media schedule calls for a buildup of intensity over time. In such a case, the effort *increases* and reaches peak level in the last time period of the campaign (see patterns 2, 6, and 10). Increasing levels of intensity are appropriate for campaigns that seek to develop market response systematically. For example, a campaign for a major movie starts with low-level efforts (teaser ads, announcements of coming events, promotion of sneak previews) to initiate interest. Then, when the movie premièrs, advertising saturates the media—television, radio, and newspapers alike.

A media schedule may call for maximum intensity at the outset with effort *tapering off* as time goes by. Ad campaigns for many household products follow such a pattern. A burst of advertising begins the campaign. This burst heightens awareness and familiarity and may lead to purchase, but then a reduction to the level of reminder advertising may be in order.

Schedules with *varying levels of intensity* are called *flighting*, *pulsing*, or *wave patterns*. In essence, these patterns call for intensified efforts in some periods and reduced efforts in others. Retail store advertising illustrates a flighting pattern. Major campaigns will start up immediately preceding shopping periods such as Valentine's Day, Mother's Day, Back-to-School, or Christmas. During other times, advertising will occur with less intensity.

In sum, then, the effectiveness of media strategy depends in equal measure on the selection and the use of vehicles. The timing of media use depends on such considerations as vehicle characteristics, the target audience, and competitors' schedules.

A media schedule can assume one of a number of different patterns, described in terms of vehicle usage over time and the intensity of effort when media are used. Our schema set forth twelve of these patterns.

SUMMARY

Our discussion of the media-planning process in this chapter included these activities: preparatory analysis, identification of media alternatives, evaluation of media alternatives, selection of the vehicles, and scheduling.

Proper preparation requires an understanding of the communications objectives, the target audience, competitors' programs, and the company's own message strategy.

After identification of the available media, evaluation of each follows. Evaluation may respond to quantitative criteria such as reach, frequency, and cost-per-thousand and may also take shape from such qualitative factors as vehicle audience characteristics, vehicle-message compatibility, and advertisement perception changes.

After selection of the vehicles comes scheduling of the appearance of the advertisements. The major objectives in scheduling are to maximize audience exposure to the ad and to maximize the impact of the ad.

Clearly, media planning involves several activities, each dependent on the other for maximum effectiveness. By its very nature, media planning is complex and requires a systematic approach. To do a good job, one must know what kinds of media are available, what they can and cannot do, and when to use each medium. We now turn to a description of the various media.

REVIEW AND DISCUSSION QUESTIONS

1. Identify and describe the major steps in the development of a media strategy.
2. What is meant by the term reach when applied to media? What does frequency mean?
3. What types of circulation figures are used for evaluating the reach of print media? How do they differ?
4. How can the advertiser benefit from the ABC reports? Explain.
5. A television program is frequently described by its rating and its share. What does each figure tell the advertiser?
6. The reach for a package of vehicles is sometimes described as an unduplicated audience. What is meant by the term unduplicated audience?

7. What is a gross rating point (GRP)?

8. A media package has a net reach of 42 percent with an average frequency of 5. What is the GRP?

9. Measures such as cost-per-thousand, milline rate, and cost-per-GRP are often used in evaluating vehicles. What do these figures say about a vehicle and why are they useful in comparing vehicles? What limitations do you see in such measures?

10. "An advertiser that describes its audience principally on psychographic dimensions may encounter difficulty in selecting the right media vehicles." Comment.

11. Describe three television commercials that would not have the same impact if other media such as radio or magazines were used to deliver the messages. Explain your selections.

12. What factors determine the appropriateness of a vehicle for carrying an advertising message? Explain each factor. Give an example of each factor.

13. If an advertisement is placed in a magazine with a net circulation of 200,000, it will be seen and read by that many persons. Do you agree or disagree? Why?

14. Developing a media plan is a complicated task. What are the benefits and limitations of using quantitative techniques such as linear programming?

15. Identify and explain the major techniques of media selection. What are the advantages and limitations of each?

16. In developing the media schedule, what major factors must be considered? Explain.

17. Under what conditions would you use a flighting pattern in your media schedule?

18. You manufacture an innovative small household appliance (list price $60) which slices and dices vegetables in seconds. It is now January 1 and you must outline a media schedule through December 31. Would you use a flighting or a continuous schedule? Would your advertising be intermittent? When would you intensify your advertising? Explain the factors that you considered.

NOTES

1. The term *medium*, or its plural form *media*, refers to a category of communications sources such as newspapers, magazines, radio, television, and outdoor advertising. The term *vehicle* usually refers to a specific publication, channel, station or

the like under a media class. For example, *Time* and *The Wall Street Journal* are vehicles. In practice, the terms *media* and *vehicles* are often used interchangeably, and the meaning of a term must be inferred from the context.

2. Nancy Stephens, "Media Use and Media Attitudes Change with Age and with Time," *Journal of Advertising,* 10, No. 1 (1981) 38–47.

3. "That Creative Edge in Media," *Marketing and Media Decisions,* December 1983, pp. 49ff.

4. Dennis Gensch, "Media Factors: A Review Article," *Journal of Marketing Research,* May 1970, pp. 216–25.

5. William Weilbacher, *Advertising* (New York: Macmillan, 1984), pp. 266–67.

6. Henry Assael and Hugh Cannon, "Do Demographics Help in Media Selection?" *Journal of Advertising Research,* December 1979, pp. 7–11; and Hugh Cannon and G. Russell Merz, "A New Role for Psychographics in Media Selection," *Journal of Advertising,* 9, No. 2 (1980), 33–36.

7. Gensch, "Media Factors," pp. 219–21.

8. William Bearden, Robert Headen, Jay Klompmaker, and Jesse Teal, "Attentive Audience Delivery of TV Advertising Schedules," *Journal of Marketing Research,* May 1981, pp. 187–91.

9. H. A. Zielske, "The Remembering and Forgetting of Advertising," *Journal of Marketing,* January 1959, pp. 239–43.

10. For a review of research concerning frequency and advertising effectiveness, see Michael Naples, *Effective Frequency: The Relationship between Frequency and Advertising Effectiveness* (New York Association of National Advertisers, 1979).

11. For a detailed example of the application of linear programming to media planning, see Anthony McGann and J. Thomas Russell, *Advertising Media, a Managerial Approach* (Homewood, Ill.: Richard D. Irwin, 1981), pp. 275–308.

12. For example, see William Moran, "Practical Media Decisions and the Computer," *Journal of Marketing,* July 1963, pp. 26–30.

13. For example, see Dennis Gensch, "A Computer Simulation Model for Selecting Advertising Schedules," *Journal of Marketing Research,* May 1969, pp. 203–14.

14. Philip Kotler, *Marketing Management: Analysis, Planning, and Control,* 5th ed. (Englewood Cliffs, N.J.: Prentice-Hall, 1984), pp. 653–54.

9

Media
Descriptions

We have seen that media planning is a complex task, chiefly because of the many aspects of the media. Chapter 8 provided a general framework of quantitative and qualitative dimensions for media selection.

In this chapter we set forth each medium's strengths and weaknesses in consideration of those quantitative and qualitative characteristics. We begin with coverage of the print media (newspapers and magazines) and then follow with the broadcast media (television and radio). Finally, we come to the outdoor, transit, and direct mail media.

AN OVERVIEW OF MEDIA
CHARACTERISTICS

Let us begin our overview of the general media differences with a look at the monies spent to buy space or time for advertising, over $75 billion in 1983. As shown in Exhibit 9-1, the distribution is not uniform across media.

EXHIBIT 9-1   U.S. Media Expenditures in 1982 and 1983

Medium	1983 $ billions	% of total	1982 $ billions	% of total	Percent change
U.S. AVERTISING VOLUME					
Newspapers					
National	2.734	3.6	2.452	3.7	+11.5
Local	17.848	23.5	15.242	22.9	+17.1
Total	20.582	27.1	17.694	26.6	+16.3
Magazines					
Weeklies	1.917	2.5	1.659	2.5	+15.5
Women's	1.056	1.4	904	1.4	+16.8
Monthlies	1.260	1.7	1.147	1.7	+9.9
Total	4.233	5.6	3.710	5.6	+14.1
Farm publications	163	0.2	148	0.2	+10.0
Television					
Network	7.017	9.3	6.210	9.3	+13.0
Spot	4.796	6.3	4.360	6.6	+10.0
Local	4.323	5.7	3.759	5.6	+15.0
Total	16.136	21.3	14.329	21.5	+12.6
Radio					
Network	296	0.4	255	0.4	+16.6
Spot	1.038	1.4	923	1.4	+12.5
Local	3.876	5.1	3.492	5.2	+11.1
Total	5.210	6.9	4.670	7.0	+11.6
Direct mail	11.795	15.6	10.319	15.5	+14.3
Business papers	1.990	2.6	1.876	2.8	+6.0
Outdoor					
National	512	0.7	465	0.7	+10.0
Local	282	0.4	256	0.4	+10.0
Total	794	1.1	721	1.1	+10.0
Miscellaneous					
National	7.951	10.5	7.067	10.6	+12.5
Local	6.996	9.1	6.046	9.1	+15.7
Total	14.947	19.6	13.113	19.7	+14.0
Total					
National	42.525	56.1	37.785	56.8	+12.5
Local	33.325	43.9	28.795	43.2	+15.7
Grand total	75.850	100.0	66.580	100.0	+13.9

Reprinted with permission from the May 28, 1984 issue of *Advertising Age*. Copyright 1984 by Crain Communications, Inc.

Total expenditures for newspapers were more than four times those for radio. The differences in media expenditures reflect differences in the willingness and ability of advertisers to use media in their campaigns. Some media may be suitable for the campaign's needs but exceed budget constraints. Some media may charge relatively attractive rates but are not effective in communicating the message.

Each medium has its own personality with a unique set of characteristics. As we can see from the sampling of characteristics in Exhibit 9-2, a very large number of qualities produces a medium's personality. Exhibit 9-2 discloses that media differ in three major areas:

> The costs charged for delivering the advertising message
>
> The audience that is attracted
>
> The technical capacities (printing process, program timing, etc.) to deliver messages

Basic rates vary considerably. Thirty seconds of prime time network television can cost over $60,000. An advertiser will pay more than $40,000 to display a full-page, color ad in a top national magazine. A full-page ad may generate over $10,000 in revenues for a major metropolitan newspaper.

There is considerable variation in the cost-per-thousand measures across media.[1] Exhibit 9-3 presents cost-per-thousand data for media to reach a national audience. Spot or locally broadcast radio offers the lowest cost to contact one thousand audience members. Nationwide newspaper coverage with ads measuring about two-fifths to one-half page has the highest cost-per-thousand.

Media charges vary because of differences in production costs (personnel, equipment, and materials), differences in audiences, and differences in ability to communicate a message. For example, national television time is very expensive because of the technical skills and sophisticated equipment needed for broadcast. Networks can also ask for high fees from national advertisers because no other medium can reach millions of households across the country at one time. The strengths and weaknesses of a medium determine its worth to an advertiser.

Different media reach different audiences because of the conditions under which the media operate, by design or not. For example, most magazines concentrate publishing energies on specific areas such as science and technology or skiing, and they attract readers with those interests. Newspapers, by contrast, appeal to a general audience. Because they are widely read, newspapers do not offer much differentiation of audiences beyond the geographical. The advertiser that knows and understands the differences across media audiences is more likely to reach its market than the advertiser that does not.

EXHIBIT 9-2 Media Comparisons along Selected Dimensions

	TV	RADIO	MAGAZINES	NEWSPAPERS
Total population reach	Very strong	Good	Fair	Good
Upscale adult selectivity	Fair	Good	Very strong	Good
National coverage	Very strong	Poor	Good	Poor
Local market selectivity	Good	Good	Poor	Very strong
Cost per thousand ratios	Fair, good	Very strong	Strong	Good
Ability to negotiate rates	Good	Fair	Poor	Poor
Brand name registration	Very strong	Good	Fair	Fair
Product demonstration	Very strong	Poor	Fair	Fair
Ability to convey detail	Fair	Fair	Very strong	Very strong

Adapted from *The Media Book, 1978* (New York: Min Publishing, 1978), pp. 433–36. Used with permission.

EXHIBIT 9-3   Estimated Cost-Per-Thousand Media Comparisons

	PRIMETIME NETWORK TV	DAY SPOT RADIO	DAILY NEWSPAPER	CONSUMER MAGAZINE
	30-second announcement (per 1,000 households)	25 adult GRPs per week (per 1,000 adults)	1,000 B/W lines every daily in the U.S. (per 1,000 circ.)	1 page, 4 color in top 50 (per 1,000 circ.)
1972	$2.17	$1.65	$ 6.71	$ 6.00
1973	$2.41	$1.73	$ 7.07	$ 5.93
1974	$2.54	$1.82	$ 7.71	$ 6.11
1975	$2.61	$1.88	$ 9.20	$ 6.59
1976	$2.93	$1.94	$10.17	$ 6.77
1977	$3.48	$2.02	$11.09	$ 7.53
1978	$3.86	$2.15	$12.00	$ 8.05
1979	$4.43	$2.28	$12.90	$ 8.70
1980	$5.05	$2.46	$14.06	$ 9.66
1981	$5.40	$2.56	$15.33	$10.72
1982	$6.70	$2.79	$16.86	$11.58
1983	$7.37	$3.01	$18.55	$12.27

Adapted from *Marketing and Media Decisions*, August 1980, pp. 70–71; and *Marketing and Media Decisions*, Special Issue, Fall 1983, p. 36.

The operating characteristics of media can serve as strengths or weaknesses in the delivery of a message. Radio is an audio medium. A message relying on a range of sound effects would use radio, but a message relying on visual effects such as vibrant colors or dramatic movements of people or objects would not.

People get different information from different media and expect to do so.[2] Some media, including newspapers and radio, are good information sources for day-to-day activities. Other media, including magazines and certain television programming, are good sources for special topics such as fashion or cooking. Familiarity with the information habits of different media is essential to the development of a media strategy.

In the remainder of this chapter we will look at the major media's strengths and weaknesses. We will discuss the audiences they reach, the technical characteristics that affect message delivery, the manner in which the audiences use their information, and their rate structure.

NEWSPAPERS

Newspapers are the number-one advertising medium in the United States with expenditures topping those for all other media by a wide margin. In 1983 newspaper space commanded $20.6 billion in comparison with $16.0 billion for the second-largest medium, television. The newspapers's ability to attract the largest share of media dollars is a reflection of the medium's ability to deliver a commercial message to its audience.

Advantages of Newspapers

The major advantages of newspapers are market coverage, widespread readership, timeliness of coverage, and short closing dates for advertisements.

Market Coverage

Newspapers are virtually incomparable in their ability to reach people. In almost any geographical region of the country, and for any of a number of special-interest groups, there is a newspaper—over 1,700 dailies, about 650 Sunday papers, over 7,500 weeklies, over 16,000 shopper newspapers, about 2,000 college newspapers, over 260 foreign language papers, and over 3,000 suburban editions.[3]

Newspapers provide the advertiser with excellent coverage of a local market. Of the $20.6 billion of newspaper ad revenues, local establishments, food stores, department stores, furniture and appliance stores, automotive businesses, and entertainment services spent some $17.8 billion.

Although the newspaper is overwhelmingly a local medium, it is useful to the national and major regional advertiser. National marketers such as R. J. Reynolds (for its tobacco products) or General Motors can approximate national coverage by buying space in major metropolitan newspapers. And they often support their local distributors and agents with cooperative advertising programs in which the national advertiser underwrites some of the local advertising costs of its retailers. Large regional marketers such as Coors Brewery or Eastern Airlines can direct their messages to specific geographical markets through newspapers.

Widespread Readership

Newspapers are excellent for reaching a geographical audience. Over 77 percent of all households claim that they read a newspaper daily. In a one-week period, almost 90 percent of all adults will have read at least one newspaper.[4]

Newspaper reading is an ingrained habit of the American household. Seventy-three percent of readers make it a point in their daily activities to go through the newspaper at a specific time of day. These figures prove that people consider newspapers an important source of information every day.

Timeliness of Coverage

People read newspapers for the current, important information they convey. Newspapers lend an authoritative and immediate nature to their content. By association, the advertisements may contain a sense of news value and urgency. We respond, as we do to news stories, to an ad announcing a two-day-only sale at a local retailer or to a supermarket advertisement for weekend food specials.

Sometimes an advertiser will use the news content of a newspaper to complement an advertisement. When RCA launched the ad campaign for its videodisc player, many newspaper articles flowed from the news value of the technology. The stories sensitized readers to RCA's ads because of heightened interest in videodisc players—readers were more perceptive of the ads than if there had been no concurrent news articles.

Short Closing Dates

The *closing date*, the time when the advertisement must be in the hands of the publisher in order to appear in a particular edition, is very short. An advertiser can place an ad on a day very close to the desired issue date.

The principal advantage of a short closing date is that an advertiser can take advantage of recent events that may increase the attractiveness of the product or service. An appliance store can quickly place an ad for air conditioners when a humid heat wave strikes during a week in August. When then-Presidential candidate Jimmy Carter received national publicity for a controversial interview with *Playboy* magazine, *Playboy* quickly exploited the situation by placing ads in major newspapers throughout the country.

Disadvantages of Newspapers

This section describes the following major disadvantages of newspaper advertising: short life, high expenditure for extensive use, unreliable color production, and clutter of competing advertisements.

Short Life

People read newspapers for an up-to-the-minute overview of events on the day of issue—and then they discard them. As the old saying goes, there are few things with less value than yesterday's newspaper.

This short life means that advertisers cannot count on advertisements to have impact beyond the appearance date. If an ad does not capture attention on the reader's initial pass, that ad will probably not get it at all. If the ad does capture attention, there is little chance of repeat exposure because that day's issue soon goes on the discard pile.

Creative execution of the advertisement, by means of attention-arresting layouts, headlines, visuals, copy, and the like, can offset the disadvantage of short life. And advertisers can induce the reader to retain the ad or some portion of the message through such devices as cents-off coupons or useful information, recipes, and household tips that readers may wish to clip and file.

High Cost of Extensive Coverage

Marketers pay heavily for the attractive spot coverage of newspapers, especially if they want to cover several markets at once. The absolute cost for a national campaign is extremely high. Thus many advertisers with a national newspaper campaign often buy space only in the leading newspapers of major markets, where they find, however, that rates for them are usually higher than the rates for local advertising. A major reason for the higher national rates is that the newspapers adjust for the commissions they give to advertising agencies, which purchase space on behalf of national advertisers, and to their media representatives, who sell space to the ad agencies.

Unreliable Color Reproduction

For advertisements that rely on color for impact, newspapers present a major problem. Color increases the chances of getting reader attention and may portray a mood surrounding the ad, but the fidelity of color production is uncertain for newspaper ads, chiefly because the quality of paper stock is poor and the printing process, although greatly improved in recent years, is still unreliable.

Advertisements requiring color for impact often appear as inserts printed on higher-quality paper stock. Or they may appear in special sections such as the Sunday magazine where the color quality is much better.

Clutter of Competing Advertisements

Advertisers have similar schedules for buying space. Newspapers overflow with advertisements on particular days, especially Wednesdays, Thursdays, Fridays, and Sundays. The high volume of advertising so overloads the reader with information that it diminishes the probability of any single advertisement getting the reader's attention.

Why the clutter? Many areas of the country have only one newspaper, surely no more than two, and the demand for ad space concentrates on these limited vehicles. Furthermore, consumers have distinctive shopping patterns during the week. Most consumers shop for food on Friday nights or Saturday. If they plan, they may do it Wednesday or Thursday. Thus food establishments place advertising on those days.

To avoid the loss of an ad among the clutter, the advertiser employs such tactics as large space, use of color, or preferred position in the newspaper. These tactics make an advertisement stand out from the rest, increasing its chances of perception.

Rate Structure

Newspaper advertising space usually costs so much per *agate line*, which measures one column wide by $\frac{1}{14}$ inch deep. The number of agate lines within the requested space dictates the total cost of the ad. Suppose you brought an ad measuring 500 lines to your local newspaper. If the rate were $4 per agate line, your bill would be $2,000.

Detailed rates and requirements for ad placement are in the newspaper's *rate card*, which contains all the essential information for buying space: rates, publisher policies regarding ad content, availability of special-interest sections such as Sports and Business, closing and cancellation dates, mechanical requirements for submitted ads, and the like.

For major advertisers that use many newspapers, the maintenance of up-to-date rate card information for a large number of newspapers is costly in both time and money. For these advertisers, Standard Rate and Data Service (SRDS) provides a compilation of rate card information in volumes issued periodically. Exhibit 9-4 shows rate card information for a particular newspaper. The major determinants of the total cost of newspaper space are circulation, status as a local or national advertiser, preferred position within the newspaper, the use of color, volume, and continuity of advertising, and appearance in multiple editions.

Circulation

Circulation, the average number of copies distributed over a set period of time, affects the rate in that a higher circulation permits a newspaper to charge a higher rate. The rationale is that a higher circulation provides greater exposure.

The Audit Bureau of Circulation (ABC) and the Traffic Audit Bureau (TAB) are the principal sources of information about newspaper circulation. The bureaus audit publishers' statements about size of circulation, type of circulation (paid, subscription, and single issue), and area of circulation. The bureaus generate revenue by offering subscriptions to their services to advertising agencies.

EXHIBIT 9-4 SRDS Rate Card Information for a Newspaper

Detroit Free Press
321 W. Lafayette Blvd., Detroit, MI 48231.
Phone 313-222-6550, TWX, 810-221-1667.

newsplan
DISCOUNTS FOR CONTINUITY

Media Code 1 123 2470 2.00
MORNING AND SUNDAY
Member: INAME, NAB, Inc.

Bid 016751-000

1. PERSONNEL
President—Don O. Becker.
Advertising Director—James H. Zinn.
General Adv. Manager—Ken Swaim.
Ass't Gen. Adv. Mgr—Corky Boyd.

2. REPRESENTATIVES and/or BRANCH OFFICES
Knight-Ridder Newspaper Sales, Inc.
Metropolitan Publishers Representatives, Inc.
(Montreal and Toronto offices).
Towmar, Representaciones Profesionales, S.A.

3. COMMISSION AND CASH DISCOUNT
15% to agencies; no cash discount.

4. POLICY—ALL CLASSIFICATIONS
30 day notice given of any rate revision.
Alcoholic beverage advertising accepted.

ADVERTISING RATES
Effective January 1, 1983.
Received November 29, 1982.

5. BLACK/WHITE RATES

Open, per line	Daily 7.54	Sunday 8.17

STANDARD AD UNITS (See Front of Book)

SAU	Daily	Sunday	CLE
1	17,400.96	19,124.64	2736
2	14,764.66	16,306.92	2268
3	8,612.73	9,512.37	1323
4	14,842.80	16,393.20	2280
5	12,303.90	13,589.10	1890
6	10,895.93	11,813.17	1643
7	8,931.72	9,964.68	1372
8	4,589.34	4,960.36	686
9	11,874.24	13,114.56	1824
10	4,905.60	6,403.32	882
11	6,905.88	9,535.92	1369
12	5,900.58	6,403.32	882
13	4,428.78	4,906.12	662
14	2,480.86	2,687.93	329
15	6,101.28	6,621.12	912
16	3,933.72	4,268.88	588
17	3,325.14	3,602.97	441
18	2,216.76	2,401.98	294
19	1,651.26	1,789.23	219
20	1,108.38	1,200.99	147
21	738.92	800.66	98
22	550.42	596.41	73
23	369.46	400.33	49
24	211.12	228.76	28
25	106.56	114.38	14

BULK CONTRACT DISCOUNTS

Lines	Daily	Sunday
500	6.60	7.26
1,000	6.51	7.19
2,500	6.49	7.13
5,000	6.33	7.04
10,000	6.29	6.92
25,000	6.20	6.83
35,000	6.17	6.80
50,000	6.08	6.78
75,000	6.05	6.69
100,000	6.04	6.68
150,000	6.03	6.67
200,000	5.91	6.55
225,000	5.85	6.49
250,000	5.81	6.44

FULL PAGE DISCOUNTS
Billed for 2736 lines.

1 page	2%
2- 5 pages	3%
6-12 pages	5%
13-25 pages	7%
26-51 pages	8%
52- 64 pages	8%
65- 77 pages	9%
78- 90 pages	10%
91-102 pages	11%
104 pages and over	12%

COMBINATION RATES
Per line, per insertion:

Daily and Saturday	5.09
Daily and Sunday	5.62

To qualify ads must be run any weekday, plus Saturday within an 8 day period.
NEWSPLAN—Linage Equivalent.

LESS THAN FULL PAGE

Pages	Morn.	Sunday	Lines
8	6.29	6.92	16,416
13	6.17	6.80	35,568
26	6.06	6.78	71,136
52	6.04	6.68	142,272
104	5.81	6.44	284,544

FULL PAGE

Pages	Morn.	Sunday	Lines
8	5.98	6.57	16,416
13	5.80	6.39	35,568
26	5.65	6.31	71,136
52	5.60	6.16	142,272
104	5.51	5.87	284,544

See Newsplan Contract and Copy Regulations—Items 3, 4, 5, 6, 7, 9, 10, 13, 18, 19, 21, 22, 24, 25, 26, 28, 29.

5a. ZONE EDITIONS
Distribution is in the City & Retail Trading Zone only. Northwest, Southwest and East zone circulation areas available Monday, Wednesday, Thursday and Friday only.

	East	NW	SW
Open, per line	2.26	3.20	2.75
500	2.01	2.85	2.45
1,000	1.86	2.66	2.29
2,500	1.85	2.64	2.24
5,000	1.84	2.59	2.23
10,000	1.80	2.55	2.18
25,000	1.79	2.52	2.17
35,000	1.78	2.51	2.16
50,000	1.74	2.48	2.13
75,000	1.73	2.45	2.12
100,000	1.68	2.42	2.11
150,000	1.66	2.41	2.04
200,000	1.65	2.40	2.02
225,000	1.58	2.33	1.96
250,000	1.54	2.29	1.91

Oakland County edition (Thursday) 1.98

SPOT COLOR
Northwest or Southwest 1,104.00
East 859.00

Average net paid circulation for 6 months ending 9-30-82:

	Mon., Wed., Thurs., Fri.
East Zone	143,052
Northwest Zone	184,977
Southwest Zone	183,238
Oakland County Edition	124,850

7. COLOR RATES AND DATA
Available daily and Sunday. Full color min. 1,000 lines.
Full color daily and Sunday 2,787.00
Optional days Monday thru Saturday 2,599.00
SPOT COLOR
Spot color daily 1,497.00
Optional days Mon. thru Sat. 1,234.00
Spot color Sunday 1,687.00
Two or more ads, same issue daily, each 1,167.00
Two or more ads, same issue Sunday, each 1,293.00
Closing dates: Spot and full color reservations 5 days before publication; spot color—material 3 days publication. Cancellation: Friday preceding week of publication.

8. SPECIAL ROP UNITS
SPACE SPOTS
Commissionable.
Available Monday thru Sunday, 1 or 4 consecutive week basis. Mixed sizes available. 42 line min.; 300 line max. space. 5 ads in 1 issue or within 1 issue or within 1 week. 5 ad minimum.
1 week .... 20% 4 weeks 30%
Discount off earned line rate.

9. SPLIT RUN
Black and White (300-line minimum) extra 365.00
Non-commissionable.

11. SPECIAL DAYS/PAGES/FEATURES
Best Food Day: Wednesday.
Business: Monday; 1 Thursday: Camera, Fashions; Friday: Garden, Entertainment; Sunday: Travel, Books.

12. R.O.P. DEPTH REQUIREMENTS
1 col. x 14 lines; thereafter columns as many inches deep as columns wide. Copy exceeding 280 lines deep accepted only for full column.

13. CONTRACT AND COPY REGULATIONS
See Contents page for location of regulations—items 1, 2, 3, 5, 7, 10, 11, 13, 21, 22, 24, 25, 27, 31, 32, 33, 34, 35.

14. CLOSING TIMES
Daily: noon 2 days preceding publication. Sunday; 6:00 p.m. Thursdays. All orders non-cancellable after closing.

15. MECHANICAL MEASUREMENTS
For complete, detailed production information, see SRDS Print Media Production Data.
PRINTING PROCESS: Offset.
9/9-4/6-6 cols/ea 6 picas/ea 6 pts betw col.
Lines to col. 304; page 2736; dbl. truck 6750.

16. SPECIAL CLASSIFICATIONS/RATES
Political (cash in advance)-open rate applies. Bulk space contracts available.
Resorts, Hotels, Chambers of Commerce:

Open, per line	6.29
5 times or 250 lines	5.78
10 times or 500 lines	5.56
15 times or 2,500 lines	5.43

17. CLASSIFIED RATES
For complete data refer to classified rate section.

18. COMICS
POLICY—ALL CLASSIFICATIONS
When orders are placed through Puck-The Comic Weekly—see that listing.
Effective January 1, 1983.
Received November 29, 1982.

COLOR RATES AND DATA

Full page	13,961.00	1/3 page	6,659.00
1/2 page	11,119.00	1/4 page	5,975.00
1/2 page	8,641.00	1/6 page	4,858.00

Daily Comic Page—B/W
Maximum size 10 inches deep accepted at regular black and white rate.
SPLIT-RUN
50/50 split (non-commissionable) 548.00
SPECIAL CLASSIFICATION/RATES
STRIPS
Strip ads 7 cols. x 14 lines 1,507.00
Color: Minimum depth 14 lines; black and white 14 lines. Full page width.
CLOSING TIMES
32 days before publication.
MECHANICAL MEASUREMENTS
PRINTING PROCESS: Rotary Letterpress.
Page size: 13" wide x 20-1/4" deep.
7 cols. to page; each col. 280 lines deep.
Colors available: ANPA/AAAA: Comic.

---

19. MAGAZINES
Rotogravure Section
SUNDAY.
POLICY—ALL CLASSIFICATIONS
Alcoholic beverage advertising accepted.
When orders are placed through Metropolitan Sunday Magazine Group—see that listing.
Effective January 1, 1983.
Received December 13, 1982.
BLACK/WHITE RATES
Per line 10.52

VOLUME DISCOUNTS

6 pages	3%
13 pages	6%
26 pages	9%
39 pages	12%
52 pages	15%

FREQUENCY DISCOUNTS

6 times	2%
13 times	3%
26 times	4%
39 times	5%
52 times	6%

COLOR RATES AND DATA
Non-commissionable
Rates do not include artwork, transparencies or color positives.
3 color .... 874.00 Spot color 442.00
4 color 1,150.00
Above rates apply when full retouches positives are furnished.
SPLIT-RUN
Monotone only (minimum 340 lines), plus 418.00.
Non-commissionable.

ROP DEPTH REQUIREMENTS
Minimum: 42 lines on 1 col.; 85 lines on 1, 2, 3 or 5 cols.; 127 lines on 1, 2, or 3 cols.; 170 lines on 1, 2, 3 or 5 cols.
CLOSING TIMES
Reservation: Monotone 34 days before publication.
Color 39 days before publication.
Copy: Monotone 32 days in advance; camera-ready art 21 days in advance. Color 39 days in advance; camera-ready art 31 days in advance.
MECHANICAL MEASUREMENTS
PRINTING PROCESS: Gravure.
5 cols. to page.
Colors available: GTA Standard; 4 Colors.
Lines to col. 170; page 850.
SPECIAL CLASSIFICATION/RATES
Political (cash in advance)—general rate applies.
Centerspread using gutter bleed charged extra column.
Late copy extra charge. Color positions established on receipt of order. 8 page fold-out available in regular roto magazine of 40 pages or less. Other roto insert size sections available.
POSITION CHARGES
Back page, premium 511.00 extra. Non-commissionable.

T. V. Book
SUNDAY.
Effective January 1, 1983.
Received November 29, 1982.
BLACK/WHITE RATES
Within 1 year:

	1 ti.	6 ti.	13 ti.
1 page	2,750.00	2,640.00	2,542.00
3/4 page	2,063.00	1,980.00	1,907.00
2/3 page	1,834.00	1,761.00	1,696.00
1/2 page	1,375.00	1,320.00	1,271.00
1/3 page	918.00	879.00	846.00
1/4 page	688.00	660.00	636.00
1/8 page	318.00	330.00	318.00
	26 ti.	39 ti.	52 ti.
1 page	2,497.00	2,449.00	2,397.00
3/4 page	1,873.00	1,837.00	1,798.00
2/3 page	1,665.00	1,633.00	1,599.00
1/2 page	1,249.00	1,221.00	1,196.00
1/3 page	832.00	816.00	798.00
1/4 page	624.00	612.00	599.00
1/8 page	312.00	306.00	300.00

COLOR RATES AND DATA
Within 1 year:

	1 ti.	6 ti.	13 ti.
4-color:			
Back cover	6,942.00	6,870.00	6,786.00
Inside cover	4,400.00	4,256.00	4,194.00
2-color:			
Back cover	6,340.00	6,255.00	6,192.00
Inside cover	3,340.00	3,148.00	3,087.00

Spot Color (Inside Pages)
1/2 page minimum:

1 ti.	6 ti.	13 ti.	26 ti.	39 ti.	52 ti.
823.00	696.00	624.00	578.00	553.00	521.00

CLOSING TIMES
Offset enamel stock pages: reservations and copy 41 days before publication; cancellations 32 days before publication.
Offset newsprint pages: reservations 23 days before publication; pub-set copy and cancellations 18 days before publication; camera-ready material 11 days before publication.
Late copy subject to service charge.
MECHANICAL MEASUREMENTS
PRINTING PROCESS: Offset.
Page size 4-13/16" wide by 6-7/8".
1 col. width 1-1/2".
Lines to col. 96; page 288.
Send printing material to Satran Printing, 3939 Bellvue, Detroit, Mich. 48207.

20. CIRCULATION
Established 1831, per copy .20; Sunday .50.
Net Paid—A.B.C. 9-30-82 (Newspaper Form)

	Total	CZ	TrZ	Other
MxSat	631,969	157,881	327,212	146,896
SatM	578,931	138,330	306,309	132,292
Sun	771,063	156,552	377,816	236,715

Max-Min rate: MxSat Max 11.93, Min 9.19; SatM Max 13.02, Min 10.04; Sun Max 10.60, Min 8.35.
For county-by-county and/or metropolitan area breakdowns, see SRDS Newspaper Circulation Analysis.

Courtesy Standard Rate and Data Service, Inc., Wilmette, Ill.

National vs. Local Rates

Newspapers' rates discriminate between national and local advertisers. In general, the *national rate* is about 50 percent more than the *local rate*. As we saw earlier, newspapers justify this differential on the basis of commissions usually paid to agencies representing national advertisers and media representatives selling space for the newspapers, along with the fact that most local advertising is usually placed directly by advertisers, thus eliminating commissions.

Position

Unless specified by the advertiser, the line rate is a *run of paper* (ROP) rate, the advertisement to appear any place in the newspaper at the discretion of the editor. An advertiser may request a preferred position in a specific section of the newspaper or in a particular location on a page, the cost for which will be higher than the ROP rate.

Color

If an advertiser wants more than the standard black-and-white advertisement, color is available at additional cost. Such ads may be on an ROP basis, or they may be preprinted and then inserted during the printing of the newspaper.

The rates for color depend on the number of colors used. A full-color ad consists of black with a mixture of red, blue, and yellow; a mix of these three basic colors produces any color in the rainbow. Rates are usually quoted for black and 1-color, black and 2-color, and black and 3-color.

Discounts

Many newspapers charge *flat rates*, the same costs for all advertisers, but some newspapers also offer discounts to encourage advertisers to buy space. Discounts may be based on volume of space purchased within a time period, typically a year. Or they may be based on frequency or continuity of advertising within a time period. An advertiser that contracts for space in bulk agrees to use a specified quantity of lines. The line rate decreases with increases in contracted volume. An advertiser may qualify for time discounts by contracting for a specified number of insertions. The advertiser that commits itself to twenty-six insertions per year will pay a smaller line rate than the advertiser with thirteen insertions.

Combination Rates

When a newspaper publishes multiple editions, such as a morning and an evening edition, it may solicit additional advertising revenue by offering *combination rates* for advertisements appearing in more than one edition. The combination rate will be less than the sum of the individual rates for each edition.

The Future of Newspapers

Newspapers will continue to be an excellent medium for access to defined geographical markets, but newspapers will change as the medium adapts to the needs of advertisers and audience.

Locally, retail advertising still dominates the medium, but national advertisers are becoming more and more interested. Many metropolitan newspapers have increased the medium's attractiveness of defined geographical coverage by issuing suburban and community editions.[5] Improvement of the printing process has greatly enhanced the color quality. Advances in communications, especially satellite transmissions, allow newspapers to gather and print a greater variety of content at a faster speed. *USA Today*, the national newspaper, is able to collect information from across the country and get it into print the next day.[6]

Some observers forecast the demise of traditional newspapers.[7] Historically, the medium attracted an audience because of its distinctive competence in reporting news events the very next day. In recent years, radio and television have gained an advantage over newspapers; they report news on the same day it occurs and sometimes as it occurs. In response to such competition for their audience and their advertising business, many newspapers have recast themselves as providers not only of news but also of useful current, topical information. They have added or expanded sections on business, science and technology, sports, home improvement, travel, entertainment, and so on. In addition to delivering geographical markets to the advertiser, many newspapers now offer segments with known product and service interests.

MAGAZINES

There are three types of magazines: consumer magazines, business publications, and farm publications. Consumer magazines such as *Sports Illustrated* or *U.S. News & World Report* accounted for $4.2 billion (5.5 percent) of 1983 media expenditures.

The principal medium for business or nonconsumer advertising is the magazine. Business publications attracted almost $2 billion of advertising.

These publications include professional magazines such as the *New England Journal of Medicine*, trade magazines such as *Advertising Age*, institutional magazines such as *Laundry News*, industry publications such as *America's Textiles*, and general business magazines such as *Business Week*.

Ad revenues for farm publications were $163 million in 1983. These publications cater to the agricultural market and include such titles as *Spudman* and *Hog Farm Management*.

Advantages of Magazines

The major advantages of magazines are the precise audience selection, the complementary nature of editorial content with advertisements, the quality reproduction and relative unobtrusiveness of advertisements, and the relatively long life.

Audience Selection

A marketer that has defined the target market precisely will probably find a magazine appropriate for that market. Specifically, magazine advertising will reach a target audience that is well defined with respect to geographical area or demographic status (education, occupation) or activities (boating, photography).

Magazines offer the advertiser national and local coverage and a high degree of flexibility in audience selection. There are over 3,600 business and professional publications, over 800 consumer magazines, and 400 farm magazines. In business publications, magazines specialize in industries like chemicals or electronics, or perhaps in functional areas like purchasing or materials management. Consumer magazines range from general audience magazines like the *Reader's Digest* or *Time* to special-interest publications like the *National Geographic*.

Many of the major national magazines offer regional or demographic editions. For example, *Time* magazine offers special regional editions, state editions, and metropolitan editions, as well as editions for college students, business executives, and top-management personnel.

Since so many magazines focus on specific lifestyles, activities, and interests, a self-segmentation process has taken place within their readership. Thus a camera distributor can limit selection of magazines to a group of vehicles emphasizing photography.

Complementary Nature of the Editorial Content

A marketer of decorator window blinds will have more success promoting the product through a home furnishings publication like *House Beautiful* than in a general audience publication like *People* magazine. The content of the magazine serves as a catalyst or stimulus for related product ideas.

An advertised product may benefit by inferred association from the image of the magazine. *Boston Magazine*, a popular regional publication with an upscale audience, supports its retail advertisers with point-of-purchase display cards featuring the ad with the overlay "You Saw Us in Boston Magazine."

High-Quality, Unobtrusive Advertisements

Good media selection, as we have said, will include compatibility of editorial and advertising content. Add to this the fact that the readers control what they read and when they read it, and the result is that magazine ads obtrude on one's life far less than, say, a broadcast commercial thrust into a television program. Magazine ads do not force themselves upon readers. At the same time, however, the medium's high-quality work—the fidelity of color reproduction and the thoughtful copy—can convey, with suitable impact, the message the creators envisioned.

Long Life

Unlike newspapers, magazines have a life. People reread them, retain them, and pass them along to others. And this means that readers even beyond the original purchaser will notice and read magazine advertisements. One study reports that an average magazine issue generated 3.2 reading days per average reader.[8]

Disadvantages of Magazines

The major disadvantages in the use of magazines are the early closing date requirements, the clutter of competing materials within a particular magazine, the one-dimensional appeal to the audience, and the relatively high cost-per-thousand.

Early Closing Dates

Magazines require the submission of advertisements far in advance of publication date, usually several weeks. This lack of time flexibility restricts the advertiser's ability to modify the campaign as a result of recent feedback from the marketplace. In addition, this requirement often places pressure on advertisers to commit to space even before completion of all the details of the program.

Clutter of Competing Materials

An advertiser selects a magazine because of the audience it attracts, the nature of the editorial content, and the appearance of complementary ads, but there is the possibility that an extremely popular magazine will be a disadvantage for the advertiser. The volume of both editorial and advertising pages in the publication may make it more difficult for the advertiser's message to gain the reader's attention and interest.

One-Dimensional Delivery

The principal factor in the impact of a magazine ad is the visual aspect, although some advertisers have attempted to add the sense of smell by using scratch-and-sniff material or the sense of sound with vinyl record inserts. Where other media, radio and TV, use sound or movement to attract attention, magazines must capture attention and convey the message through sight alone, inevitably losing the opportunity to demonstrate the product fully.

High Cost-Per-Thousand

Historically, the cost-per-thousand of magazines has been higher than that of any other national media. This turns away the advertiser that simply wants to reach the most people at the least cost, but for the advertiser that wants to reach a well-defined segment of people at a reasonable cost, magazines' cost-per-thousand is not a deterrent.

The high cost-per-thousand stems from the relatively small size of special-interest audiences and the value, determined by the publishers, of the audience to the advertiser. A magazine audience with known interests will attract advertisers that see market opportunities. Publishers in turn recognize that these advertisers are willing to pay more to reach a defined target.

Rate Structure

The standard cost for magazine space is the cost of a full-page black-and-white ad. This is the basic or *open rate*, since it determines the rate of discounts or additional charges. One finds the rate for a magazine from the publisher's rate card or from Standard Rate and Data Service. The format of a magazine rate card is similar to that of a newspaper (see Exhibit 9-5). The major determinants of the rate are circulation, ad size, color usage, page position, and applicable discounts.

EXHIBIT 9-5 SRDS Rate Card for House Beautiful

HOUSE BEAUTIFUL

A Hearst Publication

ABC MPA

Media Code 8 403 1900 8.00 **Mid 000672-000**

Published monthly by Hearst Corporation, 1700 Broadway, New York, NY 10019. Phone 212-903-5000.

For shipping info., see Print Media Production Data.

PUBLISHER'S EDITORIAL PROFILE

HOUSE BEAUTIFUL is a home magazine designed for families interested in their homes and home furnishings. Architectural and decorating articles range from advance design concepts to practical home planning and maintenance information. The editorial content is primarily devoted to home furnishings, management and building; secondly, as a guide to good living, it regularly includes articles on travel, gardening, entertainment, food, liquor, music and beauty. Rec'd 5/1/78.

1. PERSONNEL

Publisher—D. Claeys Bahrenburg
Editor—Joann R. Barwick.
Advertising Director—David J. Moore.
Prod. Mgr.—Joseph A. Enterlin (212-903-5258).

2. REPRESENTATIVES and/or BRANCH OFFICES

Chicago 60606—Michael Peterson, 1 N. Wacker Dr. Phone 312-984-5150.
Charlotte, NC 28204—Donald Rose, 1 Charlottetown Center Bldg. Phone 704-376-2704.
Santa Monica, CA 90403—Sasha Lawer, 3420 Ocean Park Blvd., Suite 1070. Phone 213-452-7803.
Dallas—The Griffith Group.
Norfolk, CT—Eileen Roberts.

3. COMMISSION AND CASH DISCOUNT

15% to recognized agencies. 2% of net 22nd of month prior to issue. Bills rendered 12th of month prior to issue.

4. GENERAL RATE POLICY

As part of the consideration and to induce House Beautiful to accept and publish the advertising for the advertiser, the advertiser's agency, if there be one, and the advertiser each agrees to indemnify The Hearst Corporation against all loss, liability, damage and expense of whatsoever nature arising out of copying, printing or publishing the advertising.
Rates, conditions and space units subject to change without notice.

ADVERTISING RATES

Rates effective February, 1983 issue. (Card No. 46.)
Rates received October 27, 1982.
Card received April 20, 1983.

5. BLACK/WHITE RATES

	1 pg	2/3 pg	(*)	1/3 pg	1/6 pg
1-2 insertions	14,880.00	9,970.00	8,030.00	5,055.00	2,600.00
3-5 insertions	14,433.60	9,670.90	7,789 10	4,903.50	2,522.00
6-8 insertions	14,136.00	9,471.50	7,628.50	4,802.25	2,470.00
9-11 insertions	13,392.00	8,973.00	7,227.00	4,549.50	2,340.00
12-17 insertions	12,648.00	8,474.50	6,825.50	4,296.75	2,210.00
18-23 insertions	12,201.60	8,175.40	6,584.60	4,145.10	2,132.00
24-35 insertions	11,904.00	7,976.00	6,424.00	4,044.00	2,080.00
36 or more insertions	10,416.00	6,979.00	5,621.00	3,538.50	1,820.00

Agate Line 42.00
(*) 1/2 page or digest.

FREQUENCY DISCOUNT

Apply to national advertising only, within a 12 month period.
6 issues .... 5% 12 issues 15%
9 issues 10%
Minimum 1/3 page.

VOLUME DISCOUNT

For advertisers not using frequency discounts:
Rates:
6 pages .... 5% 18 pages 18%
9 pages .... 10% 24 pages 20%
12 pages .... 15% 30 pages 30%
Issues must be used within 12 month period. Discounts apply to national advertising only.

5a. COMBINATION RATES

Additional discounts above volume ones can be earned by House Beautiful national display advertisers who qualify for the Hearst Magazines Corporate Buy.
See listing for Hearst Magazines Corporate Buy under Classification No. 22.

6. COLOR RATES

Black and 1 color:

	1 pg	2/3 pg	(*)	1/3 pg
1-2 insertions	19,050.00	13,380.00	10,900.00	6,860.00
3-5 insertions	18,478.50	12,978.60	10,573.00	6,654.20
6-8 insertions	18,097.50	12,711.00	10,355.00	6,517.00
9-11 insertions ..	17,145.00	12,042.00	9,810.00	6,174.00
12-17 insertions ..	16,192.50	11,373.00	9,265.00	5,831.00
18-23 insertions ..	15,621.00	10,971.60	8,938.00	5,625.20
24-35 insertions ..	15,240.00	10,704.00	8,720.00	5,488.00
36 or more insertions ..	13,335.00	9,366.00	7,630.00	4,802.00

4 color:

	1 pg	2/3 pg	(*)	1/3 pg
1-2 insertions	21,750.00	15,650.00	14,650.00	10,760.00
3-5 insertions	21,097.50	15,180.50	14,210.50	10,437.20
6-8 insertions	20,662.50	14,867.50	13,917.50	10,222.00
9-11 insertions ..	19,575.00	14,085.00	13,185.00	9,684.00
12-17 insertions ..	18,487.50	13,302.50	12,452.50	9,146.00
18-23 insertions ..	17,835.00	12,833.00	12,013.00	8,823.20
24-35 insertions ..	17,400.00	12,520.00	11,720.00	8,608.00
36 or more insertions ..	15,255.00	10,955.00	10,255.00	7,532.00

(*) 1/2 page or digest

7. COVERS

4 color	2nd cover	3rd cover	4th cover
1-2 insertions	23,925.00	22,220.00	27,190.00
3-5 insertions	23,207.25	21,553.40	26,374.30
6-8 insertions	22,728.75	21,109.00	25,830.50
9-11 insertions	21,532.50	19,998.00	24,471.00
12-17 insertions	20,336.25	18,887.00	23,111.50
18-23 insertions	19,618.50	18,220.40	22,295.80
24-35 insertions	19,140.00	17,776.00	21,752.00
36 or more insertions	16,747.50	15,554.00	19,033.00

8. INSERTS

8 page 4-color Spectacular rate available—see Good Housekeeping listing in Classification No. 49.

9. BLEED

Extra 15%

10. SPECIAL POSITION

Special position other than covers not sold. Orders specifying positions other than covers not accepted.

11. CLASSIFIED/MAIL ORDER

DISPLAY CLASSIFICATIONS

WINDOW SHOPPING

BLACK AND WHITE RATES

	1 pg	2/3 pg	(*)	1/3 pg
Open rate	11,660.00	7,795.00	5,860.00	3,905.00
4 cons. issues	11,077.00	7,405.25	5,567.00	3,709.95
8 ads (including 4 cons. issues)	10,494.00	7,015.50	5,274.00	3,514.50
12 ads	9,911.00	6,625.75	4,981.00	3,319.25

	1/6 pg	1/12 pg
Open rate	1,965.00	995.00
4 cons. issues	1,866.75	945.25
8 ads (including 4 cons. issues)	1,768.50	895.50
12 ads	1,670.25	845.75

COLOR RATES:

Black and 1 color:	1 pg	2/3 pg	(*)
Open rate	16,105.00	11,275.00	8,845.00
4 cons. issues	15,299.75	10,711.25	8,402.75
8 ads (including 4 cons. issues)	14,494.50	10,147.50	7,960.50
12 ads	13,689.25	9,583.75	7,518.25

Black and 1 color:	1/3 pg
Open rate	5,805.00
4 cons. issues	5,514.75
8 ads (including 4 cons. issues)	5,224.50
12 ads	4,934.25

4 color:			
Open rate	17,815.00	13,547.00	12,900.00
4 cons. issues	16,924.25	12,869.65	12,255.00
8 ads (including 4 cons. issues)	16,033.50	12,192.30	11,610.00
12 ads	15,142.75	11,514.95	10,965.00
Open rate			8,490.00
4 cons. issues			8,065.50
8 ads (including 4 cons. issues)			7,641.00
12 ads			7,216.50

(*) 1/2 page or digest.

RETAIL, HOTEL, TRAVEL AND NURSEY RATES

BLACK AND WHITE RATES

1 page 12,030.00
2/3 page 8,100.00
1/2 page or digest 6,510.00
1/3 page 4,055.00
1/6 page 2,040.00
Agate line (14 lines min.) 33.00

COLOR RATES:

Black and 1 color
1 page 16,610.00
2/3 page 11,630.00
1/2 page or digest 9,500.00
1/3 page 5,990.00

4 color:
1 page 18,380.00
2/3 page 13,970.00
1/2 page or digest 13,310.00
1/3 page 8,750.00

CONSECUTIVE AND FREQUENCY DISCOUNTS

A mail order advertiser must run 4 ads consecutively to reach a 5% discount. After advertisers reach the 4-time level, they will qualify for frequency discounts of 10% and 15% based on the number of ads placed within a contract year. Discounts are allowed as earned, and schedules may be of mixed size ads.

VOLUME PAGE DISCOUNTS

For advertisers not using consecutive or frequency rate discounts:
8 pages .... 20% 12 pages 25%
Volume discount advertisers may mix their schedules with any size or coloration space and need not appear in consecutive issues.
References to dealers or distributors, or soliciting agents or dealers, not permitted and requires use of general rate section in standard sizes and at general rates. All advertisers excepting those selling personalized merchandise agree to refund full price of merchandise should reader return it dissatisfied. All advertisers agree that, if shipment of merchandise ordered is not made within two weeks, the purchaser be notified of the delay with the right to have money refunded if delivery date given is not satisfactory to purchaser. To avoid shopping trips by readers, it is requested, but not obligatory, that advertisers other than retail stores include in their copy "sold by mail order only."
No merchandising nor promotion of any type to trade distribution by Window Shopping advertisers is allowed. House Beautiful reserves right to reject at any time the copy of advertisers who merchandise Window Shopping advertising as this type of activity is confined to advertisers using general rate section. A legitimate retail store or mail order advertiser may list up to five different addresses. Manufacturers, wholesalers, growers are restricted to one address. Depilatory ads, objectionable patent medicines and personal ads not accepted.
If incorrect rate is specified on order it is understood that advertiser will be billed at correct card rate. On units larger than 1/4 page of acceptable advertising for the Window Shopping Section it is understood that due to mechanical difficulties position in this section cannot always be guaranteed. All Window Shopping advertisers and/or their advertising agencies must furnish finished copy, layout and cuts. Duplicate plate material is required for ads to be repeated in successive issues. Such statements and copy as "Sold direct from factory," "50% savings buy direct from factory," or other words with the same meaning are not eligible for Window Shopping ads. Any retail store or mail order advertiser mentioning a trade-mark, brand or identifying name in heading or subcaption of ad will be charged the general rates where or when a manufacturer is contributing in any way whatsoever to part of the cost of such an ad. The Window Shopping Section is for retail mail order advertising only. The closing date for the Window Shopping advertising section is 1st of 2nd month preceding date of issue.

MECH. REQUIREMENTS

DIMENSIONS-AD PAGE

1	7 x 10-3/16	1/3	2-1/4 x 10-3/16
2/3	4-5/8 x 10-3/16	1/6	4-5/8 x 2-1/2
1/2	7 x 5-1/16	1/6	2-1/4 x 5-1/16
1/3	4-5/8 x 5-1/16	1/12	2-1/4 x 2-1/2

*RESORT, HOTEL, TRAVEL AND NURSERY RATES
(Position outside of the Window Shopping Section)

BLACK AND WHITE RATES

1 page 10,935
2/3 page 7,360
1/2 page or digest 5,915
1/3 page 3,685
1/6 page 1,855
Agate line (14 lines min.) .... 30.

COLOR RATES:

Black and 1 color
1 page 15,100
2/3 page 10,570
1/2 page or digest 8,635
1/3 page 5,445

4 color:
1 page 16,710
2/3 page 12,700
1/2 page or digest 12,100
1/3 page 7,955

BLEED:
Extra 15%
(*) Including seeds, bulbs or nursery stock sold direct or by mail order only.

Restricted to retail stores whose business is derived mainly from retail over-the-counter sales, not wholesale or mail order. Order must be placed by store or its advertising agency. Ads must be prominently signed by store or use accepted store logotypes. Use of brand names and trade marks permitted. A retailer may list up to five addresses of the same name in a single ad, but not stores of different names even though wholly owned and operated. Retail rates do not apply to national chain store operations.
All advertisers, excepting those selling personalized merchandise, agree to refund full price of merchandise should reader return it dissatisfied.

13a. GEOGRAPHIC and/or DEMOGRAPHIC EDITIONS

EAST OF MISSISSIPPI
COLOR RATES:
1 page 15,760
ISSUE AND CLOSING DATES:
Closes 10 days prior to usual close.

WEST OF THE MISSISSIPPI
COLOR RATES:
1 page 9,480
ISSUE AND CLOSING DATES:
Closes 10 days prior to usual close.

NORTHEAST
COLOR RATES.
1 page 7,160
ISSUE AND CLOSING DATES.
Closes 10 days prior to usual close.

SOUTH
COLOR RATES:
1 page 6.625
ISSUE AND CLOSING DATES:
Closes 10 days prior to usual close.

MIDWEST
COLOR RATES:
1 page 7,500
ISSUE AND CLOSING DATES:
Closes 10 days prior to usual close.

WEST & SOUTHWEST
COLOR RATES:
1 page 7,500
ISSUE AND CLOSING DATES:
Closes 10 days prior to usual close.

14. CONTRACT AND COPY REGULATIONS

See Contents page for location—items 2, 4, 8, 10, 12, 14, 15, 24, 30, 36.

15. MECH. REQUIREMENTS

For complete, detailed production information, see SRDS Print Media Production Data.
Printing Process: Offset.
Trim size: 8-1/4 x 10-7/8; No./Cols. 3.
Binding method: Perfect.
Colors available: Matched, 4-Color Process (AAAA/MPA)
Cover colors available: 4-Color Process (AAAA/MPA)

DIMENSIONS-AD PAGE

1	7 x 10-3/16	1/3	2-1/4 x 10-3/16
2/3	4-5/8 x 10-3/16	1/3	4-5/8 x 5-1/16
1/2	3-1/2 x 10-3/16	1/6	2-1/4 x 5-1/16
1/2	7 x 5-1/16	Sprd	8-1/4 x 10-7/8

16. ISSUE AND CLOSING DATES

Published monthly; on sale at newsstands Tuesday or Thursday nearest to 20th of month preceding date of issue.
Black and white closing date 25th of the 3rd month preceding date of issue.
Window Shopping closing date 25th of the 3rd month preceding date of issue.
OK, one week earlier.
Color closing date 25th of 3rd month preceding date of issue. Orders for cover pages must be received no later than 1 month prior to rate card closing date and are non-cancellable 1 month prior to rate card closing date.
Cancellations: Orders for cover pages are non-cancellable 1 month prior to rate card closing date. Other color pages are non-cancellable 5 days prior to rate card closing date. No black and white cancellations accepted after rate card closing date.

17. SPECIAL SERVICES

A.B.C. Supplemental Data Report released February 1982 issues.

18. CIRCULATION

Established 1896. Single copy 1.50; per year 13.97
Summary data—for detail see Publisher's Statement.

A.B.C. 12-31-82 (6 mos. aver.—Magazine Form)

Tot. Pd.	(Subs)	(Single)	(Assoc.)
817,062	550,822	266,240	

Average Total Non-Pd Distribution (not incl. above)
Total 13,936

Courtesy Standard Rate and Data Service, Inc., Wilmette, Ill.

Circulation

Size of circulation determines the basic rate for a magazine, together with certain indicators (income, occupation, education, and so on) of the audience's market value to the advertiser. As a rule, a magazine with a larger circulation or one with a higher market value is able to charge more.

Consider readership when selecting a vehicle. Primary and secondary readership data provide additional details about the nature and size of a magazine's audience. *Primary readership* refers to readership among buyers of magazines. *Secondary readership* refers to people to whom the magazine has been passed. The combined primary and secondary readerships add up to the total audience for a magazine.

While the size of circulation largely determines the basic rate, the demographic characteristics of a magazine's audience may also affect it. For *Time* magazine, the cost of space for the executive edition, expressed in cost-per-thousand, is higher than the rate for the general audience edition because the executive audience has greater buying power and is worth more to certain marketers.

Ad Size

As mentioned earlier, the basic rate for magazine advertising is a full-page black-and-white ad. Additional rates are quoted on portions of a full page, usually half-page rates and quarter-page rates. Although the difference in rates is usually not proportional, smaller ads usually cost less. Specifically, a half-page ad will be cheaper than a full-page ad, but the rate for the half-page ad will probably be more than 50 percent of the full-page rate.

Color

If an advertiser wants the advantage of color in the advertisement, it incurs a charge in addition to the basic rate. As with newspapers, a color ad consists of basic black and white plus one or more of the colors red, yellow, and blue. A full-color ad typically is a four-color ad, or black and white with three colors.

Position

An advertiser may wish to pay additional charges in order to place the advertisement where reader attention is likely. The positions offering these greatest opportunities for exposure are three cover positions called second, third, and fourth covers. The second cover position is the inside front cover, the third cover is the inside back cover, and the fourth cover is the back of the magazine.

Discounts

The advertiser commonly saves money through frequency of advertising, volume of advertising, multiple-page appearance, multiple-edition contracts, and purchase of remnant space.

The number of insertions in a contract period, typically a year, determines frequency discounts. An advertiser that agrees to place twenty-four insertions in a weekly magazine will get a lower rate than one that contracts for twelve insertions over the same period.

Volume discounts depend on total dollars the advertiser contracts for. Thus, in addition to any discount received for the number of pages or insertions placed, the purchaser of space may also receive a discount based on the amount of money spent.

When an advertiser runs several pages in one issue, many magazines give what is called a *multiple-page discount*, the size of the discount depending on the number of pages.

As noted earlier, many national magazines offer editions directed toward special audiences designated by such characteristics as geography, occupation, and education. As an incentive for advertisers to purchase broad coverage, such magazines often give discounts when selling space in two or more special editions.

Sometimes magazines find that after laying out all the contracted advertisements there is unsold advertising space at press time. Publishers offer this *remnant space* at a significant discount. The publisher has a high degree of discretion in placing the ad, and since the space is on a standby basis, the advertiser must be ready to furnish the magazine materials on relatively short notice.

The Future of Magazines

Magazines attract advertisers because they offer narrowly defined, special-interest audiences.[9] The growth of special-interest magazines will continue while general readership magazines expand their vehicles to include special sections and more tightly defined geographical and demographic editions.

The cost-per-thousand will probably remain high.[10] Publishers' production costs of paper, printing, postage, and personnel are likely to increase and be passed along to advertisers. The magazines' ability to reach special segments permits the medium to command higher rates than those of general audience media such as newspapers and radio.

TELEVISION

The fact that television is only second in media revenues and constitutes about 21 percent of media expenditures is an understatement of the medium's

EXHIBIT 9-6   The Top 25 Network TV Advertisers in 1982 and 1983

RANK	ADVERTISER	EXPENDITURES ($000)			
				1983 as % of total advertising exp.	1982 as % of total advertising exp.
		1983	1982		
1	Procter & Gamble Co.	$366,663.1	$390,495.4	47.4	53.8
2	General Motors Corp.	201,350.4	164,261.5	33.8	29.9
3	Ford Motor Co.	172,308.1	128,885.4	36.0	41.1
4	General Foods Corp.	170,064.5	232,349.4	44.0	54.2
5	American Home Products Corp.	161,435.0	160,767.2	48.4	49.4
6	American Telephone & Telegraph Co.	146,603.8	95,086.2	31.7	25.5
7	Sears, Roebuck & Co.	145,006.8	102,563.8	19.8	16.2
8	Johnson & Johnson	131,265.9	121,845.3	44.4	45.1
9	Philip Morris Inc.	128,266.1	110,845.0	24.3	22.1
10	Bristol-Myers Co.	120,974.3	105,717.0	51.5	51.6
11	Anheuser-Busch Cos.	116,515.2	95,676.5	40.1	39.3
12	Unilever U.S.	110,302.6	111,811.7	34.0	36.7
13	General Mills	100,279.1	93,628.5	37.3	38.3
14	Coca-Cola Co.	95,888.7	87,208.5	34.0	34.2
15	Ralston Purina Co.	94,438.5	82,570.7	33.1	37.5
16	Beatrice Cos.	88,563.6	N/A	14.7	N/A
17	Dart & Kraft	87,414.8	61,743.6	41.6	31.0
18	Warner Communications	84,243.6	75,533.0	33.6	32.5
19	Chrysler Corp.	84,193.7	68,219.5	36.6	39.4
20	Sterling Drug	82,660.0	66,383.7	48.1	47.4
21	Nabisco Brands	82,018.0	66,578.8	22.3	19.9
22	McDonald's Corp.	80,930.9	59,875.9	26.0	22.5
23	Beecham Group p.l.c.	78,806.6	66,725.1	58.8	55.3
24	Gillette Co.	75,285.5	74,025.4	40.6	45.4
25	Warner-Lambert Co.	74,638.9	81,015.4	21.7	27.5

Reprinted with permission from the September 14, 1984 issue of *Advertising Age*. Copyright 1984 by Crain Communications, Inc. *Source*: Broadcast Advertisers Reports.

impact in the marketplace. Television is dominated by major marketers of consumer products (see Exhibit 9-6), and it accounts for approximately 75 percent of these marketers' advertising budgets. Thus, although television does not enjoy wide use across all industries and companies (unlike newspapers, magazines, and radio), the limited number of organizations that do commit heavily to television are national sponsors of significant size and each sponsor spends enormous sums in the medium.

Since the early 1950s television has played an increasingly important role in American life and in the advertising world. In 1950 television ad revenues were only $58 million and accounted for approximately 1 percent of total media expenditures.[11] By the early 1980s television revenues exceeded $14 billion and accounted for about 21 percent of total media spending.

Advantages of Television

Television offers four major advantages: extensive reach, dynamism in message delivery, selective geographical coverage, and low cost-per-thousand.

Reach

Television is truly a medium to reach the masses. Ninety-eight percent of all U.S. households have at least one set, more than 50 percent of the television households have two or more sets, and 85 percent have a color set (see Exhibit 9-7).

Household television usage has been increasing over the years (see Exhibit 9-8). In the 1965–66 viewing season an average household spent five and one-half hours daily in front of the set, and in the early 1980s that figure had risen to almost seven hours daily. For the major advertiser, these data show the reach advantage inherent in television, especially for the national advertiser. No other medium but prime-time television (8:00 P.M.–11:00 P.M.) offers a reach of close to 60 percent of households across the country.

Dynamism

Television's audio and video characteristics give it a unique ability to deliver commercials using movement and sound. Advertisements that

EXHIBIT 9-7 TV Set Ownership in the U.S.

	TV HOUSEHOLDS (MILLIONS)	% WITH COLOR SET	% WITH MULTIPLE SETS
1965	53.8	22%	7%
1970	60.1	41	35
1975	69.6	74	43
1978	74.5	81	48
1979	76.3	83	50
1980	77.8	85	51
1981	81.5	86	52

Source: The 1982 Nielsen Report on Television (New York: A. C. Nielsen Company).

EXHIBIT 9-8   Average Daily Household TV Usage

VIEWING SEASON	TIME (HOURS: MINUTES)
1965–66	5:30
1970–71	6:01
1975–76	6:11
1979–80	6:35
1980–81	6:44

Source: The 1982 Nielsen Report on Television (New York: A. C. Nielsen Company).

are broadcast through television are alive with action, more exciting and entertaining than those in any other medium. Television can generate attention-grabbing scenes, establish moods to complement a product's image, or fully demonstrate a product's benefits.

Selective Geographical Coverage

National advertisers often wish to concentrate advertising efforts in selected areas rather than cover the entire country. The limited geographical coverage can serve the purposes of test marketing, selective product distribution, a desire to boost sales efforts in a particular region, and the like. An advertiser that does not wish to pay for the superfluous audience of network advertising can elect specific geographical areas through the purchase of "spot advertising." A brewery with franchises only in selected cities on the West and East coasts may opt for spot or limited geographical coverage rather than network advertising.

Low Cost-Per-Thousand

When we analyze television rates to discover how much it costs to reach a thousand persons, we conclude that television is very competitive with other media. The reason for the relatively low cost-per-thousand is, of course, that a single broadcast, especially in prime time, reaches a vast number of households. As Exhibit 9-3 shows, the cost-per-thousand for a thirty-second network prime-time ad is about half that for a one-page color ad in the top fifty consumer magazines.

Disadvantages of Television

This section looks at television's four major disadvantages: absolute cost, availability of commercial time, short life of the broadcast messages, and lack of defined segments.

High Absolute Cost

While the cost-per-thousand for television is relatively low, the absolute cost for air time is high. With costs of $80,000 to $100,000 for thirty seconds on popular prime-time shows, and even higher rates for special programs (e.g., $500,000 for thirty seconds on the 1985 Super Bowl), we can see why the bulk of television advertising revenues comes from very large organizations.

High ad rates reflect television's costly production efforts. The production cost of a thirty-second television commercial has been increasing over time and can sometimes require a budget exceeding $1 million. In 1983 the average thirty-second spot cost $75,000.[12] In that year Pepsi-Cola spent $7 million for its thirty-second and sixty-second "New Generation" commercials: $5 million for the right to identify itself with entertainer Michael Jackson and $2 million for production.[13] We can expect, by 1990, the average half-minute spot to cost in excess of $100,000.

Limited Availability of Time

As a matter of principle, the National Association of Broadcasters (NAB) has established that during any hour of prime-time broadcasting, nonprogram material may occupy no more than nine and one-half minutes. In 1982 the NAB relaxed the guidelines, but the time available for advertising in a prime-time hour is scarce, given the number of possible sponsors. Frequently the desired times are simply not available even to an advertiser willing and able to pay.

Short Advertisement Life

A major disadvantage of the use of television is that once a commercial has been aired, it is gone. There is no remnant or tangible evidence. Unlike a print advertisement, which a reader may pass over several times or actually clip and save for reference, the opportunity for additional exposure beyond the initial transmission does not exist. Consequently, to ensure maximum exposure, an advertiser must compensate for this deficiency with costly repetition.

Lack of Well-Defined Segments

Television's capacity to reach a wide audience is a disadvantage to those advertisers that wish to focus on one group. In contrast to the magazine medium, the audience for television is not well segmented. With the exception of special programming like weekend sports, television does not deliver special-interest segments in any reliable manner. Television's distinctive competence is in the extensive reach across the general public. If the advertiser's audience is not the general public, the advertiser that uses television may be paying a considerable amount of money for an audience of little value to the campaign.

Rate Structure

The major determinants of television rates are audience characteristics, extent of geographical coverage, length of commercials, and discounts.

Audience Characteristics

As shown in Exhibit 9-9, the number and makeup of television households vary during the day and evening. Broadcasters establish rates for air time according to the time of day or *day part*, which attracts different audiences with different market potential.

The day parts for television generally run as follows:

DAY PART DESIGNATION	TIME PERIOD
Early morning	7 A.M.–10 A.M.
Daytime	10 A.M.– 4 P.M.
Fringe	4 P.M.– 7 P.M.
Prime time access	7 P.M.– 8 P.M.
Prime time	8 P.M.–11 P.M.
Late night	11 P.M.– 1 A.M.

Although day parts set the general rate levels, costs will fluctuate with specific programming. Programs vary in popularity and composition of attracted audience. In the fall of 1981, the "60 Minutes" and "Dallas" programs were the two most popular among U.S. households. But for males 18 years and older, football broadcasts were more popular than "Dallas." The advertising rate is usually the highest during prime time with highly popular programs, as determined by rating and share figures.

Both rating and share of audience determine the cost of air time. While the rating score gives an estimate of a program's penetration of a television

EXHIBIT 9-9 **Weekly Viewing Activities**

VIEWING PERIOD	WOMEN				MEN				CHILDREN	
	12–17	18–34	35–54	55+	12–17	18–34	35–54	55+	2–5	6–14
Mon.–Sat. 8:00–11:00 P.M. Sun. 7:00–11:00 P.M.	33%	31%	35%	31%	35%	33%	36%	33%	20%	30%
Mon.–Fri. 4:30–7:30 P.M.	18	13	14	16	16	13	13	17	21	21
Mon.–Fri. 10:00 A.M.–4:30 P.M.	15	20	15	20	8	8	7	12	18	10
Sat.–Sun. 7:00 A.M.–1:00 P.M.	7	4	3	3	8	5	4	4	13	13
Sat. 1:00–8:00 P.M. Sun. 1:00–7:00 P.M.	12	11	11	10	14	16	16	15	10	12
Mon.–Sun. 11:00 P.M.–1:00 A.M.	7	9	10	8	8	12	12	8	1	2
Other	8	12	12	12	11	13	12	11	17	12
	100%	100%	100%	100%	100%	100%	100%	100%	100%	100%
Weekly time (hours:mins.)	18:19	30:09	32:37	39:20	22:28	26:30	27:41	35:43	24:48	27:04

Adapted from *The 1982 Nielsen Report on Television* (New York: A. C. Nielsen Company).

market, the share of audience reflects the program's ability to compete head on with other programs in pulling in an audience. Top shows generally have ratings greater than 20 with shares over 30. Ad rates for special television programming are based on expected audience ratings and shares. For the most part, expectations are not far from actual performance. Occasionally, however, audience levels do not reach projections. ABC's experience with the 1984 Winter Olympics is an example.[14] The average cost of a thirty-second spot was $185,000. The rate was established by ABC and accepted by advertisers based on the expectation that 1984 audience levels would match those of the 1980 Winter Olympics, a 23.7 rating with a 37 share. The 1984 audience was a disappointment; broadcasts over the first nine days averaged a 17.8 rating with a 27 share. Although no guarantees were made, ABC made restitution to advertisers with special consideration for ad time during the 1984 Summer Olympics and/or fall programming.

Network, Spot, and Local Rates

Rates vary with the geographical coverage of the commercial when broadcast. An advertisement may be broadcast on a network with the ad shown on all affiliated stations picking up a network program. An advertisement may be transmitted instead to selected television markets across the country (spot coverage) or an advertisement may have only local transmission. Of course, network advertising commands the highest absolute rate among the three.

Commercial Lengths

The standard unit is a minute or a portion of a minute with the common lengths being ten-, twenty-, thirty-, and sixty-second spots. In network advertising the thirty-second spot is the most popular length, replacing the sixty-second spot, a development arising from the high costs incurred by advertisers in producing commercials and acquiring time to broadcast them.

Discounts

Discounts may attach to bulk, volume, or continuity of advertising. An advertiser qualifies for a bulk discount by purchasing a specified number of spots in a given time period. Volume discounts apply to specified levels of dollar purchases, and continuity discounts apply to advertising over consecutive periods.

Discounts may also result from preemptibility. An advertiser may buy preemptible time at a lower rate, but if another advertiser is willing to pay more, then the former advertiser's commercial is rescheduled.

EXHIBIT 9-10   *List of Common Television Services and Terms*

Advertiser-supported television:

The traditional, free television service transmitted over the air waves. Programming costs are supported by advertisers.

Community antenna television (CATV):

Subscription service bringing signals into the home by cable. Early name for cable TV.

Direct broadcast satellite (DBS):

A satellite service which directly delivers a signal to the viewer's, set by way of viewer's own earth station or dish.

Pay cable:

Any number of services like HBO, for which the cable subscriber pays a charge in addition to the basic cable fee.

Pay per view:

Pay TV for which there is a charge on a program basis rather than a regular monthly fee.

Pay TV:

Any service for which the viewer pays. It is distinct from the traditional advertiser-supported service.

Subscription TV:

A pay TV service which transmits scrambled, over-the-air signals to a standard broadcast channel. The viewer must use a decoding device.

Superstation:

A copyrighted term by WTBS, Atlanta. Now a term generally applied to a station whose signal is available to cable systems via satellite transmission.

Two-way cable:

Cable TV system capable of sending signals in both directions along a cable.

Videotext:

System which is capable of delivering text and/or graphic information.

Courtesy A. C. Nielsen Company.

The Future of Television

Until recent years television consisted of 750 commercial broadcasting stations, the majority of which were affiliates of the American Broadcasting Company (ABC), the Columbia Broadcasting System (CBS), or the National Broadcasting Company (NBC). During the past few years, however, the industry has seen many changes, and there is potential for more changes principally because of deregulation and developments in telecommunications technology.[15] Exhibit 9-10 lists and defines the major services that now deliver signals to the television receiver.

In 1979 cable TV served approximately 20 percent of U.S. households. By 1990 almost 50 percent of the TV households will be hooked to cable. Although the early purpose of cable television was to serve communities with poor reception, a major stimulus currently for the growth of cable television among households is the desire for alternative programming. In 1979 almost 40 percent of the 15 million cable households had pay cable and paid a fee for special programming. By 1990 perhaps 24 million households will be linked with pay cable television (see Exhibit 9-11).

The growth of cable and other television industries implies potential loss of ad revenues for traditional network television. Additional programming fragments the viewing audience.[16] Network television, accounting for about 86 percent of viewing time in 1980, will drop to less than 73 percent by 1990 (see Exhibit 9-12).

For the advertiser, the emergence of pay TV may hold great promise. As commercial time becomes available on pay cable television, a more efficient television buy may emerge. First, the audience is screened in that they turn to programs that are of interest to them, and thus there is segmentation such as occurs in any subscription process.[17] Second, studies have shown that the pay cable TV household watches more television than the noncable household, and that means a greater opportunity for commercial exposure.

Concurrent with the growth of pay cable is the emergence of subscription television. Subscription television is also pay television. Programming comes over the airwaves, and a device at the subscriber's home decodes

EXHIBIT 9-11 Household Penetration (% of TV Homes)

	1979	1990
Network stations	100%	100%
Independents	71	80
PBS	90	92
Cable	20	50
Pay cable	7.5	35
Subscription TV	.9	7.7
Direct broadcast satellite	—	5

Adapted from *Marketing News*, July 10, 1982, p. 4.

EXHIBIT 9-12 Competition for the Video Audience

	1980 AVERAGE WEEKLY VIEWING PER HOUSEHOLD (HOURS)		PROJECTED 1990 AVERAGE WEEKLY VIEWING PER HOUSEHOLD (HOURS)	
Network stations	39.0	85.9%	35.0	72.8%
Independents	5.0	11.0	6.4	13.3
Public broadcast stations	.9	2.0	.8	1.8
Cable-originated	.1	.2	1.0	2.1
Pay cable	.3	.7	2.1	4.4
Subscription TV			.3	.6
Direct broadcast satellite			.1	.2
Other*	.1	.2	2.3	4.8
	45.4	100.0%	48.0	100.0%

* Videocassette, videodisc, home computers, videograms, teletext/viewdata.

Adapted from *Marketing News*, July 10, 1982, p. 4.

it. Such television is especially attractive in areas where people want alternatives to traditional TV and no cable system is present.

Cable and subscription systems offer attractive advertising alternatives to the current broadcasting system. Although the advertising income for cable television was less than $100 million in 1980 compared with $8 billion for broadcast television, cable ad revenues will probably approach $2 billion in 1990. Cable and subscription television are attractive media for three reasons. First, they offer commercial time with relatively little clutter from competing advertisements. Second, cable has proved to be effective in targeting specific audiences, especially in geographical segments. Finally, the cost for air time is low compared with that of standard broadcast television. For example, rates for a thirty-second cable spot in New England ranged from $3 to $50 in 1980, compared with $80 to $5,000 for equivalent time on local broadcast television during prime-time viewing hours.

Rapid advancements in technology are creating opportunities and uncertainties for the television industry. New methods of signal transmission and reception are paving the way to reach new and different audiences. At the same time, these technological developments have produced instability for traditional broadcasters, especially in terms of audience share. The advent of the videocassette recorder has given the audience greater control over *what* they watch and *when* they watch it. With timing devices, the audience can choose to record one broadcast while ignoring others. The audience could watch shows and the accompanying commercials days, even weeks, after broadcast. This behavior is obviously troublesome for the media scheduler attempting to coordinate advertising with other promotional efforts like sales promotion. Additionally, many who follow the technical development in television foresee major inroads by cable into television markets. However, recent research suggests that the marketplace is not quite as enthusiastic. One study reported that 27 percent of subscribers in one cable market, disappointed with the programming, have disconnected their systems.[18] It seems that the only certainty about the industry's future is that there will be significant change.

RADIO

Radio ad revenues were over $5.2 billion in 1983. Only 5.6 percent of this amount was network advertising. Local advertisers dominate radio. National advertisers use it chiefly to reach specific geographical markets.

Advantages of Radio

The major advantages of radio are reach and audience selectivity, coverage of the out-of-home audience, low costs for air time, and inexpensive production requirements.

Reach and Selectivity

Even more than television, radio has become an ubiquitous medium with approximately 99 percent of American households owning at least one set. With approximately 77 million radio households and 450 million sets, there is an average of over 5.8 sets per household. Close to 27 percent of these are out-of-home, chiefly in automobiles. There are also over 4,500 AM stations and 4,000 FM stations to cover the radio sets.[19] Clearly, radio is capable of providing excellent coverage in virtually all areas of the country.

One often characterizes radio stations by the format of their programming: Rock, Top 40, Middle of the Road, Contemporary, Country and Western, All News. Different formats attract different audiences. Rock stations have a strong following among the 18-years-and-under population while the 65-and-older group constitute a sizable portion of an all-news audience. Formats are reliable indicators of audience segments, and they facilitate the advertiser's vehicle selection decision.

Radio audiences are segmented, too, according to time of day. The audience during the 10:00 A.M. to 3:00 P.M. period consists largely of homemakers. From 3:00 P.M. to 7:00 P.M., the size of the audience increases as workers travel home by car and listen to the radio.

Finally, radio offers the advertiser precisely defined geographical segments. The broadcast range, in comparison with television, is smaller. The advertiser does not pay for unwanted exposure and gets a high degree of flexibility in targeting its message.

Out-of-Home Audience

Many of the major media reach an audience at home, and as a result the advertiser faces substantial competition for the audience's attention. Since more than a quarter of the radio sets are out of the home, radio provides the advertiser additional opportunities to reach the audience. The most significant out-of-home audience is the automobile commuter in the morning (7:00 A.M. to 9:00 A.M.) and in the afternoon (5:00 P.M. to 7:00 P.M.). During drive time, car radios account for over 20 percent of the audience.

Low Insertion Cost

Radio advertising is the cheapest of all major media. Since a station's production expenses are low, the cost to the advertiser is correspondingly low. One sixty-second insertion during the morning rush hour on a popular Boston station cost between $300 and $350 in 1982. The cost-per-thousand is the lowest of all major media. As indicated in Exhibit 9-3, radio delivers more audience for fewer dollars.

Inexpensive Copy Production

Unlike its broadcast cousin, television, radio's copy preparation does not always require sophisticated preparation. Although sponsors may hire an agency to generate copy and produce a highly polished audiotape, it is also possible simply to supply the station with a tape recorded at the sponsor's facilities or a script taped at the station. Since radio is an audio medium, the advertiser avoids the high expenses of the visual work for television or even magazines.

Disadvantages of Radio

Although radio is pervasive in terms of population acceptance, it is not necessarily a truly national medium, nor does the population fully rely on radio as a source of information. In fact, the two major disadvantages of radio—beyond its obvious audio-only limitation—are the highly localized coverage and the low attention level of the audiences.

Limited Geographical Coverage

Radio is principally a local medium and offers little opportunity for an advertiser who would prefer a national network broadcast. Although some special events are broadcast on networks, the major network programming is the news. Consequently, it is not surprising that network advertising represents only slightly more than 5 percent of total radio revenues.

Low Attention Level

Radio requires little participation by the audience. Unlike television, which the audience must actively watch to enjoy, or magazines, which require a conscious effort to read, a playing radio is usually not the primary focus of attention. As Exhibit 9-13 shows, radio serves as background while the audience is performing other activities. Between 6:00 A.M. and 10:00 A.M., for example, 25 percent of the listeners are cleaning and over 36 percent are using the radio for background while they eat breakfast.

It is highly improbable, then, that any single commercial will achieve wide attention at the time of its broadcast. A radio advertiser must be willing to pay for high frequency in order to get the message across.

Rate Structure

Because radio is a broadcast medium, the determinants of its rates are similar to those of television audience delivered; advertiser's desire for

EXHIBIT 9-13   Some Activities While Listening to Radio

	% OF U.S. ADULTS
6:00–10:00 A.M.	
Driving	50.1
Eating breakfast	36.6
Dressing/bathing/showering/shaving	32.0
Cleaning	25.0
10:00 A.M.–3:00 P.M.	
Driving	35.1
Preparing meals	19.9
3:00–7:00 P.M.	
Driving	41.5
Just listening	20.7
7:00 P.M.–12:00 Midnight	
Just before going to sleep	23.4
Driving	22.0
Relaxing/resting	16.8

Simmons Market Research Bureau, Inc., 1973 Target Group Index.

network, spot, or local coverage; commercial length; and appropriate discounts.

Audience Characteristics

The size and makeup of the audience determine the rate a station may charge. The measures of rating and share of audience that we defined in the television section apply to the size of a radio audience as well. Demographics such as age, income, and occupation define the makeup of the audience.

The size of an audience varies with the time of the day as people go to school, commute to work, go to the store, engage in recreational activities, and so on. Day parts determine general levels of rates. During the weekday, Monday through Friday, the day parts are as follows:

DAY PART DESIGNATION	TIME PERIOD
Drive time—morning	6:00 A.M.–10:00 A.M.
Daytime	10:00 A.M.– 3:00 P.M.
Drive time—afternoon	3:00 P.M.– 7:00 P.M.
Evening	7:00 P.M.–midnight
Late night	Midnight–6:00 A.M.

A radio station charges higher rates for the drive-time periods because they usually attract larger audiences. For the weekend, the day parts are as follows:

DAY PART DESIGNATION	TIME PERIOD
Saturday morning	6:00 A.M.–10:00 A.M.
Weekend	10:00 A.M.– 7:00 P.M., Saturday
	6:00 A.M.– 7:00 P.M., Sunday
Evening	7:00 P.M.–midnight
Late night	Midnight–6:00 A.M.

Network, Spot, and Local Rates

The air time cost to an advertiser depends on whether the air time is for network, spot, or local coverage. As with television, network advertising means a national broadcast through affiliated stations. Networks sell spot coverage for selected audiences. Network rates are of course the highest.

Commercial Length

Although sixty seconds and thirty seconds are common in radio, ten-second and twenty-second commercials are not unusual. In general, longer air time costs more than shorter; radio stations, as a matter of convenience in programming, and in the interest of higher revenues, prefer a purchase of sixty seconds. The cost differential between a sixty-second commercial and less time is not proportional; it may be that a spot of less than a minute (ten, twenty, or thirty seconds) will be 75 to 80 percent of a sixty-second spot.

Discounts

Sponsors who consistently advertise or have a sizable budget are eligible for a number of discounts off the standard rate. An advertiser that contracts for a large number of placements within a time period can qualify for a bulk or frequency discount.

An advertiser may qualify for a volume discount if the dollar expenditures in a specified time period meet or exceed a predetermined level. Package discounts are based on scheduling patterns, such as the use of certain times in a day, or the consistency of advertising broadcast over a period. Discounts may be given when the advertiser gives the station control in placing an advertisement.

Finally, discounts attach to preemptible rates. Under these rates, the advertiser pays a rate lower than the standard rate for a particular insertion. If another advertiser will pay a higher rate for that time, the former advertiser's buy is preempted.

The Future of Radio

From 1975 to 1983 the radio audience increased over 40 percent.[20] The high rate of increase will of course not continue, but an overall increase in audience will probably continue. This growth comes from the increase in the number of radio stations, especially FM, which attract many listeners who want high-fidelity stereo programming.

Radio station audiences may become smaller but better defined. As the number of stations increases, the entire radio audience will become more fragmented as stations compete for listeners. To compete, radio stations turn to distinctive programming to attract specific segments. Although the advertiser may end up paying more for fewer listeners on a station, the advertiser will get a better-defined audience.

Interest in network radio will grow.[21] Many advertisers are finding national television time too expensive. Radio is a broadcast alternative with national reach at a far cheaper rate permitting greater frequency. The radio's ability to get significant national advertising depends on the radio networks' ability to develop programming, beyond sports and news, to appeal to audiences across the country.

OUTDOOR

While outdoor advertising has the stereotypes of poster displays, it actually refers to messages displayed out in the open with a variety of devices. Messages may use neon-lit signs and mechanical or electronic displays.

Outdoor ad revenues in 1983 were $794 million. Almost two-thirds of that amount came from national advertising; the remainder came from local advertisers.

Advantages of Outdoor Advertising

The major advantages of outdoor advertising are reach and geographical selectivity, out-of-home audience, repeated exposures, low cost-per-thousand, and strong visual impact.

Reach and Geographical Selectivity

Outdoor advertising is effective for a national campaign, as it combines coverage across key metropolitan markets. The medium also provides the advertiser a high degree of precision in selecting geographical targets. An advertiser can buy coverage for an entire metropolitan area or for certain sections.

Out-of-Home Audience

Outdoor advertising, by definition, reaches the out-of-home audience. For the advertiser, this means supplementing the traditional in-residence contact through newspapers, magazines, television, or radio. Out-of-home contacts happen while people are riding in automobiles or on public transportation or simply walking. The medium intercepts people going from one place to another.

Repeated Exposures

Outdoor advertising appears along or near established traffic patterns. Displays in high-traffic areas such as highway intersections not only reach a sizable audience but reach it repeatedly. A month-long display on the edge of a major route leading into the city gives the advertiser an opportunity to catch the regular commuter about five times a week for four weeks.

Low Cost

A month-long national poster campaign cost slightly over $3.5 million in 1979.[22] For this amount, the cost-per-thousand exposure was $.55. Outdoor advertising is evidently an excellent media buy for those simply wanting the most audience contact at the least cost.

Visual Impact

Outdoor advertising wins attention through visual impact like that in Exhibit 9-14. The physical characteristics of displays allow for this. Structures stand out because of their sheer size, typically twelve feet high and twenty-five feet wide. Ads can be painted onto displays with bright, vivid colors. Or the advertiser can use what the industry calls spectaculars, using special effects such as unusual lighting, animation, and three-dimensional materials.

Disadvantages of Outdoor Advertising

The major disadvantages of outdoor advertising are its limitation to visual effects, the low attention level of the audience, and the clutter of competing signs.

EXHIBIT 9-14   The Visual Impact of Outdoor Advertising

Courtesy Arnold & Company Incorporated, Boston, Mass.

Simple and Visual Effects Only

Any message appearing on an outdoor display can only appeal to the audience's sight. What the advertiser wants to say must be seen to have an effect. Furthermore, outdoor advertising intercepts an audience while it is in movement and must deliver a message before the audience passes. An outdoor display is limited to few words, if any, and the illustrations must be simple and to the point.

Low Attention Levels

People purposely read a magazine, their exposure to newspapers is of their own volition, and when they turn on the television set, it is to enjoy the medium. Any audience exposure to outdoor advertising is by chance. A display is noticed, not because the audience sought it out, but because the ad was at the right place at the right time. The audience's attention usually concentrates on driving or reading street signs.

Clutter

Outdoor advertising must compete with a multitude of signs. They may be commercial business signs over storefronts, or they may be noncommercial traffic signs. The abundance of displays, public and advertising, distracts attention from outdoor ads.

Rate Structure

The rate charged for outdoor advertising is determined by audience size, display characteristics, and intensity of market coverage.

Audience Size

The size of the circulation or audience dictates the basic rate for outdoor display—the number, that is, of pedestrians, automobile passengers, and riders of surface mass transportation who pass by the display locations. The greater the traffic, the higher the rate.

Display Characteristics

Presentation of the ad affects the cost. The most common and least expensive display is the printed poster on a 12' by 25' structure. A painted bulletin, usually measuring 14' by 48', costs more than a poster. And a spectacular is the most expensive because the size and design come from advertiser specifications.

Intensity of Coverage

In outdoor advertising, two terms describe the intensity of area coverage: *showing*, used less and less since 1973, and *gross rating point* (GRP).

Although the term showing is losing its popularity for describing intensity of message display, it is still being used periodically and thus warrants some explanation. The standard unit was a showing of #100, coverage reaching at least 90 percent of the market with an average exposure of at least once a day for approximately one month. Space would be sold in units of 100 or in multiples of 25, such as #75, #50, and #25.

The term showing has fallen into disuse because of the lack of standardization in defining a showing unit, and the difficulty in interpreting the meaning of showing. The definition of showing varies with the seller of the advertising space. While one seller may define a #100 showing as 100 percent reach, another seller may define it as only 90 percent reach. There is also difficulty in understanding the relationship between #100 and #50. While a #50 show means that there will be half the number of displays as in the #100, there is not necessarily half the audience coverage, the space buyer's real interest.

The gross rating point has become an increasingly popular measure because of its standardized definition and its intuitive appeal. A gross rating point means reaching 1 percent of the market per day. A 100 GRP coverage means reaching 100 percent of the population daily. In general, the more GRPs for which one contracts, the higher the total outdoor advertising cost.

The Future of Outdoor Advertising

In comparison with the outlook for other media, the future of outdoor advertising is uncertain for three reasons: the legal and administrative restrictions, the medium's inability to segment its audiences beyond geographical areas, and the rising costs of space.[23]

Efforts to control and eliminate commercial clutter in public spaces have restricted the number of outdoor structures. Where other media can simply add space or time to accommodate additional ads, the outdoor medium cannot. Industry growth through additional display space is very unlikely.

While other media compete for advertiser dollars by offering defined, special-interest audiences attracted by their content, outdoor can only offer audiences that are reached through opportunistic location of its displays. The medium has no editorial content or programming to modify and thus has no basis for segmenting its audience beyond the geographical areas in which they operate. The medium is in a difficult position when competing for advertiser interest based on audience characteristics.

Finally, the costs of outdoor advertising have been increasing at a rate greater than all other media except evening network television. From 1977 to 1983, outdoor ad costs increased 87 percent, compared with 40 percent for radio, 66 percent for newspapers, and 70 percent for magazines.[24] The increase relates to the rise in energy costs for the lighting of the displays and fueling of the service trucks. If costs continue to rise at such a rate and the medium does not have more to offer the advertisers, such as better-defined segments, it will be difficult for the medium to attract additional advertising revenues.

TRANSIT ADVERTISING

Transit advertising, the display of commercial messages inside and outside transportation vehicles and at terminal locations, accounted for over $70 million in media expenditures in 1983. Considering the $75 billion of total media expenditures, transit advertising obviously plays a secondary and supplementary role in an advertising campaign.

Advantages of Transit Advertising

The three major advantages of transit advertising are geographical selectivity, large audience, and low cost-per-thousand.

Geographical Selectivity

Transit systems operate locally. Any purchase of space with a specific system means that advertising coverage concentrates on a geographical market. The advertiser that has a particular geographical market finds that transit advertising allows precise targeting.

Large Audience

Transit advertising permits the advertiser to reach a large number of people. Over 40 million people ride transit vehicles in a month, with the average rider taking twenty-four trips in that period. Most of these riders are in major markets such as New York City, Chicago, Boston, and San Francisco.[25]

Low Cost-Per-Thousand

Transit advertising is an excellent buy in cost-per-thousand. Ads inside vehicles cost between fifteen and twenty-five cents-per-thousand riders, whereas exterior ads average between seven and ten cents-per-thousand.

Disadvantages of Transit Advertising

There are two major disadvantages of transit advertising: limited availability of space and uncertainty of audience characteristics beyond geography.

Limited Availability

The number of vehicles and terminal locations delimits the space. Whatever space exists is often committed by long-term contracts, and an advertiser may have difficulty in scheduling space.

Uncertainty of Audience Characteristics

The principal disadvantage of the medium is that audience segmentation is strictly by geographical areas. Transit advertising gives the advertiser little or no opportunity to select audiences on other bases. There is little research available describing the audiences, but beyond that the riders of transit systems are primarily urban residents who may be quite different from the nonriders in the advertiser's target market.

Rate Structure

The major determinants of transit advertising rates are circulation, type of display, and discounts.

Circulation

A system's basic rate depends on circulation, the number of fares collected. The Transit Advertising Association gathers circulation figures, and a six-month average of passengers dictates the rates for the system.

Type of Display

An advertiser that engages in transit advertising can select from three forms—interior, exterior, and station displays. For example, interior advertising uses bus cards or car cards with standard sizes of 11" × 21", 11" × 28", 11" × 42", 11" × 56", 16" × 44", and 22" × 21".

Discounts

Discounts attach to volume and continuity. Volume discounts accrue with the purchase of large amounts of showings or GRPs. Continuity discounts are based on the number of months contracted.

The Future of Transit Advertising

The expected growth of public transportation contributes to a positive outlook for transit advertising. The energy crisis of the 1970s led to plans for the improvement and expansion of existing systems and the development of new systems. These in turn attract more ridership, increasing the attractiveness of the medium to advertisers.

There is a negative note. Transit advertising's growth will stop if it cannot reach beyond urban dwellers. In many major metropolitan areas, the inner-city population ranks on the low end of demographic dimensions such as income, education, and home-ownership characteristics compared with the rest of the population. This ranking lowers the audience's market value to the advertiser.

DIRECT MAIL ADVERTISING

Direct mail advertising is the transmission of commercial messages from marketer to target audiences through the postal service. Such advertising is direct in that it is essentially under the control of the marketer and not any intermediary.

In 1983 direct mail advertising expenditures totaled $12 billion, making this means of advertising the third largest.

Advantages of Direct Mail

The major advantages of direct mail advertising are audience selectivity, personalized communication, timing, and design flexibility.

Audience Selectivity

Of all the media available, direct mail advertising offers the best opportunity for precision in reaching target audiences. This precision comes from the nature of the mailing lists, containing names and addresses of individuals classified according to relevant characteristics. A marketer could obtain a list of college students enrolled in women's colleges, or one with the names of the chief executive officers of the Fortune 500 companies.

Personalized Communication

Addressing someone in a personal manner increases interest. Where the personal approach works best, direct mail advertising, with the use of word-processing technology, is the only large-scale medium that can do the job.

Timing

Direct mail advertising schedules are flexible because they are under the marketer's direct control. Advertisers can be sure that mailings will arrive when they want them to arrive. The obvious implication of such control is that the coordination of this approach with other components of the marketing effort may be easier.

Design Flexibility

Since direct mail advertising is a custom medium, the advertiser has flexibility in the presentation of the message. There are few technical constraints in space, format, and materials in a mailing. The major limitations in design of a mailing piece are primarily creative and budgetary.

Disadvantages of Direct Mail

The major disadvantages of direct mail advertising are cost and receptivity.

High Cost

Depending on how elaborate the mailing is, the costs of direct mail advertising can run anywhere from $150 to $300 per thousand. This cost-per-thousand is exceptionally high when we consider that the costs for other media—television, radio, newspapers, magazines—run from $6 to $25 per thousand. This higher cost-per-thousand can be attributed to the relatively small audience among whom the total costs are to be allocated and to the relatively high production and mailing costs per piece.

Poor Audience Receptivity

A major problem in direct mail advertising is the public's characterization of such pieces as "junk mail." An advertiser should realize that there must be a serious effort (creative and financial) to gain attention and credibility to ensure that people do not just throw the piece away without opening it.

Rate Structure

Because direct mail is a custom medium, there is no standard rate structure. The costs of direct mail come from fees for mailing lists, production costs, distribution costs, and postage fees.

Mailing List Costs

The advertiser can assemble its own list, consulting various sources such as internal customer records, telephone directories, or membership rosters of associations. Developing its own list, while relatively cheap, is time consuming. The advertiser must locate the sources of names, then evaluate and screen the names to determine whether they fit the target characteristics.

Mailing list brokers facilitate the planning of a direct mail campaign by providing lists of names according to the advertiser's specifications.

The cost of a list typically depends on the quantity of names and their market value. As a simple rule, the cost of a list increases with its size, but lists containing names of persons or organizations with greater buying power generally command a greater fee. A list of Rolls-Royce owners costs more than an equivalent-size list of Chevrolet owners.

Production Costs

The production costs include all the expenses incurred in the development of the mailing package.

The basic costs depend on the paper and the printing requirements. Larger mailing pieces using higher-quality paper stock add to expenses. Large-volume printing, along with special processes such as unusual colors or custom paper cutting, folding, or handling, affect the production costs.

Distribution Costs

The advertiser incurs costs not only in delivering the mail package to the target but also in providing the target an opportunity to respond.

Postage Fees

The United States Postal Service (USPS) usually delivers the mailing package, although private postal services may sometimes serve. The USPS fees depend on weight and the levels of service.

The levels of service provided by the USPS vary by

Speed of delivery
Efforts to deliver to the addressee
Disposition of mail if not deliverable

First-class mail provides the advertiser with the highest level of service with the speediest methods of delivery. It will forward the mailing to the addressee if that person has moved, and it will return the piece to the advertiser if it is undeliverable.

First-class rates are therefore the highest of all rates. The advertiser can save costs by giving up some of the services. For example, the advertiser can get a lower rate by forgoing the forwarding services, or the advertiser can save by undertaking some of the services normally done by the USPS. Presorting and bundling by zip code can mean significant savings for the postal patron with large mailings.

Finally, postage fees in a direct mail campaign may include the provision for customer reply. Although it may take the form of a stamped, first-class envelope, the reply card or envelope often uses "business reply" mail. The advertiser obtains a special permit number from the postmaster. This number appears on the reply card or envelope and allows the USPS to track the returns to the advertiser, which then pays on the basis of the volume of replies.

The Future of Direct Mail Advertising

The outlook for direct mail advertising rests on its ability to deliver to selected markets with a precision unmatched by any other medium. As communications technology advances, the medium should be able to compile lists much more quickly and tailored to the advertiser's target specifications.[26] A clear indication of the growing importance of direct mail advertising is the sales volume it generates. Catalog sales in 1983 were $40 billion, up 10 percent from those in 1982.[27]

Costs pose a major deterrent to the medium's use. The costs are reasonable when targeting limited numbers such as industrial markets that cannot be reached cost-effectively through mass media. For extensive coverage, however, the cost may be too high. A trend in recent years is to use agencies that get advertisers together with other advertisers to distribute a package of ad materials to a targeted list. This is a way to share a considerable amount of the costs.

Audience receptiveness to direct mail advertising poses problems now and in the future. Proliferation of commercial literature has been an irritant to many recipients. Direct mail advertising is often treated as "junk mail" and recipients pay very little attention, perhaps none. This means wasted advertising dollars. The industry has recognized this problem. The Direct Marketing Association has offered the public an opportunity to be on a list of those *not* to receive advertising materials, thereby identifying and screening the unreceptive audience before mailing.

SUMMARY

The underlying theme of this chapter has been that the media differ in their costs, the audiences they attract, their technical capacities for message delivery, and their use by audiences for information. Given certain conditions of costs, target specifications, message characteristics, and audiences' use of information, we can now understand why some media are more effective than others.

Newspapers cover specific geographical audiences well. Their content sets a tone of currency and importance for ads. They are an expensive medium in cost-per-thousand. And since an issue has such a short life, an ad may require a number of insertions for any effect.

Magazines can deliver tailored markets. Their special content not only segments the audience but also complements the ads. Magazines are read in a leisurely way and thus have a long life. On the negative side, magazines are costly, appeal to readers only visually, and may contain a considerable amount of material competing for reader attention.

Television provides the broadest geographical coverage of all media and is attractive for major advertisers. Its cost-per-thousand is one of the lowest, and it projects a message in a dynamic manner. The medium's major disadvantages are its costs, its limited availability of time, and its nondiscriminating reach.

Radio reaches selected geographical areas at a reasonable rate. It covers the out-of-home audience well. Its major weaknesses are the low-attention levels of its audience and its inability to segment its audience much more than by geographical markets.

Outdoor and transit advertising reach the mobile audience outside the home. Advertisers who are fortunate enough to buy available space find that the cost-per-thousand for these media is the lowest. The limitations of outdoor and transit advertising stem from their opportunistic coverage. Both provide ad exposure only by intercepting traffic as it goes from one destination to another.

Direct mail is potentially the best medium for audience contact. The cost depends very much on the advertiser because of the added advantage of controlling the preparation and distribution of direct mail pieces.

Having looked at the different media, we will now focus on the development of the message. Included in our discussion of the message will be considerations of vehicle characteristics.

REVIEW AND DISCUSSION QUESTIONS

1. What are the implications of cable TV for the advertiser?

2. What are the advantages and disadvantages in using television?

3. What factors are considered by a television station in setting advertising rates?

4. What is the difference between network and spot TV rates?

5. What are the advantages and disadvantages in using radio?

6. "A lot of people have the radio on but they don't really listen." Comment.

7. What are the advantages and disadvantages in using newspapers?

8. Two major characteristics of a newspaper are its "timeliness of coverage" and its "closing date" requirements. Give examples that illustrate these advantages.

9. The life of a newspaper is very short, usually twenty-four hours. Why is this a disadvantage and how might an advertiser get around this problem?

10. What factors determine the cost of placing a newspaper ad?

11. Compare and contrast the major characteristics of magazines with those of newspapers.

12. The cost-per-thousand figure for a magazine is generally the highest among the major media. Why, do you think, is this so? Why would one select magazines over other media that may be less costly?

13. "A magazine, unlike other media vehicles, may offer an audience that actively pays attention to ads." Under what conditions do you think this is true?

14. How does the life of a magazine ad compare with the life of ads in newspapers, radio, and television?

15. *What factors determine the cost of a magazine ad?*

16. *How is the audience figure for outdoor advertising determined?*

17. *The advertisements on outdoor displays are simple. That is, the copy, if any, is brief and the illustrations are straightforward. Why?*

18. *What are the advantages and disadvantages of transit advertising?*

19. *Compare and contrast the characteristics of transit advertising with those of outdoor displays.*

20. *What are the major costs in a direct mail campaign?*

21. *What advantages does direct mail have over mass media? What are the disadvantages?*

22. *Of all the advertising media available, which do you think is the most effective when used properly? Why? Which do you think is the least effective? Why?*

NOTES

1. For detailed information on comparative media costs, see *Marketing and Media Decisions*, August 1980; and *Marketing and Media Decisions*, Fall 1983, Special Issue.

2. For a summary of research on information sources used in consumer decision making, see James Engel and Roger Blackwell, *Consumer Behavior*, 4th ed. (New York: Dryden Press, 1982), pp. 333–49. Findings on information sources in industrial buying decisions can be found in John Martilla, "Word-of-Mouth Communications in the Industrial Adoption Process," *Journal of Marketing Research*, May 1971, pp. 173–78; and Charles Patti, "The Role of Advertising in the Adoption of Industrial Goods: The Raw Materials Industry," *Journal of Advertising*, 8, No. 4 (1979), 38–42.

3. David Nylen, *Advertising: Planning, Implementation, & Control* (Cincinnati: South-Western Publishing, 1980), p. 273.

4. *1982 Study of Media and Markets* (New York: Simmons Market Research Bureau, 1982), Vol. M-5, p. 3.

5. Robert Goldsborough, "Challenges Continue for Metro Dailies," *Advertising Age*, August 16, 1984, p. 11.

6. Bill Granger, "An In-Depth Look at USA Today," *Advertising Age*, January 30, 1984, pp. M10ff.

7. Harold Zeltner, "Agency Media Heads Approach '84 with Caution," *Advertising Age*, November 7, 1983, p. M30.

8. *A Study of Magazine Page Exposure* (New York: Magazine Publishers Association, 1982), p. 4.

9. *A Study of Media Involvement* (New York: Magazine Publishers Association, 1982), p. 4; and *Magazine Fact Book* (New York: Magazine Publishers Association, 1982), p. 2.

10. Robert Coen, "Next Year's Cost Increases May Average Only 6%," *Advertising Age*, November 7, 1983, p. 7; and Zeltner, "Agency Media Heads," p. M22.

11. *Advertising Age*, April 30, 1980, p. 262.

12. "Will My Mother Know the Difference?" *Marketing and Media Decisions*, Fall 1983, Special Issue, p. 117.

13. Fred Danzig, "Pepsi-Cola Gambles on the Young," *Advertising Age*, March 5, 1984, p. 3.

14. James Forkan, "Winter Olympics Sold Out: ABC," *Advertising Age*, November 14, 1983, p. 6; Forkan, "ABC '88 Rights Fee a Stunner," *Advertising Age*, January 30, 1984, p. 88; Forkan, "Olympics Downhill for ABC," *Advertising Age*, February 13, 1984, pp. 1ff; and Diane Mermigas, "NBC Ratings Golden as ABC Olympics Lag," *Advertising Age*, February 20, 1984, pp. 2ff.

15. A. C. Nielsen, Jr., "The Outlook for Electronic Media," *Journal of Advertising Research*, December 1982-January 1983, pp. 6–19.

16. William Katz, "TV Viewer Fragmentation from Cable TV, Evidence from the Canadian Experience," *Journal of Advertising Research*, December 1982-January 1983, pp. 27–30.

17. Dean Krugman and Donald Eckrich, "Differences in Cable and Pay-Cable Audiences," *Journal of Advertising Research*, August-September 1982, p. 23.

18. "Can Cable Stem Tide of Disconnects?" *Marketing and Media Decisions*, January 1984, p. 52. For an in-depth look at cable television, see "The Cable Outlook," *Marketing and Media Decisions*, February 1985, pp. 70–96.

19. Nylen, *Advertising*, p. 323.

20. *Marketing and Media Decisions*, Special Issue, Fall 1983, p. 34.

21. Zeltner, "Agency Media Heads," p. M22.

22. *Marketing and Media Decisions*, August 1980, p. 71.

23. "What It Will Cost to Go Outdoors," *Marketing and Media Decisions*, Fall 1983, Special Issue, pp. 102–6; and Zeltner, "Agency Media Heads," p. M30.

24. *Marketing and Media Decisions*, Fall 1983, Special Issue, p. 34.

25. Otto Kleppner, Thomas Russell, and Glenn Verrill, *Advertising Procedure* (Englewood Cliffs, N.J.: Prentice-Hall, 1983), p. 244.

26. Zeltner, "Agency Media Heads," p. M30.

27. Lori Kesler, "Marketing's Stepchild Comes into Its Own," *Advertising Age*, November 28, 1983, pp. M9–M11; and Pat Sloan and Robert Reed, "Fate of Catalogs Rides on Santa's Sleigh," *Advertising Age*, November 28, 1983, p. 98.

10

The Advertising Message

Audience response does not come merely from its exposure to an ad. Its response comes from *what* the ad said and *how* the ad said it. To explain the nature of an effective message and the major considerations in its execution or expression, we will first survey the relationship between the advertising message and the different types of consumer decision making to be influenced. We will then discuss the major determinants of the theme or message, the various approaches to the presentation of the message, and the expression of the theme through the creative elements of words, graphics, and sound. Finally, we will look at the role of research in selecting an ad.

THE ADVERTISEMENT
AND CONSUMER DECISION
MAKING

The message of an advertisement is the impression that the advertiser wants to leave in the audience's mind. Since it is what the advertiser believes is necessary to influence people in the marketplace, the ad addresses the decision process it is seeking to influence. Some ads may contain considerable product information while others draw the audience's attention to the mood of the setting in which the product appears.

In Chapter 4 we discussed two types of decisions: low-involvement and high-involvement. Simply stated, product choice with low-involvement results not from any extended information processing about product attributes but from brand familiarity; trial of the product shapes attitudes toward it. Product choice in a high-involvement decision depends on attitudes formed through the processing of information. How might the theme differ across these decisions?

Product information in a theme can be simple or complex. With low-involvement products where information processing, if any, is simple, the message can be a simple and memorable one such as Miller Lite's "Less filling, tastes great" theme.[1] Ads for such products often produce enjoyable, entertaining settings through music, humor, and the like, for their simple messages. With high-involvement products where there is extended decision making, the theme can be more complex, as in an economy car ad suggesting more cargo room, easier maneuverability, front-wheel-drive handling, durable power-train, and a low price. The theme may seek to influence product perceptions, which in turn affect attitudes toward the product and then purchase decisions.

Lutz has suggested that advertising themes for both high- and low-involvement products may aim toward changing attitudes, although the nature of the attitude change is probably different.[2] Advertisements promoting high-involvement products are more likely to influence marketplace decisions by stressing product attributes. Such messages endeavor to influence audience beliefs about product performance, which then change attitudes toward the product. The business computer ad that talks about product performance and superiority over competitors' hardware presents a theme promoting product attributes. The decision maker needs, wants, and is very interested in product information so as to make a correct selection.

With a low-involvement product, lack of interest in the product decision means that active processing of product information is unlikely. The low-involvement decision maker, however, may find *interest in the advertising itself*, especially if it appeals to central values or self-concept. Repeated exposure to such advertising may increase product familiarity, have a positive effect on these broader attitudes, and then relate them to the product.[3] In other words, attention is paid to an ad because of interest in the ad setting rather than in the product; it may be a humorous scene that is enjoyable or a dramatic moment that is absorbing. The good feeling evoked by the ad may then carry over to the product. American Telephone & Telegraph ads encouraging long-distance calling do cite attributes of their service such as price and convenience, but the underlying message of the ads emerges from the imagery of the people and situations (the doting parents calling their lonely daughter starting a career in a big city). With AT&T's telephone service, the decision maker may not care to know about product attributes beyond the cost, and even then cost is relatively unimportant in the decision to make phone calls. The interesting ad setting that attracts attention, and repeated exposures, may produce positive impressions leading to use of AT&T services.

In summary, we can say that the development of ads across consumer decisions differs in the balance between stress on product attributes and stress on advertising mood. The accompanying graph suggests that mood and product information are basic elements in advertisements. However, the ad for a low-involvement item is more likely to rely on imagery for its impact than the ad for a high-involvement item.

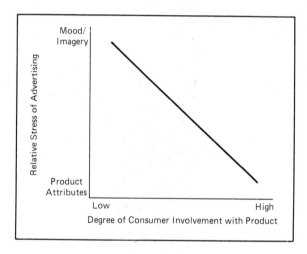

MESSAGE DETERMINANTS

With that overview of the relationship between message and marketplace, we will now consider three major elements in the development of a message: the target audience, the product or service being advertised, and the competitive positioning.

Target Audience

A logical focus for any message is the group with which the advertiser wishes to communicate. This audience will receive the message, and this group's attitude is the matter of concern. The developers of the message should understand the target audience thoroughly. They must know what the audience looks like (age, income, occupation, and so on), they must appreciate the audience's general lifestyle (its activities, interests, and opinions), and they must know the decision process for the product at hand.

Demographic and psychographic profiles together give the advertiser an understanding of how to appeal to the audience. Demographics essentially describe the audience, while psychographics tell us the manner in which the audience lives and perhaps give insights into the reasons for their behavior. Consider the shapes that an ad for financial-planning services could assume for different markets. If the audience consisted of single, 21-to-25-year-old, college-educated persons who spend most of their discretionary income on leisure, recreation, and travel activities, the ad might present financial-planning services as a means for greater enjoyment of life and the presentation might be in the context of an exciting, youthful setting. On the other hand, if the audience consisted of married couples, 55 years of age and older, the ad might stress long-term financial security and express this idea in the context of a retirement setting.

Knowledge of the audience's decision process gives the advertiser an idea of the opportunities for advertising to influence product choice. As mentioned earlier, some decisions (those for relatively unimportant and simple products) come chiefly from product familiarity, others (high-risk products) require considerable product information.

The Product

Some products do not have especially distinctive attributes. For these, the product information may be of little interest to the audience and the message should not be devoted to communicating it. A message dwelling on the characteristics of a brand of beer would be uninteresting to most audiences. As a result, most beer ads are devoid of product information but full of imagery.[4]

Some products are different from others because of performance. For a high-involvement product, the message should present appealing information on product attributes. To achieve this, bear in mind two basic points. First, the advertiser must understand the important features of the product. Proper presentation of the product requires comprehension of what it does and how it does what it does. Second, the product features are the springboard for message ideas. The message does not stop with the straightforward presentation of product characteristics. The message should concentrate on benefits that can come from those features. A prospective customer seldom judges the worth of a product by the value of its materials or the labor required for its creation. The worth of a product actually lies in the benefits that come from its ownership and use. A person buys an expensive lawn tractor not just for the sake of owning features such as a 12-horsepower engine, the grass mower, and the electric-start mechanism. That person really wants the convenience offered over standard lawn mowers, the time savings, and a range of utilities such as hauling and plowing snow with the appropriate attachments.

Whether the product is low- or high-involvement, we should remember that the message is an expression of the advertiser's offer to the target audience. And audience acceptance depends on the offer's attractiveness, quickened by reference to product benefits or by the ad's imagery. To present this attractiveness, we repeat, a full understanding of the product must be the foundation for the message.

Competitive Positioning

In a competitive environment, the audience is likely to experience hundreds of commercial messages a day. It is virtually impossible for the audience to attend to all messages. The mind just does not have the storage capacity. As a result, a selective attention and retention process occurs. Only the distinctive and the useful information get through the perceptual defenses to make an impression.[5]

As we pointed out in Chapter 5, positioning is important in a competitive environment. In the *positioning* process, an image is selected for product benefits that are not only considered desirable by the target audience but also considered superior to those of competitors. If such an impression comes across, there is a good chance that market choice will move toward the promoted product.

The advertising message should present an image sufficiently distinctive to stand out in the consumer's mind. The product should occupy a unique place in the audience's mind so that on those occasions when a choice arises, the advertised product comes up quickly and in a favorable light. IBM dominates the minds of business computer buyers, Xerox dominates the consumer's mind when it comes to copiers, and many people invariably ask for Jell-O.

APPROACHES TO MESSAGE PRESENTATION

Effective communication results not only from *what* an advertisement says but also from *how* it says it. Having seen something of the message and its determinants, we will now move to the tone or manner of message presentation. Simon has classified the following approaches:[6]

1. Informative approach
2. Argument approach
3. Psychological appeal
4. Repeated assertion

5. Command approach
6. Symbolic association
7. Imitation approach

The Informative Approach

In the *informative* approach, the audience receives an objective statement of facts or evidence. No evaluative statements color the facts. The intent is that only the features of the product or service will appear.

This approach is successful if the audience is actively seeking information from that advertiser, the assessment of facts is relatively straightforward for the audience, and the judgment is favorable to the advertiser. For example, the weekly supermarket advertisements directed toward the interested shopper take an informative approach. A specific cut of meat may be advertised at a special price per pound. This advertisement will be successful if we can assume there is an audience who will seek out the ad, notice the advertised price, and immediately judge that it is a good deal.

The Argument Approach

The *argument* approach presents not only facts but also judgments or evaluations of those facts. Rather than presenting *just* the facts and hoping for a favorable evaluation, the argument approach takes the reader through a structured process of recognizing features and then understanding the merits of those features (see Exhibit 10-1).

The argument approach is desirable in a situation in which the benefits from features are not that obvious to the reader and the advertiser cannot be reasonably confident that the receiver will deduce those benefits without help. Benefits of features are not always obvious when the advertisement is presenting an innovative product or the particular audience has not had experience in evaluating the product. Furthermore, the argument approach is appropriate in high-involvement decisions where the consumer wants to evaluate the information; in such situations, the advertiser guides the evaluation. The argument approach delivers to the receiver a "reason why" the sponsor's offer should be accepted.

Psychological Appeal

A *psychological* appeal is to the emotions, distinguished by its secondary emphasis on product attributes and by its primary emphasis on the mood that the ad's setting conveys. The use of psychological appeals rests on the premise that an ad's influence on the audience is more likely through an emotional appeal than through an objective, rational highlighting of product features. This may be appropriate with low-involvement products where

EXHIBIT 10-1 Using an Argument Approach

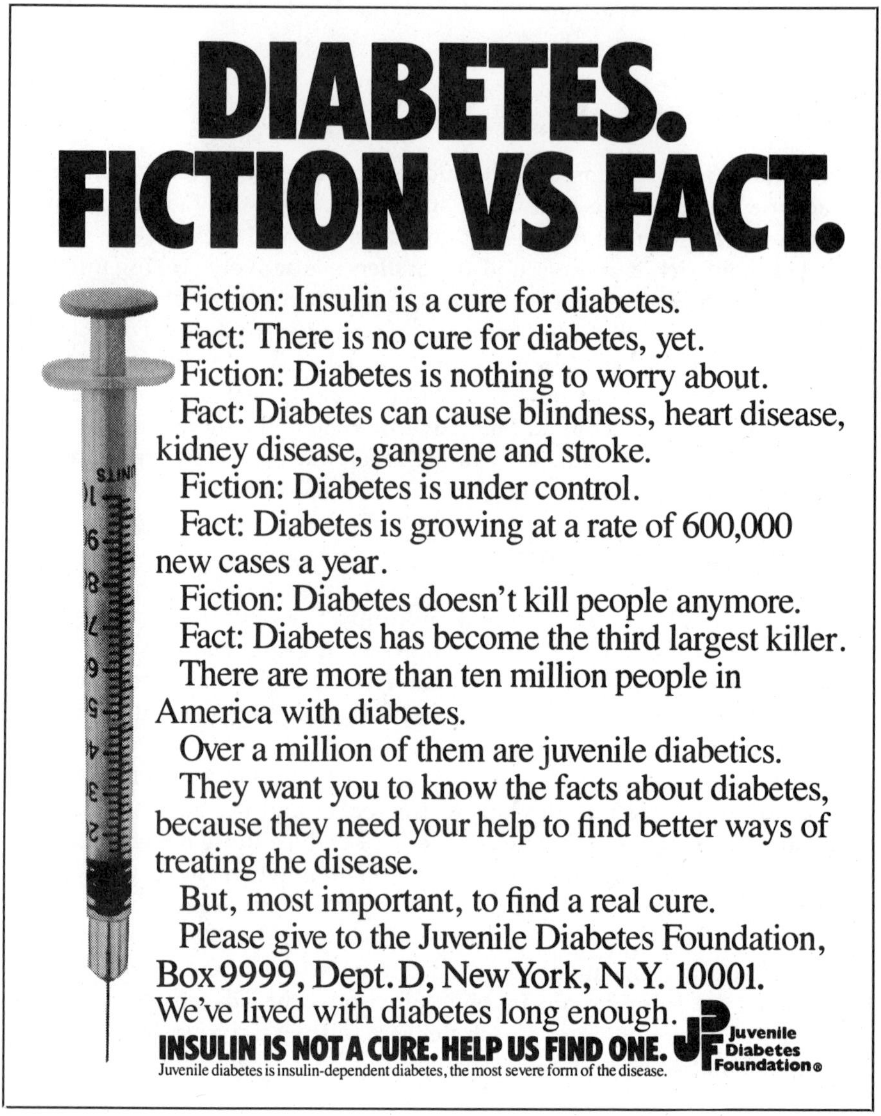

DIABETES. FICTION VS FACT.

Fiction: Insulin is a cure for diabetes.

Fact: There is no cure for diabetes, yet.

Fiction: Diabetes is nothing to worry about.

Fact: Diabetes can cause blindness, heart disease, kidney disease, gangrene and stroke.

Fiction: Diabetes is under control.

Fact: Diabetes is growing at a rate of 600,000 new cases a year.

Fiction: Diabetes doesn't kill people anymore.

Fact: Diabetes has become the third largest killer.

There are more than ten million people in America with diabetes.

Over a million of them are juvenile diabetics.

They want you to know the facts about diabetes, because they need your help to find better ways of treating the disease.

But, most important, to find a real cure.

Please give to the Juvenile Diabetes Foundation, Box 9999, Dept. D, New York, N.Y. 10001.

We've lived with diabetes long enough.

INSULIN IS NOT A CURE. HELP US FIND ONE. **JF** Juvenile Diabetes Foundation®

Juvenile diabetes is insulin-dependent diabetes, the most severe form of the disease.

Courtesy Juvenile Diabetes Foundation.

interest is low. To convey product information to an uninterested audience, the message may have to appeal to audience values and interests through the setting. In Exhibit 10-2, for example, a direct request for money would probably not have had as much effect as the strong emotional appeal in the headline.

EXHIBIT 10-2   Using an Emotional Appeal

Here's your chance to achieve a small moral victory.

Gabriel Cortez
Colombia
Age 4

What would you do if you saw a lost, frightened child?

You'd probably stop, pick him up, brush away his tears, and help him find his way. Without even thinking about it. And there's a reason.

You know what's right.

And right now, you can do just that. You can act on instinct...by reaching out to *one* desperately poor child, thousands of miles away.

Through Foster Parents Plan, you'll be helping a child who almost never has enough to eat. A decent place to sleep. Medical care. The chance to learn. Or hope.

It's your choice.

You can even choose the child you'd like to sponsor. A boy or girl. In a country where *you'd* like to help. You'll be helping that child within his own family. And more, helping that family to work with other families to make a better life for their children.

In return, you'll receive pictures of the child. Detailed progress reports. And letters written in the child's own words. You'll see for yourself just how much you're changing your Foster Child's life for the better. Forever. And for so little.

In fact, for just $22 a month, you'll make it possible for a child to have food, medical care, schooling—and hope. That's only 72¢ a day. Imagine. Your spare change could change a child's life.

Foster Parents Plan was founded in 1937 and this year will aid over 223,000 Foster Children and their families in more than 20 countries. We are non-profit, non-sectarian, non-political, and respect the culture and religion of the families we assist. Of course, your sponsorship is 100% tax-deductible, and a detailed annual report and financial statement are available on request.

Please don't wait.

If you saw a helpless child on the street, you wouldn't wait. You'd help that instant. Please don't wait now, either. Send in the coupon—or call toll-free 1-800-556-7918.

And achieve a small moral victory that can make a big difference to a needy child.

To start helping even faster, call toll-free:

1-800-556-7918

In R I call 401-738-5600

Send to: D361
Kenneth H. Phillips, National Executive Director
Foster Parents Plan, Inc.
157 Plan Way, Warwick, RI 02887

I wish to become a Foster Parent to a: ☐ Boy ☐ Girl ☐ Either
Age: ☐ 3-6   ☐ 7-10   ☐ 11-14   ☐ Any age 3-14
☐ **Wherever the need is greatest,** or as indicated below:
☐ Africa   ☐ Egypt   ☐ Honduras   ☐ Nepal
☐ Bolivia   ☐ El Salvador   ☐ India   ☐ The Philippines
☐ Colombia   ☐ Guatemala   ☐ Indonesia   ☐ Thailand
☐ Enclosed is a check for $22 for my first month's support of my Foster Child. Please send me a photograph, case history, and complete Foster Parent Sponsorship Kit.
☐ I am not yet sure if I want to become a Foster Parent, but I am interested. Please send me information about the child I would be sponsoring. Within 10 days I will make my decision.
☐ Mr.   ☐ Mrs.
☐ Miss ☐ Ms.

Address   Apt. #

City   State   Zip

Foster Parents Plan.®
It's the right thing to do.

Detach and mail or call toll-free today

Two common emotional appeals in advertising are fear and humor. A *fear* appeal stresses in a moderate manner the negative consequences of not accepting the advertiser's offer. The communicator assumes that the desire to avoid problems is a stronger motivator than any positive benefits the audience may see in the product.[7] Humorous appeals are increasingly evident. *Humor* draws audience attention because of its entertainment quality (important in consumer advertising), and it sets a positive mood for presenting the product.[8]

Repeated Assertion

In the *repeated assertion* approach, the basic message is usually very simple and appears repeatedly throughout the ad. This approach typically contains one idea continually restated in words, graphics, or sound. An advertisement for the premium scotch whiskey Johnny Walker Red sets forth a simple message—the whiskey has a distinctive premium taste. The headline "Red Stands Out When It Pours" is reinforced throughout the ad. Two young couples, obviously having a good time with drinks in hand, sit on the terrace of an outdoor café in the rain. Both wear a bright red rain poncho. One wears red sneakers; the other, red socks.

Simple repeated assertion is appropriate where the frequency of a message idea is more apt to influence consumers than is the substance of the message, particularly with low-involvement products.

The Command Approach

The *command* approach explicitly states the course of action the audience is expected to undertake and leaves no question as to what that is. United Air Lines' "Fly the Friendly Skies of United." American Express Company's "Don't Leave Home Without It." McDonald's "You Deserve a Break Today, So Get Up and Get Away, to McDonald's." A command approach promotes familiar products or services where the directed behavior is intuitively appealing and acceptable.

Symbolic Association

Very often an ad's message draws upon connotations from its association with a symbol. The object of the *symbolic association* approach is to trigger ideas through the use of a symbol. When the audience encounters the symbol—a word, an illustration, a person, music, anything that is perceptible—the product or some characteristic related to it registers in the audience's mind. The golden arches in fast foods, the blimp in the tire industry, "It's the real thing" in soft drinks, and Mr. Goodwrench in auto service are symbols readily linked to specific products and services.

With symbolic association, the advertiser must be certain that a link does indeed exist between the symbol and the ideas. The use of symbols to present a message generally occurs with reminder advertising for familiar products. And symbols are frequently used for low-involvement products where easy product recall is important for the sale.

Imitation Approach

The *imitation* approach assumes that the principal motivation for behavior is the desire to associate with or emulate a person or group. This approach often appears in ads containing endorsements or testimonials from presumably admirable individuals. Exhibit 10-3 contains an example of such an approach. Advertising that uses such an approach assumes there is social influence on the consumer decision. It in effect provides the audience with information on the appropriate behavior.

The Approach That Works

Having looked at several ways in which an advertiser can approach the audience, it is now logical to address the question, Which approach works best? The answer is simple, We don't know. As suggested earlier in this chapter and throughout preceding chapters, effective communications is determined by many factors including the audience, the product, the message idea, and the vehicle to be used. What has worked well earlier may not be effective now because the advertising conditions have changed. For example, the advertising of the 1970s presented products in bold, graphic ways with an impersonal approach. The advertising for many of those same products has now turned toward emotional approaches where the products in the context of human experiences are portrayed (good times with old friends over glasses of beer, intimate chats late in the evening over a cup of freshly brewed coffee, nostalgic family picnics where food and soft drinks are plentiful).[9] Undoubtedly, the effective approaches of the 1990s will differ from what exists today.

An effective approach should be based on research and analysis. Research can identify trends for the advertiser.

THE CREATIVE EXECUTION

The message and the message approach must translate into some perceptible and significant form for the audience. The advertiser must combine the individual elements of an ad (the words, sights, sounds, and so on) into a total impression consistent with the message.

EXHIBIT 10-3   Using an Imitation Approach

In this section we consider the creative process that gives life to the message. Our purpose is to give a sense of the elements and activity necessary to fully express a message. You will not have the technical skills to produce an ad after reading this section, but you will have an appreciation of the work entailed.

Since the relevant medium affects the final form that an advertisement assumes, our discussion of the creative process will take up each major medium. We begin with the print ads, followed by broadcast, then outdoor, transit, and direct mail. A fuller description of media constraints on advertisements appears in the preceding chapter.

Print Advertising

We will discuss three basic elements that could appear in a print ad:

The headline: the prominent word or set of words used to get attention
The copy: the words that tell the advertiser's story
The visuals: the illustration or pictures

Exhibit 10-4 contains an ad identifying these elements and others.

Any one ad may omit one or more of these elements. Or any one ad may give one element more prominence than another. The decision to use only particular elements or to stress one element over the other depends on the communication situation the advertiser faces. For example, ads promoting simple or well-known brands like Marlboro cigarettes or Pepsi Cola have very little copy. Ads for new or complex products like personal computers or microwave ovens have extensive copy explaining the product.

We will now look at the role each element plays in a print ad. By understanding the contribution of each component of the advertisement's communication with the audience, the advertiser can mix the components for the most effective presentation of the message.

The Headline

For the moment, let us consider why most people read a magazine or a newspaper. Not surprisingly, most people pick up a magazine or a newspaper to read the stories reporters write and editors edit. People do not usually buy a publication to read advertisements. In fact, the reading of advertisements is perhaps the furthest thing from the audience's mind.

The headline must attract the reader's attention, convey the message's essence, and stimulate sufficient interest so that the reader will go on to the rest of the advertisement. Since the reader's attention leans toward the editorial content of the medium rather than the sponsored messages, the first task of an advertisement is to capture some of that attention whenever it can. Frequently, the headline presents the first and only chance for the advertiser to communicate with the audience. If, as some think, 80 to 90 percent of an audience do not go beyond the headline,[10] then it must carry the burden of communicating as much of the advertiser's message as possible.

EXHIBIT 10-4   *The Components of a Print Ad*

Headline — ## "My Maytag Washer has been so great, I got a Maytag Dryer and Dishwasher, too," states Mrs. Whitehead.

Subhead — *Now going on 12, it still washes two loads a day, six days a week.*

Visuals —

Susan. 7; Jimmy, 10½; James and Nancy Whitehead.

Copy —

"I'm hoping we'll enjoy as many happy years with our Maytag Dishwasher as we have with our other Maytags," says Mrs. Nancy Whitehead, Oak Ridge, N.J.

"Our Maytag Washer was a housewarming gift from my parents in July of 1969," she continues. "This machine has been doing approximately two loads a day, six days a week, ever since. It has also washed diapers for two babies."

As hard as that washer has been working all these years, the repairman is still practically a stranger, according to Mrs. Whitehead. That's because Maytag Washers are built to last longer and save you money with fewer repairs.

"Later we purchased a Maytag Dryer," she states, and it has also proved to be a faithful workhorse. "Since our other Maytags have given us such great service, we natu-rally turned to Maytag for a dishwasher in 1979. I am delighted with my Maytag Dishwasher and hope to enjoy it a long time," concludes Mrs. Whitehead.

Naturally, we don't say all Maytags will equal that record. But long life with few repairs is what we try to build into every Maytag product. See our washers, dryers, dishwashers, and disposers.

Logo —
Slogan —

Mrs. Whitehead got her Maytag Dishwasher in 1979. "It's a pleasure to use, and it does a marvelous job of getting my dishes clean," she states.

MAYTAG
THE DEPENDABILITY PEOPLE
The Maytag Company, Newton, Iowa 50208

Courtesy The Maytag Company.

What is a good headline? The good headline causes the reader to stop and examine the ad, perhaps by arousing curiosity or provoking thought with clever combinations of words or ideas:

"Forty Years without a Sale!"
"We Have the Most Expensive Water on the Block"
"Insulin Can't Cure Diabetes"
"One of the Best Things about a Midas Brake Job Is the Part That Goes into the Glove Compartment!"

Thought-provoking headlines raise important or interesting issues in the reader's mind:

"Resale Value Is Only Interesting If You're Interested in Reselling"
"If You Fail This Simple Test, You May Be at Risk for Diabetes"

The good headline contains only enough words to convey the advertiser's point and no more. It is virtually impossible to specify an exact length that makes a headline good. A headline is too long or too short not because of the number of words used but because it catches (or fails to catch) the reader's attention. The headline should be as short as possible consistent with producing its effect.

The good headline focuses on the interests of the targeted audience. The advertising message is not for everyone, and therefore the headline is not responsible for attracting every reader. It is selective about its audience and often appears personalized toward a special group by use of the word *you*.

Finally, the good headline reflects the essence of the sponsor's message and encourages further reading. Since the likelihood of the reader's stopping at the headline and not reading the remainder of the advertisement is high, the headline should convey to the reader a statement focusing on a benefit or benefits important to him or her. The statement of benefits should be such that the reader takes the initiative to investigate beyond the substance of the headline by reading further into the copy.

The Copy

If the headline has been effective, the reader will give the advertisement an opportunity to develop and support the impressions of the headline. Advertisements for high-involvement products are likely to contain copy responding to the audience's information needs. The object of the copy is to present the advertiser's story and convince the reader to accept the message. The copy is an opportunity for the advertiser to stimulate the reader's interest in the offer and persuade the reader to accept or otherwise act on the offer.

Good copy. Prior to the development of the copy, the writer must thoroughly understand both the background of the audience and the intent of the advertiser. There must be a familiarity with the audience's decision process and the influence that advertising exerts on that process. The writer should know the most important points the advertiser wishes to deliver to the audience. In order for the writer to come up with the appropriate vocabulary and prose, he or she must understand the salient points of the advertiser's message.

The copywriter not only understands the level at which the targeted audience reads but strives to keep the copy on that level. Since the writer of advertising acts as a translator of ideas, the words and the organization of words must correspond to the reading habits of the audience. The sophistication of the vocabulary and grammatical structure should arise not from the writer's background but from the reader's. Copy that uses overly technical words or expresses concepts with a highly complex sentence structure turns off readers not comfortable with that kind of expression.

Unless there is inherent product interest, the longer it takes the copy to make its point, the more likely the audience will turn away. The writer who supposes more audience interest than really exists is likely to lose readership before the complete story is told. Print advertisements may get from five to thirty seconds of reading attention, with most experiences falling into the shorter time periods. The copy must not be tedious reading.

Good copy may increase the time the reader is willing to spend on an advertisement by having a lively, short, and interesting opening. The first words or sentence of short copy or the opening paragraph of longer copy gives the reader a glimpse of what is to come. The opening tantalizes, heightens the desire to read on, builds upon the initial interest or curiosity the headline has aroused. It should cause the reader to want more information, contained of course in the remainder of the copy. The opening lines of the copy stimulate interest by focusing on the promise of benefits, in effect saying, "Here's what you could get for yourself if you read on."

Good copy is specific and concise. After reading the copy, the audience comes away with specific points about the ad offer. If it is about a product, the copy should contain statements describing characteristics of the product's performance and the resulting benefits. Furthermore, the copy should deliver its message as quickly as possible; rather than test the limits of the reader's patience or attention, the copy should get directly to the points to be made.

Visuals and Layout

The full impact of a print ad is a function of what the audience sees, encompassing not only the written copy but also the accompanying visual elements. Words represent one means of communication, pictures and artwork another. The layout is the integration of these two in a satisfactory whole.

Effective visuals and layout. An effective visual captures reader attention, embodies the basic message, creates a mood, and complements whatever headline and copy there are.

The use of visuals as the dominant element in an ad may be due to the complexity of the message to be delivered or the simplicity of the product offer. For example, ads for luxury automobiles are usually short on copy. The basic messages of such ads revolve around abstract psychological ideas. The use of copy to convey those messages would be cumbersome if not tedious; illustrations convey the message quickly and perhaps better than words can.

For products with features that are relatively straightforward or widely understood, visuals may again be preferred over copy, since a written story is unnecessary.[11] For example, visuals rather than copy dominate many advertisements for liquor because the reader knows the characteristics of the product itself.

The visuals and the copy should go hand in hand to make an ad effective. The nature of the message is such that illustrations and words combine for a total effect, since neither one by itself actually expresses the advertiser's thoughts. Exhibit 10-5 shows an ad where the visuals and words both play integral and essential communication roles. In the Crown Royal ad, neither the headline nor the illustration by itself could fully communicate the idea, but their combination results in something meaningful.

Broadcast Advertising

There are two types of media broadcast advertisements: television and radio. Since their technical characteristics are sufficiently different from one another, we will discuss them separately.

The Television Commercial

The television commercial can be effective or ineffective in conveying the advertiser's message. Its dynamic qualities make possible a very effective expression of a message. The opportunities for creative visual techniques are superior to those for print, and when these opportunities join with audio elements, the sponsor's message comes fully alive. On the other hand, the television commercial may be quite ineffective in delivering a message, since the message has virtually no sustained life and there is inherent audience apathy (even dislike) toward advertising.[12] The life of the commercial is

EXHIBIT 10-5   An Ad Where Words and Visuals Work Together

Courtesy Seagram Distillers Co.

only as long as the broadcast time.[13] If the audience is not paying attention (and it often is not), then that advertising opportunity is gone. Unlike print advertising, which can be saved or passed on, television ads cannot.

An effective television commercial attracts audience attention, holds that attention, and registers the advertised product or service in the audience's mind. The first and most important task of a commercial is that it capture the audience's attention within the first three to five seconds.[14] Without this, the remaining commercial time has no effect. How tough is this task? Very tough. Few members of an audience turn on the television to watch ads. Ads intrude on the audience's entertainment. If the ads are not annoyances, they are at best viewed as welcome opportunities to attend to other activities while waiting for the programming to resume. Interest must be captured at the outset because it is unlikely to build over the course of the commercial.

The next task of a television commercial is to hold the audience's interest so that the advertiser's message can be told. The interest may stem from product interest (if you are in the middle of a search for a new automobile, you will probably be interested in the automobile commercials), or if interest in the product is not high, the story in the commercial must hold the interest. Most products advertised on television are low-involvement products, and the commercials' entertainment qualities must capture the audience. Entertainment can be effective in communicating product information.

Finally, the end result of audience interest in the ad must be an awareness of the product or service. A viewer may remember the ad but must remember the product. The impression the ad makes should not be at the expense of the product's impression. A few years ago Alka-Seltzer broadcast a series of humorous commercials showing scenes where people experienced severe discomfort from overeating. They expressed the common lament "I can't believe I ate the whole thing." The series was extremely popular for its entertainment value but had little impact in persuading the audience to buy the product.

The visual element. Television is a visual medium, and a commercial should use the medium's distinctive competence. With television, the advertiser can present the message dramatically by changing scenes, whereas the print ad's visuals amount to one shot or frame. The opportunity to change scenes gives the advertiser the ability to use the right settings in the right sequence to communicate the main idea. The opportunity to control the sequence of visuals is an opportunity to control the development of the advertiser's story. Such control means that the advertiser takes an active part in determining the manner in which the audience sees the message and the conclusion they draw from the story. For example, many "slice of life" television commercials start with the scene where the "problem" comes about in a setting the audience recognizes. Then comes a scene with a solution, usually in the form of the advertiser's product. And finally there is a scene showing the benefits from that solution.

The visual techniques in a television commercial can take many forms. Some of the more common involve the use of a spokesperson, demonstration of the product, portrayal of a real-life situation, narrated story, customer interview, product comparisons, humor, and animation. See Exhibit 10-6 for guidelines in the evaluation and selection of techniques.

The audio element. Although the distinctive competence of television advertising is the visual element, the audio element is nonetheless an essential

EXHIBIT 10-6   *Guidelines for Evaluation and Selection of Techniques for Television Ads*

- Does your promise of benefit and supporting evidence suggest a particular technique? Do you intend to demonstrate your product? Could it win in a side-by-side comparison with other brands? Is any of your copy based on reports of satisfied users? Is your sales story simple and direct enough to warrant the personal touch a speaker may provide?
- What techniques are your competitors using? Although no law prevents you from following their lead, you may want to choose a different direction in order to give your product its own television image.
- From previous advertising, has your product or service established a special personality that may suggest continuing a technique?
- Do consumer attitudes discovered in research interviews suggest any problems to be met or any special advantages to be stressed for your product?
- Does your campaign already exist in print advertisements? If so, you will probably want your television effort to bear a visual resemblance. Often the reverse is true; many print techniques follow the lead set by TV commercials.
- How much money is available for production of your commercial? If your budget is modest, you will want to give serious thought to closeups, artwork, simple sets, or locations with a minimum of personnel.
- What production facilities are available? If you plan to produce your commercial in a large city, facilities will probably be at hand. Otherwise, the nearest television station or a free-lance filmmaker may be your best choice.
- What techniques are used in other commercials? Make it your practice to view television often and to analyze techniques. This will sharpen your own familiarity with the subject, and you may see techniques that suggest new directions for your product.

Kleppner/Russell/Verrill, *Otto Kleppner's Advertising Procedure*, 8th Ed., © 1983, p. 411. Reprinted by permission of Prentice-Hall, Inc., Englewood Cliffs, N.J.

and integral part of a commercial. The visual can seldom convey the message alone. It is the spoken word, the music, and the sound effects that bring out the meaning of the picture.

The primary purpose of the audio is to develop the thought behind the visual. The visual gives the audience a picture or impression, and the audio presents and emphasizes details of that picture.[15] Feelings from the sight of a festive Fourth of July celebration are amplified when accompanied with the patriotic sounds of a marching band. Nostalgic scenes of a family reunion have greater impact when there is music with lyrics evoking emotional memories.

The Radio Commercial

Selective attention and selective retention operate to screen out many transmitted messages. With radio broadcasts, the barriers of selectivity are difficult to hurdle. Radio broadcasts are generally a background to activities receiving most of the audience's attention. Therefore the communications task of the radio commercial is not an easy one. Unlike newspaper and magazine readers and television viewers, who are interested in the editorial or program content (if not the ad content), the radio audience often treat the medium as nothing more than a source of pleasant sounds. Additionally, the radio commercial stands a good chance of being ignored because it intrudes into whatever regular programming is being broadcast. And if all that were not enough, the radio commercial has the handicap of appealing only to the audience's hearing. Sound effects alone must produce the desired impressions in the mind.

According to Runyon, a good radio commercial has the following characteristics:[16]

> The opening seconds are dramatic and provocative.
> It is specific about the product benefits.
> It speaks to the audience in understandable terms.
> The message is simply expressed.
> The product or service name is repeated.
> The basic points are asserted throughout.

The most important characteristic is the first. Unless the opening seconds capture attention and maintain interest, the other characteristics of the commercial do not have an opportunity to influence the audience.[17] The opening seconds must be dramatic and provocative to the point that the commercial purposely intrudes into the mind momentarily without being annoying. It is quite likely that audience thinking is elsewhere, and a radio broadcast must break the train of thought. Once the train of thought has momentarily been broken, it must be switched toward the commercial. The commercial must immediately create a mental picture that holds audience interest.

Other Media

So far we have discussed the development of advertisements as adjuncts to editorial materials of the communications vehicles. We now consider advertisements that stand alone, that appear independently.

Outdoor and Transit Advertising

Outdoor displays and advertising on public transportation vehicles aim at an audience that is mobile. The audience is going from one destination to another, and the aim of outdoor and transit advertising is interception. Unlike print or broadcast audiences that are stationary, this audience is literally on the move. The execution of the message must adapt to this situation.

Effective outdoor and transit advertisements. The first task is to capture the traveler's attention by breaking his or her concentration momentarily. The traveler is intent on getting from one location to another and does not have the slightest interest in looking at advertising signs. The single element for getting attention is the visual element. Visual impact may come from colors, illumination effects, and artwork. One element of outdoor advertising that gets attention is the enormous size of the display, generally twelve feet high and twenty-five feet across.

Once it has gained attention, the advertisement must convey the message in a matter of a few seconds (some say eight seconds or less). In contrast to the viewing or reading environment for other media, the advertisements do not have the opportunity to build audience interest. The audience looks at the advertising while in motion. The advertising must deliver the message before the audience has passed the display. To do this, there should be very little copy and simple but bold visuals.

Direct Mail

For marketers who do not wish to risk having their messages lost among the general content of magazines, newspapers, television, and radio, and for advertisers who have a special story to relate to a special audience, there is direct mail advertising. Unlike the forms of advertising we discussed in the preceding sections, direct mail advertising actively seeks out a designated reader and creates its own opportunities rather than passively waiting to be noticed at an opportune moment.

For many direct mail recipients, the initiative of the direct mail advertiser may seem undesirable, aggressive intrusion. Consequently, the development of a direct mail advertising program must concentrate on pieces that stand out and do not become quickly prejudged by recipients as "junk mail."

Effective direct mail advertising. Direct mail advertising calls for the development of several pieces constituting the mailing package. The package may consist of the envelope, a letter, a selling piece, an order form, and a reply envelope.

The envelope is the first opportunity for communication with the audience, and its principal task is to persuade the reader to open it rather than discard the package without even having looked at the contents. The envelope must arouse interest and curiosity. It must convey the sense that there is something worthwhile inside for the recipient. In developing the envelope format (distinctive color, unusual size, tantalizing one-liners, commemorative postage stamp, and the like), the sponsor should ask, Does this envelope make my audience want to look inside?

A good letter establishes rapport with the reader, explains the sender's intent, and generates interest about the enclosed selling pieces. After reading the letter, the recipient should say to himself or herself, "The sender's proposition seems to fit my particular needs and wants. Let me find out how to take advantage of the proposition by reading the enclosed literature." A good letter attempts to be as personal as possible, addressing the reader with his or her name and using the second-person "you" whenever appropriate. A good letter tantalizes by suggesting the benefits to be gained if the reader merely gives attention to the mailing's enclosures.

If the letter has been effective, the enclosed materials are ready to undertake the selling job. Whether the materials are booklets, brochures, pictures, or charts, the materials must expand on the promises of benefits made in the letter and be persuasive while doing so, using both written copy and visual effects. A major difference between the advertisements in a direct mail package and those in the traditional print media is that there is much greater latitude in direct mail in the use of production elements to express the advertiser's message. Where ads in magazines and newspapers are restricted in the use of paper stock and page dimensions, that is not true of direct mail advertising. In putting together the selling piece, the vehicle for conveying a message is limited only by the creativity of the advertiser. Messages have been expressed through the traditional vehicles of paper booklets or brochures. More-creative advertisers have used specialty items: calendars, appointment books, puzzles, fortune cookies, and so forth.

An essential part of the direct mail package is the provision of a means for recipient response. Assuming that the selling piece has accomplished its task of persuasion, the direct mail package must then make it convenient for the recipient to respond as requested. If there is no response vehicle, the marketer will miss many sales opportunities. The inclusion of a reply form and a self-addressed, prepaid envelope facilitates the process of customer response.

TESTING IN AD SELECTION

So far we have discussed the major considerations in determining what to say and how to say it. The target audience, product, competition, and media characteristics determine the possible advertisements. The number of possibilities stems from the many trade-offs of the determinants' strengths and weaknesses. As trade-offs are being made, variations in the message and its expression occur. The variations may be quite obvious (one ad uses humor while the other uses a serious tone), or they may be subtle (one alternative uses a lighter color shade as background than another). How does one choose among ad alternatives? Here is David Ogilvy's view:

> The selection of the right promise is so vitally important that you should never rely on guesswork to decide.[18]

Research helps the advertiser to sort out the ad alternatives. It can provide an approximation of the communications effect of each alternative. Of course, research cannot guarantee selection of the best ad. But it can, at the least, separate the bad from the not-so-bad. Research can help the advertiser avoid serious mistakes and can point out the general direction the advertisement should take.

Adaptation of research designs to meet the needs of the advertiser means that ad testing can take a variety of forms. The variety of approaches to ad pretesting, the testing of ads prior to campaign launch, can be described along two dimensions:

1. The extent to which the test measures audience responses to advertisement elements compared with responses to the product advertised
2. Whether the test takes place in the marketplace or a simulation of the marketplace

In the remainder of this section we will discuss each of these.

Measures of Effectiveness

The measures of advertising effectiveness are essentially the same for pretesting or posttesting ads. This section presents a brief overview of these measures. The chapter on evaluation of results, Chapter 18, gives a more-detailed description.

What measures will assess the effectiveness of an ad? Should the test focus on audience *reaction to the ad elements* themselves (headline, visuals, graphics, and the like)? How accountable should an ad be for the audience's *receptiveness to the product*? Is an ad effective if it heightens *awareness of the product*, or should the ad's effectiveness be judged by *changes in attitudes* toward the product?

The measures should refer to the communications objectives for which the advertising work is undertaken. The accompanying graph gives an overview of the balance in emphasis between measurement of reaction to advertising and reaction to the product.

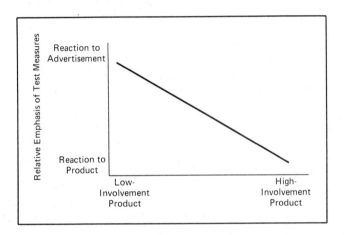

In the case of low-involvement products, audience interest in the advertising execution is critical. Since the audience is basically uninterested in product information, any product information must come across right at the time the audience scrutinizes the advertisement. Thus a greater emphasis in testing may be placed on audience reaction to the advertisement itself. On the other hand, advertising for high-involvement products, while not demeaning the importance of engaging the audience in the creative execution, is more responsible for influencing perceptions of such products. And there is the assumption that audience interest in the product information will offset any weaknesses in creative execution.

Response to the Advertising Elements

Measures of effective creative expression include the following: attention getting, interest holding, attitude formation, and the durability of impressions. An ad must get the notice of the audience to have any effect. Research can test for the attention-getting ability of single elements like the headline, the visual, and the music. More specifically, research can determine what, if any, ad element caused a reader, viewer, or listener to stop and take notice.

For an ad containing more than a simple headline or visual, one usually measures audience involvement by the amount of an advertisement read or the time spent watching or listening to a broadcast. The assumption underlying the use of these measures is that the effective creativity occupies the audience's mind and that the effort and time spent are an indication of the degree of involvement. It is assumed that the greater the number of minutes or seconds spent watching or listening to advertising, the greater the interest.

Effective advertisements should be pleasant experiences for the audience. Pretesting may identify annoying or offensive elements like a jingle, a word, or a particular celebrity spokesperson. It may also identify those elements that the audience will enjoy. Pleasant ads are assumed to set a positive mood for the audience's reception of product information.

Finally, an ad must leave a durable impression in the audience's mind. A measure of effectiveness is the extent to which the audience comprehends certain portions of the ad. Frequently, a selected sample of the audience are asked what specific points (headline, copy points, slogan, sponsor name, and the like) they can recall from an ad they have seen in the past. Accuracy of recall over time is a measure of an ad's communication ability. Furthermore, for low-involvement items, recall ability reflects familiarity, which in turn is essential to influencing product choice.

Response to the Product

We have just looked at measures of reaction to and feelings toward the ad itself. In this section we look at measures of what an ad can do for a product. These can be classified as awareness, comprehension, or attitude measures. The accompanying graph suggests that the effect for which an ad is held accountable depends on the product that is being promoted.

Every ad must at least be able to enhance the audience's awareness of the product or service. Whether it is low-involvement or high-involvement goods, the audience's familiarity with the product's availability must be affected. Otherwise the advertiser is spending money only to entertain an audience.

Product awareness and familiarity may be the principal objectives in advertising low-involvement goods like candy bars or paper towels. With higher-involvement goods, measurement of an audience's understanding of product attributes will tell the value of an ad. These measures rest on the assumption that knowledge and comprehension are important in influencing marketplace decisions.

Finally, some pretests collect data on changes in attitudes toward the product. Audience opinions, preferences, and intentions reflect the feeling

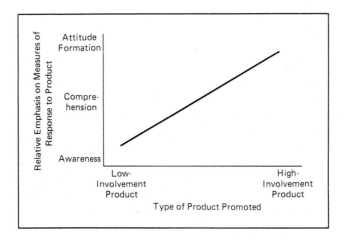

about a product. An ad aimed at shaping these elements is often for goods where the audience needs and wants product information for its decisions.

The Test Setting

Pretesting of ads can take place in the actual marketplace or in a simulation of the marketplace, often a laboratory. The decision to use an artificial market setting or to conduct a test in the field is contingent on many factors, including the type of information to be gathered and the availability of time and financial resources for testing. Whether ad tests take place in a lab or in the field, the primary objective is to obtain an accurate measure of ad performance.[19]

Artificial Market Settings

The fact that a market setting is artificial does not imply that results are less relevant than those from a field setting. A well-conceived design supplies valid insights into ad effectiveness.

Use of artificial constructs in test settings like behavioral laboratories depends on the nature of the information to be collected, time constraints, and financial limitations. Some ad effects are so subtle that a controlled environment is necessary. For example, measuring the speed of recognition of headlines and visuals is often in hundredths of a second. Only special laboratory instrumentation can achieve such measurements.

The lab offers time advantages over the field situation. Much time in field research goes to controlling influences on the measures of ad effectiveness, whereas in a lab, one can more easily manipulate such factors as economic influences, effects of competing ads, and vehicle content. This manipulation facilitates the scheduling of research activities.

Lab testing offers many financial advantages over field research. The market environment can be approximated without incurring the expense. Consider the ad to be tested for its attention-grabbing power in a clutter of editorial content and other advertisements. In field research, one must buy space and place the ad in a test market location. In a lab, one avoids the expense of media space by using a dummy magazine (but apparently real to test participants) with all the characteristics of a real magazine except for circulation.

Although pretesting in labs has many advantages, there are also major disadvantages. Let us consider two of them. First, it is extremely time consuming. The physical constraints of a laboratory and the researcher's desire to exercise control over events often means that only a few subjects can be processed at one time. To accumulate a sizable data base, the researcher has to run through a considerable number of sessions. Thus, pretesting under strict deadlines may be difficult. Second, there is the question of the extent to which generalizations about effects in the real world can be drawn from an artificial setting. In the attempt to isolate ad effects, researchers may have created settings that are not likely to exist in the real world. For example, how well does the activity of a person gazing into a scope to watch slides flashed at less than one-sixtieth of a second replicate the situation of a person leafing through a magazine filled with ads? Some would argue that there is very little replication and that conclusions drawn from such procedures and inferred to the natural setting are therefore questionable. Those who have such doubts would prefer pretests conducted in a real-world setting.

Field Settings

In artificial settings, there is the ever-present possibility that a factor critical to accurate measurement of effects will be left out, a major argument for the use of field or natural settings.

When advertisements are tested under normal market conditions, this typically means that they appear in actual vehicles. A metropolitan newspaper that publishes different editions for geographical areas can be the site for testing variations in ads. Local television broadcasts may serve to test commercials for a national campaign.

The advantages of a natural setting must be weighed against high costs, including normal operating expenses. To fit in with the natural environment, the test will incur the expenses of an actual campaign. For example, field testing of a proposed television commercial requires costs for its production as well as payment for air time. These costs must also include the expenses for a good research design that isolates advertising effects. Consider the testing of two newspaper ads. One ad appears in a newspaper run distributed to the north side of a city. The other ad appears in a same-day printing for the city's south side. Both ads have a coupon redeemable at the neighborhood stores. Although it seems that the relative effectiveness could be measured by counting the number of coupons redeemed, it is not that simple. Coupon redemption could take place not only because of the ad but because of factors like the relative participation of retail outlets in the two areas. The control of factors clouding ad performance requires time and effort that translate into substantial costs.

Testing Is Important

Testing adds an element of objectivity to a very subjective process in advertising. Testing, at the very least, can steer the advertiser away from major mistakes. We have taken a nontechnical look at the research process. Our discussion has been focused not so much on research's execution as on the critical factors underlying valid research. The most important factor is that research provide a true measure of effectiveness. No matter how well research is executed, it produces nothing useful unless it addresses the right issues.

SUMMARY

An advertisement has two components, the message idea and the manner of expressing it. Both work together to influence consumer decision making.

The message flows from characteristics of the target audience, the product, and competitive positioning. Ads for products relatively unimportant and uninteresting to the consumer and with little difference between them and the competition must get audience interest through this creative execution. We affirmed that familiarity with the product results from involvement with the ads. Where product interest is high and there is the opportunity for differentiation, advertisements stress product attributes.

The message can take a number of forms. We described the information approach, argument approach, psychological appeal, repeated assertion, command approach, symbolic association, and imitation approach.

The object of creative work is the full expression of the message. The distinctive qualities of the medium dictate the nature of the creative execution. For example, print media such as magazines and newspapers allow only the use of words and visuals. Television commercials use sight and sound, while radio commercials rely on audio appeal. Regardless of the medium, an advertisement must be able to attract attention and hold interest to communicate the message.

Research, in either a simulated or an actual market setting prior to the full-scale campaign, helps the advertiser discover the more effective ads. Valid results depend on the measures of effectiveness. There are two basic groups of measures—those that measure audience receptiveness to the advertising execution and those that measure audience reaction to the product. To communicate with an audience uninterested in the product, an ad must depend on the appeal of the advertising elements.

This concludes the section on advertising, the use of impersonal mass media. In Chapters 7–10 we discussed the major activities involved in developing and executing an advertising program. We will now consider a different communications element, personal selling. In contrast to advertising, personal selling is a highly personal communications medium where there is face-to-face contact between marketer and marketplace.

REVIEW AND DISCUSSION QUESTIONS

1. Explain the process by which a theme is developed.
2. What are the characteristics of a good theme? Give examples.
3. Identify and describe the four major components of a print ad. Explain how they have to work together.
4. What is the role of a headline in a print ad?
5. What are the characteristics of a good headline? Give some examples of good headlines.
6. Assume that you are composing an ad for a new brand of cassette recording tape. Develop a headline. Explain your choice.
7. What is the purpose of ad copy?
8. List and explain the criteria for evaluating copy.
9. Describe the major copy approaches. What are the advantages and limitations of each approach?
10. Assume that you are writing copy for a TV ad promoting a local fast-food hamburger restaurant. Compare and contrast an informative approach with an argument approach.
11. Using the repeated assertion approach, develop advertising copy (for a magazine ad) for your top-performance golf ball.
12. For each of the following, list three specific appeals you would use in your advertising: (a) a low-fat cottage cheese, (b) a sun-tanning lotion, (c) a lawn fertilizer with weed control, (d) a radio station, (e) a moving company, (f) a zoo, and (g) a minor league baseball team.
13. What is the principal objective in designing the layout of an ad?
14. What are the differences in the development of television commercials as compared with a magazine ad? Are there any similarities? Explain.
15. What is a storyboard? What is its function?

16. Develop a storyboard for a thirty-second TV commercial asking for a donation of money to the local educational channel.

17. What are some criteria for evaluating a television commercial?

18. Explain the roles of the audio and visual elements of a television commercial.

19. What are the characteristics of a good radio commercial? Explain.

20. The first few seconds of a radio commercial are the most critical. Why?

21. Write a sixty-second radio script for a local hardware store featuring a sale on Sherwin-Williams interior house paint.

22. Assume that you currently have a successful television commercial over the airwaves and you are buying radio time. Someone on your staff has suggested: "We can save money. Let's simply put the audio track of the TV commercial onto tape and use it for radio." What do you think of the idea? What are the benefits? What are the limitations?

23. What are the major components of a direct mail package?

24. What similarities and differences do you see between the rules for good ad copy and an effective direct mail package?

25. What functions does an envelope serve in direct mail?

26. What are the characteristics of a good letter in direct mail advertising?

27. As a rule of thumb, copy for outdoor advertising is readable in eight seconds or less. Is this a good rule of thumb? Why or why not?

28. You are the president of a local insurance agency and are trying to increase your business. You decide to use direct mail. Write a direct mail letter in which you want the recipient to telephone one of your agents for an appointment to discuss insurance. (You do not possess any significant differential advantage over your competitors.)

29. How would you describe the importance of creativity in advertising? Be specific.

NOTES

1. "Goal of New Product Commercials Is to Make Brand Name Memorable," *Marketing News*, January 23, 1981, p. 5.

2. Richard Lutz, "A Functional Theory Framework for Designing and Pretesting Advertising Themes," in *Contemporary Perspectives in Consumer Research*, ed. Richard Lutz (Boston: Kent Publishing, 1981), pp. 295–304.

3. Andrew Mitchell and Jerry C. Olson, "Are Product Attribute Beliefs the Only Mediator of Advertising Effects on Brand Attitudes?" *Journal of Marketing Research*, August 1981, pp. 318–32.

4. "Marketing Emphasis Is on Consistent Imagery When Selling Beer: Stroh Exec," *Marketing News*, March 4, 1983, p. 10; and John Rossiter and Larry Percy, "Attitude Change Through Imagery," *Journal of Advertising*, 9, No. 2 (1980), 10–16.

5. Jack Trout and Al Ries, "The Positioning Era Cometh," *Advertising Age*, April 24, 1972, pp. 35–38; Trout and Ries, "Positioning Cuts Through Chaos in the Marketplace," *Advertising Age*, May 1, 1972, pp. 51–54; Trout and Ries, "How to Position Your Product," *Advertising Age*, May 8, 1972, pp. 114–16; and Trout and Ries, "The Positioning Era: A View Ten Years Later," *Advertising Age*, July 16, 1979, pp. 39ff.

6. Julian Simon, *The Management of Advertising* (Englewood Cliffs, N.J.: Prentice-Hall, 1971), pp. 169–85.

7. For more information on the use of fear appeals, see Irving Janis and Seymour Feshback, "Effects of Fear-Arousing Communications," *Journal of Abnormal and Social Psychology*, January 1953, pp. 78–92; Michael Ray and William L. Wilkie, "Fear: The Potential of an Appeal Neglected by Marketing," *Journal of Marketing*, January 1970, pp. 54–62; John Stuteville, "Psychic Defenses against High Fear Appeals: A Key Marketing Variable, *Journal of Marketing*, April 1970, pp. 39–45; Brian Sternthal and C. Samuel Craig, "Fear Appeals: Revisited and Revised," *Journal of Consumer Research*, December 1974, pp. 22–34; and Michael Ray, *Advertising and Communication Management* (Englewood Cliffs, N.J.: Prentice-Hall, 1982), pp. 313–14.

8. For more information on humor, see Mervin Lynch and Richard Hartman, "Dimensions of Humor in Advertising," *Journal of Advertising Research*, December 1968, pp. 39–45; Brian Sternthal and C. Samuel Craig, "Humor in Advertising," *Journal of Marketing*, October 1973, pp. 12–18; Thomas Madden and Marc Weinberger, "The Effects of Humor on Attention Getting in Magazine Advertising," *Journal of Advertising*, 11, No. 3 (1982), 8–14; Betsy Gelb and Charles Patti, "Attitude-toward-the-Ad: Links to Humor and Advertising Effectiveness," *Journal of Advertising*, 12, No. 2 (1983), 34–42; "Humor Is Best Utilized with Established Products," *Marketing News*, September 17, 1982, p. 6; and Melvin Helitzer, "Humor Needs to Hit Home—But Not too Hard," *Advertising Age*, January 14, 1985, p. 36.

9. Hooper White, "Has the Tide Run Out on the New Wave?" *Advertising Age*, March 7, 1983, pp. M4ff.

10. Kenneth Roman and Jane Maas, *How to Advertise* (New York: St. Martin's Press, 1976), p. 31.

11. Al Ries and Jack Trout, "The Eye vs. the Ear," *Advertising Age*, March 14, 1983, pp. M27–M28.

12. Nancy Millman, "Product Claims Not Believable," *Advertising Age*, March 5, 1984, pp. 1ff.

13. William Bearden, Robert Headen, Jay Klompmaker, and Jesse Teel, "Attentive Audience Delivery of TV Advertising Schedules," *Journal of Marketing Research*, May 1981, pp. 187–91.

14. Roman and Maas, *How to Advertise*, p. 3.

15. Ries and Trout, "The Eye," p. M28.

16. Kenneth Runyon, *Advertising and the Practice of Marketing* (Columbus, Ohio: Charles E. Merrill, 1979), pp. 279–80.

17. Roman and Maas, *How to Advertise*, pp. 49–55.

18. David Ogilvy, *Confessions of an Advertising Man* (New York: Dell Pub. Co., 1963), p. 116.

19. Ray, *Advertising and Communication Management*, p. 312.

11

Personal
Selling

In sales offices across the land, the immortal phrase "Nothing happens in this country until someone sells something" blazes forth from plaques, paperweights, note pads, and other office accouterments. Yet, in this era of self-service shopping, persuasive television advertising, and sophisticated direct mail techniques, some people overlook the vital role of personal selling in an effective promotional campaign.

In this and the following two chapters we will discuss the key elements of selling and sales management that should be a part of any comprehensive and cohesive sales strategy. This chapter covers the activities, process, and self-management aspects of personal selling. Chapter 12 takes up the development of sales strategy, and Chapter 13 concentrates on the execution of the sales strategy.

ROLE OF PERSONAL SELLING

Personal selling is a highly selective form of communications that permits the marketer to tailor a persuasive message to the specific needs of an individual buyer or buying influence. It adapts to the changing circumstances of both buyer and seller, and it fosters an interaction between the parties that leads to an effective and timely resolution of a perceived buying need. In essence, it is a promotional activity that focuses on a target market of one buyer and then nurtures and encourages a rapid transition from problem recognition to purchase action.

The significance of personal selling to the marketer is widely acknowledged. It is an active effort to communicate with high-potential buyers on a direct, usually face-to-face, basis. The quotation at the beginning of this chapter expresses this idea. On the other side of it, some observers fail to recognize the importance of personal selling to the *buyer*. Salespeople are a vital source of information to various individuals contemplating a purchase. In an industrial setting the salesperson is a valuable and credible source of information to purchasing, engineering, or manufacturing personnel who make buying decisions.[1] Even as consumers we depend on salespeople to provide key information to assist us in making purchase decisions. Can you imagine buying a new car, washing machine, or living room couch without a lengthy, information-gathering discussion with one or more salespeople? Of course not!

The role of personal selling in promotional strategy varies widely from industry to industry and from firm to firm. IBM, marketing computers to large and medium-size companies, places preeminent emphasis on its personal-selling activities. The IBM salesperson and technical support team invest a considerable amount of time helping the customer. They help define the company's information needs, develop a suitable system configuration, define the software required, identify the facility specifications, and in general hold the customer's hand through a series of complex business and technical decisions. Other marketers of computers and similarly complex systems seek to do the same thing. Yet the recent introduction of less-expensive microcomputer systems for small businesses and professionals has changed the role of personal selling, with additional emphasis now on advertising and other mass-communications methods.

Conversely, the promotional strategies of Procter & Gamble, Gillette, and other marketers of well-known consumer products include heavy advertising expenditures, but they also put forward an important personal-selling effort. One part of the sales force calls on the national and regional headquarters of major supermarket and drug chains to introduce new products, to gain support for planned promotional programs, and to ensure continuing purchases of established items. Another part of the sales force provides assistance in the store by checking inventories, setting up displays, stocking shelves, and otherwise building goodwill and support among the store personnel.

As we have previously noted, the role of personal selling or any of the other three promotional elements is a function of a number of factors in the product-market environment as well as the characteristics of the firm itself. It is important to remember this as we relate the various types of selling activities to the business environment where they most frequently appear.

SELLING ACTIVITIES

There are two ways of viewing the selling activities of salespeople—by the customer served and by the sales task performed. We will look at both classifications in some detail to show the nature and scope of personal selling.

Type of Customer

While the emphasis in previous chapters has clearly been on consumer marketing, we must recognize other types of customers here and in subsequent sections of this chapter, particularly because so much of personal selling involves contact with prospects and users other than individual consumers. There are four categories of customers: trade, organizational, professional, and individual. Traditionally, salespeople serve only one of these types, since each requires a somewhat different kind of selling effort. Let us examine each to see the nature of its sales effort.

Trade

Most sales organizations established by manufacturers of consumer products aim at the trade—the buying offices of wholesale and retail outlets that currently carry or could carry the manufacturer's product line. Note that *trade* buyers are not purchasing products for their own use but are selecting items they think their clientele wants. In effect, they are resellers.

The competition for shelf space in major retail outlets is fierce, with so many more brands and sizes of merchandise being offered than can possibly be carried by any particular supermarket, drugstore, discount store, or department store. As a result, the company salesperson calling on buyers and merchandising managers has several responsibilities, among them to

> Maintain or improve the purchase level and support given to the company's products
>
> Persuade retail outlets to stock the company's new products

Solicit support for various company promotional programs

Keep track of competitive activity

Many of the larger consumer goods companies also maintain a retail sales organization (sometimes called missionary sales force) that calls on retail outlets. These individuals are responsible for ensuring that the store inventories and shelf stocks are adequate, the displays are properly set up and maintained, and the store personnel are actively supportive of the programs agreed to by the central buying office.

Together, these two separate sales organizations seek to ensure that the company receives sufficient support at all organizational levels among the retail outlets with which it does business. When we realize that the average supermarket today carries from six to eight thousand items, gaining and maintaining trade support for a few dozen selected products is not a routine task.

Industrial (Organizational) Buyers

Sales organizations directed toward *industrial* or *organizational* customers deal with purchasing agents, engineers, manufacturing managers, and other company personnel, who collectively make purchases for the organization's own use. The selling effort requires contact with several buying influences at multiple levels within the organization.[2] This forces the salesperson to be knowledgeable in the technical, operational, and economic aspects of the product offering. He or she must also be able to identify and respond to quite diverse buying needs. The buyers tend to be sophisticated and professional in their buying practices, and to be effective, the sales organization must match these capabilities. This area of selling is the most creative, most professionally demanding, and most rewarding.

Professionals

Salespeople who have *professionals* (doctors, architects, lawyers, accountants) as customers have a different sales responsibility. They must relate to these individuals, not as users or even purchasers for resale, but as specifiers or influencers of buying decisions. Drug company representatives (known as detailers in the trade), who call on doctors and distribute samples of new prescription drugs, seek to influence physicians in their role as specifiers. These representatives hope to encourage doctors to prescribe the particular drug for their patients. In addition, the pharmaceutical companies have a separate sales organization that calls on the trade (drug wholesalers and drugstores) with activities similar to those we described in the trade section. Architects are specifiers in the construction industry, though their influence may be modified by the interests and actions of consulting engineers and general contractors, as well as subcontractors. Selling to professionals requires a strong problem-solving orientation, a professional presence, and an ability to sustain personal motivation while awaiting longer-term results.

Individual Consumers

The selling environments for *individual* consumers are of two types: retail selling and direct selling (often referred to as door to door). We are all familiar with department store sales clerks, whose functions are primarily service oriented: Find the desired merchandise, assist with selection and fit, write up the order, and generally facilitate the purchase. The persuasive aspects of selling are barely present. Contrast this with the automobile or appliance salesperson, who places much greater emphasis on promoting the sale of a particular item or brand. The service aspects are still present and important, but the persuasive element is much more prominent. Retail selling tends to be passive, dependent on the customer's coming to the store and requesting sales assistance, rather than the salesperson's seeking out the prospective customer, as in the following situation.

Direct selling—Avon, Fuller Brush, encyclopedia publishers, life insurance companies, and many other marketers of consumer goods and services—is anything but passive. Direct salespeople aggressively seek out opportunities to make presentations to individuals and families in their homes and offices. Cold canvassing, advertising lead follow-up, and referral solicitations are the standard practices of the direct sales organization.

Consumers are suspicious of direct salespeople. Therefore, in the sales approach, the salesperson must develop a sense of trust within the prospective customer. At the same time, the salesperson very much wants to close the order on a single sales call. Of course, both the customer and the sales representative may feel ambivalence and stress in these circumstances. Salespeople in this field are good problem identifiers and solvers, strong sales closers, and highly self-motivated.

Sales Tasks

We can gain another perspective on the nature of sales activities by exploring the sales tasks performed, which fall into three categories.

Creative Selling

Creative selling or problem solving means that the salesperson identifies the buyer's needs and determines how the company's products can best serve those needs. Sometimes the customer does not clearly understand the need and the salesperson must identify and define it. At other times the problem is clear, but the alternative solutions are not apparent. In these environments the salesperson is a consultant, bringing specialized knowledge to bear on a client's problem. Salespeople calling on industrial and professional customers require these capabilities most frequently. Will a new integrated circuit design be less expensive or more reliable than the existing one? What formulation of adhesive will maintain the bond when the materials joined are placed under great heat and pressure? What type of grinding wheel will provide a high production rate and longer service cycles?

Service Selling

Service sales tasks, as mentioned earlier, accompany retail selling; however, similar activities can arise in other sales environments. Order preparation and processing, expediting, and arranging financing and credit are also important functions serving trade and industrial accounts. In many highly competitive fields (like printing) the service aspects are often crucial in obtaining and retaining customers. Wholesale sales organizations also attend to service tasks. The products, brands, and prices of competitive distributors are frequently the same, and only service factors distinguish between suppliers.

Missionary Selling

The manufacturer's *missionary* salesperson provides assistance to the company's direct customers (wholesale distributors) by supplying product information and support to its indirect customers (retailers). Missionary or support sales activities do not typically obtain immediate orders. They do, however, lay the groundwork for sustaining present business and developing future orders. The Merck representative, contacting physicians at Massachusetts General Hospital, is educating an important buying influence. The Alcoa salesperson and technical service representative making presentations to Ford designers about aluminum alloys perform essential missionary work; they are looking toward expanding their potential in the automotive market. A Spalding sales representative may call on sporting goods retailers and try to persuade them to order Spalding brand baseball gloves, tennis racquets, and golf clubs from the manufacturer's local distributor. The retail sales representative from Keebler, setting up and price marking an end-aisle display in the local supermarket, is also performing important support functions.

Support or missionary effort is an important part of any overall sales strategy. Some companies establish a separate sales organization to perform these functions; others incorporate these responsibilities into the tasks of a single sales force. The organizational form may vary, but the opportunities to provide substantial support for the selling effort are ever-present.

Recognizing that selling activities encompass many different aspects, the actual process of personal selling looms large. It is through the selling process that the tasks and responsibilities of the salesperson come to life. We now turn to the action part of personal selling.

SELLING PROCESS

Personal selling involves a sequential process that applies to all types of selling tasks and to all classes of customers. It is so basic to the function of selling that it has been dubbed "the anatomy of a sale." It is not only a valid conceptualization of the selling process but also a prescription for effective sales performance. Exhibit 11-1 shows the seven steps of the selling process: generating leads, qualifying the prospect, determining the buying influences, planning the presentation, making the presentation, consummating the sale, and following up. These seven steps, as the left column of

EXHIBIT 11-1 Anatomy of a Sale

	Step	Elements
Prospecting	Generating Leads	— Cold Canvass — Advertising — Referrals
	Qualifying the Prospect	— Need — Motivation — Ability to Pay — Eligibility to Buy
Planning	Determining the Buying Influences	— Influences — Spectrums — Users — Buyers
	Planning the Presentation	— Information Gathering — Information Evaluation — Information Organization
Presenting	The Presentation	— Approach — Problem Definition — Demonstration — Handling Objections — Close
Processing	Consummating the Sale	Action
	Following up	Servicing the Customer

Exhibit 11-1 shows, encompass four types of activities: prospecting, planning, presenting, and processing. Despite the obvious comparison with the now famous four *p*'s of marketing management, these elements do represent the major subtasks of the selling effort. Let us now look at each of the seven steps.

Generating Leads

The lifeblood of any selling effort is an ongoing source of new prospective customers. There is an attrition among existing customers over time, so new buyers must emerge to maintain and expand the customer base if the salesperson hopes to sustain or improve sales performance.

There is a subtle yet important distinction between suspects (leads) and prospects. A *suspect*, or *lead*, is someone who might buy; a *prospect* is someone who can or will buy from you or another supplier. Since a salesperson's time is limited and valuable, he or she must distinguish prospects from suspects as quickly as possible. We call this activity *qualifying prospects*, and we will discuss it in more detail later. Leads can come from any number of specific sources (telephone canvassing, directories, media advertising, customer referrals, friends, and so on), but these individual sources actually

EXHIBIT 11-2 Sources of Leads

```
Cold Canvass
  Door to door
  Telephone
  General directories
    Telephone Yellow Pages
    Thomas Register of American Manufacturers
    Standard and Poor's
    Dun & Bradstreet—Million Dollar Directory
  Trade directories
  Mailing lists
Inquiries from Advertising and Other Mass Communications
  Media advertising
  Direct mail
  New-product announcements
  News stories and publicity
  Contests and sweepstakes
  Coupon redemptions
Referrals
  Existing customers
  Personal contacts (business associates, friends, neighbors, professional as-
  sociations, etc.)
```

constitute three general categories of lead sources: cold canvassing, advertising and related forms of mass communication, and referrals. Exhibit 11-2 lists some of the more common sources of leads within each of the three major categories. Let us look at each of these sources to see where and how salespeople use them to develop suspects.

Cold Canvassing

Cold canvassing involves personal contact with every potential customer in a given territory, face to face or by phone. The Avon lady and the Fuller Brush salesperson canvass every house and apartment in the neighborhood; the semiconductor salesperson, using an electronics trade directory, contacts the purchasing department of every manufacturer of electronic equipment listed in the territory; the circulation department of the local newspaper calls every listing in the phone book, soliciting new subscriptions. These approaches to lead generation are time consuming and expensive. Do they make sense? The answer is frequently yes. Every firm or individual could have become a customer. In addition, the salesperson applies whatever external criteria or characteristics there are to narrow the scope of the canvass. Finally, no additional information is available to separate prospects from suspects.

Inquiries from Advertising and Other Mass Communications

In many sales situations, the number of potential customers is large, but the number of immediate prospects is a small percentage of that total. In these environments, canvassing is a costly and inefficient way of zeroing in on the most likely suspects. *Inquiries* from mass communications of all types (media advertising, direct mail, new-product announcements) are an effective means of narrowing the search. Individuals who respond to inquiries are identifying themselves as more serious potential buyers of the product. This natural self-selection helps the salesperson in planning and using the available prospecting time. It also provides a strong rationale for the initial sales call.

Referrals

Referrals are another form of prospecting that both narrows the search and provides a suitable opening for the first sales call. There are many sources of referrals (see Exhibit 11-2), but the most effective are satisfied customers. Insurance salespeople soon learn why it is important to solicit referrals from all of their customers and prospects. The greatest strength of a referral is that the prospect does not feel that he or she is dealing with a stranger. After all, the contact came by way of a mutual friend or acquaintance. In buying situations where the "perceived risk" of the buyer is high (professional services, major household items, and so on), a referral can be important in reducing the risk sufficiently to permit a decision to purchase.

Qualifying the Prospects

As we noted earlier, a salesperson's time is finite and valuable. The salesperson must determine as quickly as possible whether a suspect is in fact a prospective customer. This determination is called qualifying the prospect. There are four criteria to apply in the qualification process: the existence of the need or want, the ability to buy, the motivation to buy, and the eligibility to buy. If all four are not met, then the potential customer is still a suspect, not a prospect. Let us now briefly examine each of these criteria.

Existence of Need

The *existence of need* is paramount in all marketing activities. Salespeople and other marketers do not create needs; the needs already exist, in theory, though some customers may not recognize them until a promotional effort effects such awareness. If a need for the particular product or service offering is not evident to the salesperson, then he or she might better invest time and energy on more fruitful opportunities.

In industrial markets, some prescreening can be done by identifying standard industry classifications (SICs) where historical usage patterns have been strong. In addition, an initial sales interview will often gather more-detailed information. In many consumer markets (e.g., cosmetics, household wares), the need is widespread with virtually all households meeting the qualifying criteria.

Ability to Buy

Ability to buy is also crucial if the selling effort is going to produce a sale. It is important that the potential customer have the financial means to make the purchase. This can be in the form of either ready cash or, in today's economy, available credit. The purchase of a house, an automobile, or other major buying commitment depends essentially on the availability of credit at a reasonable interest rate. In recent times, even the most credit-worthy buyers have occasionally had difficulty securing home mortgages or new-car loans on acceptable terms.

In an industrial setting, the ability to buy may have less to do with means to pay and more to do with available budget. Purchase requirements not included in budgetary planning may face delay or even elimination because of budget considerations.

Credit agencies, Dun & Bradstreet reports, and the like, are valuable sources of financial information. Often, the salesperson makes a direct inquiry of the prospect to discover whether the budgetary or financial status sanctions a purchase.

Motivation to Buy

Since every buying decision competes with a vast array of alternative uses of the financial resources, the *degree of motivation* toward any particular purchase is a vital qualification. The new-car shopper who needs hundreds of dollars of repair work on his or her present car is a highly motivated prospect. The shopper with a two-year old vehicle in mint condition may not be. The salesperson who can underscore the importance of making the decision today may enhance motivation.

The classic mousetrap story emphasizes this and the previous points. To sell a better mousetrap, we must first find buyers who meet the three qualifications of need, means, and motivation. In other words, the buyers must have *mice*, *money*, and . . . *an intense desire to kill*.

Eligibility to Buy

Eligibility to buy means that the buyer meets the distribution policy requirements of the seller. For example, most manufacturers of consumer goods distribute through wholesalers or retailers or both. A private individual seeking to buy products directly from the manufacturer or even from the wholesale outlet would not be eligible and, therefore, would not qualify as a prospect. In the furniture business, showrooms exist in major geographical markets, but only retailers or professional decorators may purchase through these outlets. Sometimes a manufacturer will sell only through authorized dealers (retailers) who meet certain criteria of operation. Other (nonauthorized) retailers may not purchase from the manufacturer no matter how desirable the order may seem.

The effective salesperson will seek to qualify a suspect (lead) as a legitimate prospect before investing significant time, energy, or financial resources in further sales efforts. Sometimes the salesperson can do this without a personal contact; sometimes it is the main goal of the initial sales call; and sometimes it is the opening thrust of a major sales presentation. Regardless of how or when, the salesperson should make this qualifying determination as early in the selling process as possible.

Determining the Buying Influences

The determination of buying influences is critical to an effective personal-selling process. Most marketers recognize that a salesperson, selling integrated circuits to electronic equipment manufacturers, for example, has many buying influences to persuade before a sale can be consummated. The engineer who is designing the equipment specifies the type of circuit and the technical characteristics of that circuit. The purchasing agent or buyer determines the qualifications of vendors to meet the technical and volume requirements and negotiates the price and delivery terms. The manufacturing manager defines the packaging of the circuit, the product acceptance procedures, and the inventory levels for the supplier's plant. Each of these individuals is an important influence on the buying decision. Their buying criteria and areas of concern will probably vary because their roles in the buying process vary.[3] The manufacturing managers and supervisors are involved as *users* of the product. The purchasing agents participate as *buyers* of the product. The engineers contribute as *specifiers* of the product. The treasurer or controller may also be a *buying influence* if the financial commitment is large.

Buying decisions made by individual consumers and households are also subject to multiple buying influences. In some personal buying, the individual performs all the roles; in others, the buyer may lean toward the opinions of other people (a man selects a suit that his wife or girlfriend will like). In still others, the individual may act as purchasing agent for the family or a family member and therefore shares the buying decision. The mother selecting cereal for her children considers their preferences as well as her own in making a choice.

Thus an important part of the selling effort consists of obtaining answers to three key questions:

> Who are the buying influences?
> What is the role of each in the buying decision?
> What decision criteria will each be using?

Planning the Presentation

Planning is a vital yet frequently underdeveloped phase of the selling process.[4] An industrial salesperson selling a complex machine tool or a comprehensive office system may spend many days planning the presentation; a salesperson selling encyclopedias directly to consumers may do most of the planning on the walk to the front door. Most sales situations lie somewhere between these extremes. At its root, planning involves the gathering, evaluating, and organizing of information essential to making an effective sales presentation.

In an industrial environment, the information falls into three classes: the prospect's business, the buying influences as individuals, and the competition (direct or indirect). Exhibit 11-3 identifies the more important detailed information in each area.

EXHIBIT 11-3 Information Needed in the Industrial Selling Environment

ABOUT COMPETITION				ABOUT THE CUSTOMER'S BUSINESS	ABOUT THE CUSTOMER AS AN INDIVIDUAL
Direct competition			*Indirect competition*		
Who	ABC Co.	DEF Co.	RAT Co.		

Who

- How much
- Trend: up, down, no change
- The salesman
  Call patterns
  Strategies
  Entertaining
- District Sales Manager
  Who he calls on
  Frequency
- Location of the nearest office
- Service
- Pricing
- Product

Indirect competition

- Here enumerate the possible alternatives being offered to customer which, if accepted, may decrease his interest in our offering

ABOUT THE CUSTOMER'S BUSINESS

- Organizational
- Technological
- Financial
- Marketing
- Policies, procedures, buying patterns

ABOUT THE CUSTOMER AS AN INDIVIDUAL

For each customer individual having any influence on decisions re our offerings:

- What is he like?
- What are his patterns of behavior?
- How does he perceive, think, respond?
- What seems to be his set of needs, motives, or personal aspirations?

1. Purchasing agent
2. Chief engineer
3. Plant manager
4. Etc.

Source: George Downing, *Sales Management*. Copyright © 1969 John Wiley & Sons, Inc., p. 108. Reprinted by permission of John Wiley & Sons, Inc.

To the extent that the salesperson has qualified the prospects and determined the buying influences, as we discussed earlier, important aspects of the evaluation have taken place. In addition, it is essential to weigh the advantages and disadvantages of both the salesperson's product and competitive products in satisfying the prospect's needs. With this insight, the salesperson organizes the actual presentation to emphasize strengths and to overcome or minimize weaknesses. The salesperson should also assess the value of obtaining the prospect's business.

The final element of the planning effort is the organization of the information leading to the development of the presentation. The significant questions that the salesperson addresses include the following:

> Who will attend the presentation?
> What customer benefit or benefits will receive emphasis?
> What visual aids will one need?
> What sales aids and support materials are required?

Making the Presentation

The presentation is the high point of the selling process. It is here that the salesperson translates the prospecting and the planning into sales results. The presentation may be highly structured ("canned"), as in direct selling of simple consumer products, or flexible, tailored to the individual prospect's needs in a problem-solving sales environment. In either case, an organized presentation will contain five steps: the approach, the problem definition, the demonstration, handling objections, and the close. Through these steps the prospect moves logically to a purchase decision. Let us examine each of these steps, keeping in mind that clarity is a key ingredient in every part of the presentation. Unless clarity of content is achieved, buyer confusion and a reluctance to purchase can develop.[5]

The Approach

The *approach* serves two vital purposes.[6] The first is to create an environment of trust and empathy between the prospect and the salesperson. It is important that the prospect view the salesperson as a friend and adviser who will help the prospect solve problems and fulfill needs. The second is to gain the prospect's interest and to present a compelling reason for investing time and mental energy in listening to the presentation. Most professional salespeople contend that the first thirty seconds of a sales interview are critical in accomplishing these objectives. Exhibit 11-4 lists a few of the many techniques of the approach.

EXHIBIT 11-4   Typical Approaches and Examples for a Sales Presentation of Security Systems

TECHNIQUE	EXAMPLE
Ask a question	"Have you suffered unexplained inventory losses in your stockroom?"
Give the buyer some information	"Over $20 billion a year is lost due to industrial theft."
Demonstrate the product	"See how it works."
Report a case history	"Company X saved $50K in the first year with our system."
Make a provocative statement	"This little sensor can make your stockroom as secure as a bank vault."
Compliment the buyer	"Your plant is so well organized and maintained."
Promise a benefit	"How would you like to make $50K/year on a $10K investment?"
Make a personal comment	"I personally feel this is the best system available."
Offer some service	"Would you like me to send you an article on stopping inventory theft in factories?"
Arouse curiosity	"I have a piece of metal worth $50K in my shirt pocket, but I'm not afraid of being held up."

The Problem Definition

At this point in the presentation the salesperson is seeking to *identify the prospect's specific problem* or need and the particular benefit or benefits of the product or service that are most appealing. This is called finding the "hot button."[7] One effective technique for accomplishing this is to ask questions and to listen carefully to the answers. Another technique is to have the salesperson make a general statement of the problem and solicit the prospect's viewpoint. Getting the prospect to discuss his or her perception of the particular problem area or need is an essential step in defining the problem.

Both of these methods have the advantage of involving the prospect in the presentation, putting the salesperson in the role of problem solver and adviser, while communicating to the prospect that one values his or her views and opinions. With these feelings established and the specific problem and benefits now on the surface, the salesperson can proceed to the demonstration well prepared.

The Demonstration

In the *demonstration*, the salesperson offers the product as fulfilling the need and realizing the benefits identified earlier. It is the phase in which the salesperson either makes the sale or not. To achieve the desired result, the salesperson must powerfully and cogently present the benefits of the product or service. Products and services vary, but effective demonstrations have certain important characteristics in common.[8] First, they communicate through as many of the five senses as possible, particularly seeing and hearing. Show *and* tell together are more than three times as effective in communicating as either show *or* tell alone. Second, they concentrate on a *few* dominant appeals that focus on the major benefits of this product for this prospect. A few powerful ideas are more persuasive and easier to recall than a large number of less compelling ones. Third, they use drama and showmanship in demonstrating the benefits and features of the product or service. For example, the strength of a material can be better shown by trying to stretch, tear, or cut it than by statements or specifications of tensile strength. A seller of shatterproof glass might use a hammer (or, better yet, allow the prospect to use it) to whack a glass sample and thereby vividly demonstrate the shatterproof feature. Fourth, they draw the prospect closer to the product. Providing samples to inspect or test, offering use of the product (e.g., test-driving a car), and providing scale models or replicas to prospects are some of the ways to encourage involvement.

Handling Objections

Prospects raise *objections* because they are anxious about making a buying decision. They perceive that the risk of making an affirmative decision is greater than the risk of a deferred or negative one.

For the salesperson, the raising of an objection by a prospective customer is twofold. On the one hand, it is clearly a barrier to the sale, and unless it can be dealt with effectively the salesperson will lose the sale. On the other hand, it identifies the specific issue or issues that the salesperson must resolve for the prospect to enable him or her to buy.

Most salespeople consider the handling of objections an integral part of closing the sale. From experience and training, the salesperson can anticipate the objections that will probably arise. The salesperson can raise and answer these questions himself or herself in the course of the presentation and thereby nullify them as barriers to the sale. To do this, of course, requires planning and preparation.

The salesperson should respond to the objections a prospect raises.

Ignoring or deferring them implies that the salesperson cannot answer the objections. Failure to respond to an objection keeps the prospect's attention focused on the objection rather than on the rest of the salesperson's presentation.

Objections fall into five general categories representing the five major buying decisions a prospect must make in the affirmative before a sale can be made. These are need, product, source, price, and time. Exhibit 11-5 gives examples of these types of objections.

EXHIBIT 11-5   Types of Objections (Washing Machine Purchase)

TYPE	EXAMPLE
Need	"My old washing machine still gives good service."
Product	"This model doesn't have an automatic dispenser for fabric softener."
Source	"Will your store provide any warranty service I need or will I have to call the factory?"
Price	"$350 seems like a lot of money."
Time	"I think we can hold off for a few more weeks until the new models come out."

The techniques for handling objections appear prominently in salesmanship texts and professional sales-training programs.[9] There are four common techniques for handling objections: convert the objection, third-party stories, the boomerang, and comparisons. Let us look at each of them.

Convert the objection. This approach involves rephrasing the statement of objection into a question to which the salesperson can readily respond. If the prospect raises an issue about the price, the salesperson converts it into a question of value for the benefits of the product. An objection to a product's feature becomes a statement of the problem the feature solves with alternative solutions as well.

Third-party stories. This technique, as the name implies, refers the prospect to third parties (other customers) who have had similar concerns, and it then describes the solutions that they arrived at to resolve the questions. This focuses the prospect's attention on the decision of others in similar circumstances, not on the salesperson's solution.

The boomerang. This method requires the salesperson to take the objection and convert it into a benefit for the customer. An objection centered on the need for the product can be changed into the benefits of financial savings, convenience, pleasure, and the like.

Comparisons. This approach requires discretion, since the salesperson should not demean a competitor or a competitor's products. It is most effective when a prospect first mentions the competing product. Here the salesperson has an invitation to make the comparison. A highly effective procedure for showing the comparison is a side-by-side listing on paper of the features and benefits of the salesperson's product versus the competitor's. The salesperson does have some choice as to the best characteristics for this analysis.

An overview of these procedures reveals four basic principles applicable to all selling environments: (1) listen carefully and attentively to the prospect's objection and be sure to give the prospect's viewpoint a full, complete, and respectful hearing; (2) determine exactly what the objection means, by tactful questioning or by restating the objection in different words, thereby isolating the specific concern; (3) prepare the prospect to receive new information or evidence without the prospect's feeling threatened or losing self-esteem; and (4) do not argue with or directly contradict the prospect, because the objective is to make the sale, not win a debate.

Closing the Sale

The close is the final stage of the sales presentation and should flow naturally as a logical continuation of it. C. Robert Patty defines the *close* as follows:

> What is a close? A close is a question or action by the salesperson intended to evoke a favorable decision from the prospect. The decision may be a signed order, or in more sophisticated situations, it may be some preliminary decision, such as permission to have the product tested under actual use conditions or to make a survey. A close is not a high-pressure tactic or a magic panacea for rescuing an otherwise lost sale.[10]

Closing is necessary because prospects, despite their desire to buy, are ambivalent about the decision. They want the advantages and benefits of the product, but they may also be fearful that the purchase involves risks or that buying this item means forgoing something else.

Salespeople themselves are not immune to doubt, and they may be reluctant to close for fear of rejection. The experienced salesperson recognizes that on average there will be more noes than yesses. He or she builds emotional defenses against despair and learns not to take the rejection personally.

One useful way for salespeople to improve their closing effectiveness is to recognize closing clues communicated by prospects. These clues suggest a readiness to buy and can be either verbal or nonverbal. Verbal clues can be in the form of questions or comments, such as "What about installation?" "How long is the guarantee?" "I need to have it by next week." "The smaller unit would fit better."

Nonverbal signals are also important. Facial expressions are good indicators of attitudes. Belief or approval revealed by head nodding or a smile are valuable clues. Other physical actions such as handling and reading the contract, carefully examining the product, and performing calculations on scratch paper are also tip-offs to the prospect's mental state. The salesperson who uses these clues to determine when to initiate a close will undoubtedly encounter a more receptive and responsive prospect.

There are many successful closing techniques that salespeople have used over the years.[11] Though numerous variations exist, closes fall into five major groups: the direct close, the assumptive close, the summative close, the negative close, and the special concession.

The direct close. The direct close, as the name implies, is a straightforward request for the order. It is effective with decisive buyers who have received the presentation in a positive manner. Expressions such as "Shall I write up your order for ten cases?" or "Shall I have the tailor fit this for you?" are typical of this approach.

The assumptive close. The assumptive close is similar to the direct close in that it moves on the assumption that the prospect has decided to buy. This is particularly successful with indecisive or insecure buyers. Typically, this approach presents the prospect with a choice on a minor decision: "Will this be cash or charge?" "Shall I have it delivered Tuesday or Wednesday?" "Shall I put it in a bag or will you wear it?" Other assumptive derivations may involve asking the prospect what quantity he or she would like or giving the prospect the order form to sign.

The summative close. In the summative close (also called "numerous agreements"), the salesperson summarizes the benefits and recapitulates the points of agreement, touching all key elements of the decision and leaving nothing for the prospect except to commit to the purchase. A related technique is the *single-obstacle* approach. The salesperson seeks to get agreement on all points except one and then obtains the prospect's concurrence that if that point can be settled, the prospect will buy. The salesperson then works to overcome the one remaining obstacle and close the sale.

The negative close. The negative close (also known as "standing room only") attempts to put pressure on the buyer to decide now, based on some imminent negative event, an impending price increase, perhaps, or an inventory shortage. The salesperson must be careful with this close because it may increase the buyer's tension. Furthermore, the negative event must be real or the salesperson loses credibility with the customer. It is effective with prospects who are or who seem to be procrastinating.

The special concession close. In the special concession close, the salesperson offers an inducement—price concession, free merchandise, special allowance—to motivate the prospect to act now. It is a pressure close similar to the negative close. It is risky, however, as special deals and concessions may become a habit for the salesperson and repeat customers may expect them routinely.

Completing the Sale

Despite the prospect's strong affirmative response to a close, the sale may not be complete just yet. There are usually several administrative steps that the salesperson must fulfill as well, such as the following:

1. Completing the order forms or contracts, including detailed descriptions and specifications where appropriate
2. Obtaining authorized signatures of customers and company representatives on purchase orders where appropriate
3. Receiving necessary deposits from the customer
4. Arranging for financing and completion of financial paperwork
5. Forwarding the total paperwork package to the home office for approval and processing
6. Returning copies of approved paperwork to the customer
7. Ensuring that the delivery schedule planned by the factory meets the customer's needs

Some may see these as fairly routine matters; nonetheless, they are often important aspects of the total selling process. Failure to perform these tasks efficiently could result in a contentious, stressful relationship between the buyer and the seller rather than one with mutual satisfaction and benefit.

Follow-Up: Servicing the Customer

The principal objective of any sale is the satisfaction of a customer need. Professional salespeople realize they have not achieved this goal until the customer receives and successfully uses the product or service. To ensure this, the salesperson tracks the order in the company, keeps the customer advised of progress, participates in the delivery, installation, and training process, and provides fast and accurate responses to any customer questions or complaints. With this service effort, the salesperson keeps the customer sold and builds a solid relationship for future business or referrals.

IMPROVING SALES PERFORMANCE

Salespeople, more than most other business professionals, are measured and rewarded by results. It is therefore important for the individual salesperson to seek out ways to improve sales performance. Four areas of concentration are most productive: building customer relations, increasing selling skills, developing personal attributes, and exercising self-management. Let us examine them.

Building Customer Relations

In business environments where one anticipates an ongoing relationship between the customer and the salesperson, the establishing and building of sound customer relations is paramount. Even in those situations where infrequent dealings are the norm, the value of positive customer relations can be significant. The specific benefits are manifold. Customers return and buy again from salespeople they like and in whom they have confidence. This certainly enhances the salesperson's earnings and recognition within the firm. Favorable words from customers can also enhance the salesperson's reputation in the field. In addition, referrals, testimonials, and other forms of cooperative effort can expand the salesperson's business base.

Given these values, how does a salesperson create and enhance positive customer relations? The salesperson's relationship with customers depends on one basic human ingredient—*trust*. To develop trust, salespeople must deal with their customers in a straightforward, truthful, and dependable manner. They should be considerate and respectful of each customer's preferences and tastes. They should strive to provide efficient and timely service to enhance customer satisfaction. In addition, there has to be an atmosphere of friendliness and concern for the customer's welfare. These efforts are long-term activities that will bear fruit over time. Establishing and expanding positive customer relations is a worthy and valuable task, and there are no shortcuts.

Increasing Selling Skills

The salesperson, like all professionals, should be learning constantly, growing and developing. There are four areas where increased knowledge and insight will enhance the selling skills of the individual salesperson.

Customer Knowledge

Knowledge of the customer is the foundation of successful selling. The more the salesperson understands the customers—their needs and desires, their characteristics such as anxiety, self-esteem, or intelligence (which inhibit or facilitate a sale), their buying habits and motivations, their organization structures, decision process, and buying influences—the more effective and efficient the salesperson becomes.

Customers, particularly organizational buyers, change over time as they introduce new products and eliminate old ones, hire, promote, and dismiss employees, and modify their organization structures to achieve changing company objectives. The successful salesperson keeps up to date on these changes and adjusts selling strategy to the new environment.

Company Knowledge

Knowledge of the company is also a vital ingredient for sales success. Understanding the company's goals and plans, its philosophy and culture, its strengths and limitations, its policies and procedures, and its performance record can be a valuable asset in seeking to fulfill customer needs and expectations.

Just as customer organizations change, so does the salesperson's organization. The salesperson keeps abreast of these developments within his or her own organization in order to use the most up-to-date information to enhance customer satisfaction.

Product Knowledge

Knowledge of the product also contributes to superior sales performance. A thorough knowledge of a product's features and characteristics, its applications and benefits, and its competitive advantages and weaknesses can only enhance the salesperson's role as adviser and problem solver for the customer.

Selling, like all skills, improves with practice and experience. Senior sales personnel can share their insights and perspectives with newer members of the sales team; individuals who have some specialized knowledge about certain types of customers or applications can help others with less experience. The sharing of product knowledge among the members of the sales force is an efficient personnel development technique.

Selling Knowledge

Knowledge about selling is the keystone for all the other elements of sales accomplishment. Uncovering efficient prospecting techniques, developing concrete and concise presentations, handling objections effectively, mastering closing techniques, and providing good follow-up service are some of the selling skill areas that improve sales results.

Achieving selling knowledge is not a one-time task. It evolves as the company's business evolves. Products come and go; competitors enter and leave. Such events place increasing demands on the salesperson to continue to learn and grow. It is not surprising that periodic refresher courses on sales knowledge and techniques are the rule for most organizations.

Developing Personal Attributes

Listening

The stereotype of the salesperson is the glib talker. The successful salesperson, however, is an attentive listener. We do not hear as much about this essential characteristic. We have indicated, at several points throughout this chapter, the value of information to an effective selling effort. One important avenue for information gathering is the sales interview. Skillful questioning, coupled with attentiveness, can produce valuable insights into customer needs, the decision criteria, and the decision process. In addition, buyers develop positive attitudes toward salespeople whose actions indicate a sincere interest in the buyer's problem. Careful listening is a personal skill that the salesperson can learn and develop.

Ego-fulfillment and Empathy

Ego-fulfillment and empathy are attributes that should be in reasonable balance if the salesperson is to attain superior performance. Ego-fulfillment generates the desire that motivates salespeople to win. The satisfaction of getting the order, beating the competition, and persuading the customer to move in one's direction produces that fulfillment. Remaining optimistic— "hanging in" when sales are slow—comes from and reinforces a strong sense of self. The successful salesperson recognizes his or her importance as a knowledgeable problem solver for the customer and will strive to bring the customer to a "proper" point of view. On the other hand, if this attribute dominates the salesperson's personality, the customer's needs will be sacrificed to the salesperson's desires in the transaction, resulting in a less-than-satisfactory relationship.

The balancing attribute, empathy, enables the salesperson to put himself or herself in the customer's position and see the problem or need from that perspective. This capacity empowers the salesperson to understand the customer's constraints and biases, to identify with the customer's reluctance to act, and to find solutions most acceptable to the customer. The salesperson and the buyer then jointly seek a buying solution rather than take part in a combative relationship. As with ego-fulfillment, too much empathy can produce unsatisfactory results: the salesperson allows the buyer to procrastinate or seeks inappropriate compromises or commits the supplier to unrealistic performance.

The developing salesperson seeks his or her own balance between these two motivations—the desire to serve and the desire to win. The outstanding salesperson finds it.

Self-Management

Field salespersons, unlike most other company employees, operate essentially on their own, without the framework of company working hours, a plant or office to attend, or a superior nearby to structure the work or the workday. The field salesperson must personally establish an appropriate time schedule and effort.[12] Obviously this requires substantial self-discipline and significant attention to self-management. The successful salesperson has these attributes and as a result manages that most vital and limited resource, *time*, effectively.[13]

Management, whether of oneself or of an organizational unit, involves four basic elements: analysis, planning, execution, and control. Let us see how salespeople can apply these steps in self-management.

Analysis

The salesperson analyzes the sales territory to determine the number and type of current and potential customers. He or she evaluates each of these customers and prospects with regard to short- and long-term sales potential, products needed, competitive position and activity, buying attitudes and procedures, and the like. With these data, the salesperson assesses the relative importance of accounts and therefore the amount of effort to be spent on each.

Planning

The salesperson is now in a position to plan the daily, weekly, and monthly routing and call patterns. These should reflect both the assessment of the account's value to the salesperson and the firm and the current activity of the customer. This planning should provide time to serve existing accounts, actively pursue new business, and develop new prospects and leads.

Execution

The salesperson then implements the plan as well as possible, makes and keeps appointments for sales interviews, establishes and maintains account contact records, and calls in specialists for support. Occasional diversions arise, of course, because of requirements for service calls, changes in customers' schedules and plans, travel conditions, and other unavoidable occurrences.

Control

Personal sales performance and activities are regularly checked against the plan to identify discrepancies in both directions and to consider remedial or enhancement actions for execution in the ensuing periods.

The most efficient and effective salespeople follow this guideline and improve their performance. Unfortunately, not all who might benefit from the discipline of rigorous self-management employ these procedures. Many operate on an ad hoc basis, responding to the pressure of the moment without adequate consideration of long-term requirements. Experience has shown that this is inadequate. A successful personal-selling effort demands the marriage of two kinds of capabilities—communication and management.

SUMMARY

Personal selling is a major part of the promotional program. We looked at the different kinds of selling tasks: creative selling, service selling, and missionary selling. We saw that selling activities are directed at several different types of customers: trade, industrial, professional, and individual (household) consumers. Personal selling is a highly selective form of communication in that the sales message addresses a specific audience. It is a process involving several stages: generating leads, qualifying prospects, determining the buying influences, planning the presentation, making the presentation, completing the sale, and providing for follow-up after the sale. Finally, we discussed the several factors affecting the overall performance of a salesperson and how to sharpen the skills for successful performance. With this background we now turn to the subject of developing sales strategy, in which the personal-selling function takes on added meaning.

REVIEW AND DISCUSSION QUESTIONS

1. *Compare and contrast personal selling and advertising as means of marketing communications. Under what conditions is each most appropriate?*

2. *The cost per customer contact for advertising is usually a few cents, but the cost per customer contact for personal selling could average well over $100. How then do you justify the extensive use of personal selling by some companies?*

3. *The role of personal selling varies from industry to industry and from firm to firm. Why?*

4. *What are the major categories of customers? Specifically, in what ways does each require a different type of selling job?*

5. Describe the similarities and differences among the following types of customers: (a) trade, (b) industrial (organizational), (c) professionals, and (d) individual consumers.

6. Identify the different types of selling tasks. How are they similar? Different?

7. You are developing promotion plans for a new manufacturer of stereo systems. How important is personal selling? What types of selling tasks must be performed? Who would be called on by the sales force?

8. The selling process consists of several stages. What are they? Explain the relationship among the various stages in the process.

9. What are the sources of sales leads? Give examples of each type.

10. Compare and contrast the advantages and disadvantages of the various sources of sales leads.

11. What criteria should be used in qualifying prospects? Explain.

12. Can you identify some significant costs incurred by the company if salespeople do not effectively qualify prospects?

13. Distinguish between the following: (a) users, (b) buyers, (c) specifiers, and (d) influencers.

14. Explain the importance of planning the sales presentation. What kind of information is needed to plan a sales presentation effectively?

15. A sales presentation may be "canned" or flexible. Which is the better approach? Why?

16. What are the elements of a sales presentation?

17. What functions does the approach serve? Explain.

18. What is meant by "hot button" selling? Give examples.

19. Discuss the several characteristics of an effective demonstration.

20. Identify various types of objections that might be raised in a sales presentation.

21. Identify and define the techniques for handling objections. Under what conditions is each most appropriate?

22. Do you think objections should be responded to immediately when they are raised or should they be postponed for treatment later in the presentation? Why?

23. What makes closing a sale so difficult?

24. Distinguish between the following techniques for closing a sale: (a) the direct close, (b) the assumptive close, (c) the summative close, (d) the negative close, and (e) the special concession.

25. Before a sale can be considered complete, certain administrative steps must be taken. What are they?

26. *Explain the importance of the follow-up.*

27. *How would you go about building and maintaining customer relations?*

28. *Explain the importance of the following:* (a) *customer knowledge,* (b) *company knowledge,* (c) *product knowledge, and* (d) *selling knowledge.*

29. *What personal attributes are important to a successful salesperson? How does he or she go about acquiring these skills?*

30. *"Effective self-management is critical to successful selling." Comment.*

NOTES

1. Rowland T. Moriarty and Morton Galper, *Organizational Buying Behavior: A State of the Art Review*, MSI Working Paper No. 78-101 (Cambridge, Mass.: Marketing Science Institute, 1978), p. 16.

2. Frederick E. Webster, *Field Sales Management* (New York: John Wiley, 1983), pp. 68–71.

3. Ibid.

4. Carlton A. Pederson, Milburn D. Wright, and Barton A. Weitz, *Selling: Principles and Methods*, 7th ed. (Homewood, Ill.: Richard D. Irwin, 1981), pp. 234–35.

5. Danny N. Bellenger and Thomas N. Ingram, *Professional Selling* (New York: Macmillan, 1984), p. 189.

6. Paul J. Micali, *The Lacy Techniques of Salesmanship* (New York: Hawthorne Books, 1971), pp. 58–60.

7. Ibid., pp. 8–9.

8. Ibid., pp. 85–86.

9. Ibid., pp. 109–23; C. Robert Patty, *Managing Salespeople* (Reston, VA: Reston, 1979), pp. 435–43; and Howard Bonnell, *How to Give Yourself a Raise in Selling* (New York: Frederick Fell, 1980), pp. 75–87.

10. C. Robert Patty, *Managing Salespeople*, 1979, p. 444. Reprinted with permission of Reston Publishing Company, a Prentice-Hall Company, 11480 Sunset Hills Road, Reston, VA 22090.

11. For an excellent discussion of the importance of the close and a detailed description of the several closing techniques, see Charles M. Futrell, *Fundamentals of Selling* (Homewood, Ill.: Richard D. Irwin, 1984), pp. 305–28.

12. Ibid., pp. 412–23.

13. Bellenger and Ingram, *Professional Selling*, pp. 263–71.

12

Developing the Sales Strategy

In this chapter and the next, we discuss the various aspects of the development, execution, and ongoing management of the company's sales strategy. Developing an effective sales strategy involves five stages of decision making. First, the company must determine who its target customers will be. Second, it must identify the type or types of sales personnel required to reach its target market. Third, it must create the structure of the sales organization. Fourth, it must determine the size of the sales force. Fifth, it must establish the sales territories. Let us now look at each of these five decision-making stages.

DETERMINING THE TARGET CUSTOMERS

Initial efforts to develop the company's sales strategy begin with a determination of the company's target customers. Management must identify the various subdivisions or segments of the total market for the company's products and decide which segment or segments possess the highest potential for successful cultivation. An understanding of the concept of market segmentation can facilitate the effective formulation of sales strategy. It suggests that the total market for a generic product category comprises many smaller, more homogeneous components, each with its own specific characteristics.[1] And from this earlier understanding flow the later decisions, not only about sales strategy but about the kind of people and the kind of structure that will best carry out that strategy.

DETERMINING THE TYPE OF SALES PERSONNEL REQUIRED

Perhaps no other aspect of the development and execution of a company's sales strategy is as critical to the success of the entire endeavor as the proper identification of the specific type or types of salespeople to implement it. Just as the ordinary combat soldier holds the key to the success of military strategy, so too is the field sales representative a material factor in the ultimate success or failure of the company's sales and marketing strategy. Therefore it is essential that the vice-president of sales carefully determine the qualifications of the company's salespeople by conducting detailed job analyses, developing detailed job descriptions, and determining the required job specifications.

Conducting Job Analyses

Before management can prepare job descriptions and identify specific qualifications, it must conduct a detailed *job analysis* for each position. This job analysis is the critical foundation on which to build the entire sales force development. An inaccurate or incomplete evaluation of the requirements of the sales position can be costly to the company in both sales force turnover and lost business opportunities. Conducting a job analysis involves collecting and analyzing data to determine what activities and responsibilities will constitute the specific sales position. The base information emerges in response to the following questions:

What are the specific objectives for this position?
What are the general responsibilities and duties for this position?
What are the specific sales activities?
  Products sold?
  Sales promotion activities?
  Customer service activities?

Territorial assignments?

Customer relations activities?

What is the position's relationship in the formal organization, i.e., to whom does this position report *and* who reports to this position?

With what other areas or departments within the company will this position interact?

What executive or administrative duties are required?

Many of the answers will come from surveying the company's existing sales personnel. In addition, sales management should seek responses not only from other executives within the company but from a sampling of the company's customers. Analysis of the data then ensues. (The reader might wish to refer again to Chapter 11 for a perspective on some of the detailed requirements of various types of sales positions.)

Developing Detailed Job Descriptions

Once the manager is satisfied with the analysis of the data, he or she is ready to act on the findings by preparing detailed *job descriptions*. Accurate job descriptions are necessary to ensure that all parties (prospective sales personnel as well as the individuals in the recruiting and selection process) clearly understand the exact nature of a position's duties and responsibilities. Otherwise confusion and conflict may arise, which could inhibit the sales recruitment process, affect sales force morale, and ultimately have a negative impact on sales performance.

A typical job description for a sales position will include the following:

1. Job title
2. Statement of job objectives
3. Relationship of the position within the organization
4. Detailed description of duties and responsibilities including identification of specific activities to be performed
5. Nature of authority
6. Identification of individuals supervised, if any
7. Nature of compensation plan with salary range, if appropriate
8. Measures of job performance
9. Opportunities for promotion

Exhibits 12-1, 12-2, and 12-3 present examples of typical job descriptions for a territory sales representative, district sales manager, and field sales manager, respectively.

EXHIBIT 12-1   Job Description: Territory Sales Representative

POSITION TITLE: Territory Sales Repre-   LOCATION: Field
                        sentative
DIVISION: Personal Care Products   DEPARTMENT: Sales
EFFECTIVE DATE: July 1, 1985   POSITION REPORTS TO: District Sales
                                                Manager

SUMMARY:

The territory sales representative contributes to the sales and profits of the division by
- Achieving sales objectives established for the territory
- Communicating effectively with management, sales personnel, and the trade
- Developing knowledge and skills to improve personal performance

SPECIFIC RESPONSIBILITIES:

A. Achieve territory sales objectives

  1. Achieve or exceed territory objectives for
     - Promotional dollar /unit sales (against assigned objectives)
     - Total dollar sales (against assigned quotas)
     - Distribution of new and established products

  2. Establish key account objectives for dollar volume, distribution, and promotional support including advertising, pricing, and merchandising and display.

  3. Prepare, present, and gain acceptance by accounts for promotional plans to achieve objectives.

  4. Monitor account performance and follow up at headquarters and retail to ensure
     - Implementation of promotional plans
     - Maintenance of proper shelf space, position, pricing, and sufficient inventory to avoid out-of-stocks

  5. Establish and achieve objectives for direct and indirect call activity; plan schedules and routing to gain maximum benefit from time invested.

B. Maintain effective communication

  1. Advise management about market conditions, brand performance, and administrative situations affecting territory sales.

  2. Inform the trade about in-store activity, competitive conditions, and market trends affecting sales of personal care products.

  3. Share knowledge with other salespersons.

C. Develop knowledge and skills

  1. Review and understand brand marketing and promotional goals and plans.

  2. Study the operations and performance of key accounts and analyze competitive activity.

  3. Maintain territory and key account files.

  4. Establish (with management) job and development objectives and carry out plans to achieve them.

  5. Review personal progress with management and revise objectives as needed.

EXHIBIT 12-2 Job Description: District Sales Manager

POSITION TITLE: District Sales Man-
              ager
DIVISION: Personal Care Products
EFFECTIVE DATE: July 1, 1985

LOCATION: Field

DEPARTMENT: Sales
POSITION REPORTS TO: Field Sales
                        Manager

SUMMARY:

The district sales manager contributes to the sales and profits of the division by

- Contributing to the formulation of the regional sales plan and converting the regional sales plan into a set of objectives and plan for district execution
- Establishing objectives and strategies for managing the district's contribution to divisional objectives and assisting district personnel to achieve those objectives
- Building and maintaining an effective district sales organization
- Maintaining effective communication and operating efficiently
- Developing knowledge and skills to improve personal performance

SPECIFIC RESPONSIBILITIES:

A. Contribute to regional sales planning
 1. Provide input to the regional sales-planning effort by transmitting to the field sales manager and regional planning manager information on trade-buying trends and brand strength in the district.
 2. Prepare district sales objectives and plan for execution of the regional sales plan at the district level.
B. Establish and achieve district sales objectives
 1. Achieve or exceed district objectives for
    - Total dollar sales (against semiannual quota)
    - Distribution of new and established products
 2. Direct efforts by sales personnel to achieve territory and account objectives in terms of
    - Dollar volume
    - Distribution
    - Promotional support, including advertising, pricing, display, and multibrand merchandising
 3. Review key account performance on past promotions and establish district objectives by promoted item.
 4. Monitor sell-in and sell-through and assess factors contributing to achievement of key account objectives.
 5. Evaluate and communicate to division management the results of promotional strategies and activities.
 6. Maintain contact with executives in at least the top twenty accounts and make key account calls with salespersons to measure the level of promotional and merchandising support and to provide personal leadership to these accounts toward a higher standard of performance.
 7. Plan and monitor sales call activity, both direct and indirect, to achieve objectives for district call activity and to ensure effective merchandising in retail stores.

EXHIBIT 12-2 (Continued) Job Description: District Sales Manager

8. Negotiate, with the local retail merchants sales force area supervisor, specific action plans in support of district objectives and priorities.

C. Build and maintain an effective district sales organization

1. Project needs for sales personnel and plan job progression in the district.
2. Direct the regional training supervisor and district training supervisor in recruiting, using specified procedures for interviewing, selection, and new-employee administration.
3. Select and hire salespersons screened by the regional training supervisor and the district training supervisor.
4. Work with regional training managers to develop training plans for salespersons and schedule regional training supervisor time and activities in the district.
5. Train and develop the district training supervisor and sales personnel to meet job and development objectives.
6. Evaluate performance and progress of the district training supervisor and sales personnel and conduct, at minimum, semiannual reviews, annual appraisals, and career path discussions.
7. Maintain a district working environment that fosters motivation, development, and team spirit by
   - Conducting effective district meetings
   - Recognizing and rewarding significant achievements
   - Working in the field with sales personnel to help them improve performance

D. Maintain effective communication and operate efficiently

1. Transmit data on the market, accounts, and sales personnel to the regional planning manager. Recommend appropriate action.
2. Control district expenses and selling costs.
3. Establish with all district personnel a clear understanding of policies and procedures.

E. Personal development

1. Establish, with the field sales manager, job and development objectives.
2. Develop personal skills and knowledge and improve personal performance.
3. Review progress with the field sales manager frequently; obtain guidance and revise objectives and plans as needed.

F. Matrix reporting relationships

The district manager reports directly to the field sales manager and is accountable to him for performance against agreed objectives. In addition, the district manager is responsible to the regional planning manager for sales-planning and reporting functions and works with the regional training supervisors on personnel development functions.

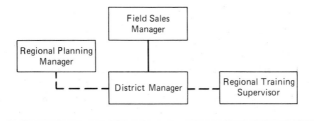

EXHIBIT 12-3   Job Description: Field Sales Manager

POSITION TITLE: Field Sales Manager   LOCATION: Field
DIVISION: Personal Care Products   DEPARTMENT: Sales
EFFECTIVE DATE: July 1, 1985   POSITION REPORTS TO: V.P.–Sales

SUMMARY:

The field sales manager contributes to the sales and profits of the Division by

- Contributing to the formulation of a national sales plan and converting the national sales plan into a set of objectives and plan for regional execution
- Achieving sales objectives established for the region
- Building and maintaining an effective regional sales organization
- Directing the activities of the regional training supervisors
- Maintaining effective communication and operating efficiently
- Developing knowledge and skills to improve personal performance

SPECIFIC RESPONSIBILITIES:

A. Contribute to sales planning

1. In conjunction with sales planning and marketing, provide input to the brand review process by transmitting information on trade buying trends and brand strength in the region.
2. Participate in the formulation of the national sales plan.
3. Prepare regional objectives and plan for execution of the national sales plan at the regional level.

B. Achieve regional sales objectives

1. Achieve or exceed regional objectives for
   - Total dollar sales (against semiannual quota)
   - Distribution of new and established products
2. Direct efforts by district managers to achieve district objectives in terms of
   - Dollar volume
   - Distribution
3. Develop and maintain rapport with executives in the top twenty key accounts, and make key account calls with salespersons to measure the level of promotional and merchandising support and to provide personal leadership toward a higher level of account performance.
4. Establish standards for, and work with, district managers to set their objectives for sales call activity, both direct and indirect, to achieve regional call activity objectives, and to ensure effective account coverage.
5. Work with the retail merchants sales force area manager to make plans and establish priorities for retail merchants sales force activity in the region.

C. Build and maintain an effective regional sales organization

1. Work with district managers to project needs for sales personnel and plan job progression in the districts and region.
2. Train and develop the regional planning manager and district managers to set job performance and development objectives.
3. Provide specific leadership in preparing annual development plans for district managers and participate in their formal training.
4. Evaluate performance and progress of the regional planning manager, regional

EXHIBIT 12-3 (Continued) **Job Description:** *Field Sales Manager*

training supervisors, and district managers and conduct, at minimum, semiannual reviews, annual appraisals, and career path discussions.

5. Maintain a regional leadership and working environment that fosters motivation, development, and team spirit by
   - Conducting effective regional meetings
   - Recognizing and rewarding significant achievement
   - Working in the field with regional personnel to help them improve performance

D. Direct regional training supervisors

1. Work with regional training supervisors to establish objectives and set priorities for their activities.
2. Monitor regional training supervisors' allocation of time to effectively meet district needs.
3. Assign regional training supervisors as necessary to monitor sales support activities such as retail drives and contests.

E. Maintain effective communication and operate efficiently

1. Direct regional planning manager in transmitting data on markets, accounts, and promotional activity to the appropriate headquarters sales-planning managers and other division and sales department personnel. Recommend appropriate action.
2. Transmit data on personnel including training and development programs and needs, compensation, and other administration.
3. Build and control regional sales budget designed to achieve optimum performance efficiency.
4. Establish with all regional personnel a clear understanding of policies and procedures.

F. Personal development

1. Establish, with the vice-president of sales, job and development objectives.
2. Develop personal skills and knowledge and improve personal performance.
3. Review progress with the vice-president of sales frequently, obtain guidance, and revise objectives and plans as needed.

G. Matrix reporting relationships

The field sales manager reports directly to the vice-president of sales and is accountable to this vice-president for performance against all agreed-upon objectives. In addition, the field sales manager is responsible to the director of sales plans for sales-planning functions including plan preparation, sales meeting and printed communication, and sales results reporting. The field sales manager is responsible to the director of sales personnel development on personnel planning, training, and development.

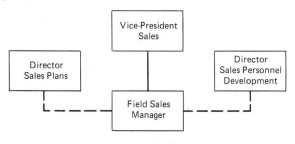

Determining Job Specifications

Job specifications identify the personal characteristics and qualifications that individuals should possess in order to function in a position. They are a product of the information generated through the job analysis and the creation of the formal job description. The following categories should appear in the identification of specific position qualifications:

> Level and type of educational background required
> Basic intelligence level required
> Necessary personality characteristics
>> Interests
>> Ambition and motivation
>> Emotional stability
>> Initiative
>> Self-confidence
>> Ability to get along with others
> Type of previous sales experience required
>> Product
>> Territory
>> Customer
> Physical attributes
>> Health and general stamina
>> Appearance

Job specifications indicate the minimum requirements necessary for a particular job. They are essential for the effective recruitment and selection (and eventual training) of sales personnel and ultimately for the successful execution of the company's sales strategy.

DETERMINING THE STRUCTURE OF THE SALES ORGANIZATION

The formal sales organization consists of activities and individuals arranged in such a fashion as to permit effective coordination of their efforts toward the accomplishment of common objectives. The key to successful management and organization is the efficient use of both human and financial resources.

The following are general characteristics of a good sales organization:[2]

1. *The sales organization structure reflects a market orientation*. The organizational design begins with a consideration of the market and those sales activities

necessary to succeed in that market. Once one identifies the basic sales tasks, one then adds the necessary supervisory and support structures.

2. *Organize activities, not people.* The organizational framework should address and define functions. Consideration of individuals is separate.

3. *Responsibility and authority relate properly.* Individuals with various sales responsibilities in the organization should have authority commensurate with those responsibilities. Responsibility for each activity should be spelled out and the accompanying authority clearly communicated to all.

4. *Span of executive control is reasonable.* There is an optimum number of individuals that an executive can manage effectively. How large a number this will be depends on a variety of factors including how routine and similar the sales duties of the individuals are, what the level of ability of the executive or sales personnel is, and so on.

5. *Organization is stable but flexible.* The organization must be stable enough to withstand losses of supervisory personnel yet maintain maximum effectiveness. At the same time, it must remain flexible enough to adjust to a variety of conditions that may affect the firm in the short run such as fluctuating market conditions and changes in manpower needs and availability.

6. *Activities are balanced and coordinated.* Good balance requires that no activity should be given undue emphasis at the expense of another. Activities such as sales and advertising should be balanced according to their relative importance in the organizational mission. What's more, in order for the organization to function effectively, close coordination among all departments (sales and nonmarketing) must occur.

Basic Types of Organizational Structure

Although the particular configuration of the sales organization varies from company to company, most sales structures have one of the following three forms of organization: basic line, line and staff, and functional.

Basic Line Organization

The *basic line* organizational structure is the least-complex type and makes no provision for staff or auxiliary positions, and the chain of command is both general and direct with authority running from the top executive position down through each successive level of subordinates. Accountability, therefore, runs vertically upward through the organization.

An example of a simple line sales organization appears in Exhibit 12-4. In this example, authority flows directly from the general manager to the sales manager and from the sales manager to each of the four salespersons. Conversely, responsibility for carrying out sales activities rests with the

EXHIBIT 12-4 Basic Line Sales Organization

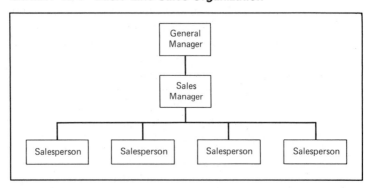

sales personnel, who then report to the sales manager. This position, in turn, is accountable to the company's general manager. In its most basic form, the line structure provides for a high degree of centralized authority with the chief executive responsible for all planning and operational activities.

This form of organization can promote swift decision making, quick execution of plans, and effective discipline. The basic line organization is both a simple and a cost-effective structure for small companies; it is not well suited for medium-sized or large companies. The line organization places considerable responsibility on the top executive. As the company grows and the size of the sales force increases, the top executive may lack both the time and the managerial specialization to function effectively in all the areas requiring attention. When this occurs, the simple line structure will cease to be appropriate. The company will find it necessary to add additional management personnel to maintain control over its operations and be effective in the marketplace.

Line and Staff Organization

The *line and staff* organizational structure is the preeminent type for companies with large sales forces serving wide geographical areas and marketing a varied product line. The line and staff structure, unlike the simple line organization, has a number of staff specialists who report directly to senior executives. Individuals operating in staff roles have no direct authority over line managers. Their chief responsibilities are planning and analysis, and providing advice and recommendations in their areas of expertise.

Exhibit 12-5 illustrates a line and staff sales organization. In this exhibit, the chief marketing executive (marketing vice-president) is ultimately responsible for the functioning of the company's entire marketing organization and supervises the general sales manager, director of market research, and director of marketing communications. Four managers report directly to the

EXHIBIT 12-5   Line and Staff Sales Organization

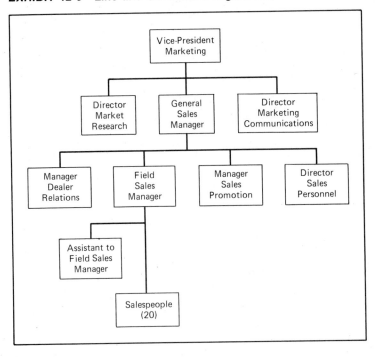

general sales manager including one line manager (field sales manager) and three staff personnel (manager of dealer relations, manager of sales promotion, and director of sales personnel). The three staff executives are responsible for their own specific areas of specialization and proffer advice and recommendations to the general sales manager and the field sales manager. This structure also includes the position of assistant to the field sales manager. This is also a staff position, but unlike the previous three, it is a source of administrative assistance and support for the field sales manager rather than one of specialized expertise. Again, the sales force does not report to this individual, nor does he or she exercise authority over the field sales personnel, since it lies outside the sales line structure.

The major advantage of the line and staff organization form is that it provides sales management with expert knowledge through specialization but relieves it from excessive immersion in detail. In this way, the company's top executives can achieve a better balance between day-to-day operational responsibilities and broader long-term issues facing the company.

The line and staff organizational structure is not without drawbacks. The addition of more executives to the structure rapidly increases administrative costs; furthermore, some confusion and conflict can arise over the role of staff personnel in relation to line managers. A key to the effective use of staff lies in clearly communicating, throughout the organization, their specific functions and the range of their authority.

Functional Organization

Exhibit 12-6 illustrates a sales organization with a functional configuration. The *functional* organization is an extension of the line and staff format. In this type, functional specialists have authority over particular functional areas throughout the organization. For example, a manager of sales promotion will have authority over the sales force when these people engage in sales promotion activities.

Let us compare the functional sales organization in Exhibit 12-6 with the line and staff format in Exhibit 12-5. In our discussion of the line and staff structure, we indicated that the sales personnel report only to the field sales manager, who has line authority over them. The manager of dealer relations, the manager of sales promotion, and the director of sales personnel serve in staff capacities and have no direct authority over the sales force but rather function only in an advisory role. In a functional organization, however, these same managers exercise direct line authority over their specialized areas, and sales personnel report to these individuals when the sales force's activities involve the specific function. Therefore, in a functional organization, sales personnel find themselves reporting to a number of executives simultaneously.

The obvious risk in this organizational format is that sales personnel will occasionally receive conflicting orders from two or more of the functional managers to whom they report. They may also become deluged with multiple assignments, all requiring attention at the same time. There is obviously a

EXHIBIT 12-6 Functional Sales Organization

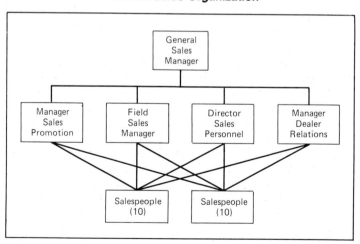

need for close coordination of the various functional areas by top management in order to make the functional structure efficient.

There are, on the other hand, significant advantages in the use of the functional structure. The major benefit lies in the execution of specialized tasks. Since functional managers exercise direct line authority over their areas, there is a greater probability of carrying out their plans and ideas in the field. By contrast, in the line and staff structure, the plans of functional specialists only carry the weight of a recommendation and will come to life only if the general sales manager actively supports them. In theory (less often in practice), the functional structure should mean better performance, since those who have expertise in a particular area also have authority over those who use that expertise.

Further Subdivision of the Sales Organization

As the company's sales force continues to expand, the top-line executives may have too many supervisory responsibilities and effectiveness may be at risk. Because of the rapid growth of the sales force, products, or markets, a further subdivision may be necessary along additional lines of specialization, according to one of the following formats: geographical, customer, or product subdivision.

Geographical Subdivision

Geographical subdivisions are characteristic of expanding organizations with a substantial number of customers and a large, widely dispersed sales force. Exhibit 12-7 illustrates such a sales organization. A regional division has devolved further into district subdivisions. Companies with this format usually market a line of closely related products and have expanded the sales organization to a size where the company's top sales executive cannot manage it effectively. Such companies will subdivide the sales management responsibility. The sales executive in charge of each region will have responsibility for the sales activities within the region and occasionally will also be responsible for other marketing actions within the territory.

There are several advantages to the company in structuring its sales organization according to a geographical subdivision. For one thing, it frees top executives' time and it places decision-making responsibility in the hands of a local manager who has firsthand knowledge of the affected area and can make decisions more quickly. Geographical territories make better market coverage possible and enhance supervision and control of the sales force, permitting greater flexibility and adaptability to competition or special marketing situations at the local level. Finally, geographical territories provide for more effective communication between management and sales personnel.

EXHIBIT 12-7   Sales Organization: Geographical Subdivision

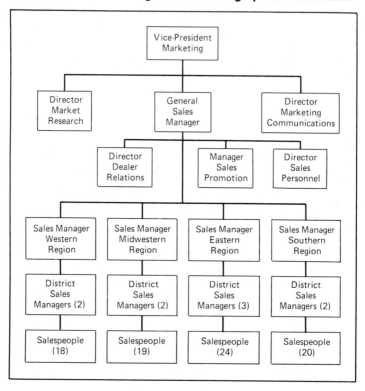

All these advantages account for the popular practice of organizing a sales force by geographical territories.

The use of geographical territories has some disadvantages. Territorial specialization by function cannot generally be used, meaning that each district manager, in addition to managing his or her sales force, will have to do some work in recruitment, training, advertising, or sales analysis. Furthermore, there is the overhead expense that comes with establishing more levels of territorial executives.[3]

Customer Subdivision

Companies marketing similar products to diversified customers often structure their sales organizations by *customer* type, a particularly useful format where the company's customer segments have distinct sets of needs, purchasing criteria, and problems requiring markedly different sales approaches and treatments. Exhibit 12-8 illustrates a sales organization structured in this manner. It is easy to envision (from this example) where individual homeowners, commercial users, and governmental agencies might require

EXHIBIT 12-8   Sales Organization: Customer Subdivision

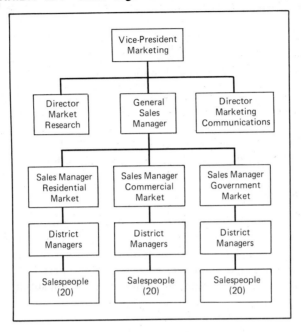

different sales approaches, since each of these customer types will have different buying decision criteria and methods of purchasing. Marketers of building materials and supplies might use this sales structure.

Other forms of customer subdivision of the sales force are also possible—some by the size of the customer; others where customers buy direct rather than from distributors or dealers. Still others subdivide into national and local accounts.

The major advantage of subdividing the sales organization by type of customer is that it allows for a better understanding of customer needs. And as a salesperson becomes more familiar with specific customer requirements, he or she can provide greater marketing assistance. A customer subdivision, however, may lead to overlapping territories, causing different salespeople to call on different customers in the same territory.[4] This duplication of effort is costly in selling and administrative expenses.

In industrial selling, there is growing interest in the management of *national accounts*, defined in a study by Shapiro and Moriarty as accounts that are both large and complex.[5] The size characteristic is determined by purchasing potential, not just current sales. Complexity comes from three sources: multiple geographical buying points, multiple buying influences, and multiple business units. Shapiro and Moriarty also emphasize that there are a variety of ways to organize the national account manager's job in dealing with these conditions:

Because of its complexity and size, the national account requires and justifies special attention. The account manager is the person responsible for insuring that the selling company provides the necessary care in an efficient and effective manner. There are a wide variety of approaches to structuring and organizing the national account manager's job. Accordingly, national account managers do different things in different companies. There can be a wide range in the number and size of accounts for which the national account manager is responsible, the size of the sales team and support staff working under the manager, and whether the national account manager has line responsibilities or is a coordinator of other people.[6]

The character of the market will actually be a major factor in determining what form of customer subdivision will be appropriate.

Product Subdivision

A final method for structuring the sales organization is to subdivide it along *product* lines. This format is most common in companies that market many products of varying degrees of complexity or in companies that produce a number of unrelated products, each requiring special attention. Exhibit 12-9 illustrates a simple version of a sales organization subdivided according to product type.

EXHIBIT 12-9   Sales Organization: Product Subdivision

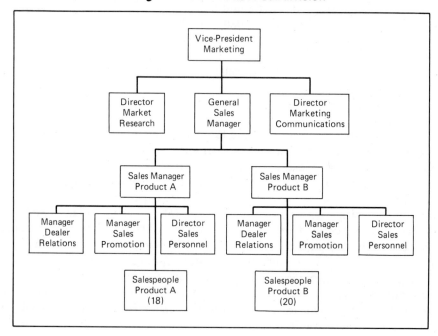

The major advantage of the product subdivision is the greater attention given to one or a few products. The salesperson can become a specialist in the product's technical attributes and its applications. The product also receives more executive attention because one person is responsible for a particular product or product group.

The limitations of organizing by products relate to duplication of coverage. More than one salesperson may call on the same customer, resulting not only in greater expense but also in possible customer confusion from dealing with more than one company sales representative.

Subdividing on More Than One Base

Few companies subdivide their sales organization on one base only. Most use some combination of the several structures we have discussed. For example, a sales organization may use geographical subdivision in combination with a customer specialization, or it may use a combination geographical-product structure. The important thing is to be aware of the several alternatives for organizing the sales effort and to use the structure that is most compatible with the company's position, resources, and marketing mission. It is also important to know that the sales organization structure has an impact on the size of the sales force.

DETERMINING THE SIZE OF THE SALES FORCE

The number of sales personnel a company deploys in the field derives from four fundamental considerations: the number of prospective customers for the company's products; the sales potential of each of these prospective customers; the geographical concentration or dispersion of these customers; and the financial resources available to the company. Much mixing and matching of these factors take place to determine the right size for the field sales force. We will examine three common approaches.

Buildup Method

One popular approach, the *buildup*, or *workload*, method, entails an analysis of the amount of activity a salesperson normally exhibits in a given time and then dividing this factor into the company's estimate of the total effort necessary to serve its market. The result will define the number of salespeople needed to cover the company's market area. Here is a step-by-step description (with an example) of this approach.

STEP 1 *Determine the amount of time available per salesperson on an annual basis.*

Calculate the total number of hours available per salesperson excluding such items as vacation time, holidays, illness, and personal time off. Assuming that the typical salesperson takes a total of five weeks off per year for vacation, holidays, and other absences, the annual number of hours available amounts to 1,880 hours (52 weeks × 5 days × 8 hours per day = 2,080 hours − (5 weeks × 40 hours) = 200 hours).

STEP 2 *Estimate the percentage of a salesperson's time devoted to selling compared with travel and other nonselling duties.*

Obviously, salespeople cannot devote all of their available time exclusively to face-to-face selling. There must be time for travel from one client to another. Clearly, if the customers are geographically concentrated, travel time will be less; conversely, if they are widely dispersed, travel time will be more significant. Other nonselling duties such as filing reports and expense forms, attending sales meetings, and participating in training programs will also demand the salesperson's time. In this example assume that the average salesperson spends 50 percent of the time selling, 30 percent traveling, and 20 percent on other nonselling duties.

STEP 3 *Determine the number of hours available per salesperson for selling.*

We can easily determine from this example the amount of time available during the year for selling by multiplying the time available per salesperson by the percentage of time devoted to actual selling. Thus 1,880 hours × 50% = 940 hours available for selling.

STEP 4 *Categorize customers and prospects by level of sales effort needed.*

Not all customers and prospects require the same amount of attention and selling effort. A few brief sales calls during the year will serve some companies, whereas others may require constant attention. The company's current and potential customers should be classified in a manner that recognizes the differences in the amount of sales effort necessary. These categories usually take shape according to the size of the account. Current sales volume or sales potential customarily relates to the amount of selling effort required. However, the analyst can use whatever system of classification identifies the necessary levels of selling effort. Assume that the manager has developed the following classifications and has estimated the number of current potential customers from within the total market area in each of these categories:

Extremely heavy sales effort required = 140
Heavy sales effort required   = 80
Medium sales effort required   = 420
Light sales effort required   = 900

STEP 5 *Determine the call length and frequency for each classification.*

For each classification of customer or prospect in step 4, the sales manager should establish the average amount of time for an effective sales call. The manager should also determine the necessary annual call frequency. Assume that the following table has been developed for the categories in step 4:

	Length	Frequency
Extremely heavy effort	60 min.	48 annually
Heavy effort	45 min.	24 annually
Medium effort	30 min.	12 annually
Light effort	30 min.	6 annually

STEP 6 *Calculate, on an annual basis, the amount of time necessary to serve current customers and prospects.*

From the data above, here is our tabulation:

Category	Time Per Call	×	Call Frequency	=	Annual Time Needed Per Account	×	No. of Accounts	=	Annual Time Per Category
	(in min.)		*(annually)*		*(in hrs.)*				*(in hrs.)*
Extremely heavy	60	×	48	=	48	×	140	=	6,720
Heavy	45	×	24	=	18	×	80	=	1,440
Medium	30	×	12	=	6	×	420	=	2,520
Light	30	×	6	=	3	×	900	=	2,700
Total hours needed annually									13,380

STEP 7 *Determine the number of salespeople required.*

Recall that we said (step 3) that each salesperson has 940 hours a year available for selling efforts. We can now use this information to calculate the needs for sales personnel. We divide the total annual hours required for selling efforts by the number of hours available per salesperson. Thus 13,380 divided by 940 = 14 sales personnel for the company to cover its market area adequately.

The buildup method of determining sales force size is easy to understand, and it takes into consideration the reality that different accounts require different levels of effort and call frequencies. This method relates sales force size to the amount of activity required. Among the weaknesses of the buildup method are that it assumes sales personnel are equal in terms of efficiency and effectiveness, differences in sales response among customers receiving the same level of sales effort go unnoticed, and there is no tie between call frequencies and profitability. On balance, the buildup method has much to offer and is the most common way of determining sales force size.

Breakdown Method

A second technique, the *breakdown* method, is also popular for determining the appropriate number of sales personnel. Here the company follows three steps:

1. Determine the company's potential sales volume for its entire market area.
2. Determine the minimum sales volume to support one salesperson.
3. Calculate the number of sales personnel by dividing item 1 by item 2.

For example, assume that the company has forecast annual sales at $10 million. Moreover, company management requires a minimum annual sales volume of $500,000 per salesperson. Twenty salespeople will answer the company's needs.

The major advantage of the breakdown method is its simplicity. However, it treats sales force size as a result of sales, rather than the opposite. Furthermore, the breakdown method requires a productivity estimate for each salesperson, which is extremely difficult because many factors affect a person's productivity, it does not allow for sales force turnover, and, like the buildup method, it does not relate to profitability.

Budgetary Method

The company's financial resources will often circumscribe the number of salespeople that go into the field. Here, management must set the budget for personal selling before deciding on the size of the sales organization. The reader should review the section entitled "Determining the Promotional Budget" in Chapter 6 to examine the full process.

There are three steps in the *budgetary* method: (1) determine the personal selling budget; (2) determine the full costs of maintaining one salesperson in the field; and (3) calculate the number of sales personnel permitted by dividing item 1 by item 2. For example, imagine that the budget for personal selling is $500,000, and it costs $50,000 in salary, commission, travel and entertainment expenses, and support services to keep one salesperson in the field. Ten salespeople would fit within this established budget.

The budgetary method of determining sales force size is easy to understand and implement. In addition, sales force size is related to the company's financial ability. The method's weaknesses are that it does not allow for differences in productivity among members of the sales force and there is no allowance for profitability.

Often, what the budget justifies does not in fact translate into the size of sales force that the manager may want, given the product's market potential. When this occurs, the structure of the sales territories and the deployment of the sales force become vital issues. We will examine that aspect next.

ESTABLISHING SALES TERRITORIES

A sales territory consists of a number of current and prospective customers assigned to a specific salesperson. These customers and prospects are within a geographical area designed for efficient, convenient, and economical access by the salesperson. But a sales territory is more than geography. The shape of it may assert itself, but the essence of a sales territory is the current and potential customers there, not the geographical boundaries that surround them.

The Need for Sales Territories

The establishment of sales territories is an essential part of the planning and execution of a company's sales strategy. It allows managers to make specific responsibility assignments to each member of the sales organization, thereby improving direction and control.

Several advantages arise when the company has clearly defined and adequately staffed the sales territories. There is greater assurance of proper attention to the market because territories permit organized and systematic market coverage. Well-defined territories can facilitate the evaluation of performance by sales personnel, particularly because sales, costs, and profits can be compared among territories. The company can achieve substantial savings by the elimination of overlapping travel routes and duplication of customer contact by two or more salespeople. Higher morale and effectiveness of sales personnel will result from a well-conceived sales territory plan, especially because salespeople will consider a territory "their own" responsibility and will do their best with the customers and prospects in their territory.[7] Sales territories provide for improved integration of personal-selling efforts with other promotional and marketing activities.

Structuring Sales Territories

Here is what the manager must do to establish or revise sales territories:

Identify a geographical base or control unit for use in establishing territorial boundaries.

Determine the relative sales potential of each control unit.

Establish sales territories by combining control units.

Selecting Control Units

The initial step is the selection of a geographical control unit that will model the eventual territorial design. *Control units* are small segments of the total market, building blocks for territories. They should have clear boundaries, be easy to pinpoint, and have sufficient statistical data available to permit accurate measurement.[8] Sales managers usually select control units from such configurations as states, counties, cities, identifiable trading areas, standard metropolitan statistical areas (SMSAs), or regions identified by a ZIP code. Control units should be small because that makes it easier to isolate sales or profit potential, and it facilitates the adjustment of territories if necessary.[9] The final territories come about through combinations of the basic geographical control units selected by the company's management.

Determining Relative Sales Potential in Each Control Unit

Once the manager has identified the type of control unit to use, the next step is an analysis of the sales potential within each control unit. Management should first identify the number and size of current and prospective customers for the company's products within each control unit. From these data, the management can create estimates of the total market potential as well as the company's market share for each unit. Finally, from the market share estimate, management projects the potential level of sales for each control unit. With these data, the management can then engage in analyses leading to the combination or subdivision of control units into sales territories.

Developing Sales Territories

To construct sales territories from the selected control units, the sales vice-president must consider three important factors: the sales potential within each territory, the travel pattern to serve the territory, and the number of sales personnel available.

Sales Potential. Sales potential is a significant factor in the structuring of sales territories.[10] On the one hand, it would be uneconomical to lock in a sales territory where the potential was insufficient to cover the salesperson's costs. On the other, if the territorial potential is enormous, the salesperson may not have time to develop it fully, opting for a "cream-skimming" approach. This would leave a substantial number of customers unserved and the territory underdeveloped.

Another aspect of sales potential is the equality of opportunity and fairness among the sales personnel. Great disparity in the potential across territories can easily lead to morale problems, high turnover of personnel, increased costs, and a reduction of overall sales performance.

Travel Patterns. With proper planning, sales territories can mean maximum selling time by sales personnel and minimum time wasted in travel to and from sales calls. Sales territories should be laid out in such a way as to reduce the distance a salesperson must travel as well as the number of nights away from home. The right design can add to the salesperson's volume and at the same time reduce selling expenses. These considerations actually generate the possible shape of the sales territory. Consider these common territorial shapes:

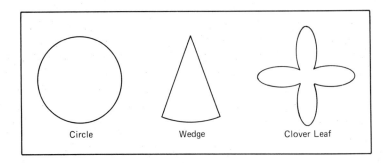

A *circular* shape seems best in those situations where customers and prospects are somewhat evenly distributed in an area with no specific concentration in any particular segment. A salesperson near the center of the circular territory will be relatively close to the majority of accounts and able to reach any of them on short notice. This shape is particularly useful when the need exists for a uniform degree of frequency in sales calls.

The *wedge* shape is best for areas where there is both a densely populated urban segment and a number of accounts in suburban areas. The urban segment is at the point of the wedge, with the territory expanding outward through the suburban areas.

Finally, the *clover-leaf* shape is best in those instances where accounts are dispersed throughout an area. The relationship of the salesperson's home base to the territory in general is similar to that found in the circular territory. That is, home base is at the center of the clover leaf, with the salesperson traveling periodically out through each of the leaves according to some precise timetable. One leaf could be covered each week, and the entire territory once each month. As with the circular territorial design, location at the center of the territory reduces the amount of time spent away from the salesperson's home and thus reduces the expense of out-of-town lodging, and it may therefore also enhance the salesperson's motivation and morale.

Number of Sales Personnel. As mentioned earlier, the number of sales personnel available within budgetary constraints may often be less than the ideal. The territory structure must be developed with this in mind. It may be necessary to structure territories to ensure coverage of all *prime* prospects, giving less attention to other customers. On the other hand, the company may choose to redefine its target customers, which would result in a substantial change in sales potential in the control units. Other approaches might involve the decision to serve a more-limited geographical area for a time or to hire manufacturers' representatives on commission to cover certain territories.

The establishment of sales territories, which enhances the accomplishment of the company's business goals, is not a simple task. It involves the consideration of a number of related factors. Effective sales managers give high priority to the appropriate structuring of sales territories.

SUMMARY

One of the important aspects of promotional programs is the development of a sales strategy, which comprises five major components: identifying target customers, determining the type of sales personnel, formulating the sales organization structure, determining sales force size, and establishing sales territories.

The process of developing sales strategy necessarily begins with determining target customers. Deciding which segments within the total market to pursue sets the stage for the crucial sales strategy decisions. Determining the type of sales personnel needed involves conducting detailed job analyses, developing the job descriptions, and enumerating the job specifications.

Another critical sales strategy decision is determining the structure of the sales organization. Management must bear in mind the characteristics of a good sales organization to ensure that the specific sales structure decided upon will be appropriate for the company's situation. Management must also explore the major alternatives in sales organization—basic line, line and staff, and functional—to see which makes the best sense. In addition, management should investigate ways to further subdivide responsibility and line authority in the sales organization, the most common methods being geographical, customer, or product subdivisions.

When the appropriate sales organization structure is in place, management next determines the number of sales personnel. This involves three approaches: the buildup method, breakdown method, and budgetary method.

Finally, we looked at the development of a sales strategy as it relates to sales territories, which are necessary to give direction to and permit control of the sales force. Establishment or revision of territories follows certain well-developed procedures.

Successful execution of a sales strategy depends on the thorough and sound formulation of strategy and the exercise of great care. With the key aspects of sales strategy development in mind, let us now consider the major factors in the actual execution of the sales strategy.

REVIEW AND DISCUSSION QUESTIONS

1. The process of developing an effective sales strategy involves five major decisions. What are they? Explain.

2. What kinds of activities are required in determining the types of sales personnel required by a company?

3. Identify the kinds of information needed to conduct a job analysis. Where can you obtain such information?

4. What is a job description? What are the major components of a typical sales position description?

5. What are job specifications? How are they used? Explain.

6. This chapter suggests several characteristics of a good sales organization. What are they? How do you go about ensuring that the formal sales organization is the "best" one for a particular organization?

7. What are the benefits of a sound organization structure? Be specific.

8. What are some signs pointing to a need to revise the sales organization?

9. Explain fully the advantages and limitations of each of the following types of organizational structure: (a) basic line organization, (b) line and staff organization, and (c) functional organization.

10. Because of rapid growth in a company's markets, product lines, or sales force, it often becomes necessary to further subdivide the sales organization along additional lines of specialization. Three major types of subdivision are used. What are they, and under what conditions is each most appropriate?

11. What are the advantages and limitations of a geographical subdivision of the sales organization? Customer subdivision? Product subdivision?

12. What are "national accounts"? Why are they complex to manage?

13. Several factors determine the number of sales personnel a company will use. What are they?

14. Identify and explain the steps involved in using the buildup method for determining sales force size.

15. As a new sales manager, you wish to determine the proper sales force size. The average salesperson puts in forty hours a week during the year except for a two-week vacation period. During a typical workday, a salesperson will spend 30 percent of the time doing direct selling.

   There are currently twelve hundred accounts. Industrial, government, and commercial customers represent 65, 10, and 25 percent of the accounts, respectively. An industrial account requires about twenty calls per year, a government account about twenty-five, and a commercial customer about fifteen. The typical visits to industrial, government, and commercial customers last sixty, forty-five, and thirty minutes, respectively.

   What is an appropriate sales force size?

16. What are the steps in the breakdown method of determining the size of the sales force? In the budgetary method?

17. Why are sales territories needed? Specifically, what purposes do they serve?

18. What procedure do you recommend for establishing sales territories? Explain.

19. What would be some indicators of poorly designed sales territories?

20. You have been asked to give some advice on the "most effective approach to developing a sales strategy." What do you suggest? Give reasons.

NOTES

1. See Chapter 5 for a more complete discussion of market segmentation and target market selection.

2. William J. Stanton and Richard H. Buskirk, *Management of the Sales Force*, 6th Ed., © 1983, pp. 49–55. Used with permission from Richard D. Irwin, Inc. Homewood, Ill.

3. Ibid., p. 62.

4. Gilbert A. Churchill, Jr., Neil M. Ford, and Orville C. Walker, Jr., *Sales Force Management* (Homewood, Ill.: Richard D. Irwin, 1981), p. 96.

5. Benson P. Shapiro and Rowland T. Moriarty, *National Account Management: Emerging Insights,* Report No. 82-100 (Cambridge, Mass.: Marketing Science Institute, March 1982).

6. Ibid., p. 7.

7. Thomas R. Wotruba, *Sales Management* (Santa Monica, Calif.: Goodyear, 1981), p. 99.

8. Ibid., pp. 109–10.

9. Stanton and Buskirk, *Management of the Sales Force*, p. 444.

10. For an excellent discussion of sales potential and other important aspects of sales territory design, see Frederick E. Webster, *Field Sales Management* (New York: John Wiley, 1983), pp. 134–51.

13

Executing the Sales Strategy

We have discussed the several aspects of planning and developing a sales strategy, and we will now look at the various actions necessary to execute that strategy. In Chapter 12 we established the framework; in this chapter we fill in the details. For example, in Chapter 12 we described how management determines the types of salespeople required; now we will describe how management goes about getting personnel with those characteristics and assimilating them into the sales force, through recruiting, selecting, and training programs.

We discussed procedures for establishing sales territories; now we will explain how salespeople are assigned to those territories. The primary focus, then, will be on these and other specific activities (such as compensating, motivating, and supervising) required to build the sales organization systematically and manage it effectively. In addition, we will examine the evaluating and controlling of the sales effort, another integral part of sales management.

BUILDING THE SALES ORGANIZATION

Building an effective sales organization starts with a variety of efforts aimed at securing applicants for the sales positions top management has created. Once the company has generated a sufficient pool of qualified individuals, the process of selecting and hiring those best suited to the company's needs begins. Following this, it is necessary to train the new salespeople to prepare them for entry into the field. The initial phase of training will deal with selling skills and familiarity with the company's products and its policies and procedures. The final stage in constructing the sales organization is determining the actual sales assignments for each salesperson and placing them into sales territories best suited to their talents and training. Let us look at each of these steps.

Recruiting

Once the sales manager has determined the appropriate type of sales personnel, developed position descriptions and detailed job specifications, and reached a decision on the structure and size of the sales force, he or she is ready to begin the recruitment process, those activities undertaken to secure applicants for open positions.

The organizational apparatus and focus of responsibility for recruiting activities will vary from company to company depending on a number of factors, such as the size of the company and sales force, rate of turnover of sales personnel, departmental structure, and degree of centralization within the organization. Companies with large sales departments and a high degree of turnover, for example, will generally place the primary responsibility for recruitment with a first-level sales manager or sales force recruitment specialist, whereas in other companies the principal responsibility may rest with the company personnel office. As a general rule, company personnel departments seldom have exclusive responsibility for recruiting sales personnel, instead they share this responsibility with some component of the internal sales organization.

Companies seeking applicants for sales positions have a number of possibilities available. The nature and scope of recruiting sources vary from the formality of the career placement office of a large university to the informality of approaching a close personal business contact. Which source or combination of sources is best to use depends on a number of factors, including what the recruiter wants in the way of experience and level of education. The number of positions to be filled, size and structure of the recruiting staff, time constraints, and size of the recruiting budget clearly play their part, too. Both internal and external sources are used. *Internal sources* include the company's own sales personnel, internal transfers by nonsales personnel, and company managers and executives. *External sources* include educational institutions, employment agencies, sales forces of competing and noncompeting companies, customers' employees, unsolicited applications, professional sales clubs and organizations, and advertisements. We will look briefly at each source.

The Company's Own Sales Personnel

Company sales personnel may be sources of leads to new recruits. Salespeople usually have numerous business acquaintances (including sales representatives from other companies) and, through these contacts, are in an excellent position to know when individuals from other companies are considering job changes. Members of the sales force are acutely aware of their company's position requirements. They are also sensitive to those special attributes that are desirable in new recruits, and they are therefore able to discourage unqualified applicants while aggressively encouraging applications by individuals they feel would meet their company's requirements. Although the use of present sales force personnel for recruiting purposes is generally beneficial to the company, the management must guard against members of the sales force expending excessive amounts of time and effort in recruiting activities at the expense of the primary selling mission.

Internal Transfers by Nonsales Personnel

It often makes good sense for companies to seek recruits for sales positions among other departments within their organizations. One advantage is that these individuals are already familiar with not only the company's products but also the company's policies and philosophy. Transfer of production or engineering personnel into the sales force is particularly advantageous where technical knowledge of the product line is essential to sales success. Given this advantage, companies frequently seek sales recruits from within their own organization when it is necessary to add *quickly* to the field sales force and time for lengthy training sessions is not available. On the other hand, individuals who are good technical personnel will not necessarily become good salespeople. Note that internal recruiting can also cause animosity within the company if other managers feel that their best employees are being pirated by the sales department.[1]

Company Managers and Executives

As a result of their many business contacts and intimate knowledge of the company's needs, company managers and executives can make useful recommendations regarding potential sales recruits. Those who make the selection decision, however, must carefully evaluate candidates from these sources. Company executives may feel compelled, through a variety of external political and business pressures, to recommend recruits based on less-than-objective criteria, such as personal friendships or obligations to return prior favors.

Educational Institutions

Colleges and universities are a valuable source for companies that view initial sales positions as an entry-level training ground for future managers or for those companies marketing highly sophisticated products where the selling effort is complex.

Most colleges and universities have career counseling and placement offices to assist both students and businesses. In addition, such educational institutions as community and junior colleges, high schools, and certain technical-vocational schools are useful sources of sales recruits. Sales force recruiters consider the dimensions of the positions for which they seek applicants and match them with the known output of educational institutions. Recruiters work with detailed job specifications accurately reflecting the optimum amount and type of education the job requires.

Employment Agencies

Employment agencies get mixed reviews as vehicles for recruiting sales personnel. Some sales executives believe that employment agencies, at best, produce only marginal applicants who use the agency's services as a desperation measure when all other efforts at obtaining employment have failed. On the other hand, many sales force recruiters have found their experiences with employment agencies to be successful and rewarding. The key to an effective relationship with employment agencies lies with the employing company itself. The company must make its specific requirements absolutely clear to the employment agency and provide it with comprehensive position descriptions and sets of job specifications. This helps to avoid misunderstandings and enables the agency to prescreen applicants.

Sales Forces of Competing and Noncompeting Companies

By virtue of their selling experience, sales personnel in other companies are very suitable potential recruits. This is particularly true of salespeople in competing companies, since these individuals are already familiar with the company's products and the market in which it operates. Hiring sales personnel away from competing businesses is especially advantageous when a company does not have sufficient time for training new recruits and needs immediate placement of personnel into the field. These salespeople already possess comprehensive product knowledge and will require only a brief orientation covering the company's philosophy and policies. Although experienced sales personnel require a higher level of initial compensation, the added cost is generally justified, since these salespeople are productive sooner and the expenses of initial training are minimal or nonexistent. The attractiveness of hiring a member of a competing company's sales organization is still greater when the new salesperson can "carry over" a number of clients from the competing company.

Customers' Employees

Many excellent sales recruits have come from the ranks of a company's customers. Companies should be especially cautious in approaching the employees of a customer, however, since the risk of creating ill feelings and eventually losing the customer may be high. It always makes good sense to bring any interest the company may have in hiring a customer's employee to the attention of the customer's management first and receive approval before contacting the individual.

Unsolicited Applications

Companies are always looking for individuals who demonstrate initiative and self-confidence. For this reason, many companies are very interested in unsolicited or "walk-in" job applicants. Unfortunately, these individuals are frequently unqualified and the number of recruits from this source is small. Nevertheless, this activity should be encouraged through the use of screening forms and immediate interviews, since this source bears only minimal costs.

Professional Sales Clubs and Organizations

Professional sales clubs and organizations are useful in both a formal and an informal way in securing sales force recruits. Some sales and marketing executives clubs maintain formal ongoing placement activities for their members. They disseminate information pertaining to openings within member firms as well as résumés of members seeking employment changes. On a more informal level, the "old boy" network among the membership of such organizations may quickly pass along information regarding openings and professionals available for new positions.

Advertisements

The placement of advertisements for sales position openings in newspapers and trade publications produces the largest volume of applicants at the lowest cost per applicant. Since the number of potential applicants is that large, however, the chances of generating an unmanageable avalanche of responses from unqualified applicants is also quite high. Companies seeking qualified and experienced sales personnel should consider placing announcements of sales openings in trade publications for their industry; on the other hand, newspaper advertisements work best for companies not looking for experienced talent but hoping to select from the largest applicant pool possible.

Selection and Hiring

Selection systems measure the extent to which applicants for sales positions meet the qualifications the company has set. (See Chapter 12 for a review of job descriptions and specifications.) The selection process should provide managers with as much information as possible upon which to judge candidates and should screen them so as to have in the final selection pool only those who have strong qualifications. The selection process may be a simple informal interview, or it may include a lengthy series of activities. While it is important for companies to design selection systems that best serve their unique conditions, the typical selection process comprises several stages, with each serving as a screening device for progression to the next: preliminary screening, formal application, personal interviews, background checks, psychological testing, physical examination, and the selection decision.

Preliminary Screening

The preliminary or initial screening process reduces the number of recruits to be closely scrutinized to a more manageable number through the early elimination of individuals who are clearly unqualified for the particular sales position. Usually there is preparation of a short application form, followed by a brief interview with a lower-level staff member, and sometimes a simple qualifying examination. This information demonstrates quickly whether a recruit has or lacks the minimum qualifications for the position. A large number of recruits will usually be screened out at this level.

Formal Application

Once the candidate has passed through the preliminary screening, he or she will normally complete a formal application. The application form procures factual data about the candidate, and it becomes the primary record for all information pertaining to the candidate gathered during the remainder of the selection process. While formal applications usually suit the specific needs of a particular company, most application forms, as a minimum, include the following items: present and past employment history, level of educational attainment, earnings history, professional organization memberships, reasons for leaving previous employment positions, physical condition, personal interests and hobbies. Besides providing information about candidates and their qualifications, completed applications are useful guides during the personal interview process.

Personal Interviews

Ordinarily the company calls in for personal interviews those candidates who survive the screening of formal applications. The interview is an essential step in the selection process and is the most effective device for judging a candidate's suitability for a sales position. Through the face-to-face contact in the interview setting, the interviewer (usually a sales manager) can evaluate the candidate's personal attributes. In particular, personal appearance, oral communication and presentation ability, personal mannerisms, motivation, confidence, poise, and, in general, how the applicant handles himself or herself are all on display. The interview enables the manager to seek amplification of certain information found on the candidate's application, as well as to gain additional data.

The personal interview also gives company representatives an opportunity to mildly "sell the company" to the candidate and to respond to the candidate's specific questions about the nature of the position, the compensation and benefits package, the training program, and the company philosophy. Interviewers should, however, guard against letting the interview session become too one-sided in these attempts to interest the candidate in the company. This might be better accomplished through such means as company brochures, policy manuals, annual reports, and other materials specifically designed for this purpose. The interviewer should persist in the objective of evaluating the candidate's appropriateness for the position.

Many interview techniques are available, ranging from informal and unstructured formats to those that are quite rigid and directive. Here are some of them.[2]

Patterned interview. In the patterned interview, the interviewer uses a prepared outline of questions to elicit a basic core of information. The interviewer may work directly from the outline, recording answers as they are given, but sometimes this tends to make the conversation stilted and the applicant nervous. Greater spontaneity results when the interviewer memorizes the outline and records the answers after the interview. Among other things, use of the patterned interview ensures that each interviewer will ask the same questions and that the right questions will be asked (assuming the list of questions is appropriate for the situation). The patterned interview is inherently inflexible, although well-qualified interviewers may make slight modifications when circumstances dictate.

Nondirective interview. In the nondirective interview, the applicant is encouraged to speak freely about his or her experience, training, and future plans. The interviewer asks few direct questions and says only enough to keep the interviewee talking. The nondirective interview does not provide answers to standard questions, and much time is spent on outwardly irrelevant subjects. Some personnel experts say that a nondirective technique yields maximum insight into an individual's attitudes and interests. Expert interpretation reveals much about the applicant—often including things of which the individual is not consciously aware. This technique's proponents claim that it is the best method for probing an individual's personality in depth. The main drawback is that administering the interview and interpreting the results demand specialized instruction.

Interaction (stress) interview. The interaction interview simulates the stresses the applicant would meet in actual selling situations and provides a way to observe the applicant's reactions to them. This interviewing technique has long been used by sales executives who, in interviewing prospective sales personnel, might hand the applicant an ashtray or other object and say, "Here, sell this to me." The objective is both to see how the applicant will react to the surprise situation and to size up the candidate's probable selling ability.

Interaction interviewing has recently become a more complex and sophisticated technique. In one version, two interviewers are required—one uses psychological techniques to set up the simulated situations, and the other, who is present but is not an active participant in the interview, observes and records the applicant's reactions. Because of their subtlety, the delicacy involved in their application, and the importance of expert interpretation, the newer kinds of interaction interviews should be planned, administered, and interpreted by trained psychologists.

Rating scales. One shortcoming of the personal interview is its tendency to lack objectivity, a defect that can be reduced through rating scales. These are so constructed that the interviewer's ratings are channeled into a limited choice of responses. In evaluating an applicant's general appearance, for instance, one much-used form forces an interviewer to choose one of five descriptive phrases: very neat, nicely dressed, presentable, untidy, slovenly. Experience indicates that this results in more comparable ratings of the same individual by different interviewers. One drawback of the rating scale is that its very objectivity restricts precise description of many personal qualities. It is good practice, therefore, to encourage interviewers to explain ratings in writing whenever they feel comments are needed. Companies using rating scales as a technique for assessing job suitability must keep in mind—in accordance with the guidelines issued by such agencies as the Equal Employment Opportunity Commission (EEOC) and the Office of Federal Contract Compliance Programs (OFCCP)—that they also need empirical data to demonstrate that the technique is predictive of or significantly correlated with successful job performance and does not result in discrimination on the basis of race, color, religion, or national origin.

There is no set rule for the correct number of interviews that must take place following the initial screening and the filing of the formal application. It is, however, safe to assume that candidates in whom the company is seriously interested will be subjected to a number of interviews during the selection process. Rarely will a company depend on the results of a single interview or the reactions of a single interviewer.[3]

Background Checks

After a candidate has survived the interviewing process, the company will conduct a background investigation, which normally includes checking both employment and credit references. Since it is unlikely that candidates will offer as employment references the names of individuals who will not speak highly of them, the company should develop its own list for each applicant and contact these individuals as well as the candidate's references. Former employers and customers not listed as references by the candidate are ideal informational sources, since they have had the opportunity to observe the candidate on a firsthand basis in the work setting. These sources may validate information provided by the candidate on his or her application, as well as offer personal judgments of the candidate's suitability for the particular position.

Psychological Testing

Perhaps the most controversial aspect of the selection process involves the use of psychological testing to gather information about an applicant. Many companies avoid the use of psychological tests for two reasons: the difficulty of validating these instruments and the growing fear of legal exposure evidenced by the increasing number of complaints of discrimination filed under Title VII of the Civil Rights Act of 1964. This is not to say that the use of psychological tests in the selection process is illegal or even ill advised. In fact, quite to the contrary, the use of professionally developed, properly validated psychological tests is legal and acceptable as part of the company's selection of candidates.

Companies interested in using psychological testing as part of their selection process should ensure that the testing instruments are relevant and tailored to the positions at hand. This works best if the manager contracts with a professional psychologist for the development of tests that address the needs of the particular position.

Companies normally use a battery of psychological tests rather than a single instrument in their evaluation of candidates for sales positions. The more common include those that measure intelligence, aptitude, interest, and personality.

Intelligence tests. Intelligence tests measure an individual's general mental abilities, including such areas as analytical ability, logical reasoning, and language comprehension and usage. While the use of intelligence tests may not be relevant for all types of sales positions, they are particularly valuable for those positions with a high degree of intensive and complex training where one must master a considerable amount of difficult material in a short time.

Aptitude tests. Aptitude tests measure the specific knowledge or special abilities of an individual, such as mechanical, spatial, or artistic ability. For example, tests of reaction time, controlled movement, or hand-eye coordination may be important for measuring potential for certain kinds of production jobs. Tests of aptitude for selling positions will include such areas as communications ability, problem solving, and social aptitude. The specific nature and content of sales aptitude tests will depend on the job specifications for the particular selling position as well as those special abilities identified as leading to successful job performance. The company must buy or construct aptitude tests valid for its particular sales positions. Unfortunately, the high costs of test construction and validation make it difficult for many small companies to justify the inclusion of such instruments in their selection process.

Interest tests. A number of tests measure specific interests, including such items as hobbies and leisure-time activities. Many managers feel that there is value in measuring an applicant's interests against the interests demonstrated by successful sales personnel within the organization; unfortunately, no conclusive evidence exists that clearly correlates interests with subsequent performance in sales positions. In addition to not being valid indicators of future success in selling, these instruments readily lend themselves to false responses by the individual being tested. It is often easy to select the response felt to be important to the hiring company even when the particular response is not a true reflection of the respondent's interests. Consider the following typical question:

STATEMENT: "Monetary reward and financial well-being are
                  of prime importance to me!"

INSTRUCTION: Relative to this statement, do you (select the
                  response that best reflects your personal views)
                  a. Strongly agree?
                  b. Agree?
                  c. Have no opinion?
                  d. Disagree?
                  e. Strongly disagree?

In this example, the respondent may select response *a* because he or she feels that the hiring firm is seeking sales personnel who are highly motivated by money and personal income, whereas the respondent may actually care very little about a substantial income or a great deal of money. Interest tests may have some value in vocational counseling with employees, but caution and skepticism should accompany their use as selection devices.

Personality tests. Personality tests measure personal characteristics such as aggressiveness, dominance, stability, and persistence. Again, as with interest tests, proper validation of such instruments is quite difficult, and their best use is as screening devices to identify those individuals possessing abnormal personality traits. Any use beyond this is, in fact, suspect as to its value.

Stanton and Buskirk suggest that a testing program has the best chance of success when the firm hires a relatively large number of salespeople; when it is hiring young, inexperienced people about whom little is known; if the executives responsible for interviewing the recruits are not adept at discovering personality traits and selling aptitudes; or when the firm is willing to spend the time and money for the development of a sound program.[4]

In summary, because of legal considerations and the difficulty of developing tests with a high degree of validity, the use of psychological tests should have at most an auxiliary role in the selection process. Under no circumstances should psychological tests be the *only* factor upon which the management makes selection decisions, but they may be useful in conjunction with other selection procedures.

Physical Examination

Before employment, most sales candidates must have a complete physical examination. The hiring company will want to be sure that the applicant possesses general good health and the degree of stamina necessary for a fast-paced sales force position. Failure to require a physical examination may result in an abnormally high degree of turnover. Problems with workmen's compensation insurance may also arise in the event of illness or injury.

The Selection Decision

Once a candidate has survived the various steps in the selection process, the company must then decide whether to offer the applicant a position. The individuals within the company who are part of the selection process should conduct a thorough review of each candidate's entire package of qualifications, considering carefully not only whether the candidate will fit into the company's plans and meet its expectations but also whether the company will meet the candidate's requirements for a challenging and rewarding employment experience. Should the managers conclude that a professional relationship with the candidate would be mutually beneficial, they make a formal offer in writing and give the candidate a reasonable amount of time to consider it and to make a response. Once an offer has been accepted and employment begins, the candidate usually enters a company sales force training program.

Training

Objectives of Training

There are two broad objectives in the development and execution of sales-training programs: to prepare new salespeople for entry into the field and to enhance the job effectiveness and sales performance of veteran sales personnel on a continuing basis. Training programs may also accomplish such specific goals as the following:

Reducing sales force turnover
Enhancing job satisfaction
Increasing morale
Improving sales force efficiency
Familiarizing sales personnel with new products
Reducing sales costs
Increasing sales force service capabilities
Introducing new selling techniques or promotion programs

While we could say much about training the sales force in an ongoing way, our purpose here is to address the needs of new sales personnel. To identify the training needs of new salespeople and develop specific objectives for an initial training program, the company will need to project the abilities of its sales trainees against the job specifications for their sales positions. The initial training program, as shown in the diagram below, follows from this projection:

Content of the Training Program

Initial training programs for new members of the company's sales team provide trainees with a general introduction to the company and its policies and practices; knowledge of the company's industry, markets, and customers; detailed knowledge of the company's products; and the development of appropriate selling skills and techniques.

General company orientation. In the orientation phase, the trainee learns the company's history, organizational structure, and overall objectives, both short and long term. The initial program should also include detailed information about sales policies and practices, that is, such items as procedures for submitting orders, pricing policies, volume discounts, expense report preparation, customer service, credit policies, handling customer complaints, and special company promotions.

Industry, market, and customer information. If sales personnel are to do well, they must know the industry and market within which they will operate. The initial training program should provide participants with information about the industry in general, as well as specific data about the company's competition, with emphasis on the competitors' marketing and promotional strategies, product characteristics, market shares, and strengths and weaknesses. The trainee pays considerable attention to a description of the company's customers during these initial phases, especially to their needs, buying habits, product preferences, and service requirements—indispensable information for an understanding of the customer.

Knowledge of the company's products. For obvious reasons, a major portion of the initial training program will educate the trainees in all aspects of the company's product line. New sales personnel will need to develop expertise in the full range of products the company offers, including product characteristics and specifications as well as alternatives, availability, and service. Trainees will need to develop a talent for aiding customers in making informed buying decisions. The amount of time and effort for this portion of the initial training program will depend, to a large extent, on the nature and complexity of the company's product line and its applications. Clearly, more time and money will go for training a computer salesperson than for training someone selling storm windows.

Selling skills. Instruction in selling techniques also constitutes an important segment of the company training program. The content of this phase of training will normally include discussions of effective procedures for prospecting customers, following up on leads, making sales presentations, holding demonstrations, and closing sales. Depending on the degree of flexibility afforded sales personnel by the company, initial training may include intensive preparation on standard company sales presentations, used by all the company's salespeople. Conversely, if greater flexibility is allowed, it may involve discussions of a variety of generally successful sales presentation techniques, permitting the trainee to decide which approach he or she will find most comfortable.

Training Methods and Techniques

There are many training methods for presenting the content of the initial training program to the participants. Which method will work best is a function of the specific areas to cover, the talent of the program instructors, and the nature and degree of sophistication of the participants. Generally, the trainer will use no one method exclusively throughout the entire program but will select the most appropriate approach for the best fit with each information component. For instance, lectures, visual displays, and handouts seem to work well in explaining preparation of company expense reports; role playing may be more suitable in dealing with material on sales presentations. The various training techniques, taken singly or in combination, include lectures, group discussions (conference or impromptu), case analysis, business simulations, demonstrations, programmed instruction, role playing, audio-visual display, correspondence courses, and on-the-job training.

Evaluating the Effectiveness of the Training Program

Planning and executing sales-training programs involve considerable investments of time, money, and effort. Therefore it is important to measure (to the extent possible given the inherent difficulty of such evaluation) the effectiveness of the training programs in meeting their objectives. Although much disagreement exists concerning proper evaluative techniques, most people agree that the company should attempt to judge two specific areas, one dealing with the near term, the other with the long term.[5]

On a near-term basis, the company should evaluate the effectiveness of the *program's content delivery system* (lectures, group projects, cases, and so on) and the extent to which the participants have mastered the material. To measure the trainee's learning, instructors may use such devices as quizzes, instructor feedback, peer evaluation, and training staff ratings. These devices not only indicate whether trainees are absorbing the subject matter but also can raise the morale of trainees who are performing well. Evaluation is a two-way street, and one can learn a great deal about the quality of the program, the instructional staff, and the training techniques by having the participants rate each training module or session and instructor. Properly administered, these evaluations will aid the training manager in identifying areas of instruction in need of improvement for the next group of participants.

On a long-term basis, the company will want to evaluate whether the initial sales training has resulted in *successful job performance* in the field. Since many factors affect sales performance, it is difficult to determine the degree to which training has contributed to the results. One frequently used method measures the time required by a new salesperson to reach a companywide average level of sales performance; another method compares the sales productivity of untrained personnel with that of trained sales personnel. Whatever approach the company employs in its evaluation, it must bear in mind that the results derived are at best only crude estimates of the training program's effectiveness.

Assigning Salespeople to Territories

When the training of its new sales personnel is over, the company is ready for the fourth and final stage in its program of building the sales organization: assignment of new sales personnel to territories. Three factors make the process of territorial assignment a difficult and complex undertaking:

1. Sales personnel are not all alike. They differ in their personal characteristics, overall abilities, and potential for success in the field.
2. Sales territories are not all alike. Territorial sales potential differs because of such factors as varying geographical conditions, customs, customer types, and competition.
3. Performance of sales personnel will often vary as a function of their specific territorial assignment even though the territories have similar sales potential.

Under ideal conditions, given the divergence in the attributes and abilities of sales personnel and territorial sales potential, the sales manager should strive to assign salespeople to territories in a way that maximizes each salesperson's relative contribution to the company's overall profit picture. We will now apply the factors mentioned above to the development of various examples of territorial assignments for sales personnel. The illustrations that follow draw heavily on James Hauk's excellent work in this area.[6]

Before making specific assignments, the sales manager must develop a method for gauging each salesperson's potential for success in the field. This can be done through the use of an "ability/opportunity rating" to identify a salesperson's probability of achieving the maximum available sales potential within a specific territory. For example, a salesperson with a rating of 0.9 who is assigned to a territory projected to have a sales volume potential of $500,000 would be expected to achieve a level of sales amounting to $450,000 (multiplying the sales volume potential of the territory by the salesperson's ability rating):

Sales volume potential	Ability rating	Estimated sales volume
$500,000	× 0.9 =	$450,000

Ability ratings for each salesperson incorporate a number of factors, including the nature and extent of prior selling experience, results of examinations, performance in company sales-training programs, initiative, sense of motivation, and so on. These are subjective judgments for the most part, are made by management, and may vary depending on the characteristics of the salesperson's territorial assignment. In other words, a salesperson may have a high rating for an assignment in one territory but, because of differences in the types of customers, may register as a potentially weak producer in another territory.

Consider the following example of sales personnel with differing ability ratings assigned to territories of equivalent sales volume potential:

Territory	Sales volume potential	Salesperson	Ability rating	Estimated sales volume
Eastside	$ 300,000	1	1.0	$300,000
Westside	$ 300,000	2	0.8	$240,000
Uptown	$ 300,000	3	0.7	$210,000
Downtown	$ 300,000	4	0.5	$150,000
Total all areas	$1,200,000			$900,000

While it is probably unrealistic to assume that all territories will offer equal sales volume potential, this example illustrates how the ability rating may help in estimating overall sales volume. Here the accuracy of the estimated sales volume of $900,000 depends on the appropriateness of both the ability ratings for sales personnel and the territorial sales volume potentials. Note that since all the territories in the example have the same sales volume potential, changing individual sales personnel assignments will not alter the total estimated volume of $900,000.

The sales manager may decide, however, to redesign the sales territories to take full advantage of the sales abilities of the company's better salespeople. He or she may decide to expand the Eastside sales territory, where the best salesperson is assigned, while at the same time reducing the size of the Downtown territory, where the weakest salesperson has been operating. In addition, the manager might redesign both the Westside and Uptown territories so that all four territories carry a sales potential proportionate to the ability ratings of the sales force. Such a decision would result in the following:

Territory	Sales volume potential	Salesperson	Ability rating	Estimated sales volume
Eastside	$ 400,000	1	1.0	$400,000
Westside	$ 320,000	2	0.8	$256,000
Uptown	$ 280,000	3	0.7	$196,000
Downtown	$ 200,000	4	0.5	$100,000
Total all areas	$1,200,000			$952,000

The table shows an increase in productivity of $52,000. There is a natural temptation here to continue to expand the Eastside and Westside territories while contracting the Uptown and Downtown areas to take further advantage of the differentials in sales personnel ability ratings. The manager must be careful not to carry this approach to an extreme, however, because soon enough the Eastside and Westside territories will have expanded such that ideal coverage of the territory by the assigned sales personnel will no longer be possible. This, of course, will result in a reduction in their individual ability ratings and their actual performance. At the same time, the reduction in the Uptown and Downtown areas may produce better coverage by salespersons 3 and 4 with a resulting increase in their ability ratings.

Where the manager has the flexibility to rearrange sales territories and sales personnel assignments, he or she will want to examine several potential configurations of assignments and territories to select the combination offering the maximum contribution to sales volume and profit. Obviously this would be extremely cumbersome to calculate by hand, but with the use of computer-assisted linear-programming techniques, such solutions are not difficult to identify.

The key, then, in assigning sales personnel to territories lies in properly identifying both the salesperson's ability ratings and the sales territory's volume potentials. Once the territorial assignments have been made, this completes the building of the sales organization. Let us now look at how we run it.

MANAGING THE SALES ORGANIZATION

Effective management of the sales organization involves determining the appropriate compensation package, maintaining high levels of motivation within the sales organization, and providing general and ongoing supervision.

Compensation

Sales force compensation programs should have the following objectives:

1. To provide sales personnel with a fair and reasonable income
2. To provide incentive through the availability of rewards in direct proportion to performance
3. To attract and maintain a competent and motivated sales force

To achieve these objectives, the company's compensation plan should meet several criteria. It should provide a living wage, preferably in the form of a guaranteed income; fit with the rest of the motivational program; be fair, allowing sales personnel to receive equal pay for equal performance and not penalizing sales personnel because of factors beyond their control; be easy for sales personnel to understand and calculate their earnings without difficulty; provide for easy adjustments in pay when performance changes occur; be economical to administer; and, finally, help in attaining the objectives of the sales organization.[7]

Types of Compensation Plans

Compensation plans include both *direct* and *indirect* elements of compensation.[8] There are essentially three direct methods of monetary compensation: straight-salary, straight-commission, and combined salary-plus-commission. In addition, the indirect components include compensation for expenses and fringe benefits.

Straight-salary. A straight-salary compensation plan is the direct payment of predetermined, fixed sums of money for services rendered over a specified period of time. The amount of compensation, therefore, is a function of a time interval rather than the level of sales production. The primary advantage to the salesperson of the straight-salary plan is stability of income and, therefore, little financial uncertainty. The obvious disadvantage, then, is that there is no provision for near-term additional compensation flowing from high levels of productivity. Some sales managers would argue that since there are no immediate incentives for increased efforts or enhanced performance, sales personnel may put forth only the minimal effort in carrying out their responsibilities. This position is probably overstated in most instances, since good salespeople are motivated by more than money, as we will discuss later in this chapter. Furthermore, regular salary reviews are as much a part of the sales organization's wage and salary procedures as they are of other parts of the company. Certainly a successful salesperson can be rewarded for outstanding performance by a significant salary increase, just as engineers, financial analysts, and production supervisors would be.

Despite the argument that incentives are necessary in order to motivate the sales force, in some situations a straight-salary compensation format is preferable. For example, a straight-salary plan seems best where the purchase decision process is long and complex, involving multiple decision makers. It is also appropriate when the sales force must undertake considerable missionary work or customer service time. Straight-salary is also an appropriate method of compensation for new sales personnel, at least until the time that they would be attaining levels of sales volume consistent with the overall average of the veteran sales force. In addition, sales management has found the straight-salary plan advantageous where it wishes to alter the nature of the tasks of sales personnel from time to time—for example, calling upon a high-performing salesperson to leave the field temporarily to act as an instructor in a sales-training program. With straight-salary there should be little resistance from the salesperson toward this temporary assignment, since the time away from selling activities will not affect the level of compensation and may enhance his or her opportunities for promotion. On the other hand, such a move might create bad feelings if the salesperson were being paid on either a salary-plus-commission or a straight-commission basis where time away from selling efforts could result in lost income.

In addition to the increased control and flexibility provided management under this plan, a straight-salary method of compensation is easier to administer. As we mentioned earlier, firms using the straight-salary approach should be prepared to appraise sales performance regularly and to make appropriate salary adjustments.

Straight-commission. Whereas the straight-salary method compensates salespeople for activity over a specific period of time, the straight-commission method pays individuals on the basis of sales results. Thus a straight-commission compensation plan provides the salesperson with an incentive to produce, with income totally dependent on achievements.

To establish a straight-commission compensation plan, the company will need to decide on three factors: (1) the *commission base* on which to measure sales productivity, that is, the unit of measurement for which the salesperson will receive payment (for example, net sales volume in dollars or number of units of product sold); (2) the *commission rate*, which identifies the amount of compensation paid for the unit of productivity attained (for example, a 5 percent commission on net sales in dollars; in other words, a $5 commission for each $100 in net sales achieved—see the accompanying illustration for variable commission rate structures); and (3) the *specific point* where commission payments will begin (usually zero sales for those on a straight-commission basis—higher for those on a salary-plus-commission basis).

Commission rates can be progressive or constant or regressive. Consider the following examples:

Progressive rate	Constant rate	Regressive rate
2% on first $15,000	5% on all sales	6% on first $10,000
5% on $15,000–$30,000		3% on $10,000–$25,000
7% on amount over $30,000		2% on amount over $25,000

The obvious advantage of such a method is the creation of incentive toward greater accomplishments on the part of the sales force. As such, it is not unusual for the company to assume that salespeople paid on a straight-commission basis will work with greater vigor and put in longer hours than those individuals on a straight-salary plan. The straight-commission method also gives the company increased control of sales costs as a percentage of sales revenue, since selling costs will vary in direct proportion to sales activity. This is particularly beneficial for smaller companies with limited cash resources.

Of course, the straight-commission method is not without its disadvantages. One of the major difficulties is that sales personnel will tend to exercise a great deal of independence. As a result, it may be quite difficult to obtain their cooperation in altering their activities (for example, spending more time on customer service or other nonselling tasks) when they feel such activities may negatively affect near-term income. In this instance, the sales force can become somewhat difficult to control. Beyond this, a salesperson's earnings may fluctuate as a result of factors totally out of his or her direct control—a declining economy for example. Such occurrences can be demotivating to the sales force. In addition, there is potential for abuse by the salesperson in order to enhance his or her personal earnings. Selling products not suited to the customer's requirements, overstocking dealers, and making exaggerated claims are but three examples of this risk. At the extreme, fraudulent orders, later canceled, may be placed with the company through collusion between the salesperson and a customer. Companies must establish sales policies and practices to guard against these significant risks of abuse.

As we said earlier, the straight-commission method of compensation seems appropriate for companies in a weak financial condition. And this method is useful where a company uses numerous part-time sales personnel or requires very little in the way of nonselling activities of the sales force.

Combined salary-plus-commission. The majority of sales force compensation plans involve a combination of salary-plus-commission. Obviously the notion behind the merger of the straight-salary and straight-commission plans is to develop a method of payment having the advantages of each while reducing their combined disadvantages. This method is the most difficult to administer because of the large amount of reporting and clerical work necessary. Administrative complexities are compounded by plans that involve time period cutoffs, sales quota thresholds, sliding commission rates, and other provisions to make the incentive compensation fully reflective of the desired sales performance. Beyond that, the potential abuses noted earlier under straight-commission plans are possible in this environment as well.

Indirect Compensation

We said earlier that there are two methods of indirect compensation: reimbursement for expenses and fringe benefits.

Reimbursement for expenses. While reimbursement for expenses does not specifically constitute direct compensation, it is considered as part of the overall compensation agreement with the company sales force. There are three methods of handling expenses:

1. Full or partial direct reimbursement—the company pays for sales-related expenses.
2. No company reimbursement—the salesperson pays all expenses.
3. Predetermined company allowance—the salesperson uses this allowance as he or she chooses for various expenses. Expenses in excess of the allowance are the salesperson's responsibility.

The first option seems to be the most widely used method of reimbursement for sales expenses. Its major disadvantage is the potential for misuse. Companies choosing this method should develop effective methods for cost control and clear policies about which expenses will be reimbursed and in what amounts. When the company compensates its sales force on a straight-commission basis, it will usually choose the second option. Here the sales personnel essentially operate as independent businesspeople and, as such, are responsible for their own expenses. The final method requires the salesperson to control expenses carefully, since he or she is personally responsible for any expenditures beyond the allowance. From the company perspective, this establishes a known, fixed sales expense easy to budget and control. On the other hand, this method is likely to be the least popular among sales personnel.

While expense reimbursement policies should attempt to keep expenditures within reasonable limits, the company must be fair in its approach to allow the salesperson to function effectively and comfortably as well as to avoid the creation of resentment.

Fringe benefits. To be competitive for sales personnel as well as to meet certain legal requirements, the company will generally offer a comprehensive package of fringe benefits. This package could amount to as much as 30 to 40 percent of the total sales compensation. Many fringe benefits are available (the first three below are required; the rest are optional): Social Security; workmen's compensation; unemployment insurance; holidays, vacations, and leaves; profit sharing; pension plans; life insurance; hospital, dental, and medical insurance; stock options; credit unions; day care for children; reimbursement for educational expenses; discounts on company products; company social events; memberships in clubs and organizations; use of company recreational facilities; and an automobile. The choice of benefits offered is a matter of company policy, guided by financial as well as competitive considerations.

Final Stages in Developing the Sales Compensation Plan

Once the objectives, components, and methods of the sales compensation plan have been set, it is important to pretest the plan by seeing how it would have worked had it been in effect over the past three or four years. Both the cost to the company and the income that sales personnel would have earned figure in the assessment. Much like pretesting a product, pretesting the sales compensation plan should iron out any wrinkles before it becomes official. Following the pretest, management introduces the plan to the sales force, preferably in small conference groups where dialogue between management and salespeople is easier. Management explains the complete package and its rationale, and sales personnel have an opportunity to raise questions and get answers directly. Finally, management installs the plan, either for the entire sales force or by introducing it gradually in a "rollout procedure," that is, putting it into effect in one or two territories at a time (as one might introduce a new product).[9] A final note: Management must evaluate the sales compensation plan periodically. Conditions change and something as important as the compensation plan has to be up to date. Constant reappraisal helps make this a reality.

In summary, a carefully considered, well-designed, and effectively controlled compensation plan will serve a variety of purposes, not the least of which are attracting and maintaining a solid, enthusiastic sales force. Managed properly, the compensation package will stimulate sales personnel, aid control, and facilitate accomplishment of overall sales objectives.

Motivation

We have discussed the benefits of a carefully planned and executed sales personnel selection program, the need for a relevant and effective program for initial and ongoing training, and the importance of an equitable and well-designed system for compensation of sales personnel. All of these play a critical role in the motivation of the sales force. It is extremely difficult to stimulate individuals who, through improper selection or poor training, are not well suited for the positions they hold. It is equally difficult to motivate individuals if the various compensation and evaluation programs under which they operate bear no relationship to their level of performance. We will consider a number of additional ways to satisfy the motivational needs of salespeople, but first we will look briefly at this concept called motivation.

The Nature and Process
of Motivation

Admittedly, differing levels of sales performance among the various members of the sales force can be traced to a number of factors: differing skill levels, experience, territorial areas, and so on. Still, there is also strong evidence that differences in sales performance mean differences in levels of motivation among salespeople.

Psychologists and other behavioral scientists are in general agreement that all human behavior is directed toward the accomplishment of certain goals, some of which have come into existence because of some unfulfilled need in the individual. While there are several theories on motivation of the sales force, perhaps the most relevant is Herzberg's motivation-hygiene theory.[10]

Herzberg's Motivation-Hygiene Theory

Herzberg's *motivation-hygiene theory*, sometimes referred to as the *two-factor theory of motivation*, is of particular interest to sales managers, since it is directly concerned with motivation in the work environment. Based on his research in the area of needs satisfaction, Herzberg concluded that two factors (or conditions) operating in the workplace had quite different effects on an individual's level of motivation. He referred to these conditions as hygiene factors and motivational factors.

Hygiene factors. According to Herzberg, certain conditions related to one's job will cause great dissatisfaction when they are not present. But, paradoxically, adding these factors if they are not present will not result in building strong motivation. Employees require these conditions, called hygiene factors (or maintenance factors), to maintain reasonable levels of job satisfaction. Herzberg asserted that many managers falsely assume that the addition of these factors will create a high degree of motivation when in fact their addition will only tend to reduce dissatisfaction. Herzberg identified the following as hygiene factors:

Company policies	Technical supervision
Salary and fringe benefits	Personal life
Job security	Interpersonal relations with supervisor
Working conditions	Interpersonal relations with peers
Status	Interpersonal relations with subordinates

Motivational factors. Herzberg identified another set of conditions, which if not present in one's job would not necessarily create dissatisfaction, but when present in the job situation these conditions, called motivational factors, can create high levels of motivation. The following are motivational factors:

Achievement	Challenging work
Recognition	Personal growth and development
Advancement	Responsibility

The obvious distinction between the hygiene and motivational factors is that the former are environmental in nature, that is, they do not relate to the content of the job itself. Motivational factors, on the other hand, are job centered, since they directly relate to the job, its challenges, its opportunities for growth and development, its responsibilities, and the individual's actual performance in the position. The implication of this theory for the sales manager is that he or she must seek ways to make the salesperson's work more challenging and provide more opportunities for growth and advancement. While added monetary incentive may in the short run reduce employee dissatisfaction, what the employee needs is the addition of motivational factors to create a long-run environment and job situation conducive to motivation at high levels.

Activities Aimed at Motivating the Sales Force

This section will briefly review four tools commonly used to stimulate sales personnel to higher levels of performance: recognition programs, contests, promotion opportunities, and sales meetings.

Recognition programs. Recognition programs motivate sales personnel through the use of nonmonetary rewards for performance. While recognition may come because of longevity, recognition programs are most effective when they stimulate sales personnel to higher levels of performance. They aim at the creation of opportunities for recognition through achievement in the context of the sales position itself. Recognition programs bear a direct relationship to the motivational factors we mentioned above. Recognition can take many forms, including newspaper announcements of individual accomplishments, citations and plaques, presentations at annual meetings, and so on. Whatever the form, it is important to recognize self-esteem as a key determinant in job satisfaction and job performance. "Management should enhance self-esteem by regularly providing positive reinforcement in the form of personal recognition and monetary rewards, as well as socially visible acknowledgment of good performance."[11]

Contests. We discuss sales contests in detail in Chapter 16, but one preliminary point bears mentioning here. If contests are to be effective as motivators, they must provide everyone with an opportunity to win. If salespeople do not feel they have an opportunity to win, they will not expend a great deal of effort trying. There is no advantage to running a contest based on total dollar sales volume when there are great differences in the sales potential among the territories. The salesperson in the rural territory cannot realistically compete with his or her counterpart in a lucrative metropolitan market. To be equitable, contests must use such measurements as percentage of increase in sales volume, number of new accounts opened, and greatest percentage reduction in sales expense as the contest benchmarks. Contests should be used sparingly. Run too frequently, they are not apt to muster the necessary enthusiasm.

Promotion opportunities. Most salespeople find motivation in a vision of advancement within the organization. Sales managers should ensure that a clear understanding exists as to the general progression of sales personnel up through the ranks of the company. Indeed, job descriptions should indicate the positions for which the successful salesperson would probably qualify. If promotion is to serve as a motivational device, then management must spell out and communicate the opportunity for such promotion throughout the organization.

Sales meetings. Periodic sales meetings are also effective in generating enthusiasm and motivating salespeople on local, regional, and national levels. With careful planning, they can evoke high levels of excitement and enthusiasm. Sales meetings usually focus on a particular theme, such as introducing a new product, presenting new company policies and procedures, or announcing new officers and executives. Considerable motivation may also come from providing members of the sales force with an opportunity to interact with their fellow sales personnel and executives. Field selling is a lonely position, and sharing experiences and insights of either a personal or a professional nature with others who have common problems, goals, and aspirations can be an energizing event.

Additional Insights into Motivation

Until the mid-1970s there was little exploration of motivation as it touched the sales management area specifically. Now, however, such scholars as Ford, Walker, and Churchill have done considerable research on sales force motivation and the effects of different types of incentives and rewards. One study reached the following conclusions: Salespeople, both young and old, are motivated by money; personal growth and career advancement opportunities are great motivators for salespeople, especially younger ones, and for the younger salespeople, these factors are often more important than pay increases; recognition programs are not viewed as an effective motivational force; and individual psychological characteristics have no influence on the kinds of rewards desired by salespeople.[12] These findings both support and refute some of the conventional wisdom in sales management as well as the Herzberg factors we outlined above. Professional sales managers would do well to keep abreast of developments in motivational theory and research.

Supervision

The field salesperson tends to be thought of as "The Lone Ranger" of the marketing organization. This salesperson is viewed as being on his or her own time schedule, traveling the territory, making presentations, entertaining customers and prospects in fine restaurants, and handling service calls and complaints—in whatever manner seems appropriate to him or her at the time. Despite this exaggerated portrayal, there is a substantial amount of reality in this description, and many individuals actually embark on a field sales career because of the freedom of action they can enjoy.

Importance of Supervision

It is the "freedom of action" perception of the field sales position that makes the task of supervision within the field organization both essential and delicate. Stanton and Buskirk have identified six principal objectives of effective sales supervision.[13]

Training. Only a small part of the training necessary for the development of a successful salesperson can take place in classrooms and workshops.

A substantial part of this personal growth must take place on the job under the observation, direction, and guidance of a knowledgeable field sales manager.

Sales assistance. In certain selling situations, a salesperson may need technical backup or other support in the selling effort. Frequently, the field manager can provide this assistance.

Policy enforcement. One way of ensuring that company policies and procedures are being carried out is through observation and evaluation of day-to-day activities. Some field sales tasks, such as missionary and service activities, may require more frequent supervision because traditional sales performance measures may not readily reveal failures to carry out assigned responsibilities.

Improved performance. Many salespeople will improve their performance as a result of closer attention by their managers; on the other hand, too much attention may cause resentment and distract from performance. The sales manager must be sensitive to differences in individual response to supervision.

Better morale. As noted earlier, field selling can be a solitary, lonely activity. The knowledge that someone in the organization cares about the field salesperson and his or her work can have a positive effect on morale.

Field intelligence. Supervision is also a way of determining what is happening in the field. Since a field manager cannot make appropriate judgments and evaluations without this knowledge, it is an essential ingredient in the management process.

How Much Supervision?

Given the noted values derived from proper supervision of the sales force, one ought to ask how much of it is necessary. This decision is a balance among the needs and interests of the sales force, the needs and interests of the managers, and the costs to the firm of supervisory activity.

Too much or too little supervision can both be costly. Excessive supervision can alienate the sales force and at the same time incur unproductive salary and travel expenses. Insufficient supervision can mean an indifferent sales force, a management lacking in understanding of activity in the field, and weak sales results. Effective supervision is at a balance point between these extremes.

The first criterion is the quality of the sales force. Sales organizations consisting primarily of experienced, proven salespeople will require substantially less supervision than one consisting of young, inexperienced, new personnel. Another factor in the decision is the importance of the sales effort to the success of the company. In organizations marketing sophisticated technical equipment (large-scale computers for example), the role of the sales force dominates the promotional plan. Closer supervision and direction may be an essential ingredient in the company's success, as each sale has a major impact. Conversely, a company whose sales organization does primarily promotion and shelf stocking in retail outlets is far less vulnerable to the performance of an individual salesperson. The size and geographical distribution of the sales force can also influence the degree of supervision employed. Supervisory costs escalate as the sales force becomes larger or becomes dispersed across the country or the world. There is clearly a cost-benefit trade-off between more and less supervisory activity. Finally, the compensation system in use can affect supervision needs. A system with strong incentives will have less need for supervision, while one without these incentives may require more.

We have concentrated on the general characteristics affecting the need for sales supervision, but we must not forget the central importance of the personality, character, and motivation of the individual salesperson. Successful sales managers learn to temper the general guidelines with a clear knowledge and understanding of the particular needs of the individuals they supervise.

Managing the sales organization, as we have seen, involves several activities. The effectiveness with which the organization is managed, of course, directly affects overall performance. It is crucial, therefore, to monitor the sales effort continually.

EVALUATING AND CONTROLLING THE SALES EFFORT

Although evaluation and control of the promotional program, including the sales effort, are the subject of Chapter 18, it is appropriate to say a few words about this important activity here. In evaluating and controlling the sales effort, management accomplishes a number of tasks: developing sales performance standards, measuring actual performance, comparing actual performance with standards, and initiating corrective action to close the gap between established standards and actual performance.

Developing Performance Standards

The development of standards for performance is the starting point in designing an effective program for evaluation and control of the company's sales effort. Standards must reflect both the company's and the sales force's overall and specific objectives for sales volume, growth, and profitability. Individuals with responsibility for establishing standards for performance must be aware not only of what the broad objectives of the company are but also of *how* individuals can and do carry out these objectives.

Establishing Criteria

Good performance standards require accurate and precise definitions of management's expectations. There are both quantitative and qualitative performance criteria.

Quantitative performance criteria. Objective gauges of sales performance—the most widely used—measure both *effort* and *results*. Criteria related to results (output factors) include sales volume—in dollars, in units, by territory, by product, by customer, as a percentage of potential; gross margin—by product, customer, or order size, or in ratio to the number of calls; and accounts—gained and lost. Effort criteria (input factors) include calls per day; days worked; selling time versus nonselling time; direct selling experience—in dollars or as a percentage of sales volume; nonselling activities—advertising displays set up, number of service calls made, or number of meetings held with dealers.[14]

Qualitative performance criteria. In addition to the many quantitative factors in the evaluation of sales performance, it is sound practice to use a number of qualitative measures as well. Various factors, not objectively measurable like, say, sales, also affect sales performance, and the management must therefore consider them in the performance of sales personnel.[15] These subjective factors include product knowledge, customer knowledge, competitive knowledge, personal appearance, attitude, quality of sales presentations, and ability to make decisions. Since these criteria are loosely defined and do not lend themselves to objective and exact measurement, sales management sometimes hesitates to include them in the evaluation of sales performance. Which particular qualitative factors should be used depends on the nature of the sales position under review, the philosophy of company management, and that company's particular sales strategy.

Setting Specific Standards

Once management has selected the specific performance criteria it will use, it must then decide how it will determine satisfactory levels of performance. Setting performance standards presents an interesting challenge to management. It must ensure that standards are reasonably attainable but at the same time sufficiently demanding. Standards must contribute to the morale of the sales force, not undermine it. Standards must, above everything else, be equitable.

Measuring Actual Performance

Once management has decided on the standards it will apply in its analysis of sales performance, it is ready to focus its efforts on the development of a system for gathering the data it will need in that analysis. At the very minimum, the company's efforts at measuring actual sales performance will involve (1) determining the information necessary to measure performance, (2) creating a system for transmitting and receiving this information, (3) identifying the specific sources of the needed information, (4) establishing a methodology for collecting and structuring the data, and (5) developing a formal reporting system for presenting the information to the interested parties on a regular basis. The key ingredient is that a well-designed mechanism must be in place if management is to measure performance accurately. And the mechanism must be functioning smoothly for the timely acquisition and use of data. A breakdown in the measurement system could be most troublesome.

Comparing Performance
with Standards

The task of comparing actual performance with standards presents management with a major challenge because much of the comparison is what they term in football a judgment call. Management cannot apply standards across the board, since there are so many recognizable differences among territorial size and sales potential, competition, customer groupings, and the sales personnel themselves. Judgment of each individual's performance must be according to his or her own set of objectives and expectations.

For example, one salesperson may report monthly expenses significantly higher than another salesperson's; however, the differential in expense may be entirely because of territorial differences. It is even possible that the salesperson reporting the lower expenses may be spending excessively given the nature of the territory, while the salesperson with the higher expenses may in fact be thrifty. In another case, a salesperson who seems to have performed poorly on the basis of the total number of orders generated may actually have been very successful in opening a number of long-sought-after new accounts, each requiring considerable time and effort. The comparison of actual performance with standards, therefore, requires both a comprehensive knowledge of the specific market conditions that may influence performance and an informed judgment on the part of those doing the evaluating.

Comparisons of actual performance with standards are generally conducted on three major bases: analysis of sales volume, analysis of sales productivity and costs, and analysis of individual performance, using the criteria we have mentioned. To get the most value from this important activity, all three types of analysis are necessary. The results determine what, if any, corrective action to take.

Taking Corrective Action

The final stage in the evaluation and control of the company's sales efforts is the application of corrective measures to areas of unsatisfactory performance. A careful diagnosis of problem situations isolates the specific causes, and then come the development and application of appropriate remedial measures. Causes of unsatisfactory performance can usually be traced to one or a combination of the following: capability of the salesperson, time allocation of the salesperson to various tasks, poor territory potential and structure, unrealistic objectives or performance criteria. The natural inclination, faced with indications of unsatisfactory performance, is to find fault with the individual salesperson. Management should avoid the tendency to focus at once on the salesperson and should instead proceed cautiously to seek the cause or causes of substandard sales performance. The problem may not rest with the salesperson at all but with unrealistic standards. On the other hand, should the evidence indicate that the poor performance attaches to the individual salesperson, management has three alternatives: retraining the salesperson, providing close supervision, or if all else fails or is simply not feasible because of a mismatch, replacing the salesperson.

The evaluation and control of sales performance culminates in either a confirmation or a redefinition of sales objectives and methods. The economics of the company, the competition, and the marketplace are constantly changing. The company's objectives and methods must be updated to be in tune with new realities. Efforts to evaluate sales performance should always complete a circle, starting with the company's objectives, proceeding through the actions and evaluations of people in the field, and returning to a fresh understanding of the company and its place in the scheme of things.

SUMMARY

Once there is a sales strategy, it is necessary to execute that strategy. The two key components of making a sales strategy work are building and managing the sales organization.

Building the sales organization means recruiting, selecting, and training sales personnel and assigning them to territories. The recruiting process requires cultivation of both internal and external sources. The selection process consists of several different stages, each stage typically serving as a filter setting up the next stage. For those individuals who are hired by the company, training comes next. Training prepares new recruits for entry into selling and increases the effectiveness of veteran salespeople. Most training programs concentrate on company information, product information, customer information, and selling skills and techniques. Yet another aspect of building the sales organization relates to assigning salespeople to territories, a process that requires careful attention to detail.

In managing the sales organization, the major concerns are compensation, motivation, and supervision. A variety of compensation plans are available, but whatever the type of plan, it should meet the criteria of fairness, simplicity, flexibility, and compatibility with the motivational program. Motivating the sales force demands considerable attention because a highly motivated sales force is a productive one. We discussed several ways to help stimulate salespeople, beyond the compensation plan itself. Recognition programs, contests, worthwhile and clear opportunities for advancement, and the exchanges and sociability of sales meetings can be great motivators.

The nature of the sales job puts a premium on effective supervision. Sales management must try to recognize that the "right" amount of supervising is a product of the needs of the sales personnel, the requirements of management, and the costs. Making sure that there is not too much or too little supervision takes excellent judgment.

No activity is more important to sales success than evaluating and controlling the sales effort. This process comprises four stages: developing performance standards—in which management establishes the criteria to apply to sales personnel; measuring actual performance—the collecting, recording, and structuring of data to be used in measuring sales efforts; comparing actual performance with standards—which requires analysis of factors such as sales volume, sales productivity, costs, and individual performance; and taking corrective action to close the distance between actual performance and established standards—to get the sales effort on the right track.

Executing the sales strategy, therefore, encompasses many activities and requires great attention to detail by sales management. Without question, the sales effort in itself is important. However, it is only one part of the total promotional effort. The sales program's effectiveness is very much related to the quality of the advertising effort—and to the sales promotion and public relations efforts. With our detailed examination of advertising and personal selling in mind, we turn now to sales promotion and, later on, to public relations.

REVIEW AND DISCUSSION QUESTIONS

1. Explain the importance of recruiting.
2. Identify and discuss the several sources of recruits for the sales force. Which do you believe are the best sources? Why?

3. State the advantages and disadvantages of the following sources of recruits: (a) educational institutions, (b) employment agencies, and (c) sales personnel from competing companies.

4. What are the stages in the selection process? Explain each stage.

5. Discuss the importance of the personal interview in the selection process. What would you be looking for in the sales candidate's interview performance?

6. Describe the various interviewing techniques. Which would you prefer? Why?

7. Do you believe psychological testing is an important part of the selection process? Why or why not?

8. There are several objectives associated with sales-training programs. How many can you name?

9. What are the benefits of sales training?

10. Explain in detail the major content areas in the typical sales-training program.

11. What are the different methods and techniques used in sales-training programs? Explain the advantages and limitations of each.

12. Describe the specific training needs of the following:
    a. The new, inexperienced salesperson selling personal computers to small businesses
    b. The newly hired, experienced (same industry) salesperson selling construction equipment to general contractors
    c. The former industrial goods salesperson just hired to sell paper products to grocery stores
    d. The retail-selling clerk who has just accepted a position selling space for a regional magazine
    e. The former textbook publisher's sales representative just hired to sell office furniture

13. What is involved in assigning salespeople to territories? Give examples.

14. Describe the characteristics of a good sales compensation program. Also, what are the specific requirements of a sales compensation plan itself?

15. Distinguish between the different types of sales compensation plans, including the advantages and limitations of each type.

16. Describe the nature and process of motivation as applied to sales personnel.

17. Explain Herzberg's motivation-hygiene theory.

18. What are the different techniques of motivating sales personnel?

19. *Devise some guidelines for effectively motivating a sales force to excellence.*

20. *Explain the importance of supervision. What benefits can be derived from a well-conceived supervision program?*

NOTES

1. Gilbert A. Churchill, Jr., Neil M. Ford, and Orville C. Walker, *Sales Force Management* (Homewood, Ill.: Richard D. Irwin, 1981), p. 308.

2. Richard R. Still, Edward W. Cundiff, and Norman A. P. Govoni, *Sales Management: Decisions, Strategies and Cases*, 4th ed. (Englewood Cliffs, N.J.: Prentice-Hall, 1981), pp. 354–55.

3. Gordon R. Storholm, *Sales Management* (Englewood Cliffs, N.J.: Prentice-Hall, 1982), p. 118.

4. William J. Stanton and Richard H. Buskirk, *Management of the Sales Force*, 6th ed. (Homewood, Ill.: Richard D. Irwin, 1983), pp. 152–53.

5. Alan J. Dubinsky and Wilhom A. Staples, "Sales Training: Salespeople's Preparedness and Managerial Implications," *Journal of Personal Selling and Sales Management*, Fall-Winter 1981–82, pp. 24–31.

6. James G. Hauk, "Research in Personal Selling," in *Science in Marketing*, ed. George W. Schwartz (New York: John Wiley, 1965), pp. 219–28.

7. Still, Cundiff, and Govoni, *Sales Management*, p. 423.

8. For an excellent summary of the alternative sales compensation plans and other compensation-related data, see "1984 Survey of Selling Costs," *Sales and Marketing Management*, February 20, 1984, pp. 59–68.

9. Stanton and Buskirk, *Management of the Sales Force*, pp. 296–97.

10. Frederick Herzberg, Bernard Mausner, and Barbara Snyderman, *The Motivation to Work* (New York: John Wiley, 1959), pp. 113–19.

11. Richard P. Bagozzi, "Performance and Satisfaction in an Industrial Sales Force: An Examination of Their Antecedents and Simultaneity," *Journal of Marketing*, Spring 1980, pp. 65–77.

12. Neil M. Ford, Orville C. Walker, Jr., and Gilbert A. Churchill, Jr., *Differences in the Attractiveness of Alternative Rewards among Industrial Salespeople: Additional Evidence*, Report No. 81-107 (Cambridge, Mass.: Marketing Science Institute, December 1981).

13. Stanton and Buskirk, *Management of the Sales Force*, pp. 335–36.

14. Ibid., pp. 561–62.

15. Rene Y. Darmon, "Identifying Profit-Producing Salesforce Members," *Journal of Personal Selling and Sales Management*, November 1982, p. 15. Also see Joseph P. Guiltinan and Gordon W. Paul, *Marketing Management* (New York: McGraw-Hill, 1985), pp. 340–48.

14

Managing Sales Promotion

Each year marketers spend billions of dollars, beyond advertising and personal selling, to motivate sales personnel and dealers and to offer incentives to consumers. Procter & Gamble alone spends approximately $120 million annually on couponing, sampling, consumer deals, premiums, and other vehicles.[1] To accomplish these goals, marketers use a wide variety of techniques collectively known as sales promotion.

Although there are several definitions of sales promotion, two capture the essence of this important phase of marketing. The American Marketing Association defines *sales promotion* as ". . . those marketing activities other than personal selling, advertising and publicity that stimulate consumer purchasing and dealer effectiveness,"[2] while the American Association of Advertising Agencies defines it as ". . . any activity which offers an incentive to buy a product beyond its inherent benefits."[3] Whichever definition one prefers, the key point is that sales promotion is an integral component of a company's overall marketing and promotional strategy. As one authority on sales promotion puts it, "Promotion . . . properly integrated . . . plays a growing role in the marketing mix, a tactical counterpoint to the strategic brand-sell advertising . . . and it will be a frequent tie-breaker . . . requiring a marketing generalist who can orchestrate promotion with the advertising (and personal selling) for optimum harmony."[4] The point is clear: There is a critical need for proper management of sales promotion.

Management of a sales promotion program involves an understanding of the various activities that constitute sales promotion, the objectives sought in the sales promotion program, and the relationship between sales promotion and other marketing mix elements. Managers must know the factors that dictate the specific use and form of sales promotion, as well as the importance of evaluating sales promotion efforts. Let us now look at these important factors, recognizing that the greater the care in planning, the greater the likelihood that a sales promotion program will succeed.

SALES PROMOTION ACTIVITIES

In the next two chapters we will define and examine the most common sales promotion activities, including point-of-purchase advertising, contests and sweepstakes, coupons, sampling, consumer deals, premiums, and advertising specialties. In addition, there are such activities as cooperative advertising, trade deals and promotional allowances, sales meetings, sales brochures, trade shows and exhibits, and packaging.

With this wide range of options, and the complementary role that sales promotion plays with other marketing and promotional forces, managers must recognize just what sales promotion can and cannot do. When well-executed advertising and a strong sales force support the right product, sales promotion can have a very positive impact. At the same time, sales promotion is not a substitute for other promotional elements and cannot compensate for other marketing deficiencies.

Sales promotion *can*

> Gain new users and encourage repeat use
> Encourage more frequent or multiple purchases
> Introduce new or improved products or product uses
> Counter competitive activity
> Obtain feature pricing, display, or other trade support
> Capitalize on seasonal, geographical, or creative advantages
> Induce "trade-ups" to larger size or longer contract
> Reduce or increase trade inventories
> Expand or improve distribution
> Motivate dealers, brokers, sales force, or franchise holders

Sales promotion *cannot*

Turn poor shelf pricing into profitable volume

Compensate for inadequate levels of advertising

Overcome problems in packaging, quality, or performance

Reverse a downward sales trend for any length of time

Compensate for an inadequately staffed or improperly trained sales force or dealer

Overcome poor distribution[5]

"Promotion should be part of a total marketing communications program—a well planned, properly timed, carefully executed program with specific goals and objectives. It should be used as an *offensive* weapon in the brand's marketing arsenal, not just as a defensive weapon when problems arise."[6]

SALES PROMOTION OBJECTIVES

Despite the diversity of sales promotion activities, they can be grouped into three major categories according to specific target audience and promotional objectives:

1. Sales promotion designed to stimulate, support, and provide incentives for the *sales force* in its merchandising and selling efforts
2. Sales promotion designed to motivate *middlemen* toward providing active and enthusiastic support in marketing the company's products
3. Sales promotion designed to provide *consumers* with incentives aimed at stimulating trial or continued used of specific products

For maximum effectiveness, a sales promotion program should include promotional activities carefully designed, coordinated, timed, and implemented at all three levels. We will now discuss the promotion objectives associated with each of these three major audiences.

Sales Promotion to the Sales Force

Sales promotion activities directed at the company's sales force aim at motivating salespeople to expend extra effort (usually on a short-term basis) in pursuit of company sales goals. Increasing the overall level of sales is the broad goal of these efforts, but they may accomplish short-term goals as well, such as securing new dealers, promoting sales of a specific item or a seasonal item, introducing special promotions to middlemen, increasing order size, and increasing profitability and lowering sales costs.

Many sales promotion devices can provide incentives to members of the sales force: sales meetings, contests, sales letters, internal house organs, and sales brochures, among others. Each of these, as we will see in Chapter 16, has a special purpose, but they share a common goal—motivating the sales force. A motivated sales force is crucial to the success of a marketing program. Achieving that motivation requires a well-conceived and well-executed sales promotion program.

Sales Promotion to Middlemen

Middlemen are an extension of a company's own sales force and therefore have the same requirements for information, assistance, and motivation. Ultimately, the fate of a product rests with middlemen. The retailer, for example, decides whether to stock the product and how much support to give it. Consequently, promotions to the trade are essential to the success of a product as they gain the cooperation and active support of middlemen and provide the company with short-term advantages within the trade. A continuing program of trade promotions translates into such benefits as securing distribution for new or improved products, increasing sales of merchandising in the off-season, building or diminishing dealer inventories, increasing in-store shelf space, increasing multiple purchases or increasing order size, obtaining feature pricing, display, or other trade support. A good program will also help to offset competition, improve distribution of mature products, gain middleman participation in consumer promotions, provide information on new products or product development, and, overall, increase middleman loyalty.

Consider these sales promotion vehicles. Periodic dealers' meetings provide middlemen with needed information about new products, product innovations, upcoming company advertising campaigns, and special promotions. Meetings not only provide a means for disseminating literature and demonstrating products but also provide company management and sales personnel with a valuable forum for soliciting active dealer support for other company promotions. Sales seminars, another useful technique, provide retail salespeople with the necessary tools for effective selling. In general, meetings are especially valuable in enhancing good dealer-company relations.

Another method for building good relations between the company and its dealers is the use of sales contests. Dealer contests usually have the same impact on middlemen as on the company's own sales force; they tend to stimulate a high degree of activity during the contest duration but seldom lead to long-lasting increases in sales. Contests are, however, an excellent vehicle for motivating distributors and dealers over the short term.

Various trade deals for middlemen help secure retail distribution for products as well as extra promotional and merchandising support that would not occur without such incentives. Trade deals may include offers of free merchandise, special displays, buying allowances and discounts, or some combination. In return, a company hopes to receive promotional support from the dealer, superior display and shelving for its merchandise, perhaps, or larger orders. Trade deals and selected consumer promotions often combine to increase the effectiveness of each.

Cooperative advertising, or advertising shared by the manufacturer and the retailer, is a proven method for stimulating increased promotional support and cooperation among retailers. There are drawbacks, as we will see in Chapter 16, but cooperative advertising does allow the manufacturer to obtain increased advertising exposure at local rates, with a degree of control over the advertisements. On the other side, the retailer obtains professionally prepared—and affordable—advertising.

With the retailer's strategic position in the distribution channel, nothing less than the best-designed trade promotion program is acceptable. This is particularly true with the increasing concentration of the retail trade into a few dominant chains and buying groups, which has resulted in the retailer's having greater marketplace power—power to dictate to the manufacturer what must be provided in the way of sales promotion just to get the product stocked in the store.[7]

Sales Promotion to Consumers

A number of sales promotions aim at inducing consumers to make initial, continued, or increased purchases of products. Such promotion tries to achieve trial of new or improved products, gain new users or encourage repeated product usage, spark "trade-ups" to larger sizes, and encourage more frequent or multiple purchases. It may also hope to stimulate off-season purchases, encourage impulse purchases, and offset competitive promotional activities.

Sales promotions include such techniques as consumer contests and sweepstakes, coupons, sampling, premiums, packaging and price packs, and consumer refund deals—each with its own particular strengths and weaknesses. Edward Meyer, director of promotion services for Dancer Fitzgerald Sample of New York, has developed a series of three grids that define, on a scale of one to ten, the impact of selected sales promotions for both the adult's and the children's market.[8]

Exhibit 14-1 measures, for example, the effectiveness of specific sales promotions in securing the initial trial of new products by consumers. The grid shows that sampling is the most effective way to induce trial; the best way to get someone to try a new product is to give him or her a free sample. Procter & Gamble has done exactly this for years. The use of coupons, particularly free coupons, also generates trial of new products by adults. For children, on the other hand, in-store premium offers are more effective.

EXHIBIT 14-1   Promotion Impact—Trial

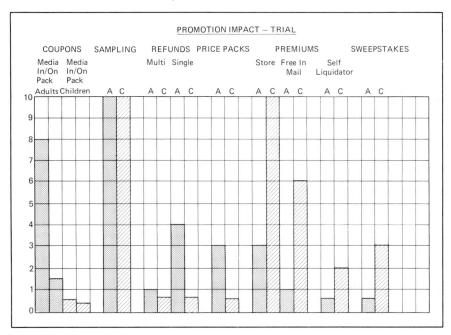

Reprinted with permission from the October 27, 1980 issue of Advertising Age. Copyright 1980 by Crain Communications, Inc. *Source*: Ed Meyer, Dancer Fitzgerald Sample.

Exhibit 14-2 rates the various sales promotion devices on their "franchise holding" impact, that is, their ability to generate repeat purchases leading to some degree of brand loyalty. Here a number of promotions have proven extremely successful in maintaining a franchise. Couponing, in addition to being a strong device for inducing trial, has considerable value in stimulating repeat purchases. Similarly, price packs (instant savings on a package or a bonus product) have been successful incentives for obtaining and holding consumers, since they induce the purchase of more than one package through the offer of immediate rewards. In-store premiums directed at children (for example, offering a different plastic toy model of a cartoon character with each flavor of a popular breakfast cereal) generate continuous purchases of particular brands.

Exhibit 14-3 shows each promotion in terms of its ability to reinforce a product's image. Sweepstakes and self-liquidating premiums (articles of merchandise available for purchase at low prices with proofs of purchase of particular products) are excellent vehicles for reinforcing a product's image.

While the grids demonstrate where individual sales promotion devices have been successful, combinations may be still more powerful. For example,

EXHIBIT 14-2 Promotion Impact—Franchise Holding

PROMOTION IMPACT – FRANCHISE HOLDING

COUPONS	SAMPLING	REFUNDS	PRICE PACKS		PREMIUMS		SWEEPSTAKES
In/On		Multi Single		Store	Free In Mail	Self Liquidator	
Adults Children	A C	A C A C	A C	A C	A C	A C	A C

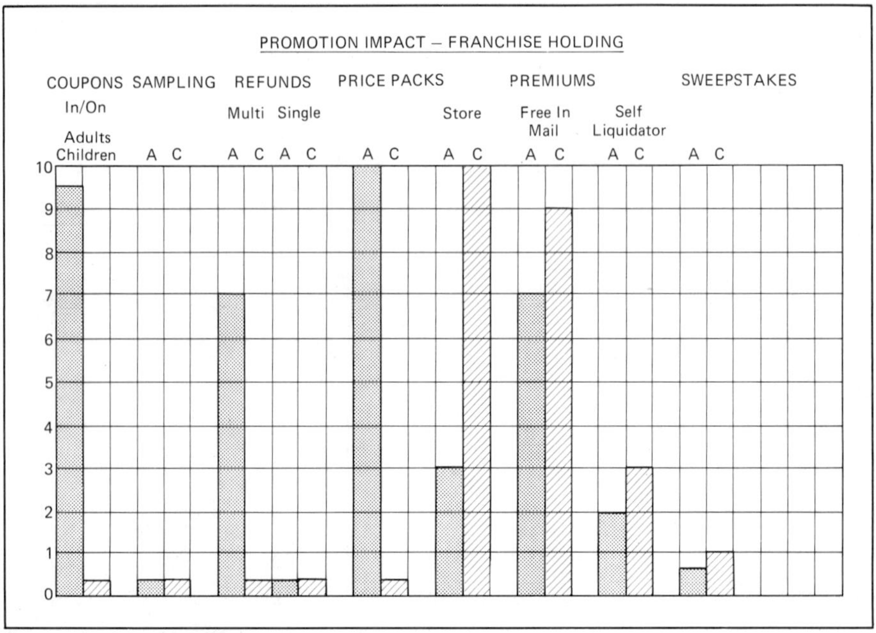

Reprinted with permission from the October 27, 1980 issue of Advertising Age. Copyright 1980 by Crain Communications, Inc. *Source*: Ed Meyer, Dancer Fitzgerald Sample.

one might include a coupon with a free sample or use a coupon that automatically enters the purchaser into a sweepstakes.

An abundance of research shows that the various promotional tools, whether used individually or in combination, can both shape new behavior and reinforce existing behavior. Sales promotion managers have to guard against the tendency to *overuse* the promotional tools because it is very possible that a dependency will develop to the point where the removal of the promotional device will cause an unwanted change in buying behavior. If long-term allegiance toward a product is desired, the promotional tools should not overshadow the product they are supporting.[9]

RELATIONSHIP BETWEEN SALES PROMOTION AND OTHER MARKETING MIX ELEMENTS

Sales promotion goals and strategies should always be tied in with a product's marketing strategy, supplementing the broader plan, but still working with the other promotional elements.[10] A company's promotional mix, as we have seen, consists of a group of activities (publicity, advertising, personal selling,

EXHIBIT 14-3   Promotion Impact—Image Reinforcement

PROMOTION IMPACT – IMAGE REINFORCEMENT

| COUPONS | SAMPLING | REFUNDS | PRICE PACKS | | PREMIUMS | | SWEEPSTAKES |

The chart shows a bar graph with a vertical scale from 0 to 10. Categories across the top:

COUPONS (All, Adults, Children — A C), SAMPLING (A C), REFUNDS (Multi A C, Single A C), PRICE PACKS (A C), PREMIUMS (Store A C, Free In Mail A C, Self Liquidator A C), SWEEPSTAKES (A C).

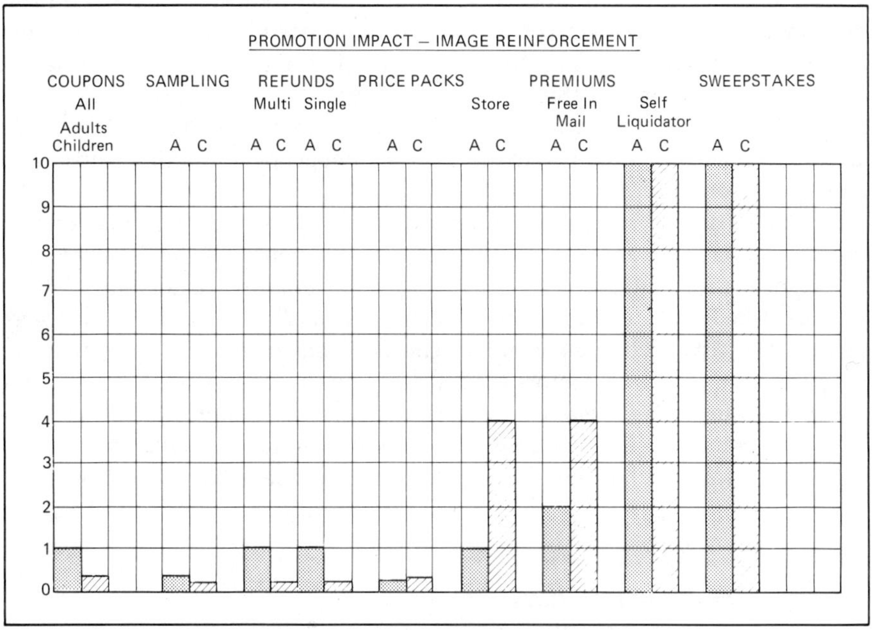

Reprinted with permission from the October 27, 1980 issue of Advertising Age. Copyright 1980 by Crain Communications, Inc. *Source*: Ed Meyer, Dancer Fitzgerald Sample.

and sales promotion) designed to produce sales by providing information, persuasion, and reinforcement regarding a product's attributes. Properly planned and coordinated, the various promotional components will complement each other to achieve maximum sales. Advertising and publicity are informational vehicles, while sales promotion serves as the persuasive element of the promotional mix. Personal selling and sales promotion likewise interrelate, since members of the sales force often serve as coordinators for various sales promotions. Beyond this, sales personnel often operate under a variety of incentives that are part of the sales promotion campaign. Therefore, because sales promotion activities support advertising, publicity, and personal selling, planning for these components should proceed together. Not everyone perceives this need.

Roger Strang has studied the relationships between advertising and promotion and has identified a number of weaknesses that may exist in the planning process.[11] First, a lack of integration frequently exists during the development of advertising and sales promotion plans, since the responsibility for planning different components usually rests with different parties. For example, advertising and promotion are complementary parts of the promotional mix; however, the planning and development of each may actually take place independently. An outside advertising agency may develop advertising themes while an in-house staff or outside independent promotion agency may work on promotions. Second, Strang indicates that all too frequently short-term budget considerations dominate planning at the expense of long-term implications. A third weakness is the shortage of information available for evaluating the impact of promotional activities. Many firms simply fail to collect adequate data about their promotional activities. Little attempt is made, for example, to discover the impact of combining advertising and sales promotion.

Strang further suggests that a number of factors affect a firm's decision to make advertising or promotion the primary element in its brand strategy.[12] In essence, these factors are (1) *corporate* considerations (availability of resources, freedom to employ certain techniques); (2) *consumer* factors (degree of brand loyalty, type of consumer, the decision process for the particular product); and (3) *market* factors (product life cycle stage, market share, competitive strategy, the existence of private labels). Basically, the stronger the brand's market position, the greater the possibility that one will favor advertising over sales promotion. We will discuss several of these factors later in the chapter.

FACTORS INFLUENCING THE USE
AND FORM OF SALES PROMOTION

This section, which draws heavily on Roger A. Strang's research on the relationship between advertising and promotion in brand strategy, will examine those factors that influence management's decision regarding the use and form of sales promotion.[13]

Stage in Product Life Cycle

Products require different promotional strategies as they move through the various stages of their *life cycles*. Since the promotional objectives are different for new products compared with mature products, for example, the stage in the life cycle of a product is a significant influence on a company's promotional mix and, in particular, its advertising and promotion strategy.

Introduction Stage

Both advertising and promotion are crucial during the *introduction stage* of a product's life cycle. Sales promotion (as in displays and allowances for example) is a key element in securing initial distribution for new products, while intense advertising informs consumers about the product and its attributes. Sales promotion devices such as consumer deals and sampling may also induce consumer trial of the new product.

Growth Stage

A product is in its *growth stage* when sales are increasing at a rate greater than 5 percent annually. Competing brands enter the market during this stage, thus making it critical for the company to stimulate demand for its own brand. Such a need should determine the company's advertising and promotion strategy. This stage may include a number of promotions (premiums, sampling, coupons) to encourage continued purchases of the product, but advertising usually surpasses sales promotion in importance as advertisers take measures to increase consumer awareness of their brand over competing brands. Aggressive competition characterizes the growth stage, and advertising is a major weapon.

Maturity Stage

Intense competition within the product's or brand's market characterizes the *maturity stage* of the life cycle. Sales during this stage may change within plus or minus 5 percent annually. Trade and consumer deals come into play to encourage brand switching by consumers as well as to load dealers in order to gain advantages at the retail level. Dealer loyalty is particularly important in the maturity stage, since shelf space and market share are now closely related. Competition is indeed intense. Consumer brand loyalty will now dictate the company's advertising and promotion strategy. Advertising will dominate when a high degree of loyalty is apparent; sales promotion will dominate when a low degree of consumer loyalty exists.

Decline Stage

Sales generally fall more than 5 percent annually during the *decline stage* of the product life cycle. Advertising and sales promotion efforts usually drop dramatically during this stage and may eventually disappear. Manufacturers want to reduce costs, seeking to keep the product viable in the market despite a shrinking demand. Sales promotion activities still in use aim primarily at the trade (e.g., allowances, discounts) to maintain distribution.

Competitive Activity

As the life-cycle analysis suggests, an awareness of the level of *competitive activity* is crucial in planning an effective sales promotion strategy. The strategy requires an assessment of what competitors are doing and a prediction as to what they are likely to do. Of course, this is no easy task. Still, management will be wise to develop this prediction before setting its own budgets for the year. Management must also ask, What are the appropriate responses to aggressive marketing tactics by both new and established competitors?

The tendency may be to combat these forces through increases in sales promotion activities, especially for their short-run effects. Management must be careful, however, to maintain an appropriate advertising and promotion mix and not to deplete advertising budgets for the sake of expanded promotional campaigns. Reliance on sales promotion alone as a combative mechanism against strong competitive forces is short-sighted and seldom successful. Marketers may counter aggressive, promotion-minded competitors with heavy sales promotion activity, but only as part of a balanced advertising and promotion program.

Offsetting a sales promotion program by an aggressive competitor at a reasonable cost can be extremely difficult. Furthermore, when all or most competitive brands are using some form of sales promotion of the same item, another problem arises: The consumer may become confused and reject all attempts at persuasion.[14] Countering a competitive sales promotion campaign takes time. It cannot be done hurriedly except at great risk. The marketer must examine the competitive program closely to determine its strengths and weaknesses. Only in this way can a marketer intelligently develop its own sales promotion program.

Industry Practice

Industry practices in recent years indicate that sales promotions have surpassed advertising in relative importance as a component of a company's brand strategy. Many companies spend more on sales promotion activities than on advertising. About $72 billion was spent on sales promotion techniques in 1983, compared with about $42 billion on advertising. And sales promotion expenditures have been rising faster than national advertising.[15]

One reason for the relative growth of sales promotion activities is the changing attitude of top management. At one time, sales promotion activities were shunned as image cheapening; now, however, successful usage has gained acceptance for them.

Two other factors contribute to the growth of sales promotion. First, the increasing number of new brands in recent years has meant increased use of sales promotion. Since the majority of new brands of consumer goods rely on extensive use of sales promotion devices to establish a market position, the number of brand introductions by itself increases the level of sales promotion activities. The greater number of brands available, new and established, places a heavier emphasis on the use of sales promotions as each brand competes for its share of limited retail shelf space, as well as for the consumer's disposable income.

Company Strategy

Corporate considerations also influence the use and form of sales promotions. Because of resource limitations, many companies now restrict the amount expended on sales promotion activities to a predetermined percentage of projected sales. Others restrict spending to a specified ratio of advertising expenditures to promotion expenditures (e.g., a 60/40 ratio of advertising to promotion outlays). Restrictions often stem from top management's view of a brand's potential as well as its relative importance to the company. Clearly, a brand with highly favorable growth prospects will receive a higher allocation of funds than a stable or declining brand. Finally, the relative importance of promotion versus advertising is usually greater for those brands with lower profit margins.

Management sometimes places constraints on the use of sales promotion when it views advertising as more beneficial for company image and sales promotion as potentially image damaging. Some managers still see promotions as "gimmicky" and cheapening. Management typically prefers consumer-directed promotions as opposed to trade-oriented promotions, believing that consumer promotions are somewhat more controllable and trade promotions are a form of subsidy to the trade. On the other hand, management will place restrictions on the use of additional consumer promotions (such as price promotions) when it feels that the frequency of use has been too great and that additional promotions may prove harmful to the brand's image.

Other corporate factors affect the degree of freedom or restraint in the use of promotions. As Strang reported:

> In general, corporate restraints on advertising/promotion spending appeared to be inversely related to the degree of actual decentralization. Where decentralization is well-established, there is less restriction, or the restrictions may be applied at division or business unit level, allowing marketing managers some freedom as to which brands will be affected. The relative power of the sales force also may affect the advertising/promotion allocation. In some companies the sales force sets the promotion requirements or makes strong recommendations. In fact, the sales force can be utilized to assist in several stages of the sales promotion planning process [see Exhibit 14-4]. The sales force may also be a powerful factor in calling for additional funds for promotion during the budget period.[16]

EVALUATION OF SALES PROMOTION

The large number of variables makes the evaluation of sales promotion particularly difficult. Sales promotion activities are usually part of a program including other elements, such as advertising, personal selling, and publicity. Given this fact, accurate measurement and evaluation of promotion components may sometimes be impossible. On the other hand, with sales promotion so costly, proponents of evaluation advocate every reasonable effort to assess its impact. Exhibit 14-5 lists some of the contrasting views.

EXHIBIT 14-4 Role of the Sales Force in the Sales Promotion Planning Process

PROMOTION PLANNING STAGE	TYPES OF SALES PROMOTION ISSUES ON WHICH SALESPEOPLE ARE QUALIFIED TO COMMENT
I. Idea Stage	1. *Competitive activity*: what promo innovations has competition tried with success?
	2. *Trade preference*: what types of promotions does the trade favor?
	3. *Defensive strategy*: will a competitor's new product launch require us to defend shelf space and/or weak items with a special promotion?
II. Budget/Planning Stage	1. *Budget*: what is the minimum amount of allowances required to receive a major price feature ad? To simply retain current distribution?
	2. *Allocation/deal structure*: what mix of off-invoice advertising and other allowances will best accomplish promotion objectives? Should consumer and trade promotions be combined to get maximum trade support?
	3. *Promotion goals*: what volume goals are realistic given current trade inventories (e.g., has the last promo sold through?) What non-volume goals—e.g., additional shelf space, off-shelf display—are realistic?
	4. *Special packs*: what special packs requiring adding a new SKU are acceptable? How many special packs should be produced for the promotion? How should these be allocated across divisions?
III. Approval Stage	Does sales management approve of plans?
IV. Implementation Stage	1. *Sales presentation details*: format of selling materials; what special pack/pricing information needed; what additional info such as GRP's in advertising, test results, will buyer require?
	2. *Timing*: what lead times do accounts require to fit us onto promo calendar?
	3. *In-store support*: what in-store activity such as setting up displays, shelf talkers, etc., can the sales force realistically provide given other priorities?
V. Promotion Evaluation	1. *Sell-through*: did promotional orders sell-through to the consumer as measured by account inventories, re-orders, store checks?
	2. *Were non-volume objectives achieved?* For example, shelf realignment, second location displays, etc.? Were special packs/displays used?
	3. *Trade reaction*: was buyer satisfied? What were problems?
	4. *Overall evaluation*: deal structure, selling materials, appropriateness of special packs, etc.

Source: Robert J. Kopp, *Improving the Effectiveness of the Sales Force Component in Sales Promotions: Directions for Sales and Marketing Management* (Cambridge, Mass.: Marketing Science Institute, 1982), p. 31.

EXHIBIT 14-5 Contrasting Views in the Great Sales Promotion Debate

SALES PROMOTION PLANNING AND EVALUATION

Point	Counterpoint
• Sales promotion is characterized by "fast growth, but faulty management."	• The sales promotion planning function has changed drastically since 1976. Firms have added specialized staff, recognizing the need for more expertise in planning. • Sales promotion is incorporated into normal planning process, not conducted as an afterthought.
• Sales promotion is a short-term fix. Sales promotion does nothing to help long-term sales and share.	• Synergy can be achieved between sales promotion and long-term franchise-building. • If share does not increase, what is effect on primary demand for the category as a whole?
• Communications effects (through advertising) build brand loyalty; price promotion tears it down.	• As product life cycle evolves toward maturity, price becomes a more important strategic weapon, all things equal. • When surveyed, consumers report that they are increasingly on the lookout for coupons, rebates, and the like. • Media-cost inflation may be shifting cost-benefit ratio toward sales promotion.
• Sales promotion spending is draining funds from the advertising budget.	• According to a Donnelly Marketing (1982) survey of consumer packaged goods marketers, the split of advertising-to-sales promotion in marketing budgets was unchanged in 1981 vs. 1979.
• Advertising is usually pretested; why aren't consumer promotions pretested?	• We didn't pretest because the value of information is not worth the cost. Rarely does a single consumer promotion involve the monetary risk of an advertising campaign. If the promotion fails from a consumer standpoint, we've probably saved money in redemptions; we can take this savings and try again.

EXHIBIT 14-5 *(Continued)*

SALES PROMOTION PLANNING AND EVALUATION

Point	Counterpoint
• Companies aren't learning from their own successes and failures in sales promotion because (thorough) post-evaluation of programs is rarely done. Many companies don't even keep good records of results. Compared to advertising, sales promotion takes a back-seat in the promotion evaluation budget.	• As firms build specialized sales promotion planning staffs, post-program evaluation is on the increase.
	• Better record-keeping is worthless without better evaluation models to make sense of the data. Models are being developed to process scanning data for consumer promotions. SPAR and Lemont Consulting have developed trade promotion evaluation models.
	• Sales promotion research lags advertising research because of the lack of research methodology for the former. The growth of UPC-scanning panels, and accompanying models, will provide the needed data and methodologies to evaluate sales promotions.
• The trade isn't passing allowances through to the consumer. Trade promotion is like wasting money!	• Are everyday margins adequate to keep the distribution channels in business? One observer says that total allowances to grocery trade are larger than the trade's total after-tax profit.
	• If trade won't promote, can "promotion" allowances be reduced to "stocking" allowances?
• Price, price, price. That's all the trade talks about.	• *Progressive Grocer* says that the trade is looking to marketers for display materials, merchandising ideas, pricing advice, shelf plan-o-grams, and the like. Perception is that fewer display and merchandising materials are being offered today ("Forty-Ninth Annual Report," 1982).
• UPC-scanning data will result in a large-scale shift in channel power to the trade. As high as 25 percent of all items will be delisted based on slow movement.	• The trade is as concerned as manufacturers with satisfying customers. Across-the-board delistings will turn off customers who want variety and wide selection.
	• Delisting isn't necessary. Better shelf space allocation will boost profits.

- The tight economy has squeezed everyone's bottom line. Confrontation with the trade on economic issues is inevitable in this environment.

- The average salesperson takes the "path of least resistance." If the buyer asks for more money, the salesperson is "on the phone" to headquarters for higher allowances.

- The sales force thinks only in terms of promotions. They don't even ask for regular "turn orders" anymore.

- It's getting so I have to bribe my own sales force with special incentives to get any attention for this brand.

- Why did the promotion fail? The sales force wasn't behind it.

- Cooperation not confrontation appears to be the sign of the times. *Progressive Grocer* states: "There is much willingness on all sides to attack problems in a cooperative spirit. Trade relations have improved appreciably in the past year" ("Forty-Ninth Annual Report," 1982).

- The salesperson is the "man in the middle." It is his job to build a long-term relationship with accounts. This entails representing the trade's interests to the manufacturer as well as selling manufacturer programs to the trade.

- Have back-to-back deals and/or crowded selling calendars caused promotions to be the sole focus of sales calls?

- Have lower list prices been considered as an alternative to frequent deals in brand marketing strategy?

- Does the regular compensation program contain incentives to push the brand?

- Are too many other brands depending on special incentives? Are sales force contests overworked?

- Can the promotion calendar be arranged to facilitate some minimum level of sales force attention—even for minor brands?

- Were the promotion objectives realistic?

- Based on the salesperson's past experience, would this promotion have been good for the trade? Or would the buyer have rejected it out-of-hand?

- Were timing and implementation details of the program in line?

- Did headquarters bother to find out why the buyer rejected the last promotion which was designed like this one?

Source: Robert J. Kopp, *Improving the Effectiveness of the Sales Force Component in Sales Promotions: Directions for Sales and Marketing Management* (Cambridge, Mass.: Marketing Science Institute, 1982), pp. 36ff.

Although the task may be difficult, some measures exist for evaluating sales promotion activities. Proposed promotions may be tested prior to general release, providing management with information so that it can address problems and select alternatives.

Once the sales promotion program has been executed, evaluation of the different activities helps management determine whether a particular promotion vehicle is achieving its objectives. For example, periodically recording the number of purchases of self-liquidating premiums shows whether this activity is reaching its desired level. Similarly, other results can be tabulated, such as the number of contest entrants or the number of coupons redeemed.

While evaluation of a consumer sales promotion program can be done by pretesting the whole plan or posttesting the results, many experts agree that pretesting deserves more attention than it has received. Basically, there are three major types of research useful for pretesting consumer sales promotion plans: qualitative research, quantitative research, and test marketing.[17] *Qualitative research* uses focus groups and panels and is concerned with open-ended probing. Such techniques permit testing of creative executions, prize structures, coupon values, delivery vehicles, and target market appeal. Weak ideas can be weeded out; good ideas, fine-tuned. Furthermore, qualitative research is the quickest and least expensive way to pretest.[18]

Quantitative research includes such techniques as street intercepts, telephone interviewing, and door-to-door surveys. Such research is well suited for confirming whether an idea is good or not so good; however, it is less useful than qualitative research for generating new ideas or modifications.

Test markets, since they come as the next-to-last step in putting the sales promotion plan into action, afford management less opportunity to make major changes, if needed, in the sales promotion program. However, a test market does put the sales promotion campaign into the marketplace for a test under actual conditions. And there is still time to make changes.

Beyond pretesting and posttesting sales promotion programs, it is important to evaluate periodically the media plan used to execute the program. Questions such as the following can be used to rate a media plan:

1. Does it fit with the sales promotion program objectives?
2. Does it yield the lowest cost per response?
3. Does it provide maximum selectivity in terms of the target audience?
4. Does it have minimum clutter?
5. Does the medium support the brand's image?
6. Does it provide adequate lead time?
7. Does the speed of response meet timetable needs?
8. Does the media plan generate trade excitement and support?
9. Does it permit measurement of results?[19]

Careful attention to questions such as these will enable promotion planners to get the most out of their media. The right promotion can increase media impact, and vice versa.[20]

These approaches provide management with information necessary for assessing sales promotion strategy and the impact of a particular sales promotion activity and determining the need for corrective action. In addition, the use of sales promotion evaluation techniques assists the company in planning future sales promotion programs, consistent with marketing objectives, strategies, and budget constraints.[21]

SUMMARY

In this chapter we looked at sales promotion and its relationship to other elements in a company's promotional mix. We emphasized the nature of sales promotion objectives and the specific short-term goals of sales promotion activities directed at the company's sales personnel, middlemen, and consumers. We examined the factors influencing the use and form of sales promotion devices, including the product's stage in its life cycle, the nature and intensity of competitive activities, industry practices, and the individual strategies of the company itself. Finally, we discussed the need for and use of sales promotion evaluation techniques. We will now explore the major sales promotion techniques, first those used for consumers and then those used for dealers and sales personnel.

REVIEW AND DISCUSSION QUESTIONS

1. What role does sales promotion play in the marketing mix? In the promotional mix?

2. Identify the major guidelines in the planning and development of a sales promotion program.

3. Explain what sales promotion can and cannot do.

4. "Sales promotion should be used as an offensive weapon in the brand's marketing arsenal, not just as a defensive weapon when problems arise." Comment.

5. Identify and evaluate the various factors affecting a company's decision to make advertising or sales promotion the primary element in a brand strategy.

6. What are some specific objectives of sales promotion when it is used for motivating a sales force? Give examples.

7. *What are some specific purposes of sales promotions directed at middlemen? Cite examples.*

8. *Identify common objectives of sales promotion directed at consumers. Give some specific examples.*

9. *You are asked to suggest three specific sales promotion activities for a new brand of deodorant soap, the first such product in your product line. What do you suggest? Why? Which is number one on your list? Give reasons.*

10. *How does the product's life-cycle stage influence the use and form of sales promotion?*

11. *How do you account for the increasing use of sales promotion to consumers? To the sales force? To dealers?*

12. *Explain the importance of evaluating the effectiveness of a sales promotion program.*

13. *"Sales promotion is a short-term fix. It does nothing to help long-term sales and market share." Comment.*

14. *For building brand loyalty among consumers, which offers more promise, advertising or sales promotion? Why?*

15. *For building loyalty among dealers, would you use advertising or sales promotion? Why?*

16. *Explain how a flow chart can be helpful in planning sales promotion programs.*

17. *Develop a set of guidelines for effectively managing sales promotion.*

NOTES

1. *Advertising Age*, September 8, 1983, p. 128.

2. *Marketing Definitions: A Glossary of Marketing Terms* (Chicago: American Marketing Association, 1960), p. 20.

3. *Sales Promotion Techniques: A Basic Guidebook* (New York: American Association of Advertising Agencies, 1978), p. 2.

4. Eugene Mahany, "Package Goods Clients Agree: Promotion Importance Will Grow," *Advertising Age*, April 14, 1975, p. 48.

5. *Sales Promotion Techniques*, p. 3.

6. Ibid.

7. Don E. Schultz, "Why Marketers Like the Sales Promotion Gambit," *Advertising Age*, November 7, 1983, p. M52.

8. Edward Meyer, "Do Your Sales Promotions Lack Impact?" *Advertising Age*, October 27, 1980, p. 74.

9. Michael L. Rothschild and William C. Gaidis, "Behavioral Learning Theory: Its Relevance to Marketing and Promotions," *Journal of Marketing*, Spring 1981, p. 77.

10. Victor P. Buell, *Marketing Management* (New York: McGraw-Hill, 1984), p. 610.

11. Roger A. Strang, *The Relationship between Advertising and Promotion in Brand Strategy* (Cambridge, Mass.: Marketing Science Institute, 1975), pp. 9–11.

12. Ibid., pp. 11–13.

13. Ibid.

14. Don E. Schultz and William A. Robinson, *Sales Promotion Management* (Chicago: Crain Books, 1982), p. 235.

15. Laura Konrad Jereski, "Marketers Fuel Promotion Budgets," *Marketing and Media Decisions*, September 1984, p. 130.

16. Strang, *Relationship between Advertising and Promotion*, pp. 34–35.

17. William A. Robinson, "Pretest for a Passing Grade," *Advertising Age*, September 5, 1983, p. M36.

18. Ibid.

19. William A. Robinson, "Fit the Medium to the Message," *Advertising Age*, March 5, 1984, p. M70.

20. Russell D. Bowman, "Add Muscle to Your Media," *Marketing Communications*, January 1984, p. 22.

21. For an excellent treatment of evaluating sales promotion efforts, as well as the issues affecting a marketer's decision to use a particular form of sales promotion, see Katherine E. Jocz, ed. *Research on Sales Promotion: Collected Papers* (Cambridge, Mass.: Marketing Science Institute, 1984).

15

Sales
Promotion
to Consumers

Sales promotion, as we have seen, involves several different activities. Choosing the right types of sales promotion for the promotional mix requires an understanding of what each type brings to the communication program. Some of the tools of sales promotion address consumers, while others address dealers or the company sales force. In this chapter we will look at the major types of sales promotion for consumers, their characteristics, and the conditions under which each is most appropriate. Chapter 16 will explore the sales promotion activities aimed at dealers and the company sales force.

Sales promotion activities directed primarily at consumers include point-of-purchase displays, coupons, premiums, sampling, and contests and sweepstakes. Some situations may dictate the use of consumer deals, advertising specialties, or distinctive packaging.

POINT-OF-PURCHASE DISPLAYS

A manufacturer uses a *point-of-purchase display* to attract the attention of the consumer in the store and, if possible, to stimulate purchase of the product. Specifically, it involves the use of display materials such as posters, racks, signs, motion displays, banners, and price cards, and it serves as a reminder of the product's media advertising. It may capitalize as well on the customer's tendency toward unplanned purchases (impulse buying).

Point-of-purchase displays have particular meanings for middlemen and for consumers.

Middleman Viewpoint

Dealers depend on manufacturers to provide point-of-purchase (POP) display materials as an aid in moving merchandise. This is particularly important to the self-service retailer, who does not rely on sales personnel to assist in making sales. These retailers substitute the use of exciting displays to stimulate consumers to purchase.

Since the retailer's primary objective is to move merchandise, a good point-of-purchase display, from the retailer's point of view, should

> Be sufficiently stimulating so as to promote impulse purchases of the displayed product as well as companion or related items
>
> Be used for products that carry high-profit margins and generate high volume
>
> Generate store traffic as well as attract the attention of consumers while shopping
>
> Be exciting
>
> Fit in with the general store character
>
> Reinforce previous national and local advertising themes
>
> Be closely related to other storewide promotions (e.g., back-to-school promotions)

Retailers are particularly interested in display materials that are simple to set up, are durable, and do not unnecessarily hinder movement of consumer traffic within the store. Generally, manufacturers using elaborate displays that require considerable time and effort to construct will dispatch detail personnel ("missionary" sales personnel) to retail outlets to help set up display materials. An additional consideration is that retailers, for the most part, have a preference for merchandise racks, trays, cases, and other display apparatus that occupy minimum space on the floor or shelf area and also provide a self-service feature. It is important to consider what retailers want in point-of-purchase materials. They can use only a small percentage of the many they receive. And it is usually a good idea to offer

Award-Winning Point-of-Purchase Displays

Courtesy Thomson-Leeds Company, Inc., New York City.

middlemen a coordinated point-of-purchase program for an entire product line rather than a collection of display materials for individual items. This can help consumer goods manufacturers achieve a competitive edge in retail outlets.[1]

Consumer Viewpoint

Two essential factors should govern the planning of point-of-purchase advertising:

1. Impulse sales dollars account for a very high percentage of all consumer purchases. A study of 53,000 purchases made by 4,000 shoppers over a twelve-year period involving 200 supermarkets found that almost two-thirds of all dollars spent resulted from decisions made by consumers while in the store as opposed to specifically planned purchases.[2]
2. A large percentage of unplanned consumer purchases occurs because a product display has attracted consumers.

Given these two factors, the role and importance of point-of-purchase advertising as a promotional device become apparent. Since many purchases are unplanned, the effective use of displays can go a long way toward lending appeal to a product at the point of purchase. Through careful planning, POP material will reflect the advertising and other parts of a promotional campaign and thereby have the best possible effect upon sales.[3]

COUPONS

Coupons have for many years been the most widely used of all sales promotion techniques. *Coupons* are certificates distributed by manufacturers to consumers, redeemable at retail outlets, giving the consumer a specified price reduction on a particular product. We regularly see examples such as a twenty-cent coupon for Minute Maid orange juice, a thirty-five-cent coupon for Aim toothpaste, a sixty-cent coupon for Hills Bros. coffee, or even a ten-dollar coupon for Midas mufflers. Coupon promotions are helpful in introducing new products as well as in attracting new users and encouraging repeat purchases for established, frequently bought products. Coupons also stimulate consumers to make more frequent or larger purchases of an article, and they help to dilute the attractiveness of competitive brands. Coupons are often especially useful when they constitute the only difference among otherwise similar products.

Annually, manufacturers distribute something over 90 billion coupons with an average redemption value of fifteen to seventeen cents. However, consumers, for various reasons, fail to redeem over 90 percent of these coupons.[4]

Methods of Distribution

Various coupon distribution methods are available, including direct delivery, media distribution, and product distribution.

Direct Delivery

Coupons can be given *directly* to consumers by direct mail delivery or by door-to-door delivery. Direct distribution enables manufacturers to achieve broad distribution or to focus on selected recipients. The major disadvantage of direct delivery is its cost. With increased postal rates and the higher costs of using distribution firms for door-to-door delivery, many manufacturers now practice cooperative couponing whereby advertisers of noncompetitive products share the cost of joint mailings of their coupons. Even this method is imperfect: Coupons tend to get lost in the clutter.

Media Distribution

Coupons can be printed in or placed in *newspapers*, *magazines*, or *Sunday supplements*. Daily newspapers, with some 56 percent of the volume, are the most widely used vehicle for coupon distribution. Daily newspapers, however, also yield the lowest average redemption rate of all vehicles carrying coupons. This is due to the extra effort required to clip the coupon, the short life of the daily newspaper, less readership per page compared with other media, and the fact that newspapers reach a less-selective audience than, say, magazines.

Many advertisers use *free-standing inserts* (FSI) to distribute their coupons. These are separate inserts in Sunday newspapers, containing a number of coupons on one sheet. Redemption rates for free-standing inserts are much higher than those for daily newspapers. Magazines are also popular vehicles for coupon distribution. A magazine *on-page* is a coupon printed as part of an advertisement appearing in the magazine; magazine *pop-ups* are coupons printed on heavy card stock and inserted into the binding of a magazine; and *tip-ins* are coupons glued to the magazine or supplement. All are popular devices and typically experience higher redemption rates than those experienced through straight daily newspaper presentation. Exhibit 15-1 shows a five-year trend in coupon distributions, and Exhibit 15-2 shows the relative importance of the various media.

Product Distribution

Many *product* coupons are also imprinted on or inserted in the package itself. They are redeemable on a subsequent purchase. Because of the direct association with the product, *in/on package* coupons have the highest redemption rate of any of the methods available.

EXHIBIT 15-1   Trend in Coupon Distributions (billions)

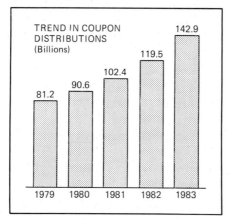

Source: NCH Reporter, No. 1 (1984), p. 3.
Courtesy A. C. Nielsen Company.

EXHIBIT 15-2   Coupon Distributions by Media (percent)

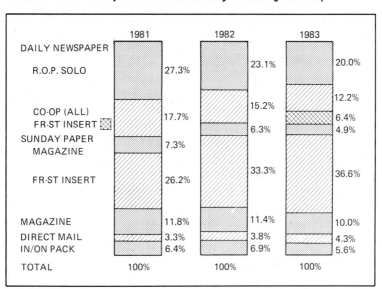

Source: NCH Reporter, No. 1 (1984), p. 3. Courtesy A. C. Nielsen Company.

Coupon Redemption

Many factors influence the *coupon redemption rate*. Among them are the method of distribution, audience reached by the coupon, consumer's need for the product, brand's consumer franchise/market share, degree of brand loyalty, brand's availability, monetary value of the coupon, whether it is a new or established brand, design of the coupon ad, discount offered by the coupon, competitive activity, size of the coupon drop, size of purchase required for redemption, level of advertising and promotion support, and demographics of consumers.[5] With these and other factors influencing coupon redemption rates, it is important that the manufacturer know the relative impact of the various factors.[6]

Coupons have captured the fancy of shoppers. Coupon clubs (members clip and trade coupons among themselves) have sprung up all over the country, as have coupon and refund bulletins (newsletters informing consumers as to the location of special bargains and the availability of the most lucrative deals). Retailers have caught the fever as well. A growing number of supermarkets, for example, offer "double-coupon days," specified days when they will honor any coupon at double its face value. (One supermarket experienced a near panic when it ran a one-time-only triple-coupon day!)

To manufacturers, coupons are both big business and big expense. Manufacturers must bear the cost of advertising and distributing coupons, redeeming their face value upon presentation by retailers, and paying retailers a coupon-handling fee (about seven cents per coupon redeemed). Perhaps the most costly of the coupon expenses comes from "misredemption." The cost of coupon fraud is over $200 million annually. For example, authorities in New York City uncovered a massive coupon fraud scheme involving twenty-one hundred retail stores. Agents raided a Brooklyn store and found stacked in piles one million coupons worth $250,000, along with hundreds of New York daily newspapers from which the store-owner and his cohorts "gang-cut" coupons. They then sent the coupons to the stores involved for kickbacks allegedly as high as 50 percent.

Both the FBI and the U.S. Postal Inspection Service investigate alleged coupon fraud. In addition, the Audit Bureau of Circulations has established the Coupon Distribution Verification service to help deal with the problem of misredemption and coupon fraud.

Despite these problems, coupon promotions continue to grow in both number and variety. (See Exhibit 15-3 for a five-year trend in coupon redemptions.) General Foods conducted the largest multibrand coupon promotion in its history when, on behalf of some twenty brands, it dropped about 500 million cents-off coupons in *Family Weekly* (12 million circulation) and 33 million free-standing inserts in some four hundred Sunday newspapers. The inserts contained between fourteen and sixteen coupons, each with a total value of $3, and reached nearly 70 percent of all U.S. households.

**EXHIBIT 15-3   Trend in Coupon
Redemptions (billions)**

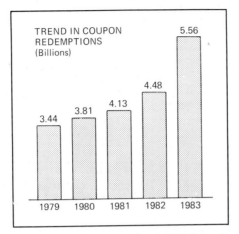

TREND IN COUPON
REDEMPTIONS
(Billions)

3.44 3.81 4.13 4.48 5.56

1979 1980 1981 1982 1983

Source: NCH Reporter, No. 1 (1984), p. 3.
Courtesy A. C. Nielsen Company.

(For each coupon redeemed, General Foods donated five cents to the Muscular Dystrophy Association.) To create awareness for its MDA effort, General Foods used a five-day, $1 million TV blitz.[7]

Many advertisers have reshaped the traditional coupons through use of combined offers to further increase their attractiveness. A number of advertisers now run coupon and sweepstakes offers in tandem. The coupon also serves as an automatic entry into a sweepstakes. The consumer simply fills out the coupon and receives both the immediate benefit of a price reduction on the article purchased and the chance of winning a prize.

Coupons are the major means by which the manufacturer presents the consumer with a price deal. They are effective in a variety of ways, and their acceptance by consumers testifies to their importance as a sales promotion medium.

PREMIUMS

Premiums are articles of merchandise provided free or at reduced prices to consumers as incentives to encourage their purchase of a specified product. While the fundamental goal of any premium campaign is to increase sales, some more specific purposes are

To offset the impact of a new competitive product

To entice consumers into switching from a competitor's product to one's own brand and become regular users

To build brand loyalty and attract repeat buyers
To offset seasonal slumps
To gain increased display area and shelf space in the store
To encourage trade-up or purchase of larger sizes
To stimulate impulse buying
To attract purchasers when product differentiation is slight

Among premium plans, these appear most often: direct premiums, self-liquidating premiums, free mail-ins, continuity coupon premiums, and free giveaways.

Direct Premiums

Direct premiums go right to the consumer, free of charge, at the time of purchase. The four major types are on-pack, in-pack, near-pack, and container premiums.

On-pack Premiums

On-pack premiums (also known as "banded" premiums) are attached to the product's package or are included in a special package holding both the advertiser's product container and the premium merchandise. Increased use of blister packaging to protect the premium from detachment and loss has stimulated the use of on-pack premiums.

EXAMPLES OF ON-PACK PREMIUMS

Kitty Clover brand potato chips has offered a free Bic ball point pen attached to its ten-ounce bag of chips.

A free salad dressing cruet has been attached to packages of Good Seasons Salad Dressing Mix.

Frito Lay has attracted home gardeners as consumers through its offer of free vegetable seeds attached to Frito's brand corn chips.

On-pack premiums achieve quick consumer response to the immediate reward and also encourage increased display by dealers. These promotions have the important advantage of eye appeal. On-pack premiums are particularly useful in increasing product usage where the premium bears a direct relationship to its accompanying product, as when Gillette offered a TRAC II razor as a premium attached to its TRAC II brand shaving cream.

A major limitation of on-pack premiums is that they lend themselves to theft. In addition, lack of proper attention to premium size during the planning process may result in a cumbersome or oversized package and possible shelf-space problems. Special packaging requirements may also materially increase product and premium costs.

In-pack Premiums

In-pack premiums are actually inside the package of the product. They may be premium merchandise or a redeemable coupon. In-pack premiums are good substitutes for "cents-off" deals and appear frequently in children's products such as breakfast cereals. In contrast to on-pack premiums, they create no shelf-space problems, since they generally require little if any package alteration, saving costs for the manufacturer. A note of caution: Food producers using this method should take care that the premium article in no way impairs the food product itself. In-pack premiums for food products must meet the strict standards of the Food and Drug Administration.

EXAMPLES OF IN-PACK PREMIUMS

The Ralston Purina Company has offered a free package of Life Savers in its Cookie Crisp brand cereal.

Specially marked boxes of Post cereals have contained Super Heroes posters, iron-ons, stickers, or comic books.

Near-pack Premiums

Because of size or bulk, some premium articles cannot be readily attached to or placed in the advertiser's product package. These items, known as *near-pack premiums*, are generally placed in separate displays close to the product. Although they have considerable display potential and allow for larger premiums, these promotions may be difficult for store personnel to administer and are subject to theft by store personnel as well.

EXAMPLES OF NEAR-PACK PREMIUMS

A plastic drink shaker and lid with the purchase of a container of Nestlé's Quik brand chocolate or strawberry milk flavoring

A free Bic ball point pen with the purchase of a Schick Super Chromium Injector

A free styrofoam cooler with the purchase of two cases of Budweiser beer

Container Premiums

A *container premium* is a reusable container that also serves as the product's package. Consumers consider these premiums extra values. Such premiums may help a product maintain a reasonable profit margin when under attack from lower-priced competitors. Container premiums appeal particularly to advertisers, since the consumer who uses them is constantly reminded of the product. They also stimulate sales, especially when the container undergoes some change of function (for example, fruit jelly in jars bearing various cartoon characters, which, following consumption of the contents, become drinking glasses with a message urging children to "collect all eight of your favorite cartoon pals").

EXAMPLES OF CONTAINER PREMIUMS

Mrs. Filbert's Soft Margarine container also serves as an eight-ounce plastic drinking cup complete with handle and lid.

Planter's Peanuts have been packaged in a decorator jar.

Paul Masson wine comes in a decorative, reusable carafe.

Self-Liquidating Premiums

A *self-liquidating premium* requires the consumer to make a payment for the premium article and provide proof of purchase of the product. The required payment generally equals the cost of the premium article to the advertiser plus postage and handling. This method is particularly advantageous to the company offering the premium, since it can provide an attractive article of premium merchandise at little or no additional cost to the company beyond that normally associated with advertising the promotion. Sale of the product may also increase, especially when the premium requires multiple proofs of purchase. In addition, the advertiser can put its brand name on the premium and get further "advertising" through the use or display of the premium.

AN EXAMPLE OF A SELF-LIQUIDATING PREMIUM

The makers of Soft-Weave bathroom tissue have offered a wallet and $1.00 of coupons for its product for a price of $2.98 and three "seals of quality" from its bathroom tissue paper.

Many advertisers also offer self-liquidating premiums at even lower prices, based on a predetermined scale that lowers consumer cost in proportion to the number of proofs of purchase received. This may stimulate additional sales.

AN EXAMPLE OF A SELF-LIQUIDATING PREMIUM WITH A SLIDING SCALE

Continental Baking, Inc., has offered a frisbee for $1.50 and one proof of purchase from its Hostess Twinkie product, a frisbee for $1.00 and two proofs of purchase, or a free frisbee for four proofs of purchase.

The major disadvantage of self-liquidating premiums is that they are not immediately available to consumers in the store. The initial impact of self-liquidators, therefore, is not as strong as with several of the direct premiums.

Advertisers look for a 0.1 percent redemption rate for self-liquidating premiums. A circulation of 10 million offers is normally expected to yield approximately ten thousand redemptions. Redemption rates for higher-priced premiums (above $25) average about one-fifth the return of the lower-priced premiums. Companies using such higher-priced premiums do not expect high redemption rates; instead their objectives are to gain increased awareness, excite the trade, and increase the product's shelf space in the store.

Self-liquidating premiums attract consumers because the cost of the merchandise is usually considerably lower than the price at which the article would sell at retail. Consumers respond to a self-liquidating premium that represents a 50 percent saving off retail price. Since manufacturers experience substantial savings through high-volume purchases of premium merchandise, they are able to offer premiums at attractively low prices. Premiums also stimulate product purchases when the consumer wishes to obtain other related premium items, as with the offer of a ring followed by a bracelet, then earrings, and so on. This is also true of "bounce-back" offers accompanying the original premium. A *bounce-back* consists of a folder or small premium catalog sent to the consumer along with the original premium item ordered. The folder or catalog offers additional premiums also available on a self-liquidating basis.

Free Mail-in Premiums

One of the most popular premiums (second only to direct premiums) is the *free mail-in*. Under this arrangement the consumer receives the premium merchandise after mailing in a request for the article along with a proof of purchase. This premium method (with a national average redemption rate of 2 to 4 percent) is one of the most effective consumer motivators, since the premium is offered free. The consumer need only purchase the required product in order to obtain proof of purchase. The free mail-in stimulates multiple purchases of the advertiser's product by requiring more than one proof of purchase from the consumer to obtain the premium. Over 80 percent of all free mail-in offers require multiple proofs of purchase. The consumer benefits as well, since the premium carries no cost of its own.

EXAMPLES OF FREE MAIL-IN PREMIUMS

Ralston Purina Company has offered a free decorative tin for twelve proofs of purchase from its Chex brand breakfast cereal.

Kellogg's has offered a free placemat with press-on initials in return for three proof-of-purchase seals from its Kellogg's Sugar Corn Pops or Apple Jacks brand cereal.

Stanley Works offers a free sports bag with the purchase of a garage door opener.

Budget car rental customers received a free Levi Strauss warmup suit as part of a special 1984 Olympics premium promotion program.

Continuity Coupon Premiums

Continuity coupon premiums are articles of merchandise for which the consumer saves by collecting coupons, proof-of-purchase seals, special labels, or some other form of product identification packed with the product or cut from its package. These offers are continuous, and the consumer selects merchandise from a catalog and then "pays" for the article with the appropriate amount of proof-of-purchase tokens. General Mills, for example, has offered redemption coupons on all of its products for many years. Continuity coupon promotions are useful in building customer brand loyalty, since the consumer must stay with the product in order to build up enough coupon value to qualify for a useful "gift."

The Premium Advertising Association of America has identified some advantages and cautions in this form of premium offer.[8] Continuity coupon premium plans are favored because they keep the customer for an extended period of time. The consumer must continually repurchase the product to accumulate the quantity of proofs-of-purchase needed to obtain the desired premium. Continuity coupon premium plans can prompt purchase of more than one product, where securing of the premium in a common catalog is shared with coupons from several different products that are combined— each having various point values. A continuity coupon plan is also well regarded by premium users because the value of the premium can be made more flexible by relating its value to the number of certificate points required for redemption. Excellent response is reported by users of these plans. Of course, the rate of redemption can vary widely, depending on the type of product, number of products offering coupons, frequency of purchase, extent of promotion, and other influencing factors.

Continuity coupon premium plans, however, also have their shortcomings. Evidently they can sometimes be confusing to many customers. These plans are aimed at the same people each time, and it may take too long to possess and enjoy the premium. Before such a plan is implemented, the following concerns must be considered: (1) setting up an efficient premium-selection and buying procedure; (2) selecting appropriate and desirable merchandise; (3) determining the mechanics of storing and redeeming the premiums; (4) selecting and scheduling the promotional media; (5) determining the possibility of providing for partial cash with fewer coupons; and (6) shortening the relatively long exposure of each premium.

Free Giveaways

In a *free giveaway*, the dealer gives certain articles to the consumer directly at the time the product is purchased. The primary objective of this plan is to increase consumer traffic into the store. A common example of giveaways would be a free piece of glassware with the purchase of a deluxe sandwich. While manufacturers or distributors sponsor most giveaway programs, local dealers may also sponsor them. Many free giveaways celebrate special events such as store openings or store anniversaries.

There are other versions of this premium program. Account openers consist of free gifts that banks give to new depositors. A branch bank may give hand calculators to customers purchasing six-month money market certificates for the first time. Or a bank may give electric frying pans or even small TV sets to individuals opening time deposit accounts with minimum initial deposits of $5,000. Referral premium offers are made to customers in an attempt to build new clientele. A gift goes to a customer referring one or more friends to the seller, who then succeeds in selling them the product or service. Many door-to-door salespeople give direct selling premiums, gifts to potential customers who permit the salesperson to conduct a product demonstration. In some instances, the individual receives a more valuable gift if he or she purchases the product after the demonstration.

Guidelines for Premium Selection

Selecting the right premium is a difficult and critical decision. Many companies hire professional premium consultants or "fulfillment firms," which handle all the tasks in a premium promotion campaign including premium selection, mailings, verification of payments, packaging, and so on.

Premium professionals and specialists recommend the selection of premiums according to these criteria:

The premium should possess an evident value that is worth considerably more than the price asked (i.e., possess a real value in both price and quality).

The premium should be a useful item to the recipient.

The premium should be of limited availability (i.e., not easily found at the retail level).

The premium should be easy to mail, attach to, or place inside the product's container.

The premium should be noncompetitive with the other products available in the same outlet or type of outlet.

The premium should be glamorous and desirable to possess.

The premium should relate, to the extent possible, to the company's advertising program.

Because selection is difficult, many companies use a prescreening and pretesting program to determine whether articles under consideration will be acceptable to consumers. Jury testing, store-level testing, and ballot mailings are three common approaches. In *jury testing*, a panel or "jury" of consumers rates each piece of merchandise under consideration and indicates whether the item is something they would purchase for themselves. *Store-level testing*, using a few stores for a short period of time to observe the movement of the test merchandise, may validate the results of the jury test. *Ballot mailings* may also be used, in which a few thousand people are selected (usually based on their previous response to mail-in offers) to receive a folder or catalog describing the premium merchandise. Since respondents must pay for any premium desired in the test, the results are quite reliable. Advertisers look for at least a 15 percent response rate for the test to be successful.

Sometimes, however, pretesting a premium program is difficult due to timing. For example, many marketers who ran a premium program as part of a 1984 Olympics promotion were faced with the inability to test any kind of new program with an Olympics theme in a non-Olympic year. Most, therefore, stayed with their standard techniques in the belief that an Olympics tie-in would add to the premium program's effectiveness.[9]

SAMPLING

Sampling is one of the most effective promotional techniques to stimulate consumer trial of new or improved products. *Sampling* places a free product in the hands of the consumer for trial, with the idea of letting the product sell itself. Samples are smaller versions of the actual product, containing a sufficient amount to enable consumers to make informed judgments of the product's attributes. We have all seen or received, at one time or another, samples containing one ounce of instant coffee, four ounces of dishwashing liquid, a small deodorant spray, or a bar of soap.

While sampling is the most effective inducement to try products, as well as an effective way to build a consumer franchise,[10] it is also the most expensive sales promotion tool, primarily because of the high costs of special packaging and distribution, not to mention the value of the product content in the sample itself. It is not unusual for the costs of a national sampling campaign for a single product to reach $5 million. Since the cost of sampling is high, only a maximum potential for success justifies its use. Sampling is particularly effective in the following situations:

The product possesses an easily demonstrated superiority over its competitors.

The product is a frequently used and frequently purchased item.

The product returns a reasonably high profit margin while selling at a fairly low retail price.

The product's primary advantage and key attributes are difficult to communicate through advertising media exclusively.

The product's promotional budget allows for sufficient advertising support for the sampling effort.

With respect to competition, sampling can be used to offset competitive marketing or sampling activity by reminding the sampling company's customers of the product's advantages and why they should continue to buy that brand. Furthermore, sampling can be used to put the product into the hands of competitors' customers in an effort to persuade them to use it versus their current brand. Whether used as a defensive or an offensive weapon, sampling can be very effective in keeping old customers or winning new users.[11]

Methods of Sample Distribution

A number of alternatives are available for the distribution of samples to potential product users. The most appropriate method depends on such factors as type, size, bulk, and perishability of the sample product; number and location of sample recipients; degree of selectivity and flexibility desired; timing constraints; and, inescapably, the costliness of the distribution method itself. Among the more common methods of sample distribution are direct mail, door-to-door delivery, and point-of-purchase giveaway, perhaps in conjunction with an in-store demonstration. Samples may also be attached to or placed in the package of another product or included in newspapers or magazines; or they may take the form of coupons (mailed, included with another product, or in print media).

Not all samples are free to consumers. The practice of distributing samples through a salable, introductory-size package has gained favor. Consumers seem more willing to take a chance on a new product if it can be purchased in small amounts for minimal cost. Retailers now support this method of distribution, since these items often carry high profit margins. Another significant advantage is that consumers are more likely to use a purchased sample than a free one. For the advertiser, of course, salable samples are desirable, since they substantially reduce the costs of sample distribution.

AN EXAMPLE OF EFFECTIVE SAMPLING

Gillette views sampling as a key element in securing consumer trial. This has been shown in the way Gillette has used sampling to market both the TRAC II and Atra shaving systems. For example, in the case of TRAC II, numerous laboratory and consumer research studies indicated that overall, TRAC II performance on all shaving attributes combined, were preferred over existing shaving systems (e.g., injector and double edge) by nearly a 9 to 1 margin. Advertising this claim to consumers would gain awareness; yet, believability might be relatively low. Additionally, with a high price tag on the razor, the number and percent of consumers willing to try the product initially would also be low. So, Gillette's strategy was to take away the barriers to trial and let consumers experience the new level of shaving performance for themselves. Hence, its sampling program. Since the introduction of the TRAC II, Gillette has sampled about 70 million consumers. For the same reasons, Gillette has used sampling for its Atra shaving system, distributing it free to over 25 million consumers. Combined, the TRAC II and Atra shaving systems account for over 35 percent of all dollar sales of blades and about 55 percent of all dollar sales of razors. In both cases, sampling deserves much of the credit.

Courtesy Stephen Shapiro, The Gillette Company, Boston.

A sampling program is usually a complex task, requiring considerable effort in planning and execution. For this reason, many companies use the services of organizations that handle the sample distribution, whether it be through mass mailings, personal handouts, or "door drops." The potential benefits of a sampling program, coupled with its costs, mean that the total effort requires coordination.

CONTESTS AND SWEEPSTAKES

Companies sponsoring a virtually endless variety of contests and sweepstakes offer over $125 million of cash and prizes (vacations, automobiles, merchandise) to consumers each year. These exciting promotions have recently regained the broad appeal they once enjoyed and are now among the most popular sales promotion devices. Three factors account for this resurgence of appeal: (1) an increased interest in and awareness of games of chance and skill brought about by a national trend toward state-run lotteries as well as the introduction of casino gambling in places such as New Jersey and its potential for legislation in a number of other states; (2) the lure of winning fabulous prizes; and (3) the fact that this type of promotion actually involves the consumer in the advertising and merchandising of the product through direct participation in the promotion.

The value of prizes and cash has increased considerably in recent years. Grand prizes consisting of new homes, $100,000 cash, and round-the-world trips, to name a few, are common. TWA, for example, through its "Win the World" game, offered a grand prize of a free round trip for two, each year of the winner's life, to anywhere the airline flies. Additional prize winners could cash in on ten thousand other free round-trip passages to any TWA city in the world. Another contest offered free groceries for the rest of the winner's life.

Sales promotions offering prizes to participating consumers fall into two major categories: contests and sweepstakes. *Contests* require the participant to apply a degree of skill judged against that of other entrants. A panel of judges makes evaluations and awards prizes. Promotions of this type involve exercises such as creating a slogan, drawing a poster related to a particular theme, writing an essay ("Cheerios is my favorite breakfast cereal because . . ."), taking photographs, and submitting recipes. Under the contest format, participants must usually submit a proof of purchase of the manufacturer's brand in order to enter and be eligible for prizes.

Sweepstakes are games of chance that, unlike contests, do not require any demonstration of skill by the entrant. Winners are selected at random through a drawing from participants' entry forms. Hence all entrants have an equal chance of winning. Unlike contests, participants need not show proof of purchase to enter. In some sweepstakes, advertisers may encourage participants to submit a proof of purchase, but to avoid breaking lottery laws, they will settle for a facsimile (printed version of the brand name or a drawing of the logo or trademark). (Most lottery laws require that no "consideration" accompany a contestant's entry form.) Advertisers choose sweepstakes over contests by a 9-to-1 margin.

Contests and sweepstakes can have several objectives. Although they do little to produce trial by new users, contests and sweepstakes can provide an excellent overlay to a basic promotion (such as a coupon). Their purpose is generally to add interest to an ad (e.g., a coupon ad) and to add visibility at the point of sale. Other objectives may be: to create an aura of excitement, to provide an extra selling tool, to revitalize the brand's image, or to tie in with some highly recognized event (e.g., the Super Bowl or the Olympics).

Contests and sweepstakes have a number of advantages. They can be directly tied to a specific creative position or product, be targeted toward a specific consumer group, help get on-floor displays, add promotion variety, enhance the brand's image, and build retail traffic. Contests and sweepstakes do have limitations. Generally, they are low-key efforts and do little to stimulate trial by themselves unless heavily advertised. Only certain types of consumers are interested in entering a contest or sweepstakes. The trade is usually reluctant to lend merchandising support for a contest or sweepstakes used alone. They are difficult, if not impossible, to test. And federal, postal, and FTC as well as state regulations make their use legally difficult.[12]

Rules are critical ingredients in running a successful contest or sweepstakes promotion and require careful planning prior to announcement of the event and then clear communication to all participants. At all events, contest rules should be as simple as possible or many problems may arise.

The American Association of Advertising Agencies suggests, at the minimum, that the game rules, communicated to all entrants, include the following: closing date of the event; judging methods and provisions for breaking ties; requirements for entry (who is eligible); the prize structure; who will judge the entries (and a note that the judges' decision will be final); the fact that all entries become the property of the sponsor; and how winners will be announced.[13]

Contests and sweepstakes are among the more-complicated and difficult sales promotion devices in use. Many companies find it advantageous to leave their planning and execution to professional firms specializing in these promotions. These firms handle all details of the promotion, checking legal requirements, setting rules, distributing entry forms, judging entries, and notifying winners.

The most successful contest and sweepstakes promotions are those with well-planned and specific objectives integrated with other advertising support and with sales force and trade promotional activities.

CONSUMER DEALS

Consumer deals are short-term promotions offering consumers a saving in the purchase of a product. Manufacturers use consumer deals to induce trial by new users and trial of new products, and to stimulate demand for mature products. They also hope to encourage impulse purchases and stimulate repurchase by current users. Finally, consumer deals may offset competitive promotional activities and stimulate off-season purchases.

The major types of consumer deals are direct price reductions, bonus packs, refunds and rebates, and combination deals.

Direct Price Reductions

Direct price reductions offer the consumer the opportunity to purchase a product at a specified saving off the regular retail price. These offers usually take the form of a "cents-off" reduction appearing on the product label or package and are popular with manufacturers of frequently purchased items in supermarkets. They are also particularly effective in stimulating sales of products during off-seasons. Many manufacturers believe that when the offer reduces a price from 12 to 15 percent, it achieves maximum impact.

Bonus Packs

A *bonus pack* deal offers the consumer an opportunity to purchase more of a product with no increase in the product's regular price. Depending on product characteristics, this increase in quantity may take the form of a greater volume of the product or an increased number of product units. Consider these examples:

> "Purchase 8 ounces of Taster's Choice brand instant coffee and get 2 ounces free." (Requires special packaging.)
>
> "Buy four bars of Ivory Soap for the price of three." (Product units are generally banded.)

A variation of the standard bonus pack deal is the combination bonus pack offer, which allows the consumer to purchase two different products (for instance, a paint brush and a gallon of paint or an oil filter and five quarts of oil) for a price lower than the total of all sold separately.

Problems may arise with the use of bonus packs, particularly those involving product units banded together. Employee theft sometimes occurs. Or the retailer may separate the pack and sell the extra units at the regular retail price. Bonus packs may also pose special handling problems as well as increased packaging costs to the manufacturer. The obvious advantage, however, is the potential for sales stimulation because of the consumer's perception of increased value and the lure of "getting something for nothing."

Refunds and Rebates

Cash refunds and *rebates* have become an increasingly popular form of consumer deal. Refunds (or "rebates" when referring to higher-price items) offer the consumer a cash payment in return for proofs of purchase for specified products. For example, Shell Oil Company has successfully used a $3 refund when a car owner buys an oil and filter change. So, too, has Lucite Paint with its refund of $1.50 per gallon of paint up to four gallons. And Mr. Coffee with its $3 refund on a purchase of its automatic coffeemaker. A single-brand refund offer involves proof of purchase for a single product, whereas a multibrand deal requires the purchase of several specified brands in order to qualify for a refund. These are extremely effective consumer incentives, especially in inducing purchase of new brands. Surveys have shown that, on average, one in three consumers will try a new or different brand because of a refund offer. And industry data indicate that requiring three proofs of purchase in order to qualify for a refund is the norm. Variable refund offers, where the size of the cash refund rises with the number of proofs of purchase, are also possible, usually only one to a family. A typical offer might include $1.00 for one proof of purchase, $1.50 for two proofs of purchase, and $2.00 for three proofs of purchase.

Combination Offers

A *combination offer* combines a refund offer with another form of consumer incentive. Consider the following variations:

"Submit three proofs of purchase and receive a $1.50 cash refund along with two 50¢ off coupons." (Referred to as a "bounce-back" coupon.)

"Submit one proof of purchase and receive a $3.00 cash refund and an entry into a contest."

Some refund deals give the consumers a choice as to the disposition of the refund. The makers of Bayer Aspirin, for example, offered the following alternatives in return for one proof of purchase from a Bayer 200- or 300-size package:

Alternative 1—The consumer receives a $1.00 cash refund check.

Alternative 2—A refund of $1.00 is sent by Bayer Aspirin to the Arthritis Foundation as a donation.

The consumer merely checks the appropriate box on the offer form to indicate preference.

While most refund offers amount to $5 or less, some may run as high as $500–$800 or more. American auto makers, in a effort to stimulate a troubled new-car market and offset foreign competition, have used rebates to attract new-car buyers in times of high inflation and increasing consumer interest rates.

In summary, these are the points to remember when considering consumer deals:

1. Price-off promotions should be used only on an infrequent basis so as not to cheapen the brand's image.
2. Price incentives should be spaced at wide intervals since the closer together the incentives, the more cost-conscious and less brand-loyal the consumer will become.
3. Consumer deals are more effective for newer brands than for older ones.
4. Deals are not substitutes for advertising. The two should complement each other.[14]

ADVERTISING SPECIALTIES

Specialty advertising involves the distribution of useful articles of merchandise (usually of nominal monetary value), often bearing the advertiser's name, logo, and promotional message. They are given, without cost or obligation, to preselected recipients as goodwill gestures. Typical gifts include pens, calendars, ashtrays, T-shirts, keychains, and the like. Specialty advertising is big business, comprising some fifteen thousand articles of merchandise and annual sales near $3 billion.[15] To maximize the benefits of specialty advertising, many companies hire professional specialty advertising counselors to assist in setting objectives, determining strategies, identifying target recipients, and developing distribution plans.

Specialty advertising can be effective by itself or as a supplement to a broader, multimedia promotional campaign. It is well suited for a variety of objectives, including promoting branch openings, introducing new products, image building, introducing new sales personnel, changing names or products, developing trade show traffic, and opening new accounts or activating inactive ones.

A major benefit, along with the goodwill created, is that the advertiser's name, logo, and message achieve considerable exposure through repetitive use of the specialty item by the user. Gifts such as pens, keychains, and calendars are prime specialty items for precisely this reason, since recipients will retain them for extended periods.

Distribution of advertising specialties occurs in several ways, including the common method of direct mail, dissemination by sales personnel and dealers, or as tie-ins with point-of-purchase displays or in-store demonstrations. Specialty advertising may not, however, be best in mass circulation, since the cost of the specialty item itself and the expense of distribution may be quite high. Its best application is highly selective with considerable thought given to the identification of recipients.

PACKAGING

The *package* is a product's "battle dress" as it wages war against legions of competing brands on the battlefield of the retailer's shelves. The package's *basic function* is to protect the product as it moves from producer to consumer; however, the package's *job* goes well beyond product protection to include the vital role of sales stimulation.

The package is the most visible part of the product and is crucial to the success of many products. It is a major influence on the consumer's buying decision and, at the same time, is a crucial factor in the retailer's decision on whether to stock the product. And although both consumers and retailers have a great interest in the package, each looks for something different.

The Consumer's Viewpoint

The consumer looks for a package that protects the product against hazards such as spoilage or breakage. The package also has to provide information to help the consumer in the purchase decision, as well as in the way to use the product. At a minimum, the following information should appear: the brand name, the manufacturer, the ingredients and the quantity, nutritional information, directions for preparation and use of the product, and any special cautions necessary. The package has to anticipate the consumer's questions and provide answers before the questions are asked.

Besides protecting the product and telling the product's story, the package should be convenient and easy to open, use, close, store, and reuse. Furthermore, it should be easy to handle under a variety of conditions, both in use and in storage.

Finally, the package should be attractive, not only to capture consumer attention and interest at the point of sale but also to enhance its surroundings at the point of use or display. Thus the package is a powerful factor in the consumer's buying decision; it can make or break the sale.

The Retailer's Viewpoint

The retailer receives, stores, prices, and displays products and therefore has a variety of concerns about packaging. Shipping cartons should be easy to handle and convenient to store, have contents clearly identified, and have adequate instructions for opening so as not to damage the merchandise. While shipping cartons should be strong and durable to protect merchandise from breakage, they should also be relatively easy to open. The package, now out of the shipping carton, should provide a prominent location where the merchant can affix a price, prior to display.

A major concern of the retailer is the efficient use of shelf space and display area. The package design should permit efficient stacking and display, occupying a minimum of shelf space. Retailers are reluctant to stock and display a product whose package design makes it difficult to handle. While the retailer's expectations of product packaging should not discourage packaging innovation, frequent package change can result in resistance by the retailer, especially when existing shelf configurations cannot easily accommodate the new package.[16] We will discuss packaging change in the next subsection.

Another important yardstick by which the retailer judges a package is its capacity for stimulating the sale of a product. Often called the "silent salesperson," the package must combine such design elements as color, shape, size, and graphics along with adequate information to answer any questions the consumer might have and to capture the consumer's attention, generate interest, and induce buying. And the package must do this better than any of its competitors.

In short, the marketer must remember that a package is a physical and psychological part of the total store environment. To be effective, it must be visible; it must reach out and arrest the consumer's attention; it must create shelf excitement.[17] For example, Nabisco and Kellogg use the same package design for many items in their product lines, creating a highly visible "billboard" effect on retail shelves.[18]

Changing the Package

One of the important decisions a marketer has to make involves package change. It is a particularly difficult decision when the existing package is well known and successful. Nevertheless, package modification is a common occurrence, conditioned by the following factors:

1. An innovation in physical packaging
2. Exploiting a reformulated product
3. Repositioning the product
4. Upgrading to more contemporary graphics
5. A change in retail selling techniques
6. Changing use of product in the home
7. Changing consumer attitudes
8. More youthful look in changing graphic environment
9. At rare times, conforming to an exploitable opportunity such as a highly successful advertising campaign[19]

Periodic evaluation of the existing package is a necessity, given the important role of the package in the consumer decision process. A change may not be required. In any proposed change, though, the marketer must know, through market research, what the important recognition factors on the package are so that any change will not harm them. For example, Quaker State, which owns more than 20 percent of the $2.5 billion motor oil market, boosted its share of the do-it-yourself market with a new plastic container that is easy to open, resealable, leakproof, and spillproof and eliminates the need for messy funnels required for regular oil containers. Based on focus group and mall intercept studies, Quaker State's bottle is used for its entire line of automobile oil. The theme for the introductory advertising campaign was "Say good-bye to America's favorite can of motor oil."[20] Whether a contemplated packaging change is minor or major, the marketer must exercise great care to preserve the existing strengths of the package, especially because the consumer's perception of the product may change when he or she perceives a change in the package.

With the impact a package can have on a product's market share, a marketer should recognize that "packaging is much more than an esthetic exercise—it is a marketing-oriented, disciplined approach to effective communication."[21] Furthermore, the package should harmonize with all other aspects of the marketing, advertising, and promotional efforts to stimulate brand recognition and purchase by the consumer.

SUMMARY

There is a broad range of sales promotional techniques shaped for consumers. Point-of-purchase displays, coupons, premiums, sampling, and contests and sweepstakes, along with consumer deals, advertising specialties, and packaging, provide the marketer with a wealth of powerful weapons for use in the battle for consumer loyalty. Management must know the strengths and limitations of these techniques, as well as the conditions under which each is most appropriate. Sales promotion is often the spark that sets the buying process in motion or provides the extra impetus sometimes needed for buying to occur. And just as sales promotion can be instrumental in motivating consumers, so too is it important for a company's dealers and sales personnel, a subject to which we now turn our attention.

REVIEW AND DISCUSSION QUESTIONS

1. Explain the characteristics of a good point-of-purchase display from the retailer's viewpoint.

2. What impact does an effective point-of-purchase display have on the consumer?

3. Under what conditions might a marketer use coupons?

4. "There is no difference in effect on sales between a direct ten-cent price reduction and a ten-cent coupon." Comment.

5. Identify and explain the different methods used to distribute coupons. What are the advantages and disadvantages of each method?

6. Although the basic purpose of premiums is to increase sales, there are several specific objectives for which premiums are used. What are they?

7. Distinguish between the following: (a) direct premiums, (b) self-liquidating premiums, (c) free mail-ins, (d) continuity coupon premiums, and (e) free giveaways. Give examples of each type.

8. You market low-price, easy-to-use cameras and wish to offer a premium during the summer vacation season. What type of premium would you offer? What guidelines would you use for premium selection?

9. When is the use of sampling appropriate? Explain.

10. Identify and discuss the common methods of sample distribution.

11. If you were directing a sampling program, would you use a specialist firm to handle the program or would you do it yourself? Give reasons.

12. What is the philosophy underlying sampling?

13. *Distinguish between* contests *and* sweepstakes. *What are the similarities? The differences?*

14. *To what do you attribute the popularity of contests and sweepstakes?*

15. *What are the advantages and disadvantages of contests? Sweepstakes?*

16. *Explain the objectives behind consumer deals.*

17. *Identify and discuss the major types of consumer deals.*

18. *A home computer manufacturer wishes to reduce the purchase price of its machines by $100 in order to stimulate sales. What are the advantages and disadvantages of using a direct price reduction or using a rebate offer?*

19. *To what purposes might advertising specialties be used? Give some examples of specialties.*

20. *What are some characteristics of effective advertising specialties?*

21. *Explain the role of packaging in the promotional mix.*

22. *From the retailer's viewpoint, what constitutes a "good" package? From the consumer's viewpoint?*

23. *Do you consider the package as part of the product? Why or why not?*

24. *What factors might lead a marketer to consider a packaging change?*

25. *"The package is the most visible part of the product, and it is a critical factor in the success of many products." Comment.*

26. *Of all the major forms of sales promotion directed to consumers, which do you consider the most effective? Why?*

NOTES

1. John A. Quelch and Kristina Cannon-Bonventre, "Better Marketing at the Point of Purchase," *Harvard Business Review*, November-December 1983, pp. 162–69.

2. Point-of-Purchase Advertising Institute, New York, 1978.

3. For an in-depth evaluation of the effectiveness of point-of-purchase displays, see "Display Effectiveness: An Evaluation—Part I," *The Nielsen Researcher*, No. 2 (1983), pp. 2–8; and "Display Effectiveness: An Evaluation—Part II," *The Nielsen Researcher*, No. 3 (1983), pp. 2–11. Also see "Pepsi Tops Honor Role of 1983's Best Point-of-Purchase Displays," *Marketing News*, April 27, 1984, pp. 14–15.

4. *Advertising Age*, December 15, 1980, p. 41.

5. David J. Reibstein and Phyllis A. Traver, "Factors Affecting Coupon Redemption Rates," *Journal of Marketing*, 46 (Fall 1982), 104. Also see "Coupon Distribution and Redemption Patterns," *NCH Reporter*, A. C. Nielsen Company, No. 1,

1984, p. 7; and "Inside Report: Couponing and Sampling," *Marketing News*, September 28, 1984, pp. 12–15.

6. Reibstein and Traver, "Factors Affecting Coupon Redemption Rates," pp. 102–13.

7. *Advertising Age*, June 15, 1981, p. 90.

8. *Marketing with Premiums* (New York: Premium Advertising Association of America, 1975), p. 11.

9. Louis J. Haugh, "Get Ready, Get Set, Promote!" *Advertising Age*, January 30, 1984, p. M54.

10. Philip Kotler, *Principles of Marketing*, 2nd ed. (Englewood Cliffs, N.J.: Prentice-Hall, 1983), p. 466.

11. Don E. Schultz and William A. Robinson, *Sales Promotion Management* (Chicago: Crain Books, 1982), pp. 245–46.

12. *Sales Promotion Techniques—A Basic Guidebook* (New York: American Association of Advertising Agencies, 1978), pp. 36–37.

13. Ibid., p. 38.

14. Charles L. Hinkle, "The Strategy of Price Deals," *Harvard Business Review*, July-August 1965, pp. 75–85.

15. Specialty Advertising Association International, Irving, Tex.

16. Quelch and Cannon-Bonventre, "Better Marketing," p. 166.

17. Jerome Gould, "Libby Libby's New Look Look Look," *Advertising Age*, April 29, 1974, p. 32.

18. Quelch and Cannon-Bonventre, "Better Marketing," p. 166.

19. Reprinted with permission from the February 19, 1979 issue of *Advertising Age*. Copyright by Crain Communications, Inc.

20. "Quaker State Expects Sales Gains with New Packaging System for Oil," *Marketing News*, February 3, 1984, p. 7.

21. "Packaging Design Seen as Cost-Effective Marketing Strategy," *Marketing News*, February 20, 1981, p. 1.

16

Sales Promotion to Dealers and Sales Personnel

Sales promotion activities often address those who are responsible for selling the manufacturer's product. Dealers and sales personnel are the targets of sales promotion as the manufacturer tries to provide incentive for its sales force and its dealers to give a stronger push to the product. Our exploration of sales promotion activities continues with discussion of the major types of sales promotion for dealers and sales personnel, including such measures as trade deals and promotional allowances, cooperative advertising, contests, sales meetings, sales brochures, and trade shows and exhibits.

TRADE DEALS AND PROMOTIONAL ALLOWANCES

Trade deals are sales promotion devices that a manufacturer uses in the short term to secure retail distribution for a product or to generate extra promotional support from middlemen. Trade deals usually take the form of discounts, allowances, or free merchandise, and they can achieve such objectives as the following:

Gaining distribution for a new product or improving the quality of distribution for a mature product

Obtaining better or more shelf space for products

Increasing retail merchandising support and special display activity

Increasing order sizes

Offsetting the competition

Increasing off-season sales

Trade promotions require careful monitoring and control, since manufacturers must depend on the cooperation of the retailer. In the absence of adequate policing, the manufacturer runs the risk that dealers will not comply with the trade-deal agreement.[1]

The major types of trade deals include the buying allowance, count and recount, buy-back allowance, free goods, and advertising and merchandising allowances.

Buying Allowance

Under a *buying allowance* agreement, the manufacturer gives a specific sum of money (or discount) to the middleman in return for a specific quantity purchased during a specified time period. This incentive (usually paid in the form of cash, a reduction in invoice amount, or a credit memorandum) generates larger-than-normal orders from wholesalers and retailers (with no special merchandising effort asked in return). To capitalize on the "back-to-school" buying season, for example, a stationery manufacturer might offer middlemen, for a limited time, say from August 1 through September 15, a reduction of seventy-five cents off the carton price of notebooks for each carton purchased during that period. The advantages to the stationery manufacturer are (1) quick execution because there are no special handling, packaging, or other arrangements; and (2) a possible block of the competition because of the increased order size. The dealer benefits from the price reduction, with no special considerations attached.

Count and Recount

To move merchandise out of a dealer's warehouse and into the store's selling space (thereby reducing the likelihood of a stockout), a manufacturer may offer a trade deal known as a *count and recount*. Under this plan, the retailer receives payment for each product unit (usually measured in cases) moved from warehouse storage into the store itself. Essentially, the manufacturer will pay the retailer a specified sum of money for each inventory unit moved, that is, the difference between the amount of product stored at the time of the initial count plus purchases and the amount remaining at the time of the recount at the end of a specified period, according to the following formula:

(Opening inventory + Purchases over the period)
    − Ending inventory = Number of units receiving allowance

Let us assume that General Foods Corporation offers Flanagan's Supermarket a count and recount deal on cases of its Country Time brand lemonade at $1.00 per case for the six-week period June 1 to July 15. On June 1 a General Foods sales representative counts fifteen cases of Country Time in stock. The representative returns on July 15, takes a recount of the inventory, and now finds six cases of Country Time on hand in the warehouse. Store purchases for the June 1 through July 15 period amount to twenty-five cases of the product. Calculation of the count and recount incentive:

$$\underset{\substack{\text{Open} \\ \text{inventory}}}{(15} + \underset{\substack{\text{Period} \\ \text{purchases}}}{25)} - \underset{\substack{\text{Ending} \\ \text{inventory}}}{6} = \underset{\substack{\text{Units to} \\ \text{receive allowance}}}{34 \text{ units}}$$

Consequently, Mr. Flanagan will receive a payment of $34 (the agreed-upon $1 per case) for his participation in the count and recount deal.

Besides preventing stockouts, the count and recount deal is useful when a manufacturer is anxious to deplete old products or packages from the distribution network just prior to introduction of a new, improved, or repackaged version of the product.

Buy-Back Allowance

A *buy-back allowance* is a follow-up to other trade deals. For instance, a buy-back allowance might occur immediately upon completion of a count and recount deal. The buy-back allowance is an offer of a specified monetary incentive for new or additional purchases, based on the purchase quantity in the previous trade deal. In this way, warehouse stocks depleted through the count and recount deal may be replenished through the added incentive to repurchase the product with a buy-back allowance. Under the buy-back allowance, repurchases will not usually exceed the amount of stock moved during the count and recount deal.

Recall the example used in the count and recount deal. Assume that GFC now offers Flanagan's Supermarket a buy-back allowance of $1.50 per case of Country Time lemonade for orders during the July 16 through July 30 period. The impact of the buy-back allowance, as well as both deals in combination, is as follows:

Inventory at time of initiation of count and recount deal (June 1)	15 cases
Purchases (June 1 through July 15)	25 cases
Inventory at time of recount (July 15)	(6) cases
Units receiving count and recount allowance (15 + 25) − 6 = 34 cases	
Count and recount allowance @ $1 rate	$34
Repurchases (July 15–July 30)	50 cases
Less: Excess over count and recount limitation	16 cases
Repurchases to receive buy-back allowance	34 cases
Buy-back allowance @ $1.50 rate	$51
Total allowances received	$85

Free Goods

Under the *free goods* arrangement, dealers receive free merchandise (not money as in most other trade deals) for purchasing a specified amount of that product or some other product from the same manufacturer. For example, a manufacturer may offer a free case of merchandise for each twelve cases purchased by the dealer. The dealer takes delivery of thirteen cases of the product and receives an invoice for twelve cases. This method, while providing the dealer with an opportunity to experience higher profits through the sale of the free merchandise, may not work for slow-moving products because large purchases simply cannot be justified for such items.

Advertising and Merchandising Allowances

Advertising allowances are incentives given to middlemen for advertising a manufacturer's product. These incentives usually take the form of a monetary payment equivalent to a percentage (e.g., 1.5 percent) of the amount of gross product purchases per specified time period (e.g., per quarter). To receive an advertising allowance, the middleman must provide the manufacturer with proof of performance that the advertising actually ran (tearsheets or affidavits indicating the copy of the advertisement, number of times run, cost of running the advertisement). Payment comes only after proof of performance.

Cooperative advertising (discussed in detail in the next section) also falls into this category of trade deals. Another type of advertising allowance involves a *dealer listing*, an advertisement placed by a manufacturer identifying its products and including a listing of the names and locations of retailers who carry the product. These listings are useful to dealers because they can generate store traffic. They are also useful to manufacturers, particularly those engaged in selective or exclusive distribution, because the listing identifies the retail source of the product for the consumer.

Display allowances go to retailers who build special displays for the manufacturer's products, according to specifications identified in a formal contract between the parties. Finally, *merchandise allowances* are used as incentives for retailers to feature the products of a particular manufacturer in their displays or advertising. As with any type of sales promotion, competitive analysis is important in determining which, if any, form of advertising and merchandising allowance to use.

All forms of trade deals and promotional allowances are subject to certain requirements set forth in the Robinson-Patman Act, which prohibits undue discrimination by requiring sellers to treat all competitive customers (dealers) on a proportionately equal basis regarding prices, discounts, promotional allowances, services, or facilities provided for goods of like grade and quality.

COOPERATIVE ADVERTISING

Cooperative advertising is advertising whose sponsorship and cost two or more advertisers share, customarily on a 50–50 basis, although the parties may make other arrangements. Manufacturers both large and small spend some $8 billion a year on cooperative advertising covering a wide range of product categories. While cooperative advertising can be a significant force in a promotional program, studies show that from a manufacturer's viewpoint, cooperative advertising "is most effective when it is combined with a strong national (i.e., sole-sponsored) advertising program."[2] There are two major categories of cooperative advertising: horizontal and vertical.

Horizontal Cooperative Advertising

Horizontal cooperative advertising (association advertising) is advertising jointly sponsored by groups of competitors operating within the same industry. Such mutual advertising campaigns stimulate primary demand for the industry's products. For instance, for many years the nation's dairy product producers have joined forces in an effort to convince consumers of the merits of milk and other dairy products. The nation's orange growers do the same to promote demand for fresh oranges and orange juice. The nation's egg producers use cooperative advertising to extol the virtues of the "incredible-edible egg." And so on. Horizontal cooperative advertising also occurs at the retail level where, for example, a regional group of automobile dealers, such as the Ohio Ford Dealers' Association, shares the advertising costs of promoting a particular make of automobile. Many retailers, however, are reluctant to join forces for competitive reasons.

Vertical Cooperative Advertising

Vertical (or "dealer") *cooperative advertising* is the type most manufacturers use. Under this arrangement, the manufacturer reimburses the dealer for a portion of the dealer's expenditures for local advertisements featuring the manufacturer's products. Many reimbursement plans are possible and are limited only by the creativity of the parties and their ability to reach agreement on terms. When a retailer combines a number of advertisements from various manufacturers into a single full-page advertisement ("omnibus" advertisement), each manufacturer pays a pro rata proportion of the total cost.

Usually, cooperative advertising is just one component in a program of promotional support a manufacturer offers to its retailers. "Such programs often include suggested advertising formats, materials for producing ads ('mats'), schedules of the manufacturer's national advertising to facilitate retailer tie-ins to the national program, and schedules of dollar allowances available; they may also include other related promotional materials (e.g., point-of-purchase displays)."[3] The primary vehicle for cooperative advertising is newspapers, accounting for about 70 percent of the $8 billion spent annually on cooperative advertising. Direct mail follows with 13 percent of the total, then comes radio (10 percent), and the remaining 7 percent consists of television, magazines, outdoor, and yellow pages.[4]

When a dealer places a local advertisement under a cooperative advertising agreement with a manufacturer, substantiation that the advertisement has actually run, along with proof of the cost, must go to the manufacturer for the dealer to gain reimbursement. The dealer will usually forward to the manufacturer a copy of the invoice along with a "tear sheet" (for print media) as proof that the advertisement ran. "Electronic tear sheets," that is, affidavits of performance indicating the content of the advertisement, the number of times aired, and the cost serve as substantiation of radio and television cooperative advertisements. The manufacturer, upon receipt of proof of performance, will then forward payment (or credit memo) to the dealer or dealers to complete the cooperative advertising arrangement. Many manufacturers and dealers have ongoing cooperative advertising agreements.

A note of caution: As we said earlier, the Robinson-Patman Act requires that all competitive customers be treated on a proportionately equal basis in terms of allowances, promotions, and services received from sellers. The specific agreement between a manufacturer and a dealer regarding a cooperative advertising arrangement must also be available to all other dealers within that market. Violation of these conditions may bring litigation by the Federal Trade Commission, which enforces the Robinson-Patman Act. (For a full discussion of the Robinson-Patman Act and other laws governing promotion, see Chapter 19.)

Benefits and Limitations of Cooperative Advertising

With careful planning, skillful executing, and close monitoring, the manufacturer and the retailer can accrue a number of advantages through the use of cooperative advertising. Any decision on whether to use cooperative advertising, however, must also consider the disadvantages—and cooperative advertising does have its drawbacks.[5]

Advantages to the Manufacturer

The manufacturer can buy more advertising space or time for less money because, when the advertisement is over the local dealer's signature, the ad runs at the local rate (substantially less than the national rate the manufacturer would otherwise pay). A greater amount of advertising normally results because cooperative advertising dollars motivate retailers to do more advertising (and encourage nonadvertising retailers to start advertising). A manufacturer can "localize" or custom-tailor its advertising to a specific market, thereby capitalizing on the specific local conditions. The customer learns exactly where he or she can purchase the advertised product. Improved dealer relations can result, especially as the retailer sees that the manufacturer cares enough to "help out." A retailer who feels that the manufacturer is doing what it can to increase sales at the local level will have a more positive outlook toward the manufacturer, and a more cooperative environment results. The manufacturer can use the promise of cooperative advertising assistance in recruiting new retailers to carry its products. Cooperative money can be an important factor in achieving greater distribution through added outlets.[6] A cooperative advertising arrangement provides automatic control over advertising expenditures because, generally, the greater the retailer's sales volume, the greater the amount of cooperative money it is allowed. Hence, proportionately greater funds go to the most productive dealers.

Disadvantages to the Manufacturer

The major disadvantage for the manufacturer is the lack of control it has over cooperative advertising, sometimes leading to such practices as the following:

> Nonuse or misuse of photostats (camera-ready ads) supplied by manufacturer
>
> Noncompliance with agreed-upon procedures or terms
>
> Substituting the dealer's advertisement for one required by the manufacturer

Switching media

Double-billing and duplicate claims (the newspaper or station prepares two bills for use of space or time—one legitimate, the other a falsified inflated one. The local advertiser pays the "correct" bill but submits the inflated bill to the manufacturer for the agreed-upon rate of reimbursement; hence the dealer receives a larger reimbursement than that to which it is entitled)

Claims of advertising for products not approved for co-op

Falsification of invoices, affidavits, scripts, and ad copy

Dealer relations may deteriorate, particularly with a control problem; namely, the tighter and more effective the controls, the greater the likelihood that dealers will complain. For example, if the manufacturer places stringent controls on the media to be used, the type of copy in a layout (or requiring use of a mat), or the amount to be spent, disagreements may result. A further disadvantage is that the time, expense, and paperwork needed to control a co-op program can be substantial.

Potential legal difficulties can arise if, as mentioned earlier, dealers do not receive proportionately equal treatment. When a dealer asks for a special deal, the manufacturer violates the law by going along with the demand. On the other hand, if the manufacturer refuses to grant special treatment, the dealer may become upset and threaten to change suppliers. Cooperative advertising can be a "no-win" situation for the manufacturer.

Advantages to the Retailer

The retailer has an opportunity to do more advertising than normal. Cooperative money helps the dealer to advertise regularly. The retailer may benefit from a well-designed cooperative advertising program because the manufacturer takes care of many of the details (such as supplying a mat and a media schedule). The quality of the advertising is often higher than what the retailer could afford because it is supplied by the manufacturer and its agency, not by the retailer or by an inexperienced local agency.

Disadvantages to the Retailer

Tight restrictions often accompany the cooperative advertising money. Retailers believe that manufacturers should allow them more flexibility in media, copy, layout, and the like. There may be a nagging suspicion that some dealers (especially the large ones) are getting a special deal. The larger, more powerful retailers can ignore the manufacturer's controls, and this annoys the smaller retailers.

Grey Advertising, Inc., has articulated the negative case very succinctly when it names these problems:

The first is the struggle between marketers and retailers . . . for control—control of monies, marketing strategy, of the message itself, as well as the media (type and timing) where it is to appear.

The second is the contradiction co-op introduces into the buyer-seller relationship, since the supplier must police and even possibly penalize his own best customers.

Many abuses stem from the fact that marketers have been unable or unwilling to risk damaging—by tough enforcement of co-op rules—relationships with the very retailers on whom their sales depend. . . .[7]

The decision whether to use cooperative advertising involves several factors. Proper planning, execution, and monitoring can yield many rewards. Poor design yields gross inefficiencies and the possibility of friction in important relationships.

Reviewing the Cooperative Advertising Program

Young and Greyser propose the following guidelines for strategic review of a company's cooperative advertising program.[8]

1. Establish objectives for cooperative advertising as precisely as possible.

    Decide what communications and trade objectives are being sought with the particular co-op advertising program. This review should include consideration of short-term and long-term aims. Likewise, it is important to establish the *balance* between trade-related goals and goals associated with the attitudes and behavior of ultimate consumers.

2. For most effective results, use co-op in conjunction with strong national advertising.

    In many situations it is difficult to develop product benefits or brand preference through the exclusive use of co-op. Many managers know that a co-op advertisement can frequently trigger a sale; however, co-op ads work best when the potential consumer has prior knowledge of and/or preference for the advertised brand. This "brand franchise development" is often most effectively accomplished by means of manufacturer-sponsored advertising.

3. Do not consider budget decisions for cooperative advertising and (sole-sponsored) national advertising as direct trade-offs.

    The objectives of each program, while related, are different. By treating the two decisions separately, manufacturers can make better judgments about how to achieve specific brand objectives with both the consumers and the trade.

4. Ask to what extent is the product or brand retailer-dependent.

    Executives should assess how important retailers' marketing or selling efforts are to the brand's success. Co-op is a relatively more important part of the marketing mix in situations where manufacturers are relatively more dependent on retailers' selling or merchandising activities.

5. Assess whether consumers seek product choice information from retailers' communications or from manufacturers' communications.

For products where there is a strong consumer reliance on information from retailers, co-op will tend to be relatively more important.

6. Emphasize cooperative advertising when a "linkage" with retailers' image in the local market is important.

When there is a need for image "rub-off" from the retailer to the manufacturer, the latter should address the question, Whose company do we keep? Cooperative advertising can be used to stimulate this linkage.

7. Try to understand target consumers' responses to "dual signature" advertisements.

That is, do the consumers react more to the manufacturer's brand name or to the retailer's store name in a jointly sponsored advertisement?

8. Look at why retailers are not utilizing a firm's co-op program enough.

The reimbursement rate may be too low, the rules may be too rigid or complex, or company personnel may not be facilitating co-op usage. Alternatively, the collateral materials may not be attractive or may not be tied to the company's overall merchandising campaign. *Implementation and administrative details of co-op programs are important*.

- Guidelines and rules for retailers should be as simple as possible. They should be explained clearly and often.

- Whenever possible, co-op materials should incorporate themes or copy points from national advertising campaigns. As appropriate, other marketing themes (new-product introductions, seasonal promotions, display ideas, etc.) should be used in this material. Obviously, the co-op materials should make merchandising sense.

- Sales personnel should be well versed in both the merchandising advantages and the implementation details of the program. They must help merchandise the program.

- Managers should ensure that reimbursement procedures are reasonably uncomplicated, and that company office personnel are equipped to implement them expeditiously.

9. Ask why cooperative advertising programs do not seem to be yielding results commensurate with expenditure levels.

Are the firm's funds being used

- In ways that do not fit with the firm's *product strategy*?
- In *media* that are not considered effective?
- At disadvantageous *times of the year*?
- In *creative formats* (e.g., advertisement size, content) that are inconsistent with the brand's communications objectives?

10. Consider strategies for focusing co-op programs, or for containing (or reducing) overall co-op expenditure levels.

These strategies include

- *Item-limits*, which specify that only certain products are eligible for co-op funding
- *Media-limits*, which allow only the most effective or efficient media to be employed in cooperatively funded advertisements
- *Time-limits*, which stipulate specific time periods, or seasons, for co-op reimbursement programs
- *Tightening* of the co-op guidelines and/or their enforcement

While these strategic alternatives can redirect or reduce co-op expenditures, they will probably also lessen retailers' support efforts for the brand. Thus they must be implemented with caution and only after thorough analysis.

11. Realize that to be most effective, cooperative advertising must indeed be cooperative.

Cooperative advertising represents a blending of the resources of two organizations, each with different goals, but both with certain common goals. Appreciating what each party contributes to accomplishing these shared objectives, and recognizing each party's aims, will lead to the mutual benefits to be derived from a successful cooperative advertising program.

In summary, cooperative advertising presents the marketer with an excellent opportunity to get dealers actively involved in the total marketing effort. Management would do well to explore the possibilities of a cooperative advertising program, giving close attention to the strengths and weaknesses of this promotional tool. And a strategic review is mandatory if all parties are to get the most out of their cooperative advertising efforts.

CONTESTS

Contests are useful sales promotion techniques for motivating sales personnel and distributors.

Sales Force Contests

Sales contests increase the motivation and productivity of *sales personnel* through an appeal to their competitive spirit. Incentives usually take the form of cash prizes, merchandise, paid vacations, or special awards and recognition. Although all sales contests, in one way or another, have the broad purpose of increasing the level of sales and profitability, most have specific goals as well, such as promoting slow-moving or seasonal items, securing new accounts, obtaining increased sales on high-margin products, pushing new products, gaining additional display space, and increasing order size.

Two important considerations in making a sales contest successful are (1) the duration of the contest and (2) the nature and structure of the prize format. While there are no established guidelines, contest duration should provide sufficient time to build enthusiasm, yet not run so long as to cause sales personnel to lose interest. Most contests run between one and four months.

Most sales professionals agree that contests should provide all participants with a reasonable chance for success. Consider the difficulty in stimulating interest among all sales personnel for a competition offering only a few prizes and rewarding sales volume alone when certain salespeople operate in high-volume sales territories and others are in low-volume territories still in the developmental stage. Clearly, salespeople in low-volume territories will quickly assess their chances, conclude that they have little possibility of winning, and decide not to participate in the effort. A valuable opportunity for creating motivation will disintegrate. An alternative is to base prizes not on total volume but on some other more equitable measure, such as percentage increase in sales, percentage of quota exceeded, or some other format based on improvement in performance. A number of contests have succeeded wherein sales personnel compete, not against each other, but against their own past performance. Prizes go to all the participants demonstrating improvement in sales volume—the value of the prize relating directly to the degree of improvement. In this way all the participants feel that they have a chance of winning something and all of them are more enthusiastic.

Whatever the specific nature of the contest or incentive program, it is important to remember that a contest or an incentive program alone cannot solve other management problems. For example, "using a sales contest in an attempt to eliminate a long-term motivational problem or to cure defects in a company's training or compensation program usually only prolongs the underlying problem."[9] Better management strategy is needed.

Dealer Contests

Sales contests also motivate *dealers* and *distributors*. The same logic with respect to prizes and awards applies to dealer contests; that is, the more prizes available and the greater the chance of winning something, the more effective the promotion promises to be. Similarly, contests should reward improvements over past sales performance rather than offer a few prizes to high-volume outlets.

Dealer contests often run in the automobile, appliance, marine craft, insurance, and home furnishings industries. Here their use promotes good relations with dealers as much as it raises the general level of sales to dealers. No matter what industry is involved, who participates, what criteria are used, or what kind of prizes are available, a dealer contest should have only one objective (e.g., related to sales or profits), and it should be clearly communicated and understood by all involved.[10]

Following is a useful checklist for managers planning an incentive program (note that the guidelines can apply to both sales force and dealer incentive programs):

10 TIPS TO KEEP INCENTIVE PLANS ON TARGET

1. Choose specific, realistic goals.
2. Set quotas that give every salesperson or dealer a chance to participate.
3. Establish time limits that give salespeople and dealers an adequate opportunity to cover their territories and attain maximum sell-through.
4. Keep rules easy to understand.
5. Use a theme that stresses how the program works. For example, a "world series" theme for a plan that groups people into sales teams that compete with one another, or a "savings bank" for a program that lets winners accumulate prize points.
6. Build and maintain enthusiasm by kicking off with a meeting and following up with mailings, phone calls, trade advertising, stories in the company sales letter, or whatever else is likely to spark the person's interest.
7. Issue frequent progress reports to let participants know where they stand and what they still have to do to qualify for awards.
8. Award prizes as soon as participants qualify for them.
9. Publicize results; recognition is often more important than the prize itself.
10. Have a budget based on what you can afford to spend per item, gross, new account, or whatever. Consider using a point system as the basis for awards. If you use volume, you may want to write an escalation clause into the program so that if you raise your products' prices during the incentive period, you won't end up overspending your promotion margin.[11]

SALES MEETINGS

Marketing executives try continuously to maintain a well-informed and highly motivated sales force and network of distributors and dealers. *Sales meetings* are effective as a means of disseminating information and stimulating greater effort. Sales meetings can address company sales personnel or the company's middlemen.

Company Sales Force Meetings

Sales meetings conducted for the *company's sales force* have two broad objectives: (1) to stimulate sales personnel to greater performance; and (2) to communicate up-to-date information on new products, plans, promotional programs, and procedures. Within this broad context, sales meetings are an excellent forum for the company to accomplish a variety of specific goals. For example:

To introduce a new product or products

To communicate new company policies and procedures

To launch and explain promotional campaigns for the coming year

To announce special sales force promotions and incentives such as contests (or announce previous contest winners)

To provide information about recent competitive developments

To increase sales force effectiveness through seminars and workshops on topics such as time management, records maintenance, and sales presentation methods

The sales meeting especially benefits sales personnel who spend most of their time on the road, since it provides one of the few opportunities for them to interact with each other and to exchange valuable information and ideas. Nonagenda activities may be even more valuable than the formal program for motivation (through peer pressure) and for exchange of information (through social activities and informal discussions with colleagues).

Sales meetings follow different formats and vary considerably in size. For instance, meetings may occur at the national, regional, or local levels depending on the particular objectives of the gathering, the costs, and the frequency. A *national sales meeting* entails such problems as incurring high costs for transportation and lodging, taking sales personnel out of their territories, and tying up executive time; however, there are some advantages that justify its use. The national meeting is particularly appropriate when the company sets in motion sweeping changes in policies and procedures, best explained in a uniform way to all parties at the same time. Furthermore, the introduction (with great fanfare) of a new product or incentive program may generate enthusiasm that will continue to motivate salespeople when they return to the field.

To avoid the high costs of a national sales meeting, and to cut the loss of selling time on the part of the sales force, many companies hold *regional sales meetings*. With this format, executives can focus on the particular problems and needs of each region through direct visits to the field. This approach is especially effective when material differences exist among the company's selling regions. What may be a major concern to one region may not be a problem at all for another. Sales meetings tailored to the specific characteristics of each region permit company executives and regional sales personnel to confront current problems and opportunities head on. If there is a major criticism of regional as opposed to national sales meetings, it is that the regional format may not generate the same high degree of enthusiasm. While the national meeting usually involves more excitement (business mixed with pleasure, major entertainment, prominent speakers), the regional meeting, even with the same approach, is necessarily much smaller. Critics of the regional format believe that a "watered-down" version achieves watered-down results and only short-term bursts of motivation. Of course, in the end, a company's specific objectives dictate the choice.

Sales meetings at the *local level* may occur frequently and regularly, perhaps even once a week. These informal gatherings provide sales personnel with an opportunity to present their own opinions and to interact with their colleagues. A major benefit of these frequent meetings is that sales group members get to know each other well, and a strong sense of team spirit and group identity emerges.

The key to running a successful sales meeting is planning. It is crucial that the meeting have well-defined goals: timely, relevant, attainable, justifiable in cost, tailored to the audience, and consistent with broader company objectives. The absence of these qualities may result in an uncontrolled gathering of people engaged in a variety of aimless activities. Sales meetings should follow a specific agenda, and printed summaries of all presentations should be available to participants and attendees at the end of each session. There should be a precise time schedule, and each session should start and finish promptly according to that schedule.

With the extraordinary advances in telecommunications, some companies now hold sales meetings via closed-circuit television or conference-telephone linkages. While not generating the same excitement as a formal sales meeting, they are cost-effective alternatives when broad communication is necessary on short notice.

Dealer Sales Meetings

Sales meetings of *distributors* and *dealers* may also be an important sales promotion device, particularly at the outset of a selling season. These meetings, typically regional, serve essentially the same purposes as company sales force meetings, that is, to provide information and increase motivation. Objectives for dealer sales meetings might include

Presentation of new models, products, or lines

Explanation of promotional programs involving dealer participation

Announcement of contests and other dealer incentives

Conducting dealer sales training

Discussion of dealer problems and concerns

Dealer sales meetings are a useful vehicle for maintaining interaction in a less-formal setting between company salespeople and their middlemen, facilitating discussion of new products, programs, problems, and other important issues and developments.

SALES BROCHURES

Sales brochures are another form of sales promotion. Distributed by manufacturers to their salespeople, dealers, and consumers, sales brochures are useful when the product is available in a variety of models, styles, and colors or has a number of optional features. A brochure will often present a technical explanation of the product's functions.

We are all familiar with the colorful brochures describing the latest automobiles. Tools and appliances come with booklets explaining usage and, if necessary, product assembly. Manufacturers and marketers in a variety of specialized fields offer dealers and consumers a wide selection of materials, such as food and beverage recipe booklets, do-it-yourself booklets, pet care brochures, lawn and garden care brochures, and proper automobile maintenance booklets.

To the salesforce, sales brochures serve as a way to keep up to date on new products, model changes, style changes, and the like. They also constitute a giveaway that the sales force can use in its dealer relations efforts. *To dealers*, sales brochures provide a wealth of information that store sales personnel can use to demonstrate a product adequately. Other types of brochures constitute a giveaway item (e.g., a recipe booklet), which promotes good customer relations. *To consumers*, sales brochures aid in the decision-making process by providing detailed information regarding product attributes, uses, options, and so on. The brochures enable consumers to do some of their shopping at home away from the pressure of sales personnel. They also serve as an information source for proper product use and maintenance.

TRADE SHOWS AND EXHIBITS

Each year thousands of *trade shows* and *exhibits* take place across the nation. Here manufacturers promote a virtually endless variety of products including automobiles, boats and marine equipment, computers and office machines, building supplies, restaurant equipment, furniture, appliances, tools, housewares, sporting goods, and the like. Trade shows play a dominant role within industrial markets, and they are gaining increasing favor in the consumer market. There are several reasons why exhibitors display their wares at trade shows. They may wish to introduce new products, make sales, generate sales leads, attract new distributors, promote the corporate image, conduct marketing research, observe the competition, train sales personnel, or get immediate customer feedback.

Although some immediate sales activity may happen as a direct result of trade show exposure, the fundamental reason for participation in these forums is to provide selected markets with product information and to establish contact with qualified sales prospects. Exhibitors set up booths where they can display merchandise, conduct demonstrations, distribute samples, provide product literature, and make media presentations. They are also eager to develop a mailing list of interested visitors for follow-up by company sales personnel.

Trade shows are expensive, but proper planning and execution can make them cost-effective. The exhibitor uses two basic measurements to evaluate the effectiveness of a trade show: (1) an independently verified visitor count and (2) an audience profile. An exhibitor of building supplies, for example, will want to know the number of people attending the trade show and the identification of the attendees by job title, authority to buy, type and size of company, location of the organization, and so on. Independent companies specializing in trade show audits can acquire this information. Since a trade show represents a substantial investment, a thorough job of evaluation should follow.[12]

SUMMARY

A manufacturer has several ways to provide additional support and incentives for its dealers and the company sales force. Sales promotion devices such as trade deals and promotional allowances, cooperative advertising, contests, sales meetings, sales brochures, and trade shows and exhibits are effective in a variety of conditions. Just as it must in promotion to consumers, management needs to know the strengths and weaknesses of each technique of dealer and sales force promotion. And management must know when each method will have maximum effectiveness. Sales promotion motivates dealers to push a product and gives a sales force extra incentive to get a job done. The key task for management is to determine which methods will achieve its promotional objectives.

Now that we have examined advertising, personal selling, and sales promotion, we can focus on the fourth and final major promotional activity—public relations.

REVIEW AND DISCUSSION QUESTIONS

1. What are the common objectives of trade deals?
2. Trade promotions must be policed. Why?

3. *Distinguish between the following types of trade deals: (a) buying allowance, (b) buy-back allowance, (c) count and recount, (d) free goods, and (e) advertising and merchandising allowances.*

4. *Explain how cooperative advertising works.*

5. *Differentiate between horizontal and vertical cooperative advertising. Give examples of each type.*

6. *What are the advantages of cooperative advertising from the manufacturer's viewpoint? The limitations?*

7. *What are the advantages of cooperative advertising from the retailer's viewpoint? The limitations?*

8. *"For the most effective results, cooperative advertising should be used in conjunction with strong national advertising." Comment.*

9. *"The objectives of cooperative advertising should be the same as those for national advertising." Do you agree or disagree? Why?*

10. *Two important considerations in making a sales contest successful are the duration of the contest and the nature and structure of the prize format. Discuss.*

11. *Under what conditions is a contest for the sales force appropriate? How about a contest for dealers?*

12. *"The surest way to rekindle the lost spark in a sales force is to run a sales contest." Comment.*

13. *What are the goals of company sales force meetings? Dealer sales meetings?*

14. *Which approach is better, a national sales meeting or a regional sales meeting? Why?*

15. *Set up some guidelines for running a successful sales meeting.*

16. *What can a sales brochure do for the (a) sales force, (b) dealers, and (c) consumers?*

17. *Identify the purposes of trade shows.*

18. *How would you measure the effectiveness of a trade show?*

NOTES

1. For an excellent discussion of manufacturers' perceptions of trade promotion and ways to increase the productivity of trade promotion expenditures, see John A. Quelch, *Trade Promotion by Grocery Products Manufacturers: A Managerial Perspective*, Report No. 82-106 (Cambridge, Mass.: Marketing Science Institute, August 1982).

2. Robert F. Young and Stephen A. Greyser, *Cooperative Advertising: Practices and Problems* (Cambridge, Mass.: Marketing Science Institute, 1982), p. 63.

3. Ibid., p. 3.

4. Ibid.

5. The discussion of the advantages and disadvantages of cooperative advertising closely parallels that in S. Watson Dunn and Arnold M. Barban, *Advertising*, 5th ed. (Hindsdale, Ill.: Dryden Press, 1982), pp. 621–23.

6. Michael Levy, John Webster, and Roger A. Kerin, "Formulating Push Marketing Strategies: A Method and Application," *Journal of Marketing*, Winter 1983, pp. 25–34.

7. *Grey Matter*, Vol. 47, No. 3, p. 3, New York: © 1976, Grey.

8. Young and Greyser, *Cooperative Advertising*, pp. 72–74. The guidelines also appeared in an article entitled "Follow 11 Guidelines to Strategically Manage Your Co-op Advertising Program," *Marketing News*, September 16, 1983, p. 5.

9. Thomas R. Wotruba and Donald J. Schoel, "Evaluation of Salesforce Contest Performance," *Journal of Personal Selling and Sales Management*, May 1983, pp. 1–10.

10. Don E. Schultz and William A. Robinson, *Sales Promotion Management* (Chicago: Crain Books, 1982), p. 268.

11. Sales and Marketing Management Magazine. Copyright April 7, 1975.

12. For a detailed discussion of an analytical approach to measuring trade show effectiveness, see Thomas V. Bonoma, "Get More Out of Your Trade Shows," *Harvard Business Review*, January-February 1983, pp. 75–83. Trade show effectiveness measures and several other important topics relating to trade shows can be found in *Marketing News*, March 2, 1984.

17

Public Relations

Lionel A. Weintraub, chairman of Ideal Toy Corp., has yet to figure out the solution to Rubik's Cube. But he's having no trouble figuring out the bottom line effect of the cube, which has put his company squarely in the black. Ideal Toy, headquartered in Hollis, New York, expects to sell more than ten million cubes in the fiscal year that ends on January 29, 1982, boosting revenues by $40 million to an estimated $210 million. Earnings will reach an all-time high of at least $9 million, a wide swing from a net loss of $15.5 million in the previous fiscal year.[1]

How was this remarkable marketing and financial success achieved? Let us look at some of the ways.

When U.S. marketing rights were acquired from Enro Rubik, the product suffered from poor packaging and the wrong name. The first thing Ideal did was to change the name from Magic Cube to the more personal Rubik's Cube. Next, Ideal created a round jewel-like case to project a sophisticated quality image. The stage was set to introduce the puzzle to the trade at the American Toy Fair in New York.

Buyers at the fair were encouraged to try to solve the cube, as a means of getting them personally involved with it. Rubik appeared at the fair to demonstrate how easy the solution was. Mass consumer promotion began with a press party. To boost attendance and project a sophisticated and fun image, Ideal invited Hungarian-born actress Zsa Zsa Gabor and Sol Goloub, a mathematician and cubist, to the party. Since students are often trend setters, teaser ads went out to college newspapers. First-class travelers on American Airlines' transcontinental flights, another trend-setting group, received cubes as they boarded. In-store demonstrations and materials such as T-shirts, bumper stickers, and solution books supported the consumer-teaser print campaign. National publicity reached a staggering level, with articles appearing in a wide range of publications, including *Omni*, *Scientific American*, and *Reader's Digest*. "NBC Magazine" and "CHIPs" gave the cube TV exposure. Finally, a nationwide contest, culminating in a world championship on the television show "That's Incredible," sustained interest in the media and among consumers.[2]

An effective public relations campaign was evidently a key element in the successful launch of this intriguing new product. The fourth major promotional activity an organization can employ to communicate with its target audiences, *public relations* is "the management function which evaluates public attitudes, identifies the policies and procedures of an individual or organization with the public interest, and executes a program of action to earn public understanding and acceptance."[3] In this chapter we discuss the nature and content of public relations to reveal how it contributes to the successful marketing of products and services.

Public relations (frequently referred to as *PR*) is a multidimensional field that encompasses much more than communicating with prospective buyers and buying influences. Public relations is a philosophy of corporate behavior that closely ties the well-being of the organization to the well-being of the society in which it operates. This view further suggests that there is a strong corporate responsibility to become actively involved in fostering the well-being of society. A sampling of some short-hand definitions reinforces this perspective:[4]

"Doing right and getting credit"
"P = Performance; R = Recognition"
"Good works well communicated"

This and other perspectives of public relations will be examined later in the chapter; first, though, let us consider the role of public relations.

THE ROLE OF PUBLIC RELATIONS

The primary objective of public relations is to establish and enhance a positive image of the company as a whole among its various publics. It seeks to persuade people that the company is an attractive organization with which to relate or do business. This differs from the principal goal of other promotional elements in that they seek to establish and enhance a positive product or brand image and thereby persuade buyers to purchase the particular product. Of course, a favorable corporate image among prospective buyers does assist, in a very important way, in concluding a sale. In fact, this is clearly one of the subgoals of any PR program. For this reason, PR is an indirect promotion. Conversely, effective product promotion efforts can add luster to the corporate image as well.

The close link between the corporate image and the company's various product images requires the two to be in harmony or else confusion may arise among the various publics. A buyer might come up against conflicting information about the organization and its products, making a buying decision more difficult. Prospective investors, too, could find themselves struggling with conflicting impressions. Consider the plight of the Chrysler Corporation in 1978–79, trying to market its new cars and solve its cash flow problems with outside financing, while the media carried stories daily of its dire financial condition. Would you have been confident purchasing a new automobile or corporate bonds from this organization?

If, however, the corporate image and the product image are in consonance, both the product sale and a favorable investment decision should be easier. Efforts to build corporate image, on the one hand, and strategies to expand product sales, on the other, clearly have different first-order objectives. But survival and growth of the corporation require compatibility, at the least, between these two types of external communication.

In the balance of this chapter we will examine public relations from the following perspectives: its characteristics as an element of the promotional mix, the publics it seeks to reach, the process of identifying and acting upon public relations opportunities, and, finally, the techniques of PR, with a special concentration on publicity and institutional advertising.

PUBLIC RELATIONS AS PROMOTIONAL COMMUNICATION

For communicating a persuasive message to prospective customers, public relations has many favorable attributes; yet developers of communications strategy often underestimate it or overlook it altogether.

The difficulty in integrating public relations into the overall promotional effort stems from two factors. First, PR activities aim toward many more audiences than just potential customers. A public relations program may have the financial community, materials suppliers, or local government among its primary target audience. As a result, PR practitioners may not be able to give as much time and attention to product-marketing needs as marketing managers would like. Second, the public relations function is seldom a formal part of the marketing organization and will report separately to senior management. This may, whether by intent or not, inhibit the active participation of PR specialists in the development and execution of marketing strategy. Despite these structural barriers, public relations has important contributions to make to the overall promotional effort.

Characteristics of Public Relations

Before exploring the characteristics of public relations, however, we must distinguish between two frequently confused terms: *public relations* and *publicity*. Public relations, as we have said, is essentially a philosophy of corporate behavior coupled with an extensive array of communications techniques to address a variety of audiences. Publicity, on the other hand, is simply one of the communications techniques used in public relations, but surely a most significant one. At this point, the focus is on public relations, so let us now examine its major characteristics as compared with the other three forms of marketing communications. On the positive side, PR is inexpensive, capable of targeting very specific audiences, and highly believable.

Inexpensive

The costs of developing and executing public relations programs (publicity, feature articles, special events) can be *far less per person reached* than the other three types of promotion. For example, it may cost $100 to prepare and distribute a one-page news release to twenty-five trade magazines. If published in any one of them, the release may well reach fifty thousand to one hundred thousand readers. In contrast, the equivalent advertising space in the publication would probably cost a minimum of $1,000.

Audience Specific

Even though PR activities can sometimes aim at several audiences at once, PR also can address the particular interests and attitudes of *small, specialized audiences*. In contrast to advertising, where high media and production costs require a mass audience, PR efforts can adjust to the size of the audience.

Believability

Many PR projects do not carry an obvious commercial message; audiences will therefore often assign *greater credibility* to the message, still more because of the positive image of the medium in which it may appear. This "third-party endorsement" rubs off on the company or product in the PR piece. It is credibility by association. A *Business Week* report on a new chief executive officer probably does more to influence investor confidence than a company-sponsored message. Or a report in *Runner's World* magazine on a new Nike running shoe can do more to bring about sales than a message or advertisement that the Nike company signs. A third-party endorsement is one of the strongest assets public relations enjoys.

While these are powerful strengths of PR, the marketer must recognize that public relations has certain limitations as a promotional vehicle, especially with respect to control and competition.

Lack of Control

Media editors make the decision as to what to publish or put on the air, when it will appear, and how much space or time it will get. The marketer, therefore, has *little direct control*, with PR, over these vital elements of its promotional strategy. The marketer can attempt through press relations and the news value of the event to obtain the most favorable timing and placement, but there are no assurances of success.

Competition

The public relations efforts of any one marketer face *stiff competition* from all other marketers interested in the same media. The limits of time and space place a high premium on the newsworthiness of the PR project. As a corollary, the opportunity to present a repetitive message in the same media is even more limited, clearly a significant disadvantage compared with other promotional elements. Furthermore, editors want to publish exciting or novel information. They are unlikely to accept a PR story about established or common products.

On balance, the favorable attributes of public relations make it a viable and contributory element of promotional strategy. It becomes even more valuable when the program accompanies a total promotional effort, achieving a synergistic effect.

Expenditure on Public Relations

One perspective on the significance of public relations can be gained by applying a common measure: how much money firms spend on it. With public relations, an appropriate number is difficult to come by for two rea-

sons. First, PR expenditures should be in inverse proportion to the communication objectives obtained. Second, PR is an aggregate of diverse techniques
and methods ranging from institutional advertising to news releases and
special events. Expenditures for these activities are nearly impossible to
determine in the aggregate.

O'Dwyer's Directory of Public Relations Firms does shed some light on this
question, however, by providing total public relations billings of the fifty
largest firms. Total billings for these firms in 1982 were $290 million, repre-
senting a 70 percent increase over 1979. The top ten firms in 1982 had
aggregate fees of over $190 million, with Hill and Knowlton heading the
list at $54 million.[5] Exhibit 17-1 lists the billing figures for the ten largest
PR agencies.

In one other area—corporate (institutional) advertising—estimates of
this expenditure in national measured media also exist: more than $1 billion,
representing approximately 7 percent of total media expenditures. This is
a dramatic increase from the early 1970s when such expenditures amounted
to $150 million.[6] Some organizations obviously make a strong commitment
to institutional advertising. We will have much more to say about corporate
advertising later in the chapter.

**EXHIBIT 17-1   Leading Public Relations Agencies—
Billings**

AGENCY	FEE BILLINGS ($ MILLIONS)
1. Hill and Knowlton	54.0
2. Burson-Marsteller	50.6
3. Carl Byoir and Associates	21.9
4. Ruder, Finn and Rotman	16.3
5. Daniel J. Edelman, Inc.	8.5
6. Doremus and Co.	8.3
7. Manning, Salvage and Lee	8.3
8. Ketchum, PR	7.8
9. The Rowland Company	7.5
10. Ogilvy and Mather PR	7.4

Source: O'Dwyer's Directory of Public Relations Firms, 15th ed.
(New York: J. R. O'Dwyer Company, 1983).

PUBLICS ADDRESSED

As we saw earlier, public relations, as a developer and communicator of a positive company image, addresses a wide range of audiences, potential buyers at one end and prospective suppliers at the other. It also includes government at all three levels (federal, state, and local) as well as individual employees and shareholders. Let us now identify the major publics that a PR program might seek to reach and explore why and how the company would approach each audience.

Customers

Of all the target audiences of public relations actions, *current* and *potential customers* are the most obvious. These are the people who determine the success or failure of the enterprise. Their purchase decisions are based on the perceived value of the company's offerings, which is at least in part related to the organization's overall image and reputation. Following are some of the questions that people ask:

> Does the company make quality products that hold up over time?
>
> Does the company treat its employees fairly and protect the community from the hazards inherent in its manufacturing processes?
>
> Does the company offer a good warranty and back it up with minimum hassle and dispute?
>
> Does the company meet its delivery and service commitments?

Certainly the most appropriate way for an organization to achieve a favorable reputation is to conduct its business in a straightforward and professional manner. Other supportive techniques could involve news releases about the receipt of major contracts, the fulfilling of unique applications, or the meeting of special service requirements.

Dealers/Distributors

Another group, whose interests clearly relate to those of the customers, includes the *retailers*, *dealers*, and *distributors* who carry the company's products. They are an important element in the company's marketing strategy, sharing consumers' concerns about product quality and services but also needing reassurance about the company's consistent fulfillment of its distribution policies (returns, allowances, inventory protection). Company newsletters (house organs), trade journal articles and advertisements, open houses, and special dealer meetings are all valuable techniques for guiding dealers toward favorable perceptions of the company.

Suppliers

Sometimes overlooked in the description of a company's vital resources are its *suppliers*. These organizations provide the essential materials and services from which the company fashions its market offerings. Good vendor relationships help to ensure continuity of supply, fair prices, and responsive service. The buying company's ability and willingness to meet its contractual obligations consistently, and to recognize suppliers' efforts to provide technical and administrative assistance, are the best ways to enhance vendor relationships. Another good way is to keep vendors current on business and financial conditions that may affect future needs. They should be included as recipients of annual reports, new-product announcements, and other related information.

Financial Community

Commercial and investment bankers, stockbrokers, financial analysts, and investors, both institutional and individual, are segments of the *financial community* that the company wants to cultivate. As prospective sources of capital for the company, these individuals and organizations are vital to the acquisition of financial resources. In addition to seeing a consistent pattern of growing earnings and a strong balance sheet, this public wishes to know of events that affect the company's short- and long-term viability. Annual and quarterly financial reports, presentations to meetings of financial analysts, and individual interviews with editors of financial publications are all useful and desirable PR activities. This area has become so significant that many PR agencies now specialize in this field.

Employees

The *employees* provide the operating, technical, and managerial skills to perform the tasks and meet the goals of the organization. Together with the financial and physical resources we spoke of, these people are the cornerstone of the business. Sound employee relations will of course require fair wages, satisfactory working conditions, and acceptable terms of employment. In addition, how the company's managers respond to individual problems and needs, legitimate questions or concerns, or special situations created by external events will also affect the relationship. House organs and newsletters, employee recognition activities, and open houses and plant tours for employees' families are just a few of the techniques that foster healthy employee relations.

Communities

The populace of the *cities* and *towns* where the company locates its facilities is another public with an interest in the company's actions. Among the issues for townspeople are the stability of employment opportunities and the disposal of waste materials that the company produces, as well as support for local charitable, cultural, and recreational programs. The community is interested in the company as a "good neighbor" sharing in community responsibilities. PR programs ranging from charitable contributions to sponsorship of youth league athletic teams to the maintenance of a safe and healthy work environment interest and gratify this audience.

Government

Government at all levels (federal, state, and local) is an important influence on the company's operations. Since they tax, license, and regulate, governments can restrict, encourage, or ignore the company's activities. The company's prime objective is to stay in close touch with the proceedings of legislative and regulatory bodies that may issue decisions affecting the company. Specific company actions could include testifying in support of company positions on matters under consideration, or responding to the legitimate concerns of officials with supervisory or regulatory duties. This area has become so important that in some companies separate departments now deal with questions of "public affairs," independently of the overall public relations activities.

Perhaps it is now clear why public relations covers such a diversity of activities, addressing a number of publics and using an array of tools and techniques.

THE PUBLIC RELATIONS PROCESS

As we noted at the beginning of this chapter, PR in its most streamlined form is "good works well communicated." To accomplish this objective, PR practitioners undertake a process incorporating the five steps we discuss below and diagram in Exhibit 17-2.

Determining the Public's Attitudes and Opinions

This first step in the public relations process is the essential underpinning to any PR program or effort. *Knowing initially how its various publics view the company and its products* serves several purposes. First, it is a baseline against

EXHIBIT 17-2   The Public Relations Process

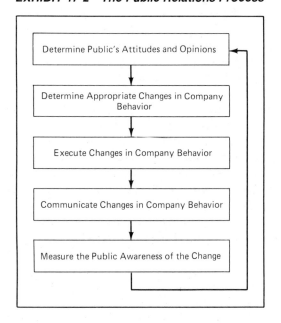

which to measure the results of future activities. Second, it can isolate the company's weaknesses and help to establish priorities for correcting them. Third, it balances the anecdotal, personal evidence of the company management with a formal quantitative assessment. Fourth, it provides an insight into not only *what* the company's publics think but *why* they think that way. With this basic information in hand, the organization is now ready for the second step.

Determining Appropriate Changes in Company Behavior

The PR specialist, in consultation with other members of management, can now *identify, evaluate, and propose appropriate changes in company behavior and activity*. The proposals could range from a more responsive posture in dealing with the press to a change in the manufacturing process or the deletion of a product line. These recommended actions should be viewed in the broadest possible context, considering the public relations impact, the company's social responsibility, and the economic implications. A company with a public relations perspective will consider a wide spectrum of alternatives.

Implementing Changes
in Company Behavior

The third step in the public relations process, *implementing changes in company behavior*, is considered separately because the individuals or departments most involved in the decisions will not necessarily be the ones to put them into practice. Planning and monitoring the implementation of change are essential. Some actions, requiring detailed plans, may have to take effect over an extended time.

A well-planned program should meet several criteria. It should be sincere in its purpose and execution. It should be enduring, and consistent with the company's mission and character. The public relations program should be positive in its approach. It should be comprehensive. The message should be simple, clear, and symbolic. Finally, the PR program should be beneficial to both the organization and the public it addresses.[7] Implementing change rarely is easy; however, strict attention to the criteria identified above will go a long way toward making any change a smooth transition from the old to the new.

Communicating Changes
in Company Behavior

To most operating managers, the *communicating of changes in company behavior* is the focal point of PR activities, the inescapable element of the public relations process. The ability to determine what and how to communicate to achieve public awareness and acceptance is the hallmark of the successful PR practitioner. Many avenues are available, and selecting and effectuating the ones appropriate for the issue at hand requires creative and analytical skill. The same kind of audience analysis and targeting that is an integral part of advertising, sales promotion, and personal-selling decisions must also be present here; but here the diverse set of direct and indirect communications opportunities makes the task of selection more challenging and more rewarding.

Consider this example. A company has recently installed some sophisticated pollution control equipment and now contemplates several public relations options: mail a news release to the local or regional press, hold a press conference at the plant, serve a luncheon to local officials in the control room, invite the public for a plant tour. Selection of the appropriate message and means of delivery will depend on a number of factors—the cost, the effect on the audience, the size of the audience reached, the opportunities for secondary communications effects, and the audience's capacities as opinion leaders or decision makers. This decision could produce results as distinct as a loud yawn or a nomination for "person of the year" by the town fathers.

In communicating with the target public, the PR practitioner should be mindful of the seven *c*'s of communication.[8] Source *credibility* is essential. The *context* for delivery of the message must be realistic and harmonious with the appeal. The message *content* must be significant to the receiver. *Clarity* is necessary if the message is to be understood as the sender intends. *Continuity* is important to achieve impact. Only those communications *channels* that the receiver uses and respects should be used. And consider the *capability* of the target audience to receive and understand the message. These guidelines for communication propel the practitioner a long way toward audience understanding and cooperation.

Measuring Public Awareness of Change and Remeasuring Public Attitudes and Opinions

To complete the circle, the PR practitioner must acquire feedback on the effectiveness of the efforts. There are two questions to answer: *Did the right audience receive and understand the message? Did the message change the public's attitudes and opinions in a direction more favorable to the company?* If the answers to both questions are positive, the company will continue to support those actions. Where the feedback is negative or ambiguous, the process we have been describing will continue until there are favorable results. The practitioner must execute the measurement process with sound research methodology, ever conscious of the issues of validity, reliability, and control.[9]

TOOLS OF PUBLIC RELATIONS

Public relations, as we stated earlier, is a wide-ranging form of communications that serves multiple purposes and reaches many divergent audiences. The tools and techniques of public relations are equally diverse. In the kit of the PR practitioner are such elements as community activities, company publications, films, displays and exhibits, special events, and the two most widely used techniques, publicity and institutional advertising.

This listing, of course, is not comprehensive or exhaustive, but it does highlight some of the more frequently used approaches. In fact, the range of PR activities is limited only by the imagination and creativity of the PR staff and the marketing managers. We will briefly describe each of the above-mentioned tools of public relations. In the case of publicity and institutional advertising, we will provide more comprehensive treatment.

Community Activities

Community activities, which contribute to the company's image in the local community, cover a range of undertakings: participation in United Fund drives; executives serving on boards of local nonprofit organizations such as the YMCA, the hospital, or private educational institutions; executive participation in service clubs (Lions, Rotary); employee involvement in local government; and sponsorship or support of youth activities such as athletic leagues, scouting programs, and high-school theatre performances.

Company Publications

Company publications, house organs, go internally to employees or externally to the distribution channel and ultimate customers. Internal newsletters keep employees informed of occurrences within the company and disseminate announcement of product introductions, personnel promotions, policy changes, and a variety of other company information.

External house organs, such as the *Saga News*, provide a communications link with current and prospective customers.[10] Articles of general interest to the over-60 audience, as well as features such as letters to Saga, make this quarterly publication a useful vehicle for building within its clientele a sense of community and identity with Saga. In this environment, the *Saga Holiday* brochure, which usually arrives in the same mailing, finds a most responsive audience.

Films

Films as a PR vehicle are limited to larger organizations because of the high cost of production. The films may provide public service information, entertainment, or background information on the company or industry. They are available to theaters and TV stations on a direct basis and to educational institutions and civic and social organizations through commercial distributors.

Although a film sponsor may derive little direct commercial benefit from the film, the indirect benefits may be considerable in terms of a favorable standing with the public. Consider Aero Mayflower Transit Company, a nationwide mover.[11] For more than twenty-five years the company has shown a film to over 200 million people, more than any other company film. The average PR film lasts three to five years and is seen by 10 million to 15 million people. Aero Mayflower's film, *The Mayflower Story*, is a documentary of the 1957 voyage of *Mayflower II*, a replica of the 1620 *Mayflower*. The film has been an invaluable public relations tool and has generated an enormous amount of goodwill among school officials, students, religious leaders, business executives, and government officials.

Displays and Exhibits

Displays and exhibits are a form of PR communications that aims at either the general public or the target audience of prospective customers. Participation in large-scale international expositions such as a World's Fair is an example at one extreme, while a float in a local Fourth of July celebration is at the other. Booths at home shows, auto shows, and other specialized exhibitions are examples of displays for both potential customers and the general public. A most original example of a display, enormously effective in building both a positive image and name recognition, is the ubiquitous Goodyear blimp. There is hardly a major outdoor event on television today without this marvelous billboard serving as a camera platform.

Special Events

The sponsoring organization often plans and stages *special events* to attract wide public attention, or a participating organization may sponsor them but leave the direction to others. Two examples of the former are open houses at company facilities and tours of U.S. and foreign ships at their ports of call. An example of the latter is the sponsorship of road races, which, because of the immense popularity of running in this country, has become a valuable PR device for manufacturers of athletic footwear (e.g., New Balance, Nike), brewers (e.g., Miller), and food producers (e.g., Dannon). The events need not relate directly to the business of the sponsoring organization (though that would be best) if they attract attendees representing the company's desired audiences (or get appropriate media coverage).

PUBLICITY

None of the tools of public relations enjoy more use than publicity. *Publicity* is a nonpaid news or information message published on behalf of an identified sponsor. Its significance as a form of marketing communications stems from the fact that it uses all the media—newspapers, magazines, radio, and television—to carry the company's message to the target audience. In doing so, the editorial or programming portion, not the advertising portion, of the media carries the message, a fact that bears certain significant advantages and disadvantages not characteristic of other promotional techniques.

Among the advantages of publicity are the following: It is inexpensive, since there is no cost for the purchase of media time or space; it reaches the mass audience of the particular medium; and it carries high message credibility, since the message sponsor appears to be the medium, not the manufacturer or marketer of the product or service. This combination of attributes suggests a powerful promotional force that might be attractive to most organizations, institutions, and individuals. And indeed it is attractive. Yet there are some disadvantages to publicity. Among them are the following: A lack of control over appearance and timing, since its use is related to its news and value and is at the discretion of media editors or directors; a lack of control over the content of communications, since it may be edited to meet space or time requirements; and there is significant competition among a variety of organizations for the available space and time, largely because the space or time is free. The extent of these disadvantages and limitations relates to the prestige and communications value of the particular medium. The town newspaper would probably accept and publish in its entirety any article about a local firm, whereas *The Wall Street Journal* would probably reject the same article. Broadcast media, specifically TV stations, have a limited amount of time available for news features. The editorial staff controls the use of this time very carefully. Yet a favorable TV story about a firm can reach millions of viewers and create a lasting and positive impression.

The principal objective of publicity is the same for all promotional communications—to present to the target audience a believable message that will persuade that audience to act as the communicator wishes. To achieve this objective, the specialist in publicity must respond effectively to its limitations in order to realize the advantages that publicity offers.

The practitioner must recognize that publicity is essentially a form of news. As such, it will attract the editor's attention if it meets the criteria of a good news story. In other words, publicity must be timely or current; it must be of interest to a significant portion of the medium's audience; and it must be accurate and true. And if the story has a dramatic content, this is an added advantage. Certainly the announcement of a medical breakthrough that will save lives is of greater interest than a news release describing an executive's promotion.

Publicity Subjects

Any occurrence within the company or organization that meets the news criteria described above and conveys a positive image of the company is a suitable subject for publicity. In general, four subject areas receive most attention.

Product Introductions

The trade publications serving particular industry or professional groups have major sections of their magazines set aside expressly for new-product announcements. Readers have shown strong interest in this kind of information, and editors are delighted to respond by providing it. Exhibit 17-3 illustrates this type of publicity.

Personnel Activities

The hiring and the promotion of executive personnel are other widely accepted publicity items. The business pages of the local newspapers as well as special sections of business newspapers and trade publications carry

EXHIBIT 17-3 New-Product Publicity

NEW PRODUCTS

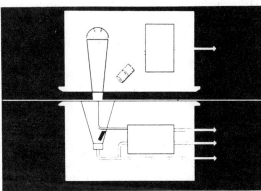

AccuRay OptiPak formation sensor

AccuRay Sensor Package Measures Opacity, Formation, and Brightness

AccuRay Corp. introduced a Microscan sensor package, OptiPak, that measures opacity, brightness, and formation.

OptiPak uses three simultaneous measurements from a scanner that is located at the reel-end of the paper machine. The sensor package displays this information at the operator station as a trend, profile, or status report.

The first measurement is performed by a 1mm diameter bundle of optic fibers. The second is done by a larger 30mm wide window. The sensor calculates the standard deviation between these two measurements and determines a formation index. The third measurement is a reflectance measurement of sheet brightness.

The OptiPak Sensor package can perform 50,000 to 100,000 measurements per second. This enables it to measure every millimeter of the sheet no matter how fast it is running.

AccuRay claims that the sensor package allows papermakers to reduce the amount of wet-end sheet breaks by helping operators to smooth out variations and improve paper machine runnability. It also claims that OptiPak can help to improve the uniformity of the sheet, thereby reducing drying costs.

The visible results provided by the sensor helps the papermaker to find the optimum speed for various papermaking parameters, such as speed, headbox consistency, jet/wire ratio, dewatering, wash content, and refining control.

Circle 201 on Reader Service Card

PROCESS CONTROL SYSTEM

Valmet Automation's Components Div. introduced its Damatic 64 distributed digital process automation system.

The compact system consists of a control terminal, one or two process stations, and a connecting interface bus. The unit provides an overview of the mill process through 64 possible display sections.

Three display formats control the process. The overview depicts the status of the entire process through bar graphs. Group display allows information to be transmitted to control units. Trend display indicates the status of the process for the last 30 minutes, 2 hours, 8 hours, or 32 hours.

Commands are entered into the system through a keyboard. The system is capable of handling both continuous control and logic operations.

Circle 202 on Reader Service Card

NEUTRAL PAPERMAKING

Hercules Inc. announced its neutral papermaking system for unbleached kraft linerboard and bag mills. The system uses Hercon UBK emulsion, a sizing and drainage chemical that does not require the use of alum. The emulsion makes it possible to eliminate paste-size storage and emulsifying systems.

Circle 203 on Reader Service Card

COMPOSITE PUMPS

Warren Pumps Div., Houdaille Industries, Inc., announced its line of Pyroite reinforced composite pumps. The vertical and horizontal centrifugal and vortex pumps are available up to 3,000 gpm. Pyroite pumps are able to handle acids, alkalines, hydrocarbons, and nearly all corrosive or erosive liquids at temperatures up to 500°F.

Circle 204 on Reader Service Card

INSTRUMENT PROTECTORS

Ronnigen-Petter Div., Dover Corp., offers Iso-ring pressure instrument protectors in two-inch increment sizes between 4 in. and 20 in. The ring isolates pressure instruments from viscous, abrasive, and corrosive liquids to prevent plugging or fouling of sensing mechanisms. The protector can be installed between pie flanges and can be used with 125 lb, 150 lb, and 300 lb design piping.

Circle 205 on Reader Service Card

CHEMICAL FEEDING SYSTEM

Nalco Chemical Co. introduced Resin Rinse, a chemical feeder designed for use with an ion-exchange maintenance program. The feeder is available in two models, can be specified for any size ion-exchange system, and is designed to feed chemicals into backwash water during resin regeneration. The feeder consists of a chemical metering pump, a calibration cylinder mounted on a skid or stand, and a control box.

Circle 206 on Reader Service Card

CLARIFIER

Infilco Degremont, Inc., introduced a high-speed clarifier-flocculator, Superpulsator. The clarifier keeps a concentrated sludge blanket in suspension by pulsation and it also recirculates internally the flocculated sludge. Recirculation uses inclined plates with deflectors located within the sludge blanket that allows the clarifier to operate at high flow rates.

Circle 207 on Reader Service Card

TEST SPECIMEN CUTTERS

Testing Machines Inc. offers a line of cutters for preparing paper test specimens. Applications include sample many such items. The story rarely appears in its full form as submitted; it is typically edited into the publication's standard abbreviated format.

Financial Activities

The reporting of financial activities, whether in the form of earnings statements, dividend announcements, or the sale of new security issues, is another type of publicity that many companies use. The business press, as well as the business sections of the general news media, is a suitable outlet for this information.

Special Events

The category involving special events is the most diverse, covering news events ranging from the acquisition or sale of a business to the opening of a new plant. In the latter, local officials may take part in special ceremonies, enhancing the news value to both the print and the broadcast media.

Most of these opportunities occur on either a repetitive or a planned basis. A successful publicity program can revolve around such known events so that the company is in regular contact with its publics and the media that serve them. A detailed calendar ensures timely preparation of stories and photographs and determines those time periods where gaps exist. Management effort can aim toward creating suitable newsworthy events to fill the holes.

Publicity Forms

In addition to subject matter, yet closely related to it, the form of the publicity is a matter for decision by the company's director of publicity. There are five main forms: news or press releases, news or press conferences, feature stories, photographs, and letters to the editor.

News or Press Release

The most frequently used type of communications, the *press release*, is usually a one- or two-page announcement of a newsworthy event (new-product development, personnel change, and the like) distributed broadly to all media of interest and including a photograph if possible. In this manner the company communicates quickly and efficiently with a large number of editors. Use of these releases by the media depends on the news content, the available space, and the policy of the media. Exhibit 17-4 shows typical formats of a release for Gillette's "For Oily Hair Only" shampoo.

News or Press Conference

News or *press conferences* are used infrequently, and usually only for major announcements. The press gathers at a central location to hear the announcement and to ask questions and explore various dimensions of the story. The president of the company should preside, with other senior executives also present. In a well-planned conference, a set of materials and a press kit should be available to attendees. These should include a news release on the announcement; photographs, if appropriate; product literature; and background information on the company and the key personnel. Saga International Holidays Ltd., in introducing its travel service to the United States, held such conferences over a three-week period. It invited the local press to attend as well as special representatives of its target market in each of its launch cities. This vehicle was an effective means to reach both the opinion leaders and the media in its selected geographical markets.

Feature Story

The type of publicity involving a *feature story* is not necessarily news. It consists of an article exploring the company or a particular aspect of its operation in some depth. The article is written by reporters or free-lancers, and its length ranges from five hundred to twenty-five hundred words. Feature stories are the exclusive property of a specific publication. Business magazines such as *Business Week*, *Forbes*, or *Fortune*, as well as trade magazines such as *Electronics* or *Iron Age*, often publish this type of story.

Photographs

When *photographs* have either a dramatic or a human interest perspective, they may be a very useful form of publicity. An eye-catching eight-by-ten-inch glossy photo with a caption may have greater appeal to some editors than a news release on the same subject.

Letters to the Editor

Letters to the editor can be a useful approach for discussing company views and positions on matters of community or company interest.

Press Relations

An important element in the success of any publicity program is the establishment and maintenance of positive relationships with the media that are expected to carry the company's publicity. While this may seem straightforward, it is not always easy to bring off.

EXHIBIT 17-4   News Release

THE GILLETTE COMPANY   NEWS

For Release: Immediate
Contact: Heidi Kane
               (212) 752-8610, Ext. 2742

Gillette to Introduce
"For Oily Hair Only"
Shampoo and Rinse System

The Gillette Company's Personal Care Division will introduce this summer "For Oily Hair Only" shampoo and rinse system, a dual product regimen exclusively tailored to the special needs of men and women with oily hair.

The new system is formulated with a unique blend of herbal extracts—birch leaf, chamomile, clover blossom, coltsfoot, horsetail, nettle, rosemary, and yarrow—and oil-controlling agents.

The shampoo thoroughly, and gently, cleanses hair by breaking down the scalp's excess sebum without overstripping hair to rinse away the oil look and leave hair softly lustrous and fresh-smelling. The conditioning rinse leaves hair free of tangles and the oily, waxy build-up consumers perceive as common among some traditional creme rinses and conditioners.

The new shampoo and rinse system is available in seven- and eleven-ounce sizes, with suggested retail prices of $2.39 and $2.99, respectively.

Gillette will support the new "For Oily Hair Only" brand with $12 million in introductory television and print advertising and $11 million in trade and consumer promotions.

Release Date: At Will   Contact: H. Kane
                                                            Burson-Marsteller
                                                            (212) 752-6500

INTRODUCING "FOR OILY HAIR ONLY"
THE SHAMPOO AND RINSE SYSTEM FOR OILY HAIR

What Is "For Oily Hair Only?"	The Gillette Company's "For Oily Hair Only" is the first brand of shampoo and rinse developed exclusively for men and women with oily hair.
How Does It Work?	"For Oily Hair Only" uses special oil-controlling agents, and a blend of eight natural herbal extracts—rose-

EXHIBIT 17-4   (Continued)

mary, yarrow, birch leaf, clover blossom, horsetail, coltsfoot, chamomile, and nettle. This unique combination works to break down sebum—the fatty lubricant matter secreted by the skin. "For Oily Hair Only" breaks down sebum more effectively than ordinary shampoos.

What Makes "For Oily Hair Only" So Special?

People with oily hair have sebaceous glands which secrete a liquid sebum that is extremely hard to remove. Therefore, a special product is needed to break this sebum down effectively, without stripping hair of its essential oils. "For Oily Hair Only" is different from other shampoos, especially formulations for oily hair. It goes beyond detergent to break down oil, and uses a unique blend of herbal extracts and non-detergent oil-controlling agents, rather than just adding extra detergent, to do so. The rinse works with a combination of light conditioners to improve manageability, and the same unique blend as the shampoo, to rinse hair clean. The special ingredients in FOHO leave hair clean, fresh-smelling and healthy-looking for a longer period of time than ordinary shampoos and conditioners.

Who Should Use "For Oily Hair Only?"

As the name indicates, these products are designed specifically for people with oily hair. In addition, they work for the occasional times when normal hair tends to be oily.

When Should It Be Used?

Every time you shampoo.

How Much Does it Cost?

The 7 oz. bottles for "For Oily Hair Only" Shampoo and Rinse will retail at $2.39; the 11 oz. bottles, $2.99.

Courtesy The Gillette Company, Boston, Mass.

When we speak of positive relationships with the press, we are not referring in the abstract to a publication or broadcast station. We are referring to individuals within the media organizations, namely, editors, reporters, columnists, commentators, and the like, who are in a position to decide whether to publish information about the company. Editors, whether they are responsible for the media as a whole or only a specialized subsection, are the gatekeepers for the media. They decide what information to communicate in the space or time they control. In this role they face four competing pressures. They are responsible for filling an editorial allocation of a certain size (number of pages or number of minutes) within their media. They do not have sufficient in-house reportorial staff to cover all the stories or to fill all the alloted space, so they need to rely, to varying degrees, on information from publicists. They cannot use all the publicity material submitted to them, so they must be selective in the material, yet be even-handed and fair to those competing for the available space. Finally, editors are judged on the editorial product they deliver to their audience. Whether the audience remains and grows over time is a function of the editor's decisions.

The skillful publicity director clearly recognizes these constraints and pressures. He or she builds sound relationships with editors by working with them, rather than adding to those pressures. To achieve this relationship, the following guidelines are a good starting point:

1. Publicity releases should emphasize the news aspects, be subtle in their promotion of the company, and be written with the specific medium's audience in mind.

2. Publicity people should respect the integrity and independence of the editorial decision process. No attempt should be made to sell a publicity story on the strength of the company's advertising commitment to the media. Editors have strong negative reactions to suggestions that editorial space is "owned" by large advertisers.

3. Publicity people should be aware of and meet deadlines. Schedules must be strictly adhered to in a complex publishing process.

4. Publicity people should keep up to date on the editor's policies and needs. Effectively responding to these requirements will make such efforts a valuable support resource that will be sought. This will require personal contact that should not be ignored.

5. Editors, like publicity directors, expect to receive fair and equitable treatment. When major stories are breaking, equal access is an appropriate doctrine to follow for building goodwill.

6. The development of positive media relations must be viewed as a long-term process. Publicity people should be persistent yet patient in their media dealings, building a reputation for integrity and fair dealings with the editorial staffs. Confidence, trust, and mutual respect are the cornerstone of effective media relations, and they are not achieved quickly.

Evaluating Results

With all forms of promotional communications, the most challenging task is to measure the results or the effectiveness of the effort. Public relations in general and publicity in particular are not exceptions. There are three approaches that will provide some measures of performance.[12]

Placements

One yardstick is the *placement* of company news stories and releases in the various media, measured by the number, the amount of space in column inches or equivalent pages (minutes for broadcast media), or the equivalent advertising cost for the space or time. These measures can come from a clipping service or they can be gathered by internal PR personnel. This approach, while useful for comparing publicity activities with advertising expenditures, discloses the number of messages, not the effectiveness of those messages in accomplishing a desired result.

Responses

The second type of measurement involves counting the *number of responses* to the publicity releases. These may be in the form of letters, telephone calls, or "bingo card" inquiries from the media. A note of explanation about "bingo cards" is warranted. Most trade publications offer a reader inquiry service. This provides the subscriber with a simple procedure to obtain information about the various products and services presented in the publication. This service is available for both the advertising and the editorial portion of the media. Each item appearing carries a separate identifying code number, which is also listed on a postage-paid, self-addressed postcard inserted in the magazine. Readers need only supply their name and address, circle the appropriate code numbers, and mail the card to receive the desired information. The cards are then sorted by the code numbers, and each company receives a listing of the names and addresses of the individuals requesting information.

These responses, as well as the direct inquiries noted above, give some indication of the persuasiveness of the messages contained in the publicity releases. This technique, however, only records those individuals who have sufficient immediate interest or motivation to take some action. It does not in any way measure the effect on those who may have read the release but had no current reason to respond. Nor does it measure, in the absence of a specific tracking system, whether those who inquired will ultimately make a buying decision.

Attitude Studies

The third approach to determining the impact of publicity on the target audience is to undertake an *attitude study*. An appropriate research project will seek to establish a base measure of attitude or opinion before undertaking certain publicity activities. It will then attempt to determine the degree of exposure to the publicity information, and finally to measure the attitudes and opinions to determine what change, if any, has taken place. This is an expensive but valuable form of performance evaluation, particularly if the organization views publicity as a major form of persuasive public communications.

Special Problem—Negative Publicity

To this point we have dealt with the positive side of publicity—the development of favorable views and attitudes toward the company. Unfortunately, an organization may occasionally have to deal with negative publicity. The occurrence of such events will often be outside of the company's control. Some examples are government investigations, plant accidents, product recalls, and lawsuits. What steps should the company take to prepare for and respond effectively to such situations?

There are two crucial steps the company must take as precautions. The first and most obvious is to try to prevent these unfavorable experiences. The second is the establishment of contingency plans to define the actions the company will take if such an event occurs. This plan will minimize the surprise and confusion that normally surround catastrophic events and will allow management to act in an efficient, controlled manner in dealing with the situation. A major aspect of the plan is defining the way in which the organization gathers information, directs it to the key executives, and then disseminates it to other interested parties internally and externally. There is no time for such planning during the coverage of unfortunate events, when relations with the press may well be strained.

An important consideration here is to establish a communications link with the press through formal press conferences, news releases, or interviews. An unresponsive organization leads to conjecture, inference, and suspicion of cover-up. This can damage the company's reputation and public relations more than the event itself. Dealing with bad news directly and candidly will enhance the organization's long-term relationship with the media.

The Tylenol incident in 1982, where capsules of Tylenol were tampered with, poisoned, and then returned to the retail shelves for purchase by unsuspecting customers, is a prime example of a potentially devastating, uncontrollable event.

To its credit, Johnson & Johnson, the marketer of Tylenol, responded in a most professional and exemplary manner. The company took the following steps:[13]

1. Recalled all Tylenol capsules in the retail and wholesale channel for full credit.
2. Advised consumers to destroy or return for credit all Tylenol capsules in their possession.
3. Instituted a testing program for capsules returned to determine the extent of the tampering.
4. Instituted a review and testing of their internal manufacturing and quality assurance procedures to confirm that no contamination risks existed in these areas.
5. Cooperated fully with federal, state, and local officials responsible for the investigation of the incident.
6. Responded fully and openly to all press inquiries and held regular press briefings to keep the public informed of actions taken and progress made in uncovering the source and responsibility for the poisoning.
7. Supported changes in FDA regulations requiring immediate modification in packaging techniques to eliminate the opportunity for undetected tampering with over-the-counter pharmaceuticals.

The investigation concluded that Johnson & Johnson was not responsible for the occurrence, that the poisoning of the capsules was by tampering and was isolated to a few bottles in a thirty-mile area, and that certain individuals were suspects and were being sought by authorities.

During and immediately following the investigation, Johnson & Johnson conducted attitude surveys and found that the public did not hold it responsible in any way for the incident. In fact, Johnson & Johnson discovered that there was still a very positive attitude toward the Tylenol brand and that the company had an enhanced reputation as an enlightened, concerned, and public-spirited corporate citizen. As a result, Tylenol was remarketed to the trade and the public within three months and is once again the established, well-respected brand it was before the events of the fall of 1982.

INSTITUTIONAL ADVERTISING

Institutional or *corporate advertising* seeks to promote the image of the organization as a whole, rather than a particular product or service. The primary objective is identical with that of publicity—to communicate the favorable attributes or position of the company in a consistent and credible manner to its various publics. The trade-offs, however, between control, cost, and credibility are quite different. With institutional advertising, the control over the message and format, as well as the timing and placement, lie with the company. On the other hand, there are significant media and production costs and an important, perhaps critical, reduction in the credibility of the message because it is clearly commercially sponsored. Institutional advertising varies depending on the primary audience. Three types deserve mention: corporate image, financial image, and advocacy advertising.

Corporate Image

Corporate image advertising, or patronage advertising as it is sometimes called, sets out to establish the company as a reputable and responsible organization to do business with. The audiences are either buyers or users of the company products. The long-running Weyerhaeuser campaign—"Weyerhaeuser, the tree growing company"—depicts the company as a competent and caring manager of the nation's forests. This is an especially valuable image in this conservation-minded age. Exhibit 17-5 shows a sample ad used in this campaign. Exhibit 17-6 contains samples from the corporate image campaigns of Whirlpool, General Motors, and United Technologies.

Financial Image

Financial image advertising has received considerable attention in recent years. Its principal intent is to convince a variety of capital sources (mutual funds, banks, individuals, investment bankers) and their advisers that the company is an attractive investment opportunity. If successful, this will allow the company to meet its capital needs at attractive rates. Indirect benefits may lie in other directions as well—in the ability to attract key personnel, for example, and the opportunity to effect acquisitions. *The Wall Street Journal*, *Business Week*, and similar business and financial publications are replete with institutional ads that carry this message (see the ITT advertisement in Exhibit 17-7). An outstanding example of this type of campaign is the one sponsored by TRW, using both TV and print media. With the theme "Tomorrow is taking shape at a company called TRW," and an objective designed to create an institutional investor-friendly image, TRW has committed more than $7 million annually for this purpose.[14]

Advocacy Advertising

Advocacy advertising, or issue advertising, is the most recent dimension of institutional advertising. It has come upon the scene surrounded by controversy. Its purpose is to present a corporation's position on a matter of social or political significance. Usually, the subject is of direct concern to the corpo-

EXHIBIT 17-5   Corporate Image Advertising—Weyerhaeuser

Weyerhaeuser. The tree growing company.

Davey and the Trees

This is Davey Marriott. Age 3. In Davey's lifetime, he'll use about 80 tons of wood and wood fiber.

In other words, about 80 mature trees.

For books to educate Davey.

Magazines that will inform him.

Cartons and boxes for Davey.

Lumber and plywood for Davey's new home.

And newsprint for the newspapers Davey will read all through life.

This is what Weyerhaeuser High Yield Forestry is all about.

Planting and managing trees in all stages of growth.

In endless cycles. Year after year.

For Davey, and all the other generations of Daveys.

Weyerhaeuser. The tree growing company.

Courtesy Weyerhaeuser Company.

EXHIBIT 17-6   Corporate Image Advertising—Whirlpool

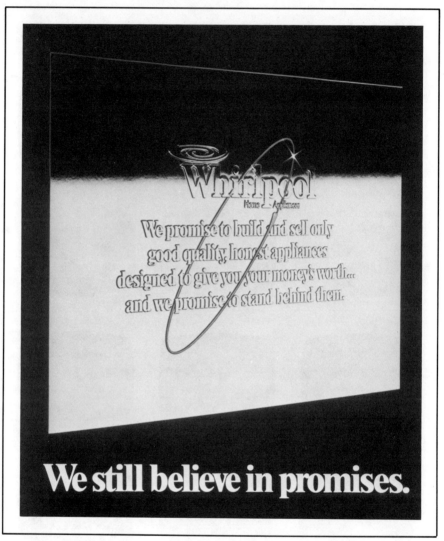

Courtesy Whirlpool Corporation.

EXHIBIT 17-6 (Continued)   *Corporate Image Advertising—General Motors*

CUSTOMER INFORMATION FROM GENERAL MOTORS

HOW TO STOP DRUNK DRIVING

TOUGH LAWS MAY HELP, BUT WE ALSO NEED TO CHANGE OUR ATTITUDES.

Do you know anyone who's in favor of drunk driving? Not likely. And yet many people have driven when under the influence of alcohol, or will do it at least once.

Take a look at some chilling statistics. One out of every two of us will be involved in an alcohol-related accident sometime during our lives. Last year alone, more than 22,000 people died in such accidents; an additional 670,000 were injured. A disproportionate number of those killed were under 25 years old.

The cost of drunk-driving accidents amounts to about $24 billion every year in property damage, loss of wages, medical and legal fees. Not to mention the emotional pain to the victims' families and friends.

What is being done about it? Over the years, many different approaches have been tried: mandatory jail sentences, stiff fines, license suspensions, alcohol-rehabilitation programs, and higher drinking-age laws.

No single countermeasure seems to do the job by itself. Tough laws, unless they are supported by equally tough enforcement and the certainty of punishment, don't seem to work over the long run. Even with all three, probably the most effective single thing we could do is to examine our own attitudes about drinking and driving.

How much do you really know about the effects of alcohol? The facts may surprise you. For example, a lot of people believe that beer and wine are less intoxicating than other drinks. In fact, a can of beer, a glass of wine, or a 1½-ounce drink of 86-proof liquor are all about equally intoxicating.

A lot of factors determine how quickly you'll get drunk. Your body weight, how much you've had to eat, and the number of drinks you have over a specified time all make a difference. That's why it's so hard to know when you've had too much.

A common legal definition of intoxication is .10 percent blood-alcohol level. For a 160 lb. person, it takes about four or five drinks in the first two hours on an empty stomach to reach the legal limit, compared with three or four drinks in the first two hours for someone who weighs 120 lbs. Of course, your judgment and reaction time will be impaired well before you reach the legal limit.

At General Motors, we're very concerned about the effects of drinking on driving. Over a decade ago, we developed a device that tests a driver's reflexes and motor responses before starting the car. The Department of Transportation is now field-testing that device.

We also strongly favor all efforts that focus attention on the problem. Make sure your friends and family know the facts about mixing alcohol and driving. Drunk driving will only stop when we all decide it isn't socially acceptable. Be self-confident enough to admit when you've had too much to drink to drive safely.

Meanwhile, seat belts are still your best protection against drunk drivers. They can't prevent an accident, but they will help save your life during a serious crash—whatever the cause.

This advertisement is part of our continuing effort to give customers useful information about their cars and trucks and the company that builds them.

Chevrolet • Pontiac
Oldsmobile • Buick
Cadillac • GMC Truck

Courtesy General Motors Corporation.

EXHIBIT 17-6 (Continued)   **Corporate Image Advertising—United Technologies**

Technology and Art

On the back of the one dollar bill is a Latin inscription: *annuit coeptis.* It means: be favorable to bold enterprise. Benjamin Franklin chose this motto because he believed initiative and innovation were singular characteristics of the people he helped forge into a new nation.

This is still true today. But like an acorn that will not grow into an oak without water, innovation must be irrigated or it will wither. Initiative needs to be nurtured or it will not take root.

That is partly why United Technologies spends more on research and development than all but six other U.S. corporations, most of them substantially larger than ours.

It also partly explains why we contribute to the arts. As with research and development, United Technologies is a leader in supporting the arts. In fact, as a percentage of total corporate giving, our corporation contributes about three times the national average to the arts.

Why is a high-technology corporation involved in the arts? Actually, the world of technology and the world of art are not that much different. Both rely on the imagination of the individual. Both strive for innovation and excellence. Both provoke our thoughts, uplift our spirits, and improve and enrich our lives.

The fruits of technology, like the best of art, sometimes puzzle us, oftentimes stir us, but always rivet our attention. Art and technology both present the uncommon marvel of daring and deliberation working together, each carried to its highest level.

Art and technology both reflect bold enterprise. Neither is a slave to tradition. Neither believes in change for its own sake. Neither is limited by what others believe possible. Both seek to explore the bounds of imagination.

Nearly 400 years ago, in the last half of the 16th century, Queen Elizabeth of England came upon Sir Walter Mildmay, one of her court favorites, whom she had not seen for some time. "Sir Walter," she inquired, "where have you been?" Mildmay, who had been away establishing Emanuel College at Cambridge, answered, "Madam, I have been away planting an acorn. And when it becomes an oak, God only knows *what* it will amount to."

Art, like research and development, begins as an acorn. Nurtured and irrigated, the acorn can grow to the fullest. And what the harvest brings from this effort will amount to a bold enterprise indeed.

Courtesy United Technologies Corporation.

EXHIBIT 17-7 Financial Image Advertising—ITT

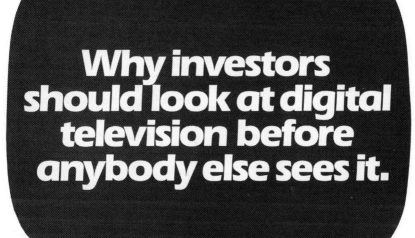

Television is about to undergo its biggest change since color.

A leading manufacturer has developed a way to replace 350 or so parts in today's TV with a unique new set of eight semiconductor chips.

In the next few years, these chips will transform your TV set into a computer. Making it a home communications center that provides such personal services as banking and shopping at home.

Plus, picture and sound quality unimaginable in today's sets.

Any investor aware of how big a market this is will want to keep an eye on the company that manufactures these remarkable chips.

(The same company will also be making its own digital TV receivers, as well as providing chips to other manufacturers all over the world.)

The company? ITT.

At ITT, we're investing in the future. What are you investing in?

Courtesy International Telephone and Telegraph Corporation.

EXHIBIT 17-8 Advocacy Advertising—Mobil

Why do we buy this space?

For more than 12 years now, we've been addressing Americans with weekly messages in principal print media. We've argued, cajoled, thundered, pleaded, reasoned and poked fun. In return, we've been reviled, revered, held up as a model and put down as a sorry example.

Why does Mobil choose to expose itself to these weekly judgments in the court of public opinion? Why do we keep it up now that the energy crisis and the urgent need to address energy issues have eased, at least for the present?

Our answer is that business needs voices in the media, the same way labor unions, consumers, and other groups in our society do. Our nation functions best when economic and other concerns of the people are subjected to rigorous debate. When our messages add to the spectrum of facts and opinion available to the public, even if the decisions are contrary to our preferences, then the effort and cost are worthwhile.

Think back to some of the issues in which we have contributed to the debate.

• Excessive government regulation—it's now widely recognized that Washington meddling, however well intentioned, carries a price tag that the consumer pays.

• The folly of price controls—so clear now that prices of gasoline and other fuels are coming down, now that the marketplace has been relieved of most of its artificial restraints.

• The need for balance between maintaining jobs and production and maintaining a pristine environment—a non-issue, we argued, if there's common sense and compromise on both sides, a view that's now increasingly recognized in Washington.

Over the years, we've won some and lost some, and battled to a draw on other issues we've championed, such as building more nuclear power plants and improving public transportation. We've supported presidents we thought were right in their policies and questioned Democrats and Republicans alike when we thought their policies were counterproductive.

In the process we've had excitement, been congratulated and castigated, made mistakes, and won and lost some battles. But we've enjoyed it. While a large company may seem terribly impersonal to the average person, it's made up of people with feelings, people who care like everybody else. So even when we plug a quality TV program we sponsor on public television, we feel right about spending the company's money to build audience for the show, just as we feel good as citizens to throw the support of our messages to causes we believe in, like the Mobil Grand Prix, in which young athletes prepare for this year's Olympics. Or recognition for the positive role retired people continue to play in our society.

We still continue to speak on a wide array of topics, even though there's no immediate energy crisis to kick around anymore. Because we don't want to be like the mother-in-law who comes to visit only when she has problems and matters to complain about. We think a continuous presence in this space makes sense for us. And we hope, on your part, you find us informative occasionally, or entertaining, or at least infuriating. But never boring. After all, you did read this far, didn't you?

Courtesy Mobil Corporation. © 1984 Mobil Corporation.

ration in question. The controversy stems in part from the obvious interest of the business enterprise in the outcome of certain public policy debates (taxation, use of national resources, regulations, and so on). Another aspect of the dispute centers on the conflict between corporate freedom of speech, embodied in the First Amendment, and the obvious economic power that permits businesses to acquire media time and space while opposition groups are not financially able to do the same.

Despite this controversy, the impact that issue advertising has on the social fabric of American life is not clear. In the first place, most of the major corporations do not engage in issue advertising. The few that do will usually allot only a small fraction of their corporations' communications budgets to it. In the second place, the persuasive power of such advertisements on the general public is limited. Given the obvious self-interest of the sponsor and the currently low credibility of business in general, the degree to which public attitudes change because of these efforts may be marginal at best.

An example that has intensified the debate over whether advocacy advertising is appropriate is Mobil's ad series advocating greater exploration of energy both offshore and on public lands (see Exhibit 17-8). The energy crisis spawned much argument, sometimes intense, over the causes of the oil shortage, whether it was real or imagined, what should be done about the crisis, what role the government and private industry should play, and other issues. Advocacy positions such as the one taken by Mobil in its advertising resulted not only in more debate over the energy crisis but also in further argument over the use of advocacy advertising.

But not all advocacy advertising has created such reactions. Warner-Swasey's campaign promoting free enterprise and other pro-business positions has been running for years, and negative reaction has been minimal. Arco, like Mobil, has taken an advocacy position on the energy issue, but one with a different approach. The petroleum company started supporting energy conservation in 1973 and has maintained that posture to date. Exhibit 17-9 illustrates the Arco approach.

RESPONSIBILITY FOR PUBLIC RELATIONS

Some people see public relations as a companywide function concerned with the organization's relationship to each of its significant publics. These individuals believe that PR should be the responsibility of a separate department, headed by a vice-president who is an active participant in the policy-making decisions of the organization. Other people believe that public relations should have a more limited scope, concentrating primarily on its role as a form of marketing communications intended to reach the company's buyers

EXHIBIT 17-9 Advocacy Advertising—Arco

Some say the answer is oil exploration. Some say the answer is conservation. For once, everybody is right.

It is exploration. It is conservation. It is alternate energy sources. And it's more.

We've also got to realize that our economic growth doesn't have to be linked with excessive energy use. And with waste. Without question, we must find more oil.

And we must learn to use the oil we have efficiently. So where do we start?

Scientists say there are billions of barrels of oil still undiscovered in the United States. We have the technology to find it.

Exploration and development will cost billions. But the money is available. Even so, the most forceful domestic program won't be enough to meet the coming demand.

Nobody uses as much oil as America. Oil provides half of our energy needs. And half of that goes into transportation.

Smaller cars help. So do mileage standards. And we're getting there. But we still have a long way to go.

Right now, there's no economical substitute for oil as a transportation fuel. So we will continue to use it. But coal, nuclear and solar are just as good for other energy needs. And they are much more plentiful.

Energy is the issue of our time. The action we take now will decide our future. At least Atlantic Richfield thinks so.

There are no easy answers.

ARCO ✦
Atlantic Richfield Company

Courtesy Atlantic Richfield Company.

and buying influences. This perspective places responsibility for the PR function within the marketing department where PR will be a separate entity reporting directly to the vice-president of marketing, or a subpart of another communications function such as advertising or sales promotion.

While these two approaches are by far the most common, where the

PR responsibility resides within an organization seems to depend on three factors:

1. *The role of public relations as perceived by the senior executives of the organization.* If it is viewed as the spokesperson for a company philosophy of social responsibility, it will be placed at the highest policy level. If it is viewed primarily as a communications vehicle, it will have a lower organizational position and be incorporated into the marketing department of some other functional area (i.e., finance, human resources, etc.).

2. *The relationship between marketing and public relations.* Kotler and Mindak define six possible relationships, which could determine where the responsibility for PR resides.[15] These possible relationships range from a posture of separate-but-equal at one extreme to a condition where marketing and PR are viewed as the same function at the other end. (Exhibit 17-10 defines these different possibilities.)

3. *The nature of the organization and the development of the PR concept within it.* For example, nonprofit organizations have tended to develop their external relationships in the context of a public relations program. As a result, the PR function has assumed a more important role as the desire to better understand and serve the organization's publics has evolved. Conversely, business organizations have vested the primary responsibility for external relations within the marketing department, and as these institutions become more sophisticated marketers, public relations evolves as another means of communicating with the marketplace.

EXHIBIT 17-10 Models of the Possible Relationship between Marketing and Public Relations

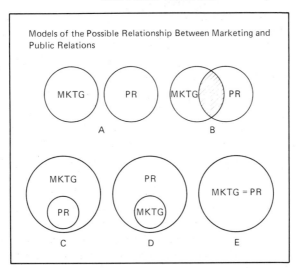

Source: Philip Kotler and William Mindak, "Marketing and Public Relations," *Journal of Marketing*, October 1978, p. 17.

Whatever responsibility structure an organization selects, a link must be forged between the PR and the marketing activities of the company. The marketing concept that acknowledges responsibilities to society as a whole as well as to the company is now more prominent in the marketing plans of many organizations. As this occurs, a closer alignment of the PR perspective and the marketing perspective will result.

Role of External PR Counsel

External PR counsel can play a major role in the development and execution of a PR program. The relationship between the company and the professional resource may be a continuing one, or it may arise with specific projects. Outside PR counsel generally provide the following advantages:

1. *Experience*. Professional counselors usually have many years of experience in the field and can expeditiously direct this experience toward the resolution of a company's PR problem.
2. *Expertise*. Professional counselors develop strong skills in particular areas. This can lead to the development of more effective and efficient approaches to the organization's PR needs.
3. *Objectivity*. Outside counsel is not emotionally committed to the company's historical decisions and can assess the company's public image and required PR actions more clearly. Bad news may come more easily from an outside source not totally dependent on the company for a livelihood.
4. *Costs*. Even though professional counsel will cost more per hour than a company employee, there are often cost advantages in the use of outside counsel. Smaller organizations can receive PR guidance and assistance, on a level commensurate with their resources, which will likely be less costly than hiring full-time personnel. Larger institutions can also take advantage of outside advisers for special projects that require either particular expertise or significant time commitments for short periods, thereby eliminating the need to hire additional employees in the PR function.

The effectiveness of outside counsel depends on the relationship between the counselor and the senior executives within the organization. An open, direct, and accessible relationship paves the way for major contributions; without such a relationship, frustration and contention will lead to disappointment and disengagement. Perhaps we can underscore the growing importance of outside PR counsel by noting again the billings of the leading PR firms, and the fact that there have been dramatic increases in PR agency billings.

SUMMARY

Public relations is a wide-ranging communications activity. Properly executed within an organization, it can help shape corporate policy as well as communicate it. We have seen the importance of having PR objectives. We have also identified the characteristics of public relations that make it an integral component of the overall communications mix. The versatility of PR has been illustrated by the different tasks assigned to it and the various publics it addresses.

Public relations is a five-stage process: discovering the public's attitudes and opinions, determining appropriate changes in company behavior, executing changes in company behavior, communicating those changes, and, finally, measuring the effects of the PR effort. To implement a PR program, many tools and techniques are available, with publicity and corporate advertising among the most popular.

A well-planned, organized public relations program not only enhances the company's overall image and facilitates the sale of products and services but also serves the organization well when unforeseen events place the company under the spotlight of intense scrutiny from the media and the public. The only true limitation of public relations is the imagination of the individuals who practice it.

Having completed our exploration of the individual elements constituting the promotional mix, we now turn to the total promotional program—specifically, the evaluation and control of the promotional program as a major component of overall marketing strategy.

REVIEW AND DISCUSSION QUESTIONS

1. What characteristics of public relations make it a unique form of promotion?

2. Distinguish between public relations and publicity.

3. A large amount of money is spent on public relations each year. In what ways is this expenditure justified?

4. The importance of public relations varies from institution to institution. What factors do you think determine the level of importance?

5. A public relations campaign can have many objectives. How many can you identify?

6. Public relations addresses a wide range of audiences. Identify them and explain the kind of public relations typically directed at each audience.

7. Describe the public relations process.

8. Prior to undertaking a public relations campaign, why is it important to determine the particular public's attitudes and opinions?

9. How would you go about measuring the effect of a public relations campaign? Be specific.

10. Identify and explain the several tools and techniques of public relations.

11. You are the administrator of a well-known metropolitan hospital. A major problem affecting the efficiency of your hospital is that the demand for elective surgery exceeds bed capacity during the weekdays while the hospital beds go virtually empty on weekends. One of your assistants has proposed a sales promotion to attract weekend patients. Any patient entering on Friday would be eligible for a weekly drawing where the prize was a Mediterranean cruise. Is the proposal good for public relations? What criteria have you used to form your opinion?

12. What are the advantages of publicity? The limitations?

13. What kinds of events are particularly suited for the use of publicity? Why are these events good subjects for publicity?

14. Publicity can take several forms. What are they? Give two examples of each.

15. If you were in charge of publicity for an organization, what would you do to establish a favorable relationship with the press?

16. You are the chief public relations officer of a large, well-known bubble gum maker. Widespread rumors have developed, alleging that your bubble gum contains impurities (e.g., spider eggs) harmful to a person's health. Sales drop off dramatically. Knowing that the rumors are completely unfounded, you have to decide how to correct the situation. What is your plan? Explain.

17. What makes institutional (corporate) advertising different from other types of advertising? What are the common purposes of institutional advertising? Give examples.

18. What is advocacy advertising? Give examples. Do you believe it is appropriate for a corporation to take a public position on matters of social or political significance, even though these matters may not be directly related to a corporation's mission? Why or why not?

19. What factors determine the way in which the responsibility for public relations is placed in the organizational structure?

20. Do you think it advisable to employ the services of an outside public relations firm, or should PR be handled entirely from within the organization? Explain your position.

21. *What are the advantages and limitations of outside public relations counsel?*

NOTES

1. *Fortune*, © 1982 Time Inc. All rights reserved.

2. "Macro Marketed Rubik's Cube Turns Around Ideal's Profit Picture with Sales of 10 Million," *Marketing News*, February 19, 1982, p. 16.

3. H. Frazier Moore and Bertrand R. Canfield, *Public Relations: Principles, Cases, and Problems*, 7th ed. (Homewood, Ill.: Richard D. Irwin, 1977), p. 5.

4. Rollie Tillman and C. D. Kirkpatrick, *Promotion: Persuasive Communication in Marketing* (Homewood, Ill.: Richard D. Irwin, 1972), p. 369.

5. *O'Dwyer's Directory of Public Relations Firms*, 15th ed. (New York: J. R. O'Dwyer, 1983).

6. Walter P. Margulies, "A Stepsister to Consumer," *Advertising Age*, July 6, 1981, pp. S2ff.

7. Scott M. Cutlip and Allen H. Center, *Effective Public Relations*, 4th ed. (Englewood Cliffs, N.J.: Prentice-Hall, 1971), p. 223.

8. Scott M. Cutlip and Allen H. Center, *Effective Public Relations*, 4th Ed., © 1971, pp. 260–61. Reprinted by permission of Prentice-Hall, Inc., Englewood Cliffs, N.J.

9. For an excellent discussion of the measurement techniques used for public relations programs, see Scott M. Cutlip and Allen H. Center, *Effective Public Relations*, 5th ed. (Englewood Cliffs, N.J.: Prentice-Hall, 1982), pp. 214–29. Also see Peter Finn, "In-house Research Catches On," *Public Relations Journal*, July 1984, pp. 18–20; Hy Mariampolski, "Qualitative Research Rebounds," *Public Relations Journal*, July 1984, pp. 21–23; Elnora W. Stuart, "The In-house Interviewer," *Public Relations Journal*, July 1984, pp. 24–27; and Albert J. Barr, "High-Technology Tracking," *Public Relations Journal*, July 1984, pp. 28–30.

10. Saga is a well-established international organization specializing in holiday tours and travel packages for people over sixty years old.

11. Leo Flores, "The Mayflower Story," *Public Relations Journal*, September 1983, pp. 23–25.

12. See Cutlip and Center, *Effective Public Relations*, 1982, pp. 214–29.

13. By permission of Johnson & Johnson, New Brunswick, N.J.

14. For further discussion of this campaign as well as other information on financial image and corporate image advertising, see "Corporate Image Advertising: A Special Report," *Advertising Age*, January 23, 1984, pp. M9–M28.

15. Philip Kotler and William Mindak, "Marketing and Public Relations," *Journal of Marketing*, October 1978, pp. 13–20.

18

The Promotional Program: Evaluation and Control

Earlier chapters focused on managing the promotional effort and the specific elements that constitute the promotional mix. In Chapter 2 we saw that execution of a promotional program is a multifaceted task requiring the integration and coordination of advertising, personal selling, sales promotion, and public relations activities. In this chapter we concentrate on the evaluation of performance and the exercise of necessary control to ensure an effective and efficient promotional effort.

The returns expected from a company's promotional campaign rest on assumptions about the operating environment and the company's ability to execute the promotional plan. When the operating environment or the execution of activities deviates from the initial plans, performance may fall short of expectations. Furthermore, the degree of disappointment for the company is positively related to the degree of discrepancy between performance and expectations.

Good promotional management will detect problems as soon as possible and will identify, with a reasonable degree of precision, the appropriate corrective action. Promotional campaigns can be very costly in time and money, and it is much less expensive to prevent major problems than to remedy those problems after the fact. To ensure that the promotional campaign is on course, management must have a system that tracks and assesses performance. To ensure that the campaign operates smoothly, that system (see Exhibit 18-1) should be capable of pinpointing those aspects of the communication effort requiring preventive or corrective action.

The organization can prevent major problems and undertake appropri-

EXHIBIT 18-1   The Evaluation and Control Process

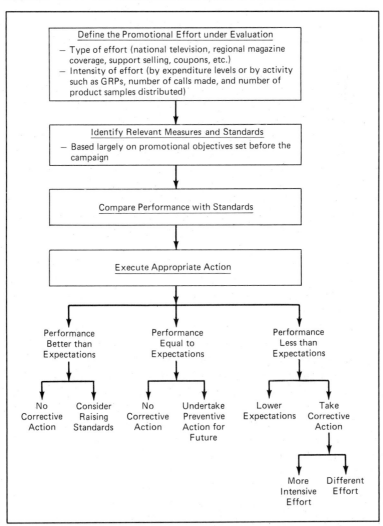

ate remedial actions only when management fully understands the underlying concepts of evaluation and control. The understanding of these two concepts focuses the manager's attention on the critical rather than trivial determinants of the campaign's success, the elements that actually reveal the direction of performance.

The value of a campaign is its ability to improve the company's competitive position. To estimate the value of a campaign, evaluation procedures must consider past efforts and performance and conclude whether or not the most recent campaign has contributed to the improvement of the company's position. The use of historical information results in the identification of long-term successes or problems that may have been too subtle to identify in the short term.

A complete evaluation of performance considers not only how an organization is doing relative to its own past but also how it is doing compared with its competitors. The assessment of competitors' performance is just as critical in future planning as the assessment of one's own performance. Consideration of the competitive efforts and performance provides data that enable the manager to make inferences as to why there are gains or losses as the result of a recent campaign. For example, if a manager has observed a significant decline in market share over several periods, it is necessary to conduct competitive analysis to determine where the share went and why it was lost.

Let us consider the concepts and procedures of evaluation and control in promotion management. By the end of this chapter, you should know what the essential components of an evaluation and control system are and what specific activities are necessary in the working of such a system.

GOALS OF AN EVALUATION
AND CONTROL SYSTEM

The *goals of an evaluation and control system* are to (1) determine what has occurred, is occurring, and will occur during the course of the campaign; (2) measure the quality of those occurrences, and (3) identify appropriate courses of action. Valid judgments of performance derive from correct measurement of performance. Consequently, the first requirement of an evaluation system is to give a true picture of activity taking place as a result of the promotional effort. The system seeks to monitor the performance and provide an accurate picture of what has developed, is developing, and will probably develop in the marketplace because of the organization's communications efforts. The evaluation system also has to measure the quality of the performance being tracked. Although merely describing what has occurred may be useful to the manager, a statement of the contribution of that performance to the attainment of promotional objectives is even more useful. The evaluation system must make a statement of the worth of the promotional performance to date.

Control activities follow up on the evaluation of performance. Once there has been a judgment on the results of the promotional effort, there must be a corresponding action from that judgment. As we will see later in this chapter, control activities can range from doing nothing, since the performance appears acceptable, to a major overhaul of the promotional plan. The basic objective of the control system, therefore, is to provide clear signals of necessary actions to ensure that the promotion program is on the right track.

CHARACTERISTICS OF AN EFFECTIVE EVALUATION AND CONTROL SYSTEM

Given the tasks of the evaluation and control system, what factors contribute to successful achievement of those tasks? A good system has the following dimensions:

1. It incorporates into its evaluation and control procedures the objectives of the promotion.
2. It measures areas of performance critical to the success or failure of the program.
3. It has the capacity to either initiate the necessary control action itself or provide indications as to the nature of those actions.

Let us look briefly at each dimension.

Understanding the Program's Goals

Statements that a performance is good or bad are comparative statements. That is, to pass judgment on the worth of promotion results, we must place a yardstick beside those results.

The benchmarks for program evaluation are the goals (like market share increase, attitude change, or increase in product awareness) established prior to the execution of the plan. As we stated in Chapter 6, properly determined goals are those performances that management can justifiably expect from the promotion effort. Therefore, in the assessment of the performance of the promotion campaign, the results should be evaluated in the context of the standards as specified in the objectives.

An evaluation system that does not fully account for the intended or desired results is susceptible to erroneous statements of the contribution (or lack of it) to the organization's welfare. A misunderstanding of the program goals may lead to a serious overestimating of achievements or to serious oversights of deficiencies. Consider the situation where a program goal is not expressed precisely and is therefore subject to misinterpretation. Let us say that the goal is loosely stated as "increased market share." Without a clear definition of the word *increased*, it is difficult to know the point at which performance is indeed acceptable or unacceptable. A market share gain of 3 percent, for example, might be viewed by an optimistic manager as a satisfactory achievement, whereas that same performance would be viewed in an opposite light by a manager with a pessimistic outlook.

Focusing on Critical Performance Measures

It is not economically feasible to track all possible results in the marketplace. Most of those factors will have no direct impact on the overall success or failure of the program. An effective evaluation system uses its financial and human resources efficiently by concentrating on the relevant rather than trivial determinants of promotion performance.

The development of appropriate measures of performance is not a simple task. Considerable thought must be given to "workable" measures. For example, an organization promoting a consumer product may have stated that the objective is to increase dollar sales in the first six months by a certain percentage. To measure performance, the manager must establish a valid working definition of sales. Should the manager count the purchase orders coming into the company to assess performance? How about actual shipments to wholesale warehouses? Should retail sales be the gauge? Each of the three definitions of sales will provide different numbers. Consequently, an incorrect selection of the performance measure may provide an incorrect assessment of achievements.

The selection of valid performance measures is a complex task. A later section of this chapter is devoted to the description of specific measures.

Putting Control Actions into Effect

A good control system minimizes the amount of time between analyzing a situation and effecting the appropriate actions. As more time passes between the recognition of an opportunity or problem situation and the taking of appropriate action, the cost goes up. The slower the company is in taking advantage of an opportunity, the greater the number of lost benefits that the company might have reaped. Conversely, if the problem means that the company is directly or indirectly experiencing losses, then the amount of time that passes before the proper remedy is administered directly affects the size of the loss.

As we will see later, there are a variety of control actions. To ensure an effective promotion program, the right course of action must be implemented.

THE EVALUATION PROCESS

So far we have established the theoretical foundations of an evaluation and control system. We have given an overview of its objectives and characterized the ideal system. In this section we will examine the sequence of activities that occurs within such a system.

An evaluation and control system is a process. The process entails stages of activities that occur sequentially or simultaneously. An evaluation and control system is not simply an accumulation of independent activities but a set of related, interdependent activities (see Exhibit 18-1):

1. Definition of the total effort and of the separate efforts of the program elements
2. Selection of the proper performance measures
3. Establishment of the appropriate standards
4. Comparison of performance with standards
5. Execution of the appropriate action

Defining the Promotional Effort

In *defining the promotional effort*, the manager's principal objective is to find *true indicators of promotional effort*. The manager needs a measure or a set of measures that accurately reflects the work actually done with advertising, personal selling, sales promotion, and public relations.

Expenditures

A common definition of effort has been the amount of money spent, a definition relatively simple to obtain if the organization has been keeping adequate accounting records. An advantage in using money to define effort is that the dollar is a standardized unit and it facilitates the comparison of effort levels across promotion elements. For example, if $100,000 were spent on advertising and $200,000 were spent on personal selling, we could say that there was twice as much effort in face-to-face communications as there was in impersonal media.

The major problem with using the dollar definition is that, realistically, a dollar spent in one promotion area does not purchase the same communications resources as a dollar spent in another area. What we get for $100,000 in advertising is different from what we get for $100,000 in personal selling. As we noted earlier, the communication and persuasion characteristics across promotion elements are different. Impersonal media budgets buy time and space, while the personal-selling expenditures acquire labor or improve its quality. Thus evaluation of effort defined by dollar levels may be invalid because of the heterogeneous nature of communication resources.

Activity by Medium

Communication activity may be a more desirable measure of communications effort than just expenditures. By *activity* we mean the type of work being done, the type of services being employed, and the amounts of such work or services. For example, we can define the effort of television advertising by the number of gross rating points purchased or the number of measured media used. We can define individual personal-selling effort by such selling activities as calls per day or advertising displays set up. Sales promotion effort can be measured by the number of samples distributed or by trade show participation. Measuring public relations effort might focus on the number of new-product announcements released or the number of films distributed to service organizations.

While the use of activity measures may not fully reflect communications effort (for example, directing sales reps to spend more time on a product provides no assurance that the quality of that selling effort is adequate), it is certainly better than merely using expenditure levels. Activity definitions tell the promotion manager how people used that expenditure. Activity definitions provide a good picture of what actually transpired in the marketplace.

The major problem with defining effort in terms of activities specific to media is that comparisons of work levels across media are difficult to derive, perhaps impossible. Can we really say with a reasonable degree of confidence that a 100 GRP ad campaign actually requires more or requires less communications effort than fifteen letters a salesperson writes to prospects? Unless we can develop rules that correspond objectively across activities of differing media, comparison is a monumental task at best. More likely than not, the promotion manager must be satisfied with knowing what the efforts of the different media are, and nothing else.

Use of Multiple Measures of Effort

Since any single measure of effort has strengths and weaknesses that other measures do not have, a single measure rarely serves to describe promotional effort. Typically, the manager will use *several measures* that collectively provide a picture of what has occurred. For example, the scope of a salesperson's work may encompass customer support visits as well as prospecting. Unless several activity measures come into play, the manager may underestimate the extent of the salesperson's effort. The manager may measure sales promotion by a combination of the dollar expenditure on cooperative advertising and the number of dealers participating, or the amount of money spent on point-of-purchase displays coupled with the number of stores using them. Such combinations yield more accurate measures of promotional efforts.

Selecting Performance Measures

Essential to the evaluation of the promotional program is the precise knowledge of what has taken place among the specified audience. *Performance measures are measures of communication and persuasion effects*. In the following sections we will discuss the relationship between performance measures and promotion objectives and describe the commonly used performance measures.

The Relationship between Performance Measures and Promotion Objectives

The determination of performance measures for the evaluation system follows a basic rule: The objectives of the promotional program are the bases for the measurement of performance.

If we can assume that the objectives emerged from extensive consideration of what one should and could achieve, then the promotional effort can be held accountable along those dimensions. Unless there have been fundamental changes in the operating environment of the program beyond the control of those charged with its management, there should be no reason not to focus on those areas of accountability set forth in the statement of objectives. Thus, if market share in units was a valid objective prior to the program and the operating environment has not changed, then management should measure the performance of promotion in terms of market share in units. Let us now look at some of the major categories of performance measures.

Specific Performance Measures

A promotion program is directed toward a defined specific audience with the intent of causing a specific response. The statement of the program's objectives reflects this; the objectives identify who is to be reached and what is to be the response (awareness, comprehension, conviction, or purchase). (See Chapter 6 for a review of the relationship between objectives and promotion elements.) Logically, then, measurement of performance should be based on the goals. In this section we describe measures of the audience reached and the effect of communications on them.

Audience analysis. Promotional programs communicate with an audience. A fundamental area of performance evaluation is whether the program in fact reached the intended audience. This is an important area for measurement because the entire promotional program has aimed at reaching a targeted audience, a group closely associated with if not the same as the target market of the overall marketing plan.

With advertising programs, the analysis of the audience proceeds through three major categories of characteristics: demographics, psychographics, and behavioristic factors. You will recall that demographic characteristics are the objective dimensions such as age, income, occupation, and education; psychographic analysis describes personality, social class, and the audience's lifestyle; behavioristic factors include the audience's loyalty status, product usage rate, purchase occasion, and the like. The specific dimensions for assessing the audience reached correspond to those for designating the target audience.

The manager often evaluates advertising performance by the number of people reached. Typically, the size of the audience is gauged by measures such as vehicle circulation or viewership. In personal selling, audience analysis may be based on the number and type of new accounts or accounts lost. The sales representative is responsible for establishing and maintaining client relationships. Growth opportunities lie in reaching new customers and expanding the business with current accounts. Noting the number of accounts and their characteristics, such as industry type, employee size, and sales volume, provides the manager with a basis for determining whether the sales force is reaching the target customers. In sales promotion, audience analysis may center on the characteristics of consumers who redeem coupons versus those who do not or the dealers who accept cooperative advertising allowances compared with those who do not participate in the program. In public relations efforts, the focus might be on those people who respond to "advertorials" or the reactions of different publics to a publicity campaign.

Awareness measures. Awareness measures determine the audience's degree of knowledge of the seller's offering, the seller's advertisement, or both. The promotion manager uses such measures when he or she is concerned about whether an ad campaign has made an impression among an audience.

An awareness measure usually concentrates on awareness of the product's existence or awareness of the product's specific attributes and could be in one of the following two forms: unaided recall or aided recall.

Unaided recall measures gauge how well the promotional campaign has instilled key ideas in the audience's consciousness, that is, the promoted ideas are at the "top of the mind" and they come forth with minimal prompting. For example, unaided recall questions might include the following:

What advertisements have you seen lately that have impressed you the most?

Can you name three products that you have seen advertised lately?

Aided recall, on the other hand, measures record awareness levels by focusing the audience's attention on a particular area. For example:

What airlines fly to New York?

Do you remember having seen in the last two weeks an advertisement about life insurance?

Can you identify the name of the bank that uses the slogan "That's my bank"?

Here is a copy of *Newsweek*. Have you seen this ad?

Note that some questioning as to the source of awareness often accompanies measurement of awareness of, say, a new-product concept. For example, if a survey respondent were to indicate awareness of the concept, there might be a follow-up question such as

Where did you hear of the idea for the first time?

This follow-up is clearly useful when the manager has several elements working in the communications program and wishes to assign proper credit.

Comprehension measures. Beyond the impact of awareness is comprehension. Specifically, comprehension measures gauge the amount of attention that the audience devoted to the promotional message.

In print advertising, readership scores are used to measure the extent to which an audience looked at an ad and read the material. Perhaps the most popular readership service is the Starch Message Report Service, which can help distinguish between awareness and interest. The service uses three categories of readership levels: noted, associated, and read most. The "noted" reader is a person who recalls having seen the ad but remembers nothing more; the "associated" reader clearly recalls having seen or read some parts of the ad, while the "read-most" reader claims to have read half or more of the written material in the ad.

While the use of readership scores has been popular for the measurement of effectiveness, this does not necessarily reflect the validity of the readership measure. The popularity of readership measures stems largely from the relative ease of administration; however, because readership measures rely heavily on the accuracy of the memory of respondents, their validity may be suspect.

Some measures of comprehension do not rely as heavily on the memory capacities of the audience. In some instances, the evaluator focuses on the behavior that immediately followed the experience and perception of a message. For some promotion plans, it is expected that message comprehension leads to product interest. The manager can then measure the interest level a message generates by the amount and sources of information the audience seeks after experiencing the message. The logic of an information-seeking measure is that if a message has had an impact, then the audience should be sufficiently excited by that message to want to learn more. Identification of an audience's sources of information provides insights into opportunities and problems in communications. For example, an audience may get information from marketer-sponsored sources like a sales representative, or it may get it from sources like friends or trade journals. Persuasion of an audience that depends largely on marketer-controlled sources may be more likely than an audience that does not have that reliance. The following matrix categorizes sources:

	Marketer controlled	Nonmarketer controlled
Personal sources	• Sales rep • Distributor	• Friends • Colleagues • Personnel from other companies
Impersonal sources	• Product brochures • Advertisements	• Trade journals • Product test reports

Sources of information can be viewed as marketer controlled or nonmarketer controlled. Marketer-controlled sources are those in which the nature of the message and its delivery is determined by the promoter. Nonmarketer-controlled sources are those that are independent of the promoter.

In addition to noting the sources of information, there should also be a focus on the type of information one seeks from these sources. The promotion planner should know whether the information the audience requested was for the purpose of clarifying the original communications or for additional information not contained in the initial communications.

Conviction measures. Conviction measures focus on the judgments or conclusions that people draw from information. Here the promotion manager's concern is not simply that the audience has received the information. The manager now wants to know what impressions the audience formed as a result of receiving the information.

Attitudinal measures reflect conviction and take several forms. One type surveys impressions about specific aspects of the offering, measuring like or dislike of the product. Another might solicit an expression of preference where a choice is possible. Let us take a closer look at these two possibilities.

A promotion manager wants to know the audience's perceptions about the extent to which specific product attributes can deliver satisfactory performance. Measurement of these opinions poses the question, How would you rate brand X's durability?

Then again, it is also valuable to obtain information on the judgment, overall, that an audience has made as a result of promotional activity. Such research information, in conjunction with the data on specific characteristics, allows the manager to draw inferences about which beliefs are most important in the determination of attitudes.

Measurement of feelings toward a product as a whole proceeds with straightforward questions, such as, Please indicate the extent to which you like or dislike the product. One assumes that a response to such a question reflects the total impact of all beliefs about the product.

A major problem in measuring only perceptions about the product is that such an approach ignores the competitive environment in which the communication may have taken place. In some instances, it may be desirable to measure the matter of choice. An audience may like our advertised product but may like someone else's product better. Here we will get a more valid picture of advertising effectiveness if we examine the audience's reaction when there are options. Preference measures provide information on the relative likes and dislikes among competing products.

Intentions measures. If interest in the marketer's offering has been sufficiently stimulated, the tendency to act accordingly should be present. More specifically, if persuasion to behave in a certain manner has been achieved, then the recipient of communications should have plans to act in that manner. Measures of such communications results are called intentions measures.

Intentions measures consider what a person or organization expects to do within a given time. Such measures often take the following forms:

> Do you intend to purchase a Maytag washer within the next twelve months?
> or
> Do you plan to visit the Bloomingdale's store during the special promotional period?

Intentions measures are often useful in situations where we cannot expect a communications campaign itself to result in purchases; this is usually the case where the decision is heavily affected by marketing factors other than communications. For example, the purchase decision involving an automobile requires serious consideration of product features, price, dealer service, and so on. Here the roles of advertising and personal selling are information dissemination and persuasion. Most consumers will not purchase strictly on the bases of advertising and personal selling alone. For automobiles, intentions measures might be more desirable than sales measures.

Purchase measures. Purchase measures such as sales are those measures that focus on actual marketplace events. They reflect a response to communication that is precisely what the promotion set out to achieve. When sales measures are used, we can justifiably expect the communications effort to have had a direct effect on action. Such a conclusion is an assumption, of course, until other measurements verify it.

Purchase measures usually take one of three forms: unit sales, dollar sales, or market share. Unit sales measures reflect the actual number of items that people have purchased; dollar sales measures report on actual revenue; market share expresses the company's sales performance relative to that of competitors.

The unit sales and dollar sales measures are descriptive measures. That is, they focus only on what the communications campaign of that company appears to have accomplished. They do not by themselves make any comparative statements of performance. The unit sales figure and the dollar sales figure, in other words, depict performance on an absolute but not relative basis. If we were only interested in the movement of goods and the revenue generated by the movement of such goods, the unit and dollar measures would be appropriate. If we wish a statement of sales performance in the competitive context, we need to have market share figures as well.

Market share figures can be computed by simply dividing the company's sales by the industry's sales figures. The result is the percentage of the industry sales that company holds. Market share reflects company achievements in a competitive environment.

Each of the three measures of sales evaluates a specific promotional activity. The key ingredient is to recognize the merits of the different measures and to use that one or combination that yields the most appropriate information.

With this detailed look at the specific performance measures, we now turn to the next aspect of promotional program evaluation: defining the standards by which to judge performance.

Establishing Standards

As we stated earlier, a company derives the expectations of performance principally from the statement of objectives. If projected conditions are similar to the actual conditions of operation, then the *objectives must be the standards on which to judge performance*. Where there are substantial unforeseen changes in the operating conditions, such as economic shifts, social pressures, or legal constraints, the company may have to adjust expectations of performance considerably from the original objectives. For example, the abrupt halt to sales of Tylenol capsules in 1982 was because of social and legal pressures, not because of problems with the communications campaign. In such an instance, a restructuring of the expectations of performance was clearly in order.

Comparing Performance with Standards

When the manager has the expectations and then has the performance, the next step is to *determine the direction and magnitude of the difference between the two*. The nature of the discrepancy dictates the judgment of good or bad. Of course, the more the actual performance exceeds expectations, the better the accomplishment.

The major difficulty in the evaluation of performance is not in determining whether there are differences between actual results and expectations, since there will almost always be differences. Instead the major difficulty is in determining whether there are significant differences, differences that exceed acceptable limits. Consequently, it is necessary to establish decision rules to define the tolerable limits of deviation.

There are both empirical and subjective bases for determining the thresholds that differentiate significant from insignificant deviations. Empirical determination of thresholds usually stems from statistical analysis of historical facts. Subjectively determined thresholds rely on opinions and expert judgment.

After the comparison of results with expectations, the manager is in a position to identify control actions that may be necessary.

CONTROL (EXECUTING APPROPRIATE ACTION)

After the launch of the promotion campaign, the manager is responsible for keeping the program on its charted course. *Evaluation of the total program and its elements* tells the manager what the effort has achieved relative to the plans; the *control system* identifies activities necessary to ensure that the program accomplishes its ultimate objectives.

There are three categories of alternative courses that the manager can take after the evaluation of performance: no action, remedial action, and preventive action.

No Action

A decision to engage in *no corrective action* may be the right decision if there is no significant deviation of actual performance from established goals. As we mentioned earlier, discrepancies between performance and expectations are likely to occur, and consequently any actual discrepancies must be tested against established acceptable limits of discrepancies. If the actual discrepancies are within acceptable limits, then no corrective action is necessary.

Therefore, when a program is going well, it is logical to take no corrective action. Sometimes, however, no corrective action is taken even though actual performance is known to differ from planned performance. How can such a situation arise? Well, good evaluation and control systems operate continually over the course of the campaign. Any specific evaluation is an assessment of performance at a given time. Sometimes there may be actual deviations from expectations in a given period. Still, no action may be taken when the performance falls below goals if the manager concludes that such a deviation is only temporary. Or no action may be taken even with known shortfalls in performance if the cost of action outweighs the projected gains in the relevant period. In such an instance, corrective action may not be taken for that period but may be unavoidable if the condition persists over several evaluation periods.

Remedial Action

A problem means that remedial action is in order. *Remedial action* directly addresses those areas of the promotions program that produce undesirable results. Some sort of remedial action will be appropriate when recall rates on advertising are very low, sales to a particular customer group are lagging well behind expectations, fewer retailers than desired are taking advantage of cooperative advertising allowances, the coupon redemption rate is abnormally low, or newspapers are printing few if any press releases on company activities. Remedial action can be directed at virtually any aspect of the promotion program, from a reassessment of the objectives to the final details of execution, such as contracting with a printing company for a sales brochure or directing sales reps on procedures in filling out call reports.

Remedial action implies a condition of significant deviation of performance from goals. If the condition does not get attention, the gulf between accomplishments and expectations will continue and perhaps widen.

Preventive Action

Corrective action is customarily remedial, but such a definition does not encompass the full nature of a control system. One of the tasks of a control system is to ensure that serious problems do not arise in the first place. *Preventive actions* do not address any immediate deficiencies in the program. Instead their purpose is to check a problem before it has developed. Let us assume that the performance measure for our promotion program is unit sales. If we discover that the actual number of units sold meets or exceeds the established quota, we may initially think that no corrective action is necessary because there is no undesirable deviation of performance from the standard. However, there may be troubling factors in existence that do not affect sales now but will certainly affect sales in the future. For example, if our sales have historically been due to repeat purchases from existing customers, we might conclude that customer satisfaction now leads to sales later. If we discover that dissatisfaction has increased dramatically in the present, we can expect poor sales results in the future. While there may be no immediate problems with sales levels, action would have to be undertaken to prevent a potential problem.

Preventive actions are usually much less costly to the company than remedial actions. When remedial actions come into play, not only is there expenditure for those actions but there may be actual costs because of the problem, or there may be opportunity costs in the form of lost sales or profits.

Focus of Attention

Corrective actions require direction toward the program as a whole or toward specific elements of the program.

Addressing the Total Effort

In conducting an evaluation of performance, the manager may conclude that the magnitude of the total effort is either insufficient or excessive for the returns, or that the general direction of the total effort is wrong. Actions that address the total effort generally result from major strategy problems and call for significant shifts in promotional strategy. There could be a major shift in resource allocation or a major change in the underlying theme of the program. Substantial changes in budget levels may of course be disruptive to other areas of marketing and the company because the budget for a department usually follows consideration of the company's overall financial resources. One department's funding requirements generally affect the budgets of other departments. A major change in the magnitude of promotional effort will generally mean a sizable budgetary adjustment, which in turn requires serious consideration as to the overall impact on the company. All things converge—at the budget.

A *change in the direction of the total effort* will affect all the individual elements of the program, since the plans for those elements are woven with the common thread of the program. This change in the direction of program effort usually means a shift in the role of the promotion program in contributing to the marketing effort. Such a change, then, would have a dramatic impact on the marketing department and would have to undergo extended examination before execution.

Reformulation of the Promotional Mix

Even though the level and direction of effort of the entire program may be acceptable, there may be corrective actions on individual elements as well as on the mix of the elements, and these may enhance the overall performance still more. For example, the total performance may be acceptable, but it may be due to satisfactory performance of all the elements or to exceptional performance by one element counterbalanced by a weak performance of another element. Here the overall performance might be satisfactory but could still be improved by upgrading the weak area.

The *reformulation of the promotional mix* involves actions to correct the intensity or direction of the individual elements of the promotional mix. Usually such actions result in improved coordination of the program elements by achieving the proper balance of individual efforts. An evaluation of the program elements may tell us that the personal selling effort is encountering difficulty because of a lack of familiarity with the company and its products among the target customers. In such an instance, we may wish to reformulate the promotion mix by increasing advertising's effort at generating awareness.

Reassessment of Expectations

Corrective actions typically concentrate on the effort, but there may be instances demanding corrective action toward the evaluation standards. When this occurs, it is an acknowledgment that the expectations used in the evaluation system were inappropriate. Expectations can be either unduly strict or easy. Expectations that cannot be met after a reasonable effort may be frustrating to those accountable, while expectations fulfilled with ease may result in serious opportunity losses for the company due to lack of effort.

The *reformulation of expectations* is usually undertaken when a significant change has occurred in the original conditions under which the promotion was planned and the objectives set, or when there is evidence that the original expectations were simply wrong. The former situation is relatively common as a result of substantial changes in the legal, competitive, social, and economic environment. The latter situation is more difficult to determine and usually comes to light when a consistent gap exists between performance and expectations over an extended period of time.

When management redefines goals, a review of the program effort is also in order. Thus, while corrective actions may not concentrate on the promotional effort itself, the change in expectations generally means that the manager must reconstruct the program effort to accommodate the new expectations.

SUMMARY

This chapter discussed the evaluation of performance and the undertaking of controls. These activities are necessary to ensure that the campaign accomplishes what it set out to do. Management wants to detect problems early and take appropriate corrective actions before incurring any serious losses of time, money, and effort.

A good evaluation system provides a true picture of the past, present, and future performance; it properly assesses the merits of performance; and it identifies the necessary courses of action. Specifically, evaluation and control should be viewed as a process involving a set of related, interdependent activities, including defining the promotional effort, selecting performance measures, establishing standards, comparing performance with standards, and taking appropriate action (control).

Performance monitoring should concentrate not only on the overall results of the total promotion mix but also on the effects of the individual elements such as advertising, personal selling, sales promotion, and publicity. If properly executed, the evaluation system ensures maximum return from the promotion campaign by identifying and eliminating weaknesses.

Any promotional program must be viewed in the context of the legal and social environments. Both serve as restraints on the structure of promotional programs, but both present the marketer with opportunities. We now turn to these important environments, which significantly affect promotional strategy. First we will look at the legal framework within which promotion operates and then consider the social aspects of promotion.

REVIEW AND DISCUSSION QUESTIONS

1. *What are the major activities involved in the evaluation and control process?*

2. *Why is it important that a promotion program be regularly evaluated? What are some of the inherent difficulties in evaluating a total promotional program?*

3. *What are the major objectives of an evaluation system? Explain.*

4. *What are three characteristics of an effective evaluation and control system?*

5. *What is the basis for standards used in judging performance?*

6. *What is meant when it is stated that a working definition of objectives is essential to accurately assessing performance?*

7. *Should action be taken by a manager only when a problem is detected? Why or why not?*

8. *Compare and contrast the major measures of promotional performance. What are the advantages and disadvantages of each?*

9. *Describe the relationship between performance measures and promotion objectives.*

10. *"Brand awareness among noncustomers should increase by 5 percent." What problems do you see with the preceding promotional standard?*

11. *Compare and contrast aided and unaided recall measures. Give examples of each.*

12. *What information is provided to the advertiser by the Starch Message Report Service? What is the value of this information? Explain.*

13. *Describe the type of information that would be gathered if attitudes among customers were to be measured.*

14. *When would intentions be an appropriate measure of promotion performance? Give examples.*

15. *Describe the specific measures of sales results.*

16. *Identify the three major alternative courses of action in the control process. Also describe the conditions under which each would be appropriate.*

17. *"Corrective action may be directed at the total program or at an individual effort such as advertising." Comment.*

18. *Sometimes action is directed not at the effort but at the expectations. When is this likely to occur?*

19

Regulation of Promotion

Because promotion has become an increasingly important marketing tool, it has also become necessary to ensure that such promotion is not being used unfairly and abusively. There is a risk, however, that in protecting against abuses of advertising, one may infringe on the right to freedom of speech guaranteed by the First Amendment to the U.S. Constitution. Governments at all levels have been cautious about expanding their powers to regulate advertising and other forms of promotion.

Still, over the years, some businesses have engaged in practices sufficiently harmful to consumers or unfair to competitors that legislation has arisen to protect both groups while preserving First Amendment rights.[1] The history of this regulation and its enforcement is illuminating.

In this chapter we will look first at federal legislation affecting promotion and then at state and local laws. We will then consider the substantial efforts the industry has made to regulate itself voluntarily, sometimes quietly producing the most effective results. Throughout this chapter we will see that while advertising and promotion are essential to the conduct of business in a free enterprise economy, the public interest must remain a primary consideration.

FEDERAL LEGISLATION

Since 1906 the federal government has passed more than a dozen important pieces of legislation affecting advertising and promotional practices in interstate commerce. The Pure Food and Drug Act appeared in 1906, followed by the Federal Trade Commission Act in 1914. After a hiatus of twenty years and in response to charges of excesses in business practices, a flurry of additional legislation arose in the 1930s. Not until the 1960s and early 1970s did new federal legislation rise to similar levels, spurred by demands from the general public and from consumer leaders for increased consumer protection.

Jurisdiction over these regulations lies primarily in three separate agencies: the Federal Trade Commission, the federal Food and Drug Administration, and the Federal Communications Commission. Later we will examine the responsibilities and remedies available to each of these bodies.

The Pure Food and Drug Act (1906)

Before the twentieth century the federal government was reluctant to pass laws dealing directly with marketing practices. Its regulatory efforts aimed at curtailing the growth of monopolies. After years of debate, however, and in response to rising consumer demands to eliminate quackery in the patent medicine business and the deception and fraud in the food-packaging industry, Congress passed the Pure Food and Drug Act in 1906. Essentially, this act called for the correct disclosure of contents on the packages of drug products and made illegal the transporting across state lines of adulterated or misbranded foods and drugs.

Passage of this act was a truly historic occurrence, since it demonstrated for the first time the federal government's willingness to protect the interests of the consumer. Until then the prevailing government philosophy had been *caveat emptor*—let the buyer beware! Although limited in its applicability, this legislation put producers and marketers on notice that the government could depart from its laissez-faire attitude. On balance, however, the Pure Food and Drug Act did not effectively control promotional abuses.

The Federal Trade Commission Act (1914)

In 1914, with the strong urging of President Woodrow Wilson, Congress created the Federal Trade Commission, chiefly in order to enforce antitrust legislation and halt the growth of monopolies.

Along with its antimonopoly provisions, Section 5 of the act states, in part, "that unfair methods of competition in commerce are hereby declared unlawful." Under this provision the FTC could take action against deceptive advertising where evidence showed that such practices resulted in injury to competition. Eventually, this authority led to the FTC's substantial involvement in the matter of advertising abuses. Note, however, that Section 5 did not extend to abuses that misled the public, only to those that impaired competition. Legislation strengthening the FTC by increasing its jurisdiction came later with acts such as the Wheeler-Lea Amendment and the Magnuson-Moss Act, to be discussed later.

The Communications Act (1934)

The Communications Act established the Federal Communications Commission to centralize the regulation of the rapidly emerging common carriers of messages: radio, wire, cable, and eventually television. Central to its purpose is the FCC's obligation to serve the public interest through its authority to grant, renew, and revoke broadcasting licenses.

In its decisions to renew or revoke licenses, the FCC considers the extent to which licensees have maintained high standards in their public service programming and in the advertisements they present. It thereby encourages broadcasters to avoid the communication of misleading messages or advertisements judged to be in bad taste. This control (indirect control, since the act does not permit the FCC to act as a censor) is supported by a full-time staff that considers and acts upon complaints from the public and other sources.

The Wheeler-Lea Amendment (1938)

As mentioned earlier, a major weakness in the Federal Trade Commission Act of 1914 was its failure to provide the commission with the authority to act against false and misleading advertising unless evidence of substantial competitive injury existed. In short, the act addressed injuries to competition but not injuries to consumers. With this in mind, Congress passed the Wheeler-Lea Amendment in 1938 to strengthen the original FTC act and to expand the FTC's jurisdiction and enforcement capability. This rewording of Section 5 was of major significance: ". . . Unfair methods of competition in commerce, and unfair or deceptive acts or practices in commerce, are hereby declared to be unlawful." This important change granted the FTC the additional authority to take action against a firm engaged in the use of unfair or deceptive advertising practices considered harmful to consumers regardless of their effect on competition.

The Wheeler-Lea Amendment provided the FTC with additional jurisdiction over false advertising of food, drugs, medical and veterinary devices, and cosmetics, which had been excluded earlier as falling under the Pure

Food and Drug Act. The act also added to the commission's enforcement capability by making possible the issuing of preliminary injunctions against the use of false advertising of food, drug, and cosmetic items when the commission anticipated that some risk to the public health might result.

The Federal Food, Drug, and Cosmetic Act (1938)

The Federal Food, Drug, and Cosmetic Act superseded the earlier Pure Food and Drug Act of 1906. It established the Food and Drug Administration, with control over the branding and labeling of foods, drugs, therapeutic devices, and cosmetic products. Specifically, the act requires the truthful and accurate disclosure of ingredients on the package or label of certain products and prohibits false or deceptive labeling and packaging of these items.

Thus the FDA is empowered, under the 1938 act, to exercise control over misbranding and false labeling of the specified products, while the FTC continues to have jurisdiction over all other forms of false and misleading advertising for these same products as well as others. A close working relationship and strong sense of cooperation between the two agencies help to prevent duplication of enforcement efforts.

Other Acts

A number of laws regulate the labeling of products not covered by the Federal Food, Drug, and Cosmetic Act. For example:

> The Wool Products Labeling Act (1939), under which items of clothing possessing wool content must be labeled accurately to indicate the type of wool included (virgin, reprocessed, and so on) as well as the percentage of each kind used in the product.
>
> The Fur Products Labeling Act (1951), which requires the identification, on the label, of the country of origin and natural name of the fur used in the garment.
>
> The Textile Fiber Products Identification Act (1958), which requires a generic or chemical description of the fiber content (including percentage by weight) of clothing, rugs, and household textiles.
>
> The Hazardous Substances Labeling Act (1960), which requires identification on the label for household products that have toxic, corrosive, irritant, or similar characteristics.

The Robinson-Patman Act (1938)

The Robinson-Patman Act was passed in response to certain promotional abuses involving the use of price discrimination and preferential treatment. Certain questionable practices, thought harmful to competition, included the granting of price concessions to large volume purchasers but not to small dealers, or providing brokerage fees to large customers when in fact no services were rendered. The act

a. Made it illegal for sellers to engage in price discrimination or alter terms of sale between purchasers of goods of "like grade and quality"
b. Prohibited discrimination by requiring sellers to treat all customers on the same proportionate basis in terms of promotional allowances, discounts, and the granting of services
c. Made it unlawful to pay brokerage fees to a broker affiliated in some way with the buyer or seller

In short, then, the act requires that all competitive customers be treated on proportionately equal terms.

The Federal Trade Commission, responsible for enforcing this act, periodically issues guidelines to help business get a better understanding of the law and its interpretation. The guidelines include such examples as the following:

Example 1: A seller may properly offer to pay a specified part (say 50 percent) of the cost of local advertising up to an amount equal to a set percentage (such as 5 percent) of the dollar volume of purchase during a specified time.

Example 2: A seller should not select one or a few customers to receive special allowances (e.g., 5 percent of purchases) to promote a product while making allowances available on some lesser basis (e.g., 2 percent of purchases) to customers who compete with them.

Example 3: A seller's plan should not provide an allowance on a basis that has rates graduated with the amount of goods purchased, as, for instance, 1 percent of the first $1,000 of purchases per month, 2 percent of the second $1,000 per month, and 3 percent of all over that.

Example 4: A seller should not identify or feature one or a few customers in its own advertising without making the same service available on proportionately equal terms to customers competing with the identified customer or customers.

The Lanham-Trademark Act (1946)

The Lanham-Trademark Act is the comprehensive federal legislation establishing the procedures for registration and protection of trademarks and other identifying marks. Registration and protection are available for the following kinds of identifying marks, as defined in Section 45 of the act:

TRADEMARK. The term "trademark" includes any word, name, symbol, or device or any combination thereof adopted and used by a manufacturer or merchant to identify its goods and distinguish them from those manufactured or sold by others.

SERVICE MARK. The term "service mark" means a mark used in the sale or advertising of services to identify the services of one person and distinguish them from the services of others and includes without limitation the marks, names, symbols, titles, designations, slogans, character names, and distinctive features of radio or other advertising used in commerce.

CERTIFICATION MARK. The term "certification mark" means a mark used upon or in connection with the products or services of one or more persons other than the owner of the mark to certify regional or other origin, material, mode of manufacture, quality, accuracy or other characteristics of such goods or services or that the work or labor on the goods or services was performed by members of a union or other organization.

COLLECTIVE MARK. The term "collective mark" means a trademark or service mark used by the member of a cooperative, an association or other collective group or organization and includes marks used to indicate membership in a union, an association or other organization.

Identifying marks may be registered in the Principal Register or a Supplemental Register. Trademarks qualifying for registration in the Principal Register are understood to have achieved primary registration and, as such, have given notice of the registrant's exclusive ownership of the trademark. Use of the trademark by others is precluded following the date of registration. On the other hand, registration in the Supplemental Register is for information purposes only, the registrant gaining no exclusive right of ownership.

The Fair Packaging and Labeling Act (1966)

The Fair Packaging and Labeling Act, also referred to as the Truth in Packaging Act, was created to ensure informative and accurate packaging and labeling of consumer products (i.e., food, drugs, devices, cosmetics). Regulation of packaging gained favor because of the added importance of the consumer package as a promotional vehicle (the "silent salesperson") and an increasing number of abuses by some marketers. During the course of the congressional hearings on deceptive and fraudulent practices in packaging, abuses such as the following were brought to light: obscure net weight designations, oversized packages resulting in nonfunctional "slack fill," multiplicity of package sizes, misleading sizes and shapes, use of misleading illustrations, and misrepresentation of package contents on the label.

The act requires certain basic information on product labels to reduce consumer confusion and to assist shoppers in making comparisons between brands of products. Information required under the act includes specific product identification; identification and location of the manufacturer, processor, or distributor; and net quantity by weight, measure, or numerical count. The Food and Drug Administration has occasionally seized shipments of goods when false or misleading labeling or packaging has created product misrepresentation.

The Magnuson-Moss Warranty—
The Federal Trade Commission
Improvements Act (1975)

The Magnuson-Moss Warranty legislation further expanded the original Federal Trade Commission Act by

    a. Requiring the strengthening and clarification of consumer product warranties through new minimum standards for disclosure

    b. Increasing the FTC's jurisdiction and authority by empowering the commission to prescribe interpretive rules regarding unfair or deceptive practices "in or affecting commerce"

This last provision is of considerable importance to professionals engaged in promotional activities in that it authorizes the FTC to issue specific Trade Regulation Rules (TRRs) that serve as broad guidelines for promotional conduct, applicable to entire industries and product categories. The establishment of TRRs has materially speeded up enforcement procedures against unfair or deceptive acts, since the FTC no longer must wait for adjudication of specific complaints on a case-by-case basis. Rather, the commission may now initiate proceedings against any firm it considers to be in violation of the broad-based industry rules it has issued.

The Federal Trade Commission
Improvements Act (1980)

The Federal Trade Commission Improvements Act of 1980 contains several major changes in the FTC's core statutory authority. The act placed a three-year moratorium on the commission's authority to use "unfairness" as the basis for promulgating trade regulations on advertising. During that period, Congress was to "hold hearings to determine if unfairness can be adequately defined and implemented and if it should be fully returned to the FTC statute."[2]

ENFORCEMENT RESPONSIBILITY
AND REMEDIES

Authority to enforce the major legislation affecting advertising and promotion is vested primarily in the three federal regulatory agencies described above: the Federal Trade Commission, the Food and Drug Administration, and the Federal Communications Commission. These agencies work indepen-

dently, but, in certain cases, in collaboration with one another. The enforcement responsibilities and the remedies available to each are quite different.

The Federal Trade Commission (FTC)

Enforcement Responsibilities

The Federal Trade Commission is the primary federal regulatory agency
controlling abuses in the areas of advertising and promotion. The FTC's
jurisdiction covering unfair methods of competition in interstate commerce
arises by virtue of its responsibility for the enforcement of laws such as
those already discussed. Again the major thrust of these acts is to provide
the FTC with broad powers and responsibility to guard against a variety
of unfair trade practices including false, misleading, or deceptive advertising.

In its role as protector of the consuming public's health, safety, and
economic well-being, the FTC combats promotion abuses such as deceptive
pricing, the use of false and unsubstantiated advertising claims, deceptive
demonstrations and fraudulent testimonials, vague warranties, illegal lotteries, and "bait-and-switch" practices.

The FTC monitors all national advertising by product category, by
medium, and by advertising technique. It also receives complaints from consumers, consumer groups, and competitors and from other governmental
bodies. In addition, the agency has introduced an advertising substantiation
program to ensure that advertising claims are truthful and fair. Under this
program advertisers must, upon request by the commission, provide substantiating documentation in support of questionable advertising claims. Firms
making such claims are further required to give evidence that the documentation provided was actually used as supporting material for the advertising
claims prior to the creation and dissemination of the advertisement. The
FTC's objective in requiring substantiation is twofold: (1) to further the
education of consumers through the public disclosure of substantiating evidence received from advertisers and (2) to provide a deterrent to the use
of unfounded advertising claims.[3]

Until the late 1970s the FTC viewed advertising substantiation as a
responsibility of the advertiser alone. In 1979, however, it took initial steps
toward involving advertising agencies in this responsibility as well. In the
1979 Annual Report of the Federal Trade Commission, it reported that it
had specifically charged ad agencies with participation in deceptive practices
and had asked them to sign consent orders agreeing to discontinue these
practices:

> . . . for the first time, the FTC attempted to transfer part of the responsibility
> of ad substantiation to the creators of advertisements. In a consent order
> with the nation's largest advertising agency, J. WALTER THOMPSON,
> the FTC provided an incentive for the agency to indicate to the advertiser

in advance of any ad campaign all claims that the agency thought the prospective advertising suggested, so that the advertiser could substantiate them.[4]

The FTC, under the authority of the Magnuson-Moss Warranty, has developed, with the assistance of representatives of the industry, a number of Trade Regulation Rules, mentioned earlier. These rules define the practices within the industry that the FTC will consider violations of legislation for which the commission bears enforcement responsibility. Incorporated within these TRRs are a variety of deceptive acts and unfair methods of competition particularly likely to occur in that industry. Firms are expected to know and comply with these TRRs. As a result, the FTC has authority to seek civil penalties against firms found to be in violation of these broad-based industry rules, even though no one has lodged a formal complaint. The FTC will also issue advisory opinions to firms interested in determining if proposed promotional programs have the potential to violate legislation or TRRs.

In late 1983 the FTC adopted a controversial policy statement in which it defined "deceptive advertising" according to a three-part test: (1) that there is a representation, omission, or practice that is likely to mislead the consumer; (2) that the consumer whose response is being examined is a reasonable consumer; and (3) that the representation, omission, or practice is material.[5] The FTC policy statement was another of the many attempts to pinpoint the meaning of "deceptive advertising."[6]

Remedies

In discharging its enforcement responsibilities, the FTC has a number of remedies to apply as the individual case seems to dictate.

Cease-and-Desist Orders. The FTC conducts preliminary investigations of each complaint against false, misleading, or deceptive advertising brought to its attention. Following such an investigation, the commission may decide to drop the matter or, if the evidence warrants it, to issue a formal complaint to the advertiser through its Bureau of Litigation. Should the alleged violation involve the advertising of food, drug, or cosmetic products, the FTC may issue an injunction to stop the advertisement or promotion if it appears that its continued use could cause harm to the public.

After a formal complaint has been filed, the advertiser is offered the opportunity to agree to a consent order issued by the FTC. If the advertiser signs such an order, it must halt the questionable practice, but it does so without admitting guilt. Consent decrees may not be appealed to the courts. The consent decree is often a desirable alternative for a firm that has only a minimum chance of being successful in its case or wishes to avoid the costs of pursuing the matter to a final judgment. Consent orders become enforceable sixty days following their issuance.

In those situations where an advertiser wishes to challenge the findings of the FTC, a trial is set before an FTC administrative law judge. If the verdict is guilty, the FTC will issue a "cease-and-desist" order to the advertiser. Under this order the advertiser must halt the stated practice within a sixty-day period or be subject to fines. The FTC has begun to use generalized cease-and-desist orders whereby an order issued against a particular advertiser is also made binding on all other firms operating within the same industry. A case involving the advertising practices of a manufacturer of children's toys, decided by a U.S. District Court, demonstrates the broadening of the FTC's enforcement capability:

FTC File No. 782 3023

United States v. General Mills Fun Group, Inc.

Complaint Filed: 5/22/79

Judgment Entered: 5/23/79

> United States District Court for the District of Minnesota; judgment in the amount of $100,000 ($90,000—Kenner Product Division, $10,000—Fun Dimensions Division). The complaint alleged that defendant had advertised toys by engaging in practices that the FTC previously had determined to be unfair and deceptive in proceedings against IDEAL TOY CORPORATION (FTC Docket No. 8530, 64 F.T.C. 297 (1064) and WALCO TOY COMPANY, INC., (FTC Docket No. 8921, 82 F.T.C. 1783).[7]

Fines. Once an advertiser has agreed to a consent order and it has become binding and enforceable, if the advertiser continues its questionable practice, it becomes subject to fines of up to $10,000 per violation. Under the broadening of the FTC's powers, a similar $10,000 fine per offense may also be levied on a firm found to be in violation of a cease-and-desist order issued to another firm. Thus an advertiser must take care not to violate these cease-and-desist orders even though it was not the original recipient of the order. The FTC also has the authority to seek civil penalties of up to $10,000 per day from firms found to be in violation of various Trade Regulation Rules. The following case illustrates the FTC's activity in securing civil penalties for TRR violations:

FTC File No. 772 3010

United States v. Dixieland Construction Company, Inc., et al.

Complaint Filed: 9/28/79

Judgment Entered: 9/28/79

> United States District Court for the Northern District of Alabama; Civil Action No. 79M 1055 S USDC ND Ala. A consent judgment in the amount of $10,000 in civil penalties and an injunction was entered

on September 28, 1979 for violations of the Commission's Trade Regulation Rule concerning a Cooling-Off Period for Door-to-Door Sales and for engaging in unfair and deceptive practices in the offering of home improvement services.[8]

Corrective Advertising. The FTC is empowered to order companies to undertake corrective advertising designed to reduce or cancel the effects of previous misleading advertising claims. This remedy is potent medicine in the FTC's cabinet of remedies. The concept of obligatory corrective advertising arose in response to the argument that merely putting an end to a deceptive advertising practice through the use of a consent decree or a cease-and-desist order was not a strong enough remedy. An advertiser would already have accumulated considerable benefits throughout the duration of the time the false advertisement had been in use. The argument was that simply halting the use of a false or misleading advertisement would in no way dissipate or correct the erroneous impressions created in the minds of consumers exposed to the advertisement.[9]

The commission responded with the remedy of corrective advertising, the objectives of which are (1) to correct false impressions created by the deceptive practice, (2) to eliminate any competitive advantage gained by the firm through its use of the false advertisement, and (3) to serve as a deterrent to misleading advertising. Under this remedy, the FTC requires advertisers to place retractions, in future advertisements, of prior claims found to be false or deceptive.

The first test case in federal courts of an FTC request for corrective advertising involved the Warner-Lambert Company, maker of Listerine. For many years this company had contended that its mouthwash could prevent or lessen the severity of sore throats or common colds. In 1975 the FTC determined these claims to be false and ordered Warner-Lambert to place corrective advertising to dispel the misleading impressions built up over time. In 1977 the manufacturer tested the FTC's authority to order corrective advertising, as well as the FTC's findings in the matter, through cases brought before the District of Columbia Circuit Court of Appeals. The court found in favor of the FTC both in its contention that the advertising claims were false and in its prescription of corrective advertising as a remedy. Later the Supreme Court refused to hear an appeal on the district court's decision. Warner-Lambert was compelled to state, in $10 million of future advertising, that "Listerine will not help prevent colds or sore throats or lessen their severity."[10] The Listerine case is a landmark decision in the use of this remedy.

Corrective advertising is a severe remedy and is used only in those special cases where beliefs will not dissipate naturally. While it is potentially an effective remedy, there is some evidence that the remedial statements may be confusing and as misleading as the advertising they are designed to counteract.[11] Some have suggested that the "FTC should investigate different procedures for executing corrective advertising, or else develop other remedies for cases of deceptive advertising."[12]

Exhibit 19-1 summarizes the FTC's remedies against deceptive advertising. Note that the FTC's investigation of alleged deceptive advertising cases involves consideration of several questions (or decision points), each leading to specific action.

The Food and Drug Administration (FDA)

Enforcement Responsibilities

The Food and Drug Administration is responsible for enforcement of the Food, Drug, and Cosmetic Act (1938) as well as the Fair Packaging and Labeling Act (1966). Under these laws the FDA has authority to exercise control over the claims appearing on product labels and packages in the food, drug, and cosmetics industries. The FDA maintains a large staff to test the safety and efficacy of food, drug, and cosmetic items. Also, as a service to manufacturers, the FDA renders preliminary opinions regarding proposed descriptive language, prior to its use on product labels. The FDA and the Federal Trade Commission, once at odds because of overlapping enforcement responsibilities, now work in close cooperation with each other.

Remedies

The FDA may initiate criminal or civil actions against manufacturers, processors, or distributors found guilty of mislabeling. Such actions may result in fines, seizure of products, and, in some instances, imprisonment.

The Federal Communications Commission (FCC)

Enforcement Responsibilities

As mentioned earlier, the Federal Communications Commission was established under the Communications Act (1934) and is charged with responsibility for regulating and controlling the communications and broadcast industries to ensure that they operate in the "public interest, convenience, and necessity." In the broadcast industry, the FCC derives its power through its authority to grant, renew, or revoke station licenses. In its decision-making process, the FCC pays particular attention to both the quality and the quantity of advertising messages broadcast by stations. It works to prevent the airing of advertisements considered to be false, misleading, deceptive, profane, or obscene. The commission monitors the broadcast advertisements

EXHIBIT 15-1 Decision Points in FTC Deceptive Advertising Matters

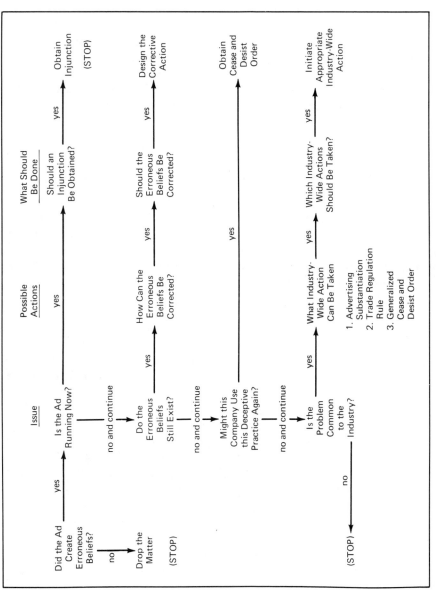

Source: H. Keith Hunt, *Advertising in Government Regulation,* a report by the Advertising and Government Panel of the American Academy of Advertising (Cambridge, Mass.: Marketing Science Institute, 1979), p. 16.

as it seeks to uncover abusive advertising practices. The FCC also maintains a staff to investigate complaints about advertising received from a variety of external sources, including the public, government agencies, and Better Business Bureaus.

The FCC works closely with the Federal Trade Commission on matters involving false, misleading, or deceptive advertising, since abuses of this nature may require FTC action against the individual advertiser. In addition, the FCC places pressure on individual stations to take corrective action with advertisers upon receipt of complaints. The commission considers the station's cooperation and performance in this regard in making its license renewal decisions.

Remedies

Although the Federal Trade Commission has jurisdiction over charges of false and misleading advertising, the FCC does have the authority, through its Complaints and Compliance staff, to issue administrative sanctions against stations, to impose fines of up to $10,000 on them, and to suspend and even refuse to extend licenses of stations transmitting messages containing profane or obscene language.

Other Agencies

Several other agencies also involve themselves with advertising regulation. For example, the Post Office Department prohibits use of the mails for illegal purposes such as fraud, obscenity, and lotteries, and it has the power to prosecute advertisers found violating the law. The Securities and Exchange Commission (SEC) regulates securities sold in interstate commerce by its authority to ensure that the advertising for securities is truthful, accurate, and nondeceptive. The Alcohol, Tobacco and Firearms Unit of the Treasury Department sets rules on the advertising, marketing, and labeling of beer, wine, and spirits. The Labor Department is involved with advertising by labor unions and employers in labor relations matters. Finally, the Interstate Commerce Commission and the Civil Aeronautics Board control advertising by regulated carriers in the trucking and airline industries.

STATE AND LOCAL LEGISLATION
AFFECTING PROMOTION

The majority of federal laws affecting the promotion and sale of products, as well as the jurisdiction of most federal agencies (excepting the FTC), apply only to interstate commerce. Therefore state and local governments must enact legislation designed to control advertising and promotion as they affect intrastate commerce.

The Printers' Ink Model Statute

Many states have adopted, in one form or another, a model statute that identifies those promotional practices considered to be "untrue, deceptive, or misleading" and proposes penalties for violations. This statute originated in 1911 with the Printers' Ink Publishing Company, publisher of *Printers' Ink*, the leading periodical of the marketing community at the time. The model statute it proposed was designed to prevent the adoption of different laws in various states that would have made compliance difficult for advertisers. This model statute is the foundation for much of the legislation dealing with false advertising in force at the state level today. Its main provisions state:

> Any person, firm, corporation or association or agent or employee thereof, who, with intent to sell, purchase or in any way dispose of, or to contract with reference to merchandise, real estate, service, employment, or anything offered by such person, firm, corporation or association, or agent or employee thereof, directly or indirectly, to the public for sale, purchase, distribution, or hire of personal services, or with intent to increase the consumption of or to contract with reference to any merchandise, real estate, securities, service or employment, or to induce the public in any manner to enter into any obligation relating thereto, or to acquire title thereto, or interest therein, or to make any loan, makes, publishes, disseminates, circulates, or places before the public, or causes, directly or indirectly, to be made, published, disseminated, circulated, or placed before the public, in this state, in a newspaper, magazine, or other publication, or in the form of a book, notice, circular, pamphlet, letter, handbill, poster, bill, sign, placard, card, label, or over any radio or television station or other medium of wireless communication, or in any other way similar or dissimilar to the foregoing, an advertisement, announcement or statement of any sort regarding merchandise, securities, service, employment, or anything so offered for use, purchase or sale, or the interest, terms or conditions upon which such loan will be made to the public, which advertisement contains any assertion, representation or statement of fact which is untrue, deceptive, or misleading, shall be guilty of a misdemeanor.[13]

This obviously comprehensive statute goes as far as one might go, perhaps, to describe the sources and kinds of promotional abuse, and it states forthrightly that such abuse is or ought to be criminal. While the statute and others like it have been somewhat ineffective in terms of dispensing punishment to violators, they do appear useful as deterrents to "untrue, deceptive, or misleading" advertising.

The Unfair Trade-Practice Acts

Many states have enacted legislation that prohibits the use of "loss leaders," declaring the practice to be an unfair method of competition. Loss-leader selling is the practice of pricing certain items at a loss so as to entice customers into a store in the hope that other such bargains exist. The store then attempts to either sell other items instead ("bait-and-switch") or make a profit by selling other items with higher margins. States that have passed unfair trade-practice acts generally consider the cost of an article to consist of its replacement cost, plus shipping cost, along with a modest percentage markup to cover other directly related business expenses. The laws make selling below this minimum price illegal.

Selected State Regulations

In addition to the Printers' Ink Model Statute and the unfair trade-practice acts, individual states have enacted a variety of laws dealing with the regulation of marketing practices such as door-to-door selling; billboards, signs, and other outdoor advertising displays; bait-and-switch tactics; endorsements; liquor sales; offers of free merchandise; contests; and sale of certain items on Sundays (so-called blue laws). Indeed the number and variety of state mandates governing advertising and promotion are considerable. A few are worth noting. For example, California's Business and Professions Code sets forth a broad prohibition of "unfair competition," which has been defined as ". . . unlawful, unfair or fraudulent business practices and unfair, deceptive, untrue or misleading advertising."[14] The plaintiff is not required to show injury to competition if there is injury to consumers (similar to Section 5 of the FTC Act). State and local prosecutors have power to sue for injunctions and civil penalties, in addition to authority to bring criminal prosecutions against violators. The New York False Advertising Statute declares deceptive acts and practices to be unlawful, and it specifically forbids false advertising. The state attorney general need not prove actual deception, only that an act has the capacity to deceive. In evaluating an advertisement's potential to deceive the public, the standard "reasonable person test" does not apply; instead, New York applies a "fool's test." This is an attempt to protect "the ignorant, the unthinking and the credulous," as well as the average consumer. (*People by Lefkowitz* v. *Volkswagen of America, Inc.*, 47 A.D. 2d 868, 366 NYS 2d 157, 1975.)[15] The attorney general has the authority to sue for civil penalties and even to bring an action for dissolution of an advertiser that operates in a persistently fraudulent or illegal manner. In Texas, the Deceptive Trade Practices–Consumer Protection Act lists twenty "false, misleading, or deceptive acts or practices" and has a "catchall" clause to include other forms of deception. The state attorney general has power to bring an injunction against violators and sue for civil penalties.

As public views evolve over time, it is certain that federal, state, and local government regulatory agencies will continue to seek more efficient and effective means to meet challenges to the public's safety and economic well-being. Rather than leave this entire process in the hands of government, many businesspeople have determined that it is more appropriate to build a partnership with government to protect the interests of the consumer and to preserve competition. These businesspeople have increased their efforts to have the business community police its own activities through industrywide programs of self-regulation. Without such efforts, there would undoubtedly be more regulation and enforcement activity logged in government, at all levels. In the next section we consider self-regulation by the advertising and promotion industry.

INDUSTRY SELF-REGULATION

> A decrease in surveillance of advertising by the Federal Trade Commission, combined with the technological revolution underway in advertising and marketing techniques . . . will increase the need for self-regulatory advertising review at both the national and local level.[16]

The advertising industry has long been engaged in voluntary efforts to regulate itself. Industry proponents of self-regulation suggest that the high level of self-regulatory activity is the direct result of a strong sense of moral and ethical obligation on the part of advertisers and the advertising industry to purge itself of abusive advertising practices and protect the health, safety, and economic welfare of the consumer. Critics of the advertising industry maintain that the degree of self-regulation activity that exists is insufficient and occurs only as a result of the industry's desire to deter further government intervention on behalf of consumers. To be sure, "a powerful motivation behind self-regulation is industry's desire to forestall government regulation."[17] While the exact motive may be uncertain, the fact is that there is a considerable attempt at self-regulation, resulting in a variety of approaches. The advertisers, advertising agencies, media, and public have joined in major efforts designed to strengthen the industry's ability to police itself effectively. The success of any self-regulatory process depends on the support of industry members and voluntary compliance with decisions rendered, as well as on the fairness, competence, and objectivity of the review panels established to pass judgment on questionable practices.

The most notable of the voluntary self-regulation efforts involves the National Advertising Review Council working with the Council of Better

Business Bureaus and its two operating arms: the National Advertising Division and the National Advertising Review Board. In addition, major self-regulation efforts are being conducted by the American Advertising Federation, American Association of Advertising Agencies, Association of National Advertisers, National Council for Consumer Affairs, various advertising media associations, and the companies that operate individual publications and stations.

The Council of Better Business Bureaus (CBBB)

Although the Better Business Bureau concept has existed for seven decades, it was not until 1970 that the current Council of Better Business Bureaus (CBBB) was organized as the result of a consolidation of the National Better Business Bureau and the Association of Better Business Bureaus. The major responsibility of the CBBB is to police advertising and other business practices. A major aim of the council is to encourage and facilitate industry self-regulation.

Some of the activities of the council include

1. Investigating inquiries and complaints from business and consumers and ruling on them
2. Providing consumer information and education through a variety of programs and publications
3. Training and development of Better Business Bureau personnel
4. Development of trade practice codes
5. Operating philanthropic advisory services

Perhaps the most significant activity of the CBBB is its role as one of the sponsors of the National Advertising Review Council and, in particular, its role as managing sponsor of the NARC's self-regulation apparatus.

The National Advertising Review Council (NARC)

The National Advertising Review Council (NARC) was established in 1971 as an administrative policy-making body to oversee the advertising industry's self-regulation mechanism. The council was formed at the initiative of the revitalized Council of Better Business Bureaus. It is composed of eight members, including the chairman and president of each of its four sponsoring organizations: the American Association of Advertising Agencies, the Association of National Advertisers, the American Advertising Federation, and, of course, the Council of Better Business Bureaus. The purpose of the NARC is ". . . to establish a self-regulatory mechanism that would respond constructively to public complaints about national advertising and would significantly improve advertising performance and credibility."[18] It was further intended that this mechanism be flexible, efficient, respected, and reliable. The National Advertising Review Council facilitates self-regulation activities for the advertising industry through its two operating arms: the National Advertising Division and the National Advertising Review Board.

The National Advertising Division (NAD)[19]

Structure

The National Advertising Division (NAD) of the Council of Better Business Bureaus, Inc. serves as the investigative mechanism of the council. Its objective is to help sustain high standards of truth and accuracy in national advertising. The NAD initiates investigations, determines the issues, collects and evaluates data, and negotiates settlements. If it is unable to resolve a controversy, an appeal can be made to a five-member panel of the National Advertising Review Board (as discussed below).

A special group within the NAD handles children's advertising. Known as the Children's Advertising Review Unit (CARU), it is discussed in Chapter 20 as part of an important social issue.

Sources of Cases

The NAD systematically monitors television, radio, and print advertising. This internal monitoring is the largest single source of cases for investigation. The majority of cases, however, arise from external sources, including competitors, individual consumers, local Better Business Bureaus, organized consumer groups, professional or trade associations, and law enforcement agencies. To encourage individuals and organizations to submit suggestions for investigation, the NAD does not reveal the source of a complaint or whether it resulted from the monitoring program or an external source, except when a competitor making a complaint agrees to an open challenge.

Procedure

The first step in an investigation is a letter addressed to the advertiser's chief executive officer specifying the claims to be substantiated. A request is made for substantiation of the questioned claims. In addition, the advertiser is asked to furnish examples of all current national advertising containing similar claims in print, radio, or television. The advertiser is asked to identify its advertising agency, and a copy of the initial inquiry is then also sent to the agency's chief executive officer. Normally, the first exchange of information is followed by a dialogue in which an advertising review specialist represents the NAD and an executive, house counsel, and specialist staff represent the advertiser. Agencies frequently contribute to the dialogue and sometimes handle the principal role. The advertiser and agency are occasionally represented by independent law firms, and independent consultants may also be brought in to advise either the NAD or the advertiser.

Since speed, informality, and modest cost are three chief benefits of a self-regulatory system, the NAD strongly requests advertisers, challengers, and complainants to strive for promptness in responding and to keep the number of participants to a minimum. Otherwise the investigations could become quite complex and drawn out.

After examination of all the facts, the NAD may determine that

1. The advertising claims have been substantiated and no further action is necessary, in which case the NAD will close its file and advise the advertiser and the complainant; or
2. The advertising claims have not been substantiated, in which case the NAD will request modification or discontinuance of the claims.

Sometimes the questioned advertising is discontinued during the inquiry; however, this is not in itself sufficient to close an investigation unless accompanied by the advertiser's formal commitment not to use the claims again without consulting the NAD or furnishing substantiation.

Public Report

Each month the NAD distributes a public report of cases resolved to contacts in the media, business, colleges, and government agencies. This report details the following for each case handled during the month:

1. Advertiser
2. Advertising agency
3. Product involved
4. Basis for questioning the advertising
5. Advertiser's response
6. NAD's decision
7. Brief statement by the advertiser if it so chooses

These reports are published in *Advertising Age* and other leading industry publications. This publication procedure places substantial pressure on advertisers and the NAD to be reasonable and responsible in the handling of complaints. (See the accompanying cases for typical NAD reports.)

National Advertising Division Case Reports (Advertising Substantiated)

NORTH AMERICAN SYSTEMS
Mr. Coffee Coffeemaker
Marketing Communications International, Inc.

Basis of Inquiry: Television advertising claimed: ". . . the only coffee-maker that precisely controls coffee brewing time and temperature for perfect coffee every time" in association with the slogan, "Mr. Coffee, America's perfect coffeemaker with a patent to prove it."

Advertiser's Response: The advertiser, prior to providing data, explained the slogan had been withdrawn. However, its patent was provided to prove the claim for precise control of coffee brewing time and temperature. The advertiser explained that the criteria had been set by the Coffee Brewing Institute (CBI) as the standard for "good coffee." NAD requested further information to support the exclusivity claim and to confirm that production models meet the specifications of the patent.

The advertiser provided an independent laboratory study indicating the typical Mr. Coffee model meets the "essentials of good brewing" as defined by CBI. Based on the combined criteria of brewing temperature, brewing time and holding temperature, the performance of Mr. Coffee came closer to the optimal than any of three leading competitive models tested. One competitive model, while demonstrating more precise control of brewing temperature in repeated uses, failed to achieve the optimal range set by CBI.

NAD felt that the term "precisely controls" can be understood to mean coming within an acceptable range of time and brewing temperature as defined by the CBI. On this basis, NAD concluded the claims were substantiated. (#2023)

FEDERAL EXPRESS CORPORATION
Package Delivery Service
Ally & Gargano, Inc. Advertising

Basis of Inquiry: Television advertising claimed: "Federal Express, when it absolutely, positively has to be there overnight." A disclaimer in the last frame of the commercial stated, "Areas served, delivery times, and liability subject to limitations in our Service Guide." This advertising was challenged by a customer who lost the chance to bid for a government contract because of late delivery by Federal Express. NAD asked for information on corporate standards and performance.

Advertiser's Response: The advertiser explained that it was committed to next-day deliveries throughout the continental U.S. with very few exceptions specified in the Service Guide. For the majority of areas the Guide indicates delivery by noon.

In respect to performance, the advertiser has set a standard of better than 99% delivery on a next-day basis, with 93.5% delivered by 12:00 noon.

NAD Case Reports (*Advertising Substantiated*) (*continued*)

Corporate quality control records in 1981/82 were supplied indicating these standards were surpassed in most months. Currently 99.8% of packages for next-day delivery are delivered prior to the close of the working day.

NAD agreed that the record demonstrated that overnight delivery was assured virtually 100% of the time. The situation which brought the ad to NAD's attention was a service failure of the type which occurs with no more than 0.2% of items.

NAD agreed the claims were substantiated. (#2002)

THE MAYTAG COMPANY
Washer
Leo Burnett Co., Inc.

Basis of Inquiry: Television and magazine advertising promoted the over-all economy of Maytag clothes washers and stated: "They're built to last longer and save money with fewer repairs."

Advertiser's Response: The advertiser explained it designs appliances with the minimum number of moving parts and manufactures the vast majority of components in its own plants. These practices ensure consistently high quality performance. To confirm this, it provided results of an extensive survey of washing machine owners, selected to be a nationally representative sample. The survey was conducted by an independent organization with no clues to the identity of the sponsor. Results indicated Maytag washers last longer before replacement and/or scrapping, perform longer before requiring repairs, require fewer service calls and impose lower annual costs for repairs and service than all other brands. The lower maintenance cost for Maytag washers was achieved both with and without the addition of service contract charges.

NAD concluded the claims were substantiated. (#2022)

National Advertising Division Case Reports (*Advertising Modified or Discontinued*)

DELTA AIR LINES, INC.
"Will Not Be Undersold/Unbeatable Fares" Promotion
BDA/BBDO, Inc.

Basis of Inquiry: A national campaign in newspapers was referred to NAD by a number of Better Business Bureaus. A typical ad contained the

NAD Case Reports (Advertising Modified or Discontinued) (continued)

headline: "Now there's no reason to settle for less! Delta will not be undersold!" A prominent explanatory statement ran adjacent to the headline: "We'll match the domestic fare on nonstop or single-plane jet service of any major airline on comparable Delta flights. Just show us any published jet fare on any other major airline and we'll sell you a Delta seat at the same price under the same travel restrictions, as long as the supply of discount fare seats lasts. That means you get the lowest jet fare you can buy."

NAD requested clarification of the terms used in the ads, details of how Delta agents handled queries and questioned whether reductions were incorporated into the general fare structure on all routes.

Advertiser's Response: The advertiser explained that Delta matched competitor discount fares for comparable service on any domestic U.S. route and to San Juan. To get these rates the customer was required to refer to the competitor's fares when making a booking. If a lower fare was not already recorded in the reservations computer, agents would accept a newspaper or similar ad as proof in order to meet their commitment. With telephone bookings, the fare was checked for comparability through an Atlanta office established for this purpose.

With this information, NAD concluded that Delta interpreted the conditions of its offer to match competitor's lower fares liberally and consistently and the claim was substantiated.

As the campaign progressed, the term "unbeatable fares" became more important; e.g. "Delta will not be undersold! Delta is unbeatable . . . Unbeatable fares . . . Unbeatable service!" For the most part, its use could be understood to reinforce the "matching" offer. However, NAD felt that when "unbeatable fares" began to dominate and the "matching" offer became secondary, a lack of clarity resulted; e.g. "New Delta Nonstops to 7 Cities. Same unbeatable Delta fares." This might cause a consumer to think that Delta's quoted fares were the lowest of any airline and discourage the comparison shopping necessary to take advantage of the "matching" offer.

While the advertiser disagreed, it pointed out that the campaign already had been discontinued with no plans to repeat it and that it would take NAD's concern into account should a similar campaign be used in the future. (#1997)

THE HERTZ CORPORATION
Rental Cars
Scali, McCabe, Sloves, Inc.

Basis of Inquiry: Advertising in the magazine of an international airline promoted the size and worldwide operations of Hertz together with claims for its Guaranteed Pricing Service and for "No charge for mileage . . . any car, anywhere, round-trip or one-way." A footnote explained that Guaranteed Pricing is available at all Hertz corporate and participating licensee locations

NAD Case Reports (*Advertising Modified or Discontinued*) (*continued*)

in the U.S. Similar claims were made in the *Official Airline Guide*. A vacationer who had read the ad in flight was surprised to be charged the equivalent of $1.50 per mile for use of a Hertz rental car in Nice, France, and complained to the National Advertising Review Board, which referred the matter to NAD.

Advertiser's Response: The advertiser explained that the standard unlimited mileage rate program is generally restricted to the U.S. where it is available at all corporate outlets and at many licensee outlets. It is not generally available in Europe and advertising of the program is therefore restricted to domestic media. A partial refund was authorized for the complainant recognizing that the terms of the rental contract may not have been clearly described by its agent in Nice.

In continuing discussions on the broader implications of the complaint the advertiser agreed that special care would be taken in the future to avoid combining, in one ad, claims for Hertz as a worldwide service with references to the unlimited mileage rate program. Wherever the program is advertised it will be explained that standard unlimited mileage rates are available in the U.S. at all corporate outlets and at many but not all licensee outlets. (#1958)

GERBER PRODUCTS COMPANY
Baby Food
J. Walter Thompson U.S.A., Inc./Chicago

Basis of Inquiry: Magazine advertising made the following claims: ". . . a baby requires a higher nutrient-to-calorie ratio than older children and adults. To ensure the necessary nutrient level Gerber specially formulates each jar of food so that every ingredient fulfills a specific purpose. Gerber foods provide more nutrients per calorie than many adult foods."

Advertiser's Response: The advertiser provided results of the research it had done, over a period of years, to learn the nutritional content and types of foods actually consumed by infants. This information provided the background for designing a range of prepared foods to meet specific nutrient needs.

In respect to the comparison with adult foods, the advertiser provided a computer print-out of analytical results for 13 major nutrients in the individual products of its line. In 31 instances it was feasible to make comparisons between Gerber products and adult foods for which detailed nutrient composition is available. Gerber products were shown richer in nutrients per calorie in the majority of these comparisons. In addition, it was plainly evident many more products in the line are richer in nutrients than the calorie-rich adult snacks that are commonly included in infants' diets.

However, NAD was concerned that the claims might be understood as applicable to every item in the line. The advertiser agreed future advertising would be qualified to indicate the claim has been confirmed in the majority of instances where detailed comparisons between Gerber products and table food are possible. (#2015)

Appeal to NARB

The NAD procedure settles most matters, including negotiations with the advertiser. In the event that the NAD and the advertiser are deadlocked in their discussions and the issue cannot be resolved, either party has the right to review by a National Advertising Review Board panel. Furthermore, at the time of the public report concluding an NAD investigation, the advertiser has ten days to file an appeal with the executive director of the NARB. And the challenger may request review of an NAD decision by filing a request within ten days of notification of the case report. This request is subject to approval by the chairman of the NARB.

Advertiser's Refusal to Participate in the Self-Regulatory Process

When an advertiser refuses to participate in self-regulation as requested by the NAD, or professes to cooperate but persistently continues a pattern of misleading or deceptive advertising, the NAD may make a finding that the advertiser is not amenable to the self-regulatory process. Accordingly, the NAD prepares a written statement of the facts for review by the chairman of the National Advertising Review Board. If the chairman agrees with the NAD finding, the NAD director files a complaint with the appropriate law enforcement agency.

The National Advertising Review Board (NARB)

The National Advertising Review Board (NARB) functions as an appeals board. As already mentioned, it goes into action when the NAD is unable to resolve a matter. The NARB membership (elected by the NARC board of directors) includes, in addition to a chairman, thirty advertiser members, ten advertising agency members, ten public or nonindustry members, and ten alternate advertising agency members.

When the NAD or an advertiser requests a review to break a deadlock, or when an appeal of an NAD-published decision by an advertiser or a complainant is granted, the NARB chairman appoints an adjudicative panel consisting of five members: three advertisers, one agency person, and one public member. The panel reviews the evidence and hears testimony from both parties in the dispute. Other witnesses may be called before the panel. Appeals are limited to the material submitted during the original hearing. If previously unavailable evidence relevant to the case comes to light after the NAD's decision, the NARB chairman may remand the case to the NAD for consideration.

On reaching a decision, the NARB panel issues a public report that details the basis for the review, the decision, and its rationale. The panel decision is binding on the NAD. If the NARB panel finds against the advertiser and the advertiser refuses to modify or discontinue the advertising in accordance with the panel decision, the NARB refers the matter to the appropriate governmental authority, duly noting the noncompliance by the advertiser. Even though the NAD and the NARB have no legal power, since the inception of the self-regulatory process in 1971, no advertiser who has participated in the complete process of an NAD investigation and an NARB appeal has refused to abide by the panel decision. Exhibit 19-2 shows the step-by-step self-regulatory procedures of the NAD and NARB.

By June 15, 1984, the NAD had processed a total of 1,873 complaints, including 175 challenges to advertising directed to children. Of this total, 869 cases (46 percent) were dismissed based on adequate substantiation of claims by advertisers. An additional 988 cases (53 percent) were dismissed following either modification or discontinuance of the questionable advertisement by the advertiser. One case was suspended pending litigation. Just 15 cases (1 percent) had been referred to the NARB for adjudication. In the thirteen-year history of the NAD ranging from July 1971 to June 1984, thirty-eight appeals had been heard by the NARB, of which twenty-six NAD decisions were upheld, eight reversed or modified, and four dismissed without prejudice. Exhibit 19-3 summarizes the NAD's regulation history for those years.

The American Advertising Federation

The American Advertising Federation is a national organization concerned with the creation and maintenance of high standards of advertising practice. Among other things, the AAF seeks to "reflect and represent industry views and concerns on public issues affecting advertising, and to prevent over-regulation of advertising."[20] Its membership is drawn from the ranks of advertisers, advertising agencies, media, advertising clubs, and other advertising service companies. As mentioned earlier, it participates in the National Advertising Review Council and, in addition, has joined with the Council of Better Business Bureaus to develop and disseminate the code of ethics for advertising practice outlined in Exhibit 19-4.

The American Association of Advertising Agencies (AAAA)

The American Association of Advertising Agencies (AAAA), consisting of over four hundred advertising agencies, represents the advertising agency business in dealings with the federal government on matters involving proposed regulation, legislation, and the setting of national policy affecting the industry. The AAAA keeps the agency business, the advertisers, and the public informed of its lobbying activities through its "Washington News-

EXHIBIT 19-2 Advertising Self-Regulatory Procedures, Step-by-Step

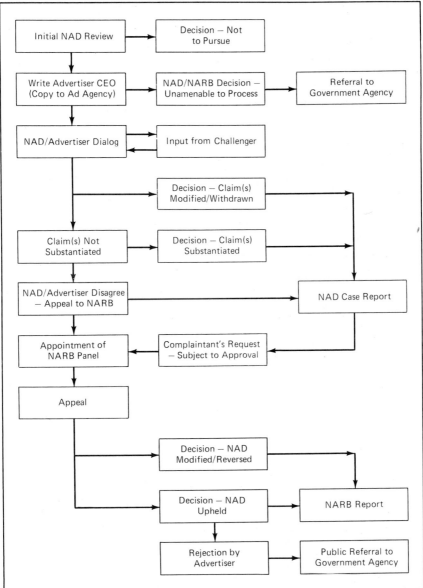

Courtesy National Advertising Division, Council of Better Business Bureaus, Inc.

EXHIBIT 19-3   NAD Case Status Report: July 1971–June 1984

SOURCES OF COMPLAINTS:

	Number	Percent
NAD monitoring program	682	36
Competitors' challenges	457	24
Referrals from local BBSs	295	16
Consumer complaints	239	13
Additional sources	200	11
Total	1,873	100

NARB DECISIONS:

NAD decisions upheld	26
NAD decisions reversed or modified	8
Dismissed without prejudice	4
Total cases handled by NARB	38

DISPOSITION OF CASES:

	Number	Percent
Claims modified or discontinued	988	53
Claims substantiated	869	46
Referred to NARB	15	1
Suspended pending resolution of FTC litigation	1	—
Total	1,873	100

SOURCES OF NARB APPEALS:

Referrals by advertiser/NAD	15
Objections by complainant after publication	23
Total	38

Source: National Advertising Division Case Status Report, June 15, 1984.

EXHIBIT 19-4   Advertising Code of Ethics

THE ADVERTISING PRINCIPLES
OF AMERICAN BUSINESS*

TRUTH

Advertising shall tell the truth, and shall reveal significant facts, the omission of which would mislead the public.

SUBSTANTIATION

Advertising claims shall be substantiated by evidence in possession of the advertiser and advertising agency, prior to making such claims.

COMPARISONS

Advertising shall refrain from making false, misleading, or unsubstantiated statements or claims about a competitor or his products or services.

BAIT ADVERTISING

Advertising shall not offer products or services for sale unless such offer constitutes a bona fide effort to sell the advertised products or services and is not a device to switch consumers to other goods or services, usually higher priced.

GUARANTEES AND WARRANTIES

Advertising of guarantees and warranties shall be explicit, with sufficient information to apprise consumers of their principal terms and limitations or, when space or time restrictions preclude such disclosures, the advertisement should clearly reveal where the full text of the guarantee or warranty can be examined before purchase.

PRICE CLAIMS

Advertising shall avoid price claims which are false or misleading, or savings claims which do not offer provable savings.

TESTIMONIALS

Advertising containing testimonials shall be limited to those of competent witnesses who are reflecting a real and honest opinion or experience.

TASTE AND DECENCY

Advertising shall be free of statements, illustrations or implications which are offensive to good taste or public decency.

*Adopted by the American Advertising Federation Board of Directors, March 2, 1984, San Antonio, Texas.

Courtesy American Advertising Federation, Washington, D.C.

letter," which features issues pertaining to federal legislation and regulation and the possible effects of such actions on advertising. The AAAA is also a sponsor of the National Advertising Review Council.

The objectives of the AAAA are

1. To promote and further the interests of advertising agencies by increasing their usefulness to advertisers, to media and to the public.
2. To collect and disseminate information and ideas affecting advertising and advertising agencies among members of the Association and others interested.
3. To cooperate with governmental, consumer and other bodies on matters affecting advertising.
4. To aid in the continued improvement in the efficiency and value of advertising by fostering and stimulating scientific research and investigation in connection with advertising.
5. To advocate informative and constructive appeals in advertising copy and, in this connection, to maintain and safeguard honesty, fairness and good taste.
6. To advise with and maintain friendly relations with associations representing advertisers, media, suppliers and consumers and with other associations and industries concerned with or related to advertising.
7. To promote and foster the continued recognition of the social responsibilities of advertising and of advertising agencies; to further efforts to lower the costs of distribution; and to cooperate with organizations marshalling advertising forces on behalf of government and patriotic activities.
8. To promote friendly relations among all advertising agencies and seek such cooperation as will promote the highest standards of service.[21]

Serving as an association of advertising agencies dedicated to the fulfillment of obligations to advertisers, advertising media, and the public, the 4A's has adopted the Standards of Practice presented in Exhibit 19-5 for its membership.[22]

The Association of National Advertisers (ANA)

The Association of National Advertisers (ANA), also an NARC sponsor, consists of members drawn from over four hundred large national corporations and is concerned with the maintenance of responsible advertising practices by advertisers. The ANA collaborates with the American Association of Advertising Agencies to sponsor the ANA–AAAA Interchange of Opinion on Objectionable Advertising. A joint ANA–AAAA Committee of the Board of Improvement of Advertising Content reviews complaints concerning advertising brought to its attention by advertising agencies. If the committee

**EXHIBIT 19-5   Standards of Practice—American Association
of Advertising Agencies**

WE HOLD THAT a responsibility of advertising agencies is to be a constructive force in business.

WE FURTHER HOLD THAT, to discharge this responsibility, advertising agencies must recognize an obligation, not only to their clients, but to the public, the media they employ and to each other.

WE FINALLY HOLD THAT the responsibility will best be discharged if all agencies observe a common set of standards of practice.

To this end, the American Association of Advertising Agencies has adopted the following Standards of Practice as being in the best interests of the public, the advertisers, the media owners and the agencies themselves.

These standards are voluntary. They are intended to serve as a guide to the kind of agency conduct which experience has shown to be wise, foresighted and constructive.

It is recognized that advertising is a business and as such must operate within the framework of competition. It is further recognized that keen and vigorous competition, honestly conducted, is necessary to the growth and health of American business generally, of which advertising is a part.

However, *unfair* competitive practices in the advertising agency business lead to financial waste, dilution of service, diversion of manpower and loss of prestige. Unfair practices tend to weaken public confidence both in advertisements and in the institution of advertising.

1. *Creative Code*

   We the members of the American Association of Advertising Agencies, in addition to supporting and obeying the laws and legal regulations pertaining to advertising, undertake to extend and broaden the application of high ethical standards. Specifically, we will not knowingly produce advertising which contains:

   a. False or misleading statements or exaggerations, visual or verbal.
   b. Testimonials which do not reflect the real choice of a competent witness.
   c. Price claims which are misleading.
   d. Comparisons which unfairly disparage a competitive product or service.
   e. Claims insufficiently supported, or which distort the true meaning of practicable application of statements made by professional or scientific authority.
   f. Statements, suggestions or pictures offensive to public decency.

   We recognize that there are areas which are subject to honestly different interpretations and judgment. Taste is subjective and may even vary from time to time as well as from individual to individual. Frequency of seeing or hearing advertising messages will necessarily vary greatly from person to person.

   However, we agree not to recommend to an advertiser and to discourage the use of advertising which is in poor or questionable taste or which is deliberately irritating through content, presentation or excessive repetition.

**EXHIBIT 19–5 Standards of Practice—American Association
of Advertising Agencies** (*continued*)

Clear and willful violations of this Code shall be referred to the Board of
Directors of the American Association of Advertising Agencies for appropri-
ate action, including possible annulment of membership as provided by
Article IV, Section 5, of the Constitution and By-Laws.

2. *Contracts*
   a. The advertising agency should where feasible enter into written contracts
      with media in placing advertising. When entered into, the agency should
      conform to its agreements with media. Failure to do so may result in
      loss of standing or litigation, either on the contract or for violations of
      the Clayton or Federal Trade Commission Acts.
   b. The advertising agency should not knowingly fail to fulfill all lawful con-
      tractual commitments with media.

3. *Offering Credit Extension*
   It is unsound and uneconomic to offer extension of credit or banking service
   as an inducement in solicitation.

4. *Unfair Tactics*
   The advertising agency should compete on merit and not by depreciating
   a competitor or his work directly or inferentially or by circulating harmful
   rumors about him, or by making unwarranted claims of scientific skill in
   judging or prejudging advertising copy, or by seeking to obtain an account
   by hiring a key employee away from the agency in charge in violation of
   the agency's employment agreements.

finds a complaint to be valid, it will place pressure on the advertiser as
well as the agency to cease use of the objectionable advertising. Should
the agency and advertiser refuse to cooperate, the ANA and AAAA may
take steps to expel the violator or violators.

The National Council
for Consumer Affairs

In 1971 President Nixon established the Office of Consumer Affairs
to coordinate the activities of a large number of government agencies involved in consumer matters. As part of this action, the president also created
the National Council for Consumer Affairs as a mechanism for providing
the White House with advice and up-to-date information pertaining to consumer issues. A major objective of the council has been to facilitate the
voluntary creation of industry programs designed to resolve consumer problems. The organization's Sub-Council on Advertising and Promotion has

issued a "Report on Corporate Policies and Procedures on Advertising and Promotion" in which it encourages corporations to exercise self-initiative in establishing internal policies to ensure high standards for advertising and promotional practices.

Advertising Media

Along with advertisers and the creators of advertisements, the media jointly share the responsibility for controlling advertising and protecting the public from false or deceptive practices. Both the print and the broadcast media have exercised their prerogative to reject advertisements that they believe contain false and misleading claims as well as to exclude advertisements for those products they consider to be in poor taste. Some magazines, such as *Good Housekeeping*, actually guarantee the accuracy of advertising claims contained in their publications. Other magazines require mail-order advertisers to provide suitable backup support to advertising claims through money-back guarantees. Many individual media have established their own internal advertising codes. Entire classes of media have adopted codes of good practice as well.

For many years the radio and television industry engaged in self-regulation through the National Association of Broadcasters (NAB), the industry's leading trade group with its 660 television and 4,500 radio station members. This organization established a series of guidelines, called "The Radio Code" and "The Television Code," which specified a variety of standards for the industry, including standards related to advertising. The NAB issued a Seal of Approval to each station subscribing to the NAB Code of Good Practice. However, due to an antitrust suit brought by the U.S. Department of Justice, the NAB television and radio codes have been dissolved since 1982. Therefore the NAB can neither review commercials, guidelines, or policies nor interpret, comment, or offer opinions on the codes' advertising standards. Furthermore, the NAB can no longer disseminate materials pertaining to code authority policies. Until this matter is resolved, the NAB's role in monitoring advertising is limited. Beyond that, in many cases, local broadcasters' individual standards—dictated by public opinion and marketplace competition—are more stringent than either the NAB codes or the FCC guidelines.

Over the years there has been a strong attempt by the advertising industry to regulate itself. Advertisers, advertising agencies, industry associations, and the media have established guidelines for good conduct, and despite their lack of legal power, they have brought pressure to bear on actual and potential violators of sound advertising practice. Self-regulation should be viewed as a complement rather than a substitute for government regulation.[23] Self-regulation alone will not correct abuses, but it will go a long way toward making advertisers aware of the need for advertising that is defensible on legal, ethical, and moral grounds.

REGULATION OF COMPARATIVE ADVERTISING

One particular form of advertising has drawn considerable attention in recent years: *comparative advertising*, where the advertiser makes direct or indirect reference to a competitor or competitors (e.g., Pepsi vs. Coke, Ford vs. Chevrolet, Burger King vs. McDonald's and Wendy's, Emery Worldwide vs. Federal Express). There is little doubt that "when used truthfully and fairly, comparative advertising can provide the consumer with needed and useful information."[24] By its very nature, however, comparative advertising "can distort facts and, by implication, convey to the consumer information that misrepresents the truth."[25] Several groups, such as the American Association of Advertising Agencies, Council of Better Business Bureaus, and National Association of Broadcasters, recognizing that extreme caution is necessary, have issued policy statements and guidelines governing comparative advertising. The 4A's guidelines statement is a good example of the attempt to self-regulate in this area.

GUIDELINES FOR COMPARATIVE ADVERTISING (AAAA)

1. The intent and connotation of the ad should be to inform and never to discredit or unfairly attack competitors, competing products or services.
2. When a competitive product is named, it should be one that exists in the marketplace as significant competition.
3. The competition should be fairly and properly identified but never in a manner or tone of voice that degrades the competitive product or service.
4. The advertising should compare related or similar properties or ingredients of the product dimension to dimension, feature to feature.
5. The identification should be for honest comparison purposes and not simply to upgrade by association.
6. If a competitive test is conducted it should be done by an objective testing source, preferably an independent one, so that there will be no doubt as to the veracity of the test.
7. In all cases the test should be supportive of all claims made in the advertising that are based on the test.
8. The advertising should never use partial results or stress insignificant differences to cause the consumer to draw an improper conclusion.
9. The property being compared should be significant in terms of value or usefulness of the product to the consumer.
10. Comparatives delivered through the use of testimonials should not imply that the testimonial is more than one individual's thought unless that individual represents a sample of the majority viewpoint.[26]

Among the several ways to resolve a comparative advertising dispute (e.g., taking it to the NAD or the FTC) is to use the Lanham-Trademark Act. In 1976 the Lanham act was used to rule in the American Home Products versus Johnson & Johnson case, paving the way for it to be used in other such disputes. Using Section 43(a) of the act, the injured competitor does not have to prove actual damage resulting from the comparative advertising, only a "reasonable" likelihood that such damage will occur. With the popularity of comparative advertising, "a growing body of law requires advertisers to support what they say about their own products and the products of competitors."[27]

SUMMARY

Many promotional activities require regulation in the interests of consumers and competitors. We have seen that several means exist—legislative, voluntary, and combinations of the two—to achieve this regulation. There are several federal laws that control promotional activities, and these laws are enforced by separate agencies, primarily the Federal Trade Commission, the Federal Food and Drug Administration, and the Federal Communications Commission, each with different enforcement responsibilities and remedies available to it. Besides federal regulation, there is a wide range of state and local legislation affecting promotion.

Recognizing its obligation to police itself, as well as a desire to forestall government regulation, industry, particularly the advertising industry, has for many years engaged in self-regulatory activities. Several industry organizations such as the National Advertising Review Council and its affiliated National Advertising Division and National Advertising Review Board, the American Advertising Federation, the American Association of Advertising Agencies, and the Association of National Advertisers, not to mention the advertising media, have generally been effective in dealing with promotional abuses and have fostered the notion of industry's responsibility to regulate itself in the best interests of all parties involved with promotional activities.

Advertising and promotion are vital parts of the free-enterprise system, but protection of the public interest generates the need for regulation of the kind we have discussed in this chapter. Very much related to the legal framework of promotion is the social responsibility of marketers, particularly that dealing with promotion. We will now consider the social aspects of promotion.

REVIEW AND DISCUSSION QUESTIONS

1. To what extent do you believe advertising and promotion should be regulated?

2. Legal restraints seem to regulate advertising considerably more than personal selling, sales promotion, or publicity. Why? Explain your reasons.

3. What are the similarities and differences between federal and state laws in regulating promotional activities?

4. Identify any major federal law and explain its purpose, its methods of dealing with promotional activities, and its effectiveness.

5. Suppose you were asked to establish some criteria for what constitutes false and misleading advertising. What would your list look like?

6. Generally speaking, are the laws governing promotional abuses effective? Why or why not?

7. Explain what is meant by corrective advertising. Is it an effective deterrent to deceptive advertising? State your reasons.

8. Do you think that the Fair Packaging and Labeling Act does an effective job in regulating packaging? Explain.

9. How effective is industry self-regulation?

10. Describe the relationships that exist among the following: (a) Council of Better Business Bureaus, (b) National Advertising Review Council, (c) National Advertising Division, (d) National Advertising Review Board, and (e) Children's Advertising Review Unit.

11. Describe the procedure followed in an NAD investigation of a complaint about advertising.

12. Explain the role of the 4A's in regulating advertising.

13. How do the media control advertising?

14. Discuss the philosophy underlying comparative advertising.

15. What are the advantages and limitations of comparative advertising from the advertiser's viewpoint? From the consumer's viewpoint?

16. Name what you consider to be three deceptive promotional practices (e.g., misleading advertising, deceptive packaging). Be specific as to the reasons why you consider the practices deceptive.

17. Devise some guidelines for an advertiser to follow to ensure truthful nondeceptive advertising (i.e., a "code of practice" for good advertising).

NOTES

1. See Dorothy Cohen, "Advertising and the First Amendment," *Journal of Marketing*, July 1978, pp. 59–68; and Gerald J. Thain, *Development of the "Commercial Speech" Doctrine by the Supreme Court—Its Implications for the Regulation of Advertising by the Federal Trade Commission*, Paper No. 10 (Urbana: University of Illinois, July 1981).

2. Dorothy Cohen, "Unfairness in Advertising Revisited," *Journal of Marketing*, Winter 1982, p. 73.

3. For an excellent discussion of the FTC advertising substantiation program, as well as a description of a study designed to measure what changes occurred in print advertisements as a result of the FTC program, see John S. Healey and Harold H. Kassarjian, "Advertising Substantiation and Advertiser Response: A Content Analysis of Magazine Advertisements," *Journal of Marketing*, Winter 1983, pp. 107–17.

4. FTC, *Annual Report*, 1979, p. 5.

5. *AAF Washington Report*, No. 84-1 (Washington, D.C.: American Advertising Federation, January 1984), p. 2.

6. Patricia P. Bailey and George W. Douglas, "Does the New FTC Deception Policy Fill the Bill?" *Advertising Age*, February 13, 1984, pp. M27–M28.

7. FTC, *Annual Report*, 1979, p. 38.

8. Ibid., p. 39.

9. For a more-detailed treatment of the background, theory, and application of corrective advertising, see Debra L. Scammon and Richard J. Semenik, "Corrective Advertising: Evolution of the Legal Theory and Application of the Remedy," *Journal of Advertising*, 11, No. 1 (1982), 10–20.

10. Warner-Lambert vs. Federal Trade Commission, CCH #61, 563 (CA-D.C., August 1977) and CCH #61 646 (CA-D.C., September 1977).

11. Jacob Jacoby, Margaret C. Nelson, and Wayne D. Hoyer, "Corrective Advertising and Affirmative Disclosure Statements: Their Potential for Confusing and Misleading the Consumer," *Journal of Marketing*, Winter 1982, pp. 61–72. This article also contains a comprehensive list of references dealing with the subject of corrective advertising. The reader is also directed to the following excellent article on corrective advertising: William L. Wilkie, Dennis L. McNeill, and Michael B. Mazis, "Marketing's 'Scarlet Letter': The Theory and Practice of Corrective Advertising," *Journal of Marketing*, Spring 1984, pp. 11–31.

12. Gary M. Armstrong, George R. Franke, and Frederick A. Russ, "The Effects of Corrective Advertising on Company Image," *Journal of Advertising*, 11, No. 4 (1982), 42.

13. Copyright, 1959, by Printers' Ink Publishing Corporation.

14. State of California, *Business and Professional Code*, Section 17200.

15. Leroy Richie and Harvey I. Saferstein, "Private Actions for Consumer Injury under State Law—The Role of the Federal Trade Commission," in *FTC Trade Regulation: Advertising, Rulemaking, and New Consumer Protection*, ed. Christopher Smith and Christian S. White (New York: Practicing Law Institute, 1979), p. 429.

16. Council of Better Business Bureaus, *Annual Report*, 1980, p. 2.

17. Priscilla A. LaBarbera, "The Diffusion of Trade Association Advertising Self-Regulation," *Journal of Marketing*, Winter 1983, p. 58.

18. Charles W. Yost, National Advertising Review Board, *Annual Report*, 1972, p. 2.

19. This section is excerpted, by permission, from the *NAD Guide for Advertisers and Advertising Agencies*. © December, 1983 by the Council of Better Business Bureaus, Inc.

20. American Advertising Federation, *A Key Role in Advertising Progress*, Annual Report, 1981–1982 (Washington, D.C.: American Advertising Federation, June 1982), p. 1.

21. *Roster and Organization* (New York: American Association of Advertising Agencies, 1978), p. 9.

22. Ibid., p. 10.

23. LaBarbera, "Diffusion of Trade Association," p. 65.

24. *Policy Statement and Guidelines for Comparative Advertising* (New York: American Association of Advertising Agencies, 1974), p. 1.

25. Ibid.

26. Ibid.

27. Debra L. Scammon and Blake Wade, "Lanham Act Provides Quick Relief from Comparative Ads," *Marketing News*, July 22, 1983, p. 8.

20

Social Aspects of Promotion

Promotion is the most visible of all the business disciplines and is an important influence on our society. Billions of dollars are spent annually on promotion-related activities alone. However, the significance of promotion goes well beyond its economic aspects. Its effects range from providing information to help consumers make intelligent buying decisions to changing attitudes toward cigarette smoking, to determining the style of dress for fashion-conscious women, to creating job opportunities by fostering business growth. These are among the results most observers view as positive, socially beneficial aspects of promotion. Yet there is persistent criticism of promotion for its perceived negative influences on society: the creation and fostering of materialistic values, the pressure to buy unneeded goods, the deception in promotional presentation to fool unsophisticated buyers, and so on. This major activity undoubtedly stirs emotions and controversies. Let us now look at several of the key social aspects of promotion.

PROMOTION AND SOCIAL RESPONSIBILITY

Like most of society's activities, promotion has the opportunity to contribute to the social well-being or to abuse it by the actions of self-centered individuals and unscrupulous con artists. Here is the critical philosophical question for the marketing profession: How can marketers in the 1980s and beyond make sure that the common good and corporate success turn out to be the same thing rather than, as some see it, at odds with each other? Three major schools of thought set forth the spectrum of possibilities marketers can consider as they contemplate the matter of social responsibility.

Letter of the Law

The first school of thought maintains that the law defines the marketer's responsibility to society. The marketer is free to pursue the goals of the firm, abiding by the strict letter of the law. An occasional legal entanglement is the price to be paid for testing the true position of the boundary.

Spirit of the Law

The second school of thought also believes that the law should determine the limits of business' social responsibility, but its adherents insist on a broader interpretation of the legal holdings. They would feel bound by the intent of the law and the interpretations, if any, by courts and enforcing agencies. This is a less contentious position than the one noted above, but its operating philosophy still rests on a legalistic premise.

Moral Imperative

The third school of thought contends that a solely legal perspective is insufficient to determine the marketer's societal conduct. Its adherents argue that business's social responsibility must have moral and ethical dimensions as well as legal ones. The law is a laggard in codifying and interpreting the views of society on any particular issue. It is a political process and, as a result, is subject to pressures from many directions, which produces delays and renders final outcomes as compromise solutions. This group believes that marketers—all businesspeople—must weigh and consider their actions for their impact on society as well as on the value for the firm. In addition, they maintain that marketers must also address the specific current concerns of society. If this results in somewhat lower performance expectations for the firm, it is an acceptable and necessary trade-off.

With these broad categories as a foundation, the rest of this chapter will discuss five major social issues challenging marketers to create a balance between the interests of the firm and the interests of society. We will consider the effects of promotion on the consumer, the economic activity, the environment, the self-concept of women, and the sensibilities of children. We will conclude with a look at two emerging and insistent social questions: (1) promotion and personal privacy and (2) the impact that the growth of telecommunications has on promotion and society. None of these issues—present or future—lend themselves to quick, convenient, or comfortable answers. They demand that the marketer or businessperson make difficult judgments in the face of competing values. These issues are raised to challenge you to develop a greater awareness of and sensitivity to marketing's social responsibilities.

PROMOTION AND THE CONSUMER:
SOME CRITICISMS

Critics of marketing raise questions about what one may call the unwanted effects of aggressive promotional activity. Webster[1] has summarized these effects:

1. Marketing communications make people buy things they do not need.
2. Marketing communications have created materialistic values in our society that are not sufficient as goals for national policy and personal life style.
3. Marketing communications are often deceptive and misleading, especially for disadvantaged consumers.
4. Marketing communications are often annoying and in poor taste.
5. Marketing communications often provide inadequate information to assist the consumer in making buying decisions about complex products.[2]

Let us now look at these criticisms to see them as a reflection of our central concerns—the power of promotion to shape society's values and to direct its actions.

Marketing Communications Make
People Buy Things They Do Not Need

Many critics believe that marketing communications make people buy things they do not need. Galbraith, in *The Affluent Society*, expressed it this way:

> The fact that wants can be synthesized by advertising, catalyzed by salesmanship, and shaped by the discrete manipulations of the persuaders shows

that they are not very urgent. A man who is hungry need never be told of his need for food. If he is inspired by his appetite, he is immune to the influence of Messrs. Batten, Barton, Durstine & Osborn. The latter are effective only with those who are so far removed from physical want that they do not already know what they want. In this state alone men are open to persuasion.[3]

Critics refer to the purchase of designer jeans, pet rocks, and the fancy trim and plush seats in our automobiles to show that advertisers influence people to make frivolous purchases.

Toynbee carries this perspective further, offering distinctions between needs, genuine wants, and unwanted demand:

Needs—the minimum material requirements of life.

Genuine wants—wants that we become aware of spontaneously, without having to be told by Madison Avenue that we want something that we should never have thought of wanting if we had been left in peace to find out our wants for ourselves.

Unwanted demand—demand created by advertising above and beyond genuine wants.[4]

Implicit in these criticisms is a value judgment about the nature of consumer wants that says that certain purchases are less desirable or less necessary than others. One wants to ask, in response, Who should make this value judgment and on what basis? Most professional marketers will argue that the ultimate arbiter is the individual consumer using whatever criteria he or she deems appropriate.

Toynbee argues that genuine wants arise spontaneously from the consumer without external stimulus. One wants to ask here, How will consumers find out what their options are if not from some external source?

The monolithic position that says promotion is a powerful force in shaping consumer needs and wants overlooks the reality that consumers reject as well as accept products. For every phenomenon like Rubik's Cube or Cabbage Patch Kids, there are ten puzzles, dolls, or board games that only gathered cobwebs on retailers' shelves.

Marketing Communications Create Materialistic Values

The criticism that marketing communications create materialistic values relates to the previous one except that the first reflects a concern about the individual consumer and this one focuses on the impact on society as a whole. Webster pinpoints the key elements of this issue:

> There can be little debate over whether marketing communication relies heavily upon materialistic values; of course it does, as does virtually all marketing activity. Disagreement comes when the direction of causation is considered: does marketing communication create materialism or does it simply appeal to already existing materialistic values in order to sell goods and services? Further disagreement comes when consideration is given to whether materialism is a legitimate value for society and for the individuals.[5]

On the question of whether marketing communications create or reflect materialistic values, the conclusions of scholars in various disciplines—history, economics, and psychology—articulate the distinction between short-term and long-term effects. In the short term, promotion is a reflection of society's values, including, in the United States, the acquisition of more and better goods and services. Over the long run, the materialistic appeals of marketing communications serve to reinforce these values. We accept this point of view while recognizing that the precise credit or blame accruing to the marketer for the values of the American people can only be a matter of conjecture.

Another question relates to the acceptability of materialism as a value for society and the individual. In many ways, this issue reaches to the core of the nation's political and economic philosophy that large policy decisions will be matters the voters will address, in both the polling booth and the marketplace.

Among many observations, these two seem particularly germane:

> First, it is clear that materialistic values are being seriously questioned as the primary goal and criterion of social progress. United States economic and social policy has been guided almost exclusively by Gross National Product and National Income as indicators of social and economic progress. A search for indicators better able to express the multidimensional nature of the quality of human life is actively underway;

> Second, the issue is not absolute but relative. The question is not materialism versus something else but how much materialism. More is not always better but how much is enough? These are questions that must be carefully weighed and answered by each individual before they can be expressed in meaningful fashion through political and buying action. A resolution of the debate may occur on pragmatic rather than philosophical grounds as environmental deterioration from production and consumption forces a halt to the growth of materialism.[6]

Here are all the ingredients of a "chicken and egg" issue. Marketers have the choice of playing leader or follower. The decision, as with most social issues, should not rest primarily on legalistic grounds; it should rest on the individual marketer's personal formula for balancing society's well-being against the interests of the marketer's firm.

Marketing Communications Are
Often Deceptive, Especially
for Disadvantaged Consumers

Deception is a particularly damaging form of market conduct. It deprives consumers of their expected satisfaction from a purchase, it transfers sales and profits from fair-dealing competitors to unethical practitioners, and it casts a shadow of doubt and suspicion over all business activities. As a result, the issue of deception in the marketplace—the act of convincing someone to buy or sell through falsehood and misrepresentation—has been of concern since the earliest days of commercial activity. A variety of laws and regulations governing labeling, weights and measures, composition of products, and the like, seek to eliminate or at least minimize this problem. Chapter 19 set forth the legal remedies from the perspective of current legislation and regulation as well as the appropriateness and effectiveness of enforcement. As we said in the introduction to that chapter, the marketer must decide whether a solely legal perspective is sufficient to guide the behavior of the business executive and the organization in dealing with social issues.

The *issue of deception in marketing communications has five dimensions*: the intent of the communicator, the capacity of the message to deceive, the capacity of the person to be deceived, the fact of a person's being deceived, and the standard to determine the extent of deception. All of these elements contain a high degree of subjective judgment. This condition is further clouded by the recognition that nearly all marketing communications have as their primary intent the persuasion of prospective customers to take a buying action; as a result, it is often unclear, in a given situation, where the boundary line between persuasion and deception actually lies.

A key consideration in this discussion of deception is the question, Deceptive to whom? Recipients of messages vary in their ability to draw correct conclusions and inferences from communications because of differences in age, experience, or education. Should we classify an advertisement aimed at well-educated adults as deceptive because it is misleading to children? Conversely, should a message intended for an audience of preteens be considered unacceptable because adults understand its persuasive content?

Clearly, the potential for deception exists in promotion because the marketer seeks to persuade potential customers to take buying actions. The marketer and society must make the judgment, fully cognizant of the target audience of the message. Even then, there may be a fairly wide gray area. Webster summarizes many of the issues with the following series of questions:

> Should a manufacturer of room air conditioners be required to provide evidence in support of its advertising claim that its product provides the clean freshness of clear cool mountain air?

Is an advertisement that describes a hair coloring product as "permanent" deceptive because although it does not wash out, it will not change the color of hair as it grows and must be used intermittently as new "roots" appear?

Should automobile companies be required to include in their advertising comparisons of their product's safety performance with that of competitors' products?

Should the entertaining features of advertising be eliminated because these do not contribute to the consumer's information about the product?

Should different standards be applied to television advertising to be run at 7:00 P.M. and that to be shown at midnight?

All cigarette advertising must prominently show the "health warning" on the side of the package. Should similar warnings be included in advertising for alcoholic beverages? Should advertising for proprietary drugs, such as aspirin, tranquilizers, and sleeping aids, be required to contain warnings against the dangers of excessive dosage?[7]

In our judgment, the marketing professional has a responsibility to be as scrupulous in the avoidance of deceptive practices in marketing communications as is humanly possible. Such a commitment serves many ends: the enhancement of consumer satisfaction through the receipt of "full and fair value"; expansion of society's well-being by the active pursuit of a value set that fosters fair dealings. There is also an enrichment of the company's reputation through recognition of its ethical behavior. The marketing profession and businesspeople in general gain from a greater recognition of their total contribution to society's development and well-being.

Marketing Communications Are Often Annoying and in Poor Taste

The enduring criticism that marketing communications are often annoying and in poor taste is felt with the same force among large segments of the population today as it was fifteen or twenty years ago.

Bauer and Greyser, in their study *Advertising in America: The Consumer View*, provide the foundation for our assessment of this criticism.[8] They sought to uncover the reasons why people liked or disliked advertising by asking the respondents to evaluate the ads they experienced. Of the approximately nine thousand advertisements rated, 23 percent were judged to be "annoying" and 5 percent were considered "offensive." The balance of the ads reviewed received favorable ratings. Advertisements considered annoying were so judged for the following reasons: intrusive (excessively loud, interruptive, and highly repetitive), informational failure through exaggeration and untruthfulness, and insult to one's intelligence (being talked down to and the use of unreal situations). Ads considered offensive or in bad taste received complaints primarily of a moralistic nature, such as advertising feminine hygiene products, cigarettes, and alcoholic beverages, using nude and scantily clad models, and portraying couples in intimate situations, as well as depicting violence and crime in ads.

We still hear these criticisms, whether in the classroom, on the street, or in editorial sections of the media. Unfortunately, no one has updated this research on a similar scale to assess more fully the current public view. It is not surprising, given the number of advertising practitioners, and their varying backgrounds, experiences, and value sets, that some percentage of their output would be annoying and offensive. We could argue that it would be better for society if that number came closer to zero percent. At the same time, on a spectrum, advertising is closer to art than to science, and we may have to accept that some results of the creative process will press too hard on some people's sensitivities. Finally, as we examine these reactions, it is important to note that social values eventually change and that things deemed annoying, inappropriate, or offensive at one time may seem less so at another.

Marketing Communications Often Provide Inadequate Information

The criticism that marketing communications often provide inadequate information emerges from two fundamental perspectives of the current marketplace and the consumer choice process: (1) consumers encounter a vast array of increasingly complex products and services from which to choose; and (2) given this market environment, consumers will be able to make the best choices for their needs if complete and accurate information is readily available to them. To deal with the choice problem, the consumer needs help in three ways. First, the consumer needs information on availability—specifically, products, brands, outlets, prices, etc. Second, the consumer needs detailed information with which to evaluate alternatives to discover the strengths and weaknesses of each choice. Third, the potential customer needs to be able to assess the accuracy and credibility of the source of the information.

We would agree in general terms that this is an appropriate description of both the market environment and the consumer's information needs. Consumer choice, particularly in complex decisions, is an evolving process that moves from need to general awareness of product availability, through the determination of buying criteria to the assessment of detailed information on individual product offerings. Since as marketers we are unable to know the specific information required by the consumer at any given point, we must sometimes rely on the consumer to seek out the information that he or she deems necessary. And it is this very condition that has led to the development of the several different forms of marketing communications. None of this is to deny the marketer's responsibility for having available in clear and understandable language, as well as in suitable form, the significant product or service information consumers must have for safe and intelligent decisions.

The question of information accuracy has already been addressed. We need only recall the importance of the receiver in interpreting and understanding a message to realize that it is difficult to evaluate the truthfulness and accuracy of specific messages or information in absolute terms. We can only deal with it in terms of probabilities or likelihoods of particular people understanding the message or being misled. In addition, there is evidence that most consumers view marketing communications with a healthy degree of caution that we would call appropriate, given the persuasive intent of the communications and the natural bias of the seller.

PROMOTION AND ECONOMIC ACTIVITY

Traditionally, the strongest arguments for the positive influence of promotion on society are its economic effects. Neil Borden's classic work, *The Economic Effects of Advertising*, is the cornerstone of these arguments.[9] Conversely, some of the most outspoken critics have raised the same issues on the negative side. Two areas of economic consideration are the primary focus of this debate: the *impact of promotion on costs* and prices and the *impact of promotion on competition*. Let us examine briefly the arguments of each side of these two questions.

Cost and Prices

The critics argue that advertising and other forms of promotion are significant costs that figure in the determination of prices of goods and services. They contend that with less promotional activity, costs would be lower and lower consumer prices would result.

Supporters of marketing and promotion reply that promotion increases the consumer's awareness of available products, thereby expanding the total market and lowering overall cost through more efficient manufacturing and distribution of a larger volume of goods. Besides these efficiencies derived from the scale of operations, they also cite learning curve effects to support their position.

Competition

Critical analysts of economic activity—notably many industrial organization economists—maintain that heavy promotional expenditures by established firms serve as a barrier to entry in many fields, especially for small competitors. Since these organizations cannot afford to make the promotional investment required to enter the business, they are effectively precluded from competing. Thus the larger, well-established firms are able to charge higher prices and reap excessive profits.

"Au contraire," respond the proponents; rather than inhibit competition, promotion fosters it. New products can be presented to the public more efficiently and quickly, permitting smaller firms with limited resources to gain acceptance of new ideas. Without the opportunity to advertise and promote freely, new products and services advantageous to consumers would never get off the drawing board.

Some Research Findings

In reaction to these positions, we can see a logical argument for either side. How, then, can we determine where the strength of the argument really lies?

Albion and Farris, concerned with this very question, explored the issue in depth, studying both the marketing and the economic research.[10] They investigated the effects of advertising on the following economic areas: prices, profits, industry concentration, product innovation, and industry demand. In their evaluation they found conflicting evidence on each subject as well as significant methodological issues that made generalization extremely difficult. Nonetheless, with great trepidation and appropriate "caveats," they were willing to put forth the following conclusions.

Advertising and Prices

We strongly believe that advertised products charge higher prices on average, than comparable unadvertised products. However, we also believe retailers earn lower profit margins on advertised brands than on unadvertised brands. Further, advertising seems to contribute to the viability of self-service retail outlets. *Because of these non-price effects*, we do not know whether advertising contributes to higher average prices paid by consumers for products; the stage in the product life cycle and the distribution network employed seem critical. Yet, even if advertising does raise average prices, the value of advertising in reducing consumer search costs and building markets must be weighed against these higher prices to measure the true *social* costs and benefits.[11]

Advertising and Profits

We feel that most firms advertise to increase sales and profits and that in established markets, this increase is likely to come at the expense of competitors' sales and profits.

We do not know whether the correlation between industry profits and industry advertising intensity means that profitable industries advertise more, or advertising increases industry profits, or both. We do strongly believe that many industries characterized by high profits and high advertising rates are also *high-risk ventures* for competitors and entrants. The advertising-profits relationship may be a function of risk, which we believe is more

a function of product, customer, and purchasing pattern factors than anything else.[12]

Advertising, Industry Concentration, and Product Innovation
We see little evidence of *significant* scale economies in advertising and doubt
that advertising weight alone can affect industry concentration to any great
extent. New entrants without established reputations must naturally advertise at higher rates to overcome consumer inertia—consumers do not immediately forget everything, and advertising for existing products must have
some carryover effect. Thus, advertising can build consumer preference and
trust and create barriers to entry. However, without advertising, new entrants with significant product or price advantages would have a more difficult time in entering markets.

That advertising *alone* cannot achieve market penetration for a firm with
"me-too" products has been too long an established fact to question seriously. However, we do not know how to distinguish whether the product
"advantages" that firms offer are "real" or "cosmetic" innovations. The
idea that advertising may help a firm to occupy all available market niches
and keep competition at bay by brand proliferation of products with only
slight differences is a contention with serious implications and one that
appears to have validity in certain types of markets where consumer involvement is low, many product attributes are hidden, and a large variety of
slightly different preferences are manifest.[13]

Advertising and Market Size
We believe strongly that advertising, as an efficient form of mass communication can *accelerate* the growth of new markets and new entries into markets.
We doubt that advertising significantly determines the ultimate size of a
market—except in those markets that depend on "reminder" advertising
for a portion of total demand (soft drinks, perhaps).[14]

The arguments as to the impact of promotion on cost, prices, and
competition are clear, as stated earlier; the research evidence, while comprehensive in nature, is, unfortunately, not clear. Albion and Farris draw conclusions that favor both positions in the debate on advertising's economic effects. The debate and research will undoubtedly continue. As new evidence
appears, we are hopeful that it will add light as well as heat to the assessment
of this social question. (See Exhibit 20-1 for a summary of two schools of
thought about the effects of advertising: the "Advertising Is Market Power"
school and the "Advertising Is Information" school.)

PROMOTION
AND THE ENVIRONMENT

The first substantial interest in protecting the environment traces to the
presidency of Theodore Roosevelt and the initiation of national forest and
wildlife policies. President Franklin D. Roosevelt expanded and reinforced
the policies in the 1930s and 1940s with public works projects to reclaim

EXHIBIT 20-1 Two Schools of Thought on Advertising's Role in the Economy

ADVERTISING = MARKET POWER		ADVERTISING = INFORMATION
Advertising affects consumer preferences and tastes, changes product attributes, and differentiates the product from competitive offerings.	*Advertising*	Advertising informs consumers about product attributes and does not change the way they value those attributes.
Consumers become brand loyal and less price sensitive, and perceive fewer substitutes for advertised brands.	*Consumer Buying Behavior*	Consumers become more price sensitive and buy best "value." Only the relationship between price and quality affects elasticity for a given product.
Potential entrants must overcome established brand loyalty and spend relatively more on advertising.	*Barriers to Entry*	Advertising makes entry possible for new brands because it can communicate product attributes to consumers.
Firms are insulated from market competition and potential rivals; concentration increases, leaving firms with more discretionary power.	*Industry Structure and Market Power*	Consumers can compare competitive offerings easily and competitive rivalry is increased. Efficient firms remain, and as the inefficient leave, new entrants appear; the effect on concentration is ambiguous.
Firms can charge higher prices and are not as likely to compete on quality or price dimensions. Innovation may be reduced.	*Market Conduct*	More informed consumers put pressure on firms to lower prices and improve quality. Innovation is facilitated via new entrants.
High prices and excessive profits accrue to advertisers and give them even more incentive to advertise their products. Output is restricted compared to conditions of perfect competition.	*Market Performance*	Industry prices are decreased. The effect on profits due to increased competition and increased efficiency is ambiguous.

Source: Paul W. Farris and Mark S. Albion, *An Investigation into the Impact of Advertising on the Price of Consumer Products*, Report No. 79-109 (Cambridge, Mass.: Marketing Science Institute, August 1979), p. 7.

the soil and harness the waterways. We mark the beginning of the current period of environmental concern with Rachel Carson's 1962 bestseller, *Silent Spring*, which strongly documented the impact of pesticides as an environmental pollutant. In 1970 the Meadowses published *The Limits to Growth*, a study conducted under the auspices of the Club of Rome; and the two main issues of environmental concern achieved a sharp focus. These were that society, through its concentration on economic growth and production, disrupts the ecological balance and pollutes and destroys the quality of air, water, and land that we all need for a healthful, functional life. At the same time, society is rapidly consuming irreplaceable natural resources essential to the productive system, with the real hazard that depletion of known reserves of some of these critical materials might occur in our lifetime.

The first issue became increasingly evident through regular accounts of polluted water supplies; raw sewage in our harbors, lakes, and rivers; and the constant battles over past and current practices of hazardous waste disposal.

The reality and impact of the second issue came home graphically during the oil embargo of 1973. The ensuing shortage of oil, oil-based products, and energy-dependent materials and services, coupled with dramatic price increases in all these categories, were incontrovertible evidence.

At this point, the critical question for marketers has become abundantly clear, How can a discipline—marketing and, particularly, promotion—whose principal economic purpose is to expand the consumption of goods and services, reconcile that activity with the realities of shortages and manifold threats to environmental integrity and the quality of life?

Of course, there is no simple answer. But at least three alternative scenarios provide a backdrop against which the marketer projects a role for itself. First, increase the reserves of natural resources and reduce our dependence on external sources of materials by opening up for exploration and development previously restricted government lands and offshore property. This may be a solution to one part of the environmental issue, but it clearly flies directly in the face of the other. Environmentalists have steadfastly opposed this proposal. Second, accept a lower standard of living, based on a conservation and low-growth philosophy that puts a premium on the quality, not the quantity, of life. This is in essence a counterpoint to the conventional "American Dream" and is least acceptable to the disadvantaged and minorities, who find only irony in the concept of a reduced living standard. Third, seek alternative means of production that depend on renewable resources such as the sun, wind, or vegetation. To achieve this involves a significant technological effort as well as a sizable shift in resource allocation among industries. There are sizable economic interests that would welcome the transition, and others that would feel threatened by such a change. To be sure, the marketing professional has a role and a stake in this important discussion. The professional cannot be a passive observer but instead must participate in the public debate.

PROMOTION AND WOMEN

In the early 1960s, feminist critics began a vocal critique of marketing and advertising for the limited and demeaning portrayal of women in advertising and other promotional vehicles. As Courtney and Whipple noted: ". . . some critics went so far as to suggest that advertising was a conspiracy intended to keep women confined to home, as witless and hapless consumers, dedicated only to the needs of men, children, and clean floors. They contended that advertising shows women as drab, repulsive, stupid, and inadequate housewives."[15]

This critical outpouring became the catalyst for serious academic research on the subject to either confirm or refute these views. Content analysis of both TV and magazine advertising became the principal research tool. Courtney and Whipple completed a comprehensive review of the research in this area, drawing upon the marketing literature as well as the extensive reportings in the communications and social science journals.[16] Their evaluation breaks down into several major content areas, among which the major findings and conclusions in the following four areas appear to be most significant for our discussion: (1) existence of sex stereotyping, (2) effects of sex stereotyping, (3) attitudes toward sex stereotyping, and (4) preferences for sex-role portrayals. Let us look at what they had to say in order to shed some light on why critics of advertising's portrayal of women were unhappy and were demanding that something be done to present women more favorably and realistically.

Existence of Sex Stereotyping

The published studies cited here on the existence of sex stereotyping all reach similar conclusions. They confirm the criticism that advertising portrays the typical woman in a limited and traditional role, that woman's place in advertising is seen to be the home, and that her labor force roles are underrepresented. Women are typically portrayed as housewives and mothers, as dependent upon men and sometimes as unintelligent and subservient. Women are often "used" as sexual or decorative objects in advertising but are seldom shown or heard in authoritative roles, such as announcers or voice-overs. On the other hand, men are depicted as the voices of authority, the older and wiser advice-givers and demonstrators. They are shown in a wider range of occupations and roles in their working and leisure lives or as beneficiaries of women's work in the home.[17]

Effects of Sex Stereotyping

The limited evidence which does exist indicates that advertising legitimizes stereotypes of women, rather than showing women realistically in today's modern society. Research on advertising and female attitudes toward achievement, drug use among women, and social effects of sex stereotyping link it with negative attitudes and behavior. For example, some research data link stereotyping women's health problems with societal effects, in that stereotyped advertising can cause doctors to misdiagnose and over prescribe for women. Such advertising may influence some doctors to treat a woman's symptoms with tranquilizers while ignoring the real cause of her difficulties.

The effect of sex stereotyping on children is a much better research topic. There is evidence that children accept the stereotyped roles shown in advertising, select them as appropriate for males and females in general, and select stereotyped careers for themselves. Boys have been found to exhibit higher propensities to stereotype than girls, as have heavy TV watchers. Studies have also demonstrated that female children are more likely to prefer and select for themselves a wider choice of careers and more unusual occupations if they have seen women portrayed in these roles on TV. The researchers agree that advertising, and television in general, can be a relevant source of information for sex-role socialization, that incidental learning about the labor force takes place among children viewers, and that children model themselves after the characters portrayed in children's programming and advertising.[18]

Attitudes toward Sex Stereotyping

Little empirical research has been reported on the question of how the consumer in general, and women consumers in particular, view sex-role portrayals in advertising. Polls conducted by consumer magazines and government agencies consistently find that the majority of consumers agree that television advertising is insulting to women. Public support has been expressed for more authoritative roles for women in advertising, such as spokeswomen for national products. Attitude studies among advertisers have found that the majority disagree with feminist criticism and do not consider their advertising campaigns offensive.[19]

Preferences for Sex-Role Portrayals

One area of growing research interest concerns the advertising effectiveness of different kinds of role portrayals of women in advertisements. This research has examined whether, and under what conditions, more progressive, less stereotyped portrayals may be preferred to traditional ones. The findings indicate that more progressive advertising approaches can be at least equally preferred to, and possibly more preferred than, more traditional approaches. The use of working women as role models in commercials rated high with both housewives and employed women, although traditional portrayals were found to be satisfactory if the roles provided an appropriate usage environment for the product. Positive attitudes toward women's liberation tend to correlate with preference for progressive advertising approaches.[20]

The portrayal of women in promotional material will undoubtedly continue to raise both social and managerial questions for the marketing executive. The evidence supports the conclusion that great strides have been made and women now enjoy a more realistic and favorable portrayal in advertising and other promotional vehicles. This area nonetheless commands the attention of social critics as women continue to strive for equality and justice in all aspects of human endeavor. We must continue to push forward.

PROMOTION AND CHILDREN

Advertising directed to children has been a subject of great controversy. It is a very important social issue.[21] Parents, government officials, and, yes, advertisers have long been concerned about the ability of advertising, particularly television advertising, to influence children. Many people argue that this concern is warranted, "since it appears that children do not seem to have the capabilities to put the information they see on television into a realistic perspective."[22]

A good portion of television advertising to children concentrates on four product categories (candy, cereal, toys and games, and vitamins). The marketing practices of these manufacturers have been questioned by the FTC and Action for Children's Television (ACT) with regard to the safety or nutritional values of their products, their aggressive sales tactics toward this immature audience, and possible deception in their advertising. ACT went so far as to petition the FTC to establish special regulations concerning the amount and content of advertising directed at children. Although the FTC conducted a comprehensive study of the matter, it did not set forth any legislation or regulations to govern children's advertising.[23] The many interested parties (advertisers, networks, and ACT for example) put forth extensive evidence, testimony, and political lobbying muscle during the deliberations.

The argument over the extent and type of regulation necessary for children's advertising and sales promotion essentially boils down to two positions: (1) the proponents of regulation, who maintain that (a) advertising exerts a powerful influence on the behavior of children and (b) the advertised products pose potential health and safety threats to children; and (2) the advertisers, who argue that (a) advertising is not the only influence on the consumption behavior of children and (b) advertisers have rights to free speech.[24]

One of the most active groups in the controversy over children's advertising has been the aforementioned Action for Children's Television, a national nonprofit consumer organization working to encourage diversity in television programming and eliminate commercial abuses from children's television. ACT initiates legal reform through petitions to the federal regulatory agencies and promotes public awareness of the issues relating to children's programming through public education campaigns, numerous publications (such as RE:ACT, a quarterly magazine), national conferences, and speaking engagements. ACT seeks, among other things, to encourage the development and enforcement of appropriate guidelines for advertisements and programming directed to children.

Among ACT's accomplishments are the following: a 40 percent reduction of Saturday morning children's advertising; elimination of the practice of using program hosts to promote products; elimination of vitamin pill advertising on children's programs; and more diversity in TV offerings for children.[25] While ACT continues to work to achieve its stated goals, it is already clear that the organization has substantially raised the public awareness and sensitivity to the crucial issues surrounding television's impact on children, particularly its impact on children's consumption habits.

Another noteworthy organization dealing with advertising to children is the Children's Advertising Review Unit (CARU) of the Council of Better Business Bureaus (see Chapter 19). Established by the advertising industry in 1974 "to promote responsible children's advertising and to respond to public concerns, CARU's basic activity is the review and evaluation of child-directed advertising media."[26] When children's advertising is misleading, inaccurate, or inconsistent with CARU's guidelines, the organization works for changes through voluntary cooperation of advertisers.

In its *Guidelines* publication, CARU sets forth five basic principles to serve as the foundation for specific guidelines by which it judges advertising directed to children. First, CARU suggests that advertisers should take into account the level of knowledge, maturity, and sophistication of the target audience, which entails a special responsibility to protect children because of their limited capability to assess the credibility of what they see on television. Second, advertisers should take great care not to exploit the imaginations of children. Third, advertisers should communicate their information truthfully and accurately, recognizing that advertising may indeed play a major role in educating a child. Fourth, advertisers should commit themselves to communicating positive social standards such as friendship, kindness, honesty, justice, generosity, and respect for others, particularly because of advertising's potential for influencing social behavior. Fifth, advertisers should do what they can to help parents provide guidance in their children's personal and social development.[27] In carrying out these principles, CARU is governed by several specific guidelines (see Exhibit 20-2).

In summary, "because children's knowledge of the physical and social world is in the process of development, they are more limited than adults in the experience and skills required to evaluate advertising and to make purchase decisions. For these reasons, certain presentations and techniques which may be appropriate for adult-directed advertising may mislead children if used in child-directed advertising."[28]

Certainly it would seem that television at least has the potential to negatively bias children in their development as consumers. On the other hand, television also has the potential to provide children with information and vicarious experiences beneficial to their development as consumers. Television's influences, if directed in positive ways, can educate children early in life about such things as good nutrition, health habits, and norms of behavior. Much of this sort of television advertising is already being done. In summary, then, it seems clear that television does have an influence on the socialization of children, including an influence on their socialization as consumers.[29]

EXHIBIT 20-2 Guidelines Used to Evaluate Advertising to Children

A. Product Presentations and Claims
1. Copy, sound and visual presentations should not mislead children about product or performance characteristics.
2. The advertising presentation should not mislead children about perceived benefits from use of the product.
3. Care should be taken not to exploit a child's imagination.
4. The performance and use of a product should be demonstrated in a way that can be duplicated by the child for whom the product is intended.
5. Products should be shown used in safe environments and situations.
6. What is included and excluded in the initial purchase should be clearly established.
7. The amount of product featured should be within reasonable levels for the situation depicted.
8. Representation of food products should be made so as to encourage sound usage of the product with a view toward healthy development of the child and development of good nutritional practices.
9. Portrayals of violence and presentations that could unduly frighten or provoke anxiety in children should be avoided.
10. Objective claims about product or performance characteristics should be supported by appropriate and adequate substantiation.

B. Sales Pressure
1. Children should not be urged to ask parents or others to buy products.
2. Advertisements should not convey the impression that possession of a product will result in more acceptance of a child by his or her peers.
3. All price representations should be clearly and concisely set forth.

C. Disclosures and Disclaimers
1. All information which requires disclosure for legal or other reasons should be in language understandable by the child audience.
2. Advertising for unassembled products should clearly indicate that they need to be put together to be used properly.
3. If any item essential to use of the product is not included, such as batteries, this fact must be disclosed clearly.
4. Information about products purchased separately, such as accessories or individual items in a collection, should be disclosed clearly to the child audience.

EXHIBIT 20–2   Guidelines Used to Evaluate Advertising to Children
(*continued*)

D. Comparative Claims

1. Comparative advertising should provide factual information.

2. Comparative claims should be presented in ways that children understand clearly.

3. Comparative claims should be supported by appropriate and adequate substantiation.

E. Endorsements and Promotion by Program or Editorial Characters

1. All personal endorsements should reflect the actual experiences and beliefs of the endorser.

2. An endorser represented, either directly or indirectly, as an expert must possess qualifications appropriate to the particular expertise depicted in the endorsement.

3. Program personalities, live or animated, should not promote products, premiums or services in or adjacent to programs primarily directed to children in which the same personality or character appears.

4. In print media primarily designed for children, a character or personality associated with the editorial content of a publication should not be used to promote products, premiums or services in the same publication.

F. Premiums

1. If product advertising contains a premium message, care should be taken that the child's attention is focused primarily on the product.

2. Conditions of a premium offer should be stated simply and clearly.

G. Safety

1. Products inappropriate for use by children should not be advertised directly to children.

2. Advertisements for children's products should show them being used by children in the appropriate age range.

3. Adults should be shown supervising children when products or activities could involve an obvious safety risk.

4. Advertisements should not portray adults or children in unsafe acts, situations or conditions or in acts harmful to others.

5. Advertisements should avoid demonstrations that encourage dangerous or inappropriate use or misuse of the product.

Source: Excerpted from *Self-Regulatory Guidelines for Children's Advertising* (New York: Council of Better Business Bureaus, Children's Advertising Review Unit, 1983), pp. 5–10.

FUTURE DIRECTIONS:
UNANSWERED QUESTIONS

The social issues we have discussed will continue to be major concerns for professional marketers in the years ahead. Some organizations have taken an aggressive approach to dealing with the issues. For example, the American Association of Advertising Agencies, greatly concerned about consumer perceptions of advertising, launched an advertising campaign designed to change those consumer perceptions that "advertising makes people buy things they don't want, increases the cost of products and helps sell inferior products."[30] As if those matters were not enough, we foresee at least two additional questions looming on the horizon. Both of these issues are a function of the dramatic technological advances in computers and communications.

The first of these—personal privacy—is not actually a new concern. It is one that has been growing steadily over the years as computers with their ever-expanding data bases contain more and more detailed information on each of us. This of course allows marketers to define and more precisely direct messages to particular target markets. But, couple this with the skills of the direct mail specialist and the growth of telemarketing activities—fostered by sophisticated computer-based switching equipment and ever-spiraling costs of transportation—and it is not unrealistic to foresee that our vehicles for personal communication may all too soon be overflowing with commercial messages. We can certainly visualize our mailboxes loaded with personal letters that are cleverly crafted sales presentations; or telephone calls insistently disrupting our activities to promote a variety of products and services.

Is there a line we should draw? How much of our private lives do we want captured by the specialists in data manipulation? How much intrusion on our personal time are we willing to allow the mail and telephone salesperson? These are questions not only for society as a whole to come to grips with but also for the marketing profession as it seeks ways to use these new techniques.

The second issue is equally broad and pervasive. As broadcast media, through the use of cable, satellite, and microwave techniques, along with low-cost computer terminals and mass-storage facilities, become sophisticated sources of information and two-directional communications, we can foresee significant changes in the consumer buying process. Philip Harding of CBS presents this perspective:

> At whatever point that happens, it seems to me the public will have at its disposal something with the potential to facilitate dramatically the tasks involved in *being* an informed and effective consumer. A means to simplify and make more efficient the performance of these tasks—tasks which, in an era of increasingly severe constraints on time, might otherwise not be performed at all. So I think that, to the extent these electronic technologies

become widely available, one major result will be a significant increase in consumers' knowledgeability and sophistication about the marketplace and about individual products and services within it. Indeed when we get to the stage of actually *marketing* these technologies, I suspect that this is going to be a key selling point—both to the public *and* prospective advertisers.[31]

Mary Gardiner Jones adds this insight:

> The incredible ability of the new technologies to create and generate information, both independently and as a byproduct of other transactions, is at the heart of the revolutionary impacts of the new technologies. These impacts are affecting the nature of information as a public or private good and hence who ultimately will have access to it. Strong dynamics are being created for centralization of the management and control over these information systems, although the technologies could equally facilitate a wide fragmentation of information providers. In either case, what information will ultimately be provided and by whom will be directly affected by who owns and manages these systems.[32]

Our traditional institutions, both informational and distributive, will witness profound changes.[33] What will become of the supermarket or the bank when we can order our weekly groceries over a TV terminal and pay for them by means of an automatic funds transfer from the computer in the bank to the one in the supermarket? What will become of newspapers and the library when we can gain access to information, current or historical, on an unlimited menu of topics? The potential social impact of these phenomena is enormous. Is this a direction in which we want to go? Will we somehow become less human and less humane when we live so much of our daily lives by pushbuttons and computer codes? Will we be giving up too much control in the pursuit of convenience and efficiency? What are the risks to individuals and society of such an automated, integrated life? Obviously the answers are not simple, nor are they universal and applicable to everyone. Aldous Huxley's *Brave New World*, Alvin Toffler's *Future Shock*, and John Naisbitt's *Megatrends* all identify social environments manifesting these and other technological trends. All present a scenario of choice. What choices will we make?

Indeed the social implications of promotion are awesome.

SUMMARY

Management has to be aware of its large social responsibility in developing and executing promotional programs. Promotion is the most visible part of the organization and is an important determinant of how people act as consumers. By its very nature, promotion can make significant contributions to the social welfare, but it can also do considerable harm to consumers and society if advertisers and other promoters abuse it. Society sanctions business activity, but it is up to management to conduct its affairs in a socially responsible way. In few areas is this more important or difficult than in marketing, especially in its use of promotion.

There are several criticisms of promotion, suggesting that promotional activities make people buy things they do not need, create materialistic values, are often deceptive in their approach to communicating with consumers, are annoying and in poor taste, and often provide inadequate information for the consumer to make an intelligent buying decision.

Besides its touching on consumers, promotion affects economic activity by virtue of its impact on prices and competition. Furthermore, promotion has implications for the quality of the environment in which we live. We also saw that promotion has special obligations in its portrayal of women and in its communications to children.

Undoubtedly, the social responsibilities of promotion are important, and these responsibilities loom large as management plans, develops, and executes promotional programs. Management's key task is to recognize its obligation to perform in the public interest and to accomplish its promotional mission in a way that reflects the well-being of society. This is a complex order, but we cannot have it any other way.

REVIEW AND DISCUSSION QUESTIONS

1. What are the responsibilities of marketers to consumers? How about advertisers' responsibilities to consumers?

2. Promotional activities add cost to products. Are the costs justified? Why or why not?

3. "Promotion offers an opportunity to contribute to the overall well-being of society, yet it also has the potential to be detrimental to society." Comment.

4. Identify and comment on the criticisms that are directed toward marketing and, in particular, toward promotional activities.

5. "The promotional element of marketing makes people buy things they do not need." Evaluate this criticism of promotion.

6. "Promotion creates materialistic values." Comment.

7. "Promotion is often deceptive and misleading." Is this true? Defend your position.

8. "Promotion is often annoying and in poor taste." Evaluate this criticism of promotion.

9. Do promotional activities, especially advertising, foster freedom of choice in the marketplace? Why or why not?

10. *Explain the impact of promotion on prices.*

11. *What is the relationship between promotion and competition?*

12. *How do promotional activities influence innovation in marketing? Be specific.*

13. *Does promotion have a responsibility to ensure a better environment in which we live? If so, in what ways? If not, why not?*

14. *Do you believe that there is a fair and adequate portrayal of women in advertising? How about the portrayal of minorities such as blacks and Hispanics? Explain.*

15. *How has the changing role of women influenced advertising? And vice versa? Explain your answer.*

16. *What are the responsibilities of advertisers who direct their advertising to children? Do the advertisers fulfill their social obligations in this regard?*

17. *The Children's Advertising Review Unit (CARU) of the National Advertising Division (NAD) sets forth several guidelines governing advertising to children. Cite any three specific guidelines and elaborate on each as to its importance.*

18. *Where do you draw the line between the responsibilities of marketers and those of consumers in the consumer buying process? Explain your position.*

NOTES

1. Frederick E. Webster, *Social Aspects of Marketing* (Englewood Cliffs, N.J.: Prentice-Hall, 1974), pp. 29–39.

2. Frederick E. Webster, *Social Aspects of Marketing*, © 1974, pp. 29–30. Reprinted by permission of Prentice-Hall, Inc., Englewood Cliffs, N.J.

3. From *The Affluent Society* by John Kenneth Galbraith, 3rd Ed., p. 131. Copyright © 1958, 1969, 1976 by John Kenneth Galbraith. Reprinted by permission of Houghton Mifflin Company and André Deutsch, Ltd.

4. Arnold J. Toynbee, *America and the World Revolution* (New York: Oxford University Press, 1966), pp. 144–45.

5. Webster, *Social Aspects of Marketing*, p. 32.

6. Ibid., pp. 32–33.

7. Ibid., p. 35.

8. Raymond A. Bauer and Stephen A. Greyser, *Advertising in America: The Consumer View* (Boston: Division of Research, Harvard Business School, 1968).

9. Neil Borden, *The Economic Effects of Advertising* (Chicago: Richard D. Irwin, 1942).

10. Mark S. Albion and Paul W. Farris, *Appraising Research on Advertising's Economic Impacts* (Cambridge, Mass.: Marketing Science Institute, December 1979), pp. 172–74.

11. Ibid., pp. 172–73.

12. Ibid., p. 173.

13. Ibid., pp. 173–74.

14. Ibid., p. 174.

15. Alice E. Courtney and Thomas W. Whipple, *Sex Stereotyping in Advertising—An Annotated Bibliography* (Cambridge, Mass.: Marketing Science Institute, February 1980), p. vii.

16. Ibid.

17. Ibid., p. vii.

18. Ibid., p. viii.

19. Ibid., pp. viii–ix.

20. Ibid., p. ix.

21. For an excellent review of the history of television advertising to children and attempts to regulate it, see Gerald J. Thain, *Television Advertising to Children and the Federal Trade Commission*, Paper No. 9 (Urbana: University of Illinois, July 1981).

22. Gerald Zaltman and Melanie Wallendorf, *Consumer Behavior*: Basic Findings and Management Implications. Copyright © 1983 John Wiley & Sons, Inc., p. 299. Reprinted by permission of John Wiley & Sons, Inc.

23. Ibid.

24. Ben M. Enis, Dale R. Spencer, and Don R. Webb, "Television Advertising and Children: Regulatory vs. Competitive Perspectives," *Journal of Advertising*, Winter 1980, pp. 20–21.

25. *ACTFACTS*, a brochure published by Action for Children's Television, Newton, Mass., 1983.

26. *Self-Regulatory Guidelines for Children's Advertising* (New York: Council of Better Business Bureaus, Children's Advertising Review Unit, 1983), p. 10.

27. Ibid., pp. 4–10.

28. Ibid., p. 3.

29. Zaltman and Wallendorf, *Consumer Behavior*, p. 299.

30. Nancy Millman, "Four A's Tackles Ad Image with Ads," *Advertising Age*, March 12, 1984, pp. 1ff.

31. Philip A. Harding, "The New Technologies: Some Implications for Consumer Policy," in *Consumerism and Beyond: Research Perspectives on the Future Social Environment*, ed. Paul Bloom (Cambridge, Mass.: Marketing Science Institute, 1982), p. 83.

32. Mary Gardiner Jones, "Wanted: Consumer Perspectives on the New Technologies," in *Consumerism and Beyond: Research Perspectives on the Future Social Environment*, ed. Paul Bloom (Cambridge, Mass.: Marketing Science Institute, 1982), p. 86.

33. For a comprehensive collection of viewpoints on the social environment of marketing, see Paul N. Bloom, ed., *Consumerism and Beyond: Research Perspectives on the Future Social Environment*, Proceedings of a conference presented by Marketing Science Institute and Center for Business and Public Policy, University of Maryland (Cambridge, Mass.: Marketing Science Institute, April 1982).

Index